Encyclopedia of

VOCATIONAL GUIDANCE

Encyclopedia of

VOCATIONAL
GUIDANCE

EDITED BY

OSCAR J. KAPLAN

VOLUME TWO

PHILOSOPHICAL LIBRARY

NEW YORK

PRINTED IN THE UNITED STATES OF AMERICA

M

MACHINE SCORING OF VOCATIONAL GUIDANCE TESTS.

The International Test Scoring Machine provides a mechanical method which reduces the clerical burden and the time required for grading objective tests. The machine will score any objective test the answers to which may be recorded in terms of position. Examples of machine-scoreable types of test items are: multiple choice, matching, true-false, like-dislike, etc. Machine-scoring is effected through the use of separate answer sheets on which examinees record their response to the test questions. Answer sheets specifically designed for various published standardized tests are available, thus making possible repeated use of test booklets. Also available for locally constructed tests are standard answer sheets which will accommodate 150 five-choice or 300 two-choice items, all of which can be scored simultaneously. Responses may be recorded on both sides of the answer sheet and each side scored in separate runs through the machine. Extensive studies have shown that the separate answer sheet does not affect the reliability or validity of test results.

The machine may be adjusted to indicate the total number of right answers, wrong answers, $R - W$, $R - \dfrac{W}{R}$, or percentage scores. Such scores may be obtained by the machine method at the rate of approximately 500 per hour; the number of test items has no significant effect on the scoring rate. Procedures are also available for scoring tests with variable item weights, of the type commonly required by interest and personality questionnaires, and for other special scoring techniques.

Published tests adapted for machine scoring include: Interest Tests (Strong Vocational Interest Blank for Men, Kuder Preference Record, etc.); Personality Tests (Bell Adjustment Inventory, Bernreuter Personality Inventory, Minnesota Personality Scale, etc.); Mental Ability Tests (American Council Psychological Examination, Tests of Primary Mental Abilities, California Intelligence Test, Pintner General Ability Test, etc.); Achievement Test Batteries (Cooperative General Achievement Tests, Progressive Achievement Tests, Stanford Achievement Tests, etc.). Subject matter tests in English, reading, foreign languages, mathematics, science and in many other fields are also available.

Machine scoring has been found to be approximately ten times a rapid as hand scoring. The machine however is most economical for large numbers of the same test. If many different tests are being used, scoring keys must be changed frequently, with a consequent decrease in scoring efficiency. Scoring by machine is also more accurate than usual handscoring methods when properly designed answer sheets and suitable pencils are used.

The Graphic Item Counter, an attachment for the test scoring machine, is designed to provide item analysis data of objective test questions by mechanical means. By means of this attachment, it is possible to print in graphic form the responses to as many as 90 questions, for a maximum of 115 answer sheets. The counter makes it possible to obtain item data for test construction and remedial work faster and more accurately than by hand tabulation. The aggregate weighting unit (a standard part of the machine) has many practical uses in connection with rating scales in which a number of variable factors are appraised independently and then weighted to obtain a composite or final rating. The unit may also be used to obtain a weighted average of the scores for a group of performance and written tests.

In many schools and colleges, the guidance clinic or student personnel unit has made use of machine scoring in order to further their service to teachers, guidance officers and research workers. It has, in many cases, made possible a more comprehensive testing program and guidance service by furnishing a more complete record of growth and achievement over a long-time period.

The machine rents for $480 per year and the item analysis unit is available for an additional $240 per year.

References:

1. International Business Machines Corporation. *Manual of instruction for the International Test Scoring Machine*. New York: The Corporation, 1943.
2. ———. *Machine methods of test scoring: manual of procedures*. New York: The Corporation, 1940.
3. Lorge, I. Tabulating and test scoring machines: applications of International Business Machines to educational research. *Review of Educational Research,* 1942, 12, 550–557.

W. J. McN.

MALARIA. An over-simplification of malaria as a problem for vocational counselors is to state unequivocally that no individual needs to choose his occupation or place of habitat solely on the basis of the possible effect either might have on his malarial condition. Such a statement might well represent the goal towards which medical authorities in the field of tropical diseases are constantly striving, but that the goal is not yet in sight is borne out by the conclusions of Colonel Dieuaide,[4] "No known drug prevents infection with malaria," and "No reliable method has yet been found to predict relapses or to demonstrate cure of malaria." The chemicals (drugs) in current use to control or prevent acute episodes of chills, fever, sweating are quinine and atabrin. Until a chemical is discovered which will kill the malarial parasites in the blood there is always the possibility or probability of recurring attacks of malaria, and counselors should become familiar with malaria as a physical (or mental) disability.

Malaria, which was once the most feared of all tropical epidemic diseases, is defined in Stedman's Medical Dictionary, 12th Revised Edition, as "A disease caused by the presence of a protozoan parasite of the red blood corpuseles.—The disease is transmitted by the bite of a mosquito, of the genus Anopheles, which has previously sucked the blood of a person suffering from malaria.—A malarial attack or paroxysm consists of a chill, accompanied and followed by fever with its attendant general symptoms and terminates in a sweating stage." It has been suggested to the writer by competent medical authority that the term "malaria victim" be dropped. The writer is, therefore, using in this article the term "malarial" for any person who has malaria or one who is recovering or has apparently recovered from malaria relapses.

A number of questions will invariably arise when a counselor and a malarial cooperate in solving the latter's problems relative to vocational guidance and training. The answers given in this article represent the most accurate and informative data available to the author at this time.

Question number (1): Are there any major occupational fields which a malarial should avoid? Major H. H. Gordon,[4] states "As far as we know, there are no occupations which a patient who has had malaria should avoid." A break-through of clinical activity may occur in the presence of excessive fatigue or exposure to high altitudes, therefore, these conditions should be avoided where ever possible and exercise or general physical activity be reduced to a minimum during a relapse.

Question number (2): Are there any sections of this country (having special brands of climate) which are either favorable or unfavorable for the habitat of persons who may be classed as malarials? To quote Major Gordon [4] again, "There are, as far as we know, no sections of the country which they (malarials) need avoid. Sudden changes in climate, either from hot to cold or from cold to hot, may bring on malarial attacks. These attacks can be brought under control so promptly with anti-malarial drugs that no individual need choose his occupation or habitat solely on the basis of possible effects on his malaria."

Question number (3): Is there such a thing as complete cure from malaria? "No known drug" states the Manual of Tropical Medicine,[3] "is certainly lethal for sporozoites and consequently there is no true causal prophylaxis for malaria. Suppressive treatment, as the term implies, does not prevent infection. When properly utilized, however, it does suppress clinical activity and atabrin may eradicate falciparum (a type of malaria) infection as well as hold it at subclinical levels." Quinine and atabrin have been the drugs used in the suppression and treatment of malaria. An announcement was made in Washington, D. C. on January 3, 1945 by the Board for the Coordination of Malarial Studies that a new synthetic drug, SN7618, has been developed which relieves acute attacks of malaria three times more quickly than either quinine or atabrin, doesn't stain the skin as does atabrin, doesn't cause buzzing in the ears as does quinine, can be taken in weekly rather than daily doses and doesn't make the malarial sick in the stomach. The promise for a complete cure with new drugs being developed is good. A rule of thumb is that if a malarial goes six months without treatment and without an attack, the chances are about ten to one that he is cured and if he can go for an entire year without a relapse, he can consider himself cured. A malarial's chances of having no attacks beyond two years after returning to the United States are 99 out of 100, assuming that the person guards his health and abstains from excessive indulgent in alcoholic beverages.

Question number (4): Is malaria a chronically active infection such as tuberculosis or is it a more or less harmless infection which has periods of recurrent activity? The problem of explaining the significance of their disease to the malarials is an important and interesting one. It must be explained to these persons that malaria, is not an active infection, such as tuberculosis, but is a comparatively harmless infection which has varying periods of recurrent activity, with no known draining of the persons strength (mental or physical) between relapses. A veteran, who is also a malarial, may upon an attack of dizziness, headache, nervousness or mild gastro-infection, reach the unwarranted conclusion that another bout with malaria is imminent. These disorders might be attributed to overseas experiences other than the one with malaria. It is therefore important, as Major Gordon[4] has said, that these veterans "recognize the true cause of their symptoms and not use malaria as a tangible crutch for avoiding military or civilian responsibilities." This problem of assuring these veterans of the comparatively minor rôle being played by their malarial sensitivity, is one that rests with vocational counselors as well as with members of the medical profession. "This," continued Major Gordon, "requires assurance and reassurance and broad surveys of all their personal problems in order to fit malaria into its proper place as one of the causes but not the chief cause of their difficulties."

In conclusion it appears desirable that vocational counselors assure malarials that their physical handicap in no way limits their occupational opportunities nor should it prevent a shift to another occupation if opportunities fail to develop in the occupation initially trained for.

References:

1. Ash, Colonel J. E., M.C., and Spitz, Sophie, M.D. *Pathology of tropical diseases.* Philadelphia: W. B. Saunders Co., 1945, pp. 206–227.
2. Dieuaide, Lt. Col. F. R., M.C. Clinical malaria in wartime. *War Medicine* 7:7–11 (January) 1945.
3. Mackie, Colonel T. T., M.C. and others. *Manual of tropical medicine.* Philadelphia: W. B. Saunders Co., 1945, pp. 213–255.
4. *Personal Communication* from Major H. H. Gordon, M.C., Chief, Tropical Disease Section, Harmon General Hospital, Longview, Texas. December 13, 1945.

M. N. T.

MATHEMATICS, APTITUDE FOR.   Although there is no universally accepted definition for mathematical aptitude, we may paraphrase a definition for the sake of discussion here that mathematical aptitude consists of those patterns of traits or qualities which are predictive of an individual's future potentialities in mathematics, based on his present achievements or proficiencies.[4]

Aptitude for mathematics, according to Hammond and Stoddard,[2] is dependent upon the ability of the individual to visualize geometric figures and to see the relationships involved between geometric figures, upon his logic, and upon his ability to symbolize and to comprehend abstractions. Tests which purport to measure mathematical aptitude are generally constructed to include a measurement of these factors as a prediction of the individual's chances of success in undertaking the study of mathematics. That these factors do have a definite place in mathematics is readily apparent from a quick appraisal of those sciences in which mathematics is basic, such as electrical and mechanical engineering, chemistry, biology, physics, metallurgy, communications, astronomy, etc.

Ruch and Segel classify mathematics as a "semicontinuous" group of subjects, meaning that the arithmetic of the elementary schools is followed by algebra, geometry and trigonometry in which there is a continuity of certain basic skills but a discontinuity of subject names.[4] Their contention is that the best prediction of future achievement is the level of achievement attained at the time of prediction, postulating the generalization that arithmetical scores predict achievement in algebra or geometry as well as, or possibly better than, the special mathematical aptitude tests which are available at present. Seemingly, it may be assumed from this statement that we have not yet learned to measure the skills of mathematics as well as we have the results of the use of those skills. It is interesting to note here an apparent conflict in the findings of guidance experts. Ross states that [3]

". . . for a few high school subjects, aptitude tests seem to be the best single basis for predicting achievement. These subjects usually represent fields the content of which is the least like that of the elementary school. Examples of such subjects are art, music, industrial arts, *algebra, geometry,* and foreign languages."

In a study by McCoy of possible predictors of algebraic success, it was found that arithmetic, intelligence and reading success ranked in that order as indicative of aptitude in algebra. Of these, past achievement in arithmetic was by far the best indicator. The correlation between achievement in algebra with arithmetic computation and reasoning was 0.62; with the Otis Group Intelligence Scale and Terman Group Test of Mental Ability 0.49. Grover found that the Orleans Algebra Prognosis Test predicted success in algebra to the extent of a correlation of 0.61 as compared with a correlation of 0.48 with the prediction from I.Q.'s as determined by the Terman Group Test of Mental Ability.

Torgerson and Aamodt compared the value of Otis intelligence I.Q.'s, Orleans Algebra Prognosis Test and the Lee Test of Algebraic Ability, getting correlations of 0.61, 0.60, and 0.62, respectively, with the algebraic success of 236 pupils after one semester's study. Lee and Hughes experimented with the Lee Test of Algebraic Ability, Kuhlmann-Anderson I.Q.'s, teachers' ratings of mathematical ability, Terman group test I.Q.'s, character ratings on the Hughes Rating Scale and chronological age. They found that the prognosis tests predict success in algebra somewhat better than do intelligence tests and considerably better than the other projected indicators.

The relative values of three algebra aptitude tests in predicting grades in algebra were compared by Greene and Jorgenson with the following results: Iowa Algebra Aptitude Test, 0.66; Orleans Algebra Prognosis Test, 0.63; Lee Test of Algebraic Ability, 0.59. Seagoe found that according to her study it seemed that the Orleans Prognosis Test is somewhat superior to tests of general intelligence for the prediction of achievement in algebra, but the Stanford Arithmetic Test is superior to both the Orleans Algebra and general intelligence tests.

Ruch and Segel, who abstracted the above six studies, suggest that, on the basis of them,[4]

". . . special aptitude tests in algebra are more highly predictive of success in that subject than are general intelligence tests. It appears further that arithmetic tests predict as well as or even better than special aptitude measures. The reason for this becomes clear when we examine the content of the Orleans, Lee, and Iowa aptitude tests. Each contains a considerable amount of arithmetic computation, arithmetic reasoning, or exercises in simple algebraic symbols to be manipulated in terms of the pupil's background in arithmetical processes. All three are fundamentally arithmetic computation and reasoning tests, and hence, not greatly different from the straight arithmetic test used by McCoy. It might be pointed out that the prediction possible through the intelligence tests is partly explained by the fact that intelligence tests usually have one or two subtests that are purely arithmetical.

"To repeat, these findings establish a principle of much wider application than the prediction of algebraic success alone. They offer proof of the generalization previously made that, in general, the best prediction of future success is the level of achievement attained up to the present time in the same subject or in closely related underlying subjects."

Traxler agrees with Ruch and Segel that research has not yet shown that tests designed to measure specific subject aptitude have significantly greater relationship to success in those areas than do the results of tests of general academic aptitude (intelligence).[5] He warns that since tests of general academic aptitude, specific aptitude, and achievement have many elements in common, one might easily be confused by a tendency to apply different names to what in reality is the same thing.

A general survey of the field of mathematics aptitude indicates that there is yet much work to be done in constructing better measures of the skills involved in mathematical processes if mathematical aptitude tests are to be improved. Even when more accurate measurements can be made available there will still remain the question of the part personality traits, attitudes, habits and other interests play in achievement results because these might easily negate the individual's desire to make use of those skills which he possesses. However, lest it be forgotten in the melee of controversy, any instrument which enables prediction with more than chance success has a value, and where there is value there will always be an attempt to improve upon it.

Mathematical Aptitude Tests

1. *Iowa Algebra Aptitude Test,* Harry G. Greene and Alva H. Piper, Iowa City, Iowa: Bureau of Educational Research and Service, State University of Iowa, 1931. $1.00 per 25; manuals 15¢; specimen set 20¢.
2. *Lee Test of Algebra Ability,* J. Murray Lee, Bloomington, Illinois: Public School Publishing Company, 1930. $1.00 per 25 booklets; manual 15¢; specimen set 20¢.
3. *Orleans Albegra Prognosis Test,* Joseph B. and Jacob S. Orleans, Yonkers, New York: World Book Company, 1928–32. $1.60 per 25 booklets; specimen set 20¢.
4. *Iowa Plane Geometry Aptitude Test,* Harry A. Greene and Harold W. Bruce, Iowa City, Iowa: Bureau of Educational Research and Service, State University of Iowa, 1935. 90¢ per 25; specimen set 15¢.
5. *Lee Test of Geometric Aptitude,* Doris M. and J. Murray Lee, Los Angeles; California Test Bureau, 1931. 75¢ per 25; specimen set 15¢.
6. *Orleans Geometry Prognosis Test,* Joseph B. and Jacob S. Orleans, Yonkers, New York: World Book Company, 1929. $2.00 per 25 tests; specimen set 25¢.

References:

1. Greene, H. A. and Jorgenson, A. N. *The interpretation of high school tests.* New York: Longmans, Green and Company, 1938.
2. Hammond, H. P. and Stoddard, G. D. A study of placement examinations. *University of Iowa Studies in Education.* Vol. IV, No. 7, p. 41.
3. Ross, C. C. *Measurement in today's schools.* New York: Prentice-Hall, Inc., 1941, p. 517.
4. Ruch, G. M. and Segel, D. *Minimum essentials of the individual inventory in guidance.* U. S. Office of Education, Vocational Division Bulletin

No. 202. Occupational Information and Guidance Series No. 2, 1940, pp. 35, 36, 75–78.
5. Traxler, A. E. *Techniques of guidance.* New York: Harper and Bros., 1945, p. 52.

H. L.

MATHEMATICS TESTS.

Foust-Schorling Test of Functional Thinking in Mathematics. This test was prepared by Judson W. Foust and Raleigh Schorling. It is a new-type mathematics test of 80 items for high school and college. It is designed to measure ability to think in terms of concepts and symbols of mathematics independent of computational ability. The test includes exercises on (1) recognizing the value on which certain quantities depend, (2) interpreting statements on the relationship between quantities, and (3) stating relationships between quantities in algebraic symbols. End-of-first-semester percentile norms which are based on 5,969 cases are available for grades 9 through 12 for total score on the test. There are two equivalent forms, A and B. The testing time is forty-five minutes. Kuder-Richardson reliability coefficients for each grade range from .80 to .88.

This test is published by World Book Company, Yonkers-on-Hudson, New York.

B. C. W.

Schorling-Clark-Potter Hundred Problem Arithmetic Test. This test, prepared by Raleigh Schorling, John R. Clark and Mary A. Potter, is a revision and improvement of the Schorling-Clark-Potter Arithmetic Test. It is designed to survey computational abilities in the basic skills of arithmetic in grades 7 to 12 inclusive; it may also be used satisfactorily in grades 5 and 6 and for high school graduates whether in college, in industry, or some other occupation where computational facility is a requisite. Fifth- and sixth-grade students will not have studied all the processes in the test, but the difficulty level is such that it will yield satisfactory scores in these grades. There are two equivalent forms, V and W. End-of-first-semester percentile norms based on 5,955 cases are available for grades 8 through 12 for total score on the test. The testing time is 40 minutes. Kuder-Richardson reliability coefficients for each grade range from .94 to .95.

This test is published by World Book Company, Yonkers-on-Hudson, New York.

B. C. W.

MECHANICAL DRAWING TEST.

Purpose—Validity—Reliability

The Mechanical Drawing Test, devised by Charles Schoonover and edited by C. L. Jackson and H. E. Schrammel, was constructed for use as an achievement test in high school mechanical drawing classes which have had a one-year course in the subject. The test covers: lines, angles, plane and solid figures, dimensioning, duplication and reproduction, instruments and materials, methods of presentation and illustration, types of drawing, identification, and vocabulary. One form of the test is available. The working time is 60 minutes.

The test items were selected from the basic content of several leading textbooks and courses of study in the field. All items were carefully checked by teachers and supervisors and by test construction specialists.

In a study of papers written by a college class of students enrolled in mechanical drawing, this test yielded a reliability coefficient of $.92 \pm .02$.

Administering—Scoring—Interpreting

The test is practically self-administering. Scoring is accomplished with ease with a printed objective key. Percentile norms are provided for interpreting the results.

Use of Test Results

It is suggested that the test results may be profitably used in a number of ways: (1) for determining pupil achievement; (2) for checking the efficiency of instruction; (3) for assigning school marks; (4) for analyzing pupil and class weaknesses; and (5) for motivating pupil effort.

Publisher

The Publisher of this test is the Bureau of Educational Measurements, Teachers College, Emporia, Kansas.

Reference:

1. 1940 Mental Measurements Yearbook, p. 330.

H. E. S.

MECHANICAL AND MANUAL ABILITY TESTS, EVALUATION OF.
With large numbers of workers, with no previous work experience in the field, continually being called into industries re-

quiring mechanical aptitudes, tests of their potential abilities for mechanical work are essential.

Psychologists and educators have long been interested in tests of mechanical aptitudes, and many such tests were devised and standardized following the First World War. However, with the intensified emergency training programs set up throughout the country in World War II, interest in the use of these tests spread rapidly. The use of such scientific aids tended to lessen a deplorable waste of training and working time of indispensable manpower and womanpower. Some mechanical aptitude tests proved invaluable aids in the selection, rejection, and classification of prospective trainees for skilled work in war industries and in guiding returning veterans and civilians generally during the difficult postwar reconstruction period. Their extensive use resulted in a wide variety of tests designed to measure mechanical aptitudes.

Motor tests were first used extensively by psychologists interested in the study of individual differences, and in the relation of physical and motor traits to estimates of mental ability. Yet few tests for measuring mechanical aptitudes were devised previous to World War I. The pioneer in this field was J. L. Stenquist, who began work on his tests as early as 1915. He based his work on Thorndike's convenient division of general intelligence into abstract, mechanical and social intelligence. Realizing that vocational success is influenced directly or indirectly by the products of mechanical skill and genius, Stenquist attempted to devise scientific tools for discovering and measuring ability in this field. His Assembling Test was first used in 1915 and his Mechanical Aptitude Test, devised for use with groups, was published in 1921. These tests are the oldest and perhaps the best known tests in this general field. Many of the tests in use today are revisions or adaptations of the Stenquist tests.

Mechanical aptitude tests are designed to analyze the individual in order to obtain a profile of his aptitudes and limitations, and to aid in the prediction of his capacity for training in a specific field and his chances for success in the occupation after completing the course of training. Thus their main function is to help in estimating the probabilities that a person will be able to succeed in an occupation he is considering which involves mechanical information, understanding, or skills.

The elements comprising mechanical ability have not been isolated. Some research in the field indicates that highly specific elements are involved whereas other workers have found two primary factors—one for mechanical ability, the other for manual dexterity. The authors of some tests have made a provisional analysis of the mental processes which they believed to be essential for success in mechanical occupations. Others have attempted to measure the activities required as the units to be measured. From a practical standpoint the major components of mechanical ability may be grouped into three arbitrary categories which appear to be fairly distinct and which are usually required for success in mechanical work. Of these capacity for understanding mechanical relationships, spatial perception, and imagination is perhaps the most important component. It is essential for engineers. A second component required in many skilled jobs requiring manual dexterity is precise muscular coordination. Many unskilled jobs call for the third component which consists of such motor abilities as endurance, speed, and strength.

Tests designed to measure aptitudes for "mechanical" jobs, from unskilled labor to highly skilled and technical types of work, may for convenience be classified into two main groups: 1. Manual Ability Tests, and 2. Mechanical Ability Tests. No attempt will be made to describe or even to list all of the tests available in either of the groups. Fairly inclusive descriptive summaries of these tests may be found in the references listed. A few widely used tests typical of each group will be discussed very briefly.

1. *Manual Ability Tests.* Manual ability tests are largely performance tests involving the use of apparatus. Most of them demand individual administration. Some of the major abilities measured are speed, coordination, versatility and dexterity of movement and endurance.

The Minnesota Rate of Manipulation Test involves two test situations: in the placing test the blocks are transferred from a position on the table to the appropriate place in the board, while in the turning test the blocks are lifted from their holes with one hand, turned over with the other hand, and returned to the hole. This test has proved highly reliable and fairly valid for routine manipulative operations, requiring hand and finger movements.

The Pennsylvania Bi-Manual Worksample combines the elements of a relatively simple work situation which calls for a smooth, integrated work pattern. It measures rate of movement involving bi-manual coordination and bi-manual cooperation. This test has been adapted for use with the blind. It supplements the Minnesota Rate of Manipulation Test in providing measures of four motor skills of increasing complexity. Both tests are widely used in personnel work and may be administered to from one to four persons at a time.

In the O'Connor Finger Dexterity Test the applicant is asked to fill 100 holes in a metal plate—three pins to a hole—as quickly as possible. A reliability of .98 by the split-half method has been obtained for the test and a statistically reliable difference between the average scores of superior and mediocre workers in a watch factory has been found. It has been validated in several industrial situations. The test has proved of definite value in selecting electrical fixture and radio assemblers. The O'Connor Tweezer Dexterity Test differs from the test of finger dexterity in that tweezers rather than the fingers are used to place the pegs in the holes. Contrary to logical considerations, the tweezers test has not been found as satisfactory for selecting workers for a watch factory as has the finger dexterity test. This would seem to indicate that practical experimentation is essential for determining the success of a test for a given type of work, since human demands vary in quite similar jobs. The O'Connor tests are also of the worksample type.

The Purdue Dexterity Test measures two basic components of manual ability: fine finger dexterity similar to the O'Connor tests, and manual dexterity. Both measurements are obtained with the same board in a few minutes testing time for each hand separately and for both hands. Ten test boards may be operated simultaneously by a trained examiner, making it possible for one person to test fifty applicants per hour. The Hayes Pegboard measures manual dexterity similar in type to the Purdue test and also measures an element of hand and arm coordination. Highly reliable coefficients have been found for various types of machine operations using the combined scores on the Hayes Pegboard and the O'Connor Finger Dexterity Test and output during the first eight weeks on the job as the criterion of success.

The Purdue Hand Precision Test consists of a piece of apparatus with a rotating clutch which uncovers a series of holes at the rate of about two per second. The applicant is asked to punch a stylus into each hole as it is uncovered without allowing the stylus to touch the side of the hole or be caught by the rotating shutter. It is particularly designed to measure precision of hand movement.

As mentioned earlier most manual ability tests involve the use of apparatus and must be administered individually. However, the first three parts of the MacQuarrie Test for Mechanical Ability, tracing, tapping and dotting, deal primarily with manual dexterity. This is a test of the paper and pencil type which is adapted to group testing.

Manual ability tests show low intercorrelations which indicates that it is unwise to predict general manual or motor performance from any one test. The motor tests used for vocational selection should measure as nearly as possible the movements required on the job. They are of use chiefly when there is a question as to a person's manual aptitude for learning an operation closely similar to the one involved in the particular test selected, or when success in a number of tests is used as an indication of manual versatility. No single test pretends to measure the complete mechanical demands of any one job. In most instances long range prediction for motor tasks has not proved satisfactory. The tests should be administered at the time of applicant selection. Since the critical score indicative of success on any given test may vary widely for similar types of work in different industries, the standards of the job in question should be checked constantly in using tests for applicant selection. Manual ability tests are of most value in selecting workers for the semi-skilled manual occupations involving manual versatility. Extensive use of the tests here described indicates they are a definite aid in placing employees who will stay on the job longer, who will be more successful and who will progress more rapidly than workers placed without the use of tests.

2. *Mechanical Ability Tests.* There are two different types of mechanical ability tests: (a) performance tests involving the use of apparatus, most of which must be administered individually, and (b) paper and pencil type tests, which are practical with large groups. The available performance type tests comprise the assembly tests, spatial form boards, cube and block construction, puzzle boxes, and the like. Since these tests differ widely in content, emphasis, extent to which they measure aptitude or familiarity, and in certain other respects, they vary in value for different jobs of placement. In the assembly test the subject is usually asked to assemble or take apart a number of mechanical gadgets.

(a) Performance Tests of Mechanical Ability. The Minnesota Mechanical Ability Tests include a battery of several tests, some of which are of the performance type. One of these, the Minnesota Assembly Test, which is a modified and lengthened form of the Stenquist Assembling Test, consists of three boxes of unassembled mechanical items which the subject is to reassemble in a given amount of time. The time for most items is adequate so that the test measures ability to assemble rather than speed. It is considered one of the most valuable tests of mechanical assembly available at the present time. It is useful primarily with adolescent boys and untrained men. Another in the battery, The Minnesota Spatial Relations Test, is also an assembly type test. It is an extension of a similar test devised by Link for selecting factory assemblers which proved too short to give satisfactory reliabilities. It is composed of a set of four standard form boards in each of which are spaces for the placing of appropriately fitting pieces. This test measures speed and accuracy in the discrimination of size and shape. It was designed to measure ability to work rapidly and accurately in performing tasks requiring some attention to spatial details. Experience and training in mechanical occupations have little influence on the results. The complete battery of Minnesota Mechanical Ability Tests is the result of one of the most elaborate investigations of tests of mechanical aptitudes as yet devised. Its use either in whole or in part will yield a measure of varied aspects of a subject's mechanical ability. These tests are at present among the most dependable performance tests for use in measuring mechanical aptitudes.

The O'Connor Wiggly-Block Test consists of nine similar pieces of wood cut with some wavy edges to be fitted together to form a solid block. It should be used in conjunction with other tests of mechanical comprehension to yield most satisfactory results. It is not recommended for general or exclusive use.

The Kent-Shakow Industrial Form Board has been found useful for measuring spatial perception and manual versatility. It is a form board which can be fitted by eight series of insets which are graduated within a suitable range of difficulty. It appears to have some value in the selection of industrial workers for tasks requiring ability to deal with complicated mechanical situations.

Miniature or jobsample, like the worksample type tests, reproduce all, or an essential sampling of the actual operations that the job itself requires. Hazards which might be involved in operating the actual machine are eliminated in constructing the apparatus. The test involves operating the miniature machine under conditions similar to the operation of the real machine. The rating of an applicant on such a test can easily be determined by comparing his score with the norms obtained from the performance of experienced and inexperienced workers. A miniature job situation enables a personnel manager to secure a sample of the quality and speed of work that an applicant is able to perform with no danger to the applicant in the sample job performance.

(b) Paper and Pencil Tests of Mechanical Ability. For purposes of preliminary appraisal, particularly of large groups of applicants, paper and pencil tests find a place on a testing program. Such tests have been designed to measure a wide range and many levels of mechanical promise, e.g., ability to think correctly about spatial relations as well as to perceive them, mechanical comprehension and mechanical information. In some of the tests the contents are all similar, the strength of only one capacity is measured.

The estimation of strength in one capacity only is the primary concern of The Bennett Test of Mechanical Comprehension, Form AA. It measures the ability of an individual to understand the operation of various physical principles from an examination of sixty drawings or schematic diagrams. A correlation of .47 has been found between scores on the test and foreman's ratings of job performance for machine operators. Its reliability is .84. The test has proved helpful for guidance and selection in work which requires a higher type of mechanical ability than that measured by most tests of mechanical aptitudes. It is not generally suitable for women, whose average score is only about two-thirds that of men. Form BB of the test measures the same type of ability as does Form AA but at a more difficult level.

The Revised Minnesota Paper Form Board Test is a revision of the original test which was developed to increase the ease and objectivity of its scoring. It estimates the candidate's ability to make fine spatial distinctions. Consequently, the value of the test depends primarily on the extent to which a demand for such ability is essential for success on the job. The problems are graded from simple problems which most industrial applicants solve successfully to problems demanding an extremely high degree of visualization. The validity of the test is based in part on the superiority of scores made by engineering groups. A multiple correlation of .57 was found for scores on a battery of tests which included the Minnesota Paper Form Board and ratings for the quality of work for power sewing machine operators. Fairly high correlations have also been found with measures of job success for can and merchandise packers, indicating that the range of usefulness of the test is not confined to strictly mechanical jobs. Other paper and pencil tests which are designed to measure the strength of a single capacity primarily are the Thurstone Mechanical Movements Test which seems to give an estimate of the speed with which mechanical problems can be understood, the N.I.I.P. Squares and the Figure Construction Tests, and the Yale University, Department of Personality Study Tests for Spatial Visualization and for Mechanical Ingenuity.

A second group of paper and pencil tests include those in which the contents of the subtests vary in an attempt to estimate a number of different capacities. Typical of these is the MacQuarrie Test for Mechanical Ability listed earlier. The first three tests measure chiefly manual dexterity while the last four give an estimate of somewhat more complex mechanical aptitudes. The value of variations in the subtest scores is lost by using only the composite score. This test is included in the Potts-Bennett battery developed to determine aptitude for nursing. The subtests are useful in predicting efficiency in some types of mechanical work. It appears to be most useful as a first rough index of mechanical ability.

The O'Rourke Mechanical Aptitude Test, Junior Grade, is chiefly of the information type. It is easily administered and is interesting to the subjects. Correlations between test scores and ratings as machinist apprentices, in school vocational classes and in vocational training courses range from .64 to .84.

The Detroit Mechanical Aptitudes Examination consists of a battery of subtests, three of which are measures of general ability, while five are tests of special ability. Since the test surveys a number of different types of performance it should be interpreted with reference to the scores on the subtests as well as the total score. Success on the test is based upon familiarity with actual tools and machines to a much greater extent than is required for the Bennett Test of Mechanical Comprehension.

The seven subtests in the N.I.I.P. Form Relations Group Test include patterns represented in bi- and tri-dimensional space. Significant correlations have been found between this test and instructors' ratings of proficiency in the trades of carpenter, electrician, fitter and smith.

A careful analysis of most of the widely used tests of the paper and pencil type reveals that the content is primarily mechanical information. The chief value of information tests for use in guidance and selection of applicants is based on the assumption that a person with a mechanical bent will in the course of his development acquire more information about tools and mechanical processes than persons not mechanically-minded. Since the correlation between mechanical information and mechanical aptitude is far from perfect, this may not be true. As in other lines an individual may be superior in his information concerning tools and the principles governing their use and very inferior in applying this information. Group tests of mechanical ability then are useful primarily in making a preliminary survey of the mechanical aptitudes of groups of subjects. They are relatively inexpensive and ordinarily easily administered and scored. They serve as a rough screening device for differentiating the most promising applicants from the most unlikely ones. They are quite reliable and preferably should be part of a battery of tests. Low to medium correlations have been found between scores on mechanical information tests and shop grades, some measures of vocational success, and assembly type tests of mechanical ability.

In general, we may safely conclude that mechanical ability tests are useful for determining the more complex mechanical aptitudes necessary for many skilled trades, whereas tests of manual ability are of value in estimating aptness in learning to make the rapid, dexterous movements of fingers and hands demanded in many semi-skilled manual jobs. One possible shortcoming of practically all mechanical ability tests as measures of the kind of intelligence needed in learning a mechanical trade results from the fact that the score is due in part to the subject's manual dexterity as well as to his mechanical insight.

Employment and personnel officers who are eager to use all techniques that may be helpful in employee selection and placement are confronted with many problems in attempting to install a testing program. Too often the program is undertaken with inadequate information and preparation, or as a result of low sales resistance. A critical and careful study of selection and placement needs, and available labor supply is essential. A person well-trained in the theory and techniques of testing should be secured to administer the program, since mechanical aptitude tests while highly valuable are complicated tools. Their use increases the responsibility of personnel men while increasing their effectiveness in selecting better workers. A careful study of the availability of suitable and valid testing devices for the particular jobs to be filled should be undertaken. It may be necessary to adapt certain tests to the peculiar needs of the particular industry. Critical scores for successful workers should be determined and the effect of experience or/and training on test results should be studied. Frequently an industry makes the error of attempting to use tests which have been found satisfactory by another firm differing widely in the particular abilities or skills needed for success. Thoughtless or unwise selection of tests will not prove a perfect answer to that most difficult of questions, how to choose the right man for the right place. Like most tools used in selection or guidance, mechanical aptitude tests have serious limitations along with their merits. Some personnel men are highly gullible with respect to tests. They accept them as infallible and as telling all about an applicant and yet tests have demonstrated no such effectiveness. The quantitative results of some tests which appear to represent numerical measures of manpower abilities, while impressive, may be unreliable and insignificant.

Although mechanical tests in conjunction with other data cannot infallibly indicate the future proficiency of an applicant, they may help to provide a reasonably accurate estimate of his probable success. Tests chosen on the basis of familiarity with the job and experience in industrial selection can, in a very short period, be set up by a person proficient in their use in such a way as to provide appreciable help in selection. However, to study and treat each one of several hundred applicants and employees as an individual requires a large, adequately-trained personnel staff since individual mechanical ability tests are always sensitive to the conditions under which they are given. Testing conditions, schedules, and purposes must be carefully standardized if reliable and valid results are to be secured.

The choice of appropriate tests depends upon a careful preliminary study of the jobs for which applicants are to be selected. This may involve observation of operators at work on the various machines, discussion with supervisors and/or talks with the operators themselves. After selecting a test the next logical step is determining its effectiveness. The validity of a test may be checked by administering it to employees of known ability. Tests which do not yield substantially higher scores for the better workers than for less efficient operators should, as a rule, be dropped. New applicants may score lower than workers already employed who possess varying degrees of experience since the effects of training are marked on certain tests. Failure in a testing program can usually be traced to inexperienced people who lack the proper background and training for determining what tests to use, how to administer and score them, and how to interpret and use the results accurately.

Data are inadequate to prove that the innate aptitude of women for all types of mechanical work is clearly inferior to men, but it would seem that the greater social pressure on boys to make use of mechanical devices does not adequately explain their superiority on several tests and in many types of work involving mechanical ability. It appears that women can be advantageously employed primarily in tasks involving light, quick dexterous movement of the hands; or light, sedentary, routine activity, i.e. for simple inspection work or as operators of simple machines.

While studies have shown that some tests may reliably measure an important aspect or aspects of mechanical work, the low intercorrelations between most tests seem to indicate that many tests have few elements in common. Thus it would be unwise for persons interested in the selection of applicants for mechanical work to choose a test at random or on the basis of its reliability alone and expect to obtain results closely similar to those that might be obtained from another test in the same general field. Until more information is available concerning the validity of tests as indicated by correlations between test scores and criteria of success on the job, vocational counselors may do well to try out a battery of two or more tests and check the value of each as experience accumulates.

ENCYCLOPEDIA OF VOCATIONAL GUIDANCE

References:

1. Bennett, G. K. and Cruikshank, R. M. *A summary of manual and mechanical ability tests.* New York: The Psychological Corporation, 1942.
2. Moore, H. *Psychology for business and industry.* New York: McGraw-Hill, 1942.
3. Tiffin, J. *Industrial psychology.* New York: Prentice-Hall, 1942.

L. G. P.

MECHANICAL APTITUDE. Mechanical Aptitude seems to consist of three relatively independent components. These are: manual dexterity, mechanical comprehension and spatial perception. On purely logical grounds it is possible to disregard the spatial and manual aspects, but in terms of popular usage and the composition of most "mechanical" jobs these factors can not be neglected.

Mechanical comprehension is a form of intelligence. It can be defined as the capacity for learning the principles of operation of machines and devices. Persons possessing high degrees of this aptitude are likely to make more than average progress in mechanical occupations and to have superior probability of success in engineering schools. Exceptionally high levels of this ability are possessed by successful inventors and machine designers.

It is well to note that the educational and vocational significance of this form of mechanical aptitude is importantly qualified by certain collateral aptitudes. For engineering school success, facility with and knowledge of mathematics is of even greater significance than mechanical comprehension. In the case of many mechanical maintenance jobs the possession of dexterity in the use of tools is essential. The mechanical draftsman needs the ability to perceive spatial relationships and a considerable degree of fine muscular co-ordination as well as some degree of mechanical understanding.

The Measurement of Mechanical Aptitude

The first important tests of mechanical aptitude were the Assembly Tests of General Mechanical Ability by J. L. Stenquist. These were developed for Army classification purposes during World War I and consist of a series of unassembled mechanical objects which the examinee is to assemble as quickly as possible. Score is a function of time and accuracy of assembly. These tests were revised in 1930 by Paterson, Elliott, Toops and Heidbreder of the University of Minnesota and are known in the revised form as the Minnesota Assembly Test. Mechanical Assembly tests appear to involve both mechanical understanding and an important element of dexterity.

Such tests have the disadvantage of requiring equipment and individual administration.

The Stenquist Mechanical Aptitude Tests, published in 1921, consist of paper booklets involving the matching of illustrations of tools or mechanical objects and the answering of questions regarding machines. A more recent test utilizing this general type of approach is the O'Rourke Mechanical Aptitude Test, published in 1939. The Stenquist and O'Rourke tests directly measure mechanical information but are presumed to reflect mechanical aptitude on the assumption that the person who has acquired the larger fund of mechanical knowledge is also the person with the greater degree of mechanical aptitude.

One of the earliest spatial relations tests was described by H. C. Link in 1919 and subsequently revised by the Minnesota group in 1930. It is called the Minnesota Spatial Relations Test and consists of four form boards containing 58 irregular cut-outs each. The time required and the errors made in filling these apertures determine the score. A related test is the Minnesota Paper Form Board, a paper and pencil test requiring the subject to fit together the components of a geometric shape. At present the multiple choice Revised Minnesota Paper Form Board by Rensis Likert and W. H. Quasha is more frequently used.

A direct approach to the understanding of mechanical principles was made in 1928 by J. W. Cox of England. Models, diagrams and questions are used to elicit explanations of the mode of operation of mechanical equipment. More recently a series of Mechanical Comprehension Tests has been prepared by G. K. Bennett and his associates. The Mechanical Comprehension Tests, like Cox's tests, measure understanding of mechanical principles, but do so by means of pictorially presented problems with multiple choice responses, thereby overcoming the subjective element of the Cox materials. The Mechanical Comprehension tests and others patterned after the originals have been widely used in industrial, scholastic, and military selection, usually with satisfactory results.

Further research on the nature of mechanical aptitude and its relationship to other abilities is needed. Only one factorial analysis in this area has come to the writer's attention. Improvements in this field can be of considerable value particularly in a technical culture.

References:

1. Allen, P., and Smith, P. The selection and training of engineering apprentices. *Human Factor,* London, 1935, 9, 63–67.

2. Bellows, R. M. The status of selection and counseling techniques for dental students. *J. consult. Psychol.*, 1940, 4, 10–15.

3. Bennett, G. K., and Cruikshank, R. M. Sex differences in the understanding of mechanical problems. *J. appl. Psychol.*, 1942, 26, 121–127.

4. ———. A summary of manual and mechanical ability tests. New York: The Psychological Corporation, 1942.

5. Bingham, W. V. *Aptitudes and aptitude testing.* New York: Harper & Bros., 1937.

6. Blum, M., and Candee, B. The selection of department store packers and wrappers with the aid of certain psychological tests. *J. appl. Psychol.*, 1941, 25, 76–85.

7. Bronner, A. F., Healy, W., Lowe, G. M., and Shimberg, M. E. *A manual of individual mental tests and testing.* Boston: Little, Brown & Co., 1927.

8. Brush, E. N. Mechanical ability as a factor in engineering aptitude. *J. appl. Psychol.*, 1941, 25, 300–312.

9. Cox, J. W. *Mechanical aptitude: its existence, nature and measurement.* London: Methuen & Co., Ltd., 1928.

10. ———. *Manual skill: its organization and development.* London: Cambridge University Press, 1934.

11. Earle, F. M. and Kilgour, J. A vocational guidance research. National Institute of Industrial Psychology, 1935. Report 6.

12. Fryer, D. *The measurement of interests.* New York: Henry Holt & Co., Inc., 1931.

13. Garrett, H. E., and Schneck, M. R. *Psychological tests, methods, and results.* New York: Harper & Bros., 1933.

14. Harrell, W. A factor analysis of mechanical ability tests. *Psychometrika*, 1940, 5, 17–33.

15. Harris, A. J. The relative significance of measures of mechanical aptitude, intelligence, and previous scholarship for predicting achievement in dental school. *J. appl. Psychol.*, 1937, 21, 513–520.

16. Harvey, O. L. Mechanical "aptitude" or mechanical "ability"?—a study in method. *J. educ. Psychol.*, 1931, 22, 517–522.

17. Hildreth, G. H. *A bibliography of mental tests and rating scales.* (2d ed.) New York: The Psychological Corporation, 1939.

18. Holcomb, G. W. and Laslett, H. R. A prognostic study of engineering aptitude. *J. appl. Psychol.*, 1932, 16, 107–116.

19. Horton, S. P. *Relationships among nineteen group tests and their validity for freshmen engineering marks.* Technical Report No. 46. Boston: Human Engineering Laboratory, Inc., 1939. (Mimeographed)

20. Jacobsen, E. E. An evaluation of certain tests in predicting mechanic learner achievement. *Educ. psychol. Meas.*, 1943, 3, 259–267.

21. Keller, F. J. and Viteles, M. S. *Vocational guidance throughout the world.* New York: Norton Pub. Co., 1937.

22. Laycock, S. R. and Hutcheon, N. B. A preliminary investigation into the problem of measuring engineering aptitude. *J. educ. Psychol.*, 1939, 33, 280–289.

23. McCauley, W. J. The tetrahedron test of power to visualize. *Engng. Educ.*, 1932, 40, 624–627.
24. Moore, H., ed. Experience with employment tests. Studies in Personnel Policy, National Industrial Conference Board, 1941, No. 32, pp. 72.
25. Morton, N. W. *Individual diagnosis: a manual for the employment office.* Montreal: McGill University, 1937.
26. Pallister, H. American psychologists judge fifty-three vocational tests. *J. appl. Psychol.*, 1936, 20, 761–768.
27. Paterson, D. G., Elliott, R. M., Anderson, L. D., Toops, H. A., and Heidbreder, E. *Minnesota mechanical ability tests.* Minneapolis: University of Minnesota Press, 1930.
28. Paterson, D. G., Schneidler, G. G., and Williamson, E. G. *Student guidance techniques.* New York: McGraw-Hill Book Co., Inc., 1938.
29. Psychological test construction and research in the Bureau of Naval Personnel: development of the basic test battery for enlisted personnel. *Psychol. Bull.*, 1945, 10, 496.
30. Quasha, W. H., and Likert, R. The revised Minnesota paper form board test. *J. educ. Psychol.*, 1937, 28, 197–204.
31. Robinson, J. B., and Bellows, R. M. Characteristics of successful dental students. *J. Amer. Assoc. Collegiate Registrars*, 1941, 16, 109–122.
32. Schultz, R. S. The relation of general intelligence, motor adaptability, and motor learning to success in dental technical courses. *Psychol. Clin.*, 1932, 21, 226–234.
33. Seashore, R. H. Work methods: a neglected factor underlying individual differences. *Psychol. Rev.*, 1939, 46, 123–141.
34. ———. Experimental and theoretical analysis of fine motor skills. *Amer. J. Psychol.*, 1940, 53, 86–98.
35. Shuman, J. T. The value of aptitude tests for factory workers in the aircraft engine and propeller industries. *J. appl. Psychol.*, 1945, 29, 156–160; 185–190.
36. Thorndike, E. L., and associates. *Prediction of vocational success.* New York: The Commonwealth Fund, 1934.
37. Traxler, A. E. Correlations between "mechanical aptitude" and "mechanical comprehension" scores. *Occupations*, 1943, 22, 42–46.
38. Viteles, M. S. *Industrial psychology.* New York: Norton Pub. Co., 1932.
39. Wang, C. K. A. *An annotated bibliography of mental tests and scales.* Vol. I. Peiping: Catholic University Press, 1939.
40. Young, H. *Hugh Young: a surgeon's autobiography.* New York: Harcourt, Brace & Co., Inc., 1940. Cf. pp. 529–530.
41. Zyve, D. L. *Stanford scientific aptitude test. Explanatory booklet.* Stanford University: Stanford University Press, 1929.

G. K. B.

MECHANICAL TESTS

Bennett Mechanical Comprehension Tests. This test is designed to measure the capacity of an individual to understand various types of physical and mechanical relationships. This type of ability is important in physics courses, many trade school courses, and in engineering schools. Form AA of this test is suitable for use with male students in high school or trade school. Form BB is suitable for use with male candidates to engineering schools, engineering students, and adult men of comparable ability and education. Form BB has been found to be approximately 12 points more difficult than Form AA. Form W1 is suitable for use with women since the situations presented in the problems are those they are apt to encounter. It is more difficult for women than Form AA is for men, but less difficult than Form BB. Experience and education do have an appreciable influence on scores. However, most of the problems are so presented as to require understanding of the principles involved rather than rote knowledge. No time limit is used. Ordinarily, a great majority complete the test in twenty to twenty-five minutes, and little is usually gained by allowing more than thirty minutes.

The test is available with answer sheets in either a hand-scoring or a machine-scoring form. Instructions for the machine scored answer sheets are sent with special keys. The printed key for hand-scoring, furnished as standard accessory equipment, is satisfactory for small numbers of answer sheets. The score for each person tested should be evaluated in relation to the norms for an appropriate group. Students about to leave high school may be compared with candidates for engineering school or light mechanical work, depending upon their future plans. In practically every instance, other test scores and personal data must be considered.

The self-correlation of Form AA, corrected by the Spearman-Brown formula, is .84 for a single grade (9th grade boys). Standard error of a score is 3.7 points. The self-correlation of Form BB, corrected by the Spearman-Brown formula, is .80 for a class of college freshman engineers. Standard error of a score is 4.3 points. The self-correlation of the test for a group of applicants for light mechanical work, also corrected by the Spearman-Brown formula, is .84 with the standard error of a score 4.5. Immediate readministration of the same form of the test based on several thousand cases has consistently yielded test-retest coefficients of .90 to .93. The standard error of a score on this basis is approximately 3.0. The self-correlation of Form W1, corrected by the Spearman-Brown formula, is .77 for a group of enlisted WAVES. Standard error of a score is 4.8 points. Several studies have been made with Form BB as a predictor of success at engineering type occupations with validity coefficients from .3 to .6. As these applications were of a military nature, it is impossible at this time to disclose details. It is the intention of the authors to release more data on this material whenever it is permissible.

The Publisher of the test is the Psycological Corporation, 522 Fifth Avenue, New York 18 New York.

References:

1. Bennett, G. K. *Manual of directions: Test of Mechanical Comprehension,* Form AA. New York: The Psychological Corporation, 1941. Pp. 4.
2. Bennett, G. K. and Cruikshank, R. M. Sex differences in the understanding of mechanical problems. *J. Appl. Psychol.,* 1942, 26, 121–127.
3. Bennett, G. K. and Fear, R. A. Mechanical comprehension and dexterity. *Person. J.,* 1943, 22, 12–17.
4. Moore, B. V. Analysis of results of tests administered to men in engineering defense training courses. *J. Appl. Psychol.,* 1941, 25, 619–635.
5. ———. Correlation of the Bennett Test of Mechanical Comprehension, Form AA, with success in chemistry and physics courses and with other tests. Personal communication.

G. K. B.

Case-Ruch Survey of Space Relations Ability. The authors, H. W. Case and Floyd L. Ruch, have designed an instrument which measures the ability of an individual to perceive spatial relationships among objects and their parts with speed and accuracy. Such ability is a factor of major importance in a variety of mechanical occupations, such as assembly, inspection, drafting and blueprint reading, lofting, tool and die making, etc., and the mechanical professions, architecture, design engineering and mechanical engineering.

The *Survey* comprises thirty-two items arranged in order of difficulty. Each item consists of a design to be duplicated by selection of several parts from a group of ten. Each item resembles an actual blueprint with white lines on a blue background. Experience has shown this method of presentation to be beneficial to the test situation since it tends to make the examinee feel that the test is "fair" and "practical."

This *Survey* may be applied in business, industry, and schools to select employees or applicants who have ability to deal with spatial relationships sufficiently to warrant placement, or induction for training, in mechanical jobs such as those previously mentioned.

Validity has been determined by correlation *Survey* scores with instructor's ratings of quality and quantity of production in electric, radio, auto and wood shops. The coefficients of validity ranged from

.34 in the wood and auto shops and .39 in the electric shops to .62 in the radio shop.

The coefficient of reliability, obtained from 150 cases among the stated groups by the split-halves method corrected by the Spearman-Brown formula, is .93.

For giving and scoring the test, a concise Manual of Directions provides the necessary information. Specific instructions articulated with illustrated sample problems are contained on the front cover of the *Survey* booklet. The test is practically self-administering. The time limit for the test itself is fifteen minutes.

The *Survey* may be given as a hand-scored test, or by use of a special answer sheet which may be scored either by the IBM test scoring machine, or by the use of a set of special hand-scoring stencils. The scoring is completely objective and easily accomplished.

This *Survey* was standardized on 1,000 adults of both sexes whose ages ranged from sixteen to fifty years. The persons selected represented a random sampling of a cross section of the general population. The norms are presented in percentiles for interpretation of the raw scores.

This *Survey* is published by the California Test Bureau, 5916 Hollywood Blvd., Los Angeles 28, California.

W. W. C.

Crawford Spatial Relations Test.   In the author's words, "This test measures the ability to rapidly assemble a described circular disc form on an irregular base plate from nine different blocks which fit together on the plate in only one possible way. This test is probably predictive of ability to grasp tridimensional, spatial, or structural relationships, such as commonly confront the draftsman."

The test is well constructed, conveniently designed for carrying and easy demonstration. It must be individually administered and the estimated time is about five minutes per person. There is no reason why a trained clerical worker could not administer and score this test, although the establishment of critical scores and interpretation of test material require a trained psychometrist.

The standardization group is composed of 346 Employable, Industrial-Technical, male applicants tested at the United States Employment office in Pittsburgh. Norms are given in Standard Scores and in Percentiles.

The author of the test reports,[1] validity information drawn from the standardization group in which small samples of design draftsmen, (N = 29) and detailers, (N = 19) had mean scores at the 92nd percentile and 80th percentile, respectively, of the total male industrial technical population. In another study,[3] of a post-high school group enrolling in a course in machine design and detail drafting under the engineering defense training program at the Carnegie Institute of Technology, a regression equation between the Crawford Spatial Relations Test, and final marks was .410, standard error of estimate, 1.11. When combined with scores on the Minnesota Paper Form Board, revised form AA, a regression equation of .565 with a standard error of estimate of .99 resulted. Tables are included in this study to facilitate the use of raw scores from tests in various combinations and the author gives the opinion that the tables may be applied to other industrial and school situations where prediction of mechanical drafting aptitude is desired. Relationship between the Minnesota Paper Form Board and the Crawford Spatial Relations Test is reported as .258, (N = 208). When scores on the language manipulation part of the Carnegie Mental Ability Test were held constant, only a small decrease, (to .393) from the original correlation of .410 between the Crawford Spatial Relations Test and final marks was noted, indicating the relative independence of the Spatial Relations Test and verbal intelligence.

Another study [1] of high school boys reports the following correlations:

Teachers ratings in mathematics versus test form 1: (N = 48) .59 ± .06.

Teachers ratings degree of drafting insight test V. form 1: (N = 39) .91 .02.

Otis I.Q. V. Crawford Spatial Relations, (N = 39) .04 .11.

Reported reliability is .89 .02 (N = 62 cases) between form 1 and 2 administered three weeks later. SD (mean dist.) 4.6 sec.

This test is published by The Psychological Corporation, 522 5th Ave., New York 18, N. Y.

References:

1. Crawford, J. E. A test for tridimensional structural visualization. *The Journal of Applied Psychology,* 1940, 24, 482–492.
2. ———. *Measurement of some factors upon which is based achievement in machine detail drafting.* Doctoral dissertation, University of Pittsburgh, 1941.
3. ———. Spatial perception tests for determining drafting aptitude. *Industrial Arts and Vocational Education,* 1942, 31, 10–12.
4. Rusmore, J. T. Comparison of an "industrial" problem solving task and an assembly task. *The Journal of Applied Psychology,* 1944, 28, 129–131.

R. M. O'N

Detroit Mechanical Aptitudes Examination, Form A. This is a group paper and pencil test designed to measure mechanical aptitude. Its principal applicability is for school children although norms are given from 8–21 years. It is well printed, easily scored. There has been no adaptation for machine or answer sheet scoring. It was originally published in 1928 when a separate edition was released for boys and girls. A revised manual dated September 1939 reports that separate forms are not considered necessary. The time limit for the battery is 30 minutes, scoring time about 3 minutes per test. The test consists of 8 sub-tests:

	Reported Reliability:
Description	
1. Identification of tools	.778
2. "X"ing circles, (motor speed and precision)	.571
3. Discrimination of sizes	.578
4. Arithmetic	.768
5. Disarranged pictures	.875
6. General information, (tools materials-foods)	.817
7. Pulleys test	.694
8. Classification, (letter-digit substitution)	.701

P.E. of reliability coefficients above range from .01 to .03.

The test was standardized on 10,000 school children and age, grade, and letter ratings are given for each sub-test, and total score. The sub-tests were grouped into these headings: Motor Information, (tests 1, 6,) Motor Skills, (tests 2, 8,) Visual Imagery, (tests 3, 5, 7,) Educational, (test 4,) and separate norms are reported for these groups. No information is given as to the method used in the grouping. It is suggested that a Mechanical Aptitude Quotient be calculated by dividing the Mechanical Age by chronological age. The meaning of the questionable concept of M.A.Q. is not clearly discernible from the manual.

No validity information is given in the 1939 form of the manual, but examination of the original (1928) manual reveals relationship of .64 between shop grades and the earlier form of the test. A correlation of .652 between the Detroit Mechanical Aptitudes Test, form A and the Detroit Advanced Intelligence Test is reported in the 1939 manual.

Test-retest reliability with a time interval of six weeks (N= 259) is reported as .898 ± .01.

The publisher is Public School Publishing Company, Bloomington, Illinois. Tests may also be purchased from The Psychological Corporation, 522 Fifth Avenue, New York 18, N. Y.

Reference:

1. Baker, H. J. A mechanical aptitude test. *Detroit Educational Bulletin,* 1929, 12, 5–6.

R. M. O'N.

Kelley Constructive Ability Test. This test was devised by Truman L. Kelley to measure creative tendencies as expressed in connection with manual manipulation and constructive activities. The material used consists of building blocks, wooden wheels and rods, including odd pieces which require a certain ingenuity to utilize to advantage. The test is administered to individuals singly or to a small number of pupils from elementary to junior high school levels working in separate booths so that a pupil does not give or get a suggestion from any other pupil.

The performance record provides for running notes covering number of constructions attempted, time on each, purposes, persistence of purposes, symmetry, nature of interest, and merit. The merit score for each structure built is obtained by comparison of the structure with stereoscopic photographs arranged according to judged merit in three scales, one of vehicles, one of buildings, and one of things with moving parts including airplanes.

No reliability coefficient is given, but the reliability of scoring by means of the stereoscopic scales is .85.

Tentative age norms of merit scores from primary to adult levels are reported in Truman L. Kelley, "A Constructive Ability Test," *Journal of Educational Psychology,* January, 1916.

This test is handled by C. H. Stoelting Company.

T. L. K.

MacQuarrie Test for Mechanical Ability. This test, devised by T. W. MacQuarrie, is a practical instrument of measurement for estimating mechanical ability. It is intended to satisfy the demand for a standard performance test which would supply reliable indications of mechanical ability. Hence, the main purpose of this test is to provide impersonal, objective data that indicate the relative extent to which a person possesses those native abilities which may be related to, or determine, his success in mechanical pursuits. Consequently, these data may be used effectively in counseling and guidance or in selection and placement.

This test supplies the need for a standard piece of work requiring mechanical ability, manipulative skills, recognition of space relationships, speed, muscular control, sharpness of vision, etc.—accomplishments generally associated with the mechanical trades.

Seven sub-tests provide objective data definitely related to accomplishments in an extensive variety of jobs and trades ranging from the highly skilled trade of the tool and diemaker to the relatively unskilled but highly specialized machine operator or assembly line worker. A significant variety of job-aptitude patterns has been constructed from these sub-test data during twenty years' use in the measurement of the aptitudes of both sexes and ranging in age from ten years to adults.

The instrument can be given easily either to an individual or a group in a short period of time. The only materials required are the test booklet and a pencil of medium hardness. The number tested at one time is limited only by the facilities of the place of examination. People of practically all ages, girls and women as well as men and boys, can take this test. All who take the test find it interesting and stimulating. A comprehensive manual provides specific directions for giving the entire battery either as a group or as an individual test. The highly objective test results are easily scored.

The use of this test over an extended period of years has produced considerable statistical evidence to show that it is a satisfactory measure of mechanical ability; viz, eye-hand coordination, speed of finger movement, and facility in handling spatial relationships.

Norms have been established for ages from ten to adult. About one thousand cases, mostly school and college students, were used to compute the norms for the original edition. The revised edition supplies a table of percentile norms for male and female adults. These norms, based on two thousand cases, provide an opportunity for accurate analysis of each sub-test without reference to any other part of the entire battery. The results from a single sub-test have been found to be more predictive of ability in some specific occupations than those of the entire series of tests.

The publisher of this test is the California Test Bureau, 5916 Hollywood Boulevard, Los Angeles 28, California.

References:

1. Harrell, W. and Faubion, R. *Journal of Consulting Psychology,* May, 1940, May, 1941.
2. Journal of Personnel Research, January, 1927.
3. Ruch, F. *How to use employment tests.* Los Angeles: California Test Bureau, 1943.
4. Stead, Shartle and Associates. *Occupational counseling techniques.* New York: American Book Co., 1940.

W. W. C.

Mellenbruch Mechanical Aptitude Test for Men and Women (Forms A and B). The Mellenbruch Mechanical Aptitude Test for Men and Women is standardized in two equivalent forms and is intended as a prognostic and screening device. It represents an attempt to measure mechanical trainability, hence is a test of mechanical "capacity" rather than mechanical "experience." Being a test of aptitude or capacity, only those items are used which fall within the realm of common experience. Furthermore, being a mechanical aptitude test, the items selected involve "things," sampling "object-mindedness" rather than concepts which would sample "idea-mindedness." The test thus seeks to measure a degree of "at-homeness" in the sphere of objects and mechanical devices.

The following fundamental assumption underlies the test: Persons who are mechanically inclined are actively interested in a wide variety of objects, machines, devices and gadgets, and they are so definitely interested in these "things" that they rather naturally give attention to their identity, uses, parts, and relationships. An adequate and proper sampling of one's recognition of common objects and devices or their obvious parts, independent of cues resulting from similarity in size or shape, should give us an index of one's mechanical inclination and hence his or her mechanical trainability.

The test was developed by actual experimental use. Altogether some 425 pairs of items were made up in various combinations to form tests of 100 pairs of items each. These were then given to about a thousand men and women mechanical workers and trainees in shops and in shop training schools. The results from these preliminary testings served as a basis for a careful analysis of the items. Only those items were retained which bore a rather high relation to rankings of workers and trainees as indicated by success on the job or in the training programs. In addition, items were rejected or revised which unduly favored or penalized either the men or the women. In this way, items for the test were selected which by actual practice seemed best to give the desired results.

The Mellenbruch Mechanical Aptitude Test is practically self-administering, requiring only the reading of simple directions, and has an overall time limit of thirty-five minutes. Through the use of two extra lettered items on each page, and also by avoiding cues in terms of size or shape, the possibility of guessing and chance success are reduced to a minimum. It is quickly and objectively scored, the same key being used for both forms.

The reliability of the test is indicated by the following correlations:

Odd items—even items .... .88   N=550
Upper half—lower half of items on each
    page .... .82   N=482
Form A and Form B .... .87+   N=450

The validity of the test as indicated by correlations between test scores and other criteria is as follows:

Test scores—Teacher rating (Engineering-
    drawing women) .... r=.59 N= 57
Test score—Mechanical activities (general
    public) .... r=.60 N=430
Test score—Mechanical ratings (Air Force
    officers) .... r=.50 N=100
Test score—Air Force Mechanical Informa-
    tion Test (Air Force employees) ...... r=.61 N= 98

Norms for the test are based on approximately 4,000 cases, norms being provided for the following groups:

Men—General public, engineering-drawing freshmen, air-craft shopmen, and graduate mechanical engineers.
Women—General public, aircraft shop workers.
Academic—Boys, grades VI through XII.
    Girls, grades VI through XII.

As an aid in counseling and in employment involving mechanical work, the following critical scores are recommended:

Scores	*Mechanical Work Possibilities*
Under 30	None, or if necessary only the simplest tasks.
30–40	Rather simple routine mechanical work.
40–55	Complex though somewhat routine work.
55 and above	Complex mechanical work involving ingenuity, foresight, and resourcefulness in proportion to the extent that their score exceeds this amount.

Publisher

Science Research Associates, 228 South Wabash Avenue, Chicago, Illinois.

P. L. M.

Miller Survey of Mechanical Insight. The author, D. R. Miller, Psychology Department, Stanford University, of this instrument has provided a scientific instrument which is objective, and affords a new approach to the measurement of aptitude for dealing with the many types of mechanical problems involved in jobs requiring the operation, maintenance, repair, or design of various kinds of machinery.

The *Survey* is composed of thirty-five problems presented in multiple choice situations and arranged in order of difficulty. Samplings of twenty-five different elements of mechanics which comprise about three-fourths of the recognized elements are included. All of the items of the test are in accord with accepted principles of mechanics.

The *Survey* is designed for use at high school and adult levels for the selection of those individuals from the general population who have aptitude sufficient to justify their enrollment as trainees or employees in various mechanical occupations.

A brief, concise Manual of Directions supplies pertinent information and definite instructions with well-illustrated sample problems. The test is practically self-administering. The time limit for the test itself is thirty minutes. The *Survey* may be administered as the usual hand-scored test, or by the use of a special answer sheet which may be scored either by the I.B.M. test scoring machine or by the use of a set of special hand-scoring stencils. The scoring is completely objective and easily accomplished when the specific directions furnished in the Manual (and on the scoring stencils) are followed.

The *Survey* was standardized on a sample of a cross-section of the general population which included subjects from various mechanical trades, art trades, miscellaneous non-mechanical jobs, mechanical and non-mechanical night trade courses, and aircraft loftsmen and engineers. The reliability coefficient of the Survey, which was obtained with 250 male and female cases by the split-halves method corrected by the Spearman-Brown formula, is .88.

Based on present cases, data obtained when the *Survey* was used in various mechanical occupations show a range of scores varying from the 70th to the 99th percentiles. Individuals from the general population at or above the 85th percentile would be acceptable as trainees even with relation to others in advanced mechanical and engineering fields. A simple correlation secured between test results and efficiency ratings of postage meter repair workers was .47.

Percentile norms are provided in the Manual of Directions for interpretation of the raw scores. A method is indicated in the Manual whereby four types of examinees can be identified; viz., the fast and accurate, the fast and inaccurate, the slow and accurate, and the slow and inaccurate.

The *Survey* is published by the California Test Bureau, 5916 Hollywood Blvd., Los Angeles 28, California.

W. W. C.

Miller Survey of Object Visualization.   This test, devised by D. R. Miller, Psychology Department, Stanford University, requires the examinee to predict how an object will look when its shape and position are changed. Two and three dimensional objects are involved. The ability to perceive spatial relationships is a vital necessity in understanding construction projects and solving mechanical problems. Such aptitude and ability is necessary to success in various jobs such as draftsman, engineer, and loftsman; machinist, maintenance mechanic, and related occupations; also in the commercial and fine arts.

The *Survey* consists of forty-four problems, presented in multiple-choice situations and arranged in order of difficulty. The instrument is a test of aptitude and ability rather than of achievement, in order that it may be applied to the general population for predictive and selective purposes. Like the *Survey of Mechanical Insight* by the same author, it does not require motor coordination, hence it is more objective and specific than other similar tests in this field.

The *Survey* is devised for use at the adolescent or adult level for the selection of those persons from the general population who have aptitude and ability sufficient to indicate enrollment as trainees in mechanical occupations involving the ability to visualize an object in terms of its parts in different positions.

A brief, concise Manual of Directions provides the necessary information for giving the test. Definite directions articulated with illustrated sample problems are supplied on the test booklet. The test is practically self-administering. The time limit for the test itself is twenty-five minutes.

This *Survey* may be administered as the usual hand-scored test, or by the use of a special answer sheet which may be scored either by the IBM test scoring machine, or by use of a set of special hand-scoring stencils. The scoring is completely objective and easily accomplished.

The *Survey* was standardized on a sampling of a cross-section of the general population which included subjects from various mechanical trades, art trades, and miscellaneous non-mechanical jobs, night trade courses for the above trade or job groups, and aircraft loftsmen and engineers. The reliability coefficient obtained with 266 male and female cases by the split-halves method corrected by the Spearman-Brown formula is .91.

Data secured when this *Survey* was applied in various mechanical occupations show that individuals whose scores are at or above the 85th percentile would be acceptable as trainees even with relation to others in mechanical and engineering fields.

The *Survey* has validity comparable with that of other well-known tests in this field of mechanical ability.

Percentile norms are provided in the Manual of Directions for interpretation of the raw scores. Instructions in the Manual indicate a method whereby four types of examinees can be identified; viz., the fast and accurate, the fast and inaccurate, the slow and accurate, and the slow and inaccurate.

The Survey of Object Visualization is published by the California Test Bureau, 5916 Hollywood Blvd., Los Angeles 28, California.

W. W. C.

Minnesota Assembly Test.   This test is one of the outcomes of a four-year research project with the purpose of discovering and measuring mechanical ability which was organized in 1923 at the University of Minnesota. The test was developed as a revision of the Stenquist Mechanical Assembly Test by D. G. Paterson, R. M. Elliott, L. D. Anderson, H. A. Toops, and Edna Heidbreder. Principal procedures in revision were lengthening and modification of scoring. It was designed to measure mechanical ability of junior high school boys. The original publication describing it appeared in 1930 (3).

The test consists of three boxes containing parts of mechanical contrivances which are to be assembled. Examples of these articles are a bicycle bell, safety razor, monkey wrench, and push button door bell. Boxes A and B each contain 10 such articles, and box C contains 16. Three of these 36 items were omitted from a later revision. A short form consisting of boxes 1 and 2 is also available. These boxes are not the same as A and B.

The test may be given individually or as a group test. Time limits for each article are established, but these are sufficiently long so that the test may be considered one of power rather than speed. When full time is allowed or required, about one hour is needed for its administration. Degree of success in assembling each article is scored on a 10-point scale. Training and experience are required for using the scoring scale, but full directions are given in the examiner's manual.

Norms are provided by the authors (3, pp. 345-349) for boys at age levels from 11 through 21 years. There are also norms for boys and girls from the seventh grade through high school, for men in an engineering college, and arts college men and women. There are also norms for occupational groups. Only when mechanical training and experience are similar to that of boys of junior high school age may the scores be interpreted as indicative of aptitude rather than experience with such materials.

Validity coefficients have been obtained which compare quite favorably with those found for intelligence tests. The authors found a correlation (corrected for attenuation) of .63 between scores on this test (long form) and the quality of shop work done by 100 seventh and eighth grade boys (3, p. 206). Differential mean occupational scores are also evidence for its validity. Higher validity coefficients were obtained when a battery of mechanical tests, including this assembly test, was used.

Using data from the same sample of junior high school boys, an odd-even reliability of .94 was obtained. Reliability of the test when used with adults is considerably lower, so that only marked differences in performance are significant.

The authors found that, in the same group of 100 boys, the correlation between the Assembly Test and Otis I.Q. was .06, indicating that the test measures something quite different from academic intelligence.

The test is distributed by the Marietta Apparatus Company, Marietta, Ohio.

References:

1. Green, H. J., Berman, I. R., Paterson, D. G., and Trabue, M. R. *A manual of selected occupational tests for use in public employment offices.* Minneapolis: University of Minnesota Press, 1933. (Bulletins of the Employment Stabilization Research Institute, Vol. 2, No. 3.)
2. Paterson, D. G. (Ed.) *Research studies in individual diagnosis.* Minneapolis: University of Minnesota Press, 1934. (Bulletins of the Employment Stabilization Research Institute, Vol. 3, No. 4.)
3. Paterson, D. G., Elliott, R. M., Anderson, L. D., Toops, H. A., and Heidbreder, E. *Minnesota Mechanical Ability Tests.* Minneapolis: University of Minnesota Press, 1930.
4. Dvorak, B. J. *Differential Occupational Ability Patterns.* Minneapolis: University of Minnesota Press, 1935. (Bulletins of the Employment Stabilization Research Institute, Vol. 3, No. 8.)

S. S. M.

Minnesota Paper Form Board. (Revised by R. Likert and W. H. Quasha.) The Revised Minnesota Paper Form Board is an adaptation of the Geometrical Construction Test in the Army Beta and a modification of the Minnesota Mechanical Ability Tests developed by Patterson, Elliott, Anderson, Toops, Heidbreder at the University of Minnesota in 1930. It is designed to measure the ability to discriminate geometrical forms in 2 dimensional space perception and to measure the ability to manipulate such figures mentally.[2]

It was revised in 1934 by R. Likert and W. H. Quasha. It is a group paper and pencil test consisting of two forms, AA and BB, each with 64 items. The task is to find which one of 5 figures when placed together represents the forms. It is suitable for elementary school pupils up to adults.

The directions for administration and for scoring present no difficulties since they have been simplified in this revision and are available in the Manual of Directions along with percentile norms. Practice problems have been added. The format is such that examinees cannot start before the signal is given and cheating is minimized.

Scoring is simple and is accomplished by means of a key. The score is the number of correct responses minus 1/5 the number wrong. Omissions are not counted. The standard time limit is 20 minutes although 14 and 25 minute norms are available.

Norms have been established for both Form AA and BB, male and female and for various age groups 9 up to and including adults. The norms are established for Elementary public school pupils, high school graduates, liberal arts college students and Engineering students. Norms were established from sample applicants for a technical drawing course.

Reliability was achieved by the retest method. With the single series of tests the coefficient of reliability is + .85 but with both series the coefficient of reliability is + .92. It is therefore desirable to administer both series.

Validity was established by correlation with such criterion of mechanical ability as the Minnesota Spatial Relations Test + .84. The Minnesota Paper Form Board was the only test of all the Minnesota Mechanical Ability Battery of Tests to give a satisfactory correlation with a criterion of mechanical ability. The raw correlation is + .52 but corrected for attenuation it is + .61 between the Minnesota Paper Form Board Test and the quality criterion of mechanical ability. Further evidence of validity is noted in the fact that students of engineering and allied fields scored higher than students of non-mechanical groups.[1]

Otis found a multiple correlation of + .57 with the quality work of power sewing machine operators.

Correlations are relatively high and positive between scores on the test and success in Mechanical Drawing + .49 and between scores of the test and descriptive Geometry + .32. In a recent experiment mechanical ability was correlated with machine detail drafting as a criterion. The following conclusion was reached: "Of the form tests in the final battery The (Revised) Minnesota Paper Form Board Test is the best single test upon which to estimate final marks in such a course." (Manual of Directions.)

The evidence accumulated thus far appears to indicate as with the Minnesota Spatial Relations Test that high scores on this test are predictive of probable success,

1. in vocational courses of mechanical drawing and descriptive geometry.
2. in mechanical occupations, and
3. in engineering.

This test in conjunction with the Minnesota Spatial Relations Test and O'Rourke Mechanical Aptitude Test may confidently be used by vocational guidance counselors as indicative of possible success in measuring mechanical aptitude calling for discrimination of spatial perception.

Distribution of this test is by the Psychological Corporation, 522 Fifth Avenue, New York City, Series AA and BB.

References:

1. Bingham, W. V. *Aptitudes and aptitude testing.* New York: Harper and Brothers, 1937, pp. 312–314.
2. Garrett, H. E. and Schneck, M. R. Psychological tests, methods and results. New York: Harper and Brothers, 1933, pp. 84–86.
3. Greene, E. B. *Measurements of human behavior.* New York: Odyssey Press Publishers, 1941, 356–357.
4. Paterson, D. G., Elliott, R. M., Anderson, L. D., Toops, H. A., Heidbreder, E. *Minnesota Mechanical Ability Tests.* Minneapolis: University of Minnesota Press, 1930.
5. Tiffin, J. *Industrial Psychology.* New York: Prentice Hall, Inc., 1943, pp. 66–74.

P. K. G.

Minnesota Rate of Manipulation Test. The *Minnesota Rate of Manipulation Test* is designed to measure quickness of muscular motion. "Quick as a flash," "quick as lightning," "quick as a wink," "slow as molasses in January," "quick as a cat," are phrases describing this trait. It refers to sheer muscular reaction time. The Germans have a word for it in "flink." It is an adjective, and its comparison is, positive "flink," comparative, "flinker," superlative, "flinkste." This word is specific in its application to sheer quickness of action or motion, and it does not involve other factors or conditions as do such words as speed, quick, fast, rapid, rate etc.

Quickness of movement is a unique trait primarily, improvable only to a very limited extent. If speed were improvable, it would be a great boon to horse racing, and certainly industry could profit immensely by it if speed could be acquired by some over-the-counter method. Because the test is so simple and elementary, and because speed is a unique trait, it is possible for the individual to make his quickest performance after a practice trial. It is very little subject to practice effect. Errors of measurement are very small. The probable error for the hand speed test is 2.8 seconds in comparison with the mean score of 233 seconds, and for the finger speed test the probable error is 2.7 seconds in comparison with the mean score of 192 seconds, which would make the error of measurement less than one-fourth of the standard deviation for adult workers.

When a worker improves his production, it is not because he has miraculously acquired capacity for quicker motion. Time and motion studies, improving technic and technique, eliminating of unnecessary movements, etc. are responsible for the increase.

In employment, both shop and office, rapid use of hands and fingers in operations and in handling of tools and materials and apparatus, is such an important factor, that a worker's success is largely dependent upon the speed at which he can work. The following table arrays this idea.

SCORE IMPLICATIONS

Percent Placement 10% is one Q deviation	Significance
Above 75% placement $+3.5$ Q to $+5$ Q	Extremely rapid. Unusually gifted in speed trait.
60 to 75 $+2$ Q to $+3.5$ Q	Very rapid. Will probably do well in work requiring speed.
50 to 60 $+1$ Q to $+2$ Q	Upper average speed. Can probably keep up.
Median	
40 to 50 -1 Q to -2 Q	Lower average speed. Should seek employment in work where speed is a minor factor.
25 to 40 -2 Q to -3.5 Q	Very slow speed. Should work in occupation where speed is not a factor.
Below 25 -3.5 Q to -5 Q	Extremely slow. Unusually lacking in speed trait.

Validity has been established by correlation between test scores and factory rating after four months of employment. The factory rating was determined by three foremen sitting in session for that purpose, using a rating scale devised for it. The *Minnesota Rate of Manipulation Test* is one of a battery of ten items in a testing program for testing factory applicants. The correlation between test scores and factory rating is 81, and the correlation between speed scores and the average of the rest of the battery is 31. There is general satisfaction on the part of the employers in seeing test implications materialize into actual production after several years of trial. Results are readily discernible in production records.

It requires about 15 minutes to give the test. It may be given to small groups. Scoring is instantaneous.

Publishers: Educational Test Bureau, Minneapolis, Minnesota.

References:

1. Bingham, W. V. *Aptitudes and aptitude testing.* New York: Harper and Bros., 1937, pp. 278–281.
2. Green, H. J., Berman, I. R., Paterson, D. G., and Trabue, M. R. *A manual of selected occupational ability tests.* Minneapolis: University of Minnesota Press, 1933.
3. Paterson, D. G., Elliot, R. M., Anderson, L. D., Toops, H. A., Heidbreder, E. *Minnesota mechanical ability tests.* Minneapolis: University of Minnesota Press, 1930, pp. 314–327.
4. Paterson, D. G., Schneidler, G. C., and Williamson, E. G. *Student guidance techniques.* New York: McGraw-Hill Book Co., 1938, pp. 240–242.
5. Ruch, G. M. and Segal, D. *Minimum essentials of the individual inventory in guidance.* U. S. Office of Education, Vocational Bulletin No. 202, p. 57. Washington: Government Printing Office.
6. Schieffelin, B. and Schwesinger, G. *Mental traits and heredity.* New York: Galton Publishing Co., pp. 216–217.
7. Viteles, M. S. and Thompson, A. S. *Mental measurements year book, 1940.* Ed. by O. Buros, p. 438 ff.

W. A. Z.

Minnesota Spatial Relations Test. This test of mechanical aptitude is a modification and extension of Link's test. It was developed by M. R. Trabue, D. G. Patterson and others at the University of Minnesota Employment Stabilization Research Institute in 1930. It is one of several tests developed and used jointly for guidance in the choice of vocational courses as well as counseling in employment placement. It is especially designed to measure speed and accuracy in discriminating odd sizes and shapes.[3]

There are four Form Boards A, B, C, D, each constructed with 58 pieces of different odd sized and shaped figures. The task is to fit each of the pieces into like depressions in the boards.

This test is an individual test to be administered only as such. It is *not* a group test. It is suitable for testing adults and pupils of the elementary and secondary school levels. It was standardized on junior high school boys.

The directions for administration and for scoring present no difficulties. They are found along with percentile norms and letter ratings in the manual of directions. The Form Boards are presented alphabetically. They were constructed in such a manner that Form Boards A and B are presented together and Form Boards C and D follow together.

The scoring is quite simple. The number of seconds taken to fill each board is noted. The number of errors, that is, the number of times the subject tries to place a block in the wrong hole is noted too. Filling the board takes from 15 to 45 minutes. A rest of 30 seconds is recommended and only one trial is given with each board. The score of the total number of seconds required to complete all four form boards is combined and compared as well as the error score to the norms. They are for Men and Women and include elementary and secondary school pupils.[1]

Reliability was achieved by lengthening the test about eight times and by retest on a sample of 217 boys of junior high school level and high school boys. The coefficient of Reliability is + .84.[2]

There is a high Validity correlation with the Minnesota Paper Form Board + .72. This is most probably due to the similarity between these two tests in complex spatial relationships. By using Toops multiple ratio technique to form a battery of tests a correlation of + .60 with the criterion was established. This is a satisfactory index of validity.[3]

This test purports to measure keen perception of spatial relationships. A high score may be interpreted therefore as indicative of the necessary aptitude for success in such occupations as "sculptors, architects, designers, dressmakers, pattern makers, sheet metal workers, engineers, dentists, surgeons, layout men, sorters, auto mechanics."

This test may be used as an aid to:

1. ascertain an individual's aptitude for the above mentioned occupations.
2. indicate probable success in a course of training or apprenticeship for such an occupation.

3. indicate probable success in school subjects in which ability to perceive size and shape is a known asset, as geometry, machine design.[1]

Counselors should note that a more valid interpretation may be arrived at if it is remembered that the Minnesota Spatial Relations Test be given as part of a battery of tests which might well include the Revised Minnesota Paper Form Board Test and O'Rourke's Mechanical Aptitude Test.

The Minnesota Spatial Relations Test provides the examiner with excellent opportunities for observation of personality traits and or behavior patterns indicative of the individual's methods of attack of a problem, of his persistence and of his emotional control.

The distributor of this test is the Educational Test Bureau, Minneapolis, Minnesota.

References:

1. Bingham, W. V. *Aptitudes and aptitude testing.* New York: Harper and Brothers, 1937, pp. 309–311.
2. Garrett, H. E. and Schneck, M. R. *Psychological tests, methods and results.* New York: Harper and Brothers, 1933, pp. 81–82, 84.
3. Greene, E. B. *Measurement of Human Behavior.* New York: Odyssey Press, 1941, pp. 359–360.
4. Patterson, D. G., Elliott, R. M., Anderson, L. D., Toops, H. A., Heidbreder, E. *Minnesota Mechanical Ability Tests.* Minneapolis: University of Minnesota Press, 1930.

P. K. G.

O'Connor Finger Dexterity Test. The Human Engineering Laboratory defines *Finger Dexterity* as an inherent nimbleness of the fingers in performing delicate operations. The Laboratory has found success in a manipulative job to be primarily dependent upon aptitude rather than acquired skill.

Skill evolves from the repetition of a task. It is the increment by which, with no change in method, a second, third, fourth, or any subsequent trial surpasses the first in either speed or accuracy. Performance on the finger-dexterity test betters with repetition until it reaches a learning plateau beyond which even considerable practice makes comparatively little alteration. But, although skill improves execution, a difference in aptitude persists even after many trials.

Such experiments as the Laboratory has completed indicate that an equal number of repetitions does not change the original ratio of performance between two persons. More specifically, if two persons differ by, for instance, 10 per cent in their initial times, they still differ by the same 10 per cent after two, three, four, or more trials. Both improve, but the ratio of performance remains the same. With equal time devoted to practice, the grade A person (one scoring in the upper quartile) outstrips the grade D, for the grade A person performs each repetition in less time and therefore in any given period more frequently than the grade D. Given equal practice, as measured by the number of repetitions of a task, ratio of performance remains unchanged. Final excellence in performing a manipulative task demands a combination of aptitude and acquired skill.

The aptitude for finger dexterity ceases to increase beyond about the age of twenty-two; when the fiftieth percentile norms for men or women at each age beyond the age of twenty-two are compared there is no change. Women score significantly higher than men. Twenty per cent of women, those beyond the eightieth percentile, score as high as the top 5 per cent of men; those scoring above the ninety-fifth percentile. Forty-two per cent of women score as high as the top 25 per cent of men: nearly 70 per cent of women score as high as the top 50 per cent of men.

The finger-dexterity board consists of a metal board with one hundred holes in ten rows of ten holes each at one end and a shallow tray at the other. In this tray are piled inch-long metal pins. Originally examinees were asked to take the pins from the tray one at a time and place each pin in one of the drilled holes. But when the data had been accumulated and studied, it was found that this method was not sufficiently discriminative. After experimentation, it was found that more accurate results were obtained by placing three pins at a time in each of the drilled holes. At present, the examinee is asked to take the pins from the tray three at a time, and to place three pins in each one of the holes as rapidly as possible. The reliability of the form of the test currently in use is 0.78.

For further discussion see:

"Too-Many-Aptitude Woman" by Johnson O'Connor
Published 1941.

P. P. A.

O'Connor Structural Visualization Test. Structural Visualization is the term employed by The Human Engineering Laboratory for the aptitude for three-dimensional visualization found usually to be a trait with which persons are born who find success and happiness in fields of engineering, the exact sciences, architecture, medical professions, many structural fields.

The equipment for measuring structural visualization consists of a block of wood which has been cut into three dimensional wiggly sections. The examinee is presented the assembled block, and explanations of the ways in which it is cut; then it is taken apart by the administrator, so that the examinee may reassemble it as quickly as possible. Several trials are given for this worksample where factors of luck and practice are considered in computing the times for each trial. This insures a more accurate measurement than merely one trial. The Wiggly Block worksample has a reliability of 0.40 which the laboratory hopes to improve by continued research permitted by additional cases for more accurate norms.

A second worksample included in the measurement of structural visualization is a cube of twenty-seven variously painted smaller cubes to be assembled according to specific instructions. This Black Cube worksample serves as a check test which compensates to some degree for possible discrepancies in the Wiggly Block. Correlation for the Wiggly Block and the Black Cube is 0.64 which, though not perfect, allows for an indication or approximation of a person's aptitude for structural work. Other worksamples, the Pyramid and Formboard are being used developmentally as experiments in further accuracy for measuring structural visualization.

High or high average percentile scores for these worksamples indicate the possibility for success in structural work. Advice offered for various structural fields and approaches to such work depends upon the whole pattern of combined aptitudes which the Human Engineering Laboratory measures and upon the individual's personal interests and necessary specialized knowledge. If structural visualization is possessed to a high or high average rating persons may find neglect of this particular aptitude a factor in any feeling of the restlessness or discontent in their work. Conversely, there are many nonstructural fields where the lack of structural visualization is counterbalanced by abstract visualization to definite advantage where ability to cope with ideas, with more stress upon the intellectual concepts are important.

Research carried on by the Human Engineering Laboratory shows that men as a group score consistently higher in structural visualization than women. For this reason the high average rating for men starts with the fifty-first percentile; for women with the seventy-sixth percentile. The laboratory feels that structural visualization may show recessive, sex-linked characteristics and is making further study of this possibility.

For further discussion of this aptitude see:
"Structural Visualization" by Johnson O'Connor
Published 1942.

P. P. A.

O'Connor Tweezer Dexterity Test.   Tweezer dexterity statistically resembles an inherent trait. It characterizes surgeons, dentists, miniature-instrument assemblers, watchmakers, and glass blowers; anyone performing delicate operations with fine tools.

Fifteen years ago it was erroneously believed that finger-dexterity scores predicted success in any manipulative job. In administering the finger-dexterity worksample to a group of women doing miniature-instrument assembly it was proven that success at the job did not correlate with success in performing that worksample. The Laboratory then developed a test for tweezer dexterity which proved to be a statistically independent trait.

Many experiments have subsequently been made which prove the independence of the two aptitudes. In one experiment a score of factory girls tried the tweezer-dexterity test once. Half of the group, selected at random, then took the finger-dexterity test daily for ten trials, gaining thereby a significant and measurable skill in the performance. All twenty girls, the ten with finger-dexterity practice and the ten without, then repeated the tweezer-dexterity test with the result that the obvious improvement in the finger-dexterity performance failed to affect the subsequent tweezer-dexterity time. Although many factory foremen still insist that novices toil months at finger-dexterity operations before advancing, as they say, to the more intricate tweezer tasks, laboratory experiments show such preparation unavailing.

The Laboratory's original tweezer-dexterity test consisted of a metal board with a tray in one end for metal pins and one hundred rows of holes, ten holes to a row, in the other end. The examinee used tweezers to pick up the pins at random from the tray and place them in the holes. This test proved to be unreliable, as picking up pins haphazardly introduced a luck element. The present form presents the pins uniformly to each examinee.

The board now consists of one hundred holes on either side of the metal board. The holes are of such depth that the tip of each pin is exactly flush with the level of the board; countersinkings allow the top portion of each pin to be gripped by the tweezers. The pins are transferred successively from a hole on the left side of the board to the corresponding hole on the right side. The holes are spaced evenly in rows of ten so that the job of moving one pin should be practically identical with the job of moving any other pin on the board. If the worksample were of perfect reliability we should expect each examinee to move each pin across the board at exactly the same speed, so that any deviation from an examinee's own standard speed would be expected to lower the reliability of the worksample. The present reliability of the tweezer-dexterity test is 0.82.

The Laboratory has found through experimentation that the exact type of tweezer used makes a great deal of difference in scores obtained. A blunt, resilient tweezer is easier to handle in performing this task than a stiff, pointed one. A stiff tweezer introduces a larger element of fatigue in the test. There is bound to be a slight element of fatigue in a test of this sort. However, when the test is given properly, the fatigue element is offset by the practice factor.

Whereas women score considerably higher than men in finger-dexterity, men slightly excel women in tweezer-dexterity. Both aptitudes reach an adult plateau at about the age of twenty-two.

For further discussion see:
"The Too-Many-Aptitude Woman" by Johnson O'Connor
Published 1941.

P. P. A.

O'Rourke Mechanical Aptitude Test—Junior Grade. This test was constructed by Prof. L. J. O'Rourke and purports to measure mechanical perception and knowledge of a mechanical nature.

It is called a Mechanical Perception and Information Test. It is based on the premise that familiarity with tools is largely traceable to interest in mechanical devices and to an aptitude for knowledge of their correct manipulation.[1] Consequently a well selected sample of the individual's stock of information would be indicative of his mechanical aptitude.[3]

O'Rourke Mechanical Aptitude Test Junior Grade is a paper and pencil test. There are three forms A, B and C, each consisting of two parts. Part one is pictorial with twelve sets of picture items, three numbered and three lettered to be matched correctly (ex) hammer and nail, a wrench and a nut accompanied by questions asked in order to indicate to what use a tool is put (ex) "write a number or letter to show which tool in Fig. 1 you would use to tighten a nut." Part 2 consists of 60 questions and is entirely verbal. The questions are based on mechanical information presented in a multiple choice form.

The original standardization was made on 9,000 men 15 to 24 years of age of whom the majority were elementary school graduates. Some few went somewhat beyond that. A recent table is based on scores made by 70,000 workmen who applied for mechanical jobs on the Tennessee Valley Authority. Part 1 has a 30 minute limit while Part 2 has a 25 minute limit with a total administration time of 65 minutes.

Scoring is simple. One point is given for each correct answer. The final score is the number right in Part 1 plus four times the number right in Part 2. The maximum possible score is 342. The average score is 190.

Directions for administering the test are found on the test blank itself while the scoring sheet and percentile norms as well as letter ratings are available together in the one sheet. This test possesses both reliability and validity. A correlation of + .64 with ratings as machinist apprentice have been reported as well as + .84 with ratings in vocational training courses. Validity has thus been established.

The guidance counselor would do well to note the following factors. Basically this test may be called an achievement test, rather than an aptitude test, since it is a measure of the individual's knowledge and familiarity with tools and their use in work of a mechanical nature. The individual interested in tools and shopwork generally avails himself of the opportunities to better familiarize himself with the same. Therefore because of this experience the individual can obtain a more favorable score on this test. The guidance counselor is justified in using this test as an aptitude test rather than an achievement test to determine or select applicants for vocational training as well as for apprentice training.[4]

Scores made by junior high school students on the average are higher than scores made by men on T V A. Candidates for engineering training, in the vast majority, made standard scores of 6.0 or higher which is equivalent to a B+ rating. T V A mature workers averaged standard scores of 4.3 or a D+ rating. An individual who claims interest in and aptitude for work which is of an essentially mechanical nature and who shows a standard score below 5.0 equivalent to a C+ rating might well be questioned as to his possible success in a mechanical vocation. However test scores should be considered in conjunction with a well rounded out search of the examinee's educational as well as vocational experiences and opportunities.[1]

The question may arise as regards the matter of entrance standards not only among vocational and technical schools but among employers. These standards may vary in different schools as well as among different employers or different occupations. The counselor should take cognizance of these facts.

The O'Rourke Mechanical Aptitude Test plus the Revised Minnesota Paper Form Board and The Minnesota Spatial Relations Test make an excellent battery of tests with a high predictive value for measuring perception of spatial relationships.

Distributors are the Psychological Institute, 3506 Patterson

Street, N.W., Washington, D. C., and the Psychological Corporation, 522 Fifth Avenue, New York City.

References:

1. Bingham, W. V. *Aptitudes and aptitude testing.* New York: Harper
   & Brothers, 1937, pp. 318–320.
2. Greene, E. B. *Measurements of human behavior.* New York: Odyssey
   Press Publishers, 1941, pp. 354–356.
3. Patterson, D. G., Elliot, R. M., Anderson, L. D., Toops, H. A., Heidbreder, E. *Minnesota Mechanical Ability Tests.* Minneapolis: University of Minnesota Press, 1930.
4. Tiffin, J. *Industrial psychology.* New York: Prentice Hall, Inc., 1943,
   p. 66.

P. K. G.

Pennsylvania Bi-Manual Worksample.   Description of Test.—The
test consists of a board with two compartments and one hundred
holes. One compartment contains 105 $\frac{1}{4}''$ bolts and the other compartment 105 $\frac{1}{4}''$ nuts. The assembly task requires the subject to
assemble 100 bolts—one at a time—and place each assembly in one
of the holes in the board. The disassembly is the reverse operation.

The Pennsylvania Bi-Manual Worksample was developed to fill
the need in the vocational field for a test situation which would
combine certain basic elements inherent in a relatively simple work
situation. Simple tests of motor skill which tend to show native
capacity within a limited area are usually selected for their uniqueness and do not show the individual's capacity to integrate a number of these unique traits into a well organized and smooth working
pattern of performance. The assembly task of the Pennsylvania Bi-
Manual Worksample has this feature. It combines finger dexterity
of both hands, gross movements of both arms, eye-hand coordination,
bi-manual coordination, and some indication of the individual's
ability to use both hands in cooperation.

The task is sufficiently long so that qualitative observations can
be made on other aspects of the performance beside native speed and
dexterity. Certain individuals will break the Worksample into four
separate tasks, i.e., selecting the nut, selecting the bolt, turning the
bolt into the nut, placing the assembled bolt into the proper hole
in the board. Others will demonstrate levels of integration up to and
including the whole task. In a well integrated performance the
hands will work together rhythmically. Individuals who have considerable native speed, but who experience difficulty coordinating
the two hands in order to execute the precise movements required

to turn the bolt into the nut in the assembly task, will usually have higher relative scores on the disassembly where this precision is not required. Individuals who are easily distracted, or who dislike this kind of work, will give evidence of this by allowing their attention to wander.

The Worksample, as its name implies, was developed as a standard job, or a standard task. Data collected over the past few years indicate clearly its value in differentiating the good workers on manipulative tasks, similar to the way tests of general mental ability differentiate the good student from the poor student. A comparison of the distributions of the Industrial Group and the General Population, a comparison of the means of the various age groups, a comparison of the distributions of the sighted and partially sighted, etc., indicate the competitive manual ability of these groups on a standard task. Also, numerous small in-plant studies of successful workers on highly repetitive manual work have consistently yielded averages equal to a transmuted score of 6 or better when compared with the general population, and rarely do we find a single worker in these groups with a transmuted score of less than 5.

The directions for administration are accompanied by a motion analysis of the movements of the right and left hand and photographs illustrating the steps are also included.

The Worksample was standardized on 3979 unselected subjects: 1793 males and 2186 females, 16 years 0 months—39 years 11 months; 550 students, 15 years 0 months to 17 years 11 months in urban and suburban private and public schools of secondary level; 400 male and female subjects, ages 16 years 11 months to 39 years 11 months with histories of at least six months successful employment in industry at manipulative tasks. Also several groups with varying degrees of vision.

Reliability was found to be .90 for a group of vocational school boys with the split halves method, and when corrected for the whole task, .95.

Sex Differences

Men are consistently superior on the assembly task.

The test reveals no significant sex difference in performance on the disassembly.

Age and Performance

Significant differences in performance were found among the various age groups tested. Although the difference between the averages of the 17–39 year group and the older groups is significantly in favor of the younger workers, the distributions show that a few of the older male workers equal or exceed the average for the younger group.

This test is published by the Educational Test Bureau, Minneapolis, Nashville, Philadelphia. Price complete with manual is $12.50. Special supplement for the blind.

Relationship to Other Tests

	r	n
Worksample—Assembly and Disassembly	.55	214
Minnesota Rate of Manipulation		
Placing—Worksample Assembly	.46	477
Turning—Worksample Assembly	.40	473
Revised Army Beta		
Worksample Assembly	.41	98
O'Connor Finger Dexterity		
Worksample Assembly	.35	201
Bennett Mechanical Comprehension, Form WI (For women)		
Worksample Assembly	.31	379
Worksample Disassembly	.17	378

All of the above correlations are positive in the sense that good scores on one test indicate good scores on the other test to the extent of the value of the "r" given.

References:

1. Bauman, M. K. Motor skills Techniques adapted to the Vocational Guidance of the Blind. *Journal of Applied Psychology*, April, 1946. Vol. 40, #2.
2. Roberts, John R. Pennsylvania Bi-Manual Worksample, *Manual of directions, norms, distributions and critical ratios*. Educational Test Bureau, 1945.
3. Roberts, John R. and Bauman, M. K. *Motor skills tests for the blind*. Educational Test Bureau, 1945.

J. R. R.

Purdue Pegboard. The Purdue Pegboard, developed by the Purdue Research Foundation, Purdue University, was designed to provide a test of manual dexterity involving gross movements of hands, fingers and arms, and finger movements associated with "tip of the finger" dexterity. The principal purpose in view was the selection of employees for industrial jobs requiring manipulative dexterity.

The Test consists of a board approximately 12 inches by 17 inches in size, having a double row of holes down the middle and four cup-like depressions at one end to hold the small metal pins, washers and collars which are to be manipulated by the subject. In the first operation, the subject, using his right hand only, picks up the pins and places them in the holes in the right-hand row on the board, one at a time, as rapidly as possible; he is allowed 30 seconds. In the second operation, he performs a similar task with the left hand, again being allowed 30 seconds. In the third operation, he works both hands together, placing pairs of pins in the holes during the 30 seconds allowed. In the fourth operation, he works both hands continuously in a series of alternating operations, picking up and putting a pin in a hole with his right hand, placing a washer over it with his left hand, placing a collar over it with his right hand, and placing another washer over it with his left hand; the subject is allowed one minute in which to complete as many pin-washer-collar-washer assemblies as he can.

The score for each of the above operations is the number of units completed in the time allowed. Five scores are obtained: (1) right-hand pin score, (2) left-hand pin score, (3) score for both right hand and left hand used simultaneously in placing pins, (4) sum of the three pin placing scores, and (5) score on pin-washer-collar-washer assembly.

Reliability

Reliability for one trial in placing pins with right hand, left hand, and both hands is reported as .62. For the pin placing operations, reliability of scores based on two trials is estimated from this data as .77 and of scores based on three trials as .83. Reliability for one trial in the assembly task is reported as .72. Reliability of assembly scores based on two trials is estimated from this data as .84 and of scores based on three trials as .89. Emphasizing brevity of administration as desirable, the author states that the single-trial method is usually satisfactory for industrial selection purposes despite its low reliability; he argues that, with an increase in the placement ratio followed in one-trial testing, practically the same results may be obtained with this measure as might have been obtained by the use of a measure meeting the standard of reliability conventionally expected for a test of this type. It is reported that as many as 50 applicants have been tested in an hour by one administrator, employing ten pegboards for group administration.

Validity

The author reports (1) that "extensive and satisfactory use of the pegboard for the placement of operators according to dexterity demands of different jobs" has been made in large ordnance plants. Data regarding the results of validation studies have not yet been made available. It is claimed that the test measures both the fine finger dexterity of the type measured by the O'Connor Finger Dexterity Test and manual dexterity of the type measured by the Hayes Pegboard, the two tests mentioned being ones which have been found to be valid in studies of selection for certain jobs. However, no data are presented to show how much correlation there is, if any, between scores on the Purdue Pegboard and scores on these tests or on any other tests of this type.

Norms

Norms for women are provided separately for each score for one-, two-, and three-trial administration. One-trial norms are based on scores of about 950 applicants in defense industries, the two-trial norms are based on 100 cases not otherwise described, and the three-trial norms are derived by statistical estimate from the two-trial norms. In the one-trial sample, no significant differences were found among sub-groups based on previous occupation, geographic locality, or race.

Norms for men are provided for one-trial scores only and are based on 340 cases at a large aviation training center; no additional information regarding this normative group is provided.

As indicated above, the Purdue Pegboard was developed and introduced primarily as a device for purposes of selection and placement of employees. It has also been suggested for school use as an aptitude test.

According to the published information available, the test in its present form and method of administration has not been shown to meet the standards of reliability customarily expected for purposes of individual counseling with this type of test; the data made available with respect to norms and validity seem inadequate for meaningful interpretation of test scores for individual counseling purposes.

The author indicates that additional data regarding the test will be forthcoming. The test is published by Science Research Associates.

References:

1. Anonymous. *Preliminary manual for the Purdue Pegboard*. Chicago: Science Research Associates.
2. Tiffin, J. *Industrial psychology*. New York: Prentice-Hall, Inc., 1942. See p. 81.

D. E. S.

Stenquist Mechanical Aptitude Tests. The Stenquist Mechanical Aptitude Tests were constructed by J. L. Stenquist, Director of Research, Baltimore, Maryland. These tests have been found effective in detecting general mechanical aptitude. They presuppose no mechanical experience. There are two tests: Test 1 and Test 2. Test 1 contains pictures of mechanical objects with questions about relationships; Test 2 consists partly of material similar to that of Test 1 and also of questions applied to cuts of machines and machine parts. The questions are of a general nature and do not presuppose that the pupil has necessarily had actual first-hand experience with the particular machines shown. Both Tests 1 and 2 should be given whenever possible. While either test alone gives a fair sampling of ability, the average result of the two tests is always more reliable and should be used if possible. Test 2 is somewhat more difficult than Test 1 and is more the test of mechanical reasoning power, while Test 1 is more a test of mechanical information. There is one form of each test. The time for Test 1 is 45 minutes and for Test 2, 50 minutes. The Tests are designed for grades 6 to 12.

A table is provided for each test which shows: raw scores, T-score equivalents and the percentile ranks for each grade corresponding to each score. Grade norms are not provided, since they are of doubtful significance. The reliability coefficients for the tests vary from .67 to .84.

The publisher of these tests is World Book Company, Yonkers-on-Hudson, New York.

B. C. W.

Van der Lugt Manual Ability Test Series. A battery of tests designed to measure speed, coordination and motor learning. Separate norms are presented for Speed, Pressure Sensitivity, Accuracy, Motor Memory, Coordination. This battery can be used from age 6 through adult. The original standardization group consisted of 2,128 Dutch children. The test must be individually administered.

These tests are published by the Psychological Corporation, 522 Fifth Avenue, New York 18, N. Y.

Reference:

Bennett, G. and Cruikshank, R. M. *A summary of manual and mechanical ability tests* (Preliminary Form). New York: The Psychological Corporation, 1942.

R. M. O'N.

Whitman Test Series for Manual Dexterity. This was an attempt by E. C. Whitman to devise and standardize a test series governed by manual dexterity as apart from higher mental processes. Various manual tests in common use have other primary factors such as learning ability, mechanical ingenuity and reasoning, and they are often used to supplement language tests of intelligence or to take their place when language difficulties arise. A test restricted to manual skills in children might have special implications for vocational guidance.

The test is composed of seven items and takes about 15 minutes to administer. Materials, instructions, and scoring are described in the Journal of Educational Psychology, 1925, 16, pp. 118–123. The materials may be purchased from C. S. Stoelting Company, Chicago, at a cost of $12.65.

The tests were standardized on 491 school children from ages 7 to 15. Percentile scores and median scores were computed for each age and some difference was noted in the scores of boys and girls— the boys having slightly higher scores. The most striking feature of the table is the difference in the way the tasks are affected by growth. Items 1 and 2 are relatively little affected; 4 and 5 quite markedly.

Four hundred and thirty-four of these children were given the Myer's Mental Measure and the scores were correlated with the scores in the tests of dexterity. A correlation for the entire group was + .65 PE.019— a figure which is governed by the improvement in both classes of performance with age. The correlations by years is also tabulated. Intercorrelation between certain items was calculated by the percentage of cases on opposite sides of the median but is expressed in terms of r.

None of these relationships is so clear as to suggest the advisability of eliminating any of the tests concerned on the ground of duplication. In view of the marked differential effect of age on the various items, a general score for the whole test is unrepresentative in the same way that an I.Q. does not represent high or low performances among the various subtests. A profile method of presenting such results give the scores more significance.

Reference:

1. Whitman, E. C. American Journal of Educational Psychology, 1925, 16, pp. 118–123.

                                        E. C. W.

Wrightstone-O'Toole Prognostic Test of Mechanical Abilities. The *Prognostic Test of Mechanical Abilities,* devised by J. Wayne

Wrightstone, Assistant Director, Bureau of Reference, Research and Statistics, and Charles E. O'Toole, Assistant Director of Educational and Vocational Guidance, New York City Schools, is a scientific instrument intended for use with students of the junior and senior high schools and for predictive and selective purposes in industry. The several abilities measured are those generally found in varying degrees in mechanical jobs and trades. The important aspects of all mechanical training and work included in the test are: Arithmetic computation, reading drawings and blueprints, identification and use of tools, spatial relationships, and checking measurements.

Complete descriptions of the tests are included in a comprehensive Manual of Directions. The diagnostic profile provided on the front cover page of each test booklet indicates graphically the relative extent to which a person possesses mechanical abilities which may be related to, or determine, an individual's success in various types of mechanical occupations. Thus, definite, objective data, which may be utilized effectively in counseling and guidance, selection and placement, or as a basis for ability groupings for various purposes, are readily available.

The validity of the test has been established by an analysis of courses of study in such mechanical occupations as automobile mechanics, aviation mechanics, trade metal work, and the like. Prescriptions of abilities, measured by the test, which are required in various mechanical trades are provided in the Manual of Directions. The subtest scores have been correlated with the total test scores and coefficients ranging from .52 to .77 have been found. The intercorrelations of the subtests indicate a positive and fair degree of correlation among arithmetic computation, accuracy in measurement, and reading simple drawings. The validity of the entire test battery has been checked by correlation with instructors' ratings in an aviation trades course and vary from .60 to .78.

This test is so devised that it may be administered, either to an individual or a group, by any person who will carefully follow the Manual of Directions. The *Prognostic Test of Mechanical Abilities* may be given as the usual hand-scored test, or by the use of a special answer sheet which may be scored by the I.B.M. test scoring machine. The time limits prescribed for each test should be strictly observed. One period of 45 minutes is required for the entire test. Scoring is completely objective and easily done when directions given in the Manual are followed.

Standards are based on a cross-section of population comprising approximately 15,000 individuals in twenty states, and from seventh grade to adult groups. Percentile norms for interpretation of test scores are provided on the last page of the Manual of Directions for each grade and for adults.

W. W. C.

MEDICAL APTITUDE.   Success in the profession of medicine is not based upon a specific or unitary talent of an inherent or inborn nature. Medical aptitude should be thought of as a combination of traits, or pattern of traits, indicative of potential success in medical work or activities. Some of these traits are largely inherent, as basic intellectual ability; some are largely acquired, as knowledge in the sciences of chemistry, physics, and biology; and some involve both inherent and acquired elements, as suitable personality traits and interests. Any one of them taken alone may be just as conducive to success in some non-medical occupational or professional field. It is a particular combination that gives the potentiality of success in medicine and that constitutes, therefore, "medical aptitude."

The problem of defining medical aptitude and the related problem of predicting success in medicine is complicated by the fact that the medical profession has many subdivisions, specialties, and auxiliary sciences, not all of which, for success, rest upon the same combination of traits and abilities. The *general practitioner of medicine* must have an especial aptitude for dealing with people in an intimate way under difficult circumstances. He must be able to keep the confidences placed in him. Social qualifications are as important, perhaps more important, for this aspect of medicine than are intellectual attributes. Aptitudes of great importance to *surgery* as a specialty of medicine include those sensori-motor abilities which are essential to success as a skilled surgical operator—steadiness, dexterity, clearness of vision, spatial visualizing ability, and delicacy of tactile discrimination. Above the abilities necessary in other fields of medicine the *pediatrician* must have an interest in and ability to deal with children. *Public health work* requires a broad interest in community welfare and a breadth of knowledge which encompasses the scope of many social problems. The physician in public health work often needs administrative and planning capacities, and abilities fitting him for success as an educator of the public. *Bacteriology* calls for aptitude for laboratory research, and interest in details and precision. *Psychiatry* will be a logical choice for those with psychological background or interest, for those who have a good psychological insight, and for those who like the challenge of a field of work in which there are many unsolved problems. The *roentgenologist* must have aptitudes in mathematics, physics, and mechanics beyond those called for in other fields of medicine. Those who utilize medical training mainly in the training of others must have the qualities of a good *teacher*. They must be able to organize their knowledge and to present it to others; it is important that they be able to inspire others. Success in *medical research* demands aptitudes and interests in invention, discovery, statistical analysis, writing and reporting; and often, as progress upward is made, administrative ability in directing research activities of others. *Medical administration,* including the administering of medical schools, hospitals, army medical units, and medical organizations, combines the general aptitudes for medicine with those for administration. There is *private practice of medicine* for the medically trained person who is energetic, who can stand irregular demands upon his time, and who is a good manager of his own affairs, business and otherwise. On the other hand, there is *institutional, organizational practice of medicine* for the medically trained person whose own traits and preferences demand a more steady income, less irregularity of demands, less managing of his own business.

We might include for discussion in this article on medical aptitude, the abilities requisite to success in the numerous medically related professions and sub-professional medical jobs, such as those in the fields of dentistry, nursing, medical technology, and medical attendance. However, we shall limit the discussion in this article to the question of aptitude for those types of work for which the Doctor of Medicine Degree is an educational prerequisite.

One might aptly say that the abilities common to all the various specialties and fields of work in medicine are those aptitudes requisite to successful completion of a course of medical training and graduation from a medical school with an M. D. degree. If the aspirant to medical work does not possess these aptitudes he is barred from all fields of medical work no matter what other characteristics or abilities essential to some particular specialty he may possess. A considerable amount of study and progress has been made in the measurement of the abilities necessary to complete a medical school course, and in the prediction of success in medical school. The progress in such studies has probably been greater than in any other professional field. This progress has been spurred on by several factors. One is the necessity, on the part of those in charge of admissions to medical schools, of selecting only a proportion for admission from a much larger number of applicants than there are facilities for training. In the prewar- years the number of applicants for admission to medical schools each year almost doubled the number accepted by the schools for training. Since many applicants applied to several medical schools, many schools had to select for admission from three or four times as many applicants as they could accept. Another factor which has stimulated the study of prediction of medical school success is the relatively high mortality in the past among students in medical schools, with the attendant waste of training facilities and human problems produced in the students unable to attain the vocational goals set up for them. With respect to aptitudes for success beyond medical school graduation and prediction of success in the actual "practice" or other use of medical training very little study has been done and little information of scientific value is available.

It seems logical from what has already been pointed out, to approach the problem of measurement of medical aptitude through a consideration of studies that have been made of abilities related to success in medical school. Several of these factors have been studied to varying degrees.

General Scholastic Ability as Indicative of Success in Medical School. Since medical school training is in large measure a scholastic task, general scholastic aptitude will constitute a part of or an element in medical aptitude. Under present standards of admission the student going into medical school must do satisfactorily from two to four academic years of premedical college work before he enters medical school. A great importance has been placed upon this premedical work by admitting officers in medical schools, premedical scholarship being the single most frequently used admission criterion, and the admission criterion receiving the highest weight among several considered in many schools. A number of studies of the validity of this criterion have been reported. Moss [4] reported a correlation of .44 between premedical scholastic averages and four-year medical school grade averages for a thousand medical students in fourteen medical schools. Separate schools in this group yielded correlations ranging from .18 to .59. A study of relationship between three-year medical school average and premedical scholarship of George Washington University students showed a correlation of .54. A University of Minnesota study showed a correlation of .52 with premedical honor point ratio for medical school grades at the end of two years and of .53 for first year medical students. In the Moss study referred to the relationship was also presented in another way. The investigator raised the question: "How efficiently could the failures in medical school be eliminated by raising the requirements with respect to premedical scholarship?" Arbitrarily, a raising of scholastic requirements to cut off the lower one-fourth actually admitted was considered. Such a cutting point he found would eliminate 44 per cent of the failures which occurred in his group of a thousand students. The efficiency of such a raising of scholastic standards is lowered, however, by the fact that it would also exclude 25 per cent of those making high medical school averages.

It would seem from studies available that general scholastic ability as shown by premedical scholarship averages is a factor in medical aptitude. However, it is far from a perfect criterion of medical aptitude or aptitude for medical school work in particular. In many instances the correlations are too low to admit of individual prediction with any high degree of accuracy.

Ability in the Sciences. A minimum of four years of premedical science work is required of all students entering medical school (general chemistry, organic chemistry, physics, and zoology or biology). No other specified area of premedical college work is required in such large amount. Like so many other college curricular requirements, no one can find stated exactly or specifically the bases upon which the requirements developed, nor the justifications at the various stages of the history of their development. One can say that the heavy science requirements are justified, because the content of the sciences forms the foundation on which the preclinical medical studies are based. And yet preclinical medical sciences, for the most part "start at the bottom." Or one might justify the sciences as a measure of scientific aptitude or aptitude for performance in scientific studies which constitute a very high percentage of the preclinical work in the medical schools. The latter supposition is a better justification for our including the matter in the discussion of this report. Moss' study on the thousand medical students already referred to showed correlations of four-year medical school averages with the four required premedical sciences to be: .38 with general chemistry, .37 with zoology, .36 with organic chemistry, and .33 with physics. Other studies on fewer students have shown slightly higher correlations but usually not above .45. In general, premedical science grades do not predict medical school work better than grades in other standard college courses and premedical science average does not predict quality of medical school work as well as does general overall premedical scholarship. This has been borne out by a number of studies and the statement corroborated by a number of persons working with the problem of selection of medical students.[2 5 6] There is a growing tendency to emphasize broader cultural training in preparing medical students rather than to emphasize an extension of science training beyond the minimum required.

Intelligence. It is obvious that intelligence is an aspect of medical aptitude, that one cannot graduate from a medical school with intelligence below a certain minimum, and that one cannot carry on the complex duties of medical work without intelligence above a requisite minimum. Evidence as to what intellectual level is required for success in medicine is furnished principally by studies of the distribution of intelligence among persons earning their living in the occupation and among students in the curricula for training for medicine in the colleges and universities. Analyses of occupational data collected during and following World War I placed the average intelligence score for medical groups at a point surpassed by about 10 per cent of the population. To state it another way, in intelligence the average medical worker falls at about the 90th percentile for the general population. The lower quartile point for physicians is at about the 82nd percentile for the general population. If one might say that the lowest quarter of those in the occupation could be considered marginal in respect to intelligence, one should be in the upper 20 per cent of the population to be suitable in intelligence for medicine; in terms of intelligence quotient, roughly above I.Q. of 115 to 120. These levels are relatively high for occupations in general, but they are surpassed by some other professions, as engineering and college teaching. Similar indications are given by the data from intelligence testing of students in various college curricula. Students in premedical curricula usually rank somewhat above the average for all college students, but fall below those in the engineering and technical-scientific curricula.

Some warning seems necessary with respect to interpretation of findings on intelligence within occupations. It is only roughly that an occupation can be said to have an intelligence level of so much. The variability within the occupation is wide and the overlapping of occupations is great. Certainly from the intelligence level alone one could not predict success or lack of success of an individual in any given occupation, unless he be markedly below the minimum required. It is to be hoped that analysis of data available on occupational groups tested during World War II will throw light on the general problem discussed here. Unfortunately it is too early for such data to be available.

Within groups of students studying medicine or premedical courses, intelligence test scores are of some value in predicting grades in medical and premedical studies. The correlations reported have been for the most part between .40 and .50, fairly comparable to correlations reported between intelligence and college scholarship in general.

Interest. There is widespread belief that enjoyment of a type of activity plays an important part in the selection of an occupation and in occupational success. In keeping with this belief growth in vocational guidance work has stimulated the development of psychological testing devices for measurement of interests. Many of these yield measures of broad activity-interest groups. The activities of medical work fall within some of these groups, such as scientific activities, social service activities, etc. The Kuder Preference Record or the Thurstone Vocational Interest Schedule yield measures of interests in such broad groupings and may be of value in indicating suitability for medical training and medical work from the standpoint of one's likes and dislikes. A somewhat different approach is available in the Strong Vocational Interest Blank. Its ratings indicate the extent to which one's likes and dislikes (or interest pattern) are similar to those of people actually working in the occupations for which the test may be scored. Standards are available both for the men's form and the women's form for the occupation of physician. Rated for the occupation of physician one would know whether his tastes and inclinations resemble those of people in the medical profession.

Most of the uses of interest tests have been made in vocational guidance at relatively early stages of vocational careers. Little use has been made of them in the actual selection or admission of students for professional training. This is probably wise because the information available at present could not justify denying a person training opportunities on the basis of such tests. There is need for more work in the form of follow-up studies showing the relationship between interest test scores and future actual vocational choice and success. Strong made a ten-year follow-up study of 197 men given his Vocational Interest Blank in 1927 as college seniors. Those who had remained in their chosen occupation (indicated at the time of the 1927 test) showed very high ratings on the occupational scoring on the test. Those who were less adjusted vocationally or less certain of their choice as shown by changing their occupations showed less consistently high ratings on the occupations in question. Eighteen physicians were included in the group. For this group the scores on the occupation of physician showed a very high ranking, more so than for many other occupational groups in the study.

Personal Characteristics. In discussing the general nature of medical aptitude it has already been indicated that traits of personality and character are determining factors in success in the medical profession. It is generally conceded that high degrees of success in the practice of medicine are not limited to those in the upper half of their medical school classes scholastically. Personal traits seem in many instances to be the more important determining factor in success.

Certain traits of good character, as honesty and reliability, and a minimum amount of such personality traits as cooperativeness, adaptability and persistence could be considered basic to success in medicine. Such a group of traits would hardly be peculiar to the profession of medicine, however. In discussing personal characteristics in medical success, we must be reminded again of the fact that medicine is not one type of job—that private practice of medicine is not the same job as medical research, and that it does not require the same type of personality. Very little has been done in studying the relationship between personal traits and success in medicine. Many medical schools interview their applicants and still more require recommendations on personal characteristics. Beyond basic traits of good character there is little indication of what interviewing committees look for or of what weight they give to interview results. In connection with studying the comparative value of different criteria in predicting medical school failures, Moss [4] reports a study of interview ratings in two medical schools. In each school all the students admitted were given ratings by a committee of medical school officers and instructors who interviewed them. In order to compare the prediction of failures by interview ratings with the prediction of failures by other criteria, a "deadline" was drawn at the lowest quartile point of the total group of ratings on students admitted. There were in the two schools nine failures in the freshman year. If admission had been refused to those in the lowest quarter of ratings, three of these nine failures would have been eliminated, but at the same time six of twenty-six who made averages of 85 or better would have been eliminated. This showing with respect to interview ratings was much poorer than with either ability test scores or premedical scholastic average. Moss concludes from the study that interview ratings are of little value in predicting level of medical school success. Another study reported by Van Beuren [6] in 1929 indicated that relatively poor students (as judged by their premedical scholarship) admitted to the College of Physicians and Surgeons largely on the basis of personality (as judged by references, interviews, college activities, etc.) did well in medical school in a large percentage of the cases.

Other Factors in Aptitude for Medicine. The factors of age and amount of premedical college background have been studied as factors in medical school success. Neither of these factors bears any appreciable relationship to success. There is some tendency for there to be an inverse relationship between medical school success and age of admission because of the greater mental brightness of those who gain admission at a young age, and the interfering factors of family and other responsibilities present in many of the older age group.

Increased amount of premedical college work above the minimum required does not seem per se to increase chances of success in medical school. Many of those with greater amount are poorer risks since they have taken an extra year of college work since they were not accepted upon first application. They are often still marginal students even after extra premedical preparation.

The Association of American Medical Colleges Scholastic Aptitude Test for Medical Schools. At the present time, under its Committee on Aptitude Tests for Medical Students, the Association of American Medical Colleges sponsors a testing program for applicants to medical schools. The test used by this committee is one which measures several of the elements already discussed as having a relationship to medical school success and as making up a part of "medical aptitude." The test as a whole measures general intellectual ability, premedical background (through its scientific content), and interest in the direction of medical-biological things (through its terminology and general informational content). Various specific parts of the test measure (1) comprehension and retention of medical type of material studied during the test, (2) visual memory of an anatomical diagram studied, (3) logical reasoning, (4) scientific vocabulary, (5) information, and (6) understanding of printed material of medical nature. New forms of the test are constructed each year by a staff under the direction of Dr. F. A. Moss, director of studies for the Association's Committee. The tests are administered once or twice each year under the Committee's direction in the various premedical schools to applicants for admission. A report is sent to each medical school in the country, giving a rating for each student in terms of percentile rank in the whole group tested. The number of students tested has averaged about 10,000 per year over the past ten years. Eighty-five to ninety per cent of applicants to medical schools have been tested. All but a few of the medical schools in the country use the test results in admission of students. The exact use made and the standards of admission vary in different schools. The Association of American Medical Colleges does not prescribe the use to be made.

A considerable amount of data on the predictive value of this test is available, particularly from studies done during the early years of its use. The test, known as the Scholastic Aptitude Test for Medical Schools, was constructed during 1927 for use in a study by Dr. F. A. Moss of the freshman class in the School of Medicine of George Washington University. The test represented an attempt to devise an instrument which would indicate ability to pursue successfully a medical course, and which might be used as one of the determining factors in the selection of students for admission to medical school. Results on a study of the relationship between the test scores and freshman medical school work at George Washington University were reported in 1929 by Dr. David Robertson, then Associate Director of the American Council on Education, before the Annual Congress on Medical Education, Medical Licensure, and Hospitals. Following the reception of this report the American Council agreed to finance a study of the test to be carried out by Dr. Moss in a more extensive experimental set-up. Tests were administered in April or May of 1929 to a thousand medical school freshmen in fourteen medical schools agreeing to cooperate in the study. These thousand students were followed through their complete medical school course, and about half of them through internship training or State and National board examinations, in an extensive study of the value of the test in predicting medical school work, medical examination performance, and internship performance. Progress reports on this experimental study were made to the Association of American Medical Colleges. After the first year of the study the Association was sufficiently impressed with the usefulness of the test that it appointed an Aptitude Test Committee to work out plans for constructing further forms of the test and administering it to applicants for medical school training.

Final results of the study showed unusually high correlations between test scores and four-year medical school averages. For the whole group the correlation was .59; it was as high as .72 in two schools; and in only two was the correlation below .45. The data showed that if a student had a score as high as the highest tenth tested, the chances were 100 per cent that he would graduate from the medical school; and 3 to 1 that he would average 85 or over for the whole four years. On the other hand if he had a test score as low as the lowest tenth in the medical school group, the chances were 6 out of 10 that he would not be able to graduate because of failure to carry the work successfully; 9 to 1 that he would have an average below 85 if he did graduate; and 2 to 1 that he would have an average below 80.

A comparative study of the value of five admission criteria in predicting the failures occurring in the fourteen medical schools studied showed the test to be the most efficient single criterion. Setting a "critical" score at a point to cut off the lower 25 per cent of the group it would predict 53 per cent of the failures with only 5 per cent of relatively high medical school averages excluded. This was better than could be done by premedical scholarship, entrance credits, age at entrance, or interviews. The best prediction of failures could be made with a combination of test score and premedical scholarship.

Approximately five hundred of the medical students in the experimental group were followed through internship. Intern ratings from hospital superintendents and staff physicians showed those making high test scores to be superior in their hospital work to those making low scores. On a rating scale in which a "1" rating was assigned to interns coming up to the best a hospital had had, and "5" to ones among the poorest, those falling in the highest tenth of test scores had an average rating of 1.3. Those falling in the lowest tenth graduating had an average rating of 3.2.

Subsequent studies have corroborated the findings of the early experimental studies. The continued testing program of the Association of American Medical Colleges is evidence of a confidence in the value of the test as one criterion in the selection of medical students.

Other Special Tests or Test Batteries for Selection of Medical Students. The University of Minnesota, finding the predictive value of the Association of American Medical Colleges test somewhat lower than that found in most other schools, has constructed its own special test battery, used in conjunction with the Association test. Their battery includes several types of tests not included in the Moss test, but, in general, similar in nature. Correlations between medical school grades for their students and test scores are somewhat higher for their test than for the Association test.

General Conclusion. In conclusion it should be reiterated that medical aptitude represents a combination of traits indicative of potential success in medical work, and that this combination is not exactly the same for all types of medical work. Progress in measuring some of the elements has been made, particularly in measuring those elements basic to successful completion of a medical school course. For those faced with problems of vocational guidance of potential medical students, the instrument of greatest assistance will probably be the scholastic aptitude tests indicating probability of success in the medical school work, vocational interest tests indicating similarity of likes and dislikes to those of medical workers, and tests and other criteria indicating ability along scientific lines. Beyond this the prospective medical worker will probably do best to fit himself into the proper niche of the profession by knowledge gained through his own experiences.

References:

1. Bingham, W. V. *Aptitudes and aptitude testing.* New York: Harper and Brothers, 1937.

2. Cramer, W. F. A study of the selective admission of students in the medical school of the University of Chicago. *Journal of Association of American Medical Colleges*, 1933, 8.
3. Kandel, I. L. *Professional aptitude tests in medicine, law and engineering.* New York: Bureau of Publications, Teachers College, Columbia University, 1940.
4. Moss, F. A. Scholastic aptitude test for medical students: report for 1932. *Journal of Association of American Medical Colleges*, 1933, 8.
5. Thorpe, E. S., Jr. Relative value of cultural courses in premedical training. *Journal of Association of American Medical Colleges*, 1931, 6.
6. Van Buren, F. T. Correlation of grades in medical and premedical work with personality. *Journal of Association of American Medical Colleges*, 1929, 4.

T. H.

MEDICAL APTITUDE TEST. The Medical Aptitude Test of the Association of American Medical Colleges must be taken by all applicants for admission to Class A medical schools in the United States. A new form is constructed each year and is given at a large number of higher institutions offering pre-medical work. Students taking the test are never informed of their scores, so it cannot be used as a counseling aid.

Subtests consist of sections on comprehension and retention, visual memory, memory for content, logical reasoning, scientific vocabulary, and understanding of printed material, and general information.

Additional information can be obtained from Dr. F. A. Moss, Association of American Medical Colleges, Columbia Medical Building, Washington, D .C.

References:

1. Chesney, A. M. Evaluation of the Medical Aptitude Test. Journal of the Association of American Medical Colleges, 1936, 2, 15–32.
2. Moss, F. A. The Secretary Report. Journal of the Association of American Medical Colleges, September, 1931, May, 1932, January, 1933, March, 1934, June 1935, etc.
3. Paterson, D. G., Schneidler, G. G., and Williamson, E. G. *Student guidance techniques.* New York: McGraw-Hill Book Co., 1938, 242–244.

R. Z. K.

MEMORY SCALE, WECHSLER. The Memory Scale constructed by David Wechsler is a simple, rapid, practical memory examination. It was designed to meet the needs of psychologists who are frequently called upon "to appraise the patient's memory particularly as it is related to the rest of his functioning." It consists of seven sub-tests: Personal and Current Information, Orientation, Mental Control, Logical Memory, Memory Span, Visual Reproduction and Associate Learning.

Clinically this scale will be found useful in detecting aphasics, seniles and cases of organic brain disease who ordinarily would not be detected by the use of simple rote memory material. In addition, the scale should prove of value in ascertaining special memory defects in cases of specific brain injuries. It will enable the counsellor to differentiate between neurotics and organics, which, of course, will be significant from the standpoint of vocational guidance and counselling. The scale has several merits. Allowance has been made for memory variations with age. Memory quotients obtained are directly comparable to the subject's intelligence quotient which makes it possible to compare the memory impairment of the subject with his loss in other intellectual functions.

The scale is individually administered and can generally be given in approximately 15 minutes. The method of standardization is similar to that employed with the Bellevue-Wechsler Scale. Provisional norms are based on the examination of approximately 200 normal men and women between the ages of 25 and 50. Intelligence ratings with the Wechsler-Bellevue Scale were also available for about 100 cases. The Memory scores were equated against the weighted scores of the Full Scale. This was accomplished by plotting the mean memory scores for different ages against the weighted scores of the Bellevue Scale (age group 20–24 years). Various constants were then tried out which would keep the mean Memory Quotient for any age group equivalent to the mean I.Q. of that age group. The scoring is simple and entails summing up the partial sub-test scores to which is added a constant for the age group in which the subject falls. This is the corrected memory score. The Equivalent Quotient for the corrected memory score is obtained by use of a table.

The Memory Scale is published by the Psychological Corporation, 522 Fifth Avenue, New York 18, New York.

References:

1. Wechsler, D. A standardized memory scale for clinical use. J. of Psychol., 1945, 19, 87–95.
2. Wells, F. L. *Mental tests in clinical practice.* New York: World Book, 1927.

H. B. H.

MENTAL DEFECTIVES. The mental defective, or the individual of sub-normal mentality whose adjustment to work we shall discuss in this article, was selected because he has a mental age that ranges anywhere from 7 to 12 as measured by the 1938 Terman-Merrill Revision of the Binet-Simon Test of General Intelligence. A member of this group may be further described as "an individual who by reason of defect existing from birth, or from an early age, is unable to profit by ordinary schooling and cannot manage himself and his affairs without supervision." [6] In addition to this it should be noted that the essence of mental defect is that it is incurable and no special education, regardless of how elaborate it may be, can raise a case of amentia to normal standards. It is possible, however, by the application of modern psychological methods whereby individual differences are carefully studied, to make recommendations for training along lines suited to the capacity of the individual so that he may frequently approach normal standards, as demanded in the labor market, and his mental deficiency may then pass unnoticed. Educational techniques that meet the needs of members of this group are an essential if this result is to be obtained.

It is generally conceded that to be effective the methods used in the education of the subnormal should be adapted to the mental level of the individual child. Sequin, after experimenting with large numbers of mentally retarded children, found that for the majority due to their limited attention span a maximum of twenty or thirty minutes devoted to each activity proved to be the best time unit, and his school classes were based on this fact. In the vocational training of subnormal individuals, the time to be allotted to the performance of a single item has to be determined on an individual basis.

For many years it was thought that teaching the mentally retarded to command some of the simplest academic tools, to acquire very rudimentary manual skills and to develop good work habits would make him a self-supporting citizen. This has not proved to be the case, partly because of the mechanization of industry, the urbanization of society, and the increased educational standards set up for its employees by industry. Because of these growing trends, special training for specific jobs has become more and more essential even in relatively simple occupations. This does not mean that numberless subnormals may not drift into industrial jobs for which they have had no training but it does mean that if the subnormal has been trained for a definite job, he will remain longer on that job and will be able to compete successfully with other workers. Thus he will acquire a self-confidence that will, to a certain extent, assure his future.

In considering job potentialities it is important to consider what might be called an *Employability Scale*. This involves a careful survey of the physical and emotional maturity age of the boy and girl, as well as an analysis of the economic and cultural status of the family. In addition to this information, there must be included a study of his personality, his general health and physique, his intelligence, the mental efficiency with which he functions, his educational background, and his interests. It is vital that the subnormal child should not be pushed beyond his capacity. An employability scale permits the grouping of children according to their occupational potentialities.

If it is true, as has been said, that the ability to perform a service that warrants the payment of wages and the wise expenditure of the wages earned are the primary essentials for living in the world of today, it is certainly important that educators through careful training and painstaking effort prepare the subnormal to meet these standards.

Teachers in the New York City Classes for the Mentally Retarded, under the able supervision of Dr. Richard Hungerford, are concerned with the development of occupational interests. Hence each teacher chooses an occupation as the main topic, or "core," of the term's work. A scrap book containing a carefully selected series of illustrative material and an outline of the particular occupation chosen is prepared. At the end of the term a complete resumé of all jobs classified under that occupation is placed on the library shelves. The various gradations of each job are set forth; the duties involved in each phase of the work are simply and clearly described. The Department has already collected a large number of these excellent job analyses, which are on file and easily available to teachers-in-training. Often the job analyses serve to bring to the realization of the subnormal child his inability to cope with the demands of a certain job that has appealed to his fancy. When, for instance, he is shown that figuring and writing must be done by a man serving as Superintendent of an apartment house, he can be made to see that he will be incapable of doing that type of work. A discussion of the jobs that he *can* do in an apartment house may logically follow. Often a subnormal boy at this point will exclaim spontaneously, "But I can clean up. I can be a helper!"

One of the objectives of such an approach to his occupational problem is that it opens the young person's eyes to the many types of work that there are to do in the world. This gives him a wholesome attitude toward work and makes him think of the several points that should be considered before a decision as to the kind of work for which he should prepare is made.

One of the first concerted attempts to give practical systematic industrial training to mentally defective girls was initiated by Mrs. Henry Ittleson, President of the New York Vocational Adjustment Bureau, in the fall of 1931 when Unit Training Courses in one of the public schools were established. Trade teachers were furnished by the Board of Education under the immediate direction of Morris Siegel, a far-seeing supervisor of industrial education. Realizing that low-level jobs are generally seasonal and that subnormal individuals cannot acquire, without prolonged practice even the knack essential for a semi-skilled job, Unit Training Courses in tagging, packing, assembling, bottle filling, folding, pinking, sewing labels, sample mounting, foot press and electric power machine operating were set up for girls whose mental ages ranged from seven to eleven. In the clerical field, girls who were fairly stable and whose mental ages ranged from ten to twelve, were given carefully supervised practice in copy typing, alphabetical and numerical filing, folding and collating.

The material used for training was given by co-operating business firms who welcomed the idea that girls were being trained to do that firm's own special type of work so that they might later become proficient workers and thus cut down the employers' turnover problems. Though there was no actual agreement that these girls should be hired when their training was completed, there was a tacit understanding to that effect, and several placements were actually made.

The dis-assembling of all practice material was carried on in a distant room so that no girl was aware of the impermanence of her work, though of course she knew that she was being trained for a future job.

It was discovered that psychological factors played an important rôle in the conduct of these classes. When, from time to time, a girl was shown her production record, her interest, hence her speed, was increased. An effort was always made to simulate actual industrial conditions. Thus in the bottle filling course, when only plain water was used the girls worked listlessly and with indifference, but when the water was colored bright-red, blue and green, speed of performance was increased by one-third.

Volunteer workers, interested in the project, assisted in the record-keeping, in the preparation of teaching material and in the fairly constant oversight which each pupil needed during the training period. Getting the girl to settle down to work was a problem encountered each morning and after each recess. She would fuss over minor matters, gaze about the room, and allow any and every incident to divert her from the task at hand. Such lack of attention caused delays in the learning process. Placement counsellors reported that often "bad work habits" was given as the reason for discharging a girl. Obviously then in these training courses, habits of concentration and a systematic approach to the required task proved to be one of the objectives which each teacher had to bear in mind. To accomplish this end, unlimited patience on the part of the teacher was most essential.

This experiment accentuated the fact that the major goal of education is to develop the type of training for the subnormal child that is wholly suited to his capacities and which will serve as a challenge to his potentialities so that he may be encouraged to take advantage of the occupational opportunities that his community has to offer. It is generally conceded by educators that all young people today need information regarding these opportunities and advice as to how to prepare to meet the demands of industry and commerce. Hence it is unquestionably true that those whose mentality is in the subnormal bracket are in even greater need of such information and advice than are those of average intelligence.

The necessity for a concerted effort to help young persons to find the right occupation was first publicly recognized in 1908 when Frank Parsons, engineer, teacher, lawyer, lecturer and civic reformer, opened a Vocation Bureau in Civic House, Boston. At about the same time in Grand Rapids, Michigan, in New York City and in other cities, keen interest was awakened in the problems of vocational guidance and discussion groups were being formed. In 1913 members of all these groups united and established the National Vocational Guidance Association which is still the authorized organ of this large and flourishing group of nationwide agencies.

Special attention to the vocational guidance of the subnormal received its first real impetus when in 1931, Herbert Hoover, President of the United States, invited representatives of schools and social agencies from all parts of the country to attend a White House Conference to consider the problems of children. One result of this conference was the issuance of the following statement: "Serious consideration must be given to the curriculum best suited to the needs of subnormal children. The aim of the educator is to develop the mental capacities and the emotional control of the subnormal so that an adequate social adjustment may be brought about. The curriculum chosen to achieve this end must necessarily be determined in part by the requisites established by adults." It was stressed that the basic goal of the "program for the subnormal should be aimed at total adjustment of each child."

As in the guidance of normal individuals, the administration of a general intelligence test to determine the person's mental ability should be given. This should be followed by such other tests as are well-standardized and of proved value in the prognostication of success or failure in the choice of a vocation. Among these are the Girls' Mechanical Assembly Test, devised under the direction of Herbert Toops, Ph.D., and put on the market by Teachers College, Columbia Institute of Educational Research; the O'Connor Finger and Tweezer Tests; the Paper Folding Test; the Babcock Mental Efficiency Examination; and the Army Performance Test standardized by Yerkes and Yoakum for use in World War I. Each of these tests throws some light upon the occupational fitness of the subnormal boy and girl. Those that are comprised of several items, as are the Toops and Stenquist Assembly Tests, are of especial value. An analysis of the execution of each item reveals which type of manual work will be best adapted to the ability of the individual performer.

It has been found upon investigation that many occupations in workshops and factories call for little mental effort and consist of manual operations within the capacity of persons of low mental level. The earlier the limitations of persons of defective mentality are recognized and their capacities evaluated the less will be the difficulty experienced in their later adjustment.

A study of jobs open to women of low intellectual level and an analysis of the requisites for the satisfactory filling of these jobs was conducted by the Vocational Adjustment Bureau with the idea of turning into productive industrial channels human material frequently considered an economic loss. This Bureau, a non-commercial, non-sectarian organization in New York City, was engaged for many years in the study and placement of maladjusted girls. Early in its existence it had come upon the industrial loss caused by the idleness of large numbers of young women who were unemployed only because no tasks simple enough for them to perform had been found. This condition was aggravated by the deteriorating effect of this idleness upon the girls under discussion and the potential development into delinquency of many of them under the obsession of failure and incompetency. It was also found upon investigation that very simple jobs were being performed by girls mentally equipped to do more complicated tasks. By releasing these girls of normal intelligence for higher grade and better paid work, room could be found for subnormal girls and other workers hitherto felt to be a total loss to society.

H. Goddard in his "Human Efficiency and Levels of Intelligence" states that "intelligence is the chief determiner of human conduct" and advocates a study of the scientific determination of the mental level of the individual in any attempt to fit the man or woman to the job.

In considering the dividing line between probable success and certain failure, there is obviously a minimum mental level that may be set up as the lowest possible standard for any given type of work. A girl whose mental age falls below this minimum should not be directed into that work. This recommendation is made without reference to personality traits, special aptitudes or the physical stamina of the individual. Counselors are urged to consider all these factors before making any definite suggestions as to training or employment.

In summing up the findings of this survey by the Vocational Adjustment Bureau it was found that girls measuring as low mentally as five years were packing indestructible articles. Various kinds of light factory work were found within the range of girls of six mental age. At the seven year level, girls were doing assembling, errand girl jobs, examining and pasting jobs. At the eight year level, they were found engaged in electric power machine operating, stock girl work, folding, and shanking buttons. At the minimum mental age of nine years, girls were found boxing and stringing beads, doing hand sewing and press machine operating. At ten mental level there were girls engaged in the duties of simple office routine, answering the telephone, filing, doing copy typing, and successfully serving in five and ten cents stores as sales girls. At mental ages of eleven and twelve girls were found performing all the jobs we have listed and remaining longer on each job.

The principal value to be derived from knowing the approximate mental level of an individual who seeks the counselor's aid is, as Dr. Herbert Toops has said, "to guide him away from those occupations in which one may be reasonably sure that his intelligence is insufficient for him to achieve a satisfactory degree of success." In this study it was, of course, recognized that the mental level of an individual is but one factor in the total picture of the girl's abilities.

As the result of classification work carried on by the Psychology Department during World War I, an assay of the intelligence required in the performance of certain trades has been listed. This list refers only to work done by men. A few industries attempted classification in World War I, notably the experiment carried on by Elizabeth Bigelow when, because of the shortage of labor, a Connecticut Rubber Factory sought to employ girls of low grade intelligence (Mental Hygiene, April, 1921).

The imbecile group could do nothing more difficult than pick up certain parts of the rubber shoe and lay the pieces neatly together to make rows of twenty-four. As some of the girls were unable to count, they were taught to make rows of six and put four sixes together. The moron group also had its limitations. These persons could not handle any tasks that involved many operations or required judgment.

Dr. V. V. Anderson, in "A Psychiatric Guide for Employment," which was written as the result of some of his studies at R. H. Macy's, New York, says: Each job is given a certain criterion and certain set standards in the way of intelligence, or accuracy or knowledge of arithmetic, or speed, which must be met by applicants seeking employment. Thus, in giving criteria for cashiers, he would not engage anyone whose mental age rated below eleven years two months.

Psychologists engaged in the study of the inmates of institutions for mental defectives have given a good deal of attention to the types of work which can be done within the institutions. The careful and prolonged period of training possible in such a restricted set-up often proved valuable preparation for outside employment. It is interesting to find that there is almost perfect agreement between the conclusion reached by psychologists in different institutions and in the study of Minimum Mental Levels made by the Vocational Adjustment Bureau.

Much work is yet to be done in this field. When the results of the testing done by psychologists in World War II are known, there may be a more concerted effort to perfect the psychological analyses that will lead to the better adjustment of problems of vocational guidance.

In all cases of mental deficiency there is usually social inadequacy so it is especially important to consider the social maturity of each person who is to be offered vocational guidance. After several years of experimentation, Edgar Doll, Ph.D., of the Vineland Training School, has established a Scale of Social Maturity. This consists of 117 items by which the rate of progress made from below one year to adult status can be estimated. The Social Age is determined by the number of activities successfully performed, the standards having been found by examination of children of various ages and adults. The following examples are taken from the revised Maturity Scale and show the approximate ages at which the degree of maturity indicated is achieved:

Below year one:

> Grasps objects within reach
> Balances head
> Pulls self upright
> Grasps with thumb and finger
> Moves about on floor
> "Talks"; imitates sounds
> Occupies self unattended
> Drinks from cup or glass assisted

Year one:

> Walks about room unattended
> Does not drool
> Demands personal attention
> Follows simple instructions
> Marks with pencil or crayon
> Goes about house or yard
> Talks in short sentences
> Discriminates edible substances

Age two:

> Plays with other children
> Fetches and carries familiar objects
> Cuts with scissors
> Avoids simple hazards
> Walks upstairs unassisted
> Initiates own play activities
> "Performs" for others

Age three:

> Dries own hands
> Puts on coat or dress unassisted
> Relates experiences
> Walks downstairs one tread at a time
> Helps at little household tasks
> Plays cooperatively at kindergarten level

Age four:

> Washes hands unaided
> Buttons coat or dress
> Cares for self at toilet
> Goes about neighborhood unattended
> Washes face unassisted
> Prints simple words

Age five:

> Plays simple games
> Dresses except for tying
> Uses table knife for spreading
> Uses pencil or crayon for drawing
> Goes to school unattended
> Uses skates, sled, wagon

Age six:

> Bathes with some assistance
> Uses pencil for writing
> Uses table knife for cutting
> Goes to bed unassisted
> Tells time to quarter hour
> Plays cooperative exercise games

Age eight:

> Combs or brushes hair
> Disavows literal Santa Claus
> Is trusted with money
> Cares for self at table
> Does routine household tasks
> Bathes self unaided

Age ten:

> Participates in pre-adolescent play
> Writes occasional short letters
> Uses tools or utensils
> Carries out written instructions
> Makes telephone calls

Age twelve:

> Does simple remunerative work
> Goes about home town freely

Makes minor purchases
Exercises complete care of dress
Employs sixth grade literacy
Does simple creative work

Such a scale as this is of value in vocational counseling.

It is apparent that educational methods have been changing gradually. For many years the high grade mental defective was taught little other than what he was capable of acquiring of the "3Rs" and he received his instruction from the regular classroom teacher. It is now recognized that there exists a definite need for trained teachers who are competent to deal with the problems of defective persons. Today emphasis is placed upon physical exercises and preparation for work to which the "3Rs" are supplementary since practical training for community living assumes the primary place, with specialized industrial training geared to meet his level of intelligence. When this is done, it is probable that a mental defective can successfully cope with tasks that would be impossible were he not trained for them. Self-respect is instilled through work. Indeed, it is an accepted fact that human beings of subnormal mentality need not be wasted, need not necessarily be institutionalized and can, if trained for jobs they are capable of performing, become useful citizens.

References:

1. Babcock, H. *Time and the mind.* Cambridge, Mass.: Sci-Art Publishing Co.
2. Davies, S. *Social control of the feebleminded.* New York: Thomas Y. Crowell & Co.
3. Doll, E. The Vineland Social Maturity Scale. Training School Bulletin, vol. 32.
4. *Employment of mentally defective boys and girls.* Washington: U. S. Government Printing Office, Bureau Publication No. 210.
5. Hungerford, R., Director of Classes for Mental Defectives, New York City. Annual Report of New York Board of Education, 1945.
6. Tredgold, A. F. *Mental deficiency.* Baltimore: William Wood & Co., p. 8.
7. Unger and Burr. *Minimum mental levels of accomplishment.* Albany: University of State of New York, 1931.
8. Wallin, J. E. W. *Problems of subnormality.* Yonkers, New York: World Book Co., 1921.

E. T. B.

METALWORKING OCCUPATIONS, APTITUDE FOR.

Despite the basic importance of the metalworking occupations to the productive capacity and national economy of highly industrialized nations, surprisingly little work has been done to determine the aptitudes required of an individual for successful performance in occupations comprising the metal trades. By far the greatest amount of work on the development of aptitude tests for metalworking occupations has been carried on in the field of machine shop work. This activity is probably a reflection of both the skill level of the occupations involved and the rather extensive training and apprenticeship required of an individual before he is considered a fully qualified worker in this field.

Machine Shop Occupations

In the United States, Link's work on machinist apprentices, reported in 1919, appears to be the earliest. The reliability of the results obtained in this initial study may be questioned since none of the three groups studied included more than 12 subjects. Of five tests used, the three which appeared to have some value and their validity coefficients were: Form Board Test .81, Cube Test .75, and the Stenquist Mechanical Assembling Test .84. Another early study on 25 machine shop and toolmaker apprentices by another worker produced the following validity coefficients: Form Board Test .40, Cube Test .33, and the Stenquist Mechanical Assembling Test .36.

O'Connor, writing in 1928, considered a good score on his Wiggly Block Test to be indicative of potentiality for tool-and-die making, all-round machining, machine setting-up and repairing, and structural iron and sheet metal work, but the value of this test is highly questionable in view of the low reliability reported by several authors.

In a more recent study of machinists, machinists' helpers, and machinist apprentices, validity coefficients of .55 and .35 were obtained on the Purdue Mechanical Assembly Test in two different plants.

Several studies have been conducted on machine-tool operators as contrasted with the all-round machinist. One study, reported in 1943, of operators working on turret lathes, precision grinders, milling machines, and Bullard automatics produced a multiple correlation of .67 for a weighted combination of the Revised Beta non-verbal intelligence test and a hand-tool dexterity test, with individual validities of .37 and .46 respectively. Another investigator attempted to establish critical scores on tests to aid in the selection of machine-tool operator trainees. He reported that the Revised Minnesota Paper Form Board Test and the Minnesota Spatial Relations Test did not give clear-cut results for this purpose. Some attempts have been made to use tests for the differential selection of potential machine-tool operators, machine shop trainees, and machinist apprentices. This potentially valuable aid to vocational counseling has not been fully developed as yet.

The Compound Slide Rest Test has been used by many workers in many countries in this field of aptitude study. Tagg, working in England, obtained the following correlations between performance on this test and trade ability: turning .62, fitting .55, pattern-making .39, machine operation .57, and toolmaking .59. He also reports correlations of .39 and .60 respectively between estimation of lengths and drawing of lengths with turning ability on a center lathe. These tests supposedly measure the static and dynamic forms of space perception which Tagg considers important for satisfactory performance in the tool room and machine shop. He is also of the opinion that individual tests are more reliable than group tests when testing for special abilities and states that standard psychological tests give low validities with practical abilities because of the elimination of extraneous conditions which are present on the job.

Pond has done extensive work in the United States attempting to relate intelligence to aptitude for machine shop work. Her work on the development of test measures for the selection of toolmaker apprentices indicated that the non-verbal tests used were more significant than the verbal tests. Clear-cut results showed that by the adoption of a "preferred range" of test scores for toolmaking apprentices, the quality of the group selected was improved as much as formerly had been accomplished in one year's trial in the training course. Later work showed that the percentage of new hires who were considered satisfactory apprentices could be increased from 83% to 93% by addition of the MacQuarrie Test of Mechanical Ability and the O'Connor Wiggly Block Test to the Scovill Classification Test and interview formerly used for selection. These three tests had validity coefficients of .315, .369, and .364 respectively. Validity coefficients of .411 and .393 were also reported for a Homemade Paper Form Board Test and the Kent-Shakow Industrial Form Board respectively.

English reports on the value of intelligence tests for this purpose are conflicting. One group of workers describes the use of a battery of seven tests covering intelligence, mechanical aptitude, mechanical ability, and dexterity for the selection of trainees for various skilled trades in the engineering industry in Birmingham, England. They found that the exclusion of a verbal intelligence test from the battery improved its prognostic value for 149 apprentices who were followed up 2½ years after being tested. Another worker used eight different tests for the selection of engineering trade apprentices in such trades as fitting, tinsmithing, and toolmaking. His study resulted in the establishment of critical scores on a verbal intelligence test. This worker is not impressed with the value of shop grades as a criterion for evaluating tests and feels that nothing can be a substitute for a thorough careful individual study of each apprentice.

The extensive work of German investigators in the development of tests for the selection of apprentices in the metalworking industries has been reviewed in this country primarily by Viteles who has frequently pointed out that Germany was a leader in this field. As early as 1921 it was reported that one-half of the large metal works in Germany were using psychological tests in the selection of workers; and manufacturers, schools, and labor unions had combined to require the use of such tests preliminary to the acceptance of an applicant for an apprenticeship in the metal trades industry. Most of the German investigators do not report work done on specific metalworking occupations, but write generally of apprentices in the metal industry. It has been pointed out by Viteles that the methods of various German workers agree in their use of a group of tests measuring underlying abilities presumably involved in mechanical operations of the type performed by apprentices under training as machinists, toolmakers, tinsmiths, foundry workers, and in other related occupations in the metal industry. In many instances the tests are analytic in character although among them are found some tests of the analogous type. One pair of investigators found markedly lower reliability and validity figures for the sensory tests used when compared with the tests of intelligence and motor ability.

The use of tests for the selection of apprentices in the metal trades has also been reported from Switzerland, Czechoslovakia, Holland and Russia. One writer reporting on the work in Russia criticizes the assumption that it is possible to use a single series of tests for an industry including over 100 specialized activities, each of which is characterized by highly diverse operations. This assumption appears to underlie all of the European and English studies, as well as many conducted in the United States. The opposite approach has been taken by the Occupational Analysis Section of the U. S. Employment Service which initially develops all of its aptitude test batteries on specific well-identified occupations. One European worker attempted to obtain a psychological profile of the metal trade and then determine the deviations of subsequent applicants from the trade profile. His analysis of a battery of eight tests disclosed what he termed technical and sensorimotor factors.

Sheet Metal Occupations

The tinsmith, coppersmith, and sheet metal occupations have been much less frequently studied than those involving various phases of machine-tool operation. In the United States the tests used have included the Otis Self-Administering Intelligence Test, the Minnesota Paper Form Board, the Minnesota Manual Dexterity Tests, O'Connor's Wiggly Block Test, Army Alpha, and Thurstone's Primary Mental Abilities Tests. An early study reported a validity coefficient of .35 on the Minnesota Paper Form Board Test for a group of 80 sheet metal trainees with the subsequent development of a test battery with a validity coefficient of .47 for sheet metal shop work. The study using Army Alpha and Thurstone's Primary Mental Abilities Tests reported no significant correlation between these tests and grades received in a course covering elements of metal work for aviation mechanics. On the basis of factor analysis it was concluded that there was no separate factor for a mechanical ability, but there were several factors more or less prominent in mechanical work whose pattern depended on the type and complexity of the work and on the point reached on the learning curve. A verbal factor was found present in training given for more complex mechanical work, along with a space factor, knowledge of mechanical processes, and two reasoning factors. A manual agility factor was found in routine jobs where individual differences depended upon the manipulation of objects, such as nuts and bolts.

Although several English studies of sheet metal occupations are reported, none adequately distinguishes between the great variety of trades or occupations included in the various studies. One report from Germany discusses the use of four tests measuring manual dexterity for the selection of unemployed persons to receive training in metalworking for the aircraft industry.

Foundry Occupations

Studies of actual foundry workers have been done almost entirely by foreign workers. One study reports the use of tests of coordination, regularity and precision in striking with a hammer and judgment of distances in the selection of workers for Russian copper foundries. Several studies of foundry workers have also been reported from Germany. One early study in the United States used the Healy Puzzle Box on 29 senior engineers who each had six semesters of shop work including foundry, forging, bench and

804 ENCYCLOPEDIA OF VOCATIONAL GUIDANCE

machine-tool metal work, patternmaking, and woodworking. Box opening correlated .49 with the average of the six grades, and box closing correlated .17.

Ornamental Iron Workers

In a study of differential occupational ability patterns by Dvorak two groups of ornamental iron workers from different companies were tested. The two groups differed significantly in the scores made on the O'Connor Tweezer Dexterity Test. In comparing the ornamental iron workers with machine operators working on lathes, drill presses, and boring mills, it was found that the former were superior to the latter in their manipulative abilities as measured by O'Connor's Finger and Tweezer Dexterity Tests and the Minnesota Mechanical Assembly and Spatial Relations Tests. The differences were statistically significant for nearly every test. It was concluded that the test scores reflected the more skillful job performance required of ornamental iron workers as compared with that required of machine operators. When compared with office clerks, it was found that the iron workers performed much better on the tests of manipulative abilities than on those of abstract functions.

Welding Occupations

The use of a battery of tests for the selection of arc welders in an engineering works is reported from Scotland. The tests reportedly closely reproduce actual working conditions and measure steadiness of movement and speed and accuracy of aim. A German study of tests administered to workers entering a training course for acetylene welders reports that the better tests seemed to be those measuring steadiness, calmness, perseverance, and slowness.

Summary

At the present time the vocational counselor will find few tests to aid him significantly in determining an individual's aptitude for metalworking occupations. Although a variety of "mechanical ability" tests may be available, the results obtained in actual industrial use have been so equivocal that their value as a counseling tool may be questioned. Much of the difficulty lies in the unreliability and low validity of the tests. It is evident that the counselor should not rely too heavily on test results in this field but must make full use of all job and worker information and other guidance tools and techniques available to him. It is quite likely that during the recently concluded war valuable work has been done which has yet to be reported. Consequently, the vocational counselor needs to be alert to new developments in this field of aptitude testing which is still largely in the stage of exploratory investigation.

Reference:

1. Hardtke, E. F. Aptitude testing for metalworking occupations. *Psychological Bulletin,* 1945, 42, 679–694.

E. F. H.

MEXICAN-AMERICANS. Present estimates of the number of Mexican-Americans range from 1½ to 3½ million and this diversity of opinion is a good indication of our statistical ignorance about the people. Probably the higher estimates are close to the facts. In the 1940 census Mexican-Americans were again enumerated as "whites" and so we must depend upon the 1930 census for information about the population as a whole. Even in this case generalizations should be made with caution, for in some areas there was an undercount. The 1930 census listed 1,423,000 Mexican-Americans according to "race." Of these more than 43% (617,000) were foreign-born. The 1940 census gives the following figures for foreign white stock, i.e. immigrants and persons with one or both parents born in Mexico:

1940   1,077,000, of which 35% (377,000) were foreign-born.
1930 (revised figures) 1,222,000 of which 52% (639,000) were foreign-born.

The distribution by regions indicates the highly localized character of the population. In New England, the Middle Atlantic, the South Atlantic, and East South Central states, the proportion of Mexican-Americans is negligible. The largest concentration is in the West South Central states (696,000 in 1930) and most of these are in Texas (684,000). The Pacific states are second (370,000) and again almost entirely in California (368,000). The Mountain states are third (249,000) with the highest concentration in Arizona (114,000). There are also significant numbers in the East North Central region (58,000) in which Illinois (29,000) is the most populous, and in the West North Central (40,000) with nearly half (19,000) in Kansas.

The proportion of foreign born varies widely in these regions from a high in the East North Central of 71% to a low in the Mountain states of 35%.

The population is about evenly divided between urban and rural areas. The rural population is in turn about evenly divided between farm and non-farm. The proportion of urban dwellers is misleading, however, because it includes important numbers of railroad and of migratory agricultural laborers who count the city as their regular place of residence even though they only winter there. For example, San Antonio (82,000), El Paso (58,000), and Houston (14,000) would have important components of migratory workers. The highest proportion of foreign-born are to be found in urban areas (48%), the next highest in rural non-farm (45%), and the lowest in rural farm (35%). These 1930 figures may be taken as merely indicative of the current situation. During the early thirties there was a repatriation movement, especially from California and Texas, and with the development of the wartime labor shortage of the forties there was a new influx of Mexican workers.

The history of Mexican immigration is recent, in large part attendant upon World War I, the boom of the 20's, and the immigration law of 1924. Prior to World War I the bulk of the Mexican-American population was in the southwest. Although there was some immigration around the turn of the century, there was also a sizable population derived from the colonial period. For our purposes they need not be distinguished from the later immigrants. The immigration of World War I, the 1920's, and World War II was characteristically labor recruitment, and not infrequently during occasions of labor tension the recruits were exploited as strikebreakers. At first unskilled, unorganized, and incompetent in English, they were to be found at the bottom of the labor pool. They did not, and often even now do not, compare favorably with Negroes, who at least have the nucleus of institutional organizations and some sophistication for dealing with the problems of an urban technology.

The only available data pertaining to the labor force are restricted to 1930. Of 1,002,000 persons of Mexican "race" over 10 years of age, 499,000 were classified as gainful workers. 432,000 (79%) of the males, but only 67,000 (15%) of the females were gainfully occupied. The largest number (175,000) of males were to be found in agriculture, in industries, chiefly as laborers (112,000), and in transportation (70,000) principally as railroad laborers (48,000). According to the census the largest number of females were in domestic and personal service (30,000), in agriculture (14,000), and in industry (13,000). The figures for agricultural workers, especially for women, are undoubtedly low. For instance, in California less than 1% of the females over 10 years of age were classified as agricultural workers which is patently erroneous. Similarly in Texas less than 4% of the female population over 10 years of age were classified as agricultural workers.

The bulk of Mexican-Americans working in agriculture are laborers. In California, for example, of 43,000 persons engaged in agriculture, 42,000 were laborers, principally migratory. The same is true of Arizona, but in New Mexico and Texas almost 30% of agricultural workers were either operators, including share croppers, or farm managers and foremen. During World War II the practice of importing migratory workers from Mexico, which was prevalent in the 20's, was revived, but under relatively well organized government supervision. Intensive use was also made of Mexican-Americans, although industrial competition and military service drained part of this labor force out of the agricultural market. Although the Mexican-American agricultural labor pools in California and Texas will continue to play an important part in regional economy they no longer predominate as they did in the 1920's.

As in agriculture the Mexican-American's position in industry is principally as a laborer. Recent comers to such work, they occupy the lower grade classifications, and the war-time up-grading was often transitory. Taylor pointed out in his analysis of the Calumet steel plants in 1928 that 2% of Mexican-Americans were in skilled categories, and 19% in semi-skilled, compared with 37% and 26% respectively for all employees. The marginal position of Mexican-American industrial workers is clear, and even in those fields—meat packing and steel—in which they have established a foothold, their position is still quite precarious. In railroad and construction labor they appear to be more firmly established although in the lower grades.

In the public services, clerical work, and professions there is a notable dearth of Mexican-American workers. This is at once a measure of the disadvantageous bargaining position of Mexican-Americans and of the inadequacy of the facilities and services of Mexican-American communities.

The job ceiling of Mexican-Americans is still low, and is chiefly restricted to "dirty" work. The Mexican-American communities suffer from an inadequate supply of physicians, lawyers, and social workers, and few teachers are placed in the public schools. Regional variations exist in the matter of the job ceiling, but the limits are most restrictive in the areas of highest concentration. The escape from the discriminatory handicaps into work of higher status is usually an indication that the individual no longer is identified as a "Mexican." This fact illustrates the principle of class, which is the core of the Mexican-American's disadvantageous position. Relatively dark color, which of course occurs in such a highly variable people, reinforces the handicaps of class and adds the factor of visibility to the stereotyping tendencies. In the Southwest and West stereotypic names also handicap those seeking positions involving public contact.

The occupational improvement of the population is retarded by the high degree of isolation of Mexican-Americans both in rural areas and in urban ghettos, by linguistic differences, and not infrequently by segregated and inferior schools, housing, and health facilities. Failure to enforce truancy laws, retardation of Spanish-speaking pupils, inferior and often segregated school facilities, the migratory patterns, and some resistance to formal education all conspire to reduce the training and constrict the work opportunities of Mexican-Americans. The educational crisis period is at the middle grades when the economically handicapped status of the familial group makes unproductive members burdensome. The most pressing need is for trained professional persons and educated leaders to raise the level of services in the community. Such persons might provide a nucleus of sophisticated leadership so that the population might improve its occupational status by other means than occasional individual crossing of the class line.

References:

1. Gamio, M. *Mexican immigration to the United States.* Chicago: University of Chicago Press, 1930.
2. Mexican Fact-Finding Committee, *Mexicans in California.* San Francisco: State of California, October 1930.
3. Taylor, P. S. *Mexican labor in the United States. University of California Publications in Economics* (1928–1934), *6, 7, 12.*
4. Tuck, R. *Not with the fist.* New York: Harcourt, Brace and Company, 1946.

L. B.

MILITARY CAREER, APTITUDE FOR A. The term, military career, is interpreted herein as implying full-time service in the profession of arms, for the duration of the aspirant's active life. Hence the following statements are confined to candidates for the Regular Army, though most of them are also applicable to the Reserve and National Guard components. Normal peacetime conditions of admission are assumed.

A military career may include service as an enlisted man, warrant officer, flight officer, or commissioned officer. The term, enlisted man, includes non-commissioned officers, namely, corporals and sergeants. Qualifications for the different grade are lowest for enlisted men and highest for commissioned officers; though it is possible, under certain circumstances, for an enlisted man to become a warrant, flight, or commissioned officer.

A detailed enumeration of the minimum qualifications for appointment to the various grades is beyond the scope of this article. They are specified in Army Regulations, of which a list is given below. In general, the basic requirements for military service may be classified under age, physical and mental fitness, education, character and general aptitude.

The following are the age limits for initial entry into the service:
Cadet, U. S. Military Academy—Between 17 and 22 years. (If a veteran, up to 24 years old)
Flying cadet—between 18 and 27 years.
Enlisted man—between 17 and 34 years. (17–18 with parents' consent.)
Commissioned officer (2nd Lieutenant)—between 21 and 27 years.

The following are the general educational requirements. In most cases, they or their equivalent, are determined by written examination. In some exceptional cases, they may be fulfilled in other ways, such as presentation of evidence of having successfully completed certain specified courses in school or college.

Enlisted men—4th grade literacy; but a high school education is an important aid to advancement. A.G.C.T. score of 70 or better.
Warrant and flight officers—a high school education or other special qualifications. (Appointed only from among men of prior military service)
Cadets, U. S. Military Academy—a high school education. (See U.S.M.A. Information Pamphlet)
Flying cadets—a high school education plus two years of college work successfully completed. Must be able to pass such mental examinations as are prescribed by the Commanding General, Army Air Forces.
Commissioned officers—a college education.

Physical fitness is determined by medical examination. (For detailed standards, see Army Regulations and the U.S.M.A. Information Pamphlet.) A man must be in excellent condition—free from diseases, abnormalities and deformities; sound in mind and nerves. Good moral character and general aptitude are essential to success in all military grades, but especially so for officers. The following paragraphs, therefore, apply particularly to candidates for cadetship or commission.

Although a candidate may fulfill all of the minimum requirements outlined above, he still may not possess the qualities necessary for a successful military career. His body must be fully useful as well as healthy; his mind must possess powers beyond the ability to pass an academic examination; and his character must embrace more than the negative virtues.

Military character implies good morals and freedom from vice. It also includes the common virtues of honesty, truthfulness and integrity. In addition it demands loyalty. A good soldier carries out the lawful intentions of his superior to the best of his ability, regardless of his personal likes or opinions, and does not in any way compromise his superior's authority or effectiveness. He is completely trustworthy, and his sense of duty can be depended on to accomplish assigned tasks without immediate supervision.

The mental and moral qualities of a good officer are manifold and important. He must be intelligent and possessed of good judgment and balance. He should be able to learn readily, and to adapt himself to new situations and changing conditions. His resourcefulness should be equal to the solution of unforeseen or difficult contingencies. He should have an effective personality and the force to get things done. He should be able to reason to right conclusions and to exercise common sense. He should be industrious and energetic. He should have the initiative to take necessary action without prompting, and to accomplish tasks without detailed direction. He should have tact and be able to get along with other people, and to cooperate with them in joint tasks. He should also possess the mechanical sense necessary to learn to operate the many machines and devices with which modern armies are equipped. His mentality must be rugged to stand up under strain and fatigue. And finally, he must have leadership—the quality that makes others willing to follow and obey him.

The attributes that go to make up physical aptitude for military service may be classified under five headings, arranged in descending order of ability to acquire. They are: endurance, strength, gross body coordination, speed of reaction or speed of muscle application, and motor educability. By endurance is meant the ability to work hard over an extended period of time—such as running or swimming long distances. Gross body coordination means the ability to do such things as dodge, climb, jump and throw. Speed of reaction or speed of muscle application means the ability to apply the body to dynamic movements such as high jumping and running rapidly. Motor educability is the ability to learn new coordinations.

A person who is deficient in the last three of the above is not likely to possess good aptitude for military service. Strength and endurance may be cultivated, coordination may be slightly improved, but speed and motor educability appear to be fixed characteristics. Tests at the Military Academy have shown that they are not susceptible of improvement.

No individual can possess to a high degree all of the desirable qualities discussed above. However, a vocational counselor, who has formed a clear conception of the type of person likely to succeed in the profession of arms, will be able to determine from his own observation, and that of his associates, whether a young man is suitable material. The standardized intelligence, scholastic aptitude and physical aptitude tests, now in use at most schools and colleges, will provide valuable supplementary information. Favorable indications of aptitude are: effective personality, ability to get along with fellow students, participation in sports and other extra-curricular acivities; exhibition of energy, industry, initiative and leadership in school and college.

References:

WAR DEPARTMENT. *Army Regulations.* Washington:
U. S. Government Printing Office

(a) AR 40–105, Standards of Physical Examination for Entrance into the Regular Army, National Guard and Organized Reserves.
(b) AR 40–110, Standards of Physical Examination for Fying.
(c) AR 605–5, Commissioned Officers, Appointment in Regular Army.
(d) AR 610–10, Warrant Officers, Appointment in Regular Army.
(e) AR 610–50, Flight Officers, General Provisions.
(f) AR 615–160, Enlisted Men, Flying Cadets.

WAR DEPARTMENT. *Information Pamphlet, United States Military Academy, West Point, N. Y.,* Washington:
U. S. Government Printing Office.

F. B. W.

MINISTRY (and Other Church Vocations), COUNSELING CANDIDATES FOR THE. The typical church vocation is the ministry, priesthood, or rabbinate, but there is increasing diversity of unordained fields of religious work in the present century. Particularly are there openings for women in growing numbers. Thus the term "church vocation" denotes all employed work under auspices of religion—minister, missionary (medical, teaching, agricultural, etc.), parish worker, area church council executive, religious journalist, and dozens of other jobs. Pertinent data may be subsumed under these headings: The Religious "Plus" Factor, Needed Interests, and Aptitudes, Jobs and Openings, Educational Requisites, Testing and Interviewing.

The Religious "Plus" Factor

Many counselors feel that church vocations are "out of their field" because related to specific religious factors not encountered in other counseling. This is particularly true of advisers unfamiliar with religious concepts, or professing religious faith markedly different from that of the student. Such obstacles, however, should not prevent helpfulness even though they result in caution or even diffidence in such counseling. We should be equipped to (1) recognize the differentia of a church vocation, (2) commend this field to those showing proper interest and skill, (3) present suggestions as to education and as to clearance with the church group involved.

The occasion or experience known as a "call" into religious work is regarded by most people as completely mysterious, and by some as evidence of mere psychological naïveté. Yet to the religious experient, for whom it may take many forms, it is the process of becoming convinced that a certain life work is the will of God for his or her career. It may be a gradual process of decision and realization, highlighted by occasional or climactic summary. In a group of 100 Protestant seminarians recently, 60 could not point to a specific occasion (such as is illustrated in Scripture) as the sudden experience of a "call": for them it had been a gradual finding-out of the largest destiny for them, with prayer, church activity, and education. Thus generally in our day, a "call" to religious work need not be a miraculous appearance or a dated emotional process.

Again, a religious "call"—in each religious group—need not summon a person into the field of professional church work. Every person in ordinary life, according to Protestant, Roman Catholic, or Jewish doctrine, is divinely fitted for and summoned to a special sort of life work. Thus in any theistic system, one is "called" to work as a physician, a teacher, or a farmer, that summons being in most ways indistinguishable from one into the ministry. A "call" interpreted as from God does not necessarily point a young person to a church vocation, unless that young person has also special equipment for such work. Thus part of a "call" to church work is the possession of personal gifts—interpreted as also granted by God—enabling the recipient to carry out the divine summons in that particular job.

Still, the fact remains that anyone entering a church vocation should be convinced of a special religious propriety in his doing so. He should have adequate background of church life in order to know what is involved. He should be able to pray and thus to have felt direct intuitive relationship with God in his choice. He should consider this vocation in comparison with others, as being for him not only the biggest and most challenging, but that which will command most of his skills and potentialities. He should enter it without such motives as attainment of professional prestige, mere wish of his family, "course of easiest livelihood," or "I-might-as-well-try-this-as-anything-else." The person who has a "call" to a church vocation makes his choice in an atmosphere—usually recognizable to the vocational counselor at once—which is distinctive, sincere, and spiritual. Even where the young person is perplexed, and himself in doubt as to whether he has a "call" from God to this type of work, the factors involved in genuine religious experience are usually apparent.

Thus the counselor (1) should not expect modern youth to have a dramatic, distinct, dated "call" from God, but (2) may find persons "called" of God to many a task done in His name, and (3) should look for specific marks of spiritual attitudes toward vocation on the part of those considering any church vocation.

Needed Interests and Aptitudes

Anyone considering a church vocation may well be scrutinized for these characteristics: concern for people, growing religious experience, above-average intellect, ability to lead, and administrative aptitude.

In aptitude and interest tests, the same grouping as to *concern for people* usually includes church workers as well as personnel counselors, "Y" staff workers, social workers, teachers, and insurance salesmen. There is some room, doubtless, for the introspective, recessive person in the church, but such a person is usually interested in this field primarily to solve his own problem and find his own way out—not to advance the program. Rather, he should evidence not only a gregarious, normal interest in others, but definite altruistic helpfulness: these may be demonstrated in school contacts, church activities, Scouting, or even family attitudes. The man or woman more interested in self or theological study or liturgy, than in other people, can be assured of an unsatisfying future in almost any church vocation.

By the second characteristic, that he should have growing religious experience, is meant not a static or dogmatic religious position inherited or assumed years before; but a current active faith keeping pace with the rest of the balanced learning process. H. E. Fosdick says, "Most ministers I know were converted in seminary" —meaning that their prior decision for the ministry was vague and tentative compared with what they found as they really entered into the field. This is often the case. Yet the person whose religion is superficial intellectually or emotionally, external, or variously unreal, should be cautioned against too ready a decision for a church vocation.

Need for an *above-average intellect* is apparent, in this field as in any requiring ability to guide others in thinking. Most church counselors agree that generally a minimum I.Q. of 110 is a requisite. But more indicative is the cumulative school record through the years: if grades have not been average or above, the young person will probably find a church vocation involving too great mental exertion in years ahead. It is to be said, however, that intellectual persistence is often more useful than intellectual brilliance in this field.

Ability to lead is of course a complex matter, to be judged only on the basis of actual performance rather than of questionnaire or interview. Voice, presence, physical attractiveness, vigor, directness —these are important in a church vocation as in few other job areas.

The final element of *administrative aptitude* comes into the picture because those in church vocations are usually charged with financial campaigns, budgets, program details, supervision of committees and teams, and other executive functions. Those who have shown inability to handle money wisely, or who have notably fallen down on responsibility in school or community, should be cautioned as to this point if they consider a church vocation. A minister or other church worker must be a good manager if his career is to be fruitful.

Jobs and Openings

In the ministry since a time shortly after the first World War there has been a rising need for trained men. This is true of almost every religious group, those of which it is not true being largely churches which accept untrained workers. Since a date about five years prior to the second World War, there has also been a constant and growing need for women in church vocations. The picture is clear that the Church is ready for a greatly increased number of able professional workers—some of them to replace inadequate and ineffective leaders already serving in church vocations.

The 1940 census shows the need for many young workers in this field. It reveals that the median age of all ministers (133,494) is 45.8 years—higher than that of any other professional group except veterinarians (50.1). Doctors (44.1), judges and lawyers (42.), and particularly the new category of research technicians (33.6), are all younger. Thus it is plain that the ranks of ministers are not being replaced by new men as they should be—even granting that (as insurance companies agree) ministerial longevity is amazing. Salaries of church workers are modest. A survey in 1945 (112,509 clergy) showed that 51% received less than $1,200 a year and 24.4% less than $600: here a compensating factor is that many clergymen receive part of their salary in goods rather than cash, and many have other employment. Generally, the trained minister begins his professional life better paid than his colleagues in other professions; 10 years later they have largely outdistanced his rather static salary. Yet in an average community he is usually paid more than most of his parishioners. To a degree which has become proverbial, the minister in most cases does "make ends meet," educating his family and living comfortably, often because of the unextravagant tastes of his household.

Numerical needs for missionaries are qualified by the fact that post-war mission work is infinitely varied and specialized. There is need for agriculturalists, engineers, merchandisers, chemists, language teachers, foresters, hygienists, doctors, dentists, office workers, psychiatrists, recreation leaders—all to be sent to fields abroad or in the Americas under the Church auspices. The aggregate of these, numerically, is in the 1,000's—computed both according to program needs, and according to financial ability of the churches which send out workers. Economic conditions in this country readily affect the mission program, but even at low ebb it demands hundreds of men and women each year.

"Religious education" is another field, including such jobs as these: director of religious education (a "D.R.E.") in a local church or mission; week-day church-school teacher (often paid by the public schools); community workers; deaconess; church social worker (for a downtown parish or a church-related settlement house); campus worker among students; youth director in a parish, etc. Often men fill these positions, but the majority of workers are women, and the numerical need for workers here is constant and growing. Roman Catholics likewise report an acute need for nuns among various orders, especially those devoted to teaching.

A further special field is the "ministry of music," which includes workers ranging from the part-time organist or choir director, to the full employed leader of music in a parish, institution, or school. As church programs become more fully established, and as American general taste in music grows, there is a mounting demand in this field also.

Educational Requisites

There is increasing unanimity among church groups regarding required training for the ministry, but even yet the standards are decidedly varied. In certain sects no educational requirement whatever is made, especially where ecstatic gifts are regarded as important or where choice of ministers is made by lot. Some larger denominations regionally require only college training, usually combining theological courses with those in arts during the undergraduate years. Such minimum requirement, however, is giving way generally to the demand that a full college course plus three seminary years is the only full preparation for ordination.

The same diversity of standards applies to training for mission work or religious education leadership. The range is from so-called "faith missions," which sometimes appoint workers with almost no formal training, to denominations which insist upon complete graduate study in any special field. (Viz., mission teachers must have M.A.'s; chemists, Ph.D.'s; agriculturalists, a graduate degree in agriculture, etc.) Women workers in American parishes and agencies often have merely college training, or less: only in church groups which take very seriously their educational task most women workers have the Master's Degree for most jobs. The M.A. in Religious Education (or M.R.E. as the equivalent is sometimes called), is the highest degree expected, usually requiring two years' graduate study beyond college. Some schools grant a bachelor's degree in this field, the B.R.E., for the college major.

Protestant policy has traditionally been to defer until middle or late teens any decision for a church vocation, with the claim that earlier choice is immature. Roman Catholics on the other hand have encouraged this career selection by the end of grade school, enrolling candidates for the priesthood (and in some cases women's orders) for segregated study through the high school and college years. Thus for the Roman Catholic, five years of minor seminary plus five of major seminary usually parallel the Protestants' eight years of high school and college plus three years of seminary. Preparation for the rabbinate in the Reform Jewish group follows generally the Protestant pattern.

In most cases, therefore, curriculum choice in high school, as it affects preparation for a church vocation, is the normal pre-college course. Particular weight given to English and social science is helpful. But more important is normal participation in extra-curricular activities: The study-load should not be so great as to handicap the development of the integrated person. Voluntary after-school responsibilities, elective for the science technician, for example, are required for the candidate for a church vocation.

In college, upon general advice of the American Association of Theological Schools, the optimum pre-seminary major courses are history, English, philosophy, and social studies. For the student going on later to seminary, a minimum of religion courses is indicated—since he will either repeat or "unlearn" in graduate study what he has had in college, and since there are undergraduate cultural courses which he must not crowd out with religion. This is particularly true also of the girl who may wish to short-cut her liberal arts college course in order to "specialize" in religious education techniques; she is usually better advised to secure the broadest and deepest cultural equipment possible, since her work either in a large educated urban parish, or in a bleak outpost, will require depth of cultural interest even more than technical skill. Courses in music and art appreciation are especially to be recommended to either men or women intending to do church work. Specialization in church music may begin at any level of study beyond high school. Some colleges offer a major in sacred music, even granting a Bachelor of Music or a Bachelor of Sacred Music for such study. Full training for the "ministry of music" includes the further step of two years' graduate work for a Master of Music or Master of Sacred Music degree.

Choice of a graduate school or seminary may depend upon ecclesiastical requirements involved: each denomination has its own schools. But there are also inter- or non-denominational seminaries which are acceptable to most church groups. Seminary study during three years ordinarily leads to the Bachelor of Divinity degree (B.D.). Since this includes professional rather than merely academic training, it usually provides the equivalent of one year's regular academic credit toward a Ph.D. in religion. This final degree is most useful for teaching positions, rather than parish work. In this country the Doctor of Divinity (D.D.) is invariably an honorary acquisition, although in England it may be earned.

Testing and Interviewing

Because students intending church vocations are a small minority, and because the field is a complex one in counseling, most testing instruments give only marginal attention to this field. It is obvious that a cluster of aptitudes and interest similar to those leading to social work, personnel counseling, teaching ,and certain types of sales also serve church vocations. But the essential factor of religious conviction, and its intensity—upon which effectiveness in this area depends rather completely—cannot be accurately gauged by tests. Especially is this true during the teen-age period when idealism makes career intentions volatile and unpredictable.

For measuring primary interest in Church vocations long use and familiarity among counselors make the Strong *Vocational Interest Blank* still probably the best general indicator available. The "social service" category of the Kuder *Preference Record,* though ingenious, provides a selection of interests too broad to be helpful in this specific field. The same comment is true of the personal-social classification arrived at in the Lee-Thorpe *Occupational Interest Inventory.* The Allport-Vernon "Study of Values" is more explicit, but it succeeds in appraising attitudes toward religion rather than toward actual church jobs; where this is the item in question, it seems eminently useful. Church groups themselves have used the Lufburrow *Vocational Interest Locator* with satisfaction, although the categories it provides are somewhat arbitrary.

The fact is, that although work is at present being done in various places on an indicator of interest-aptitude in church vocations, nothing which has yet been brought into general use has achieved common approbation. The clearest path ahead for the counselor is apparently to use interest instruments to establish general concern within the field of personal-social relations; then to secure the results of any standard test of stability and emotional balance (such as the Bernreuter *Personality Inventory*). Judgment on the candidate's actual effectiveness in the work of church vocations is probably best judged, beyond this point, by observation of the cumulative school record and active participation in church activities.

Interviewing in regard to church vocations is conditioned by several special factors which set it apart from general counseling.

(1) Rather definite social approval or disapproval is usually directed toward the young person whose choice of a church vocation is made known in his group. Nicknames, smugness, exaggerated "piosity," subtle persecution, undeserved preferment, etc., may be involved. A counselor should be readily aware

of these possibilities, taking every care to prevent premature and superficial decisions, or their announcement.

(2) Since the specifically religious and ecclesiastical aspects of the interview are often unfamiliar ground for the counselor, there should always be cooperation with pastor or rabbi in counseling. Many ministers assume that vocational guidance advisers automatically seek to disparage church vocations, and to guide young people into alternative fields. At the same time, clergymen themselves need the special help which the counselor can give with their parish young people at this point.

(3) The advisee in this field very often has been struck by the inspiration of some conspicuously successful church leader, rather than by the actual job to be done. If this concern is genuine, the counselor may well offer details about the work itself, rather than merely questioning the initial motivating factor: *great* enthusiasms for careers today are rare, and to be encouraged if the total direction vocationally is wisely chosen.

(4) If the student shows every skill and interest fitting him for work in the field of religion, but hesitates because of an "allergy" to ecclesiasticism or church professionalism, he should be asked to "look deeper," for this reaction has characterized many of the ablest candidates for church vocations during the past several decades. The constructive insurgent—man or woman —is useful and widely sought in every church group. Such a young person may be guided, through summer church camps, conferences, "caravans," and work projects, as well as parish youth activity, to investigate the specific activity involved in church vocations rather than accepting them as a traditional career pattern.

References:

1. Eddy, S. and Page, K. *Creative pioneers.* New York: Association, 1937.
2. Lotz, P. H. *Creative personalities* III. Founders of Christian movements and communions. New York: Association, 1940.
3. Palmer, A. W. *The minister's job.* Chicago: Willett, 1937.
4. Mayer, O. and Borne, M. A. *Directors of religious education.* Chicago: International Council, 1939
5. Nelson, J. O. Leaflets on church vocations, gratis: 297 Fourth Avenue, New York 10, N. Y.
6. ———, Ed. *We have this ministry.* New York: Association Press, 1946.
7. Student Volunteer Movement. Leaflets on mission work at home or abroad. Address: 156 Fifth Avenue, New York 17, N. Y.

J. O. N.

MINORS. The group of minors with whom this article deals are the boys and girls who do not continue their education beyond high school. It includes those who drop out of school for work in the elementary or high school grades and those who combine part-time jobs with school attendance, as well as those who start work on completion of high school. Because of their immaturity, lack of prior work experience, limited educational plans, and in many cases limited mental ability, vocational guidance for this group presents different and more difficult problems than guidance for older persons or young people who plan to attend college or technical schools.

According to the Census of 1940—which presents a more accurate picture of the normal extent and nature of employment by young people in this country than do the swollen figures of the war years—the number and occupational distribution of those in the labor force, at ages which suggest that, by and large, they did not go beyond high school in their education was as follows:

EMPLOYMENT OF YOUNG PEOPLE IN THE UNITED STATES
(U. S. Census—1940)

	14-15 Yrs.	16-17 Yrs.	18-19 Yrs.
Number in labor force	249,521	1,029,291	2,645,289
Employed	209,347	662,967	1,808,321
Public emergency work . . .	2,122	77,186	218,337
Seeking work—experienced workers	15,769	116,445	325,857
Seeking work—new workers	22,283	172,693	292,774
Occupational distribution of those employed			
Professional and semi-professional	393	3,402	57,633
Farmers and farm managers	1,205	6,688	41,516
Proprietors, managers and officials, excluding farm.	261	1,734	11,263
Clerical, sales and kindred workers	21,642	77,912	384,897
Craftsmen, foremen and kindred workers	675	8,097	57,588
Operatives and kindred workers	9,398	84,112	360,354
Domestic service workers. .	15,141	78,710	166,411
Protective service workers.	53	660	42,359

EMPLOYMENT OF YOUNG PEOPLE IN THE UNITED STATES—*Cont'd*
(U. S. Census—1940)

	14-15 Yrs.	16-17 Yrs.	18-19 Yrs.
Service workers, except domestic and protective ..	6,158	40,392	134,573
Farm laborers and foremen			
Wage workers	29,806	93,406	155,403
Unpaid family workers.	111,037	212,331	232,675
Laborers, except farm and mine	7,105	40,565	132,915
Not reported	6,473	14,958	30,734
	209,347	662,967	1,808,321

These figures suggest the magnitude of the task of providing guidance for minors. Even eliminating the 556,000 rural boys and girls listed as unpaid family workers in agriculture, there remain nearly 2,000,000 young people under 20 years who were employed, either full or part time, and nearly a million and a quarter more who were seeking regular employment—all of whom were potential clients for vocational guidance, both before and after they left school.

Of those actually employed the large majority, in each age group, were not attending school and presumably were full-time workers.

YOUNG PEOPLE EMPLOYED, BY SCHOOL ATTENDANCE STATUS
(U. S. Census—1940)

Age	*No. Employed*	*Attending School*	*Not Attending School*
14 and 15 yrs. ..	209,347	75,021	134,326
16 and 17 yrs. ..	662,967	111,741	551,226
18 and 19 yrs. ..	1,808,321	114,678	1,693,643

Both the need for and the difficulties of vocational guidance for minors are increased by the fact that many of those dropping out of school for work are equipped with only an elementary school education, often less, or a year or two of high school. The following table shows the median school year completed by young people not attending school in the country as a whole and in urban communities. (This is based on the total population not in school, irrespective of whether they were employed.)

MEDIAN GRADE COMPLETED BY YOUNG PEOPLE 14–19 YEARS
NOT ATTENDING SCHOOL
(U. S. Census—1940)

Age	Total	Urban
14 years	6.7	7.8
15 years	7.5	8.2
16 years	8.2	8.8
17 years	8.7	9.5
18 years	9.8	10.8
19 years	10.6	11.6

The limited educational achievement of young workers is further
indicated by figures showing the highest school grades completed by
minors receiving employment certificates. In 1941, selected as a
more typical year than subsequent ones, the Federal Children's
Bureau received reports on the school grades completed by 205,250
minors 14 to 18 years who were issued their first regular employment certificates. (In most States regular certificates are granted
only to children engaging in full-time work.)

HIGHEST SCHOOL GRADE COMPLETED BY MINORS 14–18 YEARS
RECEIVING FIRST REGULAR EMPLOYMENT CERTIFICATES IN 1941
(U. S. Children's Bureau)

	Total Reporting	6th Grade or Lower	7th Grade	8th Grade	9, 10, 11 Grade	Grade 12 or Higher
14 and 15 yrs.	6,609	978	945	2,002	2,620	64
16 and 17 yrs.	198,641	11,511	11,851	29,132	113,893	32,254

In two-thirds of the States children are legally free to leave
school for work at 14 years. Usually they must have completed a
specified grade—in most cases the elementary course, but sometimes the 5th or 6th grade. In all States a child may leave school
for work at 16 years. Since guidance must serve these early school-
leavers as well as those who complete high school, it must begin in
the early grades. Even in the elementary school guidance—under
whatever name it is called and by whomever it is given—is needed
and should be directed to persuading the child to continue his
schooling and to helping him select the right kind of high school.
Lack of such guidance, together with low standard and poorly enforced compulsory attendance laws, is one reason that many children still leave school on, or even before, completion of the 8th
grade. It is also in part responsible for the fact that the academic
courses in high schools, designed for college preparatory work, are

crowded with boys and girls who have no intention of going to college.

For the child in high school, vocational guidance and educational guidance are inseparable and must fill many needs. One of the functions of guidance is to acquaint the child with vocational possibilities and help him in his choice of and preparation for future work. If guidance begins early enough in the school program, there is no need for the child's deciding immediately upon a vocation or beginning and following through on a specific line of preparation. There is time for experimentation and exploration, and in many cases this can continue even after school leaving. One function of guidance is to help the individual determine at what point specialization—either in education or in jobs—should begin.

Guidance must also help the high school child, and his parents, to meet the constantly recurring question as to whether he shall continue in school, leave school for employment, or combine school with part-time work, either under a school-work program controlled by the schools, or independently in an after school job of his own choosing. Many factors must be considered in reaching a decision, and the guidance worker must know the child's family and economic background, his interests, abilities and aptitudes, personality and social adjustment, progress in school, and physical condition—as well as the type of jobs open to him on a part or full-time basis. Familiarity with Federal and State laws regulating the employment of minors is essential as well as ability to judge the suitability of various types of work, the physical hazards involved, their educational values, chances for advancement, etc.

The United States Office of Education has listed six principal elements in a high school guidance program which can be summarized as follows:

1. *Occupational information*—to secure and present facts regarding local occupational requirements and opportunities as well as trends in the Nation as a whole.
2. *Personal inventory*—to secure, record and interpret information secured through reports, records, tests and measurements and personal interviews.
3. *Counselling*—to assist the individual in identifying his major problem, planning lines of action, getting a start toward carrying them out and modifying them when necessary.
4. *Exploration and use of training opportunities*—to make information available concerning training opportunities at all levels and for all educational and occupational fields.

5. *Placement*—to assist young people in securing suitable employment, full-time or part-time.

6. *Follow-up*—to maintain contact with school leavers over a period of years in order to give them further assistance, and also to check individual achievements and the school-leavers experiences as an aid in evaluating and improving both the guidance program and the general educational program of the schools.

To an increasing extent the value of work experience for high school students, including paid part-time employment, is being recognized and this has opened up new guidance opportunities. As early as 1930 the Report on Vocational Guidance of the White House Conference on Child Health and Protection stated:

"Much direction can be given through part-time jobs, before the child leaves school, if he has opportunities for consultation along the way. Part-time jobs, for some inexplicable reason, are too often regarded as ways of keeping children out of mischief, and miss the chance of being a real educative force. To some groups they offer the very best kind of tryout experience, often to groups where other opportunities at early occupational exploration are rare. To others they offer financial help which makes further attendance at school possible. Part-time work is not always plentiful, and the tendency is to snatch at what there is without selection. But just as careful attention should be given to the placement and supervision of children in part-time as in full-time work. So far as actual operations are concerned, the opportunities for learning may be meager, but there is a fund of valuable experience to be gained; how to apply for the job, what to wear, how to play fair in a bad situation, and countless other details which can be carried on to a full-time job later."

The Report of a Special Committee of the American Youth Commission and other cooperating organizations, *What the High Schools Ought to Teach,* stated in 1940:

"There is no factor of general education which is more important to consider than work. This statement should not be thought of as applying merely to a few marginal cases but should be accepted as a principle of the widest possible application. Those who are to enter the professions need to labor at some period in their lives in order to gain an understanding and appreciation of what labor is. Those who are going to earn their living by labor have a right to be trained under competent supervision so that they may enter on their careers under the most favorable conditions possible.

"If the schools are to adopt work as a genuinely acceptable part of their program they will have to be prepared to yield some of the preferred hours of the day which are now devoted to their traditional courses. They will often be obliged to make provision for instruction in such a way that it will be possible for their pupils to work a number of full days each week for employers who will take them for part-time work. . . . There are valid educational reasons for advocating a work program as an essential part of the curriculum of secondary schools. A pupil gains, through the constructive handling of tools and materials, insight into the nature of things with regard to his relations to his environment that he cannot gain in any other way. Modern psychology recognizes as one of its most fundamental principles the truth that reactions, or what are commonly called 'behavior patterns,' in technical writings, condition the development of experience far more than do impressions. It is only when an individual reacts to an object that he concentrates attention on it and becomes fully aware of its chaacter and value."

During the war, both to help meet manpower needs and to keep young people from dropping out of school, programs of part-time paid work for school students, developed under school auspices and with school credit given for employment, have developed rapidly in many parts of the country. In some cases such programs are limited to students of 16 and 17 years, but in others children of 14 and 15 may participate. Many guidance workers believe that these programs offer a new, practical and effective method of acquainting the student with problems of the working world, giving him preliminary and experimental work experience, and bridging the gap between school and work for those not enrolled in vocational courses (where part-time work had been developed to some degree even before the war).

These war-time programs and the various bases on which they have been organized in different communities are now being studied with a view to determining their value, educational and otherwise, and the desirability of continuing them as part of the postwar secondary school curriculum. Although these studies are not yet completed, it is evident that a major factor in their success or failure is the degree to which they are associated with the vocational guidance work of the schools, and the scope and quality of the guidance program. The selection of students for participation in school-work programs, the selection of employment acceptable for school credit, the supervision and follow-up given the children and the correlation of their work interests with the school program are areas in which school administrators, curriculum committees and guidance personnel must work closely together.

Despite the tremendous need for guidance of high school students and the broad range of activities included under an adequate guidance program, progress has been comparatively slow in extending such service as an integral part of the programs of the public high schools.

The President's Advisory Committee on Education reported in 1938 that "in few fields of endeavor are the existing social facilities more inadequate than in vocational guidance." It pointed out that there were no vocational guidance programs in the public schools in at least half of the cities of the United States of 10,000 or more population and that guidance was especially lacking in the larger rural high schools, despite the fact that normally many young people go to the cities for employment.

In 1944, 32 States had Supervisors of Occupational Information and Guidance in the State Departments of Education and, in 1942, 80 local school systems reported Directors of Guidance among their personnel. This does not necessarily mean adequate guidance work, however, even in those communities where such services have been established. The latest figures available on the number of guidance officers employed are those reported by the United States Office of Education in 1939. At that time there were in the United States 23,032 public high schools with an enrollment of about 7 million pupils. Only 1,297 of these schools reported having counsellors or guidance officers employed on half or more than half time basis. These 1,297 schools had an enrollment of 2,062,341 and employed 2,286 guidance officers—an average of one officer (not necessarily full-time) to about every 900 pupils.

Wide variations existed among States and 7 States—New York, California, Pennsylvania, Michigan, New Jersey, Illinois and Ohio —employed 61 per cent of all the counsellors and guidance officers in the United States high schools.

One of the basic requirements for effective guidance work is well-trained personnel. The successful guidance worker must, in a sense, have three specialties—he must know young people, education and industry. Although this is recognized by leaders in vocational guidance, and job qualifications and standards for training of guidance personnel have been recommended, the job of guidance in many communities still falls to the Latin instructor whose classes are shrinking, or the teacher, lacking a year or two of retirement, for whom a full teaching schedule is a burden.

Undoubtedly, both the extent and quality of vocational guid-

ance for minors has improved since 1938, due to the need for training war workers. There are no figures, however, to show how great
this increase has been nor anything to indicate to what extent war
created guidance services in the schools may become permanent.
There is ample evidence, however, that the need for vocational
guidance of minors will be even greater in the reconversion and
post-war years. The economic conditions and the requirements of
industry will be changing. Many young workers who left school for
work during the War may find themselves unemployed—and without any saleable skills. Many in-school youth, who normally would
leave school for work, will face the fact that there is no place for
them in an over-crowded labor market and must be persuaded to
remain in school and prepare themselves for future work. Unless
guidance work is extended rapidly both in extent and quality, boys
and girls of tomorrow may be caught on the same sea of bewilder-
ment and despair that engulfed youth during the depression years.

References:

1. *American Association of School Administrators.* Youth education today,
    1938.
2. *Advisory Committee on Education.* Report of the Committee, February,
    1938.
3. *American Council on Education.* What the high schools ought to teach.
    Report of a Special Committee, 1940.
4. *Culbert and Smith.* Counseling young workers. New York: Vocational
    Service for Juniors, 1939.
5. *United States Department of the Interior, Office of Education.* Guid-
    ance programs for rural high schools. Washington: Government Print-
    ing Office, 1939.
6. *White House Conference on Child Health and Protection.* Vocational
    guidance. New York: Century Co., 1932.

G. F. Z.

MOTION PICTURES.   Motion pictures, though based on earlier
scientific discoveries, are usually considered the invention of Thomas
A. Edison, who devised the kinematograph in 1872. Since that time
this device, improved by the addition of synchronized sound, has
had such widespread acceptance and influence that it is considered
one of the most powerful factors in producing the social changes of
the past half century. Motion pictures are now one of the two leading forms of entertainment, one of the principal visual aids in
education, and an important tool for many special purposes. In all
three of these roles motion pictures have great significance for vocational guidance.

Much research, notably the Payne Fund Studies, has indicated that motion pictures used for entertainment have profound effects upon the knowledge, attitudes, and habits of the millions of children and adults who see them. Since photoplays result in great prominence for actors, directors, and other persons connected with the film industry, and since they often portray vocational activities as incidental to the plots, it is evident that they are important, though often unrecognized, influences upon the vocational ideas of young people. Film producers are seldom concerned with this function of their products, and in addition, most photoplays glamorize, caricaturize, or otherwise distort vocations. Hence the vocational guidance worker must be prepared to counteract such undesirable influences. On the other hand there have been a number of feature pictures and short films, particularly biographical ones, which are outstandingly constructive in vocational guidance. Teachers and counsellors can often integrate the pupil's interest in such pictures with their more formal vocational guidance program. They may do this by stimulating attendance at such movies, discussing points for which to watch, having the students make reports, using them as an introduction to the school's procedures in studying careers, and in many other ways. The monthly publication, *Film and Radio Discussion Guide* provides considerable aid in this connection.

The use of motion pictures as an instructional tool has had the widespread and increasing attention of educators for some years. In teaching about occupations and vocational planning, as in other fields of education, motion pictures offer the following advantages: (1) They overcome limitations of time, space, and availability; (2) They economize time and effort; (3) They provide greater realism than other classroom devices; (4) They eliminate unimportant or distracting details and focus attention at the most significant points; (5) They utilize vividness and other dramatic devices to stimulate interest, facilitate learning, and lengthen retention; (6) They make use of close-ups, slow motion, animation, time-lapse, microphotography, flashbacks, and other special methods to visualize what could not otherwise be seen; (7) They are available at any time, may be repeated as often as desired, in whole or in part, and can reach large numbers of students, and (8) They can be readily integrated with other instructional activities because the instructor knows exactly what the motion picture will present.

On the other hand, there are certain disadvantages in the use of motion pictures in vocational guidance, such as: (1) The cost of films and projection equipment is too high for many school budgets; (2) Available films do not cover all topics, and may thus present unbalanced or distorted ideas; (3) Available films are often objectionable because of poor technical quality, advertising, propagandizing, or subordination of educational to entertainment value; (4) Obsolescence in films cannot be handled adequately because of the expense factor; (5) Unless motion pictures are thoroughly integrated into the curriculum, or other special methods employed, it is likely that previous associations will cause the student's mental set to be for entertainment rather than learning; (6) Because the film is a self-contained, popular unit that can be presented to large numbers without trained instructors in a brief period of time, it may easily lead a school to be satisfied with a very superficial type of vocational guidance, and (7) Just as much as they enrich the efforts of the good instructor, so motion pictures make it easier for the lazy instructor to get by with inadequate preparation and effort. All of these disadvantages can and are being overcome through increased understanding of the value and role of motion pictures and through the combined efforts of various vocational guidance workers and agencies.

There are several types of motion picture films which are available for vocational guidance uses. Theatrical films are 35 mm. wide and involve very expensive projection equipment and safety precautions. Most educational films are of the 16 mm. size and are printed on "safety" film which eliminates the fire hazard. Silent films are still widely used for educational purposes because of the relatively inexpensive and widespread availability of the necessary equipment. Sound films and equipment are more expensive, but are of obviously greater usefulness, particularly since sound films can be run with or without the sound (though never on silent film projectors). Either 16 mm. film or the more economical 8 mm. size may be used for school-made vocational films, or for taking pictures on occupational excursions. Closely related to motion pictures is the filmstrip, which is a strip of 35 mm. motion picture film, projected as a series of still pictures, with or without an accompanying sound recording. Special projectors are needed for filmstrips.

There are four kinds of motion pictures which are useful for vocational guidance purposes. One kind, specifically prepared for this purpose, deals with general problems involved in selecting a vocation. "Finding Your Life Work," produced by Vocational Guidance Films, Inc.; "Aptitudes and Occupations," produced by Coronet Productions; "Choosing a Vocation," an Erpi Classroom Film distributed by Encyclopaedia Brittanica Films, Inc.; and "I Want a Job," produced by Forum Films, Inc., are the best examples of this kind of film.

A second kind of vocational guidance film deals intensively with a specific occupation or occupational group, providing such information about it as the activities in which the worker engages, the training which is required, where and how the training is secured, and its advantages and disadvantages. Producers of both of the above kinds of motion pictures usually make available a teacher's manual, and sometimes student's manuals, to accompany the film.

The third kind of motion picture used a good deal by vocational guidance workers is the film intended for a different purpose, but incidentally valuable for the occupational information which it provides. Vocational training films, for example, produced in great numbers and varieties during the war period by the United States Office of Education, the military services, and industrial agencies, are useful in guiding the student or worker in his selection of an occupation as well as in entering upon it and progressing in it. Similarly there are many films produced by governmental agencies, business concerns, industrial organizations, etc. which are produced for general promotional or propaganda purposes, but which provide valuable information about careers in those fields or industries. This kind of film was the earliest available for vocational guidance purposes. Earlier films of this sort were often very objectionable because of advertising matter included, but recent productions are much less so. Still another group of films in this category consists of those educational pictures in other areas—such as geography, home economics, art, and music—which incidentally deal with the occupations in that area. Finally there are the occasional photoplays which portray careers so accurately and well that they can be used educationally as well as for entertainment.

The fourth kind of motion picture which should be mentioned is a miscellaneous group, including films designed to help develop personal characteristics useful in vocational adjustment. Though films teaching parliamentary procedure, personal grooming, courtesy, getting along with others, etc. are in the areas of personal and social, rather than vocational, guidance, they do have an indirect connection with the latter, and are certainly appropriate aids for many of the broad programs carried on as vocational guidance.

There are many agencies which aid the vocational guidance worker in selecting and securing the films which he desires. The "Educational Film Catalog," " '1000 and 1'; the Blue Book of Non-theatrical Films" and "Selected Educational Motion Pictures—A Descriptive Encyclopedia" are the most useful sourcebooks for data concerning motion pictures. State departments of education, universities, and state libraries, as well as visual instruction divisions of metropolitan boards of education are agencies through which schools may obtain films. The American Film Center and the Educational Film Library Association, both at 45 Rockefeller Plaza, New York City, serve as consultants and clearing houses for all information concerning motion picture films.

Motion pictures are used in vocational guidance in many ways, ranging from such isolated events as a P.T.A. program or a vocational assembly to complete integration in an occupations course of study. They are particularly useful in vocational guidance programs carried on by clubs and other leisure time agencies. Most effective use of motion pictures in any situation demands careful planning. The following are among the more important ways of increasing the effectiveness of films: (1) Carefulness in selecting the film, both with respect to quality and to appropriateness for the purpose for which it is to be used; (2) Preparation by the teacher, including a preview and planning; (3) Preparation of the students for intelligent observation of the significant aspects of the picture; (4) Integration with other study materials, lessons, and experiences; (5) Variation of the role which films occupy in the lesson; (6) Followup of the motion picture experience with discussions, recitations, quizzes, or other such devices; and (6) Evaluation of the film and the methods by which it has been used.

The newest use of motion pictures in vocational guidance is as a special tool in psychological testing. A series of investigations at Clark University under Dr. Super's direction, attempted to measure vocational interests by showing the subjects projected pictures of various occupational activities, then having them take a test covering the material they had seen. The assumption was made that those items would be remembered best which aroused the greatest interest, so that each student's pattern of memories would indicate his pattern of vocational interests. Though filmstrips were used for the research before it was interrupted by the war, plans to resume it will involve motion pictures. Other research is also proceeding, to take advantage of the fact that motion pictures present a richly varied, yet rigidly standardized set of stimulus values for use in testing. This method has this advantage among others, that it enables the trait being measured to be separated more completely from reading ability than is the case with most paper-and-pencil tests. Much has been done with motion pictures in psychological testing in the Army Air Forces, but at the time of this writing information on this topic is still classified as Restricted, and is not available for publication.

References:

1. Brunstetter, M. R. *How to use the educational sound film.* Chicago: University of Chicago Press, 1937.
2. Dent, E. C. *Audio-visual handbook. Revised edition.* Chicago: Society for Visual Education, Inc., 1942.
3. *Educational Film Catalog.* Standard Catalog Series. New York: H. W. Wilson Company, Annual edition and quarterly supplements.
4. Forrester, G. *Methods of vocational guidance.* Boston: D. C. Heath and Co., 1944.
5. Hoban, C. F., Hoban, C. F. Jr., and Zisman, S. B. *Visualizing the Curriculum.* New York: The Dryden Press, Inc., 1937.
6. McKown, H. C. and Roberts, A. B. *Audio-visual aids to instruction.* New York: McGraw-Hill, 1940.
7. *"1000 and one"; the blue book of non-theatrical films.* Chicago: Educational Screen, Inc., annual edition.
8. *Selected educational motion pictures—a descriptive encyclopedia.* Washington, D. C.: American Council on Education, 1942.
9. Super, D. E. and Roper, S. A. An objective technique for testing vocational interests. *Journal of Applied Psychology,* 1941, 25, 487–498.

M. A. S.

MUSIC TESTS AND MUSIC TESTING, PRESENT STATUS OF.

Although music tests have been in process of development for several decades, diversity of opinion as to their present purposes and values exists to an extent unlikely to be found in any other educational field.

Sponsors have often presented music tests without information about their reliability and validity. Most music teachers who have attempted to use these tests have done so without adequate background for interpretation and use of test data, in a field where it is especially needed. The matter has been further complicated by the fact that many music teachers, as well as school administrators, have had rather hazy or misguided ideas about the place of music in the educational scheme. For these various reasons, in the field of music guidance relatively little of practical value has been accomplished, except in a few situations. This is unfortunate, because a great need has existed, and usable, though imperfect, tools for this work have been available.

In the early history of the music testing movement, prospects were bright for a fruitful achievement. At the turn of the century the relatively young psychological laboratories were interested in studies of sensation, and the field of audition received considerable attention. Particularly was this the case at the State University of

Iowa, where Professor Carl E. Seashore and a long list of highly competent graduate students engaged in numerous studies in the field. In the course of twenty or twenty-five years quite a number of tests showing individual differences in various aspects of the musical mind had been devised, and as a result, in 1919 some of the most important and most easily recordable of these appeared as the Seashore Measures of Musical Talent. At the same time, Dr. Seashore's well-known book, *The Psychology of Musical Talent*, was published. This book, which gives a comprehensive analysis of the musical mind, not only became a classic in this field, but also served as a model for the development of vocational and avocational guidance in other fields. With such an auspicious beginning, it is to be deplored that more promising guidance programs in music have not materialized during the last quarter of a century.

Since the original Seashore Measures of Musical Talent were recorded, some additional batteries of musical talent tests have been presented. The Kwalwasser-Dykema tests were recorded in 1930; the Drake Musical Memory Test, which was announced as a test of musical talent, appeared a few years later; and a revised battery of the Seashore Measures of Musical Talent was presented by Seashore, Lewis, and Saetveit in the late nineteen-thirties, about twenty years after the Seashore tests were first recorded.

Despite attempts to improve the original Seashore tests, and while later tests have the advantage of better recording, the writer finds that the early battery of Seashore tests is superior to later tests for use in his guidance program at the Eastman School of Music. This also is found to be the case in the extensive music guidance program conducted in the Rochester Public Schools. A discussion of the relative merits of the various talent tests would involve so many details and so lengthy a discussion that it is impracticable to include it in this article.

The causes for the lack of general acceptance of music guidance programs are several in number. In the first place, musical talent tests were presented to the public without adequate validation, particularly at the various levels of musical endeavor. Considerable confusion has resulted because sponsors of tests have not been in advantageous positions to prove the validity of their tests in various musical situations. Secondly, especially in early stages, musicians did not have an appreciation of the rapidly developing testing movement with its pedagogical implications. "Music is an art which transcends objective measurement," was the response of the musician to the well-meaning psychologist. Exaggerated claims were made by the proponents of music tests; in turn, skeptical musicians ridiculed the efforts of the early music psychologists. The situation was even more precarious than that of early general guidance workers, who, sometimes wary of impending trouble after giving a slow child a mental test, would hastily assure the parent that the child was not of low mentality, but rather that he was not yet ready for regular school work. In the field of music testing, prejudices early established still have considerable effect today.

A third cause of confusion was due to the fact that some of the tests are not very high in reliability. Such a matter made little difference to the uninformed music teacher who gave them without realizing the necessity of taking due precautions with a measuring instrument so lacking in one of the fundamental virtues of a good test.

In the public schools, probably the greatest impediment to the acceptance of music talent tests was and still is the faulty interpretation of a democratic philosophy of music education as typically expressed in the slogan of the Music Educators National Conference: "Music for Every Child—Every Child for Music." "Every child is musical," says the uninformed or indifferent music educator, without reference to or thought of widely varying degrees of talent, and then, with the building of advanced performing groups predominantly in mind, he indiscriminately urges any child to purchase an instrument and to enroll in an instrumental class. But only a small percentage of those beginning this special music instruction proves to be talented enough eventually to gain membership in one of the advanced musical organizations, the promotion of which demands most of the energies of the music department. It is a very worthy and valuable course for those students who are talented enough to realize that accomplishment, but too often it is attained at the sacrifice of a great many other students, who, potentially unable to achieve what so ideally is desired, could have profited greatly had they been provided with courses in music commensurate with their levels of talent. In other words, the aim in music education often has been that of developing fine performing groups rather than that of considering the musical needs of each student. The chief aim of a guidance program is to gain an insight into the potentialities of music students with the aid of talent tests and other auxiliary data, and to direct them to proper courses in music. The dubious educational practice of unduly concentrating effort on advanced performance is often accepted by the school administrator who, while disclaiming knowledge of music and therefore feeling little responsibility for its supervision educationally, appreciates the value of fine performing groups as a social relations force between school and community.

At the college and conservatory level, music talent tests likewise have not been widely accepted, but primarily for a much different reason. In many colleges, the music department is the only one expected not only to be self-supporting but also to show a profit for the general fund of the institution. Also, if the music teacher's salary fully depends on a percentage of tuitions, or in part on a percentage of tuitions for over-time teaching, it is doubtful both from the viewpoint of the school and the teacher that a discriminatory talent measuring instrument will be very popular. Considerable rationalizing about the value of musical talent tests can result under such circumstances.

And so each of the various reasons enumerated has likely had its effect in the general failure to accept musical guidance through music talent testing, although in the best educational interests of students it has been badly needed. With the exception of a few well-organized programs, guidance in music can not be favorably considered in scope or quality with general guidance programs found in most good schools.

One of the chief difficulties in establishing the validity of available music talent tests is due to the fact that few situations in music education have exactly the same aims for musical accomplishment. Therefore, it is necessary for each music teacher, who has the necessary background for it, to analyze his own music program, and, through careful study, to adapt a testing program to meet the needs of his particular situation. Unfortunately, a music testing program, if it be comprehensive enough to be of real value, takes considerable time, and most music teachers are already overburdened with heavy teaching duties. The ideal arrangement for a large school system is to have a music psychologist for this work. The Rochester Public Schools, I believe, is the only school system which has a music guidance program with a full-time psychologist in charge. An idea of the scope of her program, which indicates the possibilities of such work, can be given by quoting from a report she gave at an Eastern Music Educators Conference.[1] A general summary of the program, taken from this report, is as follows:

[1] This report by Ruth C. Larson, entitled "The Guidance Program in Music in the Rochester Public Schools," is printed in the 1939–1940 *Yearbook of the Music Educators National Conference*. In it the reader also may find an outline of the policies and procedures of the program. An earlier report by the same author, entitled "A Brief Report of a Prediction and Guidance Program in School Music," is printed in the 1934 *Yearbook*.

(1) Aid in the placement of over one thousand school instruments in the hands of the more talented students of the public schools.

(2) Information for supervisors and teachers of music that will assist them in making recommendations to parents for the purchase of instruments for their children.

(3) Recommendations for placing homogeneous talents in vocal and instrumental music classes whenever practicable to do so.

(4) Work with music teachers in directing students of unusual musical aptitude to classes in music where special opportunities will be provided for the development of their talent. This involves follow-up work over a period of years.

(5) Work with music teachers to determine if the actual accomplishments of students in their organizations conform to what might be expected as judged by their talent ratings.

(6) Co-operation with various organizations for child guidance, such as the Child Study Department, Children's Service Bureau, Visiting Teachers Department and Special Education Department, for the purpose of readjusting the activities of the student in some musical endeavor when his musical talent warrants it.

(7) Recommendations that students shall not register for special classes in music when the talent classification is so low that it is questionable whether it will be valuable for the student to spend his time or that of the teacher for such instruction.

(8) Service to the vocal department in numerous ways.

For the past fourteen years the writer has been in charge of testing at the Eastman School of Music.[2] All new regular course students—those working for degrees, are tested during "Freshman Week." The tests given include the Seashore Measures of Musical Talent, standard intelligence tests, theory placement tests, etc. The results of tests and auditions provide information not only for the student's original assignments but also for his course throughout his attendance at the School. Information gained through a testing

[2] Those who may be interested in the writer's approach may refer to his article: William S. Larson, "Practical Experience with Music Tests," *Music Educators Journal*, March, 1938. Additional articles, dealing mainly with the controversial points in music testing, may be found in immediately preceding issues of the *Music Educators Journal*: James L. Mursell, "What About Music Tests?" October–November, 1937; Jacob Kwalwasser, "From the Realm of Guess into the Realm of Reasonable Certainty," February, 1938.

program is found to be of great value both in conserving the student's time and in wisely spending the School's funds.

The final part of this article will be devoted to brief comments about achievement tests in music. Prominent among these tests are the Beach Music Test, the Kwalwasser-Ruch Test of Musical Achievement, the Gildersleeve Musical Achievement Test, the Providence Inventory Test in Music, and the Knuth Achievement Tests in Music. The names of these tests are very misleading, for they are not measures of musical accomplishment in terms of performance or appreciation as the titles would indicate. Rather, with the exception of the Knuth test, which is a recognition test of melodic and rhythmic characteristics, they are mainly tests covering rudiments of music and facts about music. It is difficult to devise an objective test of musical accomplishment; it is much easier to use rudiments of music and facts about music in constructing objective paper and pencil tests, a reason which probably accounts for undue emphasis on such material in so-called achievement tests. But a knowledge of rudiments of music and facts about music depends more on the student's general mental powers than on his musical aptitude, and an unmusical but intelligent student would undoubtedly make a higher score in this type of music achievement test than would a musical child with lower intelligence. In the absence of satisfactory forms of objective achievement tests in music, a jury of several highly competent and trained musicians, with well-organized and well-defined criteria, still serves as the most valid means of rating musical accomplishment.

In concluding this discussion, the writer wishes to express the opinion that, although the acceptance of musical talent testing and the development of its measuring instruments have been slow, there is at present a hopeful sign of a more rapid advance in these respects in the near future. With improvements in the general pedagogical training and background of music teachers there is bound to be a better appreciation of value to be derived through an efficient direction of musical talent to those musical endeavors which that talent warrants. This increased interest in turn will lead to demands for better measuring tools, which will, no doubt, be provided when there is a real desire for them. Better tests, made easier to administer and interpret, will be helpful to a program devoted to the proper direction and guidance of music students, and, in turn, will help the subject of music to realize its proper place in the curriculum as a true vitalizing force in education.

W. S. L.

MUSICAL TALENT, THE DISCOVERY AND GUIDANCE OF

The Problem.

Guidance in music assumes three aspects: the educational, the avocational, and the vocational. Music is the most universal art, but the outlet for a professional career is relatively limited to four fields: namely, that of the composer, the conductor, the virtuoso, and the teacher.

The talent required for each of these four groups is radically different; the necessary education is different; the resultant personality is radically different. Differentiated guidance toward these fields is, therefore, of the greatest importance, as it involves not only questions of expensive preparation, but, what is more important, the making or breaking of human hearts in success or failure. Yet, from the point of view of public education, it is relatively unimportant because all these vocations together comprise less than one per cent of the normal population that craves musical guidance.

The problem of guidance in the public schools, therefore, becomes primarily one of guidance toward the appreciation of music and self-expression in music for the joy of expression in itself; that is, a problem of educational and avocational guidance, whether it be for the various degrees of amateur performance or for the general appreciation of music.

The outlets and media for expression in this large area of the musical life embrace all conceivable forms of music from the most primitive beat of drums through the countless varieties of instruments, the various gifts of voice, the power of dramatization, and the various functions and roles in the service of music in the health and the life of the home, community, church, and art.

It is, therefore, clear that musical talent is not one thing; musical education is not one thing; and the effective functioning of music in the life of the people is not one thing. Hence the problem of guidance becomes extraordinarily complicated and is full of undreamed of possibilities.

The Nature of Musical Talent.

In the popular mind, a person is either musical or non-musical just as he is supposed to be either sane or insane. The fact is that we are all more or less sane and all more or less talented; it becomes a question of degree, kind, and value.

Musical talent is not one thing, but a hierarchy of talents as varied, as interrelated, and as dependent upon soil, environment, and inherited traits as is the vegetation of the forests. There are oaks and poplars, annuals and perennials; flowers and thorns, luscious fruits and pernicious weeds; so in the musical organism and its function there is vast diversity. Yet in the kingdom of art, as in the plant kingdom, there is law and order in the relationships. As in the plant kingdom, the seed is always there. But what kind of seed is it? What chance does it have of coming to foliage and fruitage through the operation of natural laws and planful cultivation?

This concept of the variety, intricacy, and vastness of talent, however, does not discourage the scientific approach to its analysis; because musical talent has its taproots, its modes of branching, re-branching, and enfoliage, and there is a possibility of establishing classifications and making quantitative measurements which may have a wide sweep of application. This faith in possibilities springs from the psychological laboratory, where the scientist is satisfied to fractionate the problem and deal intensively with one issue at a time.

The Approach.

The fundamental challenge that the psychologist has to give to the music teacher and supervisor in this: keep each student busy at his natural level of successful achievement. The emphasis shou'd be laid on the words "each," "natural," and "achievement." To do this, the average teacher should be conversant with three fundamental findings of the psychology of individual differences in musical talent.

First is the *enormous difference in talent* of apparently similar individuals. It is a general rule that the more precisely we measure specific capacities in a group of individuals, the larger the difference that will be found. Thus, it is easy to find in a group of normal children one who has two hundred times the capacity for hearing of pitch that another equally bright child might have. Similar, but not quite so large, differences are found for tonal imagery, the sense of time, sense of rhythm, sense of loudness, musical imagination, musical thinking, and the capacity for motor skills. In ordinary observation of achievement or performance these differences are covered up, because the factor under consideration is not isolated for exact valuation.

Next to the revelation of the surprisingly large extent of individual differences is the revelation in psychology of the *relative fixity of some of the innate capacities*. We must say "relative" for two reasons: (1) the physiological capacity is often not reached in measurement; and (2) physiological capacity is itself a relative term from the point of view of genetic psychology. Yet the more we employ the rigid controls of the scientific methods of analysis, the more clearly we identify specific capacities and the better we are prepared to take the limits of possibility and variability into account.

The third finding in our experimental psychology of music lies in the *revelation of ways and means for the adjustment of talent*. Tonal memory, for example, is a talent present in vastly different degrees; but there are many kinds of tonal memory. An impediment that would be prohibitive in one situation would present no difficulty in another. The educational curriculum, the types of social activity in music, the ways of planning personal satisfaction in performance, and the methods of training are all contingent upon knowledge of the nature and extent of specific talents.

Two Schools of Thought.

There are two schools of thought in regard to the significance of talent and guidance on the basis of talent. One we may call the *omnibus theory* and the other the *specific, or laboratory, theory*. The omnibus theory is the commonest. In actual practice very little use is made of measurements but the gift of music is appraised as a whole and validated against success as a whole. The chief proponent of this point of view is Professor Mursell of Columbia University (see his "Psychology of Music," W. W. Norton Press, 1937). I have nothing further to say about it in this article. The specific theory comes from the psychological laboratory and is based on the measurement of specific talents as distinguished from talent as a whole. It hinges upon two fundamental principles.

The first principle is that we must isolate one basic factor for variation and measurement at a time and keep all other factors constant. For example, instead of asking the question, "Can this child hear music?"; we ask, "Can he hear pitch?"; "Can he hear loudness?"; "Can he hear time?"; "Can he hear timbre?"; "Can he hear rhythm?"; "Can he hear tone quality?" Each of these can be isolated for measurement; and, when we have the result, it is recordable, repeatable, verifiable, and predictive. What is true of hearing has its parallel on the side of performance as repeated by skills. We do not ask, "Can he play?"; but we ask, "Can he play a tune in time and in rhythm?"; "Can he phrase?"; "Can he produce good tone quality?" etc. Such questions have their parallels at the higher levels of imagination, memory, thought and feeling;

although the higher, and therefore the more complicated, the process becomes, the more it tends to resist analysis.

The second principle is that we must limit the conclusion to what is involved in the one factor that was varied under control. Thus, if we measure the sense of pitch and we find that the record made is in the 99 percentile, the conclusion is not that the child is musical, but that he has an extraordinary sense of pitch—that he is superior in one of the scores of talents essential to musical success. He may be utterly incompetent in other talents.

Musical Guidance in the Public Schools.

In the public school situation the measurement of specific musical talents is of value in the following respects: the placement of instruments, recommendations concerning the purchase of instruments by parents, segregation of instrumental classes, cooperation with the music teacher in the study of unusual cases, check on accomplishment, cooperation with various organizations interested in child guidance, limitation of instrumental classes through talent testing.

Measuring Instruments.

The public school system of the future will include a measurement laboratory in a guidance clinic. There are now instruments available in psychological laboratories for the measurement of twenty or thirty specific abilities or capacities which we call talent. There are measurements of all the sensory capacities and, corresponding to each of these, measurements of the motor capacity, ability, or achievement. As one instrument registers the sense of pitch, another registers the ability for the control of pitch; one instrument measures the sense of timbre, another registers the quality of timbre produced by the voice. These instruments range from tuning forks up to complicated instruments which register directly the quality of voice in terms of the number, distribution and relative dominance of its overtones. In the same manner there are now measurements of achievement available covering a wide range from the development of motor skill up to achievement in musical composition.

The Seashore Measures of Musical Talent (see article) is a series of phonograph records made from laboratory instruments and adapted for general use in the schoolroom. They are issued by the RCA Victor Company and the Manual of Instructions issued by the University of Iowa Press contains full directions for the measurement and interpretation of the records and has a comprehensive bibliography covering two hundred and six titles. There are other series of phonograph records now on the market, and for certain purposes actual musical instruments can be employed.

In conclusion, the recommendations for guidance should contain a number of "Don'ts." Don't let any guide say to any pupil, "Be this," or "Be that." Musical nature is prolific and the principal function of the guide is to reveal special abilities and to guard against serious handicaps. Don't look for any foolproof system of guidance; at the best the situation will be analogous to that of the physician who is consulted about the health of a patient. Don't assume that it is desirable to have a regimentation of vocational guidance planted upon all pupils. Don't rush a guidance program any faster than the development of competent guides will warrant.

The above article consists of extracts from the author's article on "The Discovery and Guidance of Musical Talent" in the Thirty-fourth Yearbook of the National Society for the Study of Education.

C. E. S.

MUSIC TESTS.
Beach Music Test.

Purpose and Content.

The Beach Music Test is a survey test to measure musical knowledge and achievement. It is the result of many years experimentation and revision. The first edition of the test was published in 1920. After extensive use and experimentation, the test was revised and reprinted in 1930 and in 1932. The latest revision covers the following phases of musical knowledge: musical symbols, recognition of measure, tone direction and similarity, pitch discrimination, application of syllables, time values, terms and symbols, notation, syllables and pitch names, representation of pitches, and composers and artists.

Authors and Publisher.

The authors of this test are Frank A. Beach, Late Head of Department of Music, Kansas State Teachers College and H. E. Schrammel, Director, Bureau of Educational Measurements, Kansas State Teachers College, Emporia, Kansas.

Validity of Test.

The most significant criterion for evaluating a test is its validity. The original test depended entirely on the judgment of competent teachers and supervisors of music and other musicians as to what constitutes valid items for an objective music test. In the 1932 revision, the subjective criteria were supplemented by objective criteria. The supervisors in sixteen schools of Colorado, Iowa, Kansas, and Nebraska ranked their pupils prior to administering the test on the basis of (1) knowledge of musical fundamentals and (2) general musicianship. Correlations were then computed between the pupils' ranks and their test scores. The coefficients between general musicianship ranks and test scores for the 23 classes from these 16 schools ranged from $+ .92 \pm .02$ to $+ .35 \pm .13$, with a median of $+ .65$; and between knowledge of musical fundamentals and test scores from $+ .94 \pm .03$ to $+ .14 \pm .12$, with a median of $+ .74$. With a few exceptions the coefficients were high enough to be significant, and some were markedly significant. When all ranks were statistically combined and correlations computed for the entire group of 535 pupils a coefficient of $+ .67 \pm .02$ was obtained for each of the two functional ranks test scores.

In the Emporia State College music students were given a composite rank on knowledge of musical fundamentals, sight-singing ability, and general musicianship. These ranks when correlated against test scores yielded a coefficient of $+ .87 \pm .02$.

Reliability of Test.

By combining the several parts of the test in such a manner that two scores were available, i.e. the split-half method, reliability coefficients as follows were obtained for college students: $+ .88 \pm .02$; $+.91 \pm .02$; $+.82 \pm .03$; average $+.86$. For high school pupils the coefficients were: $+.78 \pm .02$; $+.89 \pm .01$; $+.83 \pm .02$; average $+.83$.

Administering, Scoring and Interpreting.

Detailed directions for administering this test are printed in the Manual of Directions. The use of a piano is essential to giving the test correctly. It may be administered to any size group, grades IV to XII and college. Scoring is accomplished by use of a printed key. Scores are interpreted for each grade by use of percentile norms.

H. E. S.

Drake Musical Memory Test. This is an aptitude test for musical talent which can be given to anyone who is over eight years of age and without previous musical training. It consists of twelve original two-bar melodies which are the standards to which other variations are to be compared. In each of the twelve trials a melody is played, followed immediately by four possibilities: there may be a change in time, key, note, or the original melody may be repeated exactly. Testee is required to compare each possibility to the original in that trial and identify it. Only one change is ever made for any one comparison. The four variables of time, key, note, and same are arranged in serial order and when treated as separate subtests show an average intercorrelation of approximately .75, indicating the measurement of some common factor rather than independent abilities.

Percentile norms based on 1979 cases from age seven to the adult level are given for both forms of the test. Percentile norms are also given for Form A and Form B combined should anyone desire to increase the reliability by increasing the length of the test.

Two independent studies of validity have been made. One correlated the test scores with ranks given by the instructor, Stanley Chapple, in a class of 46 pupils at the London Academy of Music. This r was .67, pe .05. The reliability of the ranking was .68 with a time interval of eight months between the two rankings. When the influences of age and training were removed by partial correlation the validity coefficient was .50 for the same group. The other study correlated the test scores with two aural training classes conducted by Ernest Reed at the Royal Academy of Music with final examinations consisting of writing chords and melodies from hearing them on the piano, writing counterpoint, writing four-part harmonies, and memorizing a melody in five minutes from notation on the blackboard and then transposing it into a given key. This resulted in a validity coefficient of .66, pe .07. No attempt was made to control age or training but all were approximately eighteen years of age.

Reliabilities by the split-half method and corrected by the Spearman-Brown prophecy formula for both forms combined, range from .85 with young unmusical groups to .93 for older musical groups. Form A correlates with Form B averages about .75 for grammar and high school subjects. Corrected by the Spearman-Brown prophecy formula, this would amount to .86.

Factor analysis (7) indicates that all aural tests measure a common memory factor which may be the source of most of the validity possessed by such batteries. All experimental studies confirm the importance of memory as a factor in musical talent and biographical studies indicate it even more clearly.

The test is published by the Public School Publishing Co., Bloomington, Illinois. The objectivity of administration can be increased by using recorded test material obtainable from Raleigh M. Drake, Mary Washington College, Fredericksburg, Virginia.

References:

1. Drake, R. M. Four new tests of musical talent. Journal of Applied Psychology, 1933, 17, No. 2.
2. ———. The validity and reliability of tests of musical talent. Journal of Applied Psychology, 1933, 17, No. 4.
3. ———. What is musical talent? Journal of Musicology, 1939, 1, No. 2.
4. ———. The place and use of music tests. Education, 1939, 59, No. 9.
5. ———. How to memorize music economically. Music Educators Journal, 1939, May.
6. ———. How musical is your child? The Etude Magazine, February, 1940.
7. ———. Factor analysis of music tests. Journal of Musicology, 1939, 1, No. 1.
8. ———. The relation of musical talent to intelligence and success in school. Journal of Musicology, 1940, 2, No. 1.
9. ———. The effect of ear training on musical talent scores. Journal of Musicology, 1943.
10. Karlin, J. E. Factor analysis in the field of music. Journal of Musicology, 1941, 3, No. 1.
11. Lowery, J. E. On the integrative theory of musical talent. Journal of Musicology, 1940, 2, No. 1.

R. M. D.

Kwalwasser-Dykema Music Tests. This group of ten measures constructed by Jacob Kwalwasser, Professor of Music Education, Syracuse University, and Peter W. Dykema, Professor Emeritus of Music Education, Teachers College, Columbia University, purport to measure some of the more basic traits which condition success in music. The ten tests measure: (1) tonal memory; (2) quality discrimination; (3) intensity discrimination; (4) tonal movement; (5) time discrimination; (6) rhythm discrimination; (7) pitch discrimination; (8) melodic taste; (9) pitch imagery; and (10) rhythm imagery. Norms are provided for all tests individually and a single conversion norm for the total score.

The tests have been used widely by school music departments for the purpose of differentiating the more musical from the less musical, segregation of groups have been based upon scores yielded by these tests. Differentiation of instruction has been linked with stratification of groups on the basis of test scores.

Directions for administering the tests are to be found in the *Manual of Directions,* issued by the Carl Fischer Company, Cooper Square, New York City. The tests, themselves, are recorded by the RCA Victor Company, pressed on five ten-inch records, and sold as a unit in the Kwalwasser-Dykema Music Test Album. A mechanical or electrical phonograph must be available to the tester.

The tests have been standardized on four levels: (a) intermediate (grades four through six); (b) junior high school (grades seven through nine); (c) senior high school (grades ten through twelve); and (d) college music students. Five thousand cases each were used in computing norms for the first three levels, and one thousand cases were measured for the college level.

The tests have been validated in a number of ways, principally by comparing: musicians with non-musicians; college music students with non-music students on the college level; high school music students with non-music students on the high school level; and grade school music students with non-music students on the grade school level. Invariably, the music group earns a significantly superior score to the non-music group.

However, this battery of tests may not be considered a measure of achievement in music, for training in itself is not responsible for increased scores. The tests measure chiefly one's native capacity in music. They must be considered psychological measures dealing principally with aspects of hearing rather than measures of achievement. The tests do not correlate too well with age, sex, training or intelligence. Inter-correlations of the individual tests of the battery are especially low. The reliability of a battery, using the split-half technique, corrected by the Spearman-Brown Prophecy Formula, is .87.

J. K.

Kwalwasser-Ruch Test of Musical Accomplishment. This test was constructed by Jacob Kwalwasser, Professor of Music Education, Syracuse University, and G. M. Ruch, Federal Bureau of Education, Washington, D. C., and consists of ten measures, namely: (1) knowledge of musical symbols and terms; (2) recognition of syllable names; (3) detection of pitch errors in a familiar melody; (4) detection of time errors in a familiar melody; (5) recognition of pitch names; (6) knowledge of time signatures; (7) knowledge of key signatures; (8) knowledge of note values; (9) knowledge of rest values; and (10 recognition of familiar melodies from notation. The test is designed for use in grades four through twelve.

The Manual of Directions and test blanks are issued by the Extension Division of the State University of Iowa, Iowa City, Iowa.

The test was built upon specifications adopted by the Research

Council of the Music Educators' National Conference published in 1921 in Bulletin Number One, and titled "Standard Course in Music for Grade Schools." This course outlines the aims, materials, procedures and attainments for the first eight grades. Although the test parallels recommendations of the National Conference, it has been validated further by checking with courses of study in city school systems which have received national recognition for their work in public school music.

The reliability of the battery, using the split-half technique, corrected by the Spearman-Brown Prophecy Formula, is .97.

Norms are supplied for grades four through eight individually, and for high school nine through twelve collectively. Approximately 5,500 pupils were employed. These norms are based upon scores earned by children in: Evanston, Illinois; Oakland, California; Rochester, New York; Mason City, Iowa; Pittsburgh, Pennsylvania; Denver, Colorado; and South Bend, Indiana.

The directions for giving the test, as well as the key to correct answers for scoring, are found in the *Manual*. The test consumes approximately three-quarters of an hour. The scores on the test increase with grade levels. The test correlates with age, training and intelligence. Girls earn slightly higher scores than do boys, showing about a twenty per cent increase in grades from the fifth through the high school.

J. K.

Seashore Measures of Musical Talent.   Musical minds differ vastly in kind and degree of talent. Some of the fundamental talents can be measured scientifically before formal musical education begins. Such inventories of the child's natural abilities aid in revealing musical type, in assignment of instrument, in selection and classification of music groups, and in determining what kind and degree of musical education should be planned.

These *Measures of Musical Talent* are based on a scientific analysis of musical hearing, appreciation, and performance. They deal with basic elements which function in all music and are essential for hearing and learning of music. They are simple and economical in operation, because they replace expensive and technical instruments, and fit naturally into the musical program. They may be used with any language and at any racial, cultural or age level above the age of ten. They aid in the discovery of talent and in an analysis of difficulties in training. They are essential for the interpretation of musical case histories and musical achievement as well as in the awarding of praise and blame. They save time and increase efficiency in musical education. Indeed, they have proved a spur to the introduction of general scientific procedure in musical education.

In 1939 a revision of the *Measures* was undertaken by Seashore, Lewis and Saetveit. The first edition had enjoyed a steady growth for twenty years without revision. The term "Measure" is used on the one hand to distinguish them from actual laboratory experiments and on the other hand from paper and pencil tests. They take the form of phonograph records made with the most elaborate scientific instruments and techniques and yet are available for schoolroom use at the mere cost of phonograph records, obtainable from any RCA-Victor agency.

The *Measures* are designed for individual or group testing. There are six measures of specific musical talents capable of quantitative treatment; namely, Pitch, Loudness, Time, Timbre, Rhythm and Tonal Memory.

There are two series. The two series measure the same factors. Each is complete on three double-faced 12-inch Victor Higher Fidelity records. Series A is designed for use with unselected groups or classes in general survey or individual testing, while Series B is designed for the testing of selected musical groups. Individual records of either series may be purchased separately. If only one series is purchased, Series A is recommended.

The "Manual of Instructions" contains scientific analysis and definition of each talent, description of the instruments used in recording, data on the quantitative factors involved, full directions for procedure in the measurement, principles of interpretation, record of form blanks and report cards, keys, norms, tables of reliability, a new type of analytical treatment of validity, a bibliography of approximately two hundred titles, more than half of which pertain to these particular *Measures*.

Anyone desiring to acquaint himself with the nature and significance of these *Measures of Musical Talent* should first order a copy of the manual of instructions entitled "The Revision of the Seashore Measures of Musical Talent" by Saetveit, Lewis and Seashore, University of Iowa Press, 62 pages.

C. E. S.

Strouse Music Test

Purpose and Content.

The Strouse Music Test was constructed for the purpose of providing a practical musical achievement test for use in elementary schools, junior high schools, and senior high schools. The test covers musical aptitude, knowledge, attainment, skill, and appreciation. It includes a wide variety of exercises involving both auditory and visual reactions. While it is an excellent musical achievement test for all pupils in a school, it is particularly valuable for girls participating in musical organizations, such as bands, orchestras, glee clubs, and choruses. It is a valuable measure of achievement for grades four to twelve and college. The two forms, A and B, are equivalent.

Authors and Publisher.

The authors of the test are Catharine E. Strouse, Associate Professor of Music, and H. E. Schrammel, Director, Bureau of Educational Measurements, Kansas State Teachers College, Emporia, Kansas.

Validity of Test.

The various parts of the test, as well as the individual test items, were selected to cover essentials in this field and to meet the basic objectives in public school music work. Every part and every item was subjected to the criticisms and suggestions of competent supervisors and teachers and of test construction specialists. Both forms of the test were also administered in a number of schools and the results, after careful analysis, utilized in revising the forms. Between scores made by pupils on the Kwalwasser-Ruch Music Test and their scores on Form A of this test a correlation coefficient of .90 was obtained.

Reliability of Test.

The following reliability coefficients (self-correlation) were obtained for Form A: Grade VII, .94 ± .01; Grade IX, .95 ± .01; college students, .90 ± .01; average, .93. The probable error of measurements ranges from 2.4 to 5.2, average 3.9.

Directions for Administering and Scoring

A separate bulletin containing detailed directions for administering each form of this test is provided. Before attempting to administer the test, the examiner should be sure he has a copy of the correct directions for the form of the test to be administered. He should also familiarize himself thoroughly with the specific details for administering each part.

A key is provided, by use of which the papers may be correctly scored with comparative ease. Full directions in regard to evaluating each item and each part are provided with the key.

Interpretation of Results.

Test scores may be intelligently interpreted for individual students and classes by use of the table of percentile norms. These norms were computed from the scores made by 6,505 students of a large number of representative schools in many different states.

Use of Test Results.

The test results may be profitably used in a number of ways: for determining student achievement; for checking the efficiency of instruction; for assigning school marks; for analyzing student and class weaknesses; and for motivating student efforts.

References:

1. 1940 Mental Measurements Year Book, p. 156.
2. Strouse, C. E. *The Construction of a test in general musical knowledge for the intermediate grades.* Unpublished Master's Thesis. Evanston: School of Education, Northwestern University, 1933.

H. E. S.

N

NATIONAL TEACHER EXAMINATIONS. The National
Teacher Examinations are designed to provide objective measurement of certain of the abilities and knowledges of teachers.

They are used by many public school systems in the United
States together with estimates of other types of information regarding the candidate's qualifications, in judging the satisfactoriness of
an applicant for a teaching position. In teacher training institutions
senior students are encouraged to take the Teacher Examinations,
both with a view to future employment and as a means of better
understanding their individual strengths and weaknesses in the areas
measured by tests.

The examination program is administered by a National Committee on Teacher Examinations. This Committee was first appointed in 1939 by the American Council on Education in response
to the suggestions and requests of school teachers, superintendents,
and teacher educators who foresaw the advantages of comparable
and objective measures of some of the abilities and cultural achievements of prospective teachers. The National Committee on Teacher
Examinations was assigned the responsibility of canvassing educational authorities and providing the profession with ways and means
of learning more about teaching candidates and of applying such
information to a continuously improving program of selection and
placement.

The immediate purposes of the National Committee were to
arrange for the construction and administration of a battery of
Teacher Examinations, to carry on a continuous program for the
improvement of the tests, to study and make available information
regarding means of improving the appraisal of factors not covered
by objective examinations, and to promote long-range research programs concerned with teacher guidance and teacher selection.

The National Teacher Examinations were first administered in
1940. They have been administered once each year on designated
dates in examining centers throughout the United States.

Carefully refined techniques and procedures have been employed in preparation of the National Teacher Examinations.
Briefly, this has involved: (a) development of the outline and specifications of each examination unit by a test editor in cooperation
with authorities in the fields; (b) preparation and editing of test

items in accordance with the outline and specifications; (c) "try-out" administration of the preliminary items to determine their difficulty and to detect those that might be weak or ambiguous; (d) selection and revision of suitable items for a tentative final form of the examination; (e) criticism and assistance in editing the tentative final form by a large number of experts in teacher education, heads of departments, supervisors of teaching, and others; and (f) preparation of the final form based on the criticisms and suggestions received.

The National Teacher Examinations are constructed to cover the following areas: non-verbal reasoning ability; verbal comprehension; understanding and use of the English language; general cultural information (covering the fields of history, literature, fine arts, science, mathematics, and contemporary affairs); understanding of points of view and methods of professional education (covering the areas of education and social policy, child development and educational psychology, guidance and measurement, and general principles and methods of teaching); and the mastery of the subject matter to be taught by the particular individual. By making the examinations wide in scope each individual has an opportunity to demonstrate the unique pattern of his abilities and knowledge.

The examinations are limited to intellectual, academic, and cultural materials. Other important factors that determine teaching fitness such as health and physical energy, training, experience, leadership, and other personal characteristics are, of necessity, left to the independent judgment of the local authorities to whom the candidate applies.

All examinations are of the objective type, consisting of multiple-choice items.

Each candidate is assigned a registration number, and individual examination materials, centrally assembled and stamped with the proper registration number, are provided the local examination centers. On the days of the examination the candidates indicate their answers to the items in the test booklets by recording their answers on specially prepared answer sheets. Each candidate has previously filled out a "practice answer sheet," which accompanies a practice booklet containing sample exercises.

Following administration of the examinations, all papers are sent to the central offices of the National Committee for classification and scoring. Each answer sheet is scored on the I.B.M. Test Scoring Machine. The results are also checked by an independent scoring procedure.

In order to make readily comparable the scores on several tests with varying means and distributions of raw scores, and to enable adequate interpretation of the results, all raw scores are converted to a *common scale*. Through this device a particular Scaled Score on one test becomes similar in meaning to the corresponding Scaled Score on any other examination. This provides direct comparability among scores on different tests for the same individual or for different individuals on the same test. Each annual edition of the Teacher Examinations is also equated with the previous edition so that the Scaled Scores have the same meaning from one year to another.

The proper use of examinations in teacher selection has been one of the chief concerns of the National Committee. Emphasis has been placed continuously upon the fact that examination results should not be misused as the sole basis for teacher selection. Records of experience, ratings on various personal and social characteristics, and observed teaching skill must be considered in addition to the Teacher Examination records in the evaluation of a prospective teacher's qualification and fitness with respect to a particular position. Furthermore, variation from one community to another in available financial resources, school plant facilities, curriculum emphasis, etc. make it not only desirable but necessary that the factors involved be evaluated independently by the local school officials in selecting personnel. The use of the examination scores in the selection of teaching candidates is completely a matter of local authority. The weight given the examinations varies from one school system to another. Each local system determines the relative importance which shall be given to the examination results and other relevant data.

References:

1. Flanagan, J. C. A preliminary study of the validity of the 1940 edition of the National Teacher Examinations. *School and Society,* 1941, 54, 59-64.
2. *National Teacher Examinations: Suggestions for their use in the selection of teachers.* National Committee on Teacher Examinations of the American Council on Education, August, 1945.
3. Practice Booklet for Examinees. National Committee on Teacher Examinations of the American Council on Education, November, 1945.
4. Ryans, D. G. Measuring the intellectual and cultural backgrounds of teaching candidates. Cooperative Test Service of the American Council on Education, August, 1941.
5. Wood, B. D. Making use of the objective examination as a phase of teacher selection. *Harvard Educational Review,* 1940, 10, 277-282.

D. G. R.

NAVY. Any description of vocational guidance activities in the Navy should be considered in light of the fact that the Navy is not operated primarily as an educational agency nor as a medium for providing vocational guidance services. Sound personnel practices and a basic concern for the present and future welfare of Naval personnel, however, have given rise to the development of specific programs and practices within the Navy which give considerable emphasis to vocational guidance.

A number of factors and conditions have evidenced the need within the Navy for limited vocational guidance services. Some of these factors and conditions are: (1) The presence of large numbers of men whose education was interrupted; (2) the high proportion of volunteers for the Navy who did not complete high school, but who subsequently have become interested in continuing their formal education; (3) training and experience received in Navy service schools have expanded the vocational outlook of many men; (4) the selection of a Navy job toward which a man expects to prepare results in evaluation of his abilities and potentialities in terms of the probability of attaining that job; (5) rubbing elbows with new shipmates of advanced educational levels and extensive vocational accomplishment serves to motivate many men to consider further preparation for an advanced Navy job or return to a civilian job or school; (6) others who have never had any occupational experience prior to entering the Navy are returning to civilian life much older and more seriously concerned about what is best for them to do; (7) sickness or injury after entering service has forced some men to plan for different types of jobs after release than those previously held in civilian life.

An organized guidance program whether in the armed services or in a civilian agency should include provisions for the following areas in order to insure a balanced and complete process: (1) An accumulation and study of all essential facts about the individual man, e.g., previous educational and vocational experience, interests and personal identification items; (2) the accumulation, organization and use of educational and occupational information on national, regional and local levels; (3) the collection and use of information about present and future training opportunities; (4) assisting the individual to interpret relevant facts about himself in the light of his current problems through individual counseling; (5) placement-assisting the counselee to become placed in the next best step for him; (6) follow-up—to check constantly on the effectiveness of the entire guidance process.

In considering these areas of guidance as they function within the Navy, it is important to realize that the completeness and effectiveness of the vocational guidance process varies widely from activity to activity according to the availability of officers who are trained and experienced in counseling. The understanding and appreciation of commanding officers of the value and importance of vocational guidance also affects materially the freedom and time which the officer-counselor may have to carry on counseling activities.

In regard to the area of the individual inventory, the Navy maintains on the whole a fairly complete personnel record system. Duplicate records for enlisted men are maintained. One set follows the individual from station to station; the other set is on permanent file in the Bureau of Naval Personnel in Washington, D. C. A complete file of personal and official information about each officer is maintained in the Bureau of Naval Personnel and, in addition, a Qualification Record Jacket is maintained and follows the officer wherever he is assigned. The information in these records is extremely valuable when used in connection with counseling. Occupational information is available and used extensively in shore installations and certain ships where trained Educational Services Officers are assigned. Counseling on an informal basis is available practically throughout the Navy; on a directed basis wherever trained Educational Services Officers are located. The placement area from a vocational guidance point of view is to a great extent irrelevant in the Navy, except as regards placement in off-duty educational or training situations. Follow-up of an acceptable nature is virtually impossible except over short periods of time.

Classification, Selection and Training

Partial elements of the vocational guidance process are found at work in a number of places in the Navy. Although the needs of the service are primary and consideration for the individual's own personal preference secondary, many men do receive definite assistance in formulating educational and vocational plans through these activities and contacts.

As a part of recruit training, all men are administered a battery of classification tests and are interviewed by classification interviewers. The main objectives of classification at recruit centers are: (1) To determine and record on standard forms, aptitudes, skills, and abilities that would indicate the type of duty for which each man would be best suited; (2) to recommend each recruit for the type of training or duty for which he is best qualified; and (3) to effect his assignment to this training and duty by matching his qualifications with Navy needs. All recruits are first informed about available training schools and the general duties of Navy ratings. They are then given a battery of aptitude tests designed to evaluate their knowledge, ability to learn and aptitudes such as verbal ability, arithmetical reasoning, clerical and mechanical aptitudes. (For further information about the Navy General Classification Test see references 1 and 2.) Since test scores are recorded on the Qualification Card, they can be used at any subsequent point in the man's Naval career. It is readily apparent that these test scores and other data on the Qualification Card are of real assistance in counseling situations such as are mentioned later in connection with the Educational Services Program.

In order to facilitate the recording and evaluation of the recruit's background, abilities, and interests a standard aid-to-the-interviewer blank is completed by each man prior to the actual interview. This provides an opportunity for the men to express their interests and to list their qualifications in terms of various types of Navy jobs. Knowing that the data given will be used as a means of determining qualifications for entrance into certain types of Navy schools or for assignment in a particular Navy job, the man has a strong tendency to consider his background and ability in light of the specifications of various Navy rates. While the classification interviewer is not a vocational counselor, as such, his questions and comments frequently assist the men being interviewed in crystallizing their preferences for types of Navy assignments related to previously attained skills and ability.

In the Naval structure there are over 194 separate Navy job fields. In each field it is possible to progress through four separate Petty Officer levels each requiring the demonstration of special abilities commensurate with the Petty Officer rating achieved. If a man is not selected by the classification process for assignment to a Navy service school, leading eventually to a rate, he is assigned to a permanent ship or station where in due time he may choose a type of rating toward which he would like to work. This process is called striking for a rate. In this case, he studies under the direction of his education or training officer a definite training course prepared for this purpose. It is in regard to this procedure of "striking for a rate" that the counselor provides considerable aid to the man in making a choice of a Navy job for which he would like to prepare, and for which he is best qualified.

Those men who are selected for training in the Navy service schools undergo experiences which usually give them a much broader vocational horizon. While the training given is geared to preparing men to handle specific types of Navy jobs, the training also serves to confirm or dispel tentative ideas about trying to prepare for certain civilian jobs upon release from service.

Informal discussions of educational and vocational problems of the men may be carried on by any number of different officers. A man frequently goes to his division officer or immediate commanding officer for advice. The Chaplain or Welfare and Recreation Officer serves frequently as a counselor. The education or training officer, as previously explained, is a source of frequent aid to men desiring help on their vocational plans and problems.

Educational Services Counseling Program

Recognizing the need for offering to all of its personnel a chance to participate in voluntary educational opportunities the Navy established, early in 1943, an Educational Services program which included: Voluntary classes, self-study opportunities, language instruction, information and orientation activities, literacy training, shop and on-the-job training, and through the U. S. Armed Forces Institute extensive offerings of correspondence and self-teaching courses, end-of-course tests, standardized subject examinations, general educational development tests, an educational information service, and reports of service training and experience for purposes of accreditation. The extension of these services to men in the Navy expanded steadily and with the end of the war in August 1945, it became apparent that there was an even greater need for the Educational Services Program. In addition to a large increase of specially trained Educational Services Officers sent into the field, in September 1945 the Bureau of Naval Personnel and the Commander-in-Chief, Pacific Fleet, requested commanding officers of all ships and stations to assign more personnel to the program, to increase facilities for carrying out the program and to enable interested personnel to take part in educational activities during working hours. From the very beginning, it was recognized that the personnel assigned to carry on Educational Services must be well prepared as counselors. To offer a broad educational program to men in the service without providing definite and organized assistance to help them in the selection of proper courses and to relate those courses to Navy training or future vocational objectives would result in misdirected effort on the part of many individuals.

One factor used in selecting officers for training as regular Educational Services Officers was whether they had had previous experience in the guidance and personnel field. All of the many hundreds of regular Educational Services Officers are given specific training in the Educational Services Section of the Bureau of Naval Personnel before being assigned to a field activity. This training includes a strong emphasis on counseling with attention given to such topics as: (1) The need for a counseling program in Educational Services; (2) the kind of problems which the counselor will likely encounter; (3) the objectives of counseling; (4) counseling materials; (5) case studies regarding men who desire to complete high school while in service, prepare for college after discharge, supplement Navy training, decide on a civilian occupational field, select courses to provide refresher training relative to former civilian occupations, and selection of spare time courses for general interest; (6) the Dictionary of Occupational Titles and How to Use It; (7) use of other agencies to supplement counseling; (8) counseling the physically handicapped; (9) cooperation with other agencies; (10) the Navy's demobilization program; (11) the use and interpretation of tests; and, (12) techniques of the interview.

Trained Educational Services Officers are assigned to most of the major continental and overseas shore bases, to large combatant ships, USAFI Branches and Headquarters, Naval Hospitals, Naval Districts Headquarters, major island commands and Personnel Separation Centers. In addition to organizing Educational Services programs in the field these regular Educational Services Officers have served as trainers for many hundreds of additional officers assigned to this program on a collateral duty basis. As most of the regular Educational Services Officers return to their civilian educational jobs or other pursuits, the Educational Services program will rest with these collateral duty officers.

Insofar as information regarding the individual man is concerned, records of two kinds are available. The first consists of the regular Navy personnel records including the Qualification Card containing scores on the Navy Basic Battery of Classification Tests and other personal data useful for classification purposes and also, the file jackets (previously discussed). The second type of information is obtained in and directly related to the Educational Services Program and may consist of one or more of the following for each man: (1) Voluntary Class enrollment card; (2) copies of USAFI application forms—for courses, tests and accreditation; (3) USAFI test reports, particularly scores on the General Educational Development Test, and (4) supplementary interview forms maintained by some Educational Services Officers.

To assist Educational Services Officers in counseling about educational opportunities, both within the service and in civilian life, a wide list of material was made available. Characteristic items on this list include: (1) Catalogs and bulletins on the USAFI program, (2) descriptions of available education manuals and correspondence courses, (3) lists of university extension courses offered through USAFI, (4) material on Navy rates, (5) three of The American Council on Education's guides—(a) *A Guide to the Evaluation of Educational Experiences in the Armed Forces,* (b) *A Guide to Colleges, Universities, and Professional Schools in the United States* and (c) *American Universities and Colleges,* (6) an issue of the American Vocational Association Journal entitled *America's Vocational Schools,* and (7) numerous pamphlets and bulletins and catalogs on special types and programs of education in various states, local schools and colleges.

A number of general basic references on occupational information were made available to Educational Services Officers, including: (1) The U. S. Employment Service's *Dictionary of Occupational Titles;* (2) a Navy publication entitled *What about a job;* and, (3) an extremely important tool developed by the Billet Analysis Section of the Bureau of Naval Personnel and the War Manpower Commission entitled *Special Aids for Placing Naval Personnel in Civilian Jobs.* The bulk of the occupational information distributed and used, however, is in connection with the *Navy's Occupational and Related Information File.* Approximately 625 of these occupational information kits were prepared by the Educational Services Section and distributed to major Educational Services Centers. This file is a collection of informational materials about jobs, job fields, educational information of various kinds including apprentice training opportunities, requirements for entry in various types of academic and vocational schools, and occupational briefs, pamphlets, leaflets and books of general value to counselors as well as the varied and extensive publications of the Occupational Analysis Division of the War Manpower Commission. In its folders is included information on various branches of the armed services, Navy rate training, conversion of Navy rates to civilian occupations, colleges, guidance aids, rehabilitation, and information on veterans. Since the initial files were distributed, around 20 supplements have been sent out to keep the basic material up to date. As of May 1, 1946, the number of titles of bulletins, pamphlets, and briefs included in the file, totals around 1,800. The materials in the file are loaned to the counselees and used by the Educational Services Officers in connection with group occupational activities and individual counseling.

While most counseling problems handled by Educational Services Officers fall into either a vocational or educational pattern, the number of different specific types of cases is legion. Some of the varied counseling problems which the Educational Services Officer handles include: (1) Selection of the best method of study—correspondence, self-teaching text or voluntary classes; (2) selection of best course from all those available to meet each individual's needs; (3) helping those who want to finish high school to work out a suitable plan; (4) assisting those who have never gone to college to select suitable courses to take while in service and to secure approval in advance from the institution; (5) assisting men in applying for credit for service training and experience; (6) counseling men who do not know what they want to do when they leave the service; (7) providing help to men who want to supplement their Navy training; (8) assisting individuals in selecting courses related to the occupation they expect to return to or enter after leaving the Navy; (9) helping men to decide whether they would like to take the General Educational Development Test; (10) helping men to locate and interpret occupational information relative to their future vocational plans, and (11) helping men to plan leisure time educational activities related purely to their own personal interests.

In preparation for individual counseling and in order to save valuable time during the interview, the Educational Services Officer engages in a station program of disseminating material about educational and vocational information and training available through his office. In cases where it is known that an individual is to be interviewed, adequate preparation by checking the qualification card and other records is made. An effort is made to know or to find out, early in the interview, some personal facts which may be commented on in order to set the man at ease and to let him know that he is being considered as a separate personality and not just another "warm body." The interview itself follows very closely the pattern used by many guidance and personnel workers in civilian agencies; some of the specific procedures being as follows: (1) A brief period of free conversation so as to get from the counselee a picture of what his problem is; (2) the filling out of forms during the interview is avoided; (3) the individual is encouraged to do most of the talking; (4) the attitude of friendly consideration and helpfulness is maintained by the counselor throughout the interview; (5) the counselor injects a note of humor occasionally in order to relieve any tension which might have developed; (6) the counselor changes the subject every now and then in order to provide a stimulus for the counselee to continue when a particular topic appears to have been exhausted; (7) the counselee is made to feel that any personal information will be kept in strict confidence; (8) before the interview is terminated, the counselee is assisted in working out a definite course of action; and (9) the interview is terminated on the same friendly basis as it was begun.

Immediately following the interview the counselor records the essential data on a counseling record form which is maintained for this purpose. Special care is given to noting any action which is to be carried out by the counselor and indicating a date for following up this case. Although the follow-up of counseling problems is emphasized, it should be realized that the extremely rapid rate with which service personnel are transferred, adequate and continuous follow-up is not possible except in a limited number of cases. One of the weaknesses of the present educational program in the Navy is that no feasible provision has been worked out whereby cases begun on one station are automatically followed up when the counselee transfers to another station.

Counseling in Naval Hospitals

Further comment should be made on the counseling activities carried on in naval hospitals. Conditions existing within hospitals are more favorable for thorough counseling procedures than in general naval establishments. All of the patients are in one central location. The absence of any extensive military duties facilitates the scheduling of interviews. In addition to the usual motives of men in seeking counseling, there is the added incentive resulting from handicaps or injury. Because of the obvious need of thorough counseling in hospitals, the Bureau of Medicine and Surgery has made vocational counseling an integral part of its Rehabilitation Program. A special manual outlining the type and procedures of vocational counseling for use in hospitals has been prepared and constitutes a standard operating procedure followed by Educational Services Officers. In attempting to work out satisfactory solutions to individual problems of patients, the counselor has access to the Physio-Therapy, Civil Readjustment, Occupational Therapy, Physical Training, and Recreation Departments, as well as consultation with the Medical Officer, Psychologists and Chaplains.

The counseling program in hospitals utilizes certain specialized material not generally available in other Educational Services Centers. This material includes a special series of vocational films, the O'Rourke Work Experience Kits, a series of manipulative tests and vocational interest inventories. Certain special counseling forms are also used. One of these forms, the Physical Capacity Appraisal Form, is filled out for all men who are to be discharged from hospitals to civilian life. This form gives a clear picture of the type and extent of physical disabilities and is especially useful to employers for placement purposes. This form also provides a basis for constructive vocational counseling on the part of the Educational Services Officer. Special mention should also be made of the prevocational shops which have been set up in many Naval hospitals. The purpose of these shops is to give the patient try-out experience with one or more various types of shop equipment. The objective of the hospital counseling program is to give every patient an opportunity to work out, with the assistance of the counselor, a definite and sound plan for his future educational and vocational activity.

Counseling in Personnel Separation Centers

In connection with the Civil Readjustment Program the Navy has made a rather extensive information service available to all personnel going through Navy Separation Centers. The Civil Readjustment program endeavors to provide all separatees with the information needed to make full use of counseling facilities established by the government and civilian agencies. Each man going through a center has a complete interview with a general interviewer. In addition, each separatee may consult any or all of nine special consultants regarding problems beyond the scope of the general interviewer. Four of these special consultants are provided by the Navy: A Chaplain, an Educational Services Officer, a Benefits and Insurance Officer, and a Legal Assistance Officer. Five special consultants are representatives of government and civilian agencies; Veterans' Administration, American Red Cross, United States Employment Service, United States Civil Service Commission, and the Selective Service System. This program at personnel separation centers has the following objectives:

(1) To make it possible for a separatee to utilize the services of special consultants available to help him regarding plans for education, training, or employment.

(2) To instruct each separatee in readily understandable terms concerning his rights and benefits as a veteran.

(3) To provide each separatee with an accurate summary of his education, training, and experience, including a translation of military specialties into civilian skills, and with documents which will aid the separatee in future education and job placement such as:

1. *Notice of Separation from the U. S. Naval Service* (NavPers Form 553). This form is a one-page summary of the enlisted men's Naval career. It lists service schools attended,

off-duty classes attended, rates held, date of discharge, length of service, special skills acquired, special commendations and awards. This form is to be presented to the Veterans' Administration as proof of eligibility for Veterans' rights and benefits. It is also used by civilian educational institutions as a basis for granting academic credit, and by employers in job placement.

2. *An Officer's Qualification Record Jacket* containing a description of the various duties performed while in the Navy is given to each officer-separatee to assist him in reemployment.

3. *Navy Rating Description Booklet.* This pamphlet is designed to give prospective employers, employment service officials, educators and other interested persons an over-all picture of the technical responsibilities assumed, duties performed and knowledge and skills acquired by personnel in any one of the Navy ratings. A list of civilian occupations related to the individual's specific rate is given.

4. *What About a Job.* This is a 60-page booklet intended as a guide to the thinking of the serviceman who is faced with the problem of selecting a vocation. It provides a basis for information on the selection of an occupation, fields of possible employment, and suggestions for starting a small business.

5. *Occupational Briefs.* These are small booklets covering over 100 specific jobs in the professional, agricultural, trade and industrial fields. These contain an analysis of the job field and give sources of further information and training. Each separatee who wishes may take along copies of the briefs giving information on the job fields in which he is especially interested.

The major part of the actual counseling in regard to educational and vocational plans is carried out by Educational Services Officers as special consultants in the Civil Readjustment program. The Educational Services program at separation centers consists of the same type of activities as carried on by regular Educational Services Officers, with certain modifications. The interview with the Educational Services Officer at the separation center is designed to do two things:

(1) To aid the man in analyzing the possibilities and ramifications of using existing veterans' legislation and civilian training organizations as aids in attaining his vocational and educational goal.

(2) It is designed to "dove-tail" into counseling programs sponsored by government agencies such as the Veterans' Administration, Department of Agriculture, etc., and those of civilian educational institutions. The work of the consultants, particularly those from the Veterans' Administration, U. S. Employment Service and Civil Service Commission, should not be overlooked. All of these representatives provide valuable information and counseling assistance to many men who have special problems which are under the cognizance of these agencies.

It is obvious that the separation center counselor has very little opportunity to do any "follow-up counseling," therefore, special care is taken to insure that each separatee leaves the center with a list of addresses giving organizations and, if possible, specific names and titles of individuals whom he may contact for further aid in solving his problems. There is a District Civil Readjustment Officer in each Naval District headquarters who contacts each Navy veteran in his District from 30 to 60 days after separation. Veterans call upon their own District Civil Readjustment Officer for information and assistance on all types of problems arising after return to civilian life. In its early stages, the Civil Readjustment Program functioned mainly to facilitate demobilization. More recently, however, emphasis has changed toward the relationship of the Navy with its veterans, and the maintenance of the good-will established during the period of mass demobilization. Stimulation has been given to in-service and out-of-service publicity regarding vocational matters for the benefit of veterans; the relationship of Navy skills to civilian jobs; and the programs of other related government agencies.

Information Service of the U. S. Armed Forces Institute

In considering this topic reference should be made to the Information program of the U. S. Armed Forces Institute (USAFI). The USAFI, staffed by both Army and Navy personnel, made it possible during the war for approximately one million and a half service personnel to enroll for educational courses. A plan has been approved recently whereby the War and Navy Departments will continue the USAFI program. The USAFI provides opportunities for enrollment in approximately 200 correspondence courses and over 250 education manuals. In addition, over 80 colleges and universities offer more than 5,000 extension correspondence courses to service personnel through the USAFI.

Shortly after the USAFI had begun operations, it was recognized that some specialized assistance should be provided through correspondence to help members of the Armed Forces select proper courses in relation to their present and future educational and vocational plans. Consequently, an information service was developed and functioned as an integral part of the USAFI program. Counseling in the true sense of the word cannot be carried on by mail. The supplying of information and helpful suggestions by correspondence to thousands of service personnel who do not have immediate access to a trained and currently informed education officer does, however, prove to be a valuable personnel service.

All kinds of problems are raised in the thousands of letters and applications which come to USAFI each month. Some of the more frequently recurring questions are related to: (1) Information about detailed course content; (2) Availability of courses in particular subject fields; (3) How to plan a program of studies leading to a high school diploma; (4) how to apply for academic credit; (5) what tests are available; (6) the availability of courses related to particular vocational fields.

Because of the tremendous volume of requests it has been necessary for the USAFI to develop special types of information to be used in answering these requests. Such information includes: (1) detailed descriptions of correspondence and self-teaching courses; (2) special lists of university extension courses in subject fields such as high school English, refrigeration, and cost accounting; (3) occupational briefs such as "Preparing to Become a Radio Repairman"; (4) brief statements on "A High School Diploma" and "A College Degree"; and, (5) suggestions on how to apply for academic credit for service experience.

In addition to the information service other activities of the USAFI program embody some procedures important to vocational guidance. For example, the review of all course applications to determine if the man is qualified to take certain courses in light of his background and education is of value to many individuals. Many of the education manuals, particularly those in the field of small business and others of a vocational nature, are designed primarily to be of value from a guidance point of view.

References:

1. Staff of the Test and Research Section, Bureau of Naval Personnel, *Psychological Test Construction and Research in the Bureau of Naval Personnel: Development of the Basic Test Battery for Enlisted Personnel*. Psychological Bulletin, Vol. 42, No. 8, October, 1945, pages 561–571.

2. Staff of the Test and Research Section, Bureau of Naval Personnel, *Psychological Test Construction and Research in the Bureau of Naval Personnel: Validity of the Basic Test Battery, Form 1, for the Selection for Ten Types of Elementary Naval Training Schools.* Psychological Bulletin, Vol. 42, No. 9, November, 1945, pages 638–644.

The opinions or assertions contained herein are the private ones of the writer and are not to be construed as official or reflecting the views of the Navy Department or the naval service at large.

S. M. J.

NEGRO-AMERICANS

Current Practices

There is a keen awareness of the need for vocational guidance programs among many Negro educators. Investigations of the status of guidance activities of city-wide, state-wide, regional and national scope have been made. Many of these contain suitable recommendations for improvement.

A composite picture of these programs in the accredited secondary school shows that there is a central administration, usually in the form of a committee of teachers with the principal as chairman. Policy with regard to what data are to be collected; what shall comprise the guidance program; who shall do the counseling; when the counseling shall be done; at what grade level it will be initiated, etc., is determined by this committee.

In practice, most of the guidance is group guidance. Occupational information is presented either in an organized course of occupational information or is presented during the home-room period. The data presented are usually not especially selected as applicable to Negro youth or youth of the local or regional community. Depending upon the ingenuity, training or bias of the teacher, he may occasionally narrate inspirational stories of isolated instances of Negro success in occupations in which they are infrequently employed or from which they are ordinarily excluded.

Individual conferences occur mainly during the latter half of the senior year. The principal or teacher of the student's choice serves as counselor. Usually there is no professionally trained counselor among the personnel of the school.

The poorest of the schools record and use only course grades. In the best programs are found data concerning the pupil's home background, physical status, personal-social development, school progress, intelligence, aptitudes and interests.

In cases where the secondary school is located within the community of a Negro college or university, assistance in the selection and use of tests and their interpretation is often received from a member of the personnel staff or psychologist.

Rarely does the program include try-out experiences in offices, trades and industries. The exploratory experiences are limited largely to extra-curricula such as music, dramatics, athletics, school paper, manual training or domestic science.

Definitely formulated programs of guidance are more frequently found in the Negro college. A synoptic view shows that the greatest activity is in dispensing occupational information during the freshman year. The occupational information is given through orientation courses, lectures, conferences and interviews, forum discussions, and specially prepared printed materials.

Data about the students most often concern family status and the scholastic record. In addition, objective test results, data concerning the physical condition of the student and his personal history are often included. It is the exception rather than the rule that the information is kept in the form of a cumulative record.

Only a few of the colleges conduct placement and follow-up services. Those institutions that have a well-formulated guidance program under the direction of a professionally trained personnel worker more frequently include these phases of guidance in their programs.

Agencies other than the school that are active in the field of vocational guidance are the National Urban League, national Negro fraternities and sororities, the Negro press and institutions for adult education. These agencies are chiefly concerned with the collection and dissemination of information with regard to occupational opportunities and the techniques for securing employment. The National Urban League is fundamentally active in this area, both in its practices and its publication, *Opportunity Magazine*.

Current Negro Employment

A synoptic picture of Negro employment may be drawn from the 1940 census data. About 62% of all employed Negro men are classified as farmers, farm laborers and other laborers; about 5% as professional, semi-professional, managerial, clerical and sales workers; and about 4% as skilled craftsmen, with more than half of these as mechanics, carpenters, painters, plasterers, cement finishers and masons.

About 70% of all employed Negro women are classified as in service occupations; about 1% as in clerical and sales work; about 6% as operatives; and approximately 16% as farmers or farm laborers.

SAMPLE OCCUPATIONS IN WHICH ONLY A FEW NEGROES ARE EMPLOYED

Less than 100 workers		100 to 500 workers		500 to 1,000 workers		500 to 1,000 workers cont'd	
Architects	80*	Actors & Actresses	421	Authors, Editors, Reporters	513*	Foremen in transportation communication utilities	604
Civil Engineers	95*	Artists & Art Teachers	327	Pharmacists	769*	Structural and Ornamental metal workers	811
Electrical Engineers	79*	Chemists, Assayists & Metallurgists	254	Postmasters & miscellaneous government officials	639	Apprentices	759
Mechanical Engineers	10*	Librarians	412	Proprietors, managers & officials in transportation & communication utilities	818	Linemen & Servicemen, telegraph, telephone power	604
Other technical engineers	10*	Designers & Draftsmen	197	Proprietors, managers & officials in manufacturing	917	Operators & kindred workers in knit goods	708
Osteopaths	5*	Office Machine Operators	192	Proprietors, managers & officials in finance, insurance & real estate	907*	Firemen, fire department	519
Veterinarians	84*	Construction Foremen	331	Proprietors, managers & officials in business repair	895*	Boilermakers	506
Surveyors	47	Printing craftsmen except compositors & typesetters	266	Baggagemen, express messengers & railway mail clerks	911	Cabinetmakers & pattern makers	997
Conductors, Railroad	43	Conductors, bus & street railway	101	Telephone operators	504		
Mining, Proprietor, Manager or official	37	Power station operators	113	Canvassers & solicitors	831*		
Telegraph operators	35	Operators & kindred workers in woolen & manufacturing	270				
		Operators & kindred workers in footwear except rubber	419				
		Inspectors	343				

Jobs in which comparatively few Negroes are employed may be illustrated by data taken from the 1940 census as shown in the accompanying table.

It can be inferred from an inspection of the data that not all jobs in which only a few Negroes are employed are ones in which there are attempts at systematic exclusion because of race. It is here suggested that successful pursuit of such jobs as those marked with the asterisk (*) may in many cases be possible without racial barriers. If present, factors making for exclusion on the basis of race are remote and indirect. Non-employment may be due to self-exclusion.

Current Problems

Philosophy. The counselor of Negro youth has, in addition to his evaluation of the youth's individual qualifications of general intelligence, special aptitudes, personal-social behavior, school achievement, interests and physical capacities—to consider the peculiar social economic scene in which he lives.

The picture is one of restricted living conditions and opportunities, of which occupational restrictions is one of those causing the greatest concern. Since the range of occupations in which this minority group customarily is employed is small, the dilemma in counseling is whether to weight one's advice in terms of the frequency of usual employment or to advise strictly in terms of an evaluation of the degree to which the personal qualifications of the individual match the requirements of the job.

In this matter there is often not a unified philosophy among the counselors in individual educational institutions, much less among Negroes generally. Those who would limit the choice to those occupations most frequently followed would over-look the fact that the Negro has not found his "place" in the American scene. He does not occupy a static position. He is in the process of rising to his full stature as an American citizen. Evidence of this change in occupational status is found in the successive census reports since 1890, all showing a change in the direction of an increase in the percentage employed in business, skilled labor and the professions, and a decrease in the percentage employed in personal service and unskilled labor.

On the contrary, there are those who would encourage indiscriminately preparation for jobs in keeping with personal qualifications, that is, without consideration of barriers erected because of race. They not only fail to consider the possible economic loss of preparation to the individual, but also overlook the fact that there needs to be considered the nature of the individual's reaction to his exclusion, or differential treatment on the job if secured. The emotional maladjustment consequent upon frequent failure to be hired, social isolation on the job if secured and the real or felt need to demonstrate better than average performance in order to be considered of equal efficiency may be very serious.

A realistic philosophy of guidance of the Negro must be based on certain assumptions about the social scene. The basic assumptions here are that: the scene is changing; the trend is in the direction of the ideal of democracy, i.e., of equal opportunities for all; the trend permits of an increasing rate of infiltration of Negroes into jobs from which they are ordinarily excluded.

The realistic practice of guidance would include the advising of Negroes to prepare for *all* kinds of jobs. In cases where exclusion is the rule, special precaution and preparation are advisable. In addition to the evaluation of the individual's qualifications for the job as such, the precaution needs to be taken to appraise the individual's capacity to make wholesome personality adjustments to frustrating situations. This judgment may have to depend upon a study of the individual's life history and the clinical insights of the counselor, pending the development of reliable and valid instruments for prediction.

He should be advised of the racial trends of the occupation in his own community, state, region and the nation. He should be informed about and trained in minority group techniques for breaking down barriers to employment.

Closely related to problems resulting from restrictions directly imposed because of race are those indirectly resulting from the Negro's previous condition of servitude. As a reaction against his former status, so it is assumed, there is a too widespread tendency among Negro youth to choose the learned professions and other white collar jobs.

There are those both within and without the Negro group who oppose this trend on the assumption that the American Negro's task is to build a separate and self-sufficient economy within the general American economy. They assume that the number of professional workers must be limited to the number which can be supported by Negroes. They assume that as a counter-balance to this tendency to choose the professions, much emphasis and glorification of the skilled trades and industries should obtain. There must be a proper distribution of all kinds of workers within the group as if it existed in complete isolation. An obvious inconsistency here is that the unskilled labor and skilled techniques of Negroes are used mostly by whites.

Aside from the impracticality of developing a separate economy, the concern about the choice of white collar jobs seems unfounded. If the small number of Negro high school graduates should all complete the training of their choice, it has yet to be demonstrated that their numbers would exceed the capacity of their race to support them.

Here it is not the social economic trends of the Negro community which must concern the counselor. His concerns should be: What are the bases upon which the student has made his choice? Has the student made his choice after securing wide occupational information? Has he determined his own assets and liabilities, including financial ability to secure preparation for the job? Has he determined whether his qualifications match the requirements of the vocation?

The burden of the counselor is to find ways and means of advising individuals who do not seek entrance into the professions and other white collar jobs or who do not possess aptitudes and other assets required, to prepare for and enter upon such vocations as are within their abilities and interests.

Opportunities for Exploratory Experiences

How are Negro youth to secure a sufficient breadth of experience on the basis of which to choose a vocation wisely? Ordinarily, even in urban accredited schools there are offered only a few shop courses for try-out experiences. In the rural schools of the South, the vocational training of the boys is often limited to agriculture. This limitation to agriculture or a few shop courses amounts to propaganda for entering into only a few vocations.

For girls in the urban accredited schools the occupational experiences are largely in domestic science and office work, including typing, shorthand and filing. Rarely is there a wide range of experience with a variety of types of office machines. The girl in the rural school is largely limited to training in domestic science. As with the boys, the limited opportunities for exploratory experience amount to propaganda for entering into only a few vocations.

The problem here is two-fold. It is partly a matter of changing the philosophy of those who are responsible for the construction of the curriculum. It is partly a matter of securing proper financial subsidy for the kinds of exploratory experiences that make for a wise choice of a life work.

Improvement in the programs of financial subsidy for the segregated schools of the South awaits the enactment and better enforcement of the laws that have to do with the distribution of federal funds and increased appropriations from local, state and federal governments.

Age of Students

The average age of Negro students for a given grade is above the average for the nation at large. Special consideration must be given to adjusting curricular materials to their interest level. The use of standard materials for a given grade is often not conducive to the highest motivation of the over-age individual.

Grade Level of "Drop-Outs"

The mass of Negro youth does not complete the eighth grade. The problem arises whether vocational training should be offered in the elementary schools. If it is offered at this level, it has been argued, it is done so at the expense of training in the three R's and training for citizenship. As an alternative, it is suggested that evening school opportunities be more widely offered. Whether this is a practical alternative has to be decided in light of the fact that the mass of Negro youth lives in the rural South.

Nature of Instructional Materials

Few instances exist where the textbooks used in a public school integrate with their subject matter materials about Negro life, Negro history and achievements. The opportunity is not offered to Negro youth to broaden their horizon by identifying themselves with successful members of their race who were integral parts of social, historic, industrial and scientific or artistic developments. The only opportunity to learn of Negro accomplishment is through incidental or separate study of the Negro. This tends to foster in the youth a lack of confidence in their opportunities and to limit their ambitions to a narrow section of the world's work.

Psychometrics

The interpretation of test data is difficult. The assumptions about the samples of the populations on which norms of a test were established may not be valid for a Negro sample; hence, interpretations of a particular test score may be less valid than usual. If an intelligence test or aptitude test is standardized within a group of white school children of more or less equal opportunities and then is applied to individual Negroes for guidance purposes—

interpretation in terms of the norms may be meaningless. Adequate guidance technique here would seem to depend upon the establishment of separate critical scores for Negroes for success in various occupations. Where the *opportunity to learn factor* is heavily weighted in, say, Test of Ability A, the lower scores made by Negroes, other things being equal, would conceivably correlate as highly with the vocations which depend upon Test Ability A as the higher scores made by whites.

SOME AREAS REQUIRING IMPROVEMENT

Occupational Information

There should be an extension and an enrichment of opportunities to secure occupational information. Whereas this is the phase of guidance given most attention in the majority of schools, there is evidence that it is limited in scope and quality.

Much of the information is given incidental to the study of the social sciences and literature. Where a formal course in occupational information is offered, the books used contain mostly generalizations for the nation.

It is the task of the teachers in general and particularly of those directly charged with the guidance responsibilities, to make studies of their local communities and region. They should attempt to assemble the facts with regard to occupational trends and social and economic factors that affect the employment of their students, both graduates and "dropouts." Such studies need to be kept up to date and need to include information not only with regard to vocations in which the students most often find employment, such as service occupations, agriculture and unskilled labor, but also with regard to jobs in business, industry and the professions.

Administration of the Program

The administration of the guidance program needs examination and correction. The technique practiced is generally non-professional. It is the exception that anyone in the school has received formal training in personnel work. Despite the fact that the spirit of the counselor may be appropriate to his task, it cannot be gainsaid that with both the spirit and the tools, he would be better prepared.

In secondary schools the principal is the most active person in the guidance program; he is chairman of the guidance committee and is usually the liaison between his school and the employers of the community. He does most of the individual counseling with respect to vocational courses to be pursued and the vocation to be selected. He does whatever limited follow-up there is. Usually being associated with disciplinary problems, it is doubtful whether he should play so large a rôle in individual counseling. Where he has shown special capability in this phase of the school's program, it would seem advisable that he designate one of his faculty to administer the discipline program. When this is not considered feasible, it seems advisable that he secure the services of a qualified person or encourage a capable in-service person to secure adequate training to administer the guidance functions.

"Shot-gun" guidance seems an appropriate name for most of the guidance service. In the secondary schools, information is shot at groups of individuals during the home-room period or to a whole class during the senior year. The information presented is not adjusted to the peculiar needs of each individual. Assistance in evaluating one's assets and liabilities in terms of many vocational possibilities can adequately be given only through the individual interview, or by the individual interview following group guidance.

Placement

Although it may not be unusual for the school to try to place its graduates, it is seldom that the school either attempts to place its "drop-outs" or to follow-up the placement in either instance. Information obtained from employers with regard to the weaknesses and strengths of the school's former students might serve as a valuable basis for improving both the curricula and the guidance services.

Personal Data

More adequate data than are usually secured about each student and use of the data when secured are prerequisite to improvement of the guidance programs. School grades and intelligence test scores are most frequently found. It is the exception to find objective test data with regard to personality traits, aptitudes and interests. Rarely are the data kept in the form of a cumulative record. Such data as are kept are probably used little because of the absence of specialized personnel for their interpretation or because of a lack of confidence as to their validity.

Student Philosophy

Some observers have noted the cynical regard of many former students concerning the value of their high school or college education. The value is measured in terms of dollars. Whereas the school might well look toward improving its offerings and articulating its guidance programs with profitable job opportunities, it must not overlook the need for training the individual to rationalize the cultural advantages obtained. Though the cultural advantages may be real, most individuals must be deliberately trained to appreciate them if forced to live so niggardly an existence that actual enjoyment of the advantages is a fiction.

References:

1. Brown, A. An evaluation of the accredited secondary schools for Negroes in the South. Chicago: *University of Chicago Press, 1944.*
2. Caliver, A. *The vocational education and guidance of Negroes.* Bulletin, 1937, No. 38. Washington: U. S. Office of Education, 1938.
3. Wilkerson, D. A. Educating Negro youth for efficiency. Part I. *The National Educational Outlook for Negroes, 1937, 1, 6–9.*
4. Wilkerson, D. A. The vocational education and guidance of Negroes. *Journal of Negro Education, 1938, 7, 104–108.*
5. ———. The vocational education, guidance and placement of Negroes in the United States. *Journal of Negro Education, 1939, 8, 462–488.*

A. J. D.

NETHERLANDS. The development of vocational guidance in the Netherlands is closely connected with the increasing complexity of business life and, with it, the diversity of vocations which makes it impossible for parents and guardians to orient themselves sufficiently.

At the census of 1930, 20,000 names of vocations were registered, and although these 20,000 names of vocations do not mean that there are really 20,000 essentially different vocations it can safely be assumed that the number of vocations from among which a choice can be made certainly amounts to 3–4,000. No wonder many parents and teachers lack a general view and consequently cannot find their way in the wide field of vocational posibilities. This really excludes a good choice of vocation. The large number of schools for special vocational training with everchanging requirements that have to be met, and the perspectives that are so greatly subject to change have increased the demand for expert guidance.

Written Guidance

The first attempts to give this guidance in the Netherlands date back to 1908. In Amsterdam appeared a guide for parents by the Society of Popular Education, in The Hague the municipal labor exchange followed suit with a little book: "Choice of vocation;

information for those who wish to learn a trade or profession." Several other municipalities followed and private people and societies published writings with information on certain trainings or vocations.

One very special one that may certainly not be left unmentioned is the "Guide for Hague Girls when Choosing a Vocation" (Leidraad voor Haagse meisjes bij beroeps-Keuze), by Miss Anna Polak, director of the National Bureau for Women's Work (Nat. Bureau voor Vrouwenarbeid). It was published in 1912 and was soon followed by a guide for the girls of Amsterdam and Rotterdam and finally by a "Guide for Netherlands Girls" (Leidraad voor Nederlandse Meisjes). This guide appeared every other year in a new edition and enumerated all vocations that were considered for girls, furnished with notes on the nature of the work and with brief counsel. However special information on training, as well as examination requirements etc. had to be applied for at the Bureau for Women's Work. In the war years 1940–1945 this publication was not reprinted.

A second, also very well-known guide is "The Guide in the Choice of Vocation for Boys and Girls" (De Leidraad bij beroepskeuze voor jongens en meisjes) by J. W. van Mameren that has already run through many editions. But it only mentions the vocations for which there are examinations. There is no enumeration of the demands that the vocations mentioned make on body and mind.

A series of detailed descriptions of vocations (monographs) appeared in the vocational library of C. Morks Czn. in Dordrecht in which about 50 higher occupations are discussed in succession, mostly by insiders. In 1934 its publication was discontinued.

Origin of Guidance Institutions

Actual attempts to found institutions, offices and bureaus for vocational guidance were originally made chiefly by the Society for the Advancement of Trade-Education for Artisans in the Netherlands (Vereniging tot Bevordering van de Vak-opleiding van handwerkslieden in Nederland). The Hague division founded a Bureau for Vocational Guidance (Bureau voor Beroepskeuze) in 1912. This was the first local bureau in the Netherlands. The strongest of the motives that contributed to the foundation was to stimulate energetically the wish for vocational training in boys on leaving elementary school. In Rotterdam, too, attempts were made in 1912 to arrive at a foundation; the administration of the Labor Exchange here made proposals to the municipality. This, however, did not agree to them and so a private society founded the Bureau for Occupational Guidance (Bureau voor Beroepskeuze). In 1916 bureaus were established in Arnhem, Deventer and Groningen. In Leiden a bureau was founded in 1915 and closed again in 1917 for want of interest. The municipalities of Hilversum and Zaandam instituted a Commission for Vocational Guidance in 1917, to be followed in 1918 by Amsterdam, Alkmaar, and Hoorn, and in 1919 Almelo, Enschede, Den Helder, and Schiedam. Further, the following Roman Catholic bureaus were founded: in 1918 Venraai, Hilversum, The Hague and Amsterdam (boys); in 1919 Arnhem, Hertogenbosch, Nijmegen and Amsterdam (girls); in 1922 Tilburg for boys and girls of all denominations.

Parallel to the course of things in education in the Netherlands, where there are schools for Roman Catholic, Protestant-Christian, undenominational and Public education, the organizations of vocational guidance developed along three main lines. For instance, the Roman Catholic bureaus united in a central office: The Roman Catholic Psychological Vocational office in Utrecht (Het R.K. zielkundig Beroepskantoor te Utrecht); the Protestant bureaus had their centre in the Christian Psychological Center for School and Vocation (Christel. psychologische Centrale voor School en Beroep) and the undenominational, General and Municipal (Neutrale, Algemene en Gemeentelijke) bureaus united in a Society for the Advancement of Vocational Guidance (Vereniging tot Bevordering der voorlichting bij Beroepskeuze). Collaboration between these three groups originated in 1927 in the Central Committee for Vocational Guidance (Centraal Comité voor Beroepskeuze) which received government support.

By the end of 1925 there were municipal bureaus in Amsterdam, Rotterdam, The Hague, Utrecht and Haarlem. By the outbreak of World War II there was a total of 39 bureaus and commissions that together dealt with approximately 11,000 cases a year corresponding to 3½% of the youth that should really have had advice.

Form of Organization

The mention of this percentage really contains a criticism of the manner in which vocational guidance was organized in the Netherlands until 1940, for it is this that impeded the growth of occupational guidance in the Netherlands. This impediment was mainly due to a lack of funds, as is clear from the following.

Most of the institutions working in this field were founded by private people and had to defray their expenses out of contributions and donations. A few commissions received a small subsidy from the municipality, mostly not more than a few hundred guilders, besides, in some cases, the use of premises with heating and light for consultation hours. There was no question of paying the collaborators or assistants. The possibility of extension was therefore not great and in most cases no adequate help could be engaged to carry on a guidance program. This was only possible in the municipal bureaus where one or more official counselors studied the cases and gave the actual counsel. These bureaus soon enjoyed widespread interest mainly because they were well equipped and were able to give expert advice to great numbers of people. Another factor of significance in connection with these municipal bureaus was that the work was always in the same hands so that experience in this difficult field could be accumulated. The private bureaus and commissions, on account of their method, were really never able to do more than give advice in a few dozen cases a year. The municipal bureaus took care of the lion's share of the total number of cases in need of guidance. Also the form of the municipal bureaus prevailed in the manner of organization. The economic crisis of 1930 and later forced the municipalities to make drastic retrenchments in expenditure and so the municipal bureaus in Amsterdam, Rotterdam and Utrecht in turn became victims of these economies and The Hague bureau had to reduce its activity.

Private societies and foundations took over the work of the municipal bureaus but there was a fundamental change. Until then advice had been gratis; now a fee was charged for it. During those years an essential change was made also in the method of working. Advice was primarily based on data derived from a school doctor, the headmaster or mistress, the parents and the impression the child made on the counselor. The Director of the Municipal Bureau in Utrecht pointed out, already in 1925, that these data did not suffice for well-founded guidance. He made a plea for psycho-technical (intelligence) tests to precede the advice, and immediately introduced them in his bureau. For a long time the management of the other bureaus were not convinced of the necessity of such psycho-technical tests and a lengthy dispute regarding this problem ensued, finding expression particularly in the monthly "Youth and Vocation" (Jeugd en Beroep). Gradually, however, psycho-technics gained ground and the present situation is such that in the report of the Central Bureau of Statistics (Centraal Bureau v.d. Statistiek) of 1943 (statistics of vocational guidance) it is stated that 63% of new applicants for advice are examined psycho-technically.

At the Netherlands Foundation for Psychotechnics (Nederlandsche Stichting voor Psychotechniek) in Utrecht, which succeeded the municipal bureau for vocational guidance when this closed in 1934 no occupational guidance is given without previous individual psycho-technical tests that take approximately 5–6 hours. It was this foundation that energetically propagated the idea that the cost be borne entirely by the applicants for guidance. And not without success, for approximately 6,000 psycho-technical tests were made annually, 2,000 of which were for vocational guidance and 4,000 for business concerns. The same was true of advice given by the laboratory of the Free University (Vriji Universiteit) in Amsterdam, The Hague Psychological Institute and the Institute of the Roman Catholic University in Nijmegen. Also some individual private counselors in this field took this course. Besides this, vocational guidance was still given by a number of commissions and societies which procured the material from more or less comprehensive psycho-metric tests or made no psycho-metric tests at all. Officially there are now, that is in 1945, 28 bureaus, those in Amsterdam, Rotterdam, The Hague and Utrecht being the most important.

The above sketched development naturally had its drawbacks. It retarded a general extension of vocational guidance. On the one hand there were the small, inadequately equipped commissions that treated no more than a few dozen cases a year, on the other the great laboratories that charged pretty high prices for their advice (from fl. 25 to fl. 80) making it impossible for people of limited means to afford the luxury of such guidance. The cause of this development was the lack of initiative in this field on the part of the Government. Dr. V. d. Tempel, Minister of Social Affairs who was in office in 1939–1940 had far-reaching plans in the field of vocational guidance. His intention was to form departments for occupational guidance in connection with the local labor exchanges and to have these managed by a central division of the Government Employment Bureau in The Hague. This was opposed by the champions of private, that is "denominational" ("confessional") guidance. They were of the opinion that if guidance by the government authorities became the rule, individuality and personal liberty could suffer. The invasion of the Germans made a decision in either direction absolutely impossible. In October 1940, thus during the occupation, a decree appeared in the Official Gazette of the Reich Commissioner, placing vocational guidance in the hands of the Government Employment Bureau.

As long as no other regulation was enforced private bureaus were allowed to continue their work. Their joint centre, "the Central Cooperative Committee for Vcational Guidance" (Het Centraal Comité van Samenwerking inzake Voorlichting bij Beroepskeuze), however, was liquidated thus putting an end to the central supply of material. It soon became evident that the Germans preferred to place the management of vocational guidance in the hands of "reliable" members who would fall in with the wishes of the occupier in aid of the labor reservoir. Several N.S.B.-ers (members of the Dutch nazi party) in turn were instructed to organize vocational guidance in the Netherlands. By the departure of the Germans, however, only the training of the vocational counselors had been taken in hand. This training was to last three years and only those who would make a declaration of loyalty to the occupier could take part. At the departure of the occupiers this training collapsed because the majority of the instructors and students were interned.

After May 1945 the situation was as follows: The great laboratories and bureaus saw a chance to protract their existence and are now in full swing. From the smaller commissions and bureaus several people on whom the organization depended have disappeared and the work has consequently been discontinued. A Royal Decree has now appeared declaring vocational guidance a Government concern and instructing the Government Employment Bureau to organize it as part of the Ministry of Social Affairs. The three central societies have reconstituted themselves and the Central Cooperative Committee has also resumed its work. It has however been decided, in consultation with the Secretary of the Government Employment Bureau, that the labor market data is no longer to be compiled by this Committee but by the Government Employment Bureau. The Committee on the other hand has been instructed to draw up plans for a thorough training of vocational counselors. It is planned to permit existing private institutions to continue their work during the next few years and to gradually develop departments for vocational guidance connected with the local labor exchanges. Professional material is to be supplied regularly to private institutions and before long their equipment will have to satisfy minimum requirements. The plan is to make it possible in the course of the next few years for all boys and girls to receive vocational guidance on leaving school.

Summary

Vocational Guidance in the Netherlands originated in private initiative, supplemented by municipal efforts. This private initiative flowed into three central organizations in which the bureaus and commissions of various denominations (confessions) joined. These were:

1. The Society for the Advancement of Vocational Guidance.
2. The Roman Catholic Psychological Vocational Office.
3. The Christian Psychological Centre for School and Vocation.

These three groups collaborated in the "Central Cooperative Committee for Vocational Guidance" which received a government subsidy to collect professional data and to distribute these among the bureaus and furthermore to take in hand a thorough training for vocational counselors. In 1940 a preparatory course was begun with 92 participants (34 women, 58 men). The training was discontinued when the German occupier began to interfere with vocational guidance.

The organization of the majority of the commissions was handicapped by lack of funds. The work had to be done in leisure hours after the termination of a day's work as teacher, official, physician or clergyman. There was thus no stability in working method and views. Expansion was hampered by want of time.

Favorable exceptions were the bureaus with full-time counselors. These obviously supplied a great demand and developed into well-founded institutions. At the end of 1943 altogether 111 persons were active as vocational counselors in the Netherlands, 20 working full time (6 in Amsterdam, 4 in Rotterdam, 4 in The Hague, 4 in Utrecht, 1 in Haarlem, 1 in Groningen).

It is planned that the Government organize vocational guidance through Government Employment Bureau (Rijksar beids bureau), with departments for vocational guidance connected with the 39 local labor exchanges in the country. The first step, a centre for vocational data, is being prepared.

Concerning the working method of the existing bureaus it may be recorded that this depends on the set-up.

a. *Bureau with counselors as an extra occupation* (mostly in rural districts).

As a rule the counselor studies the case by collecting data from school, home and physician on the physical and mental constitution of the applicants. The commission, be it the executive committee or the complete commission, gives the advice to the parents.

In a certain number of cases, which are considered difficult, the opinion of a psychotechnical laboratory is asked.

b. *Bureau with full-time counselors* (thus mostly in the towns).
The counselors provide themselves with all necessary data on study and vocation possibilities in their town and environment. Moreover, the Central Committee in The Hague collects and provides additional material regarding the country as a whole. The counselors record from conversations with the parents and the applicant anything that is helpful in forming an opinion. They send an extensive questionnaire to principals of schools and teachers, and if necessary, ask the opinion of the school doctor. In a limited number of cases the applicants are sent to be tested psychotechnically.

c. *Bureaus that are subdivisions of a psychotechnical laboratory,* with full-time counselors and testers. Examples of these are:
1. Psychological laboratory of the Municipal University in Amsterdam (Director: Prof. G. Révész);
2. Psychological laboratory of the Free University in Amsterdam (Director: Prof. J. Waterink);
3. Netherlands Foundation for Psychotechniques—Utrecht (Board of Directors: Jhr. Drs. D. J. v. Lennep, H. van der Vlist, Dr. W. F. v. Peype, Ir. K. H. P. Nieukerke);
4. The Psychological Institute in The Hague (Director: Dr. J. Luning Prak);
5. The Psychological Laboratory of the Roman Catholic University in Nijmegen (Director: Prof. Rutten);
6. Foundation for Psychotechnical Tests in Groningen (Management: Prof. Dr. H. J. F. W. Brugmans and Dr. Ch. Patje);
7. The Amsterdam Psychological Institute (Director: Dr. Van der Heijden).

These bureaus test every vocational guidance applicant psychotechnically.

The methodology of these psychotechnical tests is fairly divergent. This is connected with the views that are held concerning the possibility of psychotechnical tests. For a long time natural science clung to methods that furnished as much as possible exact figure material which could be mutually compared and checked. It is called the objective school of thought. Over against that stands a more subjective method which has been propagated since 1925, especially by the Netherlands Foundation for Psychotechnique in Utrecht; a method that is based on trying to understand the personality pattern of the counselee, and that attaches importance above all to methods of character tests. This group demands 3 to 4 counselors be present at the tests in order in this way to counteract errors due to subjectivity. Although at first violently opposed, this line of thought gained more and more adherents as time elapsed, but there are still laboratories that cling to the first-mentioned principle.

In general it can be said that for intelligence tests use is made of variations of the Army-test A or B, the Terman test, etc., supplemented with new tests that are taken individually and orally. For the other talents like technical ability, dexterity, organizational talent, administrative talent, etc., use is made of problems to be set individually, giving plenty of opportunity to observe the behavior. The motorio behavior is observed during motoric tests.

In order to get insight into character, standard interviews, spontaneous narratives, so-called polyvalent-tests, graphological analysis, etc., are employed.

But as has been mentioned above, not all laboratories take this course. There are those that attach greater value to ascertaining an intelligence quotient.

Comprehensive control tests have shown that psychotechnical research can boast of 86 to 92% accuracy.

It is planned to exchange the experience of the separate laboratories so that they may in this way profit by each other's work. In connection with its vocational guidance plans the Government Employment Bureau will want to make wide use of psychotechnical tests. Simplified tests will have to be found that retain the quality now obtained by elaborate tests, for the cost of the tests is now too high to permit each of the 180,000 children leaving school annually to be subjected to such tests. Perhaps a central psychotechnical institute will have to be founded for this purpose unless the existing institutes will cooperate.

References:

1. Heyden, Dr. Ph.M. v.d. *De Culturele Betekenis der Psychotechnick* (The Cultural Significance of Psychotechnics). Groningen: J. B. Wolters, 1941.
2. Holthuizen, Dr. F. *Studie over de beroepskeuze in Nederland in 1935* (Study of Vocational Guidance in the Netherlands—1935).
3. Prak, Dr. J. L. *Mensen en Mogelijkheden* (People and Possibilities). Amsterdam: Scheltema en Holkema.
4. Vlist, H. v.d. *Beroepskeuze voorlichting.* Studieboek voor de opleiding van Maatschappelijke Werkers (Vocational Guidance. Textbook for the Training of Social Workers). Haarlem: Stitching v. Opleiding v. Maatschappelijke Werkers, Zijlstraat, 47.

H. v. d. V.

NEW ZEALAND. Vocational guidance plays an important role in New Zealand, not only in schools and colleges, but in the rehabilitation of ex-servicemen and women.

Prior to 1920 there was no organized system of vocational guidance in New Zealand, though as early as 1913, the Christchurch Y.M.C.A., in conjunction with the Canterbury Education Board, arranged for prominent businessmen to address schools about their particular professions. A booklet entitled "What About Next Year" was written and distributed free to all boys ready to leave school. In November, 1924, the Christchurch Y.M.C.A. established a department of vocational guidance which operated during November, December, January and February. A vocational guidance psychological testing clinic also was set up in the Canterbury University College, which was later extended when the University organized a committee comprising an Education Professor, a lecturer responsible for psychological testing, and a selected group of professional, business and industrial men to interview and advise boys and girls.

Official recognition of vocational guidance in schools was finally given early in 1929, when vocational guidance officers were appointed by the Minister of Education. They were, however, limited to one officer attached to each technical college at the four main centres: Auckland, Wellington, Christchurch and Dunedin, such officers being released from teaching for four halfdays each week, so they would act as Guidance Officers.

In 1937, the present Prime Minister, the Right Honourable P. Fraser, then Minister of Education, took a keen interest in the development of guidance work, and was instrumental in establishing Government youth centres in the four main cities; eight parttime officers, men and women, being appointed staffs for these posts. The National Service Department provided placement officers, clerical staff, office accommodation and equipment for the centres, and for a further five years all problems relative to vocational and educational guidance were considered jointly by officers of the Education and Labor Departments.

Although the service of vocational guidance was by this time theoretically available to the whole country, in actual practice it did not extend beyond the cities. So, at the beginning of 1943, the Education Department announced its intention of taking over complete control of Government youth centres with full-time vocational guidance officers in control of each centre. New officers were trained for further development of the work, and the service was extended to rural areas. Vocational guidance work, under the same administrative control as teaching, increased cooperation between teachers and vocational guidance officers.

During the war the Vocational Guidance Centres worked closely with the National Service Department. Under industrial manpower control the Guidance Officers acted for the District Manpower Officer for all minors in the cities. An important added responsibility now is the interviewing and advising of ex-servicemen who may require money grants for further education under the Government rehabilitation scheme.

In New Zealand social and educational conditions differ in many ways from those in other countries so vocational guidance has been shaped to New Zealand needs. It tends to lay stress on the part the schools have to play in recognizing that guidance is one of their basic functions. It can be defined as teaching the child to make wise choices, such choices being based on as full a knowledge as possible of all relevant information, not only for himself but of the world and environment in which he is living. This implies that from the beginning a child should be placed in situations that require him to make choices and it is thought that, as he grows older, he will be more and more aware of the choices he may make and the reasons for his decisions. He will to an increasing extent become independent, but when the vocational aspect of guidance becomes important, he may require and will willingly accept expert advice more than at earlier stages.

It is generally believed that most guidance work in schools should be educational rather than vocational. Emphasis should be laid on the selection of courses of study that will best prepare the pupil for his chosen profession, and that will clearly show which profession or specialized branch thereof should be considered.

It is also thought that any system of vocational guidance which is divorced from educational guidance can never be wholly successful, therefore the closest liaison is maintained between Vocational Guidance Officers and career teachers in post-primary schools. Visits to schools are made by the former from time to time. Such visits are also made to primary schools where final year students are addressed and advised to take up some form of post-primary education, stress being laid on the necessity of expert advice on the course for which they are best suited. They are informed of the facilities provided by the Vocational Guidance Centres, and those who do not intend to continue school work—usually about one-third—are recommended to interview their Guidance Officer regarding types of employment. Many schools channel suitable graduates into jobs by acting as employment agencies for employers.

Towards the end of 1939 the four Vocational Guidance Centres issued booklets on careers, mainly for distribution to children about to leave primary schools. More recently a textbook on vocational civics, "Beyond the School Gates" by K. H. O'Halloran, has been widely used.

Effective vocational guidance necessitates a considerable knowledge of child psychology, accurate information about the abilities, deficiencies, and personal characteristics of the person to be guided. It also involves a wide knowledge of the requirements of different types of work, the demands they make on the physical and mental qualifications of workers and their future prospects. A teacher is usually capable of judging the first two aspects, but knowledge of diverse occupations involves wider experience, plus numerous contacts with industrial, rural and commercial life. Industry, highly specialized and rapidly expanding, requires special attention, and falls to Vocational Guidance Centres rather than to teachers.

One of the most important tasks of vocational guidance is to assess aptitudes, so frequent use is made of psychological tests in the Centres, and to a less extent in schools. All children are tested for I.Q. whilst they are at school, both with verbal and non-verbal tests. The most used test is the Otis Group Test, partly because it is a time saver and is convenient for testing large numbers, and, partly because it was standardized to New Zealand conditions a few years ago. The Stanford-Binet individual tests are also given. It is further considered advisable that a schoolchild should be tested several times as the first results may be inaccurate. At present, however, a good deal of information on pupils is collected by means of descriptive devices arising from regular work rather than testing as the number of teachers competent to interpret results of tests and to remedy defects is very small.

Cards are prepared for all post-primary school graduates by the local career teacher and sent to the respective Guidance Centres. Such cards give information as to both parents' occupations, child's age, height, weight, health, drawing attention to any marked physical characteristics, religion, length of education, attendance, courses taken and examinations passed, general appearance, carriage, manner, dress, conversation, interest and hobbies, results of I.Q. tests—if these have been given—sports and social activities, character, temperament, home circumstances and desired vocation. In some districts a portion of the card is filled by the primary school headmasters before pupils leave for post primary schools or for work. While this is a very cumbersome arrangement, it gives the headmaster an opportunity to use his knowledge of a child's educational record to indicate the type of post-primary school he should attend, and to suggest a suitable course within the school, but, of course, he cannot as a rule make any strong recommendations that a child should prepare for any particular occupation as the work of a primary school is of too general a character to form a correct estimate of any special abilities.

For thorough individual vocational testing involving use of special aptitude and mechanical tests specially trained psychologists are required. However, as qualified personnel are limited, there is a tendency to leave such clinical examinations to really difficult cases. This service is provided mainly by the University Colleges in the four main centres which have the necessary equipment and trained personnel in their laboratories and, latterly, a similar service on a smaller scale has become available within the Vocational Guidance Centres.

One of the most important features of the work of the Vocational Centres now is guidance for ex-servicemen and women. The Rehabilitation Board has assigned the Education Department the responsibility of advising on all applications for educational assistance. Their problems include: interruption in education and vocational training, the fact that in many cases they had not even commenced their career training, and also the difficulty of adjustment to civilian life. The procedure adopted is that each applicant must interview a Vocational Guidance Officer. After discussion, testing, and enquiry, the Vocational Officer sends forward the application with a report to the Education Committee of the Rehabilitation Board. There are obviously certain matters outside the province of the Vocational Officer, such as the applicant's service, which weigh in reaching a decision, but the principal factor in the Board's selection is the opinion of the Vocational Guidance Officer. Each education grant is made conditional on the fact that the student studies diligently, and shows a degree of competence and aptitude that would indicate a successful career.

Money grants and other assistance is, therefore, not granted for longer than yearly periods. At the end of that time the grants come under review, the actual results and reports of the teachers being the primary tests on which a renewal of concessions is decided; the Vocational Officer has the responsibility of investigating and advising the Board on all cases where there is doubt that the student will succeed in a given course.

Vocational guidance, at the beginning of its history as a branch of the Education Department, has been given a vastly important assignment; but from its pre-war and war record there is every

ENCYCLOPEDIA OF VOCATIONAL GUIDANCE

indication that it will succeed, and that there will be a rapid growth
of Vocational Guidance Centres throughout New Zealand.

E. H.

NURSING, SELECTION OF APPLICANTS FOR. The nursing
profession along with other professions but somewhat more tardily
has recognized its obligation to society and to individuals to set
up selective technics in order to eliminate much of the wastefulness
which results from poor selection of applicants for schools of nursing. In the early thirties approximately fifty per cent of the students
admitted to schools of nursing failed to graduate. Since then the
percentage of students withdrawing from schools of nursing has
decreased. In the last eight years the percentage of loss has fluctuated between 27 and 31 per cent. One technic which probably
assisted considerably to decrease the percentage of withdrawals of
student nurses has been the increased use of test batteries which
help to determine the ability to succeed in the profession.

Early Use of Tests for Selection and Admission

Approximately fifteen years ago several individuals established
test services to assist schools of nursing in obtaining objective evidence concerning the ability of applicants so that schools using these
batteries could better select students for professional study. The use
of such tests, sponsored by both individuals and groups of individuals, spread and in some areas were soon conducted on a state
or wider basis. Where the examiner had an opportunity to discuss
the test results with the nursing school faculty members and could
assist them to interpret them along with other data—educational
reports and interview records—selection was improved. Too frequently, however, the test results were used as the sole basis for
recommendations made to the school as to the acceptance or
rejection of the applicant. The nursing school faculty members,
inexperienced in measurement, tended to rely too exclusively upon
the recommendations which accompanied the test report rather
than to learn to interpret the test results in light of other credentials
for the applicant. The education of the professional nursing group
in this respect was not the responsibility nor the objective of these
independent and commercial test services.

A few schools of nursing were fortunate enough to have access
to competent psychometrists and counselors who were able to give
them considerable help in the testing and in teaching faculties to
interpret the test results. Nursing educators began to recognize their
responsibility not only for setting up admission standards to profes-

sional educational programs and implementing them with tests to assist in maintaining them, but also for educating its members in the appropriate use of tests.

Profession's Responsibility for Selective Admission Batteries

The National League of Nursing Education's recognition of their responsibility resulted in the appointment of the Committee on Measurement and Educational Guidance in 1941. This Committee had two main functions: (1) To make available to any school of nursing, test services to aid in the selection of suitable applicants; and (2) To study abilities deemed necessary for success in the nursing profession. To achieve these purposes the Commitee of Measurement and Educational Guidance established the Pre-nursing and Guidance Test Service, which offers a battery of tests to help schools of nursing appraise the learning capacity, the educational achievement, and the cultural background of prospective students. The tests which comprise the battery consist of the American Council on Education Psychological Examination and a group of tests, made available to the Committee by the Cooperative Test Service under a licensure arrangement, which appraises the applicant's rate and level of reading comprehension, fundamental skills in English and arithmetic, and her achievement in the biological and social sciences. A personal data form helps to determine the prospective student's cultural and home background, her hobbies and interests, her reasons for entering nursing, and goals she hopes to realize in the profession. This information not only helps in estimating the social and emotional maturity and the adjustment of the individual but also aids in her counseling on admission to the school.

No personality test is included in the selective admission battery, but the test service provides the school with a choice of either the Bernreuter or the Minnesota Personality Scale to administer only after students are in the school of nursing. In this way schools use the personality test as a tool in guidance and counseling, but not in selection.

Since manipulative ability is important in nursing, experimental work has been done by the Committee on Measurement and Educational Guidance to measure such ability by the use of a group test. However, no valid and reliable test has yet been devised which is practical to administer to large groups of applicants.

The National Committee on Measurement and Educational Guidance works cooperatively with the State Committees on Measurement and Educational Guidance in establishing testing centers, administering the test battery, and promoting the understanding in the use of test results in the selective procedure. Individuals who qualify as psychometrists are employed to administer the examinations. In addition to administering the tests, these psychometrists frequently assist schools of nursing in interpreting test results.

The fact that all of the tests in the battery are machine scored has aided the reporting of results to schools of nursing promptly and accurately. The report consists of the percentile rank of each student on each test in the battery and a copy of each prospective student's personal data form. Along with the report the Committee sends the schools instructions and suggestions to aid the school in interpreting the test results.

The norms have been compiled on large numbers of nurse applicants in 36 states. The test battery has the added advantage of having norms based on entering liberal arts college freshmen so that nurse applicants may be conveniently compared with college freshmen. Plans have been made to prepare regional norms as well as norms for different types of schools of nursing, such as hospital schools, university schools, and schools with independent control.

Use of Pre-Entrance Data in Counseling

One major emphasis of the Committee's educational program for school nursing faculty members has been on the counseling of first the applicants and then the students on the basis of pre-entrance data. Applicants who seem unsuited for nursing should be assisted to find other professions or a vocation in which they can find personal and vocational satisfaction. Applicants whose learning capacity is below that demanded in professional nursing but who are otherwise suited for some type of nursing may be directed toward schools for practical nurses. Applicants whose educational achievements seem weak in a particular area may be assisted in supplementing their preparation and thereby increase the likelihood of success. The counseling of students entering the school is greatly facilitated by the pre-entrance data particularly by providing a basis for estimating the expected level of performance which can serve as a criterion in appraising progress.

Extent of Use of Selective Admission Batteries

Of the approximately 1300 schools of nursing in this country about half of them use some form of battery consisting of objective tests to aid in selecting student nurses. These schools now using batteries still lack uniformity in that each school determines its own "critical point" below which it does not accept students. Many schools have found, for example, that students who fall below the fortieth percentile (norms based on entering liberal arts college freshmen) in the American Council on Education Psychological Test will not succeed in their schools of nursing. Schools with lower standards of instruction and education are still accepting students below this level, and these students may be able to progress satisfactorily in poorer schools. However, several factors are tending to upgrade the standards of schools and exert particular pressure on the poorer ones. A national accrediting committee now accredits schools of nursing. A battery of state board tests prepared by the National Committee on Measurement and Educational Guidance are now being used in 32 states for licensing purposes. The results of the Pre-nursing and Guidance Test Service and the state board test battery are now identifying to the profession the schools with the lowest standards and tending to hasten improvement in the selection of students as well as in the educational program.

Problems of Supply and Demand

At the present time the nursing profession is at the horns of a dilemma. In order to supply the nursing service which the nation requires, many more nurses are needed than are now prepared or being prepared; and more are needed than the public can support on salaries which are commensurate with the time and amount of education required of professional nurses. Some types of nursing service, however, can be given satisfactorily by a subprofessional group. In order that the greatest good be done for the greatest number, it remains essential that the quality of professional service is not sacrificed for quantity. In addition to the professional workers, nonprofessional, vocational, or practical nurses should be prepared for types of nursing service which can be given safely by a subprofessional group. Increasingly, young women interested in nursing and suited by disposition and by personality but with intellectual capacity and educational preparation below the standards of professional schools should be directed into approved schools for practical nursing and preparation for a vocation in a field where the demand for well prepared workers far exceeds the supply.

References:
1. Bingham, W. V. Aptitudes and aptitude testing. New York: Harper and Brothers, 1937, pp. 190–194.
2. Kandel, I. L. Professional aptitude tests. New York: Bureau of Publications. Teachers College, Columbia University, 1940.
3. Kay, L. W. Selective techniques in medical education. Journal of General Psychology, 1944, 30, 225–235.

4. McManus, R. L. Study Guide on evaluation. New York: National League of Nursing Education, 1944.

5. ————. Vocational counseling in relation to nursing. Teachers College Record, 45, 532–542.

6. McManus, R. L. and Anderson, Marie H. Interests of nursing candidates. American Journal of Nursing, 1943, 42, 555–563.

7. National League of Nursing Education. *Manual of Information.* Pre-Nursing and Guidance Test Service, 1790 Broadway, New York 19, New York.

8. Nursing Information Bureau: Vocational information and pamphlets for distribution by counselors. 1790 Broadway, New York 19, New York.

9. Potts, E. M. The selection of student nurses. American Journal of Nursing, 1941, 41, 590–597.

10. Ranier, R. N., Richfield, F. W., Madigan, M. E. The use of tests in guiding student nurses. American Journal of Nursing, 1942, 42, 679–682.

11. Sommer, I. B. The pre-nursing and guidance test service. American Journal of Nursing, 1944, 44, 158–164.

12. Triggs, F. D. *Personnel Work in Schools of Nursing.* Philadelphia: W. B. Saunders Company, 1945.

13. Walters, R. Should number of professional students be restricted? Educational Record, 1935, 16, 412–432

R. L. McM.

NURSING TESTS, A CRITICAL EVALUATION OF

Tests Used in Programs for the Selection of Students for Schools of Nursing

A. Types of Tests:

1. *Ability Tests:* A review of the literature indicates that the one best indicator of success in a school of nursing is usually a general ability or scholastic aptitude test. A number of well-known general ability tests have been used for this purpose. In fact the tests used in schools of nursing for selection purposes have generally been those which colleges and universities use for selection of students. Various forms of the *Army Alpha,* the *Otis Test of Mental Ability* and more recently (since 1930) the *Ohio Psychological Examination* and the *American Council on Education Psychological Examination* have been used.

Judging from the literature, the first two tests named have been superseded largely by the one last named, a detailed description of which is given by Triggs.[6]

Probably the test thought of most frequently when tests purporting to measure "aptitude for or ability for the profession of nursing" are considered is the *Aptitude Test for Nurses* largely because of the title it bears. However, the author of Form II herself states in the manual that "this test might be considered of the nature of a specialized intelligence test for prospective nurses."

A detailed description of the test is given by Triggs [6] and will not be repeated here. It should be stated, however, that when considered as a "general ability test for selection of nurses" the results compare favorably with those obtained when using a test such as the *American Council on Education Psychological Examination.*

Research in the prediction of success in curricula other than nursing which is promising for nursing has utilized the measurement of "quantitative ability" and "linguistic ability." Very few reports are available for nursing on the differentiation of types of general ability but schools which can do experimental work might find this promising. The *American Council on Educational Psychological Examination* yields Quantitative and Linguistic scores as well as a total score which may be used as an over-all general ability score.

One other measure of scholastic aptitude or general ability to do successful work in schools of nursing is reported as being frequently used, i.e. high school or, if available, college grades. This criterion suffers from the fact that grades are not comparable school to school or even individual to individual within a school because of their subjective nature. However, if the truth were known, this would probably be the one most frequently used criterion for selecting students for schools of nursing, unreliable and invalid as it may be.

Many studies indicate that neither the score on a scholastic aptitude test nor high school rank alone gives the best prediction of success in nursing school but that prediction is improved by combining scores on a general ability test with high school rank or grades in high school (rank or actual grades being of about equal value) and comparing the combined score to the criterion of success being used.

2. *Achievement Tests:* Achievement testing in any field serves a number of purposes. Consideration under this heading will be given only to achievement tests as a part of the selection battery. Other uses will be discussed later.

The literature indicates that background in science adds valuable information when selecting students for a school of nursing, especially a collegiate school or a school in which the students compete with college students for grades in science courses. If the first quarter of the nursing curriculum is examined, the reason for this will be clear. Usually the student is introduced to at least four science courses and in some cases has five in the very early part of her curriculum.

The *Cooperative General Science* or *Natural Science* tests are the most frequently used tests for this purpose as reported in the literature. When these scores are combined with scores on an ability test and high school rank, the best prediction of successful achievement in schools of nursing is made.

Achievement tests in the social sciences have also been used as a part of the selection battery but no report has been found in the literature which indicates that scores on them add to the prediction score. The *Cooperative Social Science Test* has been reported as used for this purpose.

3. *Mechanical Tests:* The literature indicates that many persons thought that a score on a mechanical aptitude test would add weight to a score used to predict success in nursing. Much research has been done on it however, and while no one denies that nurses do have to do jobs which require mechanical skills, it has been found that the present tests do not seem to measure the specific skill needed by nurses. A score on a mechanical aptitude test (and many have been tried), does not improve our ability to predict success in nursing.

4. *Personality Inventories:* The use of personality questionnaires for prediction of success in nursing, as for prediction of success in other fields, has not been found to be valuable. Personality inventories are counseling instruments and contribute to a counseling situation only when used by skilled counselors. It might even be said that a counseling program might be very successful without any reference to personality inventories. Much research and study must be done on them before they can be considered reliable and valid even for the usual counseling situation. No comment has been made concerning projective techniques for measuring personality because as yet no reports appear in the literature concerning the use of these techniques with nurses. However, there are at least two such studies in progress.

5. *Interest Inventories:* The literature gives very little information concerning the use of interest inventories in the battery of tests used for selection purposes. This may be due to the fact that research done on the interests of women has not been as successful as that done on the interests of men. However, recent research comparing the interests of nurses to women in general, and interests in various fields of nursing, indicates very promising results. It might be said that interest test results contribute to the selection program in the same manner as do data from the application blank. Cer-

tainly the research which has been done to date is promising enough to include the interest test in a selection battery but the scores are not used as a part of the prediction equation.

Before an interest test is selected for use in the battery of tests given to aid in the selection process, the same careful evaluation should be made against the criteria for selection of a test as should be made for any other test. Two tests frequently used for this purpose are the *Kuder Preference Record* and the *Strong Vocational Interest Inventory*. (Some of the research in this field is too recent to be included in Triggs' book.[6])

6. *Tests Measuring Special Skills:* Research reports in the literature indicate that when scores on tests which are a part of the prediction battery are good, and attention is given to reading and arithmetic skills, prediction of success in individual cases can be improved, though scores on reading and arithmetic tests add little to the prediction equation made up of scores on a scholastic aptitude test, the high school rank, and a test of background in science.

The Aptitude Test for Nursing as revised in 1940 has tests of both reading and arithmetic which may be given as a part of that test or separately. It is probable that the relationship between the score on the test itself with the reading test score would be so high as to indicate that in most cases both tests were measuring much the same thing. It is probably true, however, that there is no more satisfactory reading test for the purpose available when cost, scoring, appropriate content, and time for administration is taken into account.

It should be stressed that unless remedial work in reading and arithmetic is to follow the administration of the reading and arithmetic tests, or at least these skills are to be considered for admission along with the combined score on general ability and background in science measures, there is no use in administering them. Remedial work in most cases in both reading and arithmetic is quite practical.[3, 5] It can be supervised by the school or can be done by the candidate herself following the procedures outlined in self-administering manuals. Sufficient motivation in most cases for the probable necessary duration of such work would be an explanation of the place of these skills in the work to be undertaken in the school of nursing and the fact that a retest would be administered after remedial work was completed.

Tests in formal English grammar also have been given as a part of the selection battery. However, except in collegiate courses, there is no provision in the nursing curriculum for formal instruction in English. This is probably a weakness of the curriculum for it is well-known that students coming from high schools now-a-days can not be presupposed to have adequate formal English skills to express themselves accurately in writing or speaking; yet we would not want to suggest that such young people be barred from becoming nurses. The problem posed is one for the nurse educators to study, but if tests in formal English were generally enough a part of the selection batteries, the data would be available to show what a really important matter this is and thus might give impetus to its careful consideration.

B. Agencies Selling Selection Services to Schools of Nursing.

Triggs [6] reviews some of the testing services which have been set up to administer, score, and report results on selection batteries for schools of nursing. The candidate bears the cost of this service herself. Tests used are largely those mentioned earlier.

It is interesting to note that these testing services do not usually make available for users names of tests in the batteries; neither do they give information concerning validity and reliability of the tests used though they do give certain limited information concerning their interpretation. Perhaps users are as much at fault for not requiring more information concerning the tests used as are the services for not furnishing it.

Each school should consider carefully especially their validity and reliability for the purpose for which the individual school needs tests before accepting them for this purpose even though they were to be administered and scored by an outside service. This is not to say that the agencies selling these services are not critical of the validity and reliability of the instruments in their batteries; whether the same tests are equally valid and reliable for all schools is an important question to be raised and should be answered by each school itself in the light of a critical examination of the objectives of its own program.

These agencies selling testing services have at once been an advantage and a disadvantage to the use of tests for selection purposes. They have served to motivate some schools to use the results of tests for selection which probably would not have done so otherwise. But in some cases they have also served to prevent school administrators and faculties from learning to use to the fullest extent objective measures for selection and educational counseling of their students.

In most cases the faculty has accepted without question the tests which these services have offered without careful examination of the objectives of their curricula, the reliability and validity of these instruments, or a study of the way in which they can be used for counseling. Research which has been done to test the validity of these instruments has been done largely as if all schools of nursing have, or should have the same objectives and aims because it has usually been done by these test services for the schools they serve as a whole, not for each individual school against its stated aims and objectives. Had the schools themselves collected the five dollars per candidate and done the research themselves, admittedly perhaps not as efficiently, they would have learned a great deal which might be directly applied to the educational process in that school. This latter plan has been adopted by some schools, using as advisers local psychologists. In these schools great profit has come from participation in the process itself.

The question may arise as to who should administer and interpret psychological tests. Gordon [2] has given a concise statement and one with which most psychologists will agree.

Today, the increased educational requirements for nursing school faculties and the increased opportunity for learning about psychological tests and measurements make it possible to expect from instructors and supervisors intelligent and open-minded use of psychological data. Since they are the persons who deal directly and constantly with student activities and student development, it seems wise to place in their hands any available information that may be helpful to them in their work.

The administration and scoring of well-constructed tests which are a part of the selection battery is no more difficult than the administration and scoring of achievement or end of the course tests. The local faculties and administrators have a great deal to contribute to the improvement of these techniques from their experience once they themselves learn to handle their administration, scoring and interpretation themselves. It could probably be said with validity that any person who cannot learn to handle these instruments sufficiently well for the results to make a contribution to the educational process should not be teaching in a school of nursing preparing young persons in whose hands the very lives of individuals will lie.

We are not optimistic enough to believe that no mistakes will be made. Has progress ever been made without error?

C. Summary.

In summary it may be said that:

1. Tests may be used to predict success in the nursing curriculum as efficiently as they can be used for prediction of success in

other curricula; and most important is the fact that any school of real professional standing can itself develop a successful program of selection of students which will greatly reduce student mortality—a fact which in itself, considering the cost of present rates of student mortality to the school, would more than pay for the cost of the prediction program if the institution bore its total cost. (As now administered, the cost of most selection programs is borne by the candidates wanting to enter schools of nursing.)

2. The extent of prediction may be indicated by validity coefficients which vary all of the way from the lower to upper sixties seldom reaching a coefficient of as high as .70.

3. The validity coefficient obtained for any selection program depends to a great extent on the criteria of success used. Teacher grades have not been found to be a very reliable criterion and clinical proficiency records less reliable. In some cases grades on State Board of Nurse Examiners licensing examinations have been found to be a valid criterion but the extent of their validity must be established before they are used. It cannot be assumed.

4. A selection program set up for one school is not necessarily directly applicable to another. Only by independent investigation can a school determine the combination of measures or the level of scores which will best predict success for that school or institution.

5. Continual research is necessary to assure the efficiency of the combination of measures (or battery of tests) from year to year. This is true because of the changes in the curriculum, type of teaching, license requirements, etc., which result both from changing sociological and economic conditions in society as a whole and the inevitable change which selection and other changes, if well-used by a staff, have on instruction within the schools themselves.

6. The accuracy of selection using objective tests increases when the tests do not stand alone but when other data are scientifically used to modify the interpretation of scores on objective tests and especially as data from both sources are used in the counseling program after the student is admitted to adapt the curriculum to the individual's needs or to help her to adapt to it.

Tests Used to Evaluate Educational Programs: Achievement Testing

There are no achievement tests in areas or specific courses in the nursing curriculum or in nursing specialties which a school can, after setting up its own aims and objectives, evaluate against the criteria of validity, objectivity, reliability, and cost of administration with a view to buying them for use in evaluating a part or all of its program. A school, therefore, has two choices: 1. Itself build the tests which it needs, or 2. Pay fifty cents per test per student tested to use tests constructed by the Committee on Measurement and Educational Guidance of the National League for Nursing Education of which three are now available.

If a school, or group of schools chooses the first alternative, it could budget annually the cost of the testing program, use local consulting service, and through committees of its staff or staffs, develop tests as needed. The experience gained through an experience of this kind using the several references on testing given by Triggs,[6] and other appropriate ones, as a guide would undoubtedly reflect favorably upon teaching techniques and the tests would meet specifically the purposes and objectives of those cooperating in their construction. In certain fields such as chemistry, nutrition, and other subjects, tests published and sold by the Cooperative Test Service might be used as guides for such purposes. Such work has been done by various schools, in fact, and reports are now available an example being *Educational Research and Nursing Education* (1944) and *What the Testing Program in Schools of Nursing has Taught Us* (1946) both available from the Medical College of Virginia, Richmond.

It is to be expected that the lack of tests in this area will be noted and achievement tests be made available for sale to schools in the not too distant future. The dangers of teachers using such tests as teaching guides rather than for evaluation purposes will disappear to the extent that they understand the purposes of objective testing. Once an instructor realizes that there is no magic about the construction of such instruments, that she herself can construct and evaluate them for use in her classes, tests will then have begun to make their most valuable contribution. As long as the school faculties accept tests without evaluation for their own purposes and without information concerning their validity, reliability, and interpretation, those staff members cannot be expected to learn to make the major use of the results of testing.

Tests Used for Licensing Purposes

In the United States, individual states have laws which govern the licensing of nurses who practice within their borders. These state laws are usually administered by a body defined in the law as the State Board of Nurse Examiners which has either a paid or volunteer secretary who actually administers the law according to policy set by the Board.

The members of the State Board of Nurse Examiners and the

secretary together set up examinations which are given to students as they graduate from schools of nursing within the state, or to nurses from other states who cannot be licensed by reciprocity from another state.

The construction of tests which are used for licensing purposes follows the same plan as construction of tests for any other purpose, viz., examination of the law for a statement of objectives and purposes of the examination, the outline of test parts necessary to meet these objectives, the individual principles and content which it is necessary to cover under each part of the test as outlined, the construction of test items to measure the principles underlying performance, the submission of these items for tryout and editing to a number of specialists in each area as many times as is necessary to get agreement on each item, the assembling and administration of the examination to candidates presenting themselves for licensure, the scoring of each item according to the answer given it by the "committee of experts," the testing of the validity of each item by determining to what extent what persons who got this item right are also the ones who got high scores on the total test (and if this is not true, the item is omitted in scoring), the determining of the extent of the reliability of the test as a whole, and finally the scoring of the test for each individual who took it and determining the point at which the passing mark should be set.

Each individual item is not reconstructed for each individual examination. The item with its possible answers is typed on a card along with a record of its value to each test in which it is used as determined by the process described above. It is filed with other items according to the heading which indicates what this item purports to measure. Each time a new examination is given, old items, appropriate to the need, are pulled and new items are added as needed and a new examination is assembled.

This process is followed by State Boards of Nurse Examiners with varying modifications and examinations which results have varying degrees of validity.

The Committee on Measurement of the National League of Nursing Education sells service on individual tests to states from its pool of tests.[4] These tests are carefully constructed in the manner which has been described. Again, however, as with service on other tests which the Committee sells, there is too little opportunity and too little necessity for State Boards of Nurse Examiners in each state to examine practices within the state and the law as it is set up, and then examine the validity of a test from the State Board Test Pool to be sure that it is valid for that state's needs. Were items covering defined areas sold or rented, and the State Board of Nurse Examiners in each state required to examine them and then assemble its own tests, the resulting tests would not only be more likely to meet the individual needs of individual states, but also the State Boards of Nurse Examiners would be required to continually re-evaluate their programs and the examinations used. Both the process of such evaluation and the actual results would be more likely to affect favorably educational practices within the states than as now set up when the whole process of construction, scoring. and evaluation of the examination is done by a group of specialists working in a national office. The personnel on each State Board of Nurse Examiners changes from year to year as required by the law. What an opportunity to educate these members of the boards in sound test construction processes that they may be applied in the local institutions in which those board members work, whether they are educational institutions or institutions giving nursing service to the public, or both. The effect on the evaluation techniques used by those institutions or agencies could be felt throughout the profession. Again it may be said that the profession is no stronger than the local agencies in which individual members of the profession serve. A national or state association or organization gives its greatest service as it strengthens directly and indirectly the local unit.

Tests Used for Selection of Personnel

Objective criteria for selection of employees are usually based on a. the description of the job to be done by the employee, and b. an objective test based on this description, and some provision for objective rating of education and experience. There may also be provision for interview which may or may not be considered an objective part of the examination.

Most agencies employing nurses do not have objective criteria for selection. More often than not, unless the agency is a governmental one, there is not even a written description of the job the nurse is to do. The selection programs in these agencies, therefore, are likely not to be well-defined. Private agencies may well follow the example of governmental agencies in this regard though, of course, the efficiency of personnel programs in these agencies varies also.

The greatest impetus to the use of objective examinations came with the passage of the amendment of the Social Security Act which provides for the establishment and maintenance of personnel standards on a merit basis for all agencies receiving funds under the provisions of this Act.

The American Public Health Association,[1] at the instigation of the Childrens Bureau and the United States Public Health Service, agencies affected by this Act both employing public health personnel, including public health nurses, set up a Merit System Unit which sells examination service to merit system units serving agencies employing public health personnel. A file of items, tested for validity and difficulty as described under the heading above, is maintained by the Merit System Unit. A merit system wanting examination material from it, sends to the APHA Merit System Unit the job descriptions of the positions being filled. The unit outlines the areas of knowledge as set by the job description as necessary to do the job and selects those items which they believe to be most appropriate for the purpose. The validity and difficulty of these items have been tested for similar situations and the coefficients noted on the cards. The examination is assembled and sent to the state. The state selects specialists in the field of the examination and they review it to determine its appropriateness for the local situation, again according to the job described. They can rearrange, add, or omit material in accordance with their judgment. The test is then administered, scored, and passing points are set by the merit system giving the examination. The items are tested for validity and the data are made available to the APHA Merit System Unit that it may have additional information on the items when they are again considered for use. Careful safeguards are set up, to assure the fact that the material is at all times appropriately protected in accordance with its confidential nature.

The scores on this test then become the basis for selection of personnel using as additional information the rating on education and experience and perhaps a personal interview.

The personnel department of any agency can set up such objective methods for selection of personnel. If then the personnel practices of the agency make working conditions attractive, the ultimate service of the agency to society is increased greatly for an efficient, stable, well-motivated staff is an agency's best assurance that high standards of service will be maintained.

Summary

As has been pointed out in this review, techniques of testing used only by a few technically trained individuals may result in overstandardization and inflexibility of the pattern followed by a profession but rightly used to stimulate evaluation and research by educational and operating programs to maintain sound, varying and flexible practices in accordance with the varying needs of the communities which they serve, objective measurement will serve any profession toward more efficient education of its personnel, and the service given by that personnel after they are educated.

References:

1. Atwater, R. M., and Long, L. D. New methods for the selection of public health personnel, 1945, 41, 1–5.
2. Gordon, P. Aptitude testing: its use in the selection of student nurses. Trained Nurse and Hospital Review, 1936, 96, 360–364.
3. Hills, E. J. and Polley, A. *Arithmetic of drugs and solutions.* Philadelphia: W. B. Saunders Co., 1945.
4. McManus, R. L. The State Board Test Pool. American Journal of Nursing, 44, 380–384.
5. Triggs, F. O. *Improve your reading.* Minneapolis: University of Minnesota Press, 1942.
6. ———. *Personnel work in schools of nursing.* Philadelphia: W. B. Saunders Co., 1945.

F. O. T.

O

OCCUPATIONAL INFORMATION. A vast amount of occupational information exists at the present time and is available to vocational counselors. Much of this material can be obtained free or at little cost from governmental agencies and professional societies; many fine publications are offered for sale by such organizations as Science Research Associates and the Institute for Research. A very large number of books have been designed for high school courses in occupations.

The Women's Bureau and the Occupational Outlook Division of the U. S. Department of Labor have prepared material of great value to counselors. The Occupational Information and Guidance Service of the U. S. Office of Education has published a series of inexpensive pamphlets on important occupations and from time to time releases comprehensive annotated bibliographies. Announcements of the U. S. Civil Service Commission and of other civil service jurisdictions provide valuable additions to information files. Newspaper clippings help to keep files up-to-date. Catalogs of colleges, trade schools, and other institutions are generally sent without cost on request (see book edited by C. V. Good, listed in the annotated bibliography at the back of this Encyclopedia).

Many professional societies, unions, and other occupational organizations have published pamphlets relating to their fields and these can be obtained on request and generally without charge. The names and addresses of the principal organizations can be found in the World Almanac. Personal contacts with employed men and women in the community afford useful information that can be written down and preserved. *The Dictionary of Occupational Titles* and job description volumes published by the Government Printing Office are indispensable tools. The National Roster of Scientific and Specialized Personnel has prepared descriptions of a large number of professions. An annotated bibliography of references to the current literature is to be found in the *Occupational Index,* published monthly by the National Occupational Conference.

The writer has found it helpful in getting information about conditions in his State to write to the presidents of State occupational groups. Frequently, local and State conditions are not identical with those prevailing nationally.

Unless information is systematically organized, it is of little use. The reader is referred to the article on the library. The article on the high school course in occupations may also be of interest.

Occupational briefs ranging in length from 250 to 1000 words are very useful media for distributing occupational information. They may contain a brief description of the occupation, educational requirements, economic prospects, psychological and physical requirements, and other pertinent information.

Economic conditions and educational requirements are constantly changing and for this reason the collection of occupational information is an unending task. However, acquaintance with a very large number of occupations is one of the most important characteristics of a good counselor.

References:

1. Forrester, G. *Methods of vocational guidance.* Boston: D. C. Heath and Co., 1944.
2. Parker, W. E. *Books about jobs: a bibliography of occupational literature.* Chicago: American Library Association, 1936.
3. Shartle, C. L. *Occupational information.* New York: Prentice-Hall, 1945.

O. J. K.

OCCUPATIONAL INFORMATION COURSES IN HIGH SCHOOL. An effective guidance program must help to provide pupils with adequate occupational information. The occupations course is one of several ways by which this information can be presented to pupils. The regular classes, assemblies, career days, career clubs and work experiences represent some of the other methods for providing for this important area of student need. The occupations course is being much more frequently used as an important method for providing more adequate information. An increasing number of secondary schools are using this type of curricular organization to provide for the occupational information needs of all of the pupils. As the school offering comes closer to the basic needs of pupils the occupations course is given a more important place in the curriculum.

Trends

The course in occupations has often been placed in the eighth or ninth grades. Because of pupil immaturity and lack of vocational readiness, several changes have been taking place in the grade placement of these classes. Increasingly, schools are beginning to offer a general orientation course in the freshman year of high school. This course provides an introductory over-view to the entire world of work. This course does not attempt to introduce the pupil to the intricacies of occupational information. It tends to provide for orientation to the school, to present information about the educational program of the school and to present a general overview of the major aspects of occupational activity. An additional and much more intensive course in occupational information is offered in the latter part of the junior or the first semester of the senior years. The material in this section is concerned with the more intensive course organized to help pupils at the time when they are most concerned and most interested in vocational planning.

School administrators are beginning to recognize the special skills and interests required by successful teachers of such courses. As a result, they are selecting teachers for this specific task. Frequently, members of the counseling staff are best able to provide the best instruction in this area. This practice makes it possible to give these counselors a group as well as an individual contact with their pupils. This arrangement is finding increasing acceptance.

The objectives of the occupations course are also being broadened. The relationship between occupational and educational planning is being recognized. Pupils are given assistance in learning about themselves in order that their occupational planning might be more realistic. Consideration is also being given to their personal problems and difficulties.

This course is also being used to utilize community resources. Studies are made of occupational activities of the local community. Local employers and employment office representatives are used as instructional resources. Pupils are assisted in a program of observation and visitation of local working activities. Efforts are made to use the instructional values inherent in the local community.

More attention is given to the process of building these courses on the real occupational needs of the pupils. The vocational interests and problems of the pupils are carefully studied so that this information may be used as the core of information to determine the directions the course should take. Follow-up studies are used to determine the patterns followed by former pupils.

Purposes

The purposes of these courses are: to help pupils learn about themselves; to learn of the range and importance of individual differences; to learn about pupil's interests, abilities, aptitudes; to learn the techniques of personal development; to gain an over-all picture of the entire occupational scene; to understand significant occupational trends; to intensively study a few occupational fields most appropriate to the individual; to survey local opportunities; to gain some actual experience on several types of employment; to locate sources of information; to learn the techniques of job getting; to learn about placement agencies and organizations; to learn about the personal traits necessary to success; to understand the relationship between education, training and occupational planning; to study educational and training opportunities; to learn about individuals and agencies that are helpful; to learn the techniques of intelligent occupational planning; to provide opportunities for personal counseling in formulating and implementing these occupational plans.

The specific purposes of such courses are determined by local circumstances. They will be conditioned by local employment opportunities, by instructional resources available in the community, by the drop-out rate in the school, by the contributions made by other classes and by the other provisions made for occupational information.

Activities

The activities of the course are planned around the purposes listed above. The following procedures indicate some of the types of activity usually undertaken. The class begins with a study of the individual. An autobiography and a background data blank are often filled out by the pupils. Studies of the nature and importance of individual differences are made. Pupils are given a battery of tests and other measuring devices. The individual begins to analyze his school record and his entire program of school activities. He also studies his interests, aptitudes, abilities, problems, and opportunities. He appraises his school ability, vocational abilities, physical and economic resources and other such items of information. He attempts an analysis of his desires, his emotional and personality characteristics. These items of information are usually recorded on charts, diagrams and profiles.

The pupil begins an analysis of the occupational scene. He studies the social and economic factors leading up to our modern industrial setting. He begins an exploratory analysis of the many different ways in which people work. An attempt is made to classify or group some of the many occupations. He develops a concept of "job families." He studies the important legislation affecting occupations. A study is made of the development of labor organizations. He studies the present role of labor organizations and learns about their procedures and policies. Community occupational surveys are made. Trends in local as well as national occupational fields are studied. Each pupil selects a few occupations for intensive study and observation. Whenever possible pupils are encouraged to visit in the community to observe workers.

The pupils relate their study of occupational information to the techniques needed for getting and progressing on the job. A study is made of placement agencies and the placement process. Letters of application are written and analyzed. Trial interviews are held and pupils are encouraged to seek experience in actual interview situations. Pupils are helped to organize their data into acceptable "personal data sheets." Attention is also directed towards the social and personality traits needed for occupational success.

The attention of the pupil is then directed into the area of planning. All of the above information is related to the school program and to possible educational activities to be followed. Some time is given to the process by which pupils can learn to plan more effectively. Tentative plans for the future are formulated and discussed. Each pupil is assisted with the immediate problems and decisions confronting him.

The pupil begins with a study of self; this is followed by an over-all analysis of the occupational scene. He then carefully studies a few occupations closely related to his abilities and interests. This is followed by a study of the techniques needed to secure and to progress on the job.

Instruments Used

A course of this kind employs a wide variety of tests, questionnaires, data blanks and other types of measuring devices. It is not possible to prescribe the specific instruments to be used in any school system. The following kinds of measures will be found helpful: mental ability tests, vocational interest inventories, mechanical ability measures, reading ability tests, subject achievement tests, clerical aptitude tests, social and personality inventories.

In addition to these measures there are several other sources of information about pupils: school records, autobiographies, anecdotal materials, self-analysis charts, records of reading interests, record of work experiences, record of extra-curricular activity participation.

In a course of this kind the teacher and the pupils will use a variety of measuring devices. It is possible for the pupils to gather and record much of the material. The pupils should learn a great deal about the methods and instruments of self-appraisal. In addition, they should learn many things which will be helpful to them in many phases of personal planning.

Resource Materials

The occupations class will draw upon the widest possible range of resource materials. The ability of the teacher is tested by his knowledge of these materials and the discriminating use he can make of them. The references presented at the close of this section should be examined by every teacher of occupations classes. The publications of the state and federal Occupational Information and Guidance Service will be found to be particularly helpful.

The teaching resources of the course can be effectively enriched through the use of films, film strips, charts and through the use of a file of occupational materials. Many of these materials are available from public and private agencies. A careful study of the materials listed at the end will reveal many free and inexpensive resources.

The Occupations teacher in cooperation with the librarian can arrange a filing plan for arranging pamphlet, newspaper and magazine materials. These materials should be arranged so that pupils can select and use them. The members of the class can collect many of these materials and can be of considerable assistance in building a comprehensive classroom library. This course cannot be properly taught without the use of a rich body of reference materials.

Teachers of these courses should also be acquainted with "Occupations" published monthly by the National Vocational Guidance Association, "Vocational Trends" published monthly by Science Research Associates and the "Occupational Index" published monthly by Occupational Index, Inc. These organizations and many others publish a great deal of useful material.

A great deal of free and inexpensive material is available for such a course. The teacher of this class should contact the state director of Occupational Information and Guidance for suggestions regarding these materials. Staff members of local colleges and universities can also be very helpful.

Counseling

The course in Occupations cannot be fully successful unless time is provided for individual counseling. The teacher's schedule should be arranged to provide opportunities for this type of individual work. A schedule should be arranged to provide for a minimum of two hours of individual conference time for each student in the class during the semester.

This conference period should take precedence over other activities so that the teacher can easily arrange to see each of the pupils. These individual planning periods are of the greatest importance and should be considered an integral part of the course.

The Occupations teacher should also encourage the pupils to confer with other teachers, employers, placement agency personnel, parents and other people who might be helpful. These conferences can be extremely helpful. The results of these meetings can be summarized in a vocational plan book. Classroom discussions should also be built around the common problems the teacher discovers in her program of individual conferences.

Teaching Requirements

The Occupations teacher must be specifically selected for this responsibility. Some of the important characteristics of the instructor include: work experience in occupations other than teaching, teaching experience, graduate training in guidance, acquaintance with the community, cooperative relationship with other staff members and a sincere interest in helping pupils.

In most schools the teacher should be a member of the counseling staff and should have an opportunity to get acquainted with the pupils before and after the contacts established during the Occupations class. In addition, the teacher should be active in helping to plan other curricular activities of the school in order that the entire school program might make a maximum contribution to the occupational planning of the pupils.

Pupil Booklets

Many schools have found the use of manuals or work-books very helpful. These materials are organized around the major topics to be covered and they provide space for pupils to record many of the things they learn. These booklets provide an opportunity for pupils to work "on their own." At the same time the content of these booklets is usually flexible enough to provide considerable individualization.

Many commercial organizations handle materials of this kind. In some cases, the booklets are organized around the major topics covered in an accompanying textbook. Counselors and teachers of Occupations courses have also developed workbooks.

Evaluating Results

Few well-developed patterns have been devised to measure the results of these courses. Some attempts have been made to measure the increase of occupational information, to measure the realism of the pupils' choices, to correlate job choices with measured abilities and interests, to evaluate the accuracy of pupils' curricular choices and to evaluate results in terms of school success and lessened failures.

The Occupations course is rapidly growing in importance and is becoming part of the required curriculum in some schools. More and more attention is being given to the occupational choices and plans of the pupils. The growth of Occupations courses is an indication of the recognition being given to this phase of pupil development.

References:

1. Billings, M. E. *Group methods of studying occupations.* Second Edition, a Revision of *Teaching about vocational life.* Scranton: International Textbook Company, 1941.
2. Munson, G. E. and Schloerb, L. J. *High school course in self-appraisal and careers.* Chicago: Board of Education, 1941.
3. Occupational Information and Guidance Service, U. S. Office of Education, Washington, D. C. (Prepares and distributes a great deal of helpful material).
4. Yale, J. R. (ed.). *How to build an occupational information library.* Chicago: Science Research Associates, 1944.

C. E. E.

OCCUPATIONAL OUTLOOK SERVICE. The Occupational Outlook Service was founded in the Bureau of Labor Statistics of the U. S. Department of Labor on a recommendation of the Advisory Committee on Education in its report in 1938. The report urged that the service be established to make studies of the economic factors which may be considered in the choice of a vocation, including the long-range outlook for employment in each occupation, earnings, regularity of employment, opportunity for advancement, working conditions and hours, industrial hazards, transferability to other occupations, and the kind of training, experience and qualifications required by employers. The information on employment outlook, it was pointed out, is needed not only by individuals making an occupational choice but also by schools planning their curricula in line with the needs of the community for workers trained in the various skills.

The need for information on prospective occupational trends in connection with vocational guidance is clearly seen in the light of historical trends in our changing economy. In the short space of a man's lifetime, the pace of technological change has been so rapid that whole industries have disappeared and new ones have developed calling for wholly different skills. The changes among occupations have been even more striking, since technological innovations have often resulted in displacing a skill rather than in changing a product. The introduction of the glass-blowing machine, linotype machine, and teletypewriter are classic examples of innovations which displaced highly skilled workers; on the other hand there were no automobile mechanics, radio repairmen, or aeronautical engineers a half-century ago. Standing on the threshold of an era which may see practical peacetime developments in such fields as electronics or atomic energy, we can readily see the need for evaluation of possible occupational trends. Less dramatic than the above changes, but of great importance in vocational guidance are the widely varying trends in demand for such occupations as carpenter, teacher, physician, machinist, or engineer.

The service was organized in 1941. After several years of exploration—interrupted by the war—the first studies were published in 1945, covering such varied fields as automobile mechanics, physicians, welders, diesel-engine mechanics, and skilled occupations in aviation, foundries and hosiery mills.

The problems faced in this type of research are those of evaluating long-range employment outlook in each occupation and industry. While forecasts of changes in the level of employment in the course of the business cycle would have been extremely useful from the point of view of job placement, such estimates are extremely difficult and hazardous. Without ignoring short-run changes, major emphasis was placed on appraising the long-run changes in the level of employment in specific industries and for specific occupations. From many points of view, the long-run trend is in any case more important than short-run fluctuations for appraising employment opportunities in connection with the individual's choice of life-time occupation. It was found possible in most cases to suggest the major trends and outlook some years in advance. Conclusions were necessarily far from precise but often good enough to answer satisfactorily the questions in the minds of those preparing for a career. While it was not possible, for example, to say in 1945 with any degree of accuracy exactly how many automobile mechanics would be employed in 1950, it was quite possible to judge whether it will be relatively difficult or easy for a trained mechanic to find employment at that time.

The problems of appraising future demand and supply were found to differ greatly among occupations, since the factors affecting the outlook for one are often quite different from those which affect another. In many cases it was found possible to follow the general approach of estimating trends in total employment in the various industries and drawing conclusions about the occupations involved from data on the occupational composition of each industry. To make estimates of the probable trends in employment for any industry which supplies products to another required knowing the interrelationships of all industries—what each one buys from and sells to every other industry. The Bureau developed methods of analyzing these complex interindustry relationships, and used them to build up a picture of the economy of the United States as it might be under various assumptions as to future economic developments. From these pictures, estimates were made of the number of workers needed in each industry and in each of a number of occupations, using data on the occupational patterns of the various industries. The Bureau has a large body of information on the occupational patterns of industries, compiled in connection with its surveys of wage rates by occupation. An important element of occupational outlook research is the study of the changes in these patterns which result from technological innovations and other causes.

There are many important occupations in which employment is not directly related to any industry. A number come to mind immediately: physicians, dentists, nurses and other medical service occupations; teachers, policemen, firemen, and other government employees; social workers, lawyers, and other positions in professional services. In the case of physicians, for example, estimates of future demand were based on population trends and other special factors affecting the use of physicians.

The estimates of trends in demand for workers in each occupation were evaluated in the light of estimates of the number who would be available. Trends in the training of persons in each occupational field had to be studied. A most significant aspect of an analysis of labor supply in each occupation was, of course, the rate of withdrawal from the field due to death, retirement, or movement to other occupations. Openings arising from such withdrawals were in many cases found to yield more opportunities for new workers than the expected net expansions in employment, and even in declining occupations many openings are created by withdrawals.

In these studies, the Bureau has had the interested and helpful cooperation of trade associations, trade unions, professional societies, individual employers, and many government agencies.

References:

Studies are published as bulletins of the Bureau of Labor Statistics, U. S. Department of Labor, after being first printed as articles in the *Monthly Labor Review.* A list of early studies follows:

Employment Opportunities for Diesel-Engine Mechanics, Bulletin No. 813 (1945).

Employment Opportunities in Aviation Occupations, Part I—Postwar Employment Outlook, Bulletin No. 837–1 (1945); *Part II—Duties, Qualifications, Earnings, and Working Conditions,* Bulletin No. 837–2 (1946).

Employment Outlook for Automobile Mechanics, Bulletin No. 842 (1945).

Employment Opportunities for Welders, Bulletin No. 844 (1945).

Employment Opportunities in Foundry Occupations, *Monthly Labor Review,* December 1945.

Postwar Outlook for Physicians, *Monthly Labor Review,* December 1945.

Employment Opportunities for Molders, *Monthly Labor Review,* April 1946.

A. F. H.

OCCUPATIONAL RATING SCALES, MINNESOTA.   Any defensible plan of vocational counseling must have a foundation in the psychology of individual differences. Ever since Parsons became interested in students who were uncertain about their vocational plans, the principles of matching human beings and job requirements have been emphasized. The manual comprising *Minnesota Occupational Rating Scales,* an early edition of which was printed in Bingham's *Aptitudes and Aptitude Testing,* and the Counseling Profile, which is the companion piece to the manual, were developed to facilitate this matching process.

In the manual four hundred thirty occupations are listed alphabetically. After each title is a summary of the ratings assigned by twenty vocational psychologists who were asked to estimate the main requirements for each occupation with respect to six human abilities: academic ability, mechanical ability, social intelligence, clerical ability, musical talent, and artistic ability. Each ability is briefly defined, and for each ability four levels (A-B-C-D) are defined operationally and statistically. These four hundred thirty occupations are grouped together again according to levels of ability, and then regrouped in terms of various ability patterns. Suggestions for use of the Counseling Profile are also included in the manual.

The Counseling Profile is perhaps best described as a kind of circular slide rule on which disks can be arranged to show either job demands or levels of abilities of the client. It "facilitates the translation of case history data into terms of occupational ability patterns." Use of the Profile may force both counselor and client to recognize that in some instances case information necessary for good counseling may not be complete. In such situations it becomes obvious that no decisions can be made until more information about the client is available.

Purposes

As counseling tools the *Minnesota Occupational Rating Scales* and the Counseling Profile are designed to serve several purposes.

First, they provide occupational information—an indication of the kinds and levels of abilities estimated essential for the satisfactory performance of each of the four hundred thirty occupations. One hundred fifty-five different ability patterns are identified. Eighty-five are unique in that each is characteristic of one of the listed occupations. Each of the other seventy patterns characterizes two or more occupations.

Second, they permit both the counselor and the client to approach problems of vocational planning on a common ground by enabling the client to understand that some important facts about job requirements can be—and, if counseling is to be based on logic, must be—describable in terms of human traits and characteristics.

Third, the *Rating Scales* and the Profile are designed to help the counselor in his often difficult task of making individual differences meaningful to the client. In addition, they help the client in his often even more difficult task of understanding that he "possesses" certain strengths and weaknesses which limit the fields of work in which he is likely to attain success and satisfaction.

Fourth, it is claimed that if students studying about occupations were familiar with a classification system based on occupational ability patterns and interest fields, their vocational choices would probably be more realistic than investigations have shown them to be. Kefauver and Hand in their book *Appraising Guidance in Secondary Schools* have indicated that high school students who complete courses in occupational information should be capable of making better vocational choices than students who have not studied such information. They show, however, that traditionally designed courses apparently do not lead to realistic self evaluation. It is interesting to contemplate the problems that might confront a school if attempts were made to provide vocational training to students whose goals were realistic.

Evaluation

The *Rating Scales* and the Profile are not substitutes for adequate counseling. The materials provide no short cuts for amateurs or untrained workers. The fact that the Profile is a "gadget" may help in obtaining rapport, but may at the same time confuse the client unless its use in a counseling situation is carefully planned for.

The *Minnesota Occupational Rating Scales* are concerned only with abilities which are broadly psychological in nature. No evaluations are made of physical and strength requirements of occupations. Even though so-called physical labor aspects of many occupations have been greatly reduced by the use of machinery, there is probably as great a range in physical demands as in "mental" demands. The Division of Occupational Analysis of the War Manpower Commission is beginning to publish materials which describe physical requirements of various occupations on a "Yes—No" scale. Such information can supplement the data provided by the *Rating Scales;* it is particularly valuable when the client is physically handicapped.

The *Rating Scales* are not concerned with the fact of compensation. Although it would doubtless be very difficult to estimate the extent to which a worker could compensate for deficiencies by high motivation or by very efficient use of another ability, this function undoubtedly must play some part in the occupational success of a considerable number of people. It is emphasized, of course, that many kinds of information about the client other than those referring to abilities are necessary before counseling can be called adequate.

The authors point out that the *Rating Scales* will become obsolete as soon as "successful workers in a host of different yet representative occupations can be tested with an extensive battery of aptitude, ability, and interest tests and the results summarized by grouping together those occupations which roughly require the same pattern of test scores." Although attempts are being made to develop more objective data on occupational ability patterns, many years of careful work will doubtless be necessary before such information will be available.

The judges whose combined ratings form the basis for the *Rating Scales* did not always agree in their estimates. On purely theoretical grounds, disagreement would be expected; that is the reason for combining the judgments of many raters. It may be presumed that even if testing and sampling were both perfect, workers in any occupation would undoubtedly make various scores on any test of any particular ability. Those differences, too, would be expected on theoretical grounds. It is possible that the range of disagreement found among the ratings of the judges with reference to any one ability for any occupation might be less than the range of ability test scores earned by people who were assumed to be competent workers in the same occupation. The median values, of course, might or might not agree very closely with the median values of the ratings.

Since tests are still non-perfect instruments and since criteria of occupational success are by and large rather unreliable, perhaps the pooled judgments of vocational psychologists may be for a long time the best estimates available of the types and levels of abilities workers in various occupations should have to be successful and happy in their work.

References:

1. Bingham, W. V. *Aptitudes and aptitude testing.* New York: Harper and Brothers, 1937.
2. Brussell, E. S. *A Revision of the Barr Scale of Occupational Intelligence.* M. A. Thesis on file in University of Minnesota Library, 1930.
3. Cisney, H. N. *Classification of occupations in terms of social intelligence, artistic ability, and musical talent.* M. A. Thesis on file in University of Minnesota Library, 1935.
4. Paterson, Donald G., Hahn, Milton E., and Gerken, Clayton d'A. *Minnesota Occupational Rating Scales* and Counseling Profile. Chicago: Science Research Associates, 1941.

C. d'A. G.

OCCUPATIONAL THERAPY.

Occupational Therapy is based upon the need of all persons to be constructively occupied and is defined as a remedial activity with work as treatment. It is a form of medical treatment prescribed by the physician according to the needs of the patient. Progress of the treatment is guided and supervised by the trained therapist by applying a variety of activities or occupations. The exercise and stimulation help to restore to as nearly normal as possible the person who has suffered disease or injury.

Scope of the Field

The two major aspects which Occupational Therapy assumes are:

(1) Medical. (It is used as a treatment adjunct in practically all forms of disability.)

(2) Psychological and sociological. (It deals entirely with individual personalities and as such must employ those precepts which consider (a) the patient as important from the neck

up as from the neck down; (b) the importance of knowing what kind of person has a disease as well as what kind of disease a person has—in short, treating the whole man.)

The purposes of this type of therapy are as follows:

(1) Diversional and Recreational—tonic therapy to aid in mental rehabilitation. (This often supplies the socializing element of good group therapy.) Includes dramatics, gardening, music, sports.

(2) Functional—prescribed activities planned to assist in restoration of articular and muscular function, to improve general condition, to build up physical endurance and work tolerance. Application of exercises where the activity is selected not only furnishes the prescribed exercise but captures the interest of the patient so that he forgets his difficulties. The creative arts are used in this fashion: bookbinding, woodworking, metalry, press printing, ceramics.

(3) Educational—that exciting trend which carries adult education into the hospital field. (Regular study courses ranging from cultural subjects through commercial and vocational are made available to patients.) Scouting for the physically handicapped, plays an important part.

(4) Pre-vocational—comprising work processes as a stepping stone or preparation for the return of the patient to his former employment or further vocational education. (This is applied in hospital or treatment shop as a therapeutic conditioning process and orientation in the materials and vigor of trade training.) Radio assembling and radio, sheet metal, machine shop, stenography.

Where Used

Departments of Occupational Therapy as an adjunct in medical treatment exist in: Mental Hospitals; General Hospitals; Government Hospitals; Children's Hospitals; Hospitals and Schools for Crippled Children, Blind and Deaf, Feebleminded; Tuberculosis Sanatoria; Penal Institutions; Home Service; Community Curative Workshops and Homes for the Aged.

Professional Education of the Occupational Therapist

The curriculum of the accredited Occupational Therapy Schools today presents well-rounded requirements in the biological, social and clinical sciences, all closely bound up with the Principles and Practice of Occupational Therapy and the applied therapeutic activities used as treatment. The background of the therapist in anatomy, physiology, pathology, kinesiology, neurology, orthopedics, general medicine, and surgery gives her the working basis of her technical knowledge in understanding the physical implications of disability. The social and economic implications, parallel in importance, are met by courses in psychology, sociology, adult education, vocational guidance, social and educational agencies, rehabilitation, etc. The therapist's primary function is to treat the physical or medical problem as it exists upon a social and economic background. She must prepare her patient for the next step, which means passing into the hands of the vocational rehabilitation service, to whom he presents an economic problem with a medical background. This means that the therapist must be cognizant of the vocational and economic trends and must be able to understand the work situations into which patients will be going—i.e., the demands of certain skills, nature and weight of tools used, required motions involved.

The curriculum prescribed by the Council on Medical Education and Hospitals of the American Medical Association sets up a minimum course length of twenty-five calendar months, including a minimum of eight months of clinical internship. There are eighteen accredited schools in the country, all of which are within or affiliated with institutions of higher education and all grant a degree in this major field. (Listing of accredited schools is attached.)

Registration

The American Occupational Therapy Association maintains a Registry of Certified Occupational Therapists, of which there are approximately two thousand in the country. Eligibility for the Registry requires graduation from an accredited training center, and successful completion of the Registration Examination.

References:

1. *Bibliography on Films and Slides.* New York: American Occupational Therapy Association.
2. Davis, Emily. *Occupational Therapy, A Means of Rehabilitation.* New York: New York Public Library, 1944.
3. *Occupational Therapy.* War Department Technical Manual TM8–291, War Department, December, 1944.
4. *Occupational Therapy Manual.* Prepared by a Committee of the American Occupational Therapy Association and Council on Physical Therapy of the American Medical Association, Chicago, 1943.
5. Willard, Helen S. *Occupational Therapists Wanted.* Philadelphia: School and College Placement, 1943, Vol. 3, No. 3.

M. F.

OCCUPATIONAL THERAPY, APTITUDE FOR WORK IN.

The prospective therapist should primarily be interested in medical study and in working with disabled and handicapped persons. Specialized training consists of study of basic medical subjects such as anatomy, physiology, psychiatry, orthopedics, neurology, pediatrics and medical and surgical conditions.

Inasmuch as all schools of occupational therapy are affiliated with or are departments of colleges or universities an applicant must be able to do work of college level and should be able to prove this not only by previous scholastic records but by successful accomplishment on standard intelligence tests.

The occupational therapists of World War I and for some years thereafter were, for the most part, persons who had training in fine arts or crafts. This resulted in a general misconception that such ability or knowledge is the best basis for success in this field. The trend of the profession has, however, been steadily toward the use of activities, such as printing, woodworking, metal work and plastics, which are more generally practical and pre-vocational or even vocational in character. Experience has shown that a scientific background of chemistry, physics and zoology is of real value to the occupational therapist. Discrimination and good taste based on a knowledge of the principles of design are necessary, but the person with creative art talent frequently does not prove to have the ability to teach the necessary projects in such a way as to attain the maximum degree of benefit for the patient. The therapist needs manual and, if possible, mechanical aptitude plus the ability to teach rather than merely to perform. The activities used in occupational therapy range from the simple crafts to educational and recreational pursuits and to industrial projects such as cobbling, gardening, hospital utilities and assembly work. The successful therapist, therefore, needs versatility, the widest possible general knowledge and intellectual curiosity, which broadens the scope of methods which may be employed to meet the varied needs of the patients treated.

The personality of the occupational therapist is of paramount importance. Qualities of leadership, executive ability, initiative, emotional stability and good social adjustment will win the patient's respect, confidence and willingness to follow directions. Tact, friendliness, understanding sympathy without sentimentality, helpfulness, cooperation and ability to adjust oneself to others are all characteristics which make for success. Good health, pleasing personal appearance, poise, good grooming, a pleasant voice and the ability to speak or write well are also necessary attributes.

The occupational therapist works as a part of the medical team consisting of the doctor, nurse, physical therapist, social worker and other hospital personnel. A willingness to accept discipline, to obey orders and to subordinate one's own ideas, interests and desires to those of others is, therefore, necessary. The "rugged individualist" who finds difficulty in this adjustment, who rebels against wearing a uniform and being an effective cog in the hospital machine, is out of place in occupational therapy. At the same time, however, the nature of the work gives great scope for originality, initiative and independence in adapting activities to the need of the individual patient.

The profession has been largely one which attracts women but opportunities are opening for men in the field. Many of the schools conduct testing programs for their students. It is, however, helpful in selecting candidates to have results of previous psychological, manual aptitude and personality tests.

Information relative to the individual schools may be obtained from the American Occupational Therapy Association, 33 West 42nd Street, New York, N. Y.

References:

1. Haas, L. J. *Practical occupational therapy for the mentally ill.* New York: Bruce Publishing Co., 1944.
2. Hudson, H. and Fish, M. *Occupational therapy in the treatment of the tuberculous patient.* New York: National Tuberculosis Association, 1944.
3. Hudson, H. and Cobb, M. R. *Joan chooses occupational therapy.* New York: Dodd, Mead and Co.
4. Willard, H. S. and Spackman, C. S., Editors. *Principles of occupational therapy.* Philadelphia: J. B. Lippincott Co., In Preparation.

H. S. W.

OCCUPATIONAL TRENDS IN THE UNITED STATES.

Changes in the occupational structure of the United States reflect technological, industrial, and institutional factors which have shaped the economy in the course of our history. The occupational composition of the Nation's labor force is simply one way of looking at, or summarizing, the basic facts of economic life in the successive phases of economic development. Because the process of growth is gradual and continuous, historical trends throw light on future occupational developments. But for purposes of vocational counseling, too much reliance ought not be placed upon interpretations, with connotations of inevitability, that may be drawn from trends shown in the available statistics of occupations in past decades.

One illustration may suffice at this point: we may achieve some approximation of full employment in the postwar decade by one of a number of general alternative economic policies. Which course of action will prevail we cannot predict, but we do know that the resulting pattern of demand for goods and services will call for different patterns of occupational skills in our labor force—and perhaps significantly different from the viewpoint of the additional or new requirements of the economy.

Generalizations interpreting occupational developments in terms of progressive evolution from simple to more complex or advanced structural forms, while illuminating, are subject to dangers of oversimplification. Historically in capitalistic countries, per capita income has increased as national economies have matured; and an increasing proportion of family incomes is devoted to less urgent needs (characteristic of a rising standard of living) as against expenditures for more primary or basic needs. From this the conclusion is drawn, with implications for vocational counseling, that an increasing proportion of the labor force is engaged in (or required for) so-called service activities as against basic production of goods. There is a great deal of truth in this, if frequently based on inadequate data. Often, however, the interpretation blurs the distinction between service industries and what may be called, functionally, service occupations. And it often blurs the importance —for occupational developments—of technological changes, diversification, the complexity of modern economic life, specialization, and what has been called generally the roundabout nature of modern production.

The economic life and the occupational activities of the people in Colonial America were determined in large measure by our position in the British colonial system. Agriculture and commerce were the major economic pursuits, with manufacturing activity restricted as a matter of British policy. For a considerable time the American economy remained a young and relatively undeveloped or immature economy. Subsequent American history affords the most successful instance to date of national economic growth, starting from scratch, and reaching a rich and highly diversified system. As a new country, with little feudal or pre-capitalist background, we skipped in effect many of the earlier forms of economic organization in which occupational status and structure possessed a different meaning, sociologically, than in a free-market type of economy. Occupational mobility which, perhaps as much as anything else, differentiates capitalist from pre-capitalist societies, has been a particularly characteristic feature of American life. Not any single factor but a fortuitous combination of forces accounts for the economic development which has shaped the broad outlines of occupational patterns to the present time.

To the extent that the growth of manufacturing activities is central in capitalist economic development, this process began in earnest in this country, if on a small scale, with the military necessity of a young nation striving to free itself from the restrictions imposed by its colonial origin. The problems of industrial growth for a young country—from the point of view of national economic policy—were discussed with unusual perception in early political controversy. Perhaps no better instance exists of the conscious weighing of alternative political, social, and economic objectives as in the contrasting positions urged by Hamilton, Jefferson, and others. Whatever the merits of the two positions, subsequent developments saw the realization of an industrial economy in which the social consequences envisioned in the original discussion remained relevant.

In 1820 at the time of the first occupational census, the 27 states were predominantly agricultural although differing considerably in economic structure. Conflicting sectional interests made it imperative for Congress to have information not only on the numbers in the population but the geographic distribution of the numbers engaged in farming, manufactures, and commerce. More detailed information was obtained with respect to the persons engaged in and the output of 230 different manufactures because of their crucial importance during the embargo and in the tariff discussions when foreign competition was resumed. As time went on, more detailed information was requested with respect to inland transportation and trade as western expansion of the states and the national market thrust such matters into the center of Congressional policy.

The major fact that stands out in the occupational changes between 1820 and 1940 is the striking decline in the proportion of the labor force engaged in agriculture—from over 70 per cent to about 20 per cent. Because population increased almost 14 times during the period, the numbers of persons actually increased from 2 millions to 11½ million in 1910 before a decline set in which reduced the agricultural labor force to about 10 million in 1940. Farming remains, however, the largest single more or less homo-

geneous occupational group—a fact of considerable political significance—even though more persons are engaged in the various manufacturing industries. The types of occupations in farming have
multiplied with the specialization which has taken place as agriculture was transformed from largely subsistence farming to production for the market. Technological innovations in manufactures
tend to overshadow the gains in productivity in agriculture resulting not only from improved mechanical tools but from improved
seeds, fertilizers, crop rotation, and advances in the agricultural
sciences. Per capita consumption of foodstuffs has increased at the
same time that a smaller part of incomes goes to expenditures for
food.

Because of vast improvements in agricultural productivity that
can still result from elimination of large numbers of marginal or
subsistence farms, as well as by technological gains already in sight,
the outlook is for a continuation of the historical trend toward a
smaller farm labor force in the years ahead. This suggests opportunity for fewer numbers of persons in agriculture but for gains in
income and standard of living for those who choose farming as a
way of life under conditions of balance and full employment in the
economy generally.

Not until the first World War did the labor force in the manufacturing industries equal that in agriculture. Over half were reported in agriculture as late as 1870, at which time only one-fifth
were enumerated in manufacturing and the mechanical trades. The
transition from household industry to the workshop and to the
factory was not completed in all lines until the Civil War. From
1870 to 1940 the proportion of the labor force in manufacturing
and the mechanical trades increased gradually from 20 per cent to
about 30 per cent. The outcome was a highly industrialized economy
despite the fact that most workers, even in the nonagricultural
sector, were employed in other than manufacturing activities. In the
public mind, quite correctly, the growth of manufacturing stands
for the dynamic factor in economic development, in an economy
in which transportation facilities had been expanded at an early
date to integrate the national market geographically.

Sectional variation has always been significant, as indicated by
the events leading up to the Civil War. Even today large parts of
the country remain relatively undeveloped and, as the Tennessee
Valley experience suggests, still afford large possibilities for industrial growth. Gradual shifts in the location of industry—e.g., in
textiles from the North to the South—continuously alter regional
occupational patterns.

Technological innovation both in the form of new products and new processes in manufacturing and in other fields have affected the job content of occupations in a revolutionary fashion. The new products have created new industries, notably in rail and air transportation, power and utilities, chemicals, and consumer durables generally, such as automobiles, radios, heating, refrigeration, and air-conditioning; and with the new industries, new occupations previously unknown became important. New processes, particularly in manufacturing, have eliminated old occupations completely or have altered them substantially, sometimes in all but name. Significant clues to the occupational requirements of the future can be discerned in the innovations of progressive and pioneering establishments.

With the gains in per capita income accompanying rising productivity, demands of consumers for a broader range of goods and services stimulated the growth of commercial services catering to old needs or meeting new needs—e.g., the repair and servicing of consumer durable goods of all kinds. The growing urbanization and complexity of the social structure gave rise to expanding governmental activities until at the present time public authorities represent the leading employers of certain types of technical, professional, and clerical workers. The importance of rising per capita income upon occupational demands both in the private and public sectors of the economy is illustrated by the regional differentials in the demands for educational, medical, and other professional and social services as between rich and poor areas of the country.

The occupational proliferation which has taken place as the American economy has matured cannot be attributed solely to technological innovation or to increasing demands for services as per capita income rises; it is the whole process of economic specialization which occurs as the market develops and the market mechanism integrates expanding economic activity within the general framework of public policy and controls. Greater specialization within the single establishment resulted from larger scale production and growing rationalization with advances in techniques of production and management. As scope of operations expanded in the modern corporation, internal integration of the firm's activities required an administrative bureaucracy of managerial, professional, and clerical workers. Further, certain distributive, service, and technical functions previously performed within the establishment have been transferred outside—to establishments in the trade and service fields. An early shoe manufacturer, for example, was his own salesman, accountant, advertising man, and deliveryman, or employed persons to perform these functions. As the scale of production increased these functions could be carried on more efficiently in many instances by independent firms in wholesale and retail trade, transportation, and in consumer and business services generally.

Technological gains have been made in service occupations (office machines, e.g.) as well as innovations in service industries (self-service markets, e.g.). Generally the gains have been more marked in manufacturing, mining, transportation, and utilities, with the result that labor requirements have been reduced relative to those in the service fields. This, taken in conjunction with the fact that the service industries are closely tied to the activities of the basic producing industries, qualifies conclusions sometimes drawn with respect to the effect of changes in income levels and consumer expenditures upon future employment trends. Whether consumers will prefer to spend their income for services rather than for durable goods, relatively speaking, will depend upon their judgment as to what represents the most for their money. The conclusion that service industries and occupations are the more promising fields, for those considering vocational choices, because of an inevitable drift toward services and away from basic production of goods, certainly requires qualification in view of lower wages which prevail in many service industries or occupations because of lower productivity or an over supply of potential workers.

Specialization and mechanization have had a significant effect, occupationally, in the changes that have occurred in the relationship between the individual worker and his job. Generally the worker has become less and less a craftsman who is responsible for, and trained in, all aspects of the production of the final product for consumption. He has become typically more and more a machine-tender or a small cog in the bureaucracy of business enterprise. This is believed to have led to a certain spiritual emptiness or lack of feeling of self-realization in work—as the price we have to pay for increasing productivity through specialization and mechanization.

There is no denial that this is a serious social phenomenon. Part of the explanation, however, lies in the whole drift toward large-scale enterprise in which a larger proportion of workers become wage earners with no prospect to become independent entrepreneurs. This explains a deep-seated desire, now so obvious, for individuals to seek work in fields in which self-employment or entrepreneurial independence is still possible, as in many of the trade and service employments. It should be noted that the feeling of frustration which is believed to be so common in the day-by-day work of the large masses of employees rests partly on the greater reality of personal experience and lack of realization of the frustrations and disappointments (not to mention misery) of workers under earlier forms of economic organization. While perhaps irrelevant, there is no doubt that real income and working conditions make the life of the modern worker incomparably more comfortable. The spiritual concomitants of craftsmanship and industrial democracy were never completely or for long realized even under the guild system. The growth of labor unions and their development toward participation with management in modern industry, or the invention of forms of industrial democracy under social ownership, would appear to be the possibilities in modern economic society that would lead to a maximum feeling of self-realization on the part of workers.

The claim that mechanization makes machines of workers and is tending to reduce the level of skills of workers in the American labor force is in any case an overstatement. Modern technology has created new jobs which require skills of a high order and which from the point of view of workers' interest may provide greater individual satisfaction than found in the continuous production of more or less the same product by early craftsmen. There is, however, some evidence in Census occupational statistics that the proportion of nonagricultural workers classified as skilled workers and foremen has tended to increase in recent decades (despite a contrary movement in the 'Thirties). More significant was the unmistakable tendency for the proportion of unskilled workers to decline through the whole period, 1910–1940. As might be expected, in view of the general nature of the industrial changes characteristic of technological developments, the proportion of semi-skilled workers increased markedly during the thirty year period—and particularly during the depression years. Instead of a general deterioration of skills there appears to be a definite tendency toward higher skill requirements on the part of the large mass of industrial workers, even with growing specialization of individual job functions. The war experience, coming after ten years of inadequate occupational training, illustrated the demand for a more highly skilled labor force under conditions of full industrial activity.

The increasing proportion of women actively engaged in the labor force is one of the persistent occupational trends observable in the course of American economic development. Obviously, the increased worker rates among women does not reflect simply a growing desire to work or an autonomous change in social mores as to the role of women in economic life. Nor does the rationalization and commercialization of household activities explain it, except insofar as women have more time for work outside of the home and families are more dependent upon money in a market economy than in a household economy. The long-run decline in the birth rate and the number of children per family is an important factor, but there is evidence that demographic changes of this kind account for only a part of the rise in labor market participation that has actually taken place.

The differences that may be observed between worker rates for women in regions of the country varying with respect to urbanization and industrialization suggest the importance of the growth in the number and variety of job opportunities available for women in modern economic life. This again reflects the declining proportion of the population engaged in farming. The statistics perhaps are misleading because of lack of comparability in reporting "labor market" participation of farm women and the inherent difficulty of defining chores and work on farms. Labor market participation, like unemployment, is a concept more relevant to nonagriculture than agriculture. There is no doubt, however, that urban and industrialized communities afford more job opportunities than rural and agricultural areas. And in the course of industrial and commercial development, it is obvious that a wider variety of jobs adapted to the employment of women—e.g., clerical—have become available for young girls and women. Moreover, with concentration of population in communities of higher density, economic functions—such as nursing and social services generally—become more regularized and afford full-time jobs rather than sporadic or voluntary activities.

Two other major labor market developments represent important secular changes: First, the declining proportions of young people engaged in gainful employment, and secondly, the declining proportions in the older-age brackets. Both developments represent the outcome of a complex variety of social and economic factors. Child labor has largely disappeared in this country, with the typical age of entry into the labor force considerably above that in other countries, including Great Britain. To some extent this reflects the diminishing importance of agriculture. More importantly it reflects higher per capita incomes and institutional developments with respect to educational and social policy. Earlier retirement is the result of similar institutional factors in part, although there is evidence (in the 'Thirties, at least) that lack of job opportunities for older workers is a factor of some importance.

World War II had profound effects upon the labor force of lasting consequence for the economic and occupational life of the

American people. Wars have always had a significant impact upon the Nation's labor force and upon industrial and social developments. Military demands have stimulated industrial development by affording opportunity for large-scale production of industrially-produced goods and for the introduction of technological innovations. Because war shocks the entire social and economic structure, changes which might otherwise work out over a long period of time occur in a relatively short period of time. In the aftermath of war, economic dislocations alter the course of normal economic development, result in business crises or depressions of varying intensity or duration.

Following years of economic stagnation, the war made for striking increases in the number of people employed and their income, in marriage and birth rates, and in the occupational status and mobility of women, as well as a resurgence of vocational training and growth of occupational experience. Advances were made in ways of work and techniques of production under the pressure of demands for speed and with improvement in the nation's capital equipment. Large-scale migration occurred within the country in response to employment opportunities in expanding centers of production and war activity. Not least important perhaps was the widespread realization of the meaning of this wartime experience for postwar economic objectives and policies.

The total number of Americans employed in civilian jobs or in the armed forces increased from $45\frac{1}{2}$ million in the spring of 1940 to more than 62 million (excluding seasonal workers) in the autumn of 1944. This gain of $16\frac{1}{2}$ million in the actively employed labor force was made possible in part by the absorption of 7 million persons who were unemployed in 1940. But the most remarkable feature of wartime manpower mobilization was the addition of $9\frac{1}{2}$ million persons to the labor force as compared with an expected peacetime growth of only 3 million.

Not only has the war resulted in a great expansion of the labor force; it required and led to vast shifts of workers from one industry to another, from occupation to occupation, and a general upgrading of the skills within industries. Altogether civilian employment expanded by more than 5 million while at the same time some $11\frac{1}{2}$ million were added to the armed force. The dominating influences were, of course, the unprecedented outlays for munitions, the resulting increases in income payments, and the restriction of activity in various segments of the economy in consequence of manpower, facilities, and materials limitations.

The particular demands of war production required larger proportions of workers as operatives in the mechanical trades than will be usable in a civilian economy. In addition, military needs of the Army and Navy resulted in the training of large numbers of men in skills for which no demand, or relatively small demand, exists in civilian life. The war demonstrated, however, the occupational mobility of workers and the speed with which workers can be trained and retrained under conditions of effective demand. Significant from a long-time point of view was the growing role of women in mechanical work which may alter social mores with respect to fields of activity for women workers. Less certain is the permanence of some of the occupational gains of Negroes except under conditions of full employment.

Occupationally, the largest changes occurred among operatives, with an influx of 2.5 million women and 1 million men. For the first time, women employed as operatives constituted the largest occupational group of women. The number of women in clerical jobs increased not much less rapidly than the number in operative jobs. Women more and more dominated the clerical field, almost doubling in the 4-year period while the number of men remained almost unchanged. In sales occupations the number of women almost doubled, with the result that for the first time more women were so engaged than men. Percentagewise, the increase in women craftsmen and foremen was the largest gain shown in any of the occupational groups, but the total number was relatively small. In this connection it may be noted that among men a larger gain occurred in the number of craftsmen than in the number of operatives, as might be expected in a period of rapid expansion and large-scale military inductions accompanied by some measure of occupational deferment.

Except for domestic service, the only broad occupational group in the civilian population to decline in numbers during the war was the professional group. While vast numbers of women, youths, and older workers more than replaced drafted men in most occupational groups, the withdrawals of professional men to the armed forces were not compensated for by sufficient numbers of women. This is explained by the length of training required in the professions and by the withdrawal of women teachers from elementary and secondary schools for higher paying jobs.

Negroes experienced gains during the war comparable to those made by the population generally. Employment of Negroes increased somewhat more than the average, with changes in the various occupational groups paralleling those shown for white workers with some exceptions. Because of migration from the farms, the number of Negro women in agriculture declined while the employment of white women increased. In domestic service the employment of white women declined substantially while the number of Negro women remained about the same. A smaller percentage of the total of employed Negro women was engaged in domestic service and a larger percentage in other services than in 1940. For both men and women, the most significant factor in the occupational redistribution of Negro workers was the exodus from the farm to the factory, where the war gave the Negro his first big chance in skilled and semi-skilled jobs. The Negro made substantial gains in employment in various crafts and in sales and clerical occupations, but the numbers involved were comparatively small.

Whatever the aggregate volume of demand after the war, the allocation of workers as between industries is expected, as in the past, to be considerably influenced by changes in industrial techniques and improvements in capital equipment. Is it true, as generally supposed, that the war accelerated the upward trend of productivity which has characterized manufacturing during the past two decades? The effect of the war upon long-term trends in output per manhour was obscured by numerous conflicting forces of a temporary nature so that it is impossible to draw more than general conclusions of a qualitative character. For the industries which continued producing civilian goods, there is evidence that the trend was almost completely halted during the war years in some industries and declined in others. The fact remains, however, that a decade or more of experience and innovation were crowded into a few years in the war industries. It is impossible to predict the ultimate effects of wartime innovations, but the reduction in labor input per unit of product following reconversion will exert a positive influence upon the industrial and occupational demands for labor.

The major economic consequence of the war is the promise that is held out for a level of economic activity and employment far above that of the 'Thirties—if not full employment. If this development should prove more than temporary, the meaning in terms of employment and occupational opportunity will color the life of every individual and the whole character of social life in America. Young people will not need to look forward to the unhappy alternative of accepting a job for the sake of a job; there will be opportunity for jobs that will demand the highest abilities of all to a degree unknown to this generation.

Under conditions of full employment, all major industries and broad occupational groups, with the probable exception of agriculture, will employ more persons than in 1940. Because employment will exceed maximum civilian employment during wartime, most industries except particular manufacturing industries and manufacturing as a whole, will employ larger numbers than during the war years. Compared to the wartime composition of the labor force, more jobs will be available for professional and semiprofessional workers, service, clerical, sales, and kindred workers, proprietors, managers, and officials, and craftsmen and kindred workers. Numerically, operatives and kindred workers will remain the largest single broad occupational group in American life, regardless of the general pattern of economic activity, but will embrace fewer workers in the postwar than in the war years.

Whether full employment is sustained for long by means of relatively high investment expenditures or, as seems as more likely for the long pull, by relatively high levels of consumer expenditures—the two general alternatives of escape from the stagnation of the 'Thirties—employment opportunities will vary among industries and occupations. In a high-investment economy, with emphasis upon expansion of industrial facilities and equipment, relatively higher proportions of workers will be engaged as craftsmen, foremen and laborers. In a high-consumption economy, relatively larger proportions of workers will be engaged in professional and semiprofessional occupations, in clerical, sales, and service occupations.

C. D. S.

OFFICE OF VOCATIONAL REHABILITATION (Federal Security Agency). Under the general direction of the Federal Security Administrator, the Office of Vocational Rehabilitation was established as a constituent unit of the Federal Security Agency on September 8, 1943 to give leadership and guidance to the States in providing a program of vocational rehabilitaton for the civilian disabled. The office is responsible for (1) certifying Federal funds for grants-in-aid to the State upon the approval of State plans for vocational rehabilitation meeting requirements of the authorizing Act of Congress; (2) establishing standards in the various areas of service; and (3) rendering technical advice and assistance to the States.

Legislative Development

Beginning in 1911 and for several years thereafter, a series of State legislative acts were passed which provided for compensation to persons disabled in industry. In 1920, Congress provided for the vocational adjustment of disabled civilians on a national basis in the Vocational Rehabilitation Act. The Social Security Act of 1935 carried the stabilizing provision for a continuous rehabilitation service. Recognizing certain restrictions of existing legislation, the 78th Congress enacted in July 1943 a series of amendments to the Vocational Rehabilitation Act in Public Law 113, known as the Barden-LaFollette Act.

Legal Authority for State Programs

In a majority of States, the basic law under which the vocational rehabilitation program is administered consists essentially of an acceptance of the provisions and benefits of the Federal Act of 1920. The State Board of Vocational Education is empowered to cooperate with the Federal government in carrying out the provisions of the Federal Act and the State Treasurer is designated as custodian of all Federal funds granted for vocational rehabilitation. Some States have enacted legislation broader in scope than the "Acceptance Act." These broader acts have provided for the State's performance of special functions, generally connected with the administration of the Workmen's Compensation laws.

The basic State laws under which vocational rehabilitation for the blind is administered are treated separately. The specific authority for the vocational rehabilitation of the blind is generally contained in State statutes which provide public assistance or welfare services to the blind. Frequently, therefore, rehabilitation services for the blind are found in State welfare agencies or in special commissions which provide other services to the blind residents of the State.

All States, Hawaii, Alaska, Puerto Rico and the District of Columbia are eligible to participate in the grant-in-aid program for rehabilitation of the physically and mentally disabled. All except Alaska are operating under plans approved by the Federal office. As of November 1, 1946, thirty-four State agencies for the blind are operating under approved plans. In other States, the State Board of Vocational Education provides for the rehabilitation of all disabled persons, including the blind, in a single agency.

Federal Reimbursement

Funds are made available to the States upon the showing of a written plan meeting requirements under the Act. Prior to 1943, the maximum Federal appropriation for purposes of vocational rehabilitation was three and one-half million dollars annually. With the provision for expanded services in 1943, fiscal limitations were removed and the Federal government was authorized to reimburse States for all administrative costs and for the cost of services to war disabled civilians, defined as merchant seamen, members of the Civil Air Patrol, Aircraft Warning Service and Citizens Defense Corps, injured in the performance of their duties. The cost of other case services may be reimbursed on a fifty per cent basis.

Organization

The Federal office has been organized into two major divisions; namely, the Rehabilitation Standards Division with four sections, Physical Restoration; Services for the Blind; Advisement, Training and Placement; and Research and Statistics; and the Administrative Standards Division composed of a Management Standards Section and a Fiscal Standards and Control Section.

Seven regional offices operate to maintain close relationships between the States and the Federal office. The regional offices are located in the following cities: Boston, Massachusetts; Washington, D. C.; Atlanta, Georgia; Chicago, Illinois; Kansas City, Missouri; Denver, Colorado and San Francisco, California.

In States where a single agency administers the entire program, the responsibility for the supervision, control and operation rests with the State Boards of Vocational Education, each having a division of vocational rehabilitation under the direction of a full-time director and a professional staff. Where a separate agency for the blind has been authorized to administer a rehabilitation program for the blind, there is generally a division within this agency responsible for the rehabilitation work.

In performing the major function of case services to applicants, consultative services are made available through physical restoration specialists and other technical and professional personnel.

Advisory Committees

The Federal office has appointed a National Rehabilitation Advisory Council composed of representatives of business and industry, labor, medicine, education, services to the blind, social welfare, and others whose interests are closely allied to the problems of the disabled; and a Professional Advisory Committee, composed of representatives from the various fields of medicine and related fields.

Regulations issued under the Act require that State plans provide for a rehabilitation advisory council and a professional advis-

ory committee in each State to advise on the development of standards of service and to aid in interpreting the program to the public.

State Plans

State plans set forth the legal basis for administering the program, a description of the organization, the policies of the agency
and the plan of operation, and certain information with respect to
the handling of funds.

Services to the Individual

The amendments to the Act, passed in 1943, provide for the
expansion of services to disabled persons. Public Law 113 authorizes
a comprehensive program of rehabilitation services which will enable handicapped persons to become self-supporting individuals.
The mentally as well as the physically disabled are included; there
is specific provision for the rehabilitation of blind persons, for war
disabled civilians, previously defined, and also for civil employees
of the U. S. Government injured in the performance of duty.

A separate program is provided by the U. S. Veterans Administration for the vocational rehabilitation of veterans whose disabilities are of service connected origin. Rehabilitation for veterans
with non-service connected disabilities, for those who incur disabilities after return to civilian life, and for the disabled members
of veterans' families is provided under the program for the civilian
disabled.

Fundamental to the State program is the development and
maintenance of a case finding system which will locate all disabled
persons eligible for and in need of rehabilitation. Such a program
operates on local and state-wide levels. Much depends upon the
cooperation of both agencies and individuals and the program is
promoted by good working relationships based upon written agreements which embody referral policies and procedures. The location
of cases as early as possible lessens the likelihood of mental and
emotional conflicts sometimes created by disabilities.

Eligibility for vocational rehabilitation services under State programs is determined by the following: a person must be of employable age; an occupational handicap must exist by reason of disability; and the individual will be rendered employable, or more
advantageously employable, through rehabilitation services.

Each individual found eligible for vocational rehabilitation is
entitled to any or all of the services authorized which may be required to minimize the disability and which will aid in developing
his special aptitudes and abilities. Available services include physical

and psychiatric examinations, vocational diagnosis and counseling, medical and surgical care, physical and occupational therapy, prosthetic appliances, vocational training, training materials and supplies, maintenance during rehabilitation, occupational tools, equipment and licenses.

The provision of certain services depends upon financial need of the individual. Physical examination, vocational counseling, training, and placement are provided at no cost to the disabled; whereas medical treatment, prosthetic appliances, maintenance, transportation, occupational tools, licenses and equipment are provided without cost in cases where well-established economic need exists.

Because of the complexity of factors influencing employability, each case requires individual treatment and a flexible program must be provided to meet the needs of the applicant. An early diagnosis and evaluation of physical, educational, vocational, and social characteristics are fundamental to the selection of an appropriate vocational objective and the planning of a program of action for attaining the selected objective. In selecting an objective for the individual, the aim is to find employment in which the handicap will not interfere with successful performance of the duties of the position. The rehabilitation plan which is formulated in cooperation with the individual, considers those personal, social, physical and vocational factors which affect the adjustment of the individual in employment.

The continuous service that integrates all rehabilitation services into an organized plan is that of vocational counseling which begins with the initial interview and follows through to placement in employment. Counseling helps the disabled person to understand his capacities, the causes of his present problems, and the steps necessary to attain vocational adjustment.

Physical restoration services must be expected to eliminate or substantially reduce an employment handicap. Treatment may include medical, surgical, and psychiatric services; physical and occupational therapy, hospitalization; dentistry; care in a convalescent or nursing home; drugs and supplies. Prosthetic appliances including artificial limbs, braces, hearing aids, eye glasses and dentures are provided as necessary to improve employability. Medical advice is used in selecting the type of training to be given in preparation for employment and in determining the work tolerance of an individual. Hospitalization is limited to a period of ninety days for any one disability. This limitation, together with the condition that a disability be relatively stable and amenable to treatment, distinguishes vocational rehabilitation from programs providing long-term care for chronic illness. It is not implied, however, that a person must await the end result of an illness before rehabilitation services can be started. For example, a person with glaucoma does not await total blindness before treatment is begun.

Vocational training includes pre-vocational, vocational, and supplementary training. Training involves preparation of the disabled person for employment or gives him additional remunerative occupational skills. Regardless of the nature of the training, it must be directed toward the achievement of an employment objective.

By the terms of Public Law 113, it is the policy of State agencies to utilize existing resources so far as possible in order to provide required services for clients. Physical restoration, training, and other services may be purchased on a contract basis. The rehabilitation agency maintains a working relationship with all community facilities that may be called upon to assist in meeting the client's needs.

The State agency assumes responsibility for the placement of disabled persons for whom rehabilitation services have been provided. This may be accomplished by the rehabilitation agency itself or through cooperative agreement with placement agencies such as the United States Employment Service and the United States Civil Service Commission. Such agreements define the activities and responsibilities of the respective agencies and include provision for the exchange of data, experience, sources of service, and labor market information.

The satisfactory placement of the disabled person in remunerative employment is the objective toward which the entire rehabilitation process is directed. Therefore, no case is closed as rehabilitated until the disabled individual has been placed in employment and is adjusted to the job. Every effort is made to see that the individual is paid the same wage as other workers in the occupation, since the occupational limitations of the handicap have been offset by rehabilitation.

Case records show that 169,794 persons received services during the fiscal year ending June, 1946. Of that number 36,106 persons were rehabilitated into employment during the period. Ten thousand of these disabled men and women, 5,734 or 16.0 per cent, had never been employed; 27,022 or 74.8 per cent, were not working at the time rehabilitation services began. Total annual earnings of the 36,106 amounted to an estimated $11,600,000 prior to rehabilitation. As against this sum—which represents the entire amount earned by this group of 36,106 disabled individuals—total annual earnings after rehabilitation rose an estimated $56,300,000, more than a four-fold increase.

Studies Related to Problems of the Disabled

A survey has been undertaken in cooperation with the National Society of Crippled Children and other private agencies on sheltered workshops and facilities with which there might be developed a broader program for severely disabled persons whose impairment prevents them permanently, or for a substantial period, from entering the usual occupations.

The study of another problem vitally related to the restoration of the disabled to employment is that of nation-wide extension of Second Injury Funds under Workmen's Compensation Laws. As a protection to both employers and employees, the enactment of such legislation will greatly encourage the use of disabled persons in peacetime employment.

Program Justification

It is evident from the statistics on the increased earning capacity of disabled persons that the program is desirable for the fullest development and utilization of the nation's human resources. The broader concept, as it affects both the individual and society, goes beyond the economic aspect of the program. The objective of vocational rehabilitation is to convert disabled persons into self-supporting citizens, to develop and utilize to the fullest their abilities and skills, and to aid them in satisfactory social adjustment.

M. J. S.

OLDER PERSONS. Counseling problems peculiar to the age group over forty will become more prominent as the number of persons in this segment of our population increases. However, individual differences in education, intelligence, personality, financial status, health, occupational history, and other factors not directly related to age, are usually of more importance in vocational advisement than the number of years a man has lived.

Pollak [8] has shown that discrimination against older workers is not as extensive as some have claimed, but that it exists cannot be denied. The reluctance of employers with regard to the hiring of the middle-aged and the elderly derives from such considerations as increased pension and insurance costs, belief that younger workers are more adaptable and physically fit than older ones, and the fact that the cost of the training period in proportion to a man's total career increases with age. Many companies recruit their executives from the ranks and find this more practical when younger employees are engaged. On the other hand, older employees have lower quit rates, are more even and dependable in their work, and frequently match or exceed the production of younger persons. The compensatory effects of greater emotional stability and experience often outweigh the consequences of small losses in basic capacity. Kossoris [5] points out that the frequency of accidents decreases with age, although the duration of disability and the severity of injury tend to increase somewhat. The longer duration of disability following injury is partly due to the lowered recuperative powers of older persons. Accident rates could be even further reduced by use of proper safeguards on machinery, better placement of workers, and insistence upon regular and thorough medical examinations.

The changing population structure of the United States will challenge the resourcefulness of personnel men in business and industry as much as it will engage the attention of public and private counseling agencies. One large industrial establishment found the average age of its employees increasing almost a year annually.[9] Pollak [8] (p. 104), arguing against the widely held view that most older workers are scrapped after reaching the age of forty-five, cites the fact that "even the highest observed unemployment ratio— that for male workers of the sixty to sixty-four group in manufacturing, 1930—left 836 persons out of 1,000 employed." Moreover, men in the twenty to twenty-four age group exhibited higher unemployment rates than the fifty to fifty-nine year olds in the two census years studied.

Bound by seniority agreements and other considerations, enterprises in this country must give increased attention to employee counseling and to in-training programs promotive of the fullest utilization of the changing abilities of older workers. In many cases, training should be instituted years or decades in advance of actual need, taking advantage of the greater adaptability of the young. Psychological studies already provide a good deal of factual information on the expectancies for various physical and mental traits, and these data should be taken cognizance of in the drawing up of vocational life plans.

No older person should be counseled who has not had a thorough physical check-up within the year prior to advisement. This is particularly necessary because of the insidious nature of many of the diseases found in the elderly. Moreover, it is well to bear in mind the important distinction between permanent but stationary defects and those that become progressively worse. Unfortunately, many of the constitutional ailments found in older persons are progressive and this must be taken into account in the selection of objectives.

Unemployment in older workers is frequently associated with

physical disability; the New York State Legislative Commission on Discrimination in Employment of the Middle-aged [7] named it as the most important single cause of involuntary idleness.

One of the great dangers confronting older persons seeking employment is the possible misuse of industrial medicine facilities. Such facilities should not be used to screen out persons with handicaps, but should be employed to insure proper placement of those with organic and other difficulties. Lack of public education with regard to the assets and potentialities of disabled older workers is still very evident. Such education is absolutely essential if the work of the vocational counselor is not to be canceled out. The reader is referred to the articles on the handicapped, particularly those dealing with lifting, circulatory and heart disorders, the deaf and the visually impaired.

Excessive promotion or improper placement of older employees sometimes produces anxiety states and constitutes a hazard to mental health. This may occur if a man of limited education is elevated to a position requiring a good deal of academic training or if a person of only average intelligence is advanced to a job requiring superior mentality. Since job security means so much more to the average older person than to his younger colleague, and since poor performance does threaten job security, it is important to assign counselees to jobs that promise a high probability of success. Bad personnel work with the elderly, as with other age groups, is reflected in poor morale, lowered production rates, and increased labor turnover. Since psychological functions are not stationary, psychological examinations should be given periodically along with physical ones. Many older persons are in need of psychiatric help and could be saved from serious breakdowns if reached in time.

Evidence on the relationship between job satisfaction and chronological age is conflicting. Several investigators (Super, Hoppock) have found an over-all tendency toward increased satisfaction with age, although fluctuations occur. Others (Kornhauser and Sharp, Fryer), have been unable to locate definite age trends. It is reasonable to assume that the results would vary with individual jobs and individual men. The professional man who is constantly winning new honors and increased financial rewards is more likely to be satisfied than the man who finds himself trapped in an uninteresting job that has no future. Blum and Russ,[1] studying attitudes toward work incentives, found the desire for security to be more important to older workers than the wish for occupational advancement. This is undoubtedly associated with the lower quit rates for advanced age groups. It is interesting to note that Kitson [4] found the peaks of employment instability to occur in the early twenties and forties. He attributes the increased restlessness in the forties to such factors as ending of financial responsibilities to children and the termination of other obligations, recognition that vocational changes must be made soon if contemplated, and physiological alterations which have work implications. Unquestionably, much of this dissatisfaction could be avoided if men were successfully counseled when young.

Strong [11] has shown that age differences in interests are far less pronounced than sex or occupational variations. Interest patterns are rather clearly defined at age twenty-five and often earlier, with little basic modification thereafter. There is a tendency for both likes and dislikes to be intensified as persons grow older. It has also been noted that older men frequently develop aversions to venturesome activities requiring great physical exertion and skill. From the standpoint of vocational counseling, Strong's data support the hypothesis that the interest patterns of young adults can be used to predict the patterns that will exist two or three decades later. This finding can be utilized in the development of life plans.

The administration of mental examinations to middle-aged and older persons presents special problems. Since older testees fatigue more easily than younger ones, it is sometimes advisable to stagger tests over several sessions, particularly if a battery is being given. Sensory defects are more numerous among the aged and must be watched for, since they may invalidate results. Old people are generally less labile and more difficult to motivate in the test situation and the psychometrist must bear this in mind in conducting examinations. Unfortunately, many tests that are suitable for young people are not relevant to the needs and experiences of the elderly. Most tests have been standardized on young subjects and norms obtained with them cannot always be used as a fair basis for evaluating the status of older adults. The Wechsler-Bellevue Intelligence Scale is one of the few exceptions. Test results must always be reconciled with other data and with common sense.

In evaluating the results of intelligence tests, attention should be given to performance on various types of items as well as to the total score. It is known that the abilities measured by our mental tests (collectively called "intelligence") do not decline at equal rates. Even persons with the same total score may differ considerably from each other in terms of their mental ability patterns. This is of particular importance in the guidance of older adults. Mental ability tests that emphasize speed are known to discriminate against the upper age groups and may unfairly represent their potentialities. Power is of more consequence than great speed in many occupations.

Most of the personality adjustment inventories described in this book are even less suitable for older persons than the intelligence tests. The adjustment problems of advanced age are not identical with the problems of young adulthood. However, existing adjustment inventories can be profitably employed if answers to individual questions are carefully scrutinized. The Minnesota Multiphasic Personality Inventory, the Rorschach, and other tests utilizable in psychiatric diagnosis are valuable.

Although technical difficulties of mensuration have somewhat clouded the results of psychological inquiries on intelligence, personality and motor abilities, it is obvious that most functions follow the form of a parabolic curve, with peaks in the late teens or early twenties, a plateau or slow decline into the forties, and more precipitous losses beyond middle life. However, it cannot be stated too often that marked individual differences exist, sometimes influenced by occupation, and there are undoubtedly exceptions to most of the observed general trends. Kuhlen [6] and the writer, [2][3] recently have summarized the literature on the psychological aspects of aging.

More than usual attention should be given to the development of very complete work histories, since they often point to marketable abilities. Avocations, past and present, frequently offer clues to latent interests and aptitudes. The Dictionary of Occupational Titles is a valuable tool to use with persons who have had varied employment experiences.

A good many oldsters wish part-time work to supplement pensions and other sources of income. Infirmities may also make full time-work undesirable. The type of job recommended must, of course, vary with the background of the individual and with prevailing opportunities.

References:

1. Blum, M. L. and Russ, J. J. A study of employee attitudes toward various incentives. Personnel, 1942, 19, 438–444.
2. Kaplan, O. J., Ed. *Mental disorders in later life.* Stanford University: Stanford University Press, 1945.
3. ———. The psychology of maturity and later maturity. In *Encyclopedia of psychology,* Harriman, P. L., Ed. New York: The Philosophical Library, Inc., 1946.
4. Kitson, H. D. *The psychology of vocational adjustment.* Philadelphia: J. B. Lippincott, 1925.
5. Kossoris, M. D. Labor Information Bulletin, 1940, 7, 11.

6. Kuhlen, R. G. Age differences in personality during adult years. Psychological Bulletin, 1945, 42, 333–358.

7. New York State Joint Legislative Commission on Discrimination in Employment of the Middle-aged. *Final report*, p. 35.

8. Pollak, D. Discrimination against older workers in industry. American Journal of Sociology, 1944, 50, 99–106.

9. Stieglitz, E. J. Aging as an industrial problem. Journal of the American Medical Association, 1941, 116, 1383–1387.

10. ———. Senescence and industrial efficiency. Scientific Monthly, 1944, 58, 410–414 and 1944, 59, 9–15.

11. Strong, E. K., Jr. *Vocational interests of men and women*. Stanford University: Stanford University Press, 1943.

O. J. K.

OPTOMETRY, APTITUDE FOR. The profession of optometry is devoted to helping people to achieve the highest measure of visual efficiency and comfort. Optometrists do not provide medical or surgical treatment, but restrict their clinical work to determining just what corrective devices or training are necessary to assure maximum visual achievement in individual cases, and to provide these aids. In addition to providing such individual care, optometrists are interested in promoting surveys designed to reveal faulty visual habits and defects at early stages of their development so that visual handicaps may be corrected before they interfere too seriously with achievement. Such preventive work is represented by visual surveys in schools and in industry. Specially qualified optometrists may also act as consultants concerning the visual requirements and visual aids needed in various industrial tasks, and concerning improvement of the visual conditions through more adequate lighting, use of color contrast, adoption of best types of protective goggles, and other measures. Other optometrists have chosen to specialize in special diagnostic techniques and the development and application of special types of visual aids, such as contact glasses.

Associated with these developments in the profession is a change in emphasis on the characteristics essential for the successful practice of optometry.

The requirements are less restrictive in some ways, since the student can plan to specialize in those aspects of his work for which he, personally, is best adapted. On the other hand, rejection of commercial aspects of optometry and emphasis on professional aspects, has been associated with a raising of educational standards and an introduction of legal qualifications which are designed to assure a certain basic competence on the part of all licensed optometrists.

Modern optometric education requires four or five years work of college level. Graduation from an approved high school or its equivalent is required for entrance to any of the nine Grade A Optometry Schools in the United States:

Columbia University School of Optometry, New York, N. Y.
Los Angeles School of Optometry, Los Angeles, California
Massachusetts School of Optometry, Boston, Mass.
Northern Illinois College of Optometry, Chicago, Ill.
Ohio State University School of Optometry, Columbus, Ohio
Pacific University School of Optometry, Forest Grove, Oregon
Pennsylvania State College of Optometry, Philadelphia, Pa.
Southern College of Optometry, Memphis, Tenn.
University of California School of Optometry, Berkeley, California

Successful students must have at least the capacity for carrying successfully the ordinary liberal arts curriculum. In addition, since mathematics, physics, chemistry, zoology, anatomy, psychology and pathology, as well as clinical procedures, are required courses in the optometric curriculum, a special enthusiasm for scientific subjects and interest in making practical application of the acquired information are highly desirable. These courses involve many hours of laboratory work, and the student must be prepared to enjoy somewhat less free time than fellow students in some other departments.

When emphasis in optometry was upon "eye measurement," as the derivation of the word "optometry" suggests, special aptitude for mathematics and physics was considered of prime importance. It is essential that the student have at least the ability necessary to meet the basic requirements of the optometry curriculum, and to pass his state board requirements later, but the demands of clinical practice do not necessarily put a high premium upon mastery of these subjects.

An ability to retain, correlate and apply the knowledge that he has gained in his studies of physiological optics, physiology and psychology may be more important to the optometrist in his task of helping each individual patient to achieve his maximum visual efficiency. Similarly, manual dexterity has been considered an asset, as a factor in the accurate grinding and mounting of lenses and the fitting of the frame to the individual patient. The relative importance of this factor, too, is diminished if the clinician chooses to delegate most of the work to others.

Academic success and success in practice are not highly correlated, for personality factors assume greatly increased relative importance when the optometrist is ready to establish himself as a professional member of his chosen community. A pleasing appearance, an ability to meet people easily, and sufficient interest in social activities to participate in various group activities, are almost essential in the early building of an independent practice, and they will always contribute to its healthy growth.

It is also important that the optometrist should not offend the community's general idea of correct professional behavior. The confidence and respect which he must inspire can be all too easily diminished by conduct not considered socially acceptable in his particular community, even though transgressions be limited to such innocent matters as eccentricities in dress, or boisterousness. The building of a successful practice in a neighborhood community thus implies a certain conformity to the habits of that community. Any optometrist who finds such conformity too irksome must either practice in a large city, or select a community in which the social code is congenial to him.

The social responsiveness which makes conformity easy, is also of greatest importance to the optometrist in his professional work. He must be sufficiently interested in his patients to listen patiently to a full account of their symptoms and complaints, to adapt his procedures to make the examination easy for the patient, to consider the various special requirements of the individual in formulating his prescription, and to satisfy the patient that he is sufficiently sympathetic and painstaking to understand his needs and to provide competent care. He must also have self-control which will enable him to deal courteously, but firmly with those occasional patients who may feel that they have reason to criticize his handling of their own problems.

Finally, some business sense, initiative and enterprise are necessary in the conduct of an independent office. If the optometrist lacks the ability and drive to handle the non-clinical aspects of his work efficiently, he will probably find it more advantageous to become associated with an enterprise where someone else takes responsibility for these matters. There are indications that industry may be increasingly interested in having salaried optometrists included in their medical departments; some clinics employ optometrists on whole or part-time basis; optometrists and ophthalmologists are frequently eager to employ optometrists as assistants. The last arrangement often is attractive to young women optometrists, and they are frequently especially well qualified by temperament to do the orthoptics and visual training which are assuming increasing importance in optometric work.

Reference:

1. Lauer, A. R. Psycho-optometry. *Optometric Weekly* (in press).

M. R. S.

ORGANIZATIONS AND ASSOCIATIONS, PROFESSIONAL

American College Personnel Association. History: In February, 1923, a group of persons interested in placement met in Chicago and as a result organized in 1924 the National Association of Appointment Secretaries with 79 members. From the beginning it was clear that placement problems were only one phase of personnel work; a need was felt for coordinating with other groups handling college students. Mrs. May L. Cheney, the University of California, was the first president. The "personnel idea" was spreading in colleges and the Appointment Secretaries' Organization seemed the logical one to help pioneer in a growing program; thus a committee was appointed in 1926 to work with other groups for joint meetings, including National Vocational Guidance Association, National Association of Deans of Women, the Department of Superintendents, Personnel Research Federation and the National Committee of Bureaus of Occupations. A spirit of cooperation prevailed between the groups with no idea of merging, but holding simultaneous meetings and joint meetings on common subjects. In 1929, the name was changed from National Association of Appointment Secretaries to National Placement and Personnel Officers. In 1930, at Atlantic City, New Jersey, a new constitution was proposed. The following year at the meeting in Detroit, the name was changed to "American College Personnel Association"; the new constitution adopted; and sectional divisions were set up in Educational Counseling, General Placement, Personal Counseling, Records and Research, Teacher Placement. In 1932–33, the Association attempted to state college personnel principles, functions and standards. Also during this period the Association became a participant in the American Council of Guidance and Personnel Association. To J. E. Walters and F. F. Bradshaw go credit for much of the thinking along lines of cooperative affiliation with groups directly or indirectly handling personnel during these formative years. In 1939, under the leadership of the Reorganization Commission of the American College Personnel Association composed of Esther Lloyd Jones, Karl Onthank, and C. Gilbert Wrenn, "College Personnel Work," a charter for the American College Personnel Association was published.

Purpose: To provide (1) for the cooperative association of those persons engaged in college student personnel service and its administration; (2) for the promotion of national and regional conferences to discuss the problems, progress and possibilities of such service; (3) for the formulation and maintenance of professional standards among workers; (4) for the promotion of research and experimentation with the exchange and discussion of reports of the results thereof; (5) for the dissemination among all educational workers of the student personnel point of view as described in the charter of this Association.

Membership: Membership in the Association includes both professionally trained persons and others who are competent in the work. The functions, and not merely titles, designate the acceptability for membership. Included in the list of titles are:

1. Persons called personnel directors or personnel officers
2. Consulting psychologists
3. Academic Deans
4. Social Deans
5. Placement officers
6. Faculty advisers
7. Special counselors
8. College Physicians
9. Directors of College and University dormitories
10. Student Union Directors
11. College and University presidents
12. Business and industrial personnel workers
13. Admission officers
14. Test makers and other research workers
15. Directors of extra curricula activity
16. Religious workers

Publications: Bi-monthly "Personnelogram." "Educational and Psychological Measurement" is the Journal with which ACPA is associated. The Journal is a quarterly devoted to the development and application of measures of individual difference.

T. M.

American Vocational Association, Inc. The American Vocational Association is the professional organization of teachers, supervisors, administrators, and other persons interested in the advancement of education for occupational and social competency and efficiency.

It is founded upon the premise that the economic stability and security of a democratic nation rests upon the stability and vocational competency of its individual citizens. It, therefore, is devoted to the advancement and improvement of education in the fields of trades and industries, business and the distributive occupations, agriculture, industrial arts, vocational homemaking, and to the services of vocational rehabilitation and occupational information and guidance.

The American Vocational Association was organized in 1925 when the National Society for Vocational Education and the Vocational Education Association of the Middle West were merged. It has a membership of nearly 24,000.

In adherence to its belief in the democratic pattern and the importance of the individual, this Association is governed by a House of Delegates which establishes plans and policies for the promotion and development of vocational and industrial arts education. An Executive Committee and special committees which it appoints, give direction and professional leadership in extending the scope and improving the quality of the work of the Association. The Executive Committee includes the vice-president for each of the seven sections comprising the membership groups.

The Association believes that vocational education should remain an integral part of the American public school system, and that this educational service should be available to all youths and adults who do not pursue their education into higher fields of learning.

The services of the Association have changed during the years, to meet the professional needs of its members. In general it furnishes leadership to the several sections which comprise the membership; makes research possible; establishes standards of service; works for adequate funds for continuance and broadening of the program; provides publications, including a monthly magazine: the *American Vocational Journal*; provides field service through its officers; holds an annual convention which is strictly educational and inspirational; increases the prestige of vocational education through the contacts maintained with other national agencies and associations; affords opportunity for its membership to participate in national committee work for improvement of methods and services; watches and publicizes trends which are of significance to vocational and industrial arts educators; sponsors essential legislation; exercises its influence and strength for movements which will benefit vocational education and the youth and adults whose interests it serves, and against any movements which might be inimical to those interests. By acting as a clearing house for all of the groups of educators working in the field of vocational education it has enabled them to broaden their individual programs and thinking and enabled them to work harmoniously and unitedly for their mutual professional advancement. Through this Association the individual members are beneficiary of the constructive work of all. Few individuals can make themselves heard in a nation of 130,-000,000 people, but through organization they are articulate and can speak with effectiveness for their combined and collective thinking, planning, and objectives.

The Association develops and maintains cooperative and professional public relations with state and national organizations which represent labor, management, business, farm, economic, educational, and civic groups. Through its committees and its Executive Secretary it endeavors to promote better understanding of its objectives, better opportunities for employment and advancement of workers in the field, better standards for vocational education, and a unity of effort among both public and private agencies which are concerned with the welfare of the people. It encourages the affiliated state associations and their members to work similarly in their own states and communities.

L. H. D.

Jewish Occupational Council. The Jewish Occupational Council was established in 1939 as an association of all national and local Jewish organizations in the United States and Canada engaged in occupational adjustment service programs. The Council's objectives, as stated in its by-laws, are: (1) to act as a clearing-house for all Jewish organizations engaged in occupational research, vocational guidance, vocational training, or job placement; (2) to provide these agencies with occupational information, and to cooperate with them in research and publication projects; and (3) to assist and guide Jewish communities and organizations in establishing or improving vocational services.

During the depression of the 1930's the career and employment problems of Jewish persons were aggravated by widespread unemployment and discriminatory barriers in many economic fields. As a consequence, vocational service programs under Jewish auspices were expanded considerably to meet the needs of Jews for adequate economic adjustment. The Jewish Occupational Council was subsequently established as the central planning body for these programs. The Council offers a three-fold program of (1) coordination, (2) publications and research, and (3) field service for Jewish organizations.

Coordination involves: (1) clearance among national member agencies to eliminate conflict, duplication, and overlapping; (2) assisting national member agencies in planning programs to meet significant needs; (3) acting as a liaison agent in behalf of national and local members in relations with federal government agencies, and representing them in Jewish social work nationally and in the general vocational guidance movement; (4) gearing national agency programs and services to the vocational needs of Jewish communities; and (5) developing and maintaining high professional standards for national and local members.

Publications and research provide: (1) *Program and Information Service,* periodic releases of technical interest to professional workers; (2) *Jewish Occupational Bulletin,* a quarterly publication of interpretation; (3) central reporting service on activities of local member agencies; (4) research studies on the work of local members; and (5) consultation and information on research projects and publications of national and local members.

Field service includes: (1) visits to communities to give direct assistance in the organization of new, or the improvement of existing, Jewish community-wide vocational agencies; (2) preparation of manuals and handbooks; and (3) provision of an employment service through which national and local members may obtain professional personnel.

The Council's national member agencies are: American Jewish Committee, American Jewish Congress, American ORT Federation, B'nai B'rith, Conference on Jewish Relations, Hebrew Sheltering and Immigrant Aid Society, Jewish Agricultural Society, Jewish Labor Committee, Jewish Welfare Board, National Council of Jewish Women, National Refugee Service, and Union of American Hebrew Congregations.

The Council's local member agencies are the Jewish employment and vocational guidance services in the following twenty cities: Baltimore, Boston, Buffalo, Chicago, Cincinnati, Cleveland, Detroit, Los Angeles, Louisville, Milwaukee, Minneapolis, Montreal, Newark, New York, Philadelphia, Pittsburgh, Springfield, Mass., St. Louis, St. Paul, and Toronto.

A list of the Council's publications follows: *Occupational Research and Informational Activities of Leading Jewish Agencies, Some Aspects of the Jewish Economic Problem, A Bibliography for Jewish Vocational Agencies, Patterns of Jewish Occupational Distribution in the United States and Canada, Job Promotion, Jewish*

Occupational Bulletin, Program and Information Service, Some Characteristics of 408 Baltimore Jewish Youth, A Guide to General Vocational Service, and *Vocational Training Facilities in the National Defense Program.*

The Jewish Occupational Council has headquarters at 1841 Broadway, New York 23, New York.

E. E. C.

National Council on Rehabilitation. It was from a realization of the need for a coordination of the activities of private agencies which are engaged in rehabilitation that the National Council on Rehabilitation was born. Formed in August, 1942, its present membership numbers sixty agencies, representing the medical profession, social service organizations, and large insurance and industrial companies which are interested in rehabilitation programs.

The Council's Executive Committee, chosen from representatives of its membership, holds monthly meetings in New York City. It is there that it maintains its office, headed by the Executive Director. Each annual meeting of the entire membership provides a forum for member organizations and guests to present views on the problems and methods of rehabilitation. It has initiated studies by special committees on such subjects as: defining the processes of rehabilitation; personnel qualifications, standards, and facilities for training; and an investigation of state compensation insurance laws in relation to second injuries and the effect of these on the employment of the handicapped. It publishes monthly the *News Letter* reporting factual material and new publications relating to rehabilitation, each issue of which contains an article of special interest on some phase of this subject.

The purposes of the Council are to study, encourage, and advise upon the development of rehabilitation programs, to study and encourage programs and services for the prevention of handicaps, to serve as a forum for the discussion of problems concerning the handicapped, to act as a medium for exchange of information, and to cooperate with all agencies, public and private, which are interested in rehabilitation. The Council provides a symposium of the ideas of those interested in the three main subdivisions of rehabilitation: medical-physical rehabilitation, social adjustment, and vocational and industrial rehabilitation. All its planning is directed toward the restoration of the handicapped of all ages, veteran as well as civilian, to the fullest physical, mental, social, educational, and economic usefulness of which they are capable.

Publications by the National Council on Rehabilitation:

Report on Rehabilitation Legislation, 1943, 17 pp.
Symposium on the Process of Rehabilitation, 1944, 32 pp.
The Rehabilitation of the Psychoneurotic, by Thomas A. C. Rennie, M.D.,
    1944, 8 pp.
News Letter, published monthly.

In Press:

Health and Employment, by Myra A. Shimberg, Ph.D.
A Study of Public Assistance Clients Attending Out-Patient Department
    Clinics in New York City.
Bibliography on Rehabilitation, containing over 3,000 titles, the majority
    of which will be accompanied by a brief summary of the contents.

Scheduled for Publication, Fall, 1946:

The Processes of Rehabilitation.
A Compilation and Revision.

                                                        C. S. T.

National Rehabilitation Association, Incorporated. Organized in
Cleveland, Ohio in 1925, the National Rehabilitation Association
has, for the past twenty years, served as a clearing house for the
efforts expended by State and Federal agencies and individuals on
behalf of all types of the disabled. The activities of the Association
include:

Journal of Rehabilitation; a professional magazine containing
articles of the medical, social, educational and employment phases
of work with the disabled.

State and National Forums where representatives of the various
agencies dealing with the disabled can meet and discuss their mutual
problems.

Promotion of legislation. Active cooperation is now being extended to a subcommittee of Congress that is studying the whole
problem of the physically handicapped.

Coordination of effort among all groups interested in the disabled.

Cooperation with State and Federal offices of Vocational Rehabilitation.

Any one engaged in work with the disabled on a professional
basis may become a Professional Member upon the payment of the
sum of five dollars ($5.00) per year.

Any person may become an Active Member of the Association
upon payment of the sum of two dollars ($2.00) per year.

The National Rehabilitation Association includes in its membership not only those who work actively in rehabilitation service and in all the related services, but it offers to every interested citizen the opportunity to contribute the best of his time and effort to the handicapped.

R. G.

National Vocational Guidance Association, Inc. (1913). Association Headquarters and Editorial Office for *Occupations,* The Vocational Guidance Journal, 82 Beaver Street, New York 5, N. Y. Membership: Individuals, approximately 4,500; organizations, 75.

Purpose: "To foster vocational guidance and occupational adjustment and to establish and improve standards of professional service in those fields"; to bring those individuals who are engaged in or interested in any phase of vocational guidance together in one national organization and into its branches; and to carry on through its Divisions and Committees, the various activities which need special emphasis or attention.

History: The National Vocational Guidance Association was organized in 1913 following three years of careful study by pioneer leaders in the vocational guidance movement. A constitution was adopted at the fourth national convention in 1914. Annual conventions have been held usually preceding the February Convention of the American Association of School Administrators. At this time the Delegate Assembly meets to transact Association business according to an agenda prepared by the Board of Trustees with the cooperation of the Policy Committee. The Association was incorporated according to the laws of the State of New York in 1933.

In 1920 the Association was organized as a federation of chartered Branches. Seventy-five Branches have been chartered and other groups are now in the process of organization. Each Branch has its own Constitution and By-Laws and is autonomous in the conduct of its own affairs consistent with the Branch Constitution and By-Laws and those of the National Association.

The By-Laws also provide for Membership-at-Large for those individuals who do not have access to a Branch of the Association. A Life Membership may be purchased by or for a member of the Association. All types of membership in the National Association entitle the individual to voting power in Association affairs, to hold office in the National Association, and to a subscription to the official Journal.

A recent development has been the establishment of Professional Membership for those who are technically qualified in the fields of guidance and personnel and who possess minimum qualifications as set forth in the By-Laws.

During the past few years when it has been impossible to have national conventions, Regional Conferences have been held. These have been planned by one or more Branches to enlarge and strengthen the Branch programs. Some of the conferences have been in cooperation with the Council of Guidance and Personnel Associations of which the National Vocational Guidance Association is a member.

Occupations, The Vocational Guidance Journal is the official publication of the National Vocational Guidance Association. It is the only periodical in the personnel field that devotes itself primarily to the problems of persons who give vocational and educational guidance on a professional level.

The journal was first published in 1911 as the *Vocational Guidance News-Letter,* a special number of the *Boston Home and School News-Letter,* edited by Frederick J. Allen of Harvard. The first national magazine was a four page monthly leaflet, *The Vocational Guidance Bulletin.* In 1918 publication was suspended for three years; then in 1921 the *National Vocational Guidance Association Bulletin* was published, edited first by Anne S. Davis of Chicago and later by Frederick J. Allen.

The *Bulletin* was taken over by the Bureau of Vocational Guidance of the Harvard Graduate School of Education in December, 1922. In March, 1924, the name was changed to the *Vocational Guidance Magazine.*

Occupations, The Vocational Guidance Journal became the name of the name of the official publication in 1933 when the National Occupational Conference was organized with funds set aside by the Carnegie Corporation. The Conference was co-publisher with the National Vocational Guidance Association during the six years from 1933 to 1939. The National Vocational Guidance Association resumed publication of the magazine in 1939. In 1944 the name was changed, by vote of the members of the Association, to *Occupations, The Vocational Guidance Journal.*

Occupations is published eight times a year from October through May. In addition to the members of the Association there is a subscription list of thousands of professional and semi-professional workers in the field of occupational adjustment. Numerous libraries, public, private, and educational, are also on the subscription list. The editorship has passed successively since 1923 from

Frederick J. Allen to Fred C. Smith in 1927, and to Harry D. Kitson, the present editor, in 1937.

The Journal carries articles which have been prepared by outstanding leaders in the profession and which cover every major point in the adjustment of the individual to occupational life. Every issue features technical aids, new books and articles, and records Association activities.

In addition to its official Journal the Association has authorized several publications, including, *Basic Units for an Introductory Course in Vocational Guidance,* 1931; *The Printing Trades and Their Workers,* 1932; *Occupations in Retail Stores,* 1937, revised 1941; *Principles and Practices of Educational and Vocational Guidance,* 1927; *Distinguishing Marks of a Good Occupational Monograph,* 1939; and the *Content of a Good Occupational Monograph —The Basic Outline,* 1940.

C. M.

ORGANIZATIONS INTERESTED IN VOCATIONAL GUIDANCE, A SELECTED LIST. (Adapted from *Occupations,* the Vocational Guidance Magazine for October 1938.)

ACGPA. *See* American Council of Guidance and Personnel Associations.

Affiliated Schools for Workers, Inc., 302 East 35th St., New York, N. Y.

Alliance for the Guidance of Rural Youth, 401–402 Grace-American Bldg., Richmond, Va.

American Association for Applied Psychology, Alice I. Bryan, South Hall, Columbia University, New York, N. Y.

National Vocational Guidance Association, 525 West 120th St., New York, N. Y.

American Association of Engineers, 8 South Michigan Ave., Chicago, Ill.

American Association of University Women, 1634 I St., N.W., Washington, D. C.

American Association to Promote the Teaching of Speech to the Deaf, 1537 35th St. NW., Washington, D. C.

American College Personnel Association, Secretary, Thelma Mills, Director of Student Affairs for Women, University of Missouri, Columbia, Mo.

American Council of Guidance and Personnel Associations, Miss Gladys Gove, National Federated Business and Professional Women's Clubs, 1819 Broadway, New York, N. Y.

American Council on Education, 744 Jackson Pl. NW., Washington, D. C.

American Federation of Labor, 901 Massachusetts Ave. NW., Washington, D. C.

American Foundation for the Blind, 15 West 16th St., New York, N. Y.

American Occupational Therapy Association, 175 5th Ave., New York, N. Y.

American Psychological Association, Willard Olson, University of Michigan, Ann Arbor, Mich.

American Society for the Hard of Hearing, 1537 35th St. NW., Washington, D. C.

American Vocational Association, Inc., 1010 Vermont Ave. NW., Washington, D. C.

American Women's Association, 353 West 57th St., New York, N. Y.

American Youth Commission of the American Council on Education, 744 Jackson Pl. NW., Washington, D. C.

Association of Colleges and Secondary Schools for Negroes, L. S. Cozart, Secretary, Barber-Scotia College, Concord, N. C.

B'nai B'rith Hillel Foundation. B'nai B'rith, 1003 K St. NW., Washington, D. C.

Boy Scouts of America, 2 Park Ave., New York, N. Y.

Boys' Clubs of America, Inc., 381 4th Ave., New York, N. Y.

Braille Institute of America, 741 North Vermont Ave., Los Angeles, Calif.

Child Study Association of America, 221 West 57th St., New York, N. Y.

Children's Bureau, United States Department of Labor, Washington, D. C.

Council of Jewish Federations and Welfare Funds, Inc., 71 West 47th St., New York, N. Y.

Engineers' Council for Professional Development, 29 West 39th St., New York, N. Y.

Federal Committee on Apprentice Training, United States Department of Labor, Washington, D. C.

Federated Council on Art Education, 745 5th Ave., New York, N. Y.

Four-H Clubs, Extension Division, U. S. Department of Agriculture, Washington, D. C.

Future Farmers of America, Division of Vocational Education, United States Office of Education, Washington, D. C.

General Federation of Women's Clubs, 1734 N St. NW., Washington, D. C.

Girls' Service League of America, 138 East 19th St., New York, N. Y.

Handicapped: (Organizations interested in the occupational adjustment of the handicapped.) *See* under American Association to Promote the Teaching of Speech to the Deaf; American Foundation for the Blind; American Occupational Therapy Association; American Society for the Hard of Hearing; Braille Institute of America; National Society for the Prevention of Blindness; National Committee for Mental Hygiene; National Rehabilitation Association.

International Association of Altrusa Clubs, Inc., 701 North Michigan Ave., Chicago, Ill.

International Association of Public Employment Services, Secretary, B. C. Seiple, 8 City Hall, Cleveland, Ohio.

Jewish Welfare Board, 220 5th Avenue, New York, N. Y.

Joint Vocational Service, Inc., 130 East 22d St., New York, N. Y.

Kiwanis International, 2225 McGraw-Hill Bldg., 520 North Michigan Ave., Chicago, Ill.

Metropolitan Junior Achievement, Inc., 16 East 48th St., New York, N. Y.

Mortar Board (national honor society for College Women), 80 East Willis Ave., Detroit, Mich.

National Association of Deans of Women, 1201 16th St. NW., Washington, D. C.

National Association of State Directors of Vocational Education, Secretary, Irvin S. Noall, State Director of Vocational Education, Salt Lake City, Utah.

National Catholic Welfare Conference, 1312 Massachusetts Ave. NW., Washington, D. C.

National Child Labor Committee, 419 4th Ave., New York, N. Y.

National Committee for Mental Hygiene, Inc., 1790 Broadway, New York, N. Y.

National Committee on Household Employment, 525 West 120th St., New York, N. Y.

National Congress of Colored Parents and Teachers, 20 Blvd. NE., Atlanta, Ga.

National Congress of Parents and Teachers, 1201 16th St. NW., Washington, D. C.

National Conference on Rehabilitation, 1790 Broadway, New York, N. Y.

National Council of Jewish Women, Inc., 1819 Broadway, New York, N. Y.

National Education Association of the United States, 1201 16th St. NW., Washington, D. C.

National Federation of Business and Professional Women's Clubs, 1819 Broadway, New York, N. Y.

National Institutional Teacher Placement Association, Secretary, Mrs. Mary B. Bondurant, University of Georgia, Athens, Ga.

National Rehabilitation Association, State Capitol, Frankfort, Ky.

National Society for the Prevention of Blindness, 50 West 50th St., New York, N. Y.

National Urban League for Social Service Among Negroes, 1133 Broadway, New York, N. Y.

National Vocational Guidance Association, 525 West 120th St., New York, N. Y.

Optimist International, 1721 Railway Exchange Bldg., St. Louis, Mo.

The Osborne Association, Inc., 114 East 30th St., New York, N. Y.

Personnel Research Federation, 29 West 39th St., New York, N. Y.

Phi Delta Kappa, a professional fraternity in education, 2034 Ridge Rd., Homewood, Ill.

Protestant Episcopal Church, The National Council, 281 4th Ave., New York, N. Y.

Psychological Corporation, 522 5th Ave., New York, N. Y.

Quota Club International, 1204 18th St. NW., Washington, D. C.

Rotary International, 35 East Wacker Drive, Chicago, Illinois.

Sons of the American Legion, 777 North Meridan St., Indianapolis, Ind.

Teachers College Personnel Association, Nora A. Congdon, Secretary, Colorado State College of Education, Greeley, Colo.

United States Civil Service Commission, Washington, D. C.

United States Department of Agriculture. *See* Four-H Clubs.

United States Department of Labor, Washington, D. C.

United States Employment Service, Washington, D. C.

United States Office of Education, Washington, D. C.

United States Office of Indian Affairs, Department of the Interior, Washington, D. C.

Western Personnel Service, 30 North Raymond Ave., Pasadena, Calif.

Women's Bureau, United States Department of Labor, Washington, D. C.

Workers Education Bureau of America, 1440 Broadway, New York, N. Y.

Young Men's Christian Associations of the United States of America, National Council of, 347 Madison Ave., New York, N. Y.

Young Women's Christian Association of the United States of
America, 600 Lexington Ave., New York, N. Y.

Zonta International, 59 East Van Buren St., Chicago, Ill.

Society for Occupational Research, Ltd. The Society for Occupational Research, Ltd., is a non-profit organization devoted to
the scientific study of problems in the field of occupational
relations. Founded in 1925 by G. Vernon Bennett at the University of Southern California, the first group of members consisted of graduate students in attendance at seminars in vocational
guidance conducted by Dr. Bennett. Formal organization of the
Society was effected in 1928, and in 1930 it was incorporated in the
State of California as a non-profit corporation with headquarters at
the University of Southern California, Los Angeles.

Purposes of the Organization

The specific aims of the Society as defined in its constitution
were:

1. To make studies in vocational education and guidance, and
   in other occupational relations.
2. To advance vocational education and guidance by publicity,
   endowments, holding of conferences, and by lectures and
   debates.
3. To finance studies and researches in vocational education
   and guidance and in other occupational relations.
4. To publish materials resulting from studies made by the
   Society, or under its direction, or acceptable to its purposes.
5. To disseminate materials resulting from studies, researches,
   and other activities of the Society.
6. To endeavor to articulate the conclusions reached by the
   studies of the Society in the curricula of schools and colleges.

Activities

Pursuant to its purposes, the Society has held regular monthly
meetings at the University of Southern California at which lectures,
reports and discussions in the field of occupational relations have
been presented. The Society has maintained a Vocational Guidance
Clinic which has offered both to youth and to adults scientific vocational adjustment at cost. Each summer it has been the practice of
the Society to sponsor a large general conference on Occupational
Orientation; and each winter, through the *American Institute of
Occupational Relations,* a subsidiary organization, it has conducted
a conference on current economic problems. Beginning in 1930, the

Society has published a monthly magazine, the *Occupational Outlook,* was suspended for the duration of the war.

Publications

In addition to the publication of the magazine, the Society has published a number of monographs, and has sponsored a series of books known as *The Occupational Relations Series.* This now includes the following titles: *Occupational Exploratory Courses* (1930), *Occupational Orientation* (1931), *Exploring the World of Work* (1937), *Youth and the World's Work* (1938), *Occupational Exploration* (1941), *You and Your Future Job* (1944), *The Veteran and His Future Job* (1946). Books now in preparation include *The Science of Vocational Adjustment, Opportunities Abroad, A History of the Labor Movement, Vocational Self-Guidance,* and *Opportunities for Women.*

Membership

Membership in the Society is open both to individuals and to institutions, and includes two forms. *Life Membership* ($50) entitles holders to the full privileges of the Society, including the right to receive all books, monographs, magazines, and other publications of the Society. *Associate Membership* is on a yearly basis and is intended for those who desire to affiliate with the Society but who do not desire the full privileges of Life Membership.

Officers

Three presidents have served the organization: E. T. Robinson (1928–1930); Thomas E. Elson (1930–1938), and James H. Bedford (1938–   ). The headquarters of the Society are now located at 608 Kimlin Drive, Glendale 6, California.

J. H. B.

ORIENTATION INVENTORIES

Burns-Spencer Surveying Your Future Vocation. *Surveying Your Future Vocation,* a vocational survey blank, was prepared by Robert K. Burns and Lyle M. Spencer to assist in organizing and stimulating the efforts of students to learn about the world of work and the places they may expect to fill in that world.

The general objectives are to help make the student job-conscious before he actually faces the problem of getting a job; to avoid a passive approach to vocational guidance by the active participation of the student; to emphasize the importance of having complete information about an occupation in making career choices; to help students to evaluate and appraise their career choices and to point out to them the necessity of job analysis and self-appraisal; and to emphasize the importance of today's employment trends and their effects upon tomorrow's jobs.

Surveying Your Future Vocation provides twelve pages for occupational and personal information, and is divided into four sections. Part I is called *Studying the Occupation*. It helps the student find out about the history of the occupation he is studying and directs him in the analysis of the duties of the work, its relation to other jobs, employment opportunities, earnings, hours, working conditions, and advantages and disadvantages. Part II, *Studying the Worker,* deals with the personal qualifications important to success in that field, such as educational requirements, training, special abilities, and personality traits.

In Part III, *Planning Your Career in This Field,* the student compares his own measured interests, abilities, aptitudes, and training with the requirements of the occupation he is surveying. Part IV, *Finding More Information on Your Future Vocation,* challenges the resourcefulness of the student in obtaining additional occupational information and also aids the teacher in building a useful bibliography for future reference.

Methods of using this vocational survey blank, and other instructional procedures are given in *School Courses and Related Careers,* by O. R. Bacher and G. J. Berkowitz, another Science Research Associates publication.

Surveying Your Future Vocation is published by Science Research Associates, 228 S. Wabash Avenue, Chicago 4, Illinois.

B. J. M.

Gentry Vocational Inventory.   The Vocational Inventory is for use from Grade VIII through graduate work in college, and in adult education classes.

It gives a general vocational picture of high school and college students based upon interest in a particular vocational area, likes and dislikes for the activities usually involved in the occupations comprised in the area, and information and knowledge of the eight general occupational groups into which the world of work is classified. The eight groups are Art, Literature, Government and Law, Social Service, Business, Mechanical Designing, Mechanical Construction, and Science.

Definite and objective data for use in educational and vocational counseling are provided. The materials are designed for use in large and small schools. Extensive knowledge of the guidance field is not necessary for deriving the benefits from and making use of the *Vocational Inventory*. The manual and accompanying accessories give necessary information for the proper use of the Inventory and the interpretation of the results.

These materials combine to form a basis for counseling and for placing graduates into industry. They also may be used for a comprehensive orientation program.

Since the Inventory covers the world of work comprehensively, it eliminates the necessity of giving separate aptitude tests in the various fields in the large majority of cases. If such individual tests are contemplated, this general inventory should be given first.

The *Individual Analysis Report* is designed for the student. It not only provides him with an understanding of the results of the Inventory, but may also be used as a guide in the study of various occupations in which he is definitely interested.

The *Personality Inventory,* which is given in conjunction with the aptitude tests in the *Vocational Inventory,* provides the counselor with a personality developmental tendency which is useful to him in the counseling interview.

Materials

       Vocational Inventory, a 30-page booklet
       Individual Analysis Report, a 16-page booklet
       Individual Score Tabulation Sheet
       Manual and Keys

The Inventory is now being revised to provide for machine scoring. Dr. Roy B. Hackman, Temple University, is collaborating with the author in the revised edition. This edition will have the additional occupational groups of Computation and Music.

Statistical studies dealing with validity and reliability, and also with norms, will be given in the new Manual to the new edition. The next printing will include two forms, No. 1 and No. 2. No. 1 is for junior high school use and for adults who have not gone far in their education. Form No. 2 will be for senior high school students and adults.

Both forms will be suitable for the use of personnel directors in business and industry. It is published by the Educational Test Bureau.

                                               C. G. G.

Kefauver-Hand Guidance Tests and Inventories. This series of Tests and Inventories was constructed by Grayson N. Kefauver and Harold C. Hand. They were devised to serve a definite need in developing a guidance service. They comprise six guidance tests and two inventories, as follows:

> Educational Guidance Test
> Health Guidance Test
> Recreational Guidance Test
> Student-Judgment Guidance Test
> Vocational Guidance Test
> Inventory of Student Plans
> Inventory of Student Self-Ratings

The five Tests measure how well students are informed concerning conditions, problems, and opportunities in society and the school. The two Inventories indicate how accurately students define their own abilities. Any one may be used alone or in conjunction with the others.

The Tests and Inventories are designed for grades 7 to 14. They are practically self-administering and may be given to large groups. There are no time limits but the working time on the Tests is approximately 20 minutes each and on the Inventories, 25 minutes. Students should understand the purpose of the Tests and Inventories as well as the value of the results to them. A preliminary discussion of the purpose is desirable.

In order to interpret conveniently the relative standing of the individual on the Tests mentioned above, a profile chart is provided on which may be shown graphically the standing of the student on each Test not only relative to the others but also relative to the average or median of his class, school, or school system. Norms have not been reported for the various Tests because of a real objection to their use in a guidance program. There is now no way of determining what scores students have before it can be said that they have attained a desirable standard. This judgment must be in the light of the goals guidance workers are striving for in a particular situation.

Each of the six Tests in the battery has been prepared in two forms, called Form A and Form B. Form A only is published at present.

The reliability coefficients for single grades range from .77 to .89 with an average value of .82. Reliability coefficients were computed by correlating the score made on Form A of each test by randomly selected junior high school, senior high school, and junior college students with those made on Form B of the same test by the same students.

The publisher of these Tests and Inventories is World Book Company, Yonkers-on-Hudson, New York.

B. C. W.

Occupational Orientation Inquiry. This four-page printed questionnaire is designed for use with high-school seniors or college students, as a basis for vocational guidance interviews and individual counseling procedures. Its purpose is to induce the student to think through his vocational problems in a systematic manner as a preparation for the interview, and to afford the counselor a rapid summary of the student's background as it affects his vocational choices.

On the first page of the questionnaire the student is directed to give a brief vocational history of his experiences and interests from childhood to the present. On the two inside pages is a list of 224 occupations ranging from unskilled to highly professional types of work, arranged in chart form with spaces for self-ratings concerning each. The student is asked to rate separately his knowledge about the work, his interest in it, his ability for it, and his probable opportunity for placement in the field, using a five-point scale (0 to 4) for each evaluation. On the last page the student is asked to evaluate his vocational problem in the light of all the considerations which the filling out of the first three pages has brought to light, and to indicate what vocational advice he would now give himself.

The author states that the blank has been found particularly useful with (1) high-school students who do not contemplate entering college; (2) college students who have or have had difficulties with their academic work; and (3) individuals who have no idea as to what they would like to do.

The 1939 form is a third revision; the earlier editions were used respectively with 178 and 565 college freshmen. The counselor's use of the blank will be chiefly qualitative and not quantitative. If desired, total scores may be obtained to indicate the number of different occupations in which the student considers that he has a high degree of knowledge, interest, ability, or opportunity. The manual presents decile norms for high-school seniors, college freshmen, and college seniors, for men and women separately, for each of these four categories.

The references below give general discussions of the value of the questionnaire in practical clinical counseling situations and are illustrated with specific case histories, but no statistical data are presented. Wallar has stated (1) that several investigations are in progress to determine (a) the intercorrelations between ratings on the blank of knowledge, interest, ability and opportunity, (b) patterns of jobs based on similarities of individual's ratings, and (c) comparison of the results of the inquiry with diagnostic tests at the freshman college level.

No time limit is set. The average college student could be expected to complete the blank within an hour.

This questionnaire is published by the Psychological Corporation, New York.

References:

1. Wallar, G. A. Occupational orientation inquiry. *School and Society,* 1937, 46, 507–510.
2. ———. Use of the occupational orientation inquiry. *Occupations,* 1939, 17, 299–302.
3. ———. Practical aid to occupational orientation. *Journal of Applied Psychology,* 1941, 25, 535–557.
4. Wallar, G. A. and Pressey, S. L. *Occupational orientation inquiry—manual of directions.* New York: Psychological Corporation, 1939.

F. A. M.

Richardson Aids to Self-Analysis and Vocational Planning Inventory. This inventory, constructed by H. D. Richardson, is a device for helping the student to inventory those elements of his experience which have a direct bearing on the character of his vocational choice and the soundness of his plan for realizing the goal he has set for himself, and to see, understand, and use this information in a careful consideration of his problem during the course of one or a series of vocational counseling interviews. It is also a device that should enable the counselor to more readily identify the individual's problems, and to bring to bear on them information and data essential to adequate understanding and treatment.

The inventory is self-administering. It is intended for use by senior high school and junior college students. It is to be filled out by the student prior to an appointment for a vocational counseling interview. A previous course in psychology, a course in occupations, or a program of group guidance activities should materially assist the student in filling out the inventory, but such experiences are not essential.

Through the inventory the student takes stock of his parentage and family background; reviews his educational history including past achievements, interests, and future plans together with the factors that have helped to determine his educational goals and plans for reaching them; expresses an occupational choice or goal; analyzes his pattern of work interests, special abilities, skills, and aptitudes; appraises his traits of character and symptoms of health and physical status; recounts his work experiences; and records his present vocational choice, the factors that have influenced that choice, the resources he has considered in making it, and those he will utilize in achieving it. This self-analysis and inventory serves to prepare the student for the vocational interview and in turn provides the counselor with the information and data for the skillful direction of it.

The extent to which the intended function of the inventory is realized, its validity, depends both upon the quantity and quality of the information supplied by the student and the experience and skill of the counselor as a diagnostician. The inventory alone will seldom furnish the counselor with all the data and information needed in a clinical approach to vocational counseling, but it will supply certain information and data essential for counseling in the typical school situation with both convenience and economy in time and effort.

The inventory is published by Science Research Associates, 1700 Prairie Avenue, Chicago, Illinois.

Reference:

1. Richardson, H. D. *Analytical devices in guidance and counseling.* Chicago: Science Research Associates, 1940, pp. 47–58.

H. D. R.

Thurstone Employment Tests.   The Thurstone Employment Tests were constructed by L. L. Thurstone, of the University of Chicago. They consist of two examinations designed to serve as supplements to the interview of an employee in order to determine the applicant's general fitness for the position. The two tests are the Examination in Clerical Work and the Examination in Typing. There is one form of each Examination. The several parts of the Examination in Clerical Work are sample clerical tasks. The last part of the test is a generally accepted intelligence test. The Examination in Typing contains samples of just the kind of work a typist will be called on to do. Ability in spelling is also tested. Tables for the interpretation of scores for both examinations are provided. Neither of the examinations is timed, but the time taken to complete the test is recorded and taken into consideration in interpreting the results.

The publisher of these Examinations is World Book Company, Yonkers-on-Hudson, New York.

B. C. W.

ORTHOPEDIC HANDICAPS.

Definitions

"Orthopedic handicap" as used in this article means any deformity or impairment of limbs or body that affects normal functioning. Disabilities included in this group are (1) amputation of finger(s), hand(s), arm(s), foot or feet or leg(s); and (2) disabled condition of hand(s), arm(s), foot or feet, leg(s) or trunk. The condition may be the result of trauma, congenital defect, or crippling disease such as arthritis, cerebral palsy, osteomyelitis or poliomyelitis. Persons with orthopedic handicaps are, therefore, those commonly referred to as "crippled." A large proportion of all physically handicapped persons fall within this general classification.

Vocational Rehabilitation is defined as the rendering of a disabled person fit to engage in remunerative employment. For the younger group that has had no work experience it means preparation for and establishment in suitable employment; for those injured or otherwise incapacitated after reaching maturity it means readjustment and restoration to employment in a type of work compatible with the impaired condition.

Vocational Rehabilitation is in effect a process of preparation for or restoration to a condition of employability. It is an art rather than a science. Its application requires the greatest skill, experience and resourcefulness. Only those who are well qualified should undertake to assist in the vocational adjustment of a disabled person, since failure may result in complete frustration of the individual concerned. The leading authorities in the field are the Federal-State Vocational Rehabilitation agencies, operated in the various states under the Barden-LaFollette Act (Vocational Rehabilitation Act, Amendments of 1943) by the respective State Boards for Vocational Education, and the U. S. Veterans Administration which is responsible for the rehabilitation of disabled war veterans.

The Counselor

The qualifications of a rehabilitation counselor in this field include a broad knowledge of the principles of vocational rehabilitation and of educational and industrial psychology, of vocational guidance and counseling techniques and procedures, of modern case-work methods, and of the principles and practices of psychiatry, psychology and mental hygiene. He must have a wide fund of occupational information and know employment conditions and opportunities in his community. He must be familiar with the etiology, effect and treatment of orthopedic defects. He must be skilled in making personal and job analyses.

The counselor must be versatile, practical, resourceful, and open minded with ability to size up persons and situations and to make adaptation to the endless variety of circumstances that affect the adjustment of his clients. He must be tactful and have a sympathetic understanding of the handicapped and their problems.

Services Required

Service is provided on the casework basis, with scrupulous attention to the individual needs of each client. Some require only one major service; others may require many adjustment aids.

The types of services required for a complete vocational rehabilitation program include morale building, medical examination, educational, social and vocational counseling or guidance, corrective surgery and other therapeutic treatment, hospitalization, provision of prosthesis, prevocational and vocational training, adequate supervision of the training program, maintenance during training or convalescence, transportation, provision of training or placement equipment, provision of occupational license, placement and follow-up to insure success on the job.

The principal steps of the individual program are (1) interview, (2) survey, (3) medical examination, physical diagnosis and prognosis, (4) vocational diagnosis, (5) counseling or guidance, including necessary psychological testing, (6) preparation of plan of services to be rendered, and (7) carrying the plan through to completion. The end result sought, in every case, is employment on a suitable job.

Interview

The recognized principles of interviewing apply, but adapted to dealing with disabled persons. Many such persons are sensitive with regard to their physical impairment. The approach should be frank and realistic, neither avoiding nor emphasizing the impairment. Acceptance of the fact of impairment on the part of the interviewer will aid similar acceptance by the client. Every interview should be constructive; emphasis should be placed on positive factors and the possibility of overcoming any handicaps involved, rather than on negative factors and limitations. This is a first step in building up the client's morale, a process that should continue throughout the program. It is only to be expected that most disabled persons, and particularly those with visible impairments, should be prone to discouragement and fear of failure. Only when they are aided to acquire a hopeful and forward-looking attitude can real progress be made in their vocational adjustment. Telling them of the accomplishment and success of others with a similar impairment is often helpful.

Survey

Essential for vocational diagnosis and for use as a basis for guidance is a comprehensive survey of the client and of all circumstances and conditions that affect his adjustment. Included are: (1) *Personal factors,* such as age, sex, race, citizenship, marital status, family status, and social status. (2) *Physical factors,* such as exact nature of disability, its origin, age at which acquired, cause, course and prominence; treatment given or needed; appliance used or needed; secondary defects, if any; general health. (3) *Mental and educational factors,* such as intelligence quotient, grade level, subject preference, special training, reading habits and preference. (4) *Economic factors,* such as compensation status, earnings, other income, savings and possible sources of financial aid. (5) *Vocational factors,* including complete work history, skills, aptitudes, interests, self-help efforts, reference. (6) *Personality factors,* such as appearance, emotional stability, behavior, attitude toward self and others.

These data may be obtained through the interview with the client, and interviews with or reports from relatives, teachers, physicians, employers and others who have knowledge of him. Verification of the data is a usual procedure.

Medical Diagnosis

A thorough physical examination and report is essential. Even though the major disability is readily apparent as in the case of amputation or ankylosed joint, there may be other conditions such as tuberculosis, heart defect or vision defect that might seriously affect the choice of the job objective. The examination may also reveal the possibility of corrective surgery. The diagnosis and prognosis further aid in determining the physical capacities of the client for various types of employment.

Vocational Diagnosis

Careful analysis of the survey data including medical diagnosis will enable the counselor to make the necessary vocational diagnosis, which is the accurate determination of the client's present condition with respect to employment; his vocational assets as well as his vocational liabilities. One liability in many orthopedic cases is the usual visibility of the impairment. This has an effect upon the client himself, upon his associates and upon prospective employers that must be given due consideration. The diagnosis, then, constitutes a concrete and definite statement of the problem. With this picture clearly in mind the counselor is prepared to begin the task of working out with the client the solution to the problem.

Counseling or Guidance

Counseling the orthopedically handicapped for rehabilitation purposes goes far beyond the choice of job objective. It is a continuous process throughout the entire program from the initial interview through placement and follow-up. It includes counseling for emotional and social adjustment, educational guidance, guidance for placement and adjustment on the job, as well as occupational choice. It is one of the most important steps in the rehabilitation process since it is the prime determinant of the individual program leading to vocational activity, which is the keystone of the client's whole structure of living.

Vocational counseling for choice of job objective reduced to simplest terms consists of three essential factors. First, assisting the client to evaluate himself, his skills, aptitudes, interests, drives, resources, and finally, his limitations. Second, providing complete occupational information concerning any proposed objective; its requirements, work conditions, opportunities for preparation and for employment. Third, the correlation of the first two factors by interpretation and objective reasoning. The client with disabled legs will be aided to realize that he has abilities equal to the performance of many of the hundreds of jobs that do not require the use of legs; those with arm disabilities can choose from many occupations within their recognized capacity and in which the impairment does not constitute a handicap. The aim should be work on the highest level of which the client is capable.

The physical demands and capacities analysis technique is one of the counselor's tools. But this method of matching workers and jobs by analyzing the job requirements as to lifting, pulling, walking, stooping, reaching, etc., and analyzing the client's capacity to meet these requirements must be used with judgment and the realization that special adaptations may be made. A man with an artificial leg may apparently be barred from operating the stitcher in the shoe repair trade by the requirement of balancing in order to operate the foot pedal, but the simple device of a supporting belt around man and machine may overcome this difficulty. An arthritic with ankylosed spine may obviate the bending requirement of instrument repairing or watch repairing by using a specially made chair permitting him to work in a reclining position on a bench extension. An amputee may drive a car by the use of special attachments now available. A job requiring carrying work material to his bench, may be adapted to a legless man by the simple expedient of having the material routed to him. Ingenuity often finds the way to overcome a seeming obstacle.

Tests constitute another tool in the counselor's kit, to assist the client in self-evaluation. For use with the orthopedically handicapped careful selection and administration is required. The usual intelligence tests and most aptitude tests are valueless in the case of persons with cerebral palsy where there is lack of muscular coordination. Similarly, clients with hand disabilities cannot be expected to measure up to established norms in the performance of tests of manipulative skill. Tests should nevertheless be used whenever applicable and as adaptation may be made, as objective measurements of aptitudes and skills or as indications of interests and personality traits.

Personality tests are of special importance in the case of persons with orthopedic handicaps. A physical disability and especially a visibly prominent one invariably has an emotional accompaniment that affects character and behavior. A suitable test will aid in revealing the extent to which the client has accepted the fact of disablement or is still rebellious and embittered. This in addition to the other values of such tests applicable to all cases.

Another tool of the counselor is the "job families" technique. Job analysis indicates the transfer values of certain skills on one job that are usable on another job. Tables of such job relationship are available. This is in conformity with the guidance principle that the client's skills on a former job should be capitalized in any necessary change to another job. Another adaptation of this principle is to raise the job level in the same field of work. A machinist who sustains a disabling hand injury may, assuming necessary qualifications, be trained as a mechanical draftsman; a carpenter with a leg amputation or spinal injury may have the capacity for training as an estimator or building contractor or foreman.

Having aided the client to complete understanding of himself and of his capacities, and having provided the necessary occupational information, the counselor aids the client to decide upon a suitable employment objective. It may be necessary to direct his thinking as to such points as capitalizing former experience, utilizing present skills, developing new skills as indicated by aptitudes and interests, and choosing the best occupation attainable, but the decision should be made by the client.

Job Objectives

Selection of the employment objective in each individual case should be based, as stated above, on an evaluation of the client's vocational assets and of the requirements of the proposed occupation, matching the two factors as nearly as may be possible. This method precludes the use of lists of feasible jobs for specific disabilities except as a source of suggestions. That one man with a double leg amputation is listed as a successful cabinet maker does not mean that another man with identical impairment may succeed in that trade. Conversely, architecture would not appear in any list as suitable for a man with multiple hand-arm-leg-back disabilities, yet at least one such case is on official record. No list should be considered as exhaustive. Of some thirty thousand job titles defined by the *Dictionary of Occupational Titles* (Government Printing Office, Washington, 1939) it is safe to say that fully one-third may represent jobs feasible for persons with some type of orthopedic disability.

Bulletin No. 96 of the Federal Board for Vocational Education entitled *A Study of Occupations at which 6,097 Physically Disabled Persons are Employed after being Vocationally Rehabilitated* (Government Printing Office, Washington, 1925), lists 311 occupations followed by persons with hand disabilities, 368 occupations followed by those with leg disabilities, and somewhat lesser numbers of occupations for those with other disabilities. Dr. Roy N. Anderson in his book *The Disabled Man and His Vocational Adjustment* (Institute for the Crippled and Disabled, New York, 1932), devotes 42 pages to listing types of jobs held by 4,404 orthopedic cases in relation to the specific disability. *The Operations Manual for Placement of the Physically Handicapped* published by the U. S. Civil Service Commission (Government Printing Office, Washington, 1943), contains a consideration of approximately 2,000 positions that could be filled by disabled persons in 105 government establishments and private establishments holding government contracts.

In view of the extremely broad range of possibilities indicated by these citations, the logical and only safe method of job selection is to consider, with the client, *any* occupation within the general range of his interests and abilities and then follow the recognized procedure of matching his capacities and the requirements of the proposed job.

Planning

The counselor works out with the client the details of the individual program of job adjustment. Factors to be considered are the possibility of return to former job or immediate placement on a new job; the possibility of physical restoration to a condition of employability; the need for prosthesis; the need for training; and provision for maintenance during the period of preparation. A definite plan is prepared outlining the services to be rendered, facilities to be used, with estimates of time and costs involved.

Physical Restoration

Many persons with orthopedic handicaps can be rehabilitated by corrective surgery or other therapeutic treatment. The physical condition of others may be so improved by such service that the rehabilitation process is facilitated. Physical restoration should therefore always receive first consideration in accordance with the fundamental principle that it is never advisable to train around a handicap that can be removed. The counselor should have recourse to expert medical advice for interpretation of the necessary specialist's report, approval of the physician's recommendation, and as to the choice of surgeons, hospitals and other facilities. He should, however, be familiar with the details of a medical care program since he is normally responsible, in consultation with technical experts, for planning and arranging the necessary services and for supervision of the client during the restoration process.

Occupational therapy is likewise of special value in orthopedic impairment cases, both as a remedial measure and as an introduction to work. The counselor should not overlook it as a possible means of restoring hope and confidence in an injured person who believes that he is incapable of earning a living. Frequently, through the medium of occupational therapy he finds that he can perform useful functions in spite of his impairment. By prescribing therapy with vocational values the activity may serve as pre-vocational training, and such a course should be followed whenever possible.

Physical therapy is often prescribed by the physician as a part of the treatment following surgery in orthopedic cases, but it may also be useful in itself for loosening joints, developing muscles and restoring functions for work activities.

Prosthesis

Provision of a suitable appliance is often the sole measure needed for the rehabilitation of a person with an orthopedic handicap, although additional services may be required. An orthopedist should be consulted in each instance both for recommendation as to type of brace or artificial limb to be provided and for check to determine proper fitting after the device has been supplied by the manufacturer. The training of the amputee in the use of his appliance, heretofore usually confined to a short period of instruction by the limbmaker, is so important that the counselor should know the details of and how to procure adequate service outlined as follows: The training of the leg amputee is a physical therapy problem and falls into two periods. The first period, before fitting of prosthesis, should begin immediately after surgery. The physical therapist supervises the bed position of each patient to prevent the formation of muscle contractures which will later hamper the achievement of a satisfactory gait. As soon as the stump is healed, exercises are started to further prevent or, if necessary, correct such contractures, and to strengthen the muscles which have been weakened by the amputation. This program is particularly important in the thigh, or above the knee amputation. The second period begins as soon as the client receives his prosthesis and involves training in gait and balance. Ten instruction periods are a minimum requirement. Many below the knee amputations are able to pass a walking test in less than the required ten lessons, but most above the knee amputations will require considerably more than ten. The length of time required is an individual matter depending upon a number of factors including the length of stump, the condition of the surrounding muscles, the existence of secondary injuries and the attitude of the patient. The training of an arm amputation falls into the same two periods, before and after fitting of prosthesis. Since most of the arm prostheses are controlled by a forward and downward motion of the shoulder girdle, it has been found advisable to institute a routine exercise program for arm amputees as soon as the stump is healed. This program includes posture training, and development of the specific muscles which are to control the prosthesis. This again is a physical therapy problem.

As soon as the man is fitted with a prosthesis, occupational therapy is instituted. The physical and psychological adaptation of a man to an artificial arm is complicated by the fact that during the period of treatment and healing of the stump, many arm amputees learn to compensate to a larger extent with the remaining arm, and become fairly self-sufficient. In many cases they are extremely reluctant to give an artificial arm a fair chance, particularly since this arm always seems at first to be heavy and cumbersome.

Training

Insofar as possible the instruction provided should be tailored to meet the individual needs of each client for adequate job preparation in the minimum necessary period of time. The type of training is determined by the particular circumstances of each case. Institutional training is preferred for most cases and particularly the younger group. It has the advantage of organized courses and trained instructors. Employment training is the best method for those who do not fit into the school situation and for those who must work quickly into employment. In the lack of instructional organization the counselor must be prepared to work out with manager or foreman a detailed step-by-step training program, to impart training methods, and to guard against any tendency to subordinate instruction to production. Related technical training may be needed to supplement on-the-job training. Correspondence instruction may be used for that purpose, as well as for providing home instruction when other facilities are not available. Tutorial instruction may be used in lieu of or to supplement either of the other types of training, and particularly the correspondence type which is seldom effective without personal assistance. The best training provision of all is a combination of institutional and employment training, insuring both sound instruction and practical application of the learning in a work setting.

Every training program should include instruction in study methods, personality development, job ethics and job finding methods. If such instruction is not provided by the training facility it is incumbent upon the counselor to provide it as a phase of supervision.

Supervision of the training program must be thorough. It is a phase of the continuous counseling process. It should include a check of the trainee's progress, any necessary adjustment of courses, helping in the solution of any instructional difficulties, inquiry into and aiding the solution of the trainee's personal problems, and counseling for emotional and social adjustment if needed.

Placement

The test of the entire program is successful placement. It should always be made on the basis of merit and ability to do the job. In orthopedic cases placement has the added difficulty of a visible handicap which often increases the employer's reluctance to hire. The counselor can overcome this in most instances by stressing the client's abilities and indicating that his disability does not constitute a handicap for the job in question.

Follow-up is essential for any needed adjustment. Even though a trainee is apparently satisfactorily placed after physical restoration or training or any combination of rehabilitation services, it has been found that further assistance in the vocational adjustment process may be necessary. Where orthopedic difficulties are involved, it may be necessary to suggest and help install special equipment such as high-stools for bench assembly or drafting or special jigs for using with shop machines. Further, it may become the job of the counselor to continue the training on the job as many schools, although proficient in teaching trades, commercial subjects and the like, give no training whatsoever in the factors of job success. The rehabilitation process is not complete until the trainee has demonstrated a reasonable level of proficiency and adjustment to the job.

Self Employment

Establishment in his own business or profession should be considered for some clients. Included are (1) those prepared for the practice of such professions as law, medicine, dentistry, and the like; (2) those with business ability who prefer to work independently; and (3) elderly clients and others not acceptable to employers. The probability of success is far greater in types of business that utilize special skills and production rather than those that involve marketing of goods only. Training in business techniques should supplement technical training for those who plan to enter business or a profession as their own employers. Follow-up and early supervision are necessary services in the rehabilitation of a self-employed individual.

Sheltered Employment

Some clients are so severely handicapped that they cannot compete with normal workers in private industry. Many of this group may, however, be prepared for and enter employment under sheltered conditions. Such employment may also be a satisfactory solution for those not badly crippled but whose handicap is aggravated by mental retardation or emotional instability. Every client placed in sheltered employment should be followed up to determine whether improvement in physical condition, in acquired skill or in emotional balance may make possible subsequent placement in industry.

Psychology of the Orthopedically Handicapped

For effective work with this group thorough understanding on the part of the Counselor of the disabled person's outlook and of the emotional effects of disablement is essential. Emotional adjustment is an important factor in successful rehabilitation. The approach is on the individual basis, since each person differs from all others in this as in other respects. The fact remains that every person is emotionally affected by disability. Some may have made a complete or at least a satisfactory adjustment before contact. This applies particularly to the younger group with congenital defects or who have incurred disability in childhood as the result of poliomyelitis, cerebral palsy, injury or other cause. But even with this group the counselor must be on the lookout for feelings of inferiority and withdrawal tendencies resulting from the child's inability to compete with other children in active sports. Some have been "spoiled" by parental over-indulgence and shielding. Some feel that they are unwanted and shunned or have developed self-pity because of the understandable but unfortunate sentimental reaction of parents to the handicap. Some try to compensate for their defects by the defense mechanism of bragging and "showing off" in order to gain attention. On the other hand, some have become well adjusted by realistic acceptance of the fact of impairment or through the satisfaction of attaining equality or superiority in some respect; e.g. in school work.

With more mature individuals, shock and depression is the natural accompaniment of an injury that results in the sudden loss of a limb or of other disablement. The disability itself is serious but the individual's reaction to it may be even more serious. Insecurity and doubt as to ability to work often result in complete loss of confidence and discouragement.

The remedy is the application of the principles of mental hygiene. The fundamental wants of the disabled person are exactly the same as those of all persons, and his motivations and mental processes are the same. Physical impairment is an added problem that increases the difficulty of satisfying the disabled person's desires, but the counselor aids him to realize that the difficulty is not insurmountable and that it is within his power to attain security, acceptance, approval and recognition that all persons seek. The first step is acceptance of the fact of impairment; the next is realization of ability to work in spite of impairment and that suitable employment is the keystone to normal living. The client is then on the road to emotional adjustment and in a favorable attitude to profit by vocational rehabilitation services.

Other Considerations

The rehabilitation process in its broadest sense should, for the younger group, begin immediately following disablement insofar as remedial treatment, care, education and emotional adjustment are concerned. The vocational phases of the rehabilitation process, however, should be deferred until the disabled child has reached the maximum level of general education it is possible for him to obtain, up to high school graduation. Counseling and pre-vocational training may well be provided in the upper grades, as preliminaries for the vocational preparation to follow. Insofar as possible cure, care, schooling, counseling, pre-vocational and vocational training should be closely coordinated.

For those who incur disablement after reaching maturity, the appropriate vocational rehabilitation services should begin during the convalescent period if possible and in any event immediately following discharge. Any period of insecurity allowed to intervene tends to lower morale and make rehabilitation more difficult. Prompt rehabilitation service is at once an excellent therapeutic medium, an aid to emotional adjustment and the basis for satisfactory vocational adjustment.

H. D. H.

OSTEOPATHY, APTITUDE FOR.   Osteopathy is a complete system of therapeutics, emphasizing manipulation in the treatment of disease. The Osteopathic profession recognizes the bacterial, chemical, nervous and psychic, as well as mechanical cause of abnormal function.

The Osteopathic physician advocates and uses all modern scientific methods and apparatus of diagnosis and treatment. The usual medical specialties are practiced within the profession.

There are six schools of Osteopathic Medicine in the United States. These schools are: Chicago College of Osteopathy, Chicago, Ill.; College of Osteopathic Physicians and Surgeons, Los Angeles, Calif.; Des Moines Still College of Osteopathy, Des Moines, Iowa; Kansas City College of Osteopathy and Surgery, Kansas City, Mo.; Kirksville College of Osteopathy and Surgery, Kirksville, Mo.; Philadelphia College of Osteopathy, Philadelphia, Pa.

While all six of the schools do not use the same techniques for student selection, a survey of these schools has been made and the following basic criteria are set forth for the guidance worker to use in his counseling of students:

Abilities in General

In the first four fields the standards for the student in Osteopathy are the same as in any other school of medicine.

Physical: Good health is of primary importance.

Mental: One must be above average in intelligence and must possess a scientific mind.

Social: One should have an inexhaustible fund of good cheer and optimism, tolerance and sympathetic understanding.

Moral: Trustworthiness is essential.

Manual Dexterity: Should be good because of type of treatment of the general practitioner as well as in other specialties. (This is of far greater importance in the Osteopathic than in other medical students.)

In addition these people should have a burning desire to be doctors.

As was stated before, all schools do not use the same techniques for student selection; however, there has been some research work done by some of the schools in the use of standardized tests for this purpose. From the studies that have been made, and from various practices used, the following battery of standardized tests is suggested to the guidance worker for his use in the counseling of prospective osteopathic students.

The Strong Vocational Interest blank scored for the occupation Osteopathic Physician and Surgeon, using scales which were constructed by Dr. E. K. Strong, Jr., of Stanford University or the Kuder Preference Record, may be used. In addition to one or the other of these interest inventories the following test battery is suggested:

Ohio State Psychological Test, The Minnesota Test for Mechanical Ability, The Personal Audit, The Chicago Test of Clerical Promise, and The Purdue Pegboard Test of Manipulative Dexterity.*

This battery of tests gives a very good profile of interests and the six abilities used in classifying an occupation.

The interest ratings from either of the interest inventories plus the six abilities, measured by the test battery, are essential to the osteopathic student in varying degrees. (At present, the Osteopathic physician is rated exactly the same as the Allopathic physician in selective ratings.) A definition of the six abilities and the grades suggested for the osteopathic physician are:

1. *Academic.* The ability to understand and manage ideas and symbols.—Grade "A."
2. *Mechanical Ability.* Includes both the ability to manipulate concrete objects, work with tools and machinery and mate-

* Can be secured through Science Research Associates, Chicago, Ill.

rials of the physical world, and the ability to deal with mechanical movements.—Grade "B."

3. *Social Intelligence.* The ability to understand and manage people; to act wisely in human relations.—Grade "B."

4. *Clerical Ability.* The ability to do rapidly and accurately detail work such as checking, measuring, computing, classifying, recording and similar activities.—Grade "C."

5. *Musical Talent.*—Requires the capacity to sense sounds, to image these sounds in reproductive or creative imagination. To be capable of sustained thinking in terms of these experiences.—Grade "D."

6. *Artistic Ability.* The capacity to create forms of artistic merit and the capacity to recognize the comparative merits of forms already created.—Grade "D"; or the so-called Pattern 3 of the Minnesota Occupational Rating Scale which pattern includes only the oculist, the osteopathic physician and the allopathic physician.

The test battery and suggested grades plus teacher evaluations of individuals should be used by the guidance worker for the purpose of screening.

The next step in the counseling procedure is that of determining entrance requirements to a particular school of osteopathy. The procedure in this is the use of college catalogues from these specific schools. Therefore, the counselor should have on file up-to-date catalogues from each of the specific schools in order to have accurate information concerning entrance requirements for each school.

It is suggested that the counselor have prospective students contact practicing osteopathic physicians in the community for conferences concerning the practice and procedures used by the physician; also that the following occupational literature be available for the use of students:

American Osteopathic Association. *Abstract of Laws Governing the Practice of Osteopathy.* American Osteopathic Association, Chicago, Ill., 1943.

——. *Osteopathy as a Profession.* American Osteopathic Association, Chicago, Ill., 1940.

——. *Osteopathy Questions and Answers.* American Osteopathic Association, Chicago, Ill., 1940.

——. *Women in Osteopathy.* American Osteopathic Association, Chicago, Ill., 1942.

Carey, Robert E., *Osteopathy as a Career.* New York State Osteopathic Society, 64 Ludlow Street, Yonkers, N. Y., 1942.

Greenleaf, Walter J., *Osteopathy, Leaflet No. 23*. U. S. Government Printing Office, Washington, D. C., 1944.

Shade, Chloris, *Osteopathy, Bulletin No. 56*. Morgan and Dillon Co., Chicago, Ill., 1940.

Thorburn, Dr. Thomas, *Osteopathy*. Bellman Publishing Co., Boston, Mass., 1941.

R. E. C.

P

PALESTINE. Although Palestine is an ancient land, modern Palestine is a pioneering country. The industrial development of Palestine and the scientific development of its agriculture, in modern times, began with the Jewish efforts to develop the country in consequence of the declaration made by Lord James Balfour, British Colonial Minister during the First World War, which pledged the establishment of Palestine as a Jewish National Home. While these developments have led to the organization of vocational curricula, almost exclusively under Jewish auspices, on the elementary, secondary and higher levels, and several vocational guidance and testing bureaus have been established, the guidance stage on a broad level has not as yet been reached.

Several factors have contributed to this situation. The Arab population has, by and large, continued its established way of life, which is patriarchal and in the main rural, with a limited town life and a low regard for labor. The Jewish population, which has grown from 60,000 immediately after the First World War to approximately 600,000 at the present time, on the other hand, consists predominately of immigrants who either acquired specific industrial or agricultural training for work in Palestine in the countries of their origin, or continued in Palestine their previous occupations. Then, too, the industrial and agricultural development of Palestine has been of such dimensions, as to leave no reserve of essential manpower. From 1922 to 1940–41, the number of industrial enterprises increased from 1850 to 6143, the number of industrial workers from 4,750 to 45,000, production from £P 500,000 to £P 15,000,000, and the invested capital from £P 600,000 to £P 15,000,000. The consumption of electric current for industrial purposes, rose from 1,427,475 kwh in 1926 to 35,830,000 kwh in 1940. In 1918, there were 43 Jewish settlements in Palestine with a total area of 421,000 dunams, and a Jewish rural population of 12,000. In 1940 there were 257 Jewish settlements in Palestine with a total area of 1,570,000 dunams and a Jewish rural population of 142,000. The available facilities for vocational training, therefore, have not been adequate for the meeting of existing needs. Such criteria, as prevail for the admission to vocational training have been of a qualifying rather than a selective nature.

Palestine's economy, moreover, has not as yet become a competing one to a point of necessitating quality training and a concern for production rates. Should this occur, the problem of the conservation and direction of human resources—in brief, vocational guidance—would become correspondingly important.

References:

1. Epstein, S. Vocational training as an economic problem. Zionist Organization, Youth Department, Information Service, January, 1944, 7–10.
2. Hartstein, J. I. Education in Palestine, in *Encyclopedia of modern education*. Edited by H. N. Rivlin and H. Schueler. New York: The Philosophical Library, 1943.
3. Hamekasher (Organ of the Palestine Contacts Office of the Habomin Movements), Rosh Pina, Palestine, Vol. IV, No. 5, September, 1944.
4. Kamievesky, I. Habituach Ha-soziali B'eretz Yisroel. Tel Aviv, 1942.
5. Nardi, N. *Education in Palestine, 1920–1945*. New York: Zionist Organization of America, 1945.
6. Stewart, W. A. Vocational training in Palestine. Palestine Post, December 14, 1942.

J. I. H.

PARENTS. More vocational guidance has probably been given to young persons by their parents than by all other classes of adults. No other adult is likely to have a more sincere interest in the success of a young person than his or her own father or mother. Parents are usually in the best possible situation to offer guidance to their children, and the home is the ideal place for guidance to be given. But many parents fail to provide their children with effective guidance, and an increasingly large number of young people find it necessary to seek guidance outside their homes.

Parents normally have an opportunity to know more about a young person's true characteristics than others, for they are intimately associated with him or her from infancy to early maturity. All too often, however, the parent does not know what characteristics to look for, nor how to interpret correctly the child's daily behavior. Perhaps the greatest handicap of a parent in giving guidance to a son or daughter is parental pride and affection, which frequently tend either to blind the parent to the child's deficiencies or to exaggerate grossly the child's minor deviations from those types of behavior which the parent would like to see. The strong emotions aroused in a parent by the words and actions of his or her own child frequently make it impossible to analyze a situation objectively. Intelligent guidance must be based upon facts regarding the individual's true characteristics, and anyone whose observation is dulled or distorted by strong emotion finds it difficult to recognize the true facts.

Another handicap of the average parent is that he or she does not know very much about the specific combinations of characteristics that are actually most helpful to successful persons in the various occupations. Even the best informed occupational-information experts do not know very much about the real requirements in many kinds of work, for the amount of careful research that has been done on these matters is distressingly inadequate. The average father could probably tell his son something about the requirements for his own job, and perhaps for a half-dozen other types of employment, but much of what he would say is likely to be general in character and not especially accurate. Parents cannot be expected to prepare themselves to give extensive occupational information in many different fields, nor even to know the names of the books, reports, and other sources from which to obtain the facts that are known. The industrial developments of the past century have narrowed tremendously the range of occupational information possessed by the average parent, and it would be unwise to ask him or her to spend the time necessary to increase that range very much merely in order to provide vocational guidance to two or three children. Every prospective parent should, however, be taught while still a student in high school how to identify an expert in the field of occupational information and guidance, as well as how to choose experts in such other important fields as law, dentistry, and medicine.

Although most parents are not as well qualified as professional guidance counselors should be, no counselor should neglect to inform himself regarding the relationships between a young client and his parents, and to estimate the probable influence of those relationships upon the client's behavior. In some instances it may be desirable to talk at length with one or both parents regarding their child's vocational problem, while in other cases such conversations might be most unfortunate. A wise counselor will size up beforehand the probabilities with regard to a parent's reactions and will avoid making frequent mistakes in this matter.

Perhaps the most tragic cases that come to the guidance worker's attention are men and women who have been dominated throughout their lives by a possessive, strong-willed parent. Many mothers have never really "weaned" themselves from their children. It seems impossible to one of these women that her child has a mind that has matured to such a degree that it is capable of making sound judgments and choices. Such a parent is always confident that she is acting for the best interests of her child, and she is almost certain to resent deeply any efforts by an outsider to encourage the "child" to think, to choose, or to act independently. In some situations of this type the counselor may be able, either personally or through some close friend of the parent, to develop in the parent's mind a clearer understanding of the real facts. In other cases there is relatively little that can be done with such a parent, even by a skillful psychiatrist, to break the strangle-hold of the parent on the child. An experienced counselor may sometimes be able to help the "child" of such a parent to understand more fully the natural source of the parent's abnormal behavior, and this better understanding may enable the victim to gently but firmly loosen the bonds which the parent has forged, or at least to endure them with less pain and resentment.

One of the false ideas that lead many parents to misunderstand and misguide their children is the belief that the child possesses exactly the same interests, abilities, and ambitions as the parent possessed in earlier years. Many a man has spent his life unhappily in an inappropriate occupation because his father had always wanted to work in that field but had been prevented by circumstances from doing so. It might possibly give satisfaction to a farmer, who had always wanted to be a doctor, for example, to see his son studying and later practicing medicine; but unless the son has most of the varied characteristics actually needed by a doctor, including a strong desire to practice medicine, he may be very unhappy in his work, irritable and dictatorial in his home, and generally unpleasant in his relations with patients and the public. Counselors should help parents to understand that children often differ from their parents, and that each human being should have an opportunity to choose his own vocation in the light of all the facts obtainable.

Another false idea that counselors should do everything they possibly can to break down is the notion that certain occupations are "superior" to others. Teachers have frequently been guilty of spreading this idea among their students by such remarks as, "You don't want to be only a farmer, do you?" or: "Don't stop going to school to get married. Make something worthwhile of your life." The notion that it is "better" to be a lawyer than to be a garage mechanic, for example, leads many parents to give their sons a type of misguidance that is most unfortunate for society as well as for the young men to whom it is given. Counselors must help everyone to understand that, so long as an occupation is one that is really needed in a modern community, one job is superior to another only in terms of the qualifications of the worker. If Mary Jones has the interests, abilities, and attitudes needed by a successful housewife, but does not have those needed by a successful stenographer, then being a housewife is the "superior" vocation for her. A particular job is "inferior" to another only when the individual doing it is less competent in performing it than he would be in performing the other, or when an individual who is equally fitted for the two tasks chooses to work at the one which is less urgently needed by the community.

Still another important fact which counselors should impress upon parents is that there is no single index to the vocation into which a young person should plan to go. Neither intelligence tests nor interest tests nor any other single index should be considered as finally indicative of the occupational field or type or work to be chosen. The whole pattern of the individual's abilities, interests, previous experiences and personality traits must be carefully considered in the light of the actual requirements of various kinds of useful work and of the world's relative needs for workers in various fields. Furthermore, the needs for different kinds of work and the requirements for success in the various vocations are constantly being modified by new conditions resulting from technology and invention. The intelligent choice a youth makes of a vocation in college may in a few years need to be changed. The guidance received by a youth, in studying his own qualifications and the requirements of occupations that make use of such qualifications, should enable him later to turn his efforts to other appropriate occupations with little loss of efficiency and satisfaction.

The most vicious use of single indices occurs when astrologers, palmists, and other fakirs are called upon by young people for aid in deciding upon a vocation. Parents should be enlisted to help eliminate from the community all such fortune-tellers and frauds. In both public and private contacts with parents, professional vocational counselors should make it clear that guidance is not fortune telling, but that it is education of an individual to understand his own qualifications in the light of the actual needs of the world of work and thereby to make his own vocational choices intelligently. Those who tell one what to do in life on the basis of an examination of tea leaves, bumps on the head, facial contours, or other magic indices are only a little more fraudulent than those who undertake to tell the same thing from examining a paper and pencil test (sent by mail for one dollar). Parents must be taught that guidance is an educational process by which the individual is helped to make intelligent decisions for himself rather than a seance during which a fortune teller pretends to reveal one's fate in return for a given number of pieces of silver.

M. R. T.

PERCENTILE RANK.   The percentile rank of an individual on a given test is the relative position on a scale of 100 to which his test score entitles him. If, for example, a subject's score corresponds to a percentile rank of 87, he stands eighty-seventh in a group of 100—that is, he excels 87% of the members of the group with which he is being compared.

Percentile rank offers a simple and ready means of interpreting performance and of defining the relative position of a member of a group with respect to the whole group. It provides a method whereby direct comparison can be made of the performances of individuals upon tests scored in different units. The method of percentile scaling has therefore been widely applied in the standardization of educational and psychological tests. A percentile scale specifies the score or level of achievement which each percent of the population failed to attain. By referring an individual's score to the percentile scale prepared for the group on which the test was standardized (i.e. to the table of norms expressed in terms of percentiles, also called percentile ranks, or centiles) it is possible to tell what percentage of the population did no better than the person whose score is to be interpreted. Often, only a table of deciles, showing the score equaled or exceeded by the top ten percent of the persons in the group tested, the score equaled or exceeded by the next ten percent, etc., is presented. In still other cases, percentiles are given only for scores in the top and lowest deciles, with deciles throughout the rest of the range.

One serious defect in percentile scales is that the units are not equal throughout the range, those at the extremes being much larger than the ones near the middle. The difference in ability between individuals obtaining percentile ranks of 5 and 10 on a given test, for example, is considerably greater than the difference between individuals with percentile ranks of 55 and 60. This follows from the fact that the distribution of measurements of most mental and social traits tends to be normal, people with average or moderate abilities being relatively numerous, whereas those at the extremes of the scale are few. This inequality of units should be kept clearly in mind when comparing the percentile ranks of two or more individuals on the same test or of a single individual on two or more tests. It also precludes the averaging of percentile ranks except in the range Q_1–Q_3, where the inequalities between units on a percentile scale are fairly small.

References:

1. Bingham, W. V. D. *Aptitudes and aptitude testing.* New York and London: Harper and Bros., 1937.
2. Garrett, H. E. *Statistics in psychology and education.* New York: Longmans, Green and Co., 1941.

I. C.

PERSONALITY AND ADJUSTMENT INVENTORIES

Adams-Lepley Personal Audit. The Adams Lepley Personal Audit is an inventory-type of questionnaire purporting to measure the nine bipolar traits described below. For each trait is given the name assigned by the authors and a sample item answered as keyed for the last-named extreme of the trait.

    I. Seriousness—Impulsiveness
       Raising money for charity—"would like it a great deal."
    II. Firmness—Indecision
       "States' rights" have little place in a democracy—"agree with the experts that the statement is true."
    III. Tranquillity—Irritability
       To miss a streetcar or bus—"it annoys me much."
    IV. Frankness—Evasion
       Rich people are often very "snooty"—"true."
    V. Stability—Instability
       Being trapped in a burning building—"usually have considerable fear."
    VI. Tolerance—Intolerance
       People who are chiselers—"dislike a great deal."
    VII. Steadiness—Emotionality
       Past: yesterday forget sorrow *hidden.*
    VIII. Persistence—Fluctuation
       Old age pensions—"feel different now than three years ago."
    IX. Contentment—Worry
       Divorce—"have done much thinking about it during the past year."

The trait names do not clearly bear a face relationship to the test. Other evidence of the meaning is to be preferred to face relationship; however, where both types of evidence are lacking, meaning is not given the trait by naming it. The fifty items measuring each trait were selected from an original sixty by item analysis against total score on the trait; each item was also cross-analyzed against other traits showing correlation coefficients above .30 with the initial trait, with selection on the basis of high internal, low external critical ratios. The items are arranged in order of descending critical ratios. Despite selection to reduce intercorrelation among the traits, coefficients of intercorrelation based on 442 college students show values of .56 for III and VI, .45 for III and V, .33 for V and VI, .30 for V and IX as well as for VI and IX. The only other coefficient of .30 or more is for II and IV (.37). Apparently traits III, V, VI, and IX form an interrelated complex. Discounting these correlations, the authors report in the Manual that "the nine parts do *not* overlap one another to any appreciable extent. Instead, nine relatively independent factors are measured."

The consensus of thirty psychologists, twelve of whom had used the scale "coincided with the descriptions which have been prepared for each trait." There is, however, no reference to definitions of the judgment called for nor to the way in which coincidence with the descriptions was determined.

Nine teachers and four upper class students were asked to identify high school students who represented extremes on twelve traits. "Although the differences found were small, they tended to support the descriptions of Audit traits as tentatively given in the Manual." There is no indication in the Manual that the differences were statistically significant; since "in no case was the number at each trait extreme less than 5, on most traits the number was 20 to 40," and the differences were small, statistical significance is doubtful.

The nine traits, studied in relation to the factors STDCR of the Guilford Inventory show nine correlations with absolute magnitude greater than .30 and eight more significant at the 1 per cent level. Correlations with Guilford-Martin Inventory I, Strong Vocational Interest Blank, Bernreuter Personality Inventory and the Allport-Vernon-Ascendance-Submission Scale are also reported. Although the authors report that "the cycloidal person . . . tends to score *low* on all Audit traits," three of the nine coefficients on which this conclusion is based are not different from zero at the 1 per cent level and only two are above .30.

Each trait is rather elaborately "interpreted" although little evidence is reported in the Manual to support the interpretations. Moreover, some fifteen patterns of traits are given ranging from "undesirable score patterns" through "delinquent persons" to patterns for "military" and "industrial leadership." The evidence for these pattern interpretations is not given in the Manual and is presumably contained in the unpublished master's theses at Pennsylvania State College. Except for three journal articles and six earlier versions of the Manual, these six unpublished studies are the only references given.

The scales show Spearman-Brown reliability coefficients of .90 or above. Norms are given by sex for high school students, college freshmen, a general college group, business and industrial groups and general adult norms. Scoring is extremely simple.

In summary we quote from the Manual, "The interpretation of the measurement involves the integration of the separate traits into a meaningful composite. Measurement is simple; interpretation requires skill." The interpretations of both made of both traits and patterns, however, are often not supported by a reference to the evidence on which they are based and when the evidence is presented, it is consistent with a number of other interpretations than the one offered.

The test is published by Science Research Associate, 228 South Wabash Avenue, Chicago 4, Illinois.

                                                        C. I. M.

Allport-Vernon Study of Values.   The *Study of Values,* constructed by G. W. Allport and P. E. Vernon, attempts to measure "the relative prominence of six basic interests or motives in personality: the *theoretical, economic, aesthetic, social, political,* and *religious*" [1] (p. 3). The classification of types is taken from Eduard Spranger.[4] The values, or evaluative attitudes, measured may be described as follows: (1) the *theoretical,* or interest in the discovery of truth (characteristic of the intellectualist, especially the scientist or the philosopher); (2) the *economic,* or interest in the useful (characteristic of the business man); (3) the *aesthetic,* or interest in form and harmony (characteristic of the artist); (4) the *social,* or interest in, and love of, people (characteristic of the philanthropist); (5) the *political,* or interest in power and prestige (characteristic of leaders in politics or other fields); (6) the *religious,* or desire for comprehension of, and unity with, the cosmos as a whole (characteristic of the mystic).

The scale consists of a number of questions based upon familiar situations, the alternative answers to which provide choices between two or more of the values listed above. The score of an individual, therefore, indicates his *order of preference* of values, not the "absolute" degree to which any given value is held. [For a discussion of this feature of the scale, see (3), pp. 606–607].

The test is self-administering. No time limit is set; most subjects require about twenty minutes to answer the questions. It is suitable for use with either sex, and may be taken individually or in a group. Since bias may affect the subject's scores, it is undesirable for him to understand in advance the significance of the questions he is to answer.

Original norms for the six values, based on tests of 800 college students and adults of both sexes, have been confirmed by several hundred additional scores derived from a wide variety of groups.[2] Consistent sex differences appear; men score relatively higher on theoretical, economic, and political values, and women on aesthetic, social, and religious values.[2]

The validity of the test is best demonstrated by examination of the test scores of groups whose interests are known. The expectation of common sense is confirmed in the test scores of different occupational groups, of individuals who score differently on the Strong Vocational Interest Blank, of students in different colleges, of students in different fields of study within the same college, and of men and women.[2, 3] Correlations with ratings have ranged from +.45 to +.59 (+.83 if corrected for attenuation). Agreement between ratings and test scores is no doubt reduced by the fact that, in the case of these six values, most raters fail to understand adequately the nature of the characteristic which they are rating.

A reliability coefficient of + .72 (based on scores of 776 subjects) was obtained by a method which is said to give results almost identical with those obtained by the ordinary split-half method.[5] Repeat-reliability for the six values (based on scores of 84 subjects on two occasions 100 days apart) are as follows: religious, .87; aesthetic, .86; economic, .79; political, .76; theoretical, .68; social, .50.[6] The religious and the aesthetic values are the most satisfactorily measured. That the social value is *not* measured satisfactorily is indicated by evidence from many sources.[2]

The demonstrated relationship between the test profile on the one hand and vocational and academic interests on the other, points to the fact that the *Study of Values* may be of use in vocational and academic guidance. Two review articles summarize, through 1939, the investigations in which this test has been employed.[2, 3]

A revision of the Allport-Vernon test, designed to make it suitable for high school students, has been prepared by Rothney.[3] The reliability of this test, however, is not so high as that of the original scale. Other tests which are designed to measure some or all of Spranger's six categories of value have been prepared by Lurie, by Van Dusen, Wimberly, and Mosier, and by Maller and Glaser.[3]

The publisher of the Allport-Vernon *Study of Values* is Houghton Mifflin Company, Boston, Massachusetts.

References:

1. Allport, G. W. and Vernon, P. E. A study of values. Manual of Directions (Revised ed.). Boston: Houghton Mifflin, 1931.
2. Cantril, H. and Allport, G. W. Recent applications of the *Study of Values. J. abnorm. soc. Psychol.*, 1933–1934, 28, 259–273.
3. Duffy, E. A critical review of investigations employing the Allport-Vernon *Study of Values* and other tests of evaluative attitude. *Psychol. Bull.*, 1940, 37, 597–612.
4. Spranger, E. Lebensformen (3rd ed.). Halle: Niemeyer, 1922; Types of men. (Trans. by P. J. W. Pigors.) New York: Stechert, 1928.
5. Vernon, P. E. and Allport, G. W. A test for personal values. *J. abnorm. soc. Psychol.*, 1931–1932, 26, 231–248.
6. Whitely, P. L. A study of the Allport-Vernon test for personal values. *J. Abnorm. soc. Psychol.*, 1933, 28, 4–13.

E. D.

Aspects of Personality. *Aspects of Personality* by Rudolf Pintner, Professor of Education, Teachers' College, Columbia University; John J. Loftus, Assistant Superintendent in Charge of Curriculum, Division of Elementary Schools, Board of Education of the City of New York; George Forlano, Assistant in Educational Psychology, Teachers' College, Columbia University; and Benjamin Alster, teacher, Public Schools, New York, is a personality test of the inventory type particularly suitable for grades 4–9 in the elementary and junior high school. The inventory consists of three sections:

Section I contains 35 items and provides a measure of *ascendance and submission*

Section II contains 35 items and affords a measure of *introversion and extroversion*

Section III contains 35 items plus 9 items which are non-significant, designed to give a measure of *emotional stability*

This inventory has several uses.

The test has been carefully checked for validity and reliability. The diction and sentence structure have been adapted to the needs of fourth year children. In safeguarding internal consistency each test item was correlated with the total score of the section of which it is a part. The Clark Item value technic and the Pearson Bi-serial r were used for this purpose. Only items which had an item value of .15 or more and a Bi-serial r of .30, .40, or .50 were included. Each item was then correlated against each of the totals of the other two sections. Each item finally included had to have a high correlation with the total score of its own section and a low correlation with the total score of each of the other two sections of the test.

Percentile norms are set up separately for grades 4, 5, and 6, and for grades 7, 8, and 9. A percentile score of 25 or less in any section indicates that a pupil falls in the lowest quarter of children in general on that section of the test. A very low score in Ascendance-Submission indicates a submissive retiring type of child who is not likely to succeed as a leader but is probably a docile follower. His attitude may be due to repression at home or to undesirable feelings of real or imaginary inferiority. In general, such a child needs opportunities for success.

Children with low percentile scores in Extroversion-Introversion presumably are too much turned in on themselves, withdrawn too much from the world, and tend too much to worry or daydream. They dodge responsibilities of the real world. They miss many of the normal satisfactions of life.

Section III provides useful clues as to the emotional problems of children.

The inventory is significant for vocational education:

1. It provides a controlled interview in regard to crucial personality factors that are related to social and self-adjustment.

2. The results of this test in conjunction with the results of tests of interest, intelligence and aptitude serve as objective evidence upon which a more adequate counseling program may be developed.

3. When employed at grade levels at or above the eighth grade it can be employed by the teacher as a means of stimulating discussions on personality differences and their implication for vocational and educational adjustment, especially in terms of ability to get along with others, in school, at work, in the home, or elsewhere.

4. It helps the teacher to understand the three aspects of personality of each pupil. When administered early in the

school year it gives the teacher a preview of three important aspects of personality of each pupil. The personality descriptions may suggest possible leaders, possible disciplinary cases, and possible emotional problem cases.

5. It furnishes a basis for recommending pupils for psychiatric advice. It may save a great deal of time for the psychological, psychiatric, or social worker.

6. The test can serve as a measuring instrument for survey, evaluation, and research purposes.

Aspects of Personality is published by the World Book Company, Yonkers, New York.

J. J. L.

Beckman's Revision of the A-S Reaction Study for Business Use. This is R. O. Beckman's adaptation of the Allport and Allport questionnaire for use with business personnel. It follows the general structure of the original and has the same purposes. The manual gives suggestions concerning the administration of the test and its usefulness in vocational guidance, selection and placement. Norms are given for 350 cases. A table comparing the scores of various groups such as managers of stores, field salesmen, junior executives, etc., is given.

This test is published by the Psychological Corporation, 522 Fifth Avenue, New York City.

H. S.

Bell Adjustment Inventory. The Adjustment Inventory, constructed by Hugh M. Bell, is published in two forms: the Student Form for use with individuals of high school and college ages; and the Adult Form for use with persons who are not attending school nor living with their parents. The Student Form provides measurements of adjustment in four areas: home life, health, social relationships, and emotional stability. The Adult Form provides measures of home, health, social and emotional adjustment, and in addition, occupational adjustment.

Both the Student and the Adult Forms have been developed to be used primarily in personal counseling and not as research tools. The scores on the various categories of the inventories and the answers to the specific questions within each category provide the counselor with information on the individual's personal and social adjustment which can be of assistance in helping the counselee find solutions to his adjustment problems.

The Adjustment Inventory is practically self-administering. Specific instructions appear on the blank which should be read aloud by the examiner. There is no time limit for the Inventories, but ordinarily not more than twenty-five minutes are required for the Student Form and thirty minutes for the Adult Form. Both forms of the Inventory are suitable for use with either sex.

The Student Form has been standardized on both high school and college groups and separate norms obtained from schools and colleges in the United States are available for men and women in each group.[3] Norms for the Adult Form were obtained from extension classes and counseling centers in various sections of the United States. Separate norms for each sex are provided.[3] It is recommended that the norms in the manuals be considered tentative and that local norms be established as soon as feasible.

For the Student Form, studies of the reliability of the various sections has been made by Traxler,[25] Tyler,[27] Turney and Fee,[26] and the author.[3] Table I is a summary of the coefficients of reliability as obtained by these studies. All the coefficients were determined by correlating the odd versus the even items and applying the Spearman-Brown formula, except the retest coefficients of Turney and Fee.

Table I. Comparison of the Reliability Coefficients on the Bell Adjustment Inventory. Student Form.

| Scale | Traxler | Tyler | | Turney & Fee * | Bell |
		Men	Women		
Home Adjustment	.84	.80	.83	.85	.89
Health Adjustment	.83	.72	.80	.74	.80
Social Adjustment	.93	.85	.88	.83	.89
Emotional Adjustment	.88	.79	.84	.79	.85
Total Score	.90	.90	.91	.82	.93

* Retest Coefficients.

The median coefficients are: Home Adjustment, .84; Health Adjustment, .80; Social Adjustment, .88; Emotional Adjustment, .84; and Total Score, .90.

The reliability coefficients, determined by the split-half method and the Spearman-Brown formula, for the five sections and the Total Score of the Adult Form are as follows: Home Adjustment, .91; Health Adjustment, .81; Social Adjustment, .88; Emotional Adjustment, .91; Occupational Adjustment, .85; and Total Score, .94.[3]

Each section of the Student Form and the Adult Form was validated through an item analysis to determine the degree to which each question differentiated between the upper and the lower fifteen per cent of the individuals in a distribution of scores. Only those items which clearly differentiated between these extreme groups were retained for the final forms.

The various sections of both forms of the Inventory were further validated through the selection of individuals who in the judgment of expert counselors were well-adjusted or poorly adjusted * in the different areas of adjustment surveyed by the inventories, and determining the degree to which the inventories discriminated between the two groups in each category. The results of such analysis indicated satisfactory agreement between the judgment of the counselors and scores on the different sections of the inventories.[3]

Studies of the validity of the Student Form in which the judgments of teachers and counselors were correlated or compared with adjustment status as measured by the Adjustment Inventory have resulted in findings some of which questioned the validity of the test and others which supported it.[5, 9, 14, 17, 22, 26]

Other studies of the Student Form have indicated that none of the sections of the Inventory is successful in predicting academic success or failure,[12, 9, 15] Other investigations have been concerned with the use of the Student Form in the prediction of success or failure in public speaking;[10, 13] in seeking to differentiate between Jewish and non-Jewish students;[24] in the selection of radio tube mounters in an industrial plant;[11] in studying the bi-linguality of youth;[23] in determining the relationship between good and poor home adjustment and other aspects of personality;[28] and in distinguishing between delinquents and non-delinquents.[16, 3]

* In the case of the Social Adjustment sections of both Forms, the differentiation was made between Aggressiveness and Timidity rather than in terms of Good or Poor social adjustment.

The Student Form has been administered to various groups in Scotland [20] in which results were obtained comparable to those secured in America. Recently this form of the Inventory was translated into French for use with French-Canadian students, and into Spanish for use in the schools of Mexico. Recently, the Inventory has been adapted to Braille for use with the blind.

The publisher of both the Student and the Adult Forms of the Adjustment Inventory is the Stanford University Press, Stanford University, California.

References:

1. Altus, W. D. and Bell, H. M. The validity of certain measures of maladjustment in an Army Special Training Center. Psychological Bulletin, 1945, 42, 98–103.
2. Bell, H. M. The Adjustment Inventory, manual of directions, and norms. (Student Form) 1934, (Adult Form) 1937.
3. ———. *The theory and practice of personal counseling.* (Revised) Stanford University Press: Stanford University, California, 1939.
4. Buros, O. K. *The 1940 mental measurement yearbook.* Highland Park, New Jersey: 1941, Sec. 1200, 1252.
5. Clark, W. A. and Smith, L. F. Further evidence of the validity of personality inventories. Journal of Educational Psychology, 1942, 33, 81–91.
6. Darley, J. G. Tested maladjustment related to clinically diagnosed maladjustment. Journal of Applied Psychology, 1937, 21, 632–42.
7. ———. Changes in measured attitude and adjustments. Journal of Social Psychology, 1938, 9, 189–199.
8. ———. A preliminary study of relations between attitude, adjustment and vocational interest. Journal of Educational Psychology, 1938, 29, 467–473.
9. Drought, N. E. An analysis of eight measures of personality and adjustment in relation to relative scholastic achievement. Journal of Applied Psychology, 1938, 22, 597–606.
10. Eckert, R. and Keys, N. Public speaking as a cue to personality adjustment. Journal of Applied Psychology, 1939, 24, 144–153.
11. Farlano, G. and Kirkpatrick, F. H. Intelligence and adjustment measurement in the selection of radio tube mounters. Journal of Applied Psychology, 1945, 29, 257–261.
12. Feder, D. and Mallet, D. R. Validity of certain measures of personality adjustment. Journal of American Association of Registrars, 1937, 13, 5–15.
13. Gilkinson, H. and Knower, F. H. A study of standardized personality tests and skill in speech. Journal of Educational Psychology, 1941, 32, 161–175.
14. Greene, J. E. and Staton, T. F. Predictive value of various tests of emotionality and adjustment in a guidance program for prospective teachers. Journal of Educational Research, 1939, 32, 653–659.

15. Griffith, G. R. The relations between scholastic achievement and personality adjustment of men college students. Journal of Applied Psychology, 1945, 29, 360–367.

16. Keys, N. and Guilford, M. Validity of certain adjustment inventories in predicting problem behavior. Journal of Educational psychology, 1937, 28, 641–655.

17. Marsh, C. J. The diagnostic value of the Bell Adjustment Inventory. Journal of Social Psychology, 1943, 17, 103–109.

18. McNamara, W. J. and Darley, J. G. A factor analysis of retest performance in attitude and adjustment tests. Journal of Educational Psychology, 1938, 29, 652–664.

19. Pallister, H. American psychologists judge fifty-three vocational tests. Journal of Applied Psychology, 1936, 20, 761–768.

20. Pallister, H. and Pierce, W. O. D. A comparison of Bell Adjustment Scores for American and Scottish groups. Sociometry, 1937, 2, 54–72.

21. Paterson, D. G.; Schneidler, G.; Williamson, E. G. *Student guidance techniques.* New York: McGraw-Hill, 1938, pp. 185–189.

22. Pederson, R. A. Validity of the Bell Adjustment Inventory when applied to college women. Journal of Psychology, 1940, 9, 227–36.

23. Sproel, D. T. Bilinguality and emotional adjustment. Journal of Abnormal and Social Psychology, 1943, 38, 37–57.

24. Sukov, M. and Williamson, E. G. Personality traits and attitudes of Jewish and non-Jewish students. Journal of Applied Psychology, 1938, 22, 487–492.

25. Traxler, A. E. The reliability of the Bell Inventories and their correlation with teachers' judgments. Journal of Applied Psychology, 1941, 25, 672–678.

26. Turney, A. H. and Fee, M. An attempt to use the Bell Adjustment Inventory for high school guidance. School Review, 1936, 44, 193–198.

27. Tyler, H. T. Evaluating the Bell Adjustment Inventory. Junior College Journal, 1936, 6, 353–357.

28. Woolf, M. D. A study of some relationships between home adjustment and the behavior of junior college students. Journal of Social Psychology, 1943, 17, 275–286.

H. M. B.

Bell School Inventory.   This inventory, consisting of 76 items concerned with the student's attitude toward his teachers, fellow-students, and the administration of his high school, was constructed by Hugh M. Bell. It is designed for senior high school students who have attended the school where the test is being given at least three months. The purpose of the Inventory is to enable the school administrator or counselor to detect students who are not well-adjusted to the school they are attending.

The items and total score can be used either as an aid to the counseling interview or as a measuring technique for determining the school morale of various student groups.

The Inventory is practically self-administering. There is no time limit, but all students should be able to complete it in twenty minutes. Space is provided at the bottom of the last page of each test blank for students to write in specific criticisms of the school. Students may be encouraged to make use of this space as the replies often provide the alert administrator with constructive suggestions for the improvement of the operation of his school.

The Inventory was standardized on high school students and norms are provided for this age group. Separate norms for boys and girls are not required since the average scores for the two groups were practically identical. Reliability was determined by the split-half method and the Spearman-Brown formula. The author reports a coefficient of .94,[1] and Traxler[3] found a coefficient of .92 employing the same method.

Validity was determined by the author[3] by comparing the judgment of high school teachers and principals with scores on the Inventory. Two groups of students were selected by school faculties: one group whom they considered to be very well-adjusted toward the school; and one group that the faculty members felt were poorly adjusted to the school. Subsequent administration of the School Inventory to these two groups revealed marked agreement between the test scores and the judgments of the teachers. A similar study has been reported by Traxler[3] but employing the correlation procedure, in which a coefficient of .54 was obtained between scores on the School Inventory and the pooled opinions of teachers.

The School Inventory has ben adapted recntly for use with college students by Ryan and Peters.[2]

The School Inventory is published by the Stanford University Press, Stanford University, California.

References:

1. Bell, H. M. The School Inventory, manual and norms. Stanford University: Stanford University Press, 1939.
2. Ryans, D. G. and Peters, E. F. An analysis and adaptation of the Bell School Inventory with respect to student adjustment in a women's college. Journal of Applied Psychology, 1940, 24, 455–462.
3. Traxler, A. E. The reliability of the Bell Inventories and their correlation with teachers' judgments. Journal of Applied Psychology, 1941, 25, 672–678.

H. M. B.

Bernreuter Personality Inventory.   The inventory is made up of
125 questions dealing with personal problems to which the subject
must answer Yes, No, or Doubtful. Its purpose is to measure with
one instrument six important traits of personality, four derived by
Bernreuter from a combination of earlier tests: emotional balance
or neuroticism (B1–N), self-sufficiency (B2–S), introversion-
extroversion (B3–I), dominance-submission (B4–D); and two
derived by Flanagan [2] by factor analysis from the other four: self-
confidence (F1–C) and sociability (F2–S). Empirically the introversion, self-confidence and neuroticism scales are highly correlated [2] and appear to be measuring much the same trait, i.e., emotional sensitivity or self-consciousness. Recently an attempt has
been made [7] to combine scores on B1–N, B2–S and B4–D to find a
more valid index of personality disorder than any trait score gives
by itself.

The test is very popular. Super [10] in a complete summary of its
uses up to 1941 remarks that no less than 135 different articles
have been written on it since it was first published. At least 25
more have appeared since. It has been used [10] to detect those who
may need counseling or psychiatric help; to analyze the personality
characteristics of various types of people such as college leaders,
husbands and wives, racial and occupational groups; to study trait
resemblances among members of a family or among friends; to
discover relations between traits and attitudes and between traits
and other measures such as school achievement, intelligence, persistence and punctuality. Findings on the traits of occupational
groups, such as the greater dominance of sales people,[4] make the
test somewhat useful in vocational guidance. Theoretical formula-
tions such as Stagner's [8] as to the fundamental traits of personality
have been based on it.

The test is self-administering and takes from twenty to thirty
minutes. Bernreuter emphasizes [2] that the subject should interpret
the questions for himself, should not know what traits are being
measured beforehand, and should want to cooperate fully in following the instructions.

Hand scoring keys are supplied for each of the six traits which
weigh each possible answer on a scale varying from + 7 to − 7.
Reliabilities for the various traits lie between .80 and .88 and have
been checked many times.[10] Because the scoring is so time-con-
suming, attempts have been made to shorten it.[1, 6] McClelland has
recently reported [6] that, if all answers weighted − 3 or more are
counted and subtracted from all answers weighted + 3 or more,
scores are obtained which correlate above .95 with the weighted

scores for B1–N, B4–D, F1–C and F2–S among college men. Practically the same results have been obtained for college women and
the reliabilities are the same as under the weighted method. Bernreuter supplies norms [3] for male and female adults, college students, and high school students. McClelland has published norms
for college men using the simplified scoring [6] and has prepared
them for college women.

The validity of the test was originally established by clinical
judgment as to the logical meaning of an answer. Weights were
assigned according to the degree to which they agreed with the
total. Attempts which have been made to see whether the test distinguishes normals from neurotic led Super [10] to the conclusions
that it does distinguish but in a less clear cut fashion than is
desirable, and that an unfavorable score is more significant than
a favorable one. Case studies have shown that the subject's answers
check with the objective facts [5] and that ratings based on thorough
knowledge of the person correlate satisfactorily with the trait scores
on the inventory. [9]

Certainly one of the most important criteria of the value of
a test is the amount which is known about it. The more that is
known the more a score can be related to other facts and interpreted to the subject. By this criterion the Bernreuter Personality
Inventory is one of the most useful personality tests available today.

Package lots complete with manual, six scoring scales and percentile norms are available from Stanford University Press, Stanford University, California. McClelland's simplified or unit weight
scoring keys may be made from the originals. Norms for these keys
for college men and women are available from the Personnel
Records Bureau, Wesleyan University, Middletown, Conn.

References:

1. Bennett, G. K. A simplified scoring method for the Bernreuter Personality Inventory. *J. Appl. Psychol.*, 1938, 22, 390–394.
2. Bernreuter, R. G. *Manual for the personality inventory.* Stanford University, Stanford University Press, 1938.
3. ———. *The personality inventory.* Tentative percentile norms. Stanford University, Stanford University Press, 1938.
4. Dodge, A. F. Social dominance of clerks and sales persons as measured
   by the Bernreuter Personality Inventory. *J. educ. Psychol.*, 1937, 28,
   71–73.
5. Landis, C. and Katz, S. E. The validity of certain questions which purport to measure neurotic tendencies. *J. appl. Psych.*, 1934, 18, 343–356.
6. McClelland, D. C. Simplified scoring of the Bernreuter Personality
   Inventory. *J. appl. Psychol.*, 1944, 28, 414–419.

7. Schmidt,. H. O. and Billingslea, F. Y. Test profiles as a diagnostic aid: the Bernreuter Inventory. *J. abnorm. soc. Psychol.,* 1945, 40, 70–76.
8. Stagner, R. *Psychology of personality.* New York: McGraw-Hill, 1937.
9. ———. Validity and reliability of the Bernreuter Personality Inventory. *J. abnorm. soc. Psychol.,* 1934, 28, 413–418.
10. Super, D. E. The Bernreuter Personality Inventory: a review of research. *Psych. Bull.,* 1942, 39, 94–125.

D. C. McC.

Body Sway Test of Suggestibility. This test, introduced by Hull,[1] is of interest mainly (1) because scores on it show a high correlation with the general personality trait of "neuroticism," and (2) because it enables the psychologist to forecast the hypnotic susceptibility of a subject.

In the standard form in which this test has been given to thousands of normal and neurotic adult subjects,[8] a gramophone record is used in order to give the suggestion in a manner not influenced by subjective differences between operators, and in order to allow the operator to concentrate on recording the sway of his subject or subjects. The operator calls the subject into the room and asks him to stand a few feet from the wall on which the recording instrument has been fixed, facing the opposite wall. The subject is then asked to put his heels close together, to form an angle of about 30 degrees with his feet, to let his arms hang down by his sides, and to close his eyes. By means of a pin, a thread is affixed to his collar; this thread runs back to a hook which is driven into the wall at a height of exactly 5 feet. At the other end of the thread a pointer is attached which travels on a scale painted on the wall, graduated in inches and half-inches. Every movement of the subject forward or backward is mirrored by a corresponding movement of the pointer.

The operator allows the subject 30 seconds to settle down, then issues the following instructions: "Just keep standing as you are now, with your eyes closed. I am going to play a record to you, and I want you to listen carefully to everything it says. While you are listening I want you to keep on standing just as you are standing now, quite still and relaxed, with your eyes closed." At this point, the record is started, and the operator notes the exact position of the pointer on the scale. The record runs as follows: "Now I want you to imagine that you are falling forward. You are falling, falling forward, you are falling forward all the time. You are falling forward, forward, you are falling forward all the time. . . ." After 2½ minutes the record is stopped, unless the subject has fallen outright at some earlier instant, in which case he is scored as a "fall," and the experiment is not continued. If the subject does not fall outright, his maximum sway forward and backward from the resting position are noted separately. Whichever of these two scores is higher is considered his score on the test.

This test has a repeat reliability of over + 0.90,[2] and correlates with other tests of "primary suggestibility," such as the arm levitation test, the Chevreul pendulum, the Press-Release test, and so forth.[2, 7] It also correlates highly with hypnotic susceptibility,[3, 7] but does not correlate with intelligence.[8] Suggestible individuals are rendered more suggestible under narcosis, while non-suggestible subjects remain unaffected.[5]

The main use of the test lies in the sphere of personality diagnosis. In several investigations, it has been shown that there are no differences between various neurotic syndromes (e.g. between hysterical and anxious or depressed patients), but that there are very large differences between normal and neurotic subjects. In one study, a correlation of + 0.66 has been reported between suggestibility and neuroticism;[4] other unpublished investigations show correlations from + 0.55 to + 0.75. Correlations between neuroticism and suggestibility have been found not only by comparing neurotic and normal populations, but also within neurotic groups, by comparing the more seriously ill with the less seriously ill.[8]

The extreme simplicity of the test, its lack of correlation with intelligence, its brevity, and the fact that it can easily be adapted to a group-test procedure, make it a useful part of any test battery for an investigation of neuroticism, or for use as a "screening" device.[6] Norms for the test are given in.[8] The record used can be obtained from the Star Sound Studio, 17 Cavendish Square, London W. 1., England; price approximately 1 dollar.

References:

1. Hull, C. L. *Hypnosis and suggestibility*. New York: Appleton Century, 1933.
2. Eysenck, H. J. Suggestibility and hysteria. J. Neurol. Psychiat., 1943, 6, 22–31.
3. ———. Suggestibility and hypnosis—an experimental analysis. Proceedings of the Royal Society of Medicine, 1943, 36, 349–354.
4. ———. States of high suggestibility and the neuroses. Amer. J. Psychol., 1944, 57, 406–411.
5. Eysenck, H. J. and Rees, W. L. States of heightened suggestibility: narcosis. Journal of Mental Science, 1945, 91, 301–310.
6. ———. A comparative study of four screening tests for neurotics. Psychol. Bull., 1945, 42, 659–662.

7. Eysenck, H. J. and Furneaux, W. D. Primary and secondary suggestibility: an experimental and statistical study. J. exp. Psychol., 1945, December.
8. ———.Dimensions of personality. London: Kegan Paul, 1946.

H. J. E.

California Test of Personality. The California Test of Personality, devised by Louis P. Thorpe, Ernest W. Tiegs, and Willis W. Clark, has been designed to identify and reveal the status of certain fundamental characteristics of human nature which are highly important in determining general success in personal, social, or vocational relations. These characteristics have usually been designated as intangibles because they cannot be measured with ordinary intelligence, knowledge, achievement, or skill tests, and cannot be estimated with any high degree of reliability in a short interview.

The major purpose of the test is to reveal the extent to which the individual is adjusting to the problems and conditions which confront him and is developing a normal and socially effective personality.

The test is divided into two sections. The purpose of Section 1, self-adjustment, is to indicate how the individual feels and thinks about himself, his self-reliance, his estimate of his own personal worth, his sense of personal freedom, and his feeling of belonging. In this section the individual also reveals certain withdrawing and nervous tendencies which he may possess. Section 2 consists of social adjustment components. Its purpose is to show how the person functions as a social being, his knowledge of social standards, his social skills, his freedom from anti-social tendencies, and his family, school or vocational, and community relationships.

An evaluation of these components discloses whether or not the individual's basic needs are satisfied in an atmosphere of security and whether he is developing a balanced sense of self-realization and social acceptance.

The diagnostic profile is so devised that it is possible to compare and contrast the adjustment patterns and habits of each individual with the characteristic modes of response of large representative groups of similar individuals by the use of percentile norms. The profile thus reveals graphically the points at which a particular person differs from presumable desirable patterns of adjustment and which constitute the points of departure for remedial guidance measures or for selection and adjustment in employment. No computations are necessary in completing the profile.

The reliability of the California Test of Personality does not suffer by comparison with many widely used tests of mental ability and achievement. The following correlations for the Adult Series were obtained by the split-halves method corrected by the Spearman-Brown formula:

		S.D. dist. score	P.E. est. score
Total Adjustment	.918	21.1	5.6
Sec. 1. Self-Adjustment	.888	12.0	3.7
Sec. 2. Social Adjustment	.898	12.1	3.6

The correlation between Section 1 and Section 2, .76, is sufficiently low to emphasize the desirability of studying the individual from the standpoint of both self-adjustment and social adjustment. The reliabilities of the component tests average about .75 and are sufficiently high to locate more restricted areas of personality difficulty.

This test is based upon a study of several hundred ways in which children, youths, or adults respond when confronted with problems which test their self-reliance, sense of personal worth, knowledge of the right thing to do, skill in using this knowledge in new situations, and other situations which test their personality characteristics. Many of these situations had previously been studied by other workers and characteristic modes of response had been determined. Before a situation (represented by a test item) was included in the test, it was evaluated in the following manner:

1. Judgments of teachers, principals, psychologists, personnel directors, or employers as to whether or not it was an indicator of adjustment and employability.
2. The reactions of competent adults as to whether or not they judged it to be an essential characteristic of a successful pupil or employee.
3. The extent to which the results of the test agreed with the known characteristics of particular adults.
4. The extent to which each item was consistent with the score on the test as a whole (Bi-serial r).

The California Test of Personality is available in five series—primary, elementary, intermediate, secondary, and adult—each of which is offered in two alternate equivalent forms, A and B. It is published by the California Test Bureau, Los Angeles 28, California.

L. P. T.

Dodge Occupational Personality Inventory. This inventory developed by Arthur F. Dodge attempts to measure the extent to which the personality of an individual is favorable for success in certain occupational fields. Scoring keys are now available for clerical work, sales work and teaching.

The scoring keys are the result of studies of the differences in personality between more successful and less successful workers in each occupational field. Thus a high score in clerical personality, for example, indicates that the individual has a personality similar to the personalities of successful workers in that occupational field, while a low score indicates a personality similar to the less successful workers in the field. This method of developing a scoring key would seem to be more satisfactory than the more common method of studying the differences between one occupational group and the general adult population. Traits, attitudes and interests characteristic of both the successful and the unsuccessful, which may have been acquired because of common influences experienced in the occupation or in preparation for that occupation, are certainly valueless for predicting success in that field.

The inventory is self-administering and no instructions are necessary except those printed on the blank. There is no time limit, but few individuals require more than fifteen minutes.

No negative weights are used in the scoring keys and no weights greater than three. As a result the average clerk can score the inventory for any one of the personality scales in less than a minute.

The coefficient of correlation between teacher personality score and expressed liking for teaching was found to be $+ .42$ for a group of 239 teachers in an air corps technical school. For the graduating class (N $=$ 377) of another air corps technical school the correlation was $+ .57$.[5] No similar studies have been made for clerical or sales personality.

For the purpose of measuring reliability, the inventory was administered a second time to a group of 92 after a period of approximately two weeks. The coefficients of correlation between the scores of the first and second applications of the inventory were found to be $+ .77$ for the teacher personality score, $+ .70$ for the clerical personality and $+ .69$ for the sales personality score.

This inventory is distributed by The Psychological Corporation, 522 Fifth Avenue, New York.

References:

1. Dodge, A. F. Social dominance and sales success. Journal of Applied Psychology, 1938, 22, 132–139.

2. ———. What are the personality traits of the successful sales-person? Journal of Applied Psychology, 1938, 22, 229–238.

3. ———. Personality measuring stick, Retailing-Executive Edition, 1939, 11, 14–15.

4. ———. What are the personality traits of the successful clerical worker? Journal of Applied Psychology, 1940, 24, 576–586.

5. ———. What are the personality traits of the successful teacher? Journal of Applied Psychology, 1943, 27, 325–337.

A. F. D.

Guilford Inventory of Factors S T D C R. This inventory, constructed by J. P. Guilford, was an outcome of factor-analysis studies of items that had been traditionally utilized to measure introversion-extraversion. The five traits measured are defined as follows: S—social introversion-extraversion—shyness, seclusiveness, tendency to withdraw from social contacts, versus sociability, tendency to seek social contacts and to enjoy the company of others; T—thinking introversion-extraversion—an inclination to meditative or reflective thinking, philosophizing, analysis of one's self and others, versus an extravertive orientation of thinking; D—depression—habitually gloomy, pessimistic mood, with feelings of guilt and unworthiness, versus cheerfulness and optimism; C—cycloid disposition—strong emotional fluctuations, tendencies toward flightiness and emotional instability, versus uniformity and stability of moods, evenness of disposition; R—rhathymia—a happy-go-lucky, carefree disposition, liveliness, impulsiveness, versus an inhibited, overcontrolled, conscientious, serious-minded disposition.

The scores are used in educational and vocational guidance, in selection and placement of personnel, in personal and marital counseling, in general clinical practice, and in research.

The test is self-administering, having simple directions. There is no time limit but most examinees finish in about 25 minutes. It is likely to give best results when administered to young adults who have some insight into their personal habits and who make an honest effort to cooperate. Scoring keys are in the form of transparent stencils. Simple scoring weights (positive only) are used. Answer sheets and machine scoring stencils are provided.

Norms are provided for senior high school and college groups and for adults, in terms of either of Guilford's C-score scale or the centile scale. The most notable age difference is a lowering of the rhathymia score (decreasing carefreeness) with advancing age. The most marked sex difference is a greater tendency toward emotionality (more depressed and cycloid) among females. Scores are also interpretable on the Guilford-Martin Temperament Profile Chart, along with eight other trait scores from two other inventories.

Reliabilities of scores are indicated by split-half coefficients of .91, .86, .92, .90, and .89 for the five factors respectively. Validities against self-ratings and ratings by others were approximately .6, .5, and .5 for factors S, D, and R, respectively.

The publisher of this inventory is the Sheridan Supply Co., Beverly Hills, Calif.

References:

1. Guilford, J. P. and Guilford, R. B. Personality factors D, R, T, and A. J. Abnor. and Soc. Psychol., 1939, 34, 21–36
2. Guilford, J. P. and Martin, H. Age differences and sex differences in some introvertive and emotional traits. J. Gen. Psychol., 1944, 31, 219–229.
3. Steinberg, D. L. and Wittmer, M. P. Etiologic factors in the adjustment of men in the armed forces. J. War. Med., 1943, 4, 129–139.

J. P. G.

Guilford-Martin Personnel Inventory I. This inventory, constructed by J. P. Guilford and H. G. Martin, was designed to detect the discontented and maladjusted employees either before or after employment, and to extend the measurement of temperamental traits into the area of paranoid disposition in its milder manifestations.

Factor analysis studies and clinical experiences have shown several traits in this area, namely: O—objectivity (as opposed to personal references or a tendency to take things personally); Ag—agreeableness (as opposed to belligerence or a dominating disposition and an overreadiness to fight over trifles); Co—cooperativeness (as opposed to faultfinding or overcriticalness of people and things).

The scores have a general clinical use as well as a selective value. Not only the troublemaker in industrial or business assignments needs attention and diagnosis. Among wreckers of marital harmony and social peace in many kinds of groups are individuals who suffer from extreme degrees of suspiciousness, criticalness, belligerence or touchiness. Only by analysis of the symptoms and of what lies behind them can peace be restored in such situations.

The test is self-administering and takes approximately 20 minutes. Good cooperation of the examinees is important, though not essential. Low scores are usually indicative of an unfavorable temperamental disposition but high scores are not complete evidence of "good" disposition without supporting evidence. Items are generally phrased so that only the sagacious suspect their intent.

Norms are provided, based on a sample of 500 employees of varied type, aged 20 to 45. The Guilford C-scale is used as a common basis for interpretation of scores. These apply where examinees are *not* under compulsion to appear well because they are applying for a position or are in similar situations. Scores are also interpretable on the Guilford-Martin Temperament Profile Chart, along with ten other trait scores from two other inventories.

The reliabilities of these scores are .83, .80, and .91 for traits O, Ag, and Co, respectively. Intercorrelations of these scores are in the neighborhood of .60.

The validity of the test in industry is indicated by the fact that it typically detects about 70% of the recognized troublemakers while falsely pointing to about 35% of the non-troublemakers. Its selective value, as for any test, depends upon the degree of selectivity that can be exercised and this depends upon the supply of applicants as compared with the demand for appointees.

The publisher of this inventory is the Sheridan Supply Co., Beverly Hills, Calif.

References:

1. Dorcus, R. M. A brief study of the Humm-Wadsworth Temperament Scale and the Guilford-Martin Personnel Inventory in an industrial situation. J. Appl. Psychol., 1944, 28, 302–307.
2. Johnson, R. H. The inheritance of personality. Education, June, 1941, 592–597.
3. Martin, H. G. Locating the troublemaker with the Guilford-Martin Personnel Inventory. J. Appl. Psychol., 1944, 28, 461–467.
4. Mosier, C. I. A factor analysis of certain neurotic tendencies. Psychometrika, 1937, 2, 263–287.

J. P. G.

Guilford-Martin Inventory of Factors G A M I N (Abridged Edition). This inventory, constructed by J. P. Guilford and H. G. Martin, in large part grew out of factor analysis discoveries with inventory questions by the senior author. The five traits, G, A, M, I, and N, form a natural cluster that might be called "dynamic" or "mastery" traits of temperament. The variables are defined as follows: G—general pressure for overt activity; A—ascendancy in social situations as opposed to submissiveness; leadership qualities; M—masculinity of attitudes and interests as opposed to femininity; I—lack of inferiority feeling; self-confidence; N—lack of nervous tenseness and irritability.

The inventory has been published in two forms, the original (270 items) and in an abridged form (186 items).

The scores are usable in general clinical and consulting practice, including educational, vocational, and personal guidance, marital counseling and personnel placement, as well as in research.

The test is self-administering, having simple directions. Best results are obtainable when examinees are cooperative and possess some insight into personal habits. There is no time limit, but most examinees complete the test in 30 minutes. Transparent stencil keys and weights of +1 only are provided.

Norms based upon college-age adults are provided in both Guilford's C-scale and the usual centile scale. Normal distributions are assumed except for trait M in which bimodality is apparent. Scores are also interpretable on the Guilford-Martin Temperament Profile Chart, along with eight other trait scores from two other inventories.

Reliabilities of scores are indicated by split-half coefficients of .89, .88, .85, .91, and .89 for the five traits, respectively, for the original form of the inventory and .80, .88, .82, .89, and .90 for the abridged form. The validity of the M score, correlated against sex, is .84. Validities of other scores are unknown as yet, owing chiefly to lack of suitable criteria.

The publisher of this inventory is the Sheridan Supply Co., Beverly Hills, Calif.

References:

1. Guilford, J. P. and Guilford, R. B. Personality factors S, E, and M, and their measurement. J. Psychol., 1936, 2, 107–127.
2. ———. Personality factors N and GD. J. Abn. and Soc. Psychol., 1939, 34, 239–248.
3. Martin, H. G. Measuring temperament with the Guilford-Martin Inventory of Factors G A M I N. J. Appl. Psychol., 1945, 29.
4. Mosier, C. I. A factor analysis of certain neurotic tendencies. Psychometrika, 1937, 2, 263–287.

J. P. G.

Harrower Rorschach Multiple Choice Test (originally published as the Harrower-Erickson Multiple Choice Test). This test was constructed by M. R. Harrower in an endeavor to meet the demands for a short modification of the Rorschach test which would (a) be capable of administration to a large group of subjects, (b) in a short time, and (c) would dispense with the detailed technical aspects of Rorschach scoring so that it could be handled by untrained assistants and recorded on a punch card system.

Needless to say such a drastic revision of the original procedure could not hope to retain all the finer shades of diagnostic information which the Rorschach method allows of in the hands of an expert, nonetheless as a screening test it has, in its own right, proved of value in certain types of problems.

The test procedure is very simple. On seeing the Rorschach card or slide the individual picks out and underlines on the printed form, the three answers which seem to him to be the best description of that blot or any of its parts (from the 30 which are offered for each inkblot). He also checks any additional answers which he finds acceptable. This procedure is repeated for each of the ten inkblots.

Scoring is done from a key which designates a number to each answer. Answers designated 1,2,3,4,5, were originally chosen from the records of "normal" subjects, answers 6,7,8,9,10 from answers given by various types of "abnormal" subjects. (Neurotics, psychotics and psychopathic personalities.)

It is suggested that those subjects who draw more than 40% of their answers from the 6–10 or "poor" range, be subjected to further psychological investigation.

The test has been modified since its initial presentation so as to include alternative choices which other investigators have found to have diagnostic value, and weighed scores have been suggested [3] [5] to sharpen the differential picture. The original form of the test contained 100 responses, whereas the present form contains 300. The additional material allows of more accurate predictions. Some investigators have used the test as a systematic testing of the limits procedure, notably Hutt.[4] Extensive studies have been made with psychotics [7] and some consideration has been given to the psychopathic personality.[6] Amongst college students the test has been used a a screening device by the department of student health [2] on a summer school population. Much additional information can be derived from the basic procedure by the qualitative methods suggested by Due, Wright and Wright.[1]

In addition to the practical demands which furthered the construction of the test the author wished primarily to call attention of Rorschach workers to the importance of the *content* both actual and symbolic of the material which is seen in the inkblot responses, a factor which has received the least attention in the original Rorschach evaluations. The theoretical assumption is made that an individual's potential emotional stability is directly related to the number of areas in the personality which are free from disturbance. Scores which are heavily weighted with poor answers reflect a personality too preoccupied with coping with his anxieties and conflicts to have sufficient psychological energy available to constructive living.

The material required for this test is available from the Psychological Corporation, 522 Fifth Avenue, N. Y. 18. The book containing instructions and the key Large Scale Rorschach Techniques is available from the publisher: C. C. Thomas, Springfield, Illinois.

References:

1. Due, F. O., Wright, M. E. and Wright, B. A. The Multiple Choice Rorschach Test in military psychiatric differentiation. *Large scale Rorschach techniques.* Springfield: C. C. Thomas, 1945.
2. Harrower, M. R., Washburne, A. C. and Jacobs, J. S. L. A preliminary screening test for disturbances in personality. *Bulletin of the Canadian Psychological Association,* 1944, 4, 4–6.
3. Harrower, M. R. and Steiner, M. E. *Large scale Rorschach techniques.* Springfield: C. C. Thomas, 1945.
4. Hutt, M. The use of projective methods of personality measurement in army medical installations. *Journal of Clinical Psychology,* 1945, 1, 134–140.
5. Malamud, R. F. and Malamud, D. I. The Multiple Choice Rorschach, a critical examination of its scoring system. *Journal of Clinical Psychology,* 1946, 21, 237–242.
6. Rotterman, W. The guardhouse inmate. War Medicine, Vol. V, No. 5, May, 1944.
7. Wittman, P. The use of the Multiple Choice Rorschach as a differential diagnostic   tool. *Journal of Clinical Psychology,* 1945, 1, 281–287.

M. H.

Humm-Wadsworth Temperament Scale. The Humm-Wadsworth Temperament Scale is a measure of the pattern or complex of tendencies which determines an individual's behavior. These tendencies cluster around general tendencies recognizable as temperamental components. Leri, Birnbaum, Kraepelin, Spratling, Davenport, Dostoyevski, and Flaubert have described these components and Rosanoff has drawn them up in an ordered description of temperament. They are:

Component		*Effect on Behavior Trends*
"Normal"	(N)	Integration and control of other components to utilize them in life situations. Improvement of the individual.
Hysteroid	(H)	Self-preservation; consideration of profit and advantage.

Component		Effect on Behavior Trends
Cycloid	(C)	Emotional reactions, production of energy, sensory orientation (attention).
Manic	(M)	Tends toward cheerfulness, activity, and alertness.
Depressive	(D)	Tends toward sadness, inactivity, and lack of concentration.
Schizoid	(S)	Imagination, idealism, philosophy.
Autistic	(A)	Tends chiefly toward inward contemplation (day dreams) with seclusiveness and narrowing of external interest.
Paranoid	(P)	Tends chiefly toward philosophical considerations with a somewhat militant defense of ideas.
Epileptoid	(E)	Tendencies toward project-making with inspiration toward achievement. (Some epileptoids have lapses in consciousness or other epileptic symptoms.)

The Temperament Scale was standardized in an industrial corporation for industrial purposes. The item analysis and original norms were determined from the responses of 436 subjects who were first carefully analyzed for possession or non-possession of these components. This analysis made possible the setting up of fourteen control groups. These groups comprised seven pairs of groups, one pair for each component; each pair was comprised of one group with strong possession of a given component (plus group) and another with very weak possession of that component (minus group). The subjects used in standardization were deliberately so treated as to cause them to endeavor to make a good impression, since this is the attitude acknowledged to be present in applicants and employees who are being tested. Complete honesty of response is not anticipated.

Since industrial test subjects are likely to be on their mettle and may respond unduly to test strain, two measures of typicality of response or relative presence or absence of suggestibility (both positive and negative) are included in the interpretative techniques. These measures are used both to determine the acceptability of subject response to the Scale and to compensate, within permissible limits, for atypicality of response.

Since the Scale anticipates the above-described attitudes in responding, it is best used in industrial testing. It may, however, be used in clinical testing if certain precautions are observed.

The Scale is reported by means of a Profile or psychograph.

THE HUMM-WADSWORTH TEMPERAMENT SCALE
EVALUATING PROFILE

From this Profile, it is possible to determine the temperamental pattern of the subject. When the subject has responded acceptably, which occurs in about 85 per cent of the cases, the temperamental pattern is indicative of the subject's mental health and predictive of his behavior. Approximately 100 frequently occurring patterns have been identified.

Because of the complicated interpretation, the Scale is furnished only to technicians specially trained. A fee is charged for training for profitable use; no fee is charged for non-profit use.

The validity of the Scale (Journal of Psychology, 1944, *18*, 55–64) is +.84 for all cases and +.94 for cases acceptably answered.

The reliability (split-half method) averages +.80. This is probably an understatement, since split-half method is difficult to apply to a complicated test such as this. (American Journal of Psychiatry, 1935, *92*, 163–200.)

The Scale itself is not sold. Instead, permission to test a certain number of persons or number of times is sold and the materials with which to do this are furnished without charge. Manuals and other necessary interpretative materials are rented (special discount to non-profit users).

A quick-scoring form is printed, which reduces scoring time to two minutes per Scale when a laboratory counter is used.

The Scale is regularly employed in vocational guidance, since it evaluates mental health and determines the presence or absence of trait patterns which may prove handicapping in some occupations. It is especially valuable in vocational readjustments, where the problem of personality maladjustment must always be considered as a factor.

D. G. H.

Johnson Temperament Analysis. This temperament test measures nine traits based on the work of Rosanoff, Guilford, and Murray and has been found to be useful in the study of marital failures. The traits fall in three syndromes. The first consisting of nervous, depression and the lower pole of self-mastery, called impulsive, is called the traumatoid as it especially results from a wide range of damages to the individual. Related are two traits, subjective (a selection from the introvert group) and critical (allied to paranoid) called here the schizoid. A third group, on the whole negatively correlated with the previous, consist of active, cordial and sympathetic. These are found with lower metabolism in general and are called the hypodynamic. The ninth trait "aggressive" is dual, bridging active to critical.

An especially valuable trait measured by this instrument is self-mastery vs. impulsive.

There are 182 questions answered in three columns. They have the irregular spiral arrangement, yet so arranged that five stencils will score the nine traits. The questions are so constructed as to be one-half positive with "yes" and one-half with "no" to avoid "yes" or "no" bias.

Scoring stencils are available on an unweighted basis to permit machine scoring but also on a weighted basis for hand scoring. The unweighted has less reliability and is planned for use as a machine scored screening test. For clinical use the weighted scores and norms should be used as they permit better discrimination at the extremes which are the more significant.

Norms are furnished for each sex for both adults and youths.

Reliability figures and intercorrelation tables are given for the weighted form in the Manual of Directions.

It has validity for marriage success especially nervous, depressed, self-mastery, active and cordial. It has validity also for hyposexual and homosexual individuals, the neuroses and even as distinguishing from students seeking counseling from others as found at Green Mountain College, Vermont.

It has been especially successful in both the temperament and sexual deviants in marital relations cases.

In vocational guidance the traits self-mastery, cordial, aggressive and subjective are of prime importance. In fact a fitting temperament is as important as interests, to which an undue proportion of attention is now being given.

The salesman needs a high aggressive score with sympathy not high. The researcher calls for high self-mastery. Cordial, sympathetic and low depressive are needed in social service occupations and in teaching.

Some temperament traits have given scores superior to observation and interview in some of the army predictions as to success in assignments.

It is useful in detecting cases for which a psychopathic test such as the Minnesota Multiphasic should be given. Very high nervous, depression, subjective and critical and very low self-mastery scores have so far always been confirmed by observation and by the Minnesota Multiphasic.

A unique and valuable feature is the avoidance of "you" in the questions. They ask about S—this person. This is to facilitate its use for self-rating and also rating by another. Both profiles should be entered on the profile grid and the zone between the two used.

Where there is a pair relation such as a marriage or a parent child relationship, we have here in some degree a sociometric measure.

The publisher of this inventory is the California Test Bureau, 5916 Hollywood Blvd., Los Angeles 28.

R. H. J.

Livingstone Rotating Hexagon Test. This test is of interest because although it was introduced as a test of dark vision it was found that scores on it show a very high correlation with neuroticism. (Correlations range from +.0.30 to +0.80 for different groups.) In consequence, the test may be used in experimental studies of neuroticism, and may be useful as a screening device, when it is important that the subjects should have no knowledge of the purpose of the testing procedure.[3] Its reliability is reasonably high for a test of this type.

The apparatus was designed for testing night vision in the Royal Air Force by Livingstone.[1] It consists of a hexagonal structure which can be rotated so as to present different panels to the subjects tested; there are altogether 96 letters and objects on its six sides. The letters are placed in various positions, and the objects are out- lines of aircraft, ships, parallel lines, etc. Preparation for the test includes 30 minutes dark adaptation with dark goggles, only admit- ting 3% light, followed by ten minutes in the dark room during which the details of the test are carefully explained. The subject is able to record his interpretations of the objects and letters in the dark by means of special Braille cards. Four routine tests are given to six subjects at a time at various levels of illumination, each deal- ing with 6 letters and 2 objects. The Hexagon test examines a mix- ture of photopic and scotopic vision, illumination during the test ranging from 0.00015 eq. foot candles to 0.0012 eq. foot candles.

Comparisons between neurotic and normal subjects, equated for intelligence, age, nutrition and motivation show large differ- ences.[2][4][5] A typical instance of the kind of difference to be expected is reported by Rees,[2] who found that while out of a possible range of scores from 0 to 32, the normal group averaged 19.3, the neurotic group only averaged 7.1. Roughly speaking, the average of the neurotic group is almost three S.D.s below the mean of the normal group.

Comparisons within the neurotic group also show very signifi- cant differences between the more seriously ill and the less seriously ill. Comparing a relatively well-scoring neurotic group with a rela- tively badly-scoring neurotic group, differences were found in the incidence of such psychiatric notations as: Poor mental health before illness; well organized personality; very anxious and highly strung; cyclothymic personality; poor work history; considerable unemployment; discharged from the army because of psychoneu- rotic disorder. Anxiety state patients tend to show poorer results than hysterics.

An interpretation of the experimental findings is attempted in,[4] where the differences between normal and neurotic subjects are linked with autonomic imbalance. Regardless of interpretation, how- ever, there is little doubt that from a practical point of view the correlation between the personality trait of "neuroticism" and the scores on the dark vision test is high enough to make the test useful in diagnosis and screening.

The apparatus may either be rebuilt from specifications pub- lished by Dr. Livingstone, or may be obtainable under certain con- ditions from the R.A.F. Physiological Laboratory, Farnborough, Hants, England. Norms are given in (4).

References:

1. Livingstone, P. C. Examination of night visual capacity in relation to flying. Brit. J. Surg., 1942, 29, 339–345.
2. Rees, W. L. L. Night visual capacity of neurotic soldiers. J. Neurol., Neurosurg., Psychiat., 1945, 8, 34–39.
3. Eysenck, H. J. A comparative study of our screening tests for neurotics. Psychol. Bull., 1945, 42, 659–662.
4. ———. *Dimensions of personality.* London: Kegan Paul, 1946.
5. Livingstone, P. C. and Bolton, B. Night visual capacity of pathological cases. Lancet, 1943, 1, 263–264.

H. J. E.

Maslow Social Personality Inventory for College Women. The "Social Personality Inventory" is a quantitative measurement of the self-esteem syndrome as manifested in college women.

High self-esteem or "ego-level" and "self-strength" is behavior which shows a greater tendency toward: self-confidence, social poise, relaxation, extroversion, self-assurance, unconventionality—"masculinity." The opposite would be true of women with low self-esteem. There we may note a greater tendency toward: timidity, shyness, more conventionality, promptness, faithfulness, introversion, more inferiority feelings—"femininity." These two categories might be designated more simply by calling the high self-esteem personality "strong," and the lower scoring group as "weak" or "quiet and retiring." In interpreting these results great care should be taken not to attach a value judgment to the score or to make the subject feel that this is an unchangeable or undesirable part of her personality.

The test was clinically derived and validated. The subjects were studied carefully by interviews before their results included in the statistical portion of the research.

The most important data are the following:

Range	−145 to −182	Sigma	55.56
Mean	−8	N of Criterion Group..	845
Median	−12	N Total	1,201

Repeat reliability ....r(rel)		
(two weeks interval)		.90 ± .01 = 100
Split-half reliability ....r(rel)	.88 ± .03 = 100
Validity for a selected group...........r(val)	.91 ± .02 = 61
Validity for an unselected group........r(val)	.90 ± .02 = 100

Primarily this test is useful as a research instrument. It is a timesaving way of establishing rapport with students. Also very frequently the personal problems of a student can be understood more easily and quickly when her score on the self-esteem has been obtained, since one very important aspect of the personality is revealed with fair accuracy by this score. It might also be emphasized that the high correlations of the test score with sexual attitudes and behaviors at once give a preliminary understanding of the "vita sexualis" that can save both time and embarrassment for the subject.

The test can be used profitably for other purposes than academic research; such as vocational guidance, social activity programs, and in group therapy (class room) where the primary aim is self-knowledge. In all these the value of this test as of all other clinical instruments is only increased if it is used in conjunction with personal interview.

Instructions for giving the Inventory:

A. It is self-administering. It may be given to groups of any size or may be used individually. The instructions printed on the form are usually sufficient to take care of questions that are asked.
B. There should be no time limit. Ninety per cent of the ordinary college class will have finished the test in about twenty minutes.
C. It is well to state orally that honesty, frankness, and sincere cooperation are required.
D. It is imperative that subjects be not told the purpose of the Inventory until they have finished.
E. Scores should only be returned after a full discussion of the self-esteem syndrome, also giving norms and means. (See References).

References:

1. Maslow, A. H. Dominance-feeling, behavior, and status. Psychol. Rev., 1937, 44, 404–29.
2. ———. Dominance-feeling, personality, and social behavior in women. J. Soc. Psychol., 1939, 10, 3–39.
3. ———. A test for dominance-feeling (self-esteem) in college women, published by Stanford University Press, Stanford University, California, 1940.
4. ———. Dominance-feeling (self-esteem) and sexuality in women. J. Soc. Psychol., 1942, 16, 259–294.

A. H. M.

Minnesota Multiphasic Personality Inventory. The Minnesota Multiphasic Personality Inventory, as developed by Starke R. Hathaway, and J. Charnley McKinley, has been designed to aid in the identification and evaluation of some of the personality factors commonly recognized in psychiatric practice. Nine scales are in use at present in either a final or preliminary stage. These are hypochondriasis, depression, hysteria, psychopathic deviate, masculinity-feminity, psychasthenia, schizophrenia, hypomania. More scales will appear later. In addition to the clinical scales several methods are provided to aid in the identification of records from subjects who are unable to comprehend the items or who for any other reason do not respond in appropriate fashion.

The Multiphasic is designed for routine use on persons 18 years or older who need not have more than a few years' education. It has also been found possible to administer the Inventory to young people as far down as 12 years of age although the validity at these ages is not yet established. There is no time limit. The time required for a subject varies widely, but usually lies between 30 and 90 minutes.

The Multiphasic is presented as a strictly clinical device in that it is not expected that it will be used as a final diagnostic instrument or as a final critical device in the selection of personnel. Rather it is presumed that the profile will be combined with interview and other data providing modifications and leads that would increase the validity of the whole picture.

The Multiphasic was derived and validated in a psychiatric clinic. The validating data show that the various scales differ somewhat in their validity but that 50 to 80 per cent of persons in the various diagnostic groups will be identified correctly with less than five per cent of persons in the general population. Many mixed types of personality deviation can be identified where they would otherwise be overlooked.

The problems of reliability have in general been shifted to the problem of validity. This was based upon the assumption that the chief effort should be directed toward providing a device that would identify new groups according to diagnosis and it was assumed that when this goal was achieved as nearly as possible, the instrument would of necessity have reasonable reliability. The usual reliability procedures are difficult to apply since several of the traits change strength in the subject within relatively short periods and since the items in the scales have various purposes and do not form a homogeneous intercorrelated group of items.

The standardization group is made up of a sample of about 700 men and women of the Minnesota population whose modal school level was eighth grade and whose socio-economic background compared rather closely to census data. These persons were in the middle ages of life and assumed to be a fair sample of persons not ill since they claimed not to be under care of a medical doctor.

The directions for administration are simple, as is the recording and scoring. The whole procedure may be carried out by a clerical worker without special training.

Several forms are provided. The authors recommend the card form in which the 550 items of the Inventory are presented in a box for sorting. For groups too large to provide card forms, a booklet form is available. Record blanks from this may be scored by the aid of IBM test scoring machines.

The distributor is The Psychological Corporation, 522 Fifth Avenue, New York, New York. For details it is suggested that one use the catalogue of tests issued by The Psychological Corporation or write to them directly.

References:

1. Hathaway, S. R. and McKinley, J. C. A multiphasic personality schedule (Minnesota): I. Construction of the schedule. Jour. of Psychol., 1940, 10, 249–254.
2. ———. A multiphasic personality schedule (Minnesota): III. The measurement of symptomatic depression. Jour. of Psychol., 1942, 14, 73–84.
3. ———. The Minnesota multiphasic personality inventory: V. Hysteria, hypomania, and psychopathic deviate. Jour. of Appl. Psychol., Vol. 28, No. 2, 153–174.
4. McKinley, J. C. and Hathaway, S. R. A multiphasic personality schedule (Minnesota): II. A differential study of hypochondriasis. Jour. of Psychol., 1940, 10, 255–268.
5. ———. A multiphasic personality schedule (Minnesota): IV. Psychasthenia. Jour. of Appl. Psychol., Vol. XXVI, 614–624.
6. ———. The identification and measurement of the psychoneuroses in medical practice. Jour. of Am. Med. Assn., Vol. 122, 161–167, 1943.

S. R. H.

Minnesota Personality Scale. The Minnesota Personality Scale, constructed by John G. Darley and Walter J. McNamara, provides five separate measures of individual adjustment: Morale, Social Adjustment, Family Relations, Emotionality and Economic Conservatism.

The Scale is the result of four years of work on problems of personality measurement in a clinical personnel program at the University of Minnesota. As a result of factor analysis of several personality tests (The Minnesota Scale for the Survey of Opinions, the Bell Adjustment Inventory, and the two Minnesota Inventories of Social Attitudes), it was found that the thirteen separate scores in the original battery could be accounted for by five psychologically meaningful factors, and that these factors were sufficiently stable from test to retest to represent significant aspects of personality. By means of item analysis the 368 items in the original battery were reduced to 290 items and administered in experimental form to 100 men and 100 women in the first two years of college. For these new samples of men and women, another item analysis was made for the further elimination of non-differentiating items. The final revision contains 199 items for the men's form and 209 items for the women's form. Intercorrelations between the five parts scored were obtained for the standardizing samples and a new group of approximately 500 men and 500 women entering college. These procedures resulted in a smaller number of tests for the counselor to interpret in diagnosing five important aspects of personality; and a smaller and more homogeneous number of items in each of these tests than in the groupings of tests from which the items were derived.

From the standpoint of validity, factor analysis establishes one form of validity in terms of internal consistency. Furthermore, none of the validity of the original scales should be lost in this greater refinement of measurement.

The Scale is self-administering on either a group or individual basis. There is no time limit, but the average length of time required is about 45 minutes. The inventory can be used in the last two years of high school, with college students, and in some adult cases. It consists of two booklets, one for men and one for women, and a special answer sheet, usable with either form.

The Scale can be scored by hand or on the International Test Scoring Machine. Each item is weighted from one to five, corresponding to the alternatives. Two tables of norms based on approximately 2,000 men and women freshmen at the University of Minnesota are provided, one for each method of scoring.

Reliability was determined by the split-half technique and ranged from .84 to .97 for the five parts of the men's scale, and from .91 to .95 for the five parts of the women's scale.

The publisher of this inventory is The Psychological Corporation, 522 Fifth Avenue, New York, New York.

References:

1. Darley, J. G. and McNamara, W. J. Factor analysis in the establishment of new personality tests. J. Educ. Psych., 1940, 31, 321–334.
2. McNamara, W. J. and Darley, J. G. A factor analysis of test-retest performance in attitude and adjustment tests. J. Educ. Psych., 1938, 29, 652–664.

W. J. McN.

Minnesota T-S-E Inventory. This inventory was constructed by the authors, Catharine Evans and T. R. McConnell, to measure three types of Introversion-Extroversion. Guilford's factor analysis of I-E yielded evidence that the available I-E tests were not measuring a single dimension of personality. Therefore, this inventory has been developed to measure not a general, undifferentiated trait, but three types of I-E which have been precisely defined as follows:

Thinking I-E

The Thinking Introvert shows a liking for reflective thought, particularly of a more abstract nature. His thinking tends to be less dominated by objective conditions and generally accepted ideas than the extrovert. In contrast, the Thinking Extrovert shows a liking for overt action, and his ideas tend to be ideas of overt action.

Social I-E

The Social Introvert withdraws from social contacts, and displays little interest in people. The Social Extrovert seeks social contacts and depends upon them for his satisfaction. He is primarily interested in people.

Emotional I-E

The Emotional Introvert tends to inhibit the outward expression of emotions. He tends not to make the typical response to simple, direct emotional appeals. On the other hand, the Emotional Extrovert readily expresses his emotions outwardly. He tends to make the expected response to simple, direct emotional appeals.

Three distinct types of items were formulated in an effort to develop relatively independent tests.[1] Ten experts sorted the original items in terms of the definitions of the three I-E types, and those items on the placement of which six of the judges agreed were retained. A technique of item analysis was then employed as the principal method for obtaining three homogeneous but relatively independent tests. This technique left only those items in each test which discriminated significantly with respect to the total score on that particular test, but not for the total scores on either of the other tests. The scores of five groups of college students were used and the results were remarkably consistent for the five samples. This simple technique yielded three tests with low intercorrelation coefficients (.13 to .27).

Indirect evidence of the validity of each test also was collected. Each test was found to differentiate significantly known groups of students which, on an *a priori* basis, seemed to be extreme in that type of I-E.[1] Test scores of 784 University of Minnesota students were employed in this study of the differentiation of known groups.

The tests seem to be sufficiently reliable for individual prediction. By the split-half technique, the coefficients of reliability based on scores of 396 college seniors were: Thinking test, .91; Social test, .88; Emotional test, .75. The coefficients between test and retest scores of 101 college students were: Thinking test, .89; Social test, .84; Emotional test, .88.[1]

The T-S-E inventory is useful as one of a battery of tests employed in the diagnosis and counseling of high school and college students. Data reveal that Thinking Introversion is related to high scholastic achievement and that Social Extroversion is characteristic of the more successful student teachers [2] and of life insurance salesmen.[3] Standard score and percentile norms based on 400 freshmen and sophomores at Indiana University are available.

Science Research Associates, Chicago, publish this inventory.

References:

1. Evans, C. and McConnell, T. R. A new measure of introversion-extroversion. *Journal of Psychology*, 1941, 12, 111–124.
2. Evans, C. and Wrenn, C. G. Introversion-extroversion as a factor in teacher training. *Educational and Psychological Measurement*, 1942, 2, 47–58.
3. Hahn, M. E. An investigation of measured aspects of social intelligence in a distributive occupation. Unpublished, Ph.D. Thesis, University of Minnesota, 1942.

M. C. E.

Moore-Gilliland Aggressiveness Test. The Moore-Gilliland Test of Aggressiveness is composed of five subtests. Subtests I and II consist in measures of the effect in increased time and the number of eye movements of adding by increments of one up to nine to a given number while staring the tester in the eye. Scoring on this and other parts of the test are deducted from 100. Five points are deducted for each eye movement in two trials, and two points are deducted for each second over three caused by staring as compared with normal adding time. Subtest III consists in writing the name and address first at normal rate and then as rapidly as possible. One point is deducted for each per cent increase in normal over rapid writing above 20 per cent. Subtests IV and V consist of word associations to "enterprise," "success," and "danger." Two points are deducted for each "negative" response and one point for each second in excess of two seconds for the reaction to each word.

Validity. The test was first validated against the 13 highest and lowest out of a class of 89 students as rated by the class. The mean score of the aggressive group was 93 and of the submissive group it was 58.5. In a later study correlations of 40 to 95 were obtained between ratings and test scores with a mean of 60.

Reliability. Three studies of reliabilities were made with small groups. These correlations were 30, 67, and 72.

References:

1. Gilliland, A. R. A revision and some results with the Moore-Gilliland aggressiveness test. J. of Appl. Psych., 1926, 10, 143–150.
2. Moore, H. T. and Gilliland, A. R. The measurement of aggressiveness. J. of Appl. Psych., 1921, 5, 97–118.

A. R. G.

Murray Thematic Apperception Test.   In the Thematic Apperception Test, also known as the TAT, the subject is asked to make up and tell to the examiner a story about each picture in a standard set shown to him; the purpose of the test is to elicit for skilled interpretation a set of stories that will be rich in significant information about the story-teller's own personality, including leads or clues to underlying tendencies which the subject may be reluctant to reveal or of which he may be unaware. The principle of the test is that the subject attending seriously to creating a story will interpret the pictured situations in conformity with his past experiences and present wants, expressing conscious and unconscious sentiments and needs, attitudes and conflicts.

The test was constructed as part of an intensive study of the personalities of 50 men of college age by Henry A. Murray and the staff of the Harvard Psychological Clinic.[4] The pictures of the most recent set of TAT cards (1943) are described in the test manual.[3] Separate sets for young boys, young girls, males over 14 years, and females over 14 years are derived from the 31 cards. Each set includes 20 pictures, administered in two one-hour sessions. The stories are written down by the examiner or otherwise recorded. In a shorter procedure, only the first session is held. The 1943 series is the third set and is regarded by the authors as to some extent still an experimental form. Some experimenters prefer cards of earlier series for their purposes. Experimentation with a form adapted for group administration is reported.[1]

In current practice with the TAT, the method of interpreting the stories and the direction and depth of interpretation vary according to the immediate purpose and according to the orientation of the interpreter with respect to personality theory. One framework for interpretation is suggested by the authors of the test. This method includes consideration of such features of the stories as the following: the character with whom the subject identifies himself; the forces in the hero's environment, to which forces the term *press* is applied; the story's outcome; the episode as a whole, i.e. the structure consisting of *hero's need—environmental press—outcome,* to which structure the term *thema* is applied.

With respect to validity, investigators report agreement of TAT interpretations with direct clinical evaluations and diagnoses, biographical data, written case histories and personality information; one study describes similarities between dreams and thematic stories; in another, unfavorable criticism during testing increased aggressive indications in the subjects' subsequent stories. The trend of these researches is to support the conclusion that TAT interpretations may reflect genuine manifestations of personality and that the test is an expeditious means of obtaining certain kinds of information about personality.

The TAT has been used in regular examinations in the psychiatric clinic, in studies of groups of mentally deficient, mentally disordered, and socially maladjusted persons, and in the general study of personality in children and adults. TAT interpretations are not used as conclusions in themselves but as hypotheses to be developed and evaluated in conjunction with other methods of studying the individual. Specific uses for vocational counselors in general have not been developed; a test of this type in its present stage might prove of pertinent interest to the vocational counselor with clinical facilities who is concerned with the more profound or pervasive effects of personality underlying occupational choice and occupational adjustment.

The TAT is a projection test. A review of this field of testing is given elsewhere.[5] As with other projection tests, the immediate advantages of greater standardization, objectivity of scoring, increased reliability, and statistically demonstrable validity for specific purposes—advantages which might be obtained by narrowing the scope of the test or restricting the free play of the subject's responses—have been considered secondary in the development of the TAT to the advantages of obtaining for study responses as rich in information as the basic technique permits. In addition to the training and experience which are important safeguards against the pitfalls of amateur interpretation, therefore, a genuine capacity for insight on the part of the interpreter is necessary if evaluation of TAT stories is to be dependable and fruitful.

The test is published by the Harvard University Press, Cambridge, Mass.

References:

1. Clark, R. M. A method for administering and evaluating the Thematic Apperception Test in group situations. *Genetic Psychology Monographs*, 1944, 30, 3–55.
2. Morgan, C. D. and Murray, H. A. A method for investigating fantasies—the Thematic Apperception Test. *Archives of Neurology and Psychiatry*, 34, 2, 289–306.
3. Murray, H. A. and Staff of the Harvard Psychological Clinic. *Thematic Apperception Test Manual*. Cambridge, Mass.: Harvard University Press, 1943.
4. Murray, H. A. et al. *Explorations in personality*. New York: Oxford University Press, 1938.
5. Sargent, H. Projective methods: their origins, theory, and application in personality research. *Psychological Bulletin*, 42, 5, 257–293.

D. E. S.

P.Q. (Personality Quotient) Test

Inventory

This test, constructed by Henry C. Link, with the assistance of G. K. Bennett, Rose G. Anderson, Sidney Roslow, and P. G. Corby, purports to measure personality defined as follows: "Personality is measured by the extent to which an individual has acquired habits and skills which interest and serve others." There are separate forms for boys and girls which have been standardized for ages between 12 and 20. The test is based on 150 items or questions regarding specific habits and activities, as contrasted with feelings and subjective beliefs. Each question is answered by checking one of three alternatives. It is constructed to be scored for the following traits, or collections of habits: 1. social initiative; 2. self-determination; 3. economic self-determination; 4. adjustment to opposite sex; 5. personality, an overall score from which the P.Q. is derived.

Norms

These cover grades 6 to 12 and college level, and are based on tests given to 3,131 individuals in about 100 schools throughout the country under the direction of cooperating psychologists and in accordance with procedures prepared by us.

Validity

The validity of this test has been demonstrated by several independent studies (see references below), including a nation-wide study in 48 high schools with 1,138 boys and girls, under the direction of 54 psychologists. The criterion in this study was leadership and non-leadership, leaders being defined as those democratically elected by their fellow students to such positions as captain or manager of an athletic team, president of the class or student body, manager of the paper, chairman of standing committees, et cetera. Leadership in these terms represents personality in a highly developed form, following our definition of personality. The members of the leadership group obtained significantly higher P.Q.'s than did the members of the non-leadership group, regardless of scholarship. Consistently, there has been no correlation between the P.Q., or personality traits, and scholarship, or performance in scholastic tests, indicating that the P.Q. Test measures characteristics quite distinct from those measured under the heading of intelligence. Validity has also been established in terms of classmate ratings on personality traits, and behavior problems as found in the Mooseheart Laboratory.

Clinical and Educational Uses

This test is a basic step in enumerating and evaluating the essential habits and skills which contribute to personality. In clinical work, aside from the significance of its scores, it serves as an interview by which the subject can enumerate many of his habits and activities. With groups it may be used as a device for developing personality building programs, since our concept of personality assumes that it is the result of habits which can be developed just as education now develops the habits measured by tests of scholastic achievement.

The Psychological Corporation, 522 Fifth Avenue, New York 18, New York, is the publisher.

References:

1. Drake, M. J., Roslow, S. and Bennett, G. K. The relationship of self rating and classmate rating on personality traits. Journal of Experimental Education, 1939, 7, 210–213.
2. Link, H. C. A test of four personality traits of adolescents. Journal of Applied Psychology, 1936, 20, 527–534.
3. ———. *The rediscovery of man.* Chapters 3 and 4: The psychodynamics of personality; Habits of personality. New York: The Macmillan Co., 1937.
4. ———. Manual for the P.Q. or Personality Quotient Test, 1938 Revision. New York: The Psychological Corporation.
5. ———. Social effectiveness and leadership. Educational and Psychological Measurement, 4, 57–67.
6. Roslow, S. Nation-wide and local validation of the P.Q. or Personality Quotient Test. Journal of Applied Psychology, 1940, 24, 529–539.
7. Thomson, W. A. An evaluation of the P.Q. (Personality Quotient) Test. Character and Personality, 1938, 6, 274–292.

H. C. L.

Psycho-Somatic Inventory. This inventory, referred to as the P-S Experience Blank and constructed by Ross A. McFarland and Clifford P. Seitz "is the result of an investigation into the psychologic and physiologic experiences which differentiate the psychoneurotic from the normal individual." A complete discussion of the concepts underlying the inventory is given elsewhere by the authors.[1]

The purpose of the inventory is to aid physicians, clinicians, social workers and school psychologists in ascertaining neurotic tendencies in late adolescents and adults and to determine whether these tendencies are predominately psychologic or physiologic. The authors hasten to add that "No questionnaire can be a final basis for classification, although it should direct attention to those cases which require investigation." This modesty is remarkable in that too many fail to note limitations in their testing devices.

The inventory consists of two scales of 46 questions each, to be answered "often," "at times," "seldom," or "never." The items composing the inventory were selected on the basis of their power to differentiate a group of normal subjects from a group of psychoneurotics. The reported reliability coefficients by the Spearman Brown method based on 100 normal subjects were .89, .86 and .80 respectively for Parts I and II, and .87 for the entire test. The reliability was also determined by retesting 52 normal males. These correlations were: Part I, .73; Part II, .75; Total, .75.

The validity of the inventory is indicated by the extent of the differences between the normal and psychoneurotic groups. These differences were from 13 to 19 times their standard errors, which would indicate unusually high validity. A study by Page[3] with Army personnel indicated such differences to be from 10 to 11 times their standard errors. In both of these studies the validating groups were the same as those used in the selection of items which tend to produce a spuriously high validity. This is mitigated in the Psycho-Somatic inventory by computing scoring weights on only a small part of the total number of subjects, and when groups containing none of the individuals used to establish scoring weights were used high CR's were still found.

A correlation coefficient between the two parts of the scale is in the order of magnitude of .70. Another study[3] reports a coefficient of .57.

The publisher of this inventory is Psychological Corporation, New York, New York.

References:

1. McFarland, R. A. and Seitz, C. P. A Psycho-Somatic Inventory. J. Appl. Psychol., 1938, 22, 327–339.
2. Mosier, C. I. On the validity of neurotic questionnaires. J. Social Psychol., 1938, 9, 3–16.
3. Page, H. E. Detecting psychoneurotic tendencies in army personnel. Psychol. Bull., 1945, 42, 645–658.

H. E. P.

Schrammel-Gorbutt Personality Adjustment Scale

Nature and Purpose

The Schrammel-Gorbutt Personality Adjustment Scale is a scale for evaluating the personal neurotic adjustment of junior and senior high school students, college students, and other adults. The scale is comprised of 117 simple situation items, all of which were carefully validated for the purposes herein presented. While the interpretation of results is to be made only on the basis of the total score, responses to individual items frequently will aid the counselor in a fuller comprehension of the adjustment problems any case may present. To have a comprehension of the degree of adjustment or maladjustment is of value, but the primary purpose of the scale is the discovery of maladjustments so that measures for improvement may be devised and applied.

In using this scale it should be kept in mind that it is not a measure of culture, personal attractiveness, or glamor, but of the personal neurotic adjustment of the individual to his environment.

When used with this in mind, the results should prove valuable for enhancing personal neurotic adjustment of individuals and groups.

Authors and Publisher

The authors of this scale are H. E. Schrammel, Director, Bureau of Educational Measurements, Teachers College, Emporia, Kansas, and Dorothy Gale Gorbutt, Clinical Psychologist, Children's center, Detroit, Michigan. The publisher is the Bureau of Educational Measurements, Kansas State Teachers College, Emporia, Kansas.

Validity of Scale

In order to validate the individual items comprising this scale, and the scale as a whole, the following procedure was followed. First, a content analysis was made of eight other reputable scales in the field. Next, an inventory was made of supplementary sources for additional suggested topics comprising the general field of neurotic adjustment. Items were then constructed to incorporate a sampling from the general areas which had been most frequently suggested by these scales and the supplementary literature.

The preliminary scale composed of these items was then administered to a random sampling of 125 college freshmen. On the basis of an item analysis of responses of this edition a revision was made and the revised edition administered to the entering class of college freshmen at the Emporia State College in September 1942. After further analysis of responses and scores, as explained in the next paragraph, the scale was printed in its present form and used in the Nation-Wide pupil Scholarship Test in April, 1943.

The process in the final selection and rejection of items just referred to was as follows. After the scores on the edition administered to the college freshmen class had been computed, the papers were divided into three groups for each sex on the basis of their adjustment scores. The total number of persons for whom papers were available was 112 men and 190 women. The number and per cent of maladjustment responses for each item for each of the three groups was next computed. Finally a comparison was made between the per cent of maladjusted responses on each item for the best adjusted third and the least well-adjusted third. Items on which the former group registered a higher per cent than the latter group were either modified or eliminated from the scale.

Between the adjustment scores made by 294 college freshmen on the Thurstone Personality Schedule, consisting of 223 items, and the Schrammel-Gorbutt Adjustment Scale which consists of only 117 items, a correlation computed by use of the Otis Correlation Chart yielded a coefficient of .88 ± .01. From the data presented it is apparent that the present scale possesses satisfactory validity for the purposes for which it was devised.

Reliability

By the split-half method of computation on the responses made by 298 college freshmen, this scale yielded a reliability coefficient of .90 ± .01. On a random sample of 100 papers written by the same group of students on the Thurstone scale, a reliability coefficient of .91 ± .01 was obtained.

On the Schrammel-Gorbutt scale a P. E. score of 1.49 was obtained for the combined group of high school and college students. This score signifies that any person's obtained raw score does not diverge from his theoretical true score by more than 1.49 score points. These data signify that in respect to reliability it is very satisfactory.

Administering, Scoring, and Interpreting

It is simple to administer this scale. Scoring is also easily and quickly accomplished. Scores are interpreted by use of percentile norms computed from scores made by 951 High School and college students.

Use of Results

The chief values accruing from use of this scale obviously are those which aid the individual in making improved adjustments to the various situations of life. During a period of attendance in a high school or college most students will enhance their adjustments without conscious effort on their part, because of the numerous and varied new contacts and experiences. If a student, however, is cognizant of his adjustment rating, he may be motivated to make conscious efforts to improve. In this manner much more will be accomplished for all but especially for those whose scores place them into the lower of the above brackets. An alert counselor should be able to give constructive advice and suggestions so that much more will be accomplished than through the ordinary incidental processes.

H. E. S.

Stott's Every-Day Life—An Inventory for the Measurement of Self-Reliance. This inventory is the result of a number of years of analytical study of the nature of self-reliance in adolescents and of work on the problem of its measurement. It was constructed by

Leland H. Stott. A factor analysis of the results from a preliminary form indicated a number of fairly distinct varieties of self-reliance.[1] The three most clearly defined of these were called "independence of decision in meeting personal problems and difficulties," "resourcefulness in group situations" and "personal responsibility." These three factors may be briefly described as follows:

I. Independence in personal matters.—An individual scoring high in this variable indicates that he prefers to make his own decisions and to rely upon his own judgment, particularly in regard to matters of a personal nature. He is inclined to meet and solve his own problems and difficulties in his own way.

II. Resourcefulness in group situations.—High scores indicate resourcefulness, together with dependability and willingness to work and lead out in the group situation. They indicate the tendency to participate actively in group discussions and to make contributions and suggestions which are acted upon by the group.

III. Personal responsibility.—A high score in this variable suggests the dependable, responsible sort of individual—one who is especially conscientious in keeping his agreements, meeting his obligations and doing his share generally in his relationships with others.

Theoretically these factors are independent of each other. However, conditions of measurement introduce sizable intercorrelations among them. They are sufficiently distinct one from another to warrant separate scorings.

The heading of the inventory—"Every-Day Life"—and the instructions to the subject were designed so as not to reveal the nature of the traits being measured. The scale is self-administering. With young subjects, however, the examiner should stress the fact that the only "right" answer is the one that describes the subject best. Five alternative answers, ranging from complete acceptance to strong denial, are provided for each item. Centile norms are available for high school students.[2]

Estimates of the reliability of the inventory have been derived by use of the split-half method. The following Spearman-Brown corrected coefficients were obtained:

I. Independence	II. Resourcefulness	III. Personal responsibility
.84	.90	
.92	.86	.94
		.94

The validity of the scores as indicators of the "factors" measured was insured by the method of item selection employed. Every item scored for a particular factor was selected, first, because it was found to be significantly correlated with a criterion score based upon the items that were highly "loaded" with that factor in the original analysis, and second, because it bore a logical relationship with the factor.

A moderate degree of relationship (r's in the neighborhood of .30) have been found between scores II and III ("resourcefulness" and "personal responsibility"), and the two adjustment scores of the California Test of Personality.[5] Studies have also indicated that certain factors in the home environment bear some relationship to self-reliance scores.[4] In a study of parental attitudes it was found that the children of the fathers who favored less strict disciplinary control tended to score highest in "independence." [3]

Every-Day Life is published by the Sheridan Supply Company, Beverly Hills, California.

References:

1. Stott, L. H. An analytical study of self-reliance. J. Psychol., 1938, 5, 107–118.
2. ———. *Every-day life: manual of directions and norms.* Beverly Hills, California: Sheridan Supply Co., 1941.
3. ———. Parental attitudes of farm, town and city parents in relation to certain personality adjustments in their children. J. Soc. Psychol., 1940, 11, 325–339.
4. ———. *The relation of certain factors in farm family life to personality development in adolescents.* Nebr. Agr. Exp. Sta. Res. Bull. No. 106, 1938, pp. 46.
5. ———. Unpublished data. University of Nebraska, Agricultural Experiment Station, Lincoln.

L. H. S.

Thorpe-Clark-Tiegs Mental Health Analysis. The purpose of the Mental Health Analysis, which was devised by Louis P. Thorpe, Willis W. Clark, and Ernest W. Tiegs (consultant), is to assist teachers, parents, and advisors in obtaining a better understanding of the subtle forces which condition and determine mental health. It is intended to clarify certain mental health concepts that may be used as tools in attacking the problems related to mental health. It provides a method of detecting and working for the elimination of causes which have been found to operate in producing various evidences of maladjustment. In short, it is an instrument which provides (1) a means for the identification of mental health difficulties, (2) assistance in the understanding of their significance and implications, and (3) suggestions for eliminating or alleviating such maladjustments.

The Analysis has been organized in two sections of five categories each: Section 1 is designed to ascertain the presence of mental health liabilities: (a) behavioral immaturity, (b) emotional instability, (c) feelings of inadequacy, (d) reaction to physical defects, (e) nervous manifestations, which should be minimized and eliminated as far as possible; Section 2 is similarly adapted to the detection of vital mental health assets: (a) close personal relationships, (b) inter-personal skills, (c) social participation, (d) satisfying work and recreation, (e) outlook and goals, which should be recognized and as far as possible amplified. It thus provides for a more adequate and constructive appraisal than is ordinarily furnished by instruments of this kind. It appraises the mental health status of pupils from the elementary grades through high school and college. It provides clinics with a convenient instrument for obtaining valuable information concerning maladjusted individuals. The adult form provides information on assets and liabilities which may be used in the selection, placement, adjustment, and up-grading of employees.

The Mental Health Analysis may be administered in about 45 minutes, either to an individual or a group, by anyone who will follow carefully the Manual of Directions, or it may be given as a "self-administering" test. The number of persons tested at one time is limited only by the facilities of the place of the examination. The test results can readily be scored by any person who will exercise care in following the directions supplied in the Manual.

The coefficients of reliability of the Total Scores and of the Assets and Liabilities scores of all series of the Mental Health Analysis are high, ranging from .92 for the Elementary Series to .93 for the Adult Series.

	Elementary	Intermediate	Secondary	Adult
Total Score....	.92	.93	.92	.93
Liabilities	.90	.91	.90	.91
Assets	.89	.90	.88	.89

The validity of any measuring instrument is dependent not only upon its intrinsic nature but also upon the manner in which it is used. Among the factors of importance that are related to the validity of the present test are (a) selection of test items, (b) the mental health categories, and (c) test item disguise.

Percentile norms are provided for each of the series, and are based on approximately one thousand cases at each level. The normative groups were carefully selected to provide a sampling of typical populations. Percentile norms make possible a comparison of a given individual's responses with those of the representative group on which the Analysis was standardized.

The various series of the Mental Health Analysis are available in hand-scoring editions. Each package of 25 inventories includes a complete Manual of Directions.

Machine scoring of all series of the Analysis may be accomplished by employing specially prepared I.B.M. answer sheets. For this purpose, the regular Analysis booklets are used.

The Mental Health Analysis is available in four series—Elementary, Intermediate, Secondary, and Adult. It is published by the California Test Bureau, Los Angeles 28, California.

L. P. T.

Vineland Social Maturity Scale. The Vineland Social Maturity Scale affords a genetic scale of social maturation from birth to senescence. It is designed to provide a developmental schedule for the measurement of social competence in terms of the behavioral expression of personal independence, social sufficiency, and social participation.

The scale consists of one hundred seventeen items of behavior performance classified for convenience in six categories, namely, self-help, locomotion, communication, occupation, self-direction and socialization. These categories are made up of detailed items in caption form, supplemented by descriptive definitions and organized as a measuring scale analogous to the Binet-Simon scale for intelligence. The items have been normatively standardized on a preliminary sample of twenty subjects of each age (ten boys and ten girls) so selected as to represent an approximation to normal social-economic distribution according to paternal occupation. The items have been calibrated as to progressive sequence by the Thomson method of scale calibration and arranged in year groups on the basis of normative total scores.

The scale represents a unique method of examination in that it is neither a rating scale nor a testing device. In standard application the skilled examiner obtains factual information by interviewing a competent informant intimately acquainted with the subject's performances. This permits examination without requiring the subject to be present and therefore affords a much wider range of application than is the case where subjects must be directly examined. It also avoids the embarrassments of rating scales by procuring concrete information regarding the subject which is then evaluated in standard definitional terms.

In addition to its standardization on normal subjects, the scale has been differentially standardized with institutionalized mentally deficient subjects. It has also been validated in many application studies with various types of cultural situations and in relation to numerous special handicaps. The method of examination also permits employing the subject as his own informant, although the use of independent informants is generally advocated.

The scale has a normative ceiling of twenty-five years. Results are expressable either in point-scale units or in year-scale units. As a year scale the average adult standardization is extended by interpolation to a maximum interpolated age score of thirty years at point score one hundred ten, leaving a balance of seventeen item points beyond this limit for the evaluation of very superior adult subjects. The scale is useful not only for the measurement of maturation, but also of deterioration or decline such as occurs in mental disturbance or incidental to senescence.

The scores by this scale are functionally related to intelligence as the major determining variable in addition to life age. The correlation is approximately $r = .85$ with 1916 Stanford-Binet for 431 institutionalized mentally deficient subjects with mental age range from one to twelve years, and life ages from six to fifty years.

The scale is published by the Educational Test Bureau, Minneapolis, Minnesota. An elaborated manual of instructions with presentation of supporting evidence is in preparation.

References:

1. Doll, E. A. *The Vineland Social Maturity Scale: revised condensed manual of directions. Publication of The Training School at Vineland, New Jersey, Department of Research.* Series 1936, No. 3, April, 1936.
2. ———. Annotated bibliography on the Vineland Social Maturity Scale. *Journal of Consulting Psychology,* 1940, 4, 123–132.

E. A. D.

Washburne Social Adjustment Inventory. The primary purpose of this test is to measure the degree of social and emotional adjustment of the individual. The current form, named the Thaspic Edition, includes 118 questions of the objective-answer type about the individual's feelings and customary behavior, and 4 free-answer questions about the individual's wishes. An over-all score for social adjustment is obtained; in addition, separate scores may be derived for sub-test groups of items classified as Truthfulness, Happiness, Alienation, Sympathy, Purpose, Impulse-Judgment, Control, and Wishes. (The name Thaspic is derived from the initial letters of the names of the sub-tests, excluding Wishes.)

The test was developed by J. N. Washburne to provide a measure of adjustment independent of intelligence for use in early identification of those students in a class likely to develop symptoms of maladjustment, for use in classification of children referred to a mental hygiene clinic because of behavior difficulties, and for use in personal counseling. Norms for total test score and sub-test scores are provided separately for junior high school, high school, and college groups.

In validation studies [3] involving 400 matched pairs of subjects, the questions in the present test ranked in the expected order with respect to adjustment, four samples consisting of (a) high school students judged exceptionally well adjusted, (b) high school students judged neither outstandingly well-adjusted nor poorly adjusted, (c) high school students judged exceptionally poorly adjusted, and (d) adolescent prisoners with records judged indicative of social maladjustment. Seventy-five per cent of the highest group scored above the upper ten per cent of the lowest group. The questions in the present test were selected in experimentation over a period of years with several earlier forms of the test. With respect to reliability, test-retest correlation for 400 college students over an interval of one semester was .92 for the test as a whole. Correlation of test score with intelligence was .07.

In a study [1] of first-year students in a girls' college, one investigator compared a group of students with good academic records who were individually judged to be well-adjusted with a group with poor academic records, including those who dropped out in their first year. The test did not differentiate the two groups effectively. The significance of this finding for purposes of generalization is obscured by the fact that individuals in the group with poor academic records were not otherwise evaluated with respect to adjustment.

The test is administered without time limit, average working time being from 30 to 50 minutes. The face-sheet of the test calls for personal information from which socio-economic status may be estimated.

The purpose of the sub-test Truthfulness is to identify papers invalidated by inaccuracies of the subject, unintentional or deliberate, in replies to 21 questions worded to imply possession of favorable traits to an unbelievable degree. The sub-test is not intended to measure any general tendency to untruthfulness and correlates .34 with intelligence.

In the three sub-tests Happiness (7 questions), Alienation (28 questions) and Sympathy (27 questions) are grouped those of the questions which seemed to pertain to emotional adjustment to other people and to the environment. In the three sub-tests Purpose (9 questions, one of them with several parts), Impulse-Judgment (9 questions) and Control (17 questions) are grouped those of the questions which seemed to be concerned with self-organization and self-regulation. The meanings of the separate sub-tests are discussed in the test manual. A guide for interpreting the sub-test "Wishes With Respect to Occupational Evaluation, Social Evaluation and Self Evaluation," is given in the manual. The test may be used without scoring the Wishes sub-test, the chief purpose of which is given as differentiation of degrees of superior adjustment. Coefficients of reliability of the sub-tests (excepting Truthfulness) are reported as ranging from .80 to .90.

The test is published by the World Book Company, Yonkers-on-Hudson, New York.

References:

1. Marsh, C. J. Prognostic value of the Washburne Social Adjustment Inventory. *Journal of Social Psychology,* 1943, 17, 287–294.
2. Washburne, J. N. A test of social adjustment. *Journal of Applied Psychology,* 19, 2, 125–144.
3. ———. *Washburne Social-Adjustment Inventory: manual for interpreting.* Yonkers-on-Hudson: World Book Company, 1940.

D. E. S.

Watson-Fisher Inventory of Affective Tolerance. This inventory, constructed by Robert I. Watson, and V. E. Fisher, purports to measure the so-called affective tolerance of an individual or group by self-rating. Affective tolerance is conceived to be the capacity to deal with affective tensions or emotional excitements. The sheer capacity to withstand or to "take" emotional disturbance is its most basic aspect. In addition, there are at least two other capacities which make relative this affective endurance. These are the individual's ability to vent or discharge his affective tensions and his ability to give a subjectively appropriate form and direction to his release of tension. A more detailed discussion of this conception is given elsewhere.[1] [2] Separate scores for these three aspects are not derived; rather, affective tolerance in general is measured.

The scores and items of this inventory may be used for the selection of those in need of personal counseling, as a tool in guidance, and for purposes of research in the fields of personality and emotion. It is not intended to be a substitute for clinical interviews; rather, it is an aid in such interviews.

The directions for administration are self-explanatory. The inventory calls for the person's own evaluation of his affective tolerance. Hence, cooperation, honesty, and some degree of insight are necessary if valid results are to be obtained. There is no time limit, but very few persons require more than twenty-five minutes. It is suitable for use with either sex. Average scores showing greater tolerance among males have been found.[4]

The inventory was standardized on college students, and centile norms are available which are based on scores obtained from schools in various areas throughout the country. The value of the development of local norms has been demonstrated.[4] It has also been administered to normal, neurotic, and psychotic adults;[2][6] student nurses;[3] and Negro college students.[6]

Validity has been demonstrated for college students and adults by the following methods: First, a preliminary selection of items was made which depended upon the progressive increase of criterion averages on each item from the lowest to the highest; i.e., the sixth scale step. Second, an analysis of variance was applied to each item surviving the preliminary selection. The average F value of the 61 items making up the final measure was 13.95 with a standard deviation of 7.70.[2] Third, the inventory, as constructed by the foregoing techniques, was applied on two occasions to clinically diagnosed neurotic and normal individuals and was found to discriminate between them.[2][5] The neurotic groups proved to be considerably less tolerant.

Reliability has been investigated by the split-half technique and found to be .93 and .94 for male and female college students respectively when corrected by the Spearman-Brown prophecy formula.

The Inventory has been found to show some degree of relationship to so-called personality inventories such as the Bell Adjustment Inventory, the Willoughby Personality Schedule, and the Bernreuter Personality Inventory, but not to the extent that would indicate its measuring the same aspect of personality.[3]

The publisher of this inventory is the Sheridan Supply Company, Beverly Hills, California.

References:

1. Fisher, V. E. Psychic shock treatment for early schizophrenia. Amer. J. Orthopsychiatr., 1944, 14, 358–367.
2. Fisher, V. E. and Watson, R. I. An inventory of affective tolerance. J. Psychol., 1941, 12, 149–157.
3 Watson, R. I. The relationship of the affective tolerance inventory to other personality inventories. Educ. psychol. Measure., 1942, 2, 83–90.

4. ———. School and sex differences in affective tolerance. Educ. psychol. Measure., 1943, 3, 43–48.
5. ———. Clinical validity of the Inventory of Affective Tolerance. J. soc. Psychol., 1945, 22, (3–15).
6. Watson, R. I. and Fisher, V. E. *Inventory of affective tolerance: manual of directions and norms.* Beverly Hills, California: Sheridan Supply Co., 1942.

R. I. W.

Weitzman Inventory of Social Behavior. This inventory, constructed by Ellis Weitzman, is designed to assess the level of social maturity of an individual or a group. Social maturity has been defined, in this case operationally, as the level of socially significant behavior attained at a given age. The social behavior characteristic of various age levels was studied, using about 900 subjects in four categories: employed persons, college students, CCC enrollees, and unemployed persons. The subjects were separated into three approximately equal age groups according to chronological age. The proportion of each group responding each way to every item was determined, scoring weights then being assigned in accordance with the direction and degree of changes accompanying increasing chronological age (the assumption having been made that social growth increases with increasing chronological age). A more detailed discussion of the nature of social growth and the method involved in its study has been presented elsewhere.[3]

An external check on the assumption of increasing score with chronological age was made by administering the test to an additional group of 100 subjects made up of employed persons and college students in states other than that of the original study. The linear correlation of the scores with chronological age was .55 with a PE of .047. The correlation ratio for the regression of age-on-scores was .54, and for the regression sçores-on-age, .61. Since there is naturally considerable spread of social maturity at any age level, higher correlations with chronological age should not be expected.

An estimate of test-retest reliability was made with a week's intervening interval with a group of university students. The coefficient of reliability was .88, with a PE of .02. The standard error of measurement was 2.34, which was 28.5 per cent of the standard deviation of the group.

Centile, age, and college norms are presented, for men and women separately, in the Manual.[1]

The inventory is self-administering and requires about fifteen minutes of the subject's time The test content emphasizes behavioral aspects characteristic of growth in social competence and adulthood. It should be especially useful in counseling and guidance in instances where it is important to determine the subject's ability to behave in a mature manner socially, or for the selection of personnel for tasks in which the social factor is important to success.

The publisher of this inventory is the Sheridan Supply Company, Beverly Hills, California.

References:

1. Weitzman, E. *Inventory of social behavior: manual of directions and norms.* Sheridan Supply Co., Beverly Hills, Calif., 1941.
2. ———. Note on a test of social competence. Jour. of Applied Psychol., 1941, 5, 595–596.
3. ———. A study of social maturity in persons sixteen through twenty-four years of age. Jour. of Genetic Psychol., 1944, 64, 37–66.

E. W

Wilson Scales of Stability and of Instability

General Statement

The Wilson Scales of Stability and of Instability consist of two divisions. Part I is a scale of stability, and Part II, a scale of instability. Each of the two scales is a complete unit in itself, but the two may be considered supplementary in the subject's self-analysis of his stability of character or personality.

The purpose of the scales is their use for self-analysis of character or personality, with the assistance of the counselor, so that suggested improvements in specific fields may be made.

The scales are designed for use by junior and senior high school students, college students, and other adult groups. Counselors, personnel directors, and other sponsors of organizations or leaders of groups will find the scales interesting and valuable.

Author and Publisher

The author of this set of scales is Matthew H. Wilson, Professor Emeritus of Psychology, Park College, Parkville, Mo. The manual of directions was provided by H. E. Schrammel, Director of the Bureau of Educational Measurements. The publisher is the Bureau of Educational Measurements, Teachers College, Emporia, Kansas.

Validity of Scales

The original scales which were tentatively constructed consisted of many more items than the present scales contain. The preliminary editions were administered to 111 college students. These students were asked to suggest additional items for each of the two scales which they felt significant in determining their own feelings of stability and of instability. At the same time they rated themselves on the scales that were provided as well as on the additional suggested items. The final items retained for the scales were those which an appreciable number checked as being significant factors in determining their stability or their instability. The final item values and the percentile scores were computed from the responses of 400 high school sophomores attending seven high schools in four different states. The college data were provided by the responses of 100 liberal arts college freshmen attending sixty-four different colleges.

Administering and Scoring

Each of the two scales is practically self-administering. No time limit is to be observed, but twenty to thirty minutes will be ample for all to complete both divisions.

Obviously there are no right or wrong answers. Hence no scoring is necessary. All that is needed is to find the sum of the numbers which the student crossed out. This is his score.

Norms for Interpreting

The norms for the Wilson Scales of Stability and of Instability are of two types. First, there are percentile norms for both scales for high school students and for college students. These are presented in Table II. These percentile norms were computed from the distribution of scores presented in Table I. As pointed out above these scores were made by 400 high school sophomores in seven representative high schools located in four states. The college scores were made by 100 liberal arts college freshmen in sixty-four colleges. The percentile norms are valuable for interpreting group and individual total scores.

The second set of norms are listed in Tables III and IV. These are the average ratings the group of students made on each item. By use of these item values, individual responses on the separate items may be given a more specific interpretation.

Use of Results

The values accruing from the application of these scales depends upon the use that the resourceful counselor or student will make of the results. For many students a knowledge of their total score rank and of their relative rank on each item will be sufficient stimulus to make efforts to effect improvements. For all, and particularly for those who possess a low degree of stability, the counselor should carefully study the total picture presented by the results on the two scales and make constructive suggestions.

To make use of the item value norms the student's score on each item should be compared with the norm values. If the student's score is average or superior, it is an indication his adjustment in regard to that situation is satisfactory. If his score, however, gives him an inferior rating, efforts should be made to enhance his adjustment in regard to the situation suggested by the item.

The counselor can be of the greatest help to the student by discussing with him his rating by items. Generally a student can tell when his score on a particular item is unsatisfactory. Then together, student and counselor, they can work together for the correction of each unsatisfactory trait.

In regard to overcoming neurotic handicaps, effective work can be done through conferences, suggested readings, and specific suggestions.

H. E. S.

PERSONALITY MEASUREMENT. Personality is widely believed to be an important factor in vocational success. In the popular meaning of the term, i.e., "influencing people," it has often been considered of greater importance than any other factor. While the vocational counselor does not accept this point of view so wholeheartedly, it is common practice to include one or more "personality tests" in the guidance battery. Such tests are intended to supplement those of intelligence, special aptitudes, interest, etc., in order to give a more complete picture of the vocational potentialities of the individual. The attempt to obtain an appraisal of personality is justified by evidence from studies of occupations and of school work. Successful accomplishment is determined, in part, by the personal characteristics of the individual, by his ability to adjust to the job or school situation, and by his ability to maintain the social relationships required of him.

When the counselor desires to use personality information in the guidance process, he is confronted with two problems: how best to secure the information; and how to interpret it. He can, of course, secure some of his knowledge of the counselee by personal appraisal, by reference to school and employment records, recommendations, and ratings, and by other informal devices. The counselor, however, seldom desires to depend entirely on such subjective evaluations for his information. His use of personality tests is an attempt to secure more objective information with results in quantitative terms. The occupational significance of such tests will depend on the aspects of personality they measure, and the relationship of those traits to vocational success and vocational satisfaction. It is profitable, therefore, to consider the traits of personality and the validities of the tests used to evaluate them.

The Definition of Personality

Personality has been defined in a variety of ways. Some definitions emphasize the general characterization of the individual, his total behavior pattern; "personality-as-a-whole" is held to be unanalyzable. Other definitions stress the reactions aroused in others by the behavior of the individual; his "social stimulus value." [4] Still others define personality as a pattern of traits or modes of behavior; while relationships may exist among the various components, they may be separated for analysis and measurement. This last point of view is the one most commonly accepted by the vocational counselor. His approach is, of necessity, analytical. He is less concerned with the integration, or total pattern, of the individual than with the nature and extent of specific characteristics. For the counselor's purpose, personality may be defined as *the pattern of traits of the individual which determine his adjustments to his environment.*

Definition of a Personality Trait

A personality trait is a characteristic mode of behaving. Aggressiveness, for example, is a personality trait of the individual if, in those situations permitting him to display some degree of aggressiveness or its opposite, he is consistently aggressive. The matter of consistency is basic to personality evaluation in that any prediction depends upon it. Argument has existed concerning the specificity or generality of traits. In the opinion of some authorities the trait is specific to the immediate situation, and the manner of behaving will change as conditions are varied. For others a trait is a generalized habit or system of reactions, which predisposes the individual to a certain mode of behavior in all situations of a similar character. The conflict between these points of view may be more apparent than real. It is obvious that the consistency with which a given mode of behavior will occur is itself a variable characteristic, both with regard to different aspects of any individual, and from one person to another. To be a trait, which can be identified and used, a characteristic must appear with sufficiently greater than chance consistency to permit the counselor to predict how the individual will behave on new occasions.

Fortunately for the field of vocational and adjustment counseling, many traits can be found within any individual which are consistent enough to permit prediction. It is probable that they become more clearly established as one grows older and, therefore, more easily predictable. This does not deny the presence of innate factors in personality development, but rather it emphasizes the importance of experience, particularly in social situations, such as family relationships. Some modes of behavior undoubtedly are established in early childhood. The experiences of adolescence, and later, result in other traits.

Identification of the Traits of Personality

The traits having vocational-guidance significance are those for which a standardized meaning or interpretation has been accepted. Allport and Odbert[2] list 17,953 trait names which have dictionary definitions. Only a small number of these terms appear in the literature on the subject of personality as conventional definitions of traits. Fewer still have been subjected to measurement by standardized testing procedures.

Trait names and definitions are derived from a variety of sources. Certain of them are arrived at by "logical analysis" of personality or of motives. This usually results in pairs of characteristics representing two extremes of the dimensions: Illustrations include introversion-extroversion, dominance-submission, etc. Other traits are stated in terms of adjustment to everyday social-personal problems, such as home adjustment, school adjustment, social intelligence, etc. A third group of traits is clinically derived. The assumption of such traits is based on the hypothesis that behavior of the sort observed in psychotics and neurotics is found to a greater or lesser degree in all persons. These trait names include hysteroid, schizoid, cycloid, and other aspects. Still another group of traits is produced by factor-analysis methods. These are identified by analysis of the correlations among tests and test items, and are defined in terms of the items involved. The trait names are commonly those used in other classifications, i.e., introversion, depression, etc.

From the vocational-guidance point of view, the lack of agreement on a system of traits is conducive to confusion. Characteristics having essentially the same behavioral basis may be given a variety of titles. Systematic exploration of personality by means of tests will produce many overlapping and non-parallel measurements, making interpretation difficult. Moreover, when the counselor investigates job descriptions and job requirements he finds a variety of characteristics described, frequently in vague or generalized terms, for which no tests exist. Part IV of the Dictionary of

Occupational Titles, for example, lists the following "personal traits" as being required in various types of work: leadership, poise, tolerance, patience, self-confidence, perseverance, showmanship, cheerful disposition, calmness, presence of mind, emotional control, and many others. It is pointed out that such traits may be estimated from observation, and from evidences of school, work, and social situations.

Tests of Personality Traits

In contrast with the nearly 18,000 trait names, the number of personality tests appears quite small. There are, however, over 500 such tests, many of them of limited use, and many not widely known. A number of different devices have been used to secure the information desired. The most popular, both in number of tests, and in frequency of use, has been the questionnaire or self-inventory test. This procedure secures, in a variety of ways, evidence of the individual's attitudes, interests, emotional behavior, adjustments, likes, and dislikes. The items may be limited to a single dimension of personality, as in Allport's Ascendance-Submission Reaction Study, or may be differentially weighted to give information about several traits, as in the Minnesota Multiphasic Test of Personality. In the latter test the responses are secured by having the subject sort cards on which the items are printed. In the majority of such inventories the items are marked "yes" or "no" to indicate the individual's description of his behavior in the situations listed. Variations of this technique include having the responses checked by someone who knows the individual being studied rather than by the subject himself. The popularity of the questionnaire test is due to the ease with which it may be administered, to its applicability to group administration, and to the objectivity with which it can be scored. Its chief weakness arises from the variations in interpretations of the items, and from the extent to which answers to them deviate from objective facts. It has been demonstrated that, with appropriate motivation, trait scores can be willfully modified by the examinee. While it is probable that the vocational-guidance situation offers less motivation for conscious influencing of scores, the problem of self-deception still remains. Some inventories attempt to secure internal evidence of objectivity of responses by the use of certain check items. It is safe to say, however, that one can never be sure that the answers to a self-inventory represent a true description of the individual's modes of behavior.

As a development of the clinical field there have appeared a number of devices for evaluating traits which are classed under the general heading of projective techniques. The most widely used of these is the Rorschach Test. In these procedures the characteristics of the subject are presumably revealed by the manner in which he responds to a photograph, an ink blot, or other abstract form. Such a test is usually administered individually but attempts have been made to devise forms for group administration. Scoring systems for these tests have become extremely intricate and a high degree of specific technical knowledge and of psychological background is usually regarded as necessary for adequate interpretation of responses. For these reasons, in part, and because of the subjective nature of the interpretations and the lack of validity data, projective tests have been relatively little used in guidance programs.

In terms of the definition of personality given above, the intellectual aspects of behavior are traits of personality; however, measures of intelligence and achievement are usually treated apart from tests of personality. It is of interest, therefore, that the use of such tests may provide indications of other personality traits. Interpretation of the sub-score pattern of the Wechsler-Bellevue Scales, for example, is said to give a basis for diagnosis of clinical characteristics such as neurotic or psychotic tendencies. Efforts have been made to develop other measures of this sort which will avoid the question of truthfulness of response, so inherent in the questionnaire. This is an undeveloped field, but one that deserves exploration if objective measurements are to be found. Other methods have been attempted in which the purposes of the test have been concealed from the subject. In the Character Education Inquiry Tests,[4] for example, honesty and deception are measured by means of "self-scoring tests of intelligence," "tests of coordination," etc. The behavior of the subject in such tests is observed or evaluated in various ways, but he is presumed to be unaware of the traits being studied.

A somewhat similar but more involved procedure has been developed for determination of other characteristics. Situations, often elaborately planned, have been presented to the subject to permit observation of his behavior. The manner in which he meets problems, accepts responsibilities, reacts to frustration, and so on, is noted. Some use of this procedure was made in the military services for selection of candidates for special training. While it is doubtful whether any elaborate situation test of this sort would be practicable for vocational counseling, within limits counselors can and do observe behavior of various sorts, such as reactions to testing, manner during interviews, etc. Informal judgments are made from such observations and frequently are made part of the guidance record.

More use is made of extended observations of the counselee as reported by means of rating scales. Letters of recommendation and anecdotal materials are also used to secure evidence of traits. Such information may be prepared by teachers, friends, employers, or by the counselor himself. The principal defects of such devices are (1) the lack of adequate opportunity for observation by the rater, (2) a tendency toward bias or prejudice on the part of some observers, and (3) variations in interpretation of trait names or descriptions. On the other hand, a well designed rating scale provides data whose reliability, at least, is satisfactory.

Validation of Personality Measures

The crucial question about any measuring device used in vocational guidance is, of course, not reliability, but validity. The reliability coefficients for the various personality tests are found ordinarily to range from .80 to .95. Validities, on the other hand, have usually been low. Moreover, validation studies have frequently been inadequate because of the lack of satisfactory criteria. Of the two kinds of criteria which are possible, the one most often used is a trait criterion; that is, the test results are correlated with some other indicator of the trait which the test is intended to measure. For this purpose the test may be correlated with a rating scale, a self-evaluation, or some other inventory. When one questionnaire is correlated with another designed to measure the same traits, the coefficient obtained is, strictly speaking, an indication of reliability rather than validity. Only when one or the other of such measures is found to be related to some objective indicator of the trait in question can validity be said to be established. Unfortunately, such criteria are very difficult to secure. For tests intended to measure adjustment, case histories, records of disciplinary action or other difficulties, etc., may be useful. Clinical diagnoses and commitment to an institution have been criteria for the tests of neurotic or psychotic tendencies. The Minnesota Multiphasic Personality Inventory, for example, was reported by its authors to discriminate, in its various phases, between hospitalized cases and those assumed to be normal.

The value of such validity information in vocational guidance depends upon the extent to which such traits can be shown to relate to vocational success. A second type of validation is, therefore, essential, i.e., a measure of the relationship between the test data and evidences of occupational success and satisfaction. This kind of validation is largely lacking. The most that can be said, in the majority of cases, is that job analyses indicate the importance of certain personality traits. On this basis the tests are assumed to have predictive value. The weakness of this assumption is apparent and accounts for the fact that in a recent poll only fifteen per cent of a sample of test experts believed the personality inventory to be even moderately useful for practical purposes. Twenty per cent of the same group credited the Rorschach Test with moderate or greater usefulness.

Relatively few validation studies against the criterion of occupational success have been made and these do not always support the *a priori* assumption often made concerning the vocational application of personality test results. Teachers, for example, have no distinguishing pattern of traits. Sales and clerical personnel have been found to differ in the traits of dominance and of extroversion. There is reason to believe, however, that this is due to the salesman's attempt to present himself in the best possible light on the questionnaires used. In one extensive study of men and women in sales work, clerical work, professions, trades, and common labor with the Bernreuter Personality Inventory it was reported that it was "impossible to find any important personality differences" between the various groups.[5] A study of Pharmacy and Accounting students by means of the Rorschach Test indicated no patterns common to either group. The evidence concerning academic achievement in various fields is not conclusive, but tends to indicate that measured personality traits have little bearing on scholastic achievements. Considering the present evidence, there appears to be little basis for the use of personality test scores in the choice of one vocation over any other.

Two reasons may be advanced to account for this conclusion. First, most occupations provide sufficiently varied opportunities and activities to permit successful achievement by persons of varied personality characteristics. This is particularly true in the professional and semi-professional fields where specialization within the occupation is common. Even at lower occupational levels considerable variation in personalities is possible without interfering with success.

The other reason for lack of complete satisfaction with personality tests for vocational guidance lies in the construction and validation of the measuring instruments. Few of them have been satisfactorily validated against outside criteria. Their relationship to vocational success and satisfaction is a matter of conjecture. For prediction of success in specific vocations, tests covering a wide variety of traits should be applied to a large sample of occupational fields. The scores should be examined to determine whether distinguishing patterns of traits can be found for the various fields. Similar studies should be made of relationships to success in various school subjects. This procedure is essential for any kind of measuring device that is to be used in counseling.

The Use of Personality Information

Although specific occupational validities of personality test results are not available, there remain other important reasons for use of the information in vocational guidance. Knowledge of certain traits may enable the counselor to aid his subject to adjust his new vocation, regardless of its specific nature. Probability of completion of extended training programs, satisfaction with training and with the occupation, and adjustment to the social requirements of the job may be evaluated. Several studies have shown that personality maladjustments, such as lack of confidence, emotional instability, and others, are major causes in job maladjustments. Friction on the job, poor morale, deficient output, and dismissal frequently result. Failure in school, confused or inadequate study habits are often attributable to personality disturbances. It is no less the counselor's duty to aid the student in adjusting his emotional and social problems in relation to his school work and his job than it is to help him make the best vocational choice.

In instances of serious personality disorders the information provided by test or by clinical diagnosis is indispensable. Not only is the over-all picture of occupational competence involved, but selection of an objective in accordance with interests, aptitudes, and abilities is an important step in adjustment therapy.

Summary

In summary, it may be said that some personality tests have been shown to possess considerable validity when correlated with clinical diagnoses, case histories, and other evidence of adjustment or maladjustment. While it is not yet possible to interpret test scores differentially in terms of specific vocations, the experienced counselor recognizes the necessity of having all possible knowledge of the characteristics of his counselee to use as basis for satisfactory guidance. Vocational guidance, in many of its aspects, is a clinical procedure and knowledge of personality traits is essential for the complete picture. As a clinical tool the personality test serves as a point of departure, as a means of focusing attention on adjustment problems, and as an aid in interpreting other data. As further research

ENCYCLOPEDIA OF VOCATIONAL GUIDANCE

is accomplished, new devices developed, and more validity data accumulated, such tests may become of practical significance in the selection of specific vocational objectives.

References:

1. Allport, G. W. *Personality.* New York: Henry Holt and Co., 1937.
2. Allport, G. W. Henry and Odbert, H. S. *Trait-Names: a psychological study. Psychological Monographs,* 1936, No. 211.
3. Guilford, J. P. *Psychometric methods.* New York: McGraw-Hill Book Co., 1936.
4. Hartshorne, H. and May, M. *Studies in deceit.* New York: Macmillan Co., 1928.
5. Paterson, D. G. and Darley, J. G. *Men, women, and jobs.* Minneapolis: University of Minnesota Press, 1936.
6. Shaffer, L. F. *Psychology of adjustment.* Boston: Houghton Mifflin Co., 1936.
7. Stagner, R. *Psychology of personality.* New York: McGraw-Hill Book Co., 1937.
8. Symonds, P. M. *Diagnosing personality and conduct.* New York: D. Appleton-Century Co., 1931.

N. D. W.

PERSONALITY TESTS, EVALUATION OF. Personality is of prime importance in one's vocational adjustment and success. Studies of job satisfaction, of factors contributing to vocational morale, of causes of vocational failure, and of qualities desired by employers in employees at the time of selection all emphasize this point. Therefore, if an individual possesses any qualities of personality which might contribute significantly either to wholesome adjustment or to maladjustment in occupations he has under consideration he might well profit by knowing this before a choice is made. It has been said that one's choice of a vocation is not merely the choice of a means of making a living but a way of life. For greatest happiness and efficiency this way of life ought not only to be consistent with the individual's present personality but ought to be such that the individual can develop the kind of personality he wants to and can become.

Optimum personality patterns for various vocations and specific jobs are as yet unknown. A beginning has been made in studying such patterns. Dodge [5] has published studies on personality traits of successful people in certain occupations. Although the more successful employees as a group in these studies are significantly differentiated from the less successful ones in certain traits, there is enough overlapping of groups to make accurate individual prediction impossible. This is not a criticism of the studies, but it is, in part, a result of inaccuracy of measurement with present scales and, possibly, of no clear-cut personality patterns which are essential for success in given vocations. This latter point is argued by Super.[17] This uncertainty as to the relationship between personality characteristics and vocational success as well as the inaccuracies of measurement cast doubt on the kinds of guidance that ought to be given in this area. It is possible that as improved measures of personality become available and as job analysis becomes more accurate, clearer patterns of personality for success will emerge.

The last decade and a half has witnessed a great deal of activity in the development of means of measuring personality. Attempts have been made to improve rating scales; factor analysis has been used to analyze personality into specific components and tests made for the purpose of measuring these components; and elaborate clinical and statistical investigations have been combined to establish and to check the validity of certain measures. Even with all this meticulous research on the part of many people, one must say that personality measurement is in a highly experimental stage and those who use such tests should do so with caution and with an awareness of their shortcomings. Some of these shortcomings will be more apparent after a critical examination of some of the common measuring instruments in use. The devices to be examined will be limited to inventories, questionnaires, tests of personality, in the restricted sense, omitting scales of attitude, measures of interest, and tests of character which, in a broad sense, are interpreted also as kinds of personality measures.

Certain tests now available for use in vocational guidance will be discussed in the paragraphs that follow. These particular measuring instruments are cited because they are among the ones now being most widely used and among those most carefully constructed. It will be recognized that any such selection is quite arbitrary when it is realized that, perhaps, five hundred devices and procedures for appraising personality have been developed during the last few decades and are referred to in psychological literature. The intention in this discussion is not to condemn or praise any particular test, but to examine critically procedures for evaluating personality status and development. There is no implication by omission that other available tests may not be just as useful as these as aids to vocational guidance.

The tests which will be used in this illustrative manner are as follows:

Adams, Clifford R. and Lepley, William M. *The personal audit*. Chicago: Science Research Associates.

Bell, Hugh M. *The adjustment inventory* (Student Form). Stanford University, California: Stanford University Press.

Bernreuter, Robert G. *The personality inventory*. Stanford University, California: Stanford University Press.

Darley, John G. and McNamara, Walter J. *Minnesota personality scale*. New York: The Psychological Corporation.

Evans, Catherine and McConnell, T. R. *Minnesota T.S.E. inventory*. Chicago: Science Research Associates.

Hathaway, Starke R. and McKinley, John C. *The Minnesota multiphasic personality inventory*. Minneapolis: University of Minnesota Press.

Humm, Dorcaster G. and Wadsworth, Guy W. *The Humm-Wadsworth temperament scale*. Los Angeles: Humm-Wadsworth Personnel Service.

Link, Henry C. *P. Q. or personality quotient test*. New York: The Psychological Corporation.

Tiegs, Ernest W., Clark, Willis W., and Thorpe, Louis P. *California test of personality* (Secondary series). Los Angeles: California Test Bureau.

A relatively new inventory for use in appraising certain personality characteristics in high school, college, and industrial situations is *The Personal Audit,* by Adams and Lepley. The areas measured by each of nine subtests, stated in abbreviated form, are: I. sociability; II. suggestibility; III. tendency to rationalize; IV. tendency to anxiety; V. tendency to personal intolerance; VI. flexibility of attitudes; VII. susceptibility to annoyance; VIII. sexual emotionality; and IX. tendency to think, possibly worry, about unsolved problems. A form is also available which includes only the first six of these subtests.

Data given in the manual indicate that it was validated chiefly on the basis of cross analysis and item analysis on pairs of subtests with a view to insuring inner consistency. What each part measures is concluded from the combined opinions of fourteen psychologists. Reliabilities of the parts based on 442 college students are all above .90. Tubbs,[18] reported reliabilities above .90 for Parts I to VI and coefficients in the 70's for Parts VII–IX. The writer can't be sure whether this is for the latest form of the test. Present norms are based upon an inadequate number of cases.

Adams [1] experimented with two forms of directions to study the influence upon the test scores of trying to represent one's self well. The results seem to show that scores can be influenced by an attempt to misrepresent; but, perhaps, the items are more indirect and the purpose more concealed than with many such tests.

The writer has found, in the use of this test with college freshmen, that it was often difficult to show them logically why their answers to certain items were indicators of the trait or adjustment in question. For example, if one thinks differently now than he did three or four years ago (and he must be able to remember) about these items, he is flexible or docile of attitudes:

15. Educational value of movies
20. Truth in advertising
30. Value of college education in life success
40. Getting regular amount of sleep

Or, again, one shows personal intolerance (Part V) if he dislikes a great deal "people who are 'chiselers,' " "a person who brags about his achievements" or "individuals who bite their finger nails constantly" but is susceptible to annoyance (Part VII) if he is much annoyed "to have a person push ahead of you in line," "to have someone read over your shoulder," or "to have a person sneeze or cough in your face." Whether these two sets of items bring about different responses because they tap different basic personality components or because of their wording, might be worthy of investigation. The correlation coefficient between Parts V and VII is .57, so there apparently is considerable overlapping from some cause. There is counseling value in having test items seem logically related to the aspects of personality they measure, although, it might be possible to find wholly disguised or illogical (on the surface) items for this purpose.

Some personality tests are designed to measure adjustment to specific elements in life situations instead of the strength of one or more unified personality traits or components. *The Adjustment Inventory* by Bell is one such device. This test purports to measure home, health, social, and emotional adjustment. It has been validated by the use of four common procedures, namely, correlating it with known tests, studying differences between widely-spaced groups, measuring internal consistency, and checking it against interviews and case data.

The size of groups whose differences were studied for validating the subtests is small, e.g., the smallest being 24 in each group in the case of social adjustment and the largest being 51 in each group for home adjustment. Other groups than these were used for validating the total score. On this type of test, however, total adjustment is of doubtful use since "unsatisfactory" adjustment in one area is not compensated for by having "satisfactory" adjustment in the total inventory. The test as a whole was checked against four hundred interviews with college students. Norms, however, are given for both high school and college students. Reliability coefficients as given by Bell on the separate sections vary from .80 to .89.

Clark [3] made a careful check of the validity of this test at the Rochester Athenaeum and Mechanic Arts Institute by comparing it with composite faculty ratings based upon a large mass of information about each of 138 students. He found that correlations between Bell's scores and the ratings varied from—.319 to .165. He concludes that this inventory is not a valid indicator of student adjustments at this school. It must be remembered, however, that there is considerable difficulty in using ratings as a valid criterion. A number of other schools have found it useful as an instrument for locating cues to maladjustment or potential difficulties to be pursued more intensively in the interview. If used this way by trained counselors it can be of value in vocational guidance. Bell [2] gives data about the construction and use of this inventory in a separate volume.

The Personality Inventory by Bernreuter undoubtedly has been the most widely used adjustment measure in recent years. It was designed to measure four personality characteristics, namely, neurotic tendency, self-sufficiency, introversion-extroversion, and dominance-submission. Studies of this test by factor analysis show that these are not unique traits and the intercorrelations between some of them show that there is great overlapping among the neurosis, self-sufficiency, and dominance scales. Flanagan contributed two more scales to the test, one measuring confidence and the other sociability. These seem to be quite independent of each other.

In the use of such a scale the counselor will need to avoid assuming that a personality trait, such as neurotic tendency, is identified merely by naming it. In general efforts to validate the test against clinical groups have not been successful. Therefore, there is uncertainty as to what is measured. It has been proposed that the test be used as an excellent check list of clinical symptoms. Although percentile norms are given for high school, college, and adult levels this writer has found the test rather difficult reading for many high school pupils.

The *Minnesota Personality Scale* gives five separate measures of adjustment: I. morale, II. social adjustment, III. family relations, IV. emotionality, and V. economic conservatism. The items were derived from a factor analysis of four scales or inventories in use at the University of Minnesota in 1935–36. Items were retained on the basis of their differential power between high and low scoring groups. Since the original scales from which the items were derived were validated on a series of group difference studies, these were not repeated. Intercorrelations of arts on the final scale range from .05 to .56 for two groups of each sex. Of forty such intercorrelations eight are in the .50's, seven are in the .40's and five are in the .30's. Parts II and IV and Parts III and IV are most closely related. Norms are only for university men and women.

The writer has found some difficulty in the interpretation of Part I, morale, with college students. The manual states that on this part, "Low scores usually indicate cynicism or lack of hope in the future." This has not seemed true with a fairly large percentage of students interviewed. Perhaps this is just a difference in clinical interpretation. One wonders, also, why Part V is called "economic conservatism" instead of "economic attitudes." The other four parts do not carry names which designate an extreme point on a scale.

An interesting investigation [4] of the form of statement in such inventories was carried on with fifty men and fifty women in the experimental stages of construction. Duplicate forms were organized, one using declarative sentences and the other interrogative ones. In each case answers were to be indicated on a five point descriptive scale. Each student answered both forms in a rotation arrangement. Eighty of the one hundred students expressed preference for the interrogative form of statement.

The *Minnesota T-S-E Inventory* differs from all those so far described in that it attempts to concentrate on a narrower range of personality and measure it more thoroughly. Guilford [9] showed through his factor analysis of introversion-extroversion items that this characteristic is not a unified trait but has several components. The *T-S-E Inventory* is designed to give a measure of introversion-extroversion in relation to thinking, social, and emotional reactions. That each test is fairly independent of the others is shown by the fact that the highest intercorrelation is $-.27$. Reliabilities for the separate parts with two groups of college students range from .75 to .91. The writer would question the statement in the manual that, "The tests seem to be sufficiently reliable for individual prediction." Such a statement needs to be qualified even if each subtest has shown a reliability of at least .88 in one or more situations, as the authors point out. However, the tests seem to differentiate fairly well between the averages of groups known to be different in these traits. Evans and McConnell [8] have described the construction of the scale.

The statement is made in the manual that the *T-S-E Inventory* "may be employed . . . in the diagnosis and counseling of senior high school and college students." No norms are given for high schools and no references to studies or investigations of its use with high school students are cited. It may be useful with high school students but it is doubtful practice to recommend such inventories for other than experimental use with groups at other levels of maturity than those for which it is known to be suitable.

The idea back of this inventory, to take a characteristic of personality which has been identified in a general way, to define it more precisely, and to invent a way to measure its components is a fruitful approach to appraisal. The aspects of personality which are measured by the *T-S-E Inventory* are important for vocational guidance.

The Minnesota Multiphasic Personality Inventory by Hathaway and McKinley [11] is a very carefully constructed instrument for the measurement of those personality characteristics often confronting the psychiatrist. These traits are hypochondriasis, symptomatic depression, psychaesthenia, hysteria, hypomania, and psychopathic deviation. The original items for the test were formulated on the basis of clinical experience, texts in psychiatry, other tests, and directions for case taking in medicine. The scale has been validated clinically, some parts of it on a small number of cases. The authors, however, do not consider it a finished scale but one which needs to be validated further in practice and in other laboratories.

Although there is at least one report [10] of the use of this scale in connection with the vocational advisement of veterans it has not, and perhaps will not, be generally used for routine vocational counseling. It seems that it is more likely to be used to identify extreme deviates who may come to a counseling center and may need psychiatric or psychological counseling and therapy before vocational guidance. Those who devise other personality tests (and those who use them) might profit greatly if similar care were taken to validate the test clinically as well as statistically.

The Humm-Wadsworth Temperament Scale measures seven components, namely, "Normal" (N), Hysteroid (H), Manic Cycloid (M), Depressive Cycloid (D), Autistic Schizoid (A), Paranoid Schizoid (P), and Epileptoid (E). The scale contains 318 items of a clinical nature. About half of these items are not scored but are retained in the scale because they are presumed to influence the manner in which other items are answered. Validity is based upon the agreement between scores and clinical records and upon intercorrelation of parts. The coefficients between the "normal" category and each of the other six parts range from .040 to .690.

Dysinger [7] published a critique of this scale and his inter-correlation coefficients for the "normal" component with the other six were all negative and ranged from — .218 to — .785. Humm and Wadsworth secured a correlation of .887 between cycloid manic and cycloid depressive categories and Dysinger reported a relationship of .853 for these same subtests. He questioned the advisability of dealing with these components separately. Kruger[15] also reported considerable overlapping of components on the basis of the test results of 437 men 20 to 30 years of age who had not found satisfactory vocational adjustment. Humm[12][13] published replies to both articles. Humm has reported several instances of the high validity of the scale as an aid in selecting public service, shop, and engineering employees. Dorcus[6] gave this scale to two groups of employees picked by management, one being made up of maladjusted discontents and the other of employees showing no such behavior patterns. The tests were scored independently by Dorcus and by Humm. It is reported that there was agreement on all cases as to the scoring. The test identified 72.8 per cent of the problem employees and 69.2 per cent of the non-problem ones.

The *P. Q. or Personality Quotient Test* was designed, so states the manual, "to provide a measure of personality in terms of a P. Q. or personality quotient. . . . The P. Q. indicates the development or growth of the individual's personality." There are five scales: (X) Personality (The Overall Score), (S. I.) Social Initiative, (S. D.) Self-Determination, (E. S. D.) Economic Self-Determination, and (S. X.) Adjustment to the Opposite Sex. The P. Q. is based on the overall score (Scale X) which includes most of the items. It is intended for secondary school students and college freshmen.

The theory proposed is that personality components are not independent, therefore, a large amount of overlapping is to be expected. Intercorrelation coefficients are relatively high. For example .704 between S. I. and E. S. D. for boys and .62 between S. I. and S. X. for boys. These coefficients are a little lower for girls, .491 and .543, respectively. Of course the coefficients between the overall score and the parts are high, .349 to .869, because the same items are involved. This raises the question of the value of the part scores, since they do not represent sharply defined patterns of behavior. Roslow[16] reports that two separate item analyses were made and two successive revisions of the scale developed after the 1936 edition. What changes were made in form or content is not described but the reliabilities given in the manual are for the boy's form for the 1936 edition. Three of these reliability coefficients are in the .80's and two in the .70's. Validity is substantiated by the fact that the test has been shown to differentiate between leaders and non-leaders and agrees with teachers' and students' judgments about the personality of pupils well known to them.

The P. Q. methods of interpretation seems to this writer to be an unfortunate procedure. The use of the I. Q. with adolescents is undesirable because of its fictitious nature and the use of various types of so-called intelligence tests have shown that there is not one but many I. Q.'s. There undoubtedly would be many P. Q.'s if all personality tests provided such derived scores. Even the same P. Q.'s of this particular test will differ in significance for different people because they may be determined by different components. It seems wiser to avoid use of the total score and use percentile interpretations, as provided, for the part scores.

The *California Test of Personality* has twelve subtests, six related to "self-adjustment: based on feelings of personal security" and six related to "social adjustment: based on feelings of social security." A study of some of the individual items causes one to wonder why they are (if they are) more indicative of the trait under which they are classified than of certain other traits. The correlation between Section 1 and Section 2 is .54 and the authors state: "The items of each component represent fundamental action patterns. The obtained correlations among components emphasize the unity or 'wholeness' of normal individuals." Of course, it could also represent "halo" or a wide range of overlapping of items. The authors seem to have thought it was unimportant to publish these intercorrelations.

The secondary series is designed for grade levels 9 to 14, yet only one set of norms is furnished. If personality does develop much from grades 9 to 14 the younger children are likely to be in the very low percentile ranges and the college sophomores in the very high ones. On some subtests a difference of one item answered correctly will raise or lower the percentile score 25 points. No evidence is given as to how many individuals are used as a basis for the norms or at what ages or grade levels they may have been in their development. Such omissions in published standard test manuals is inexcusable.

The test booklet is well arranged, easy to administer and easy to score. The profile plan of graphing scores is desirable if the separate components have validity. The symbols for the parts on the front of the profile do not seem well enough disguised to prevent pupils from understanding what is being measured. The authors have introduced words of caution at a number of places in the manual hoping to guard the user against placing too much reliance on items and specific parts of the test.

A few final comments will be made about the use of personality tests in vocational guidance. Traits do not exist or come into being merely by naming them. One must be cautious in assuming that a test measures exactly what its name may imply to any user. Authors of tests have an obligation to furnish valid and reliable supporting data and users ought to avoid purchasing tests for which such data are not easily available in the manual of directions.

No personality test now exists which can be used with the assurance that one may have in the better intelligence and achievement tests. Therefore if personality tests are to be included in vocational guidance batteries they should be employed experimentally. They should always be interpreted in the light of other supporting data from records, interviews, other tests, and case histories. This note of caution is well reflected in the replies of 79 psychologists to a questionnaire by Kornhauser [14] on the use of personality tests.

Finally, counselors should carefully guard against adding to an individual's personality difficulties through the use of such tests. Intelligence test scores have often been used to "catalogue" individuals, to limit their opportunities, and even to criticize them and their families. There are even more mental hygiene dangers in such uses of personality tests both because of ignorance as to what they measure and their very personal nature.

References:

1. Adams, C. A new measure of personality. *Journal of Applied Psychology*, 1941, 25, 141–151.
2. Bell, H. M. *The theory and practice of student counseling, with special reference to the adjustment inventory.* Stanford University: Stanford University Press, 1935.
3. Clark, W. A. and Smith, L. F. Further evidence on the validity of personality inventories. *Journal of Educational Psychology*, 1942, 33, 81–91.
4. Darley, J. G. Factor analysis in the establishment of new personality tests. *Journal of Educational Psychology*, 1940, 31, 321–334.
5. Dodge, A. W. What are the personality traits of the successful salesperson? *Journal of Applied Psychology*, 1938, 22, 132–139. . . . of the successful clerical worker? *Journal of Applied Psychology*, 1940, 24, 576–586. . . . of successful teachers? *Journal of Applied Psychology*, 1943, 27, 325–327.
6. Dorcus, R. M. A brief study of the Humm-Wadsworth temperament scale and the Guilford-Martin personnel inventory in an industrial situation. *Journal of Applied Psychology*, 1944, 28, 302–307.
7. Dysinger, D. W. A critique of the Humm-Wadsworth temperament scale. *Journal of Abnormal and Social Psychology*, 1939, 34, 73–83.

8. Evans, C. and McConnell, T. R. A new measure of introversion-extroversion. *Journal of Psychology,* 1941, 12, 111–124.

9. Guilford, J. P. and Guilford, R. B. Personality factors S, E, and M and their measurement. *Journal of Psychology,* 1936, 2, 109–127.

10. Harmon, L. R. and Weiner, D. N. Use of the Minnesota multiphasic personality inventory in vocational advisement. *Journal of Applied Psychology,* 1945, 29, 132–141.

11. Hathaway, S. R. and McKinley, J. C. A multiphasic personality schedule: I. Construction of the schedule. *Journal of Psychology,* 1940, 10, 249–254.

12. Humm, D. G. Dysinger's critique of the Humm-Wadsworth temperament scale. *Journal of Abnormal and Social Psychology,* 1939, 34, 402–403.

13. ———. Discussion of "A statistical analysis of the Humm-Wadsworth temperament scale." *Journal of Applied Psychology,* 1939, 23, 525–526.

14. Kornhauser, A. Replies of psychologists to a short questionnaire on mental test development, personality inventories and the Rorschach test. *Educational and Psychological Measurement,* 1945, 5, 3–15.

15. Kruger, B. A statistical analysis of the Humm-Wadsworth temperament scale. *Journal of Applied Psychology,* 1938, 22, 641–652.

16. Roslow, S. Nation-wide and local validation of the P. Q. or personality quotient test. *Journal of Applied Psychology,* 1940, 24, 529–539.

17. Super, D. E. *Dynamics of vocational adjustment.* New York: Harper and Brothers, 1942, 97–98.

18. Tubbs, W. R. A study of the interrelationships between the Adams-Lepley Personnel Audit and the Bernreuter Personality Inventory. *Journal of Applied Psychology,* 1942, 26, 338–358.

C. O. M.

PHARMACY APTITUDE AND INTEREST MEASUREMENT.

At the present time, there exist no tests of pharmacy aptitude. However, both the American Foundation for Pharmaceutical Education and the American Association of Colleges of Pharmacy are interested in problems of selection and are considering investigations in this field.

Although it should not be very difficult to construct a valid aptitude test for the work of the pharmacy school, it appears that there are often marked discrepancies between grades in the pharmacy curriculum and financial success in the operation of drug stores. For this reason, considerable attention must be given to personality and interest factors. However, there are many pharmacy graduates who go into manufacturing establishments, dispensaries, and research, and their interest and personality patterns may differ considerably from those of persons who are seeking store jobs.

Studies at the University of Idaho, Southern Branch have shown that pharmacy students with I.Q.'s of less than 110 have great difficult in obtaining degrees. Aptitude for science, particularly for chemistry, is extremely important. There is some correlation between interest in pharmacy as expressed by students and high ratings on the Chemist and Physician scales of the Strong Vocational Interest Blank for Men. A high rating on the Sales Manager scale of the Strong might be interpreted to mean interest in drug store work, if coupled with similar ratings on the Physician and Chemist categories. It should be remembered, however, that the interest patterns of physicians, chemists, and sales managers are by no means identical with those of pharmacists.

On *a priori* grounds, it seems reasonable to suppose that the Scientific and Persuasive categories of the Kuder Preference Record are related to interest in pharmacy. As a matter of fact, Kuder assumes this to be true in his Table for Use in Interpreting Preference Record Profiles (1944).

O. J. K.

PHILOSOPHY OF VOCATIONAL GUIDANCE. Philosophy has many meanings. In this article it means a body of principles or general concepts. For vocational guidance it is the knowledge useful in explaining the nature of the individual at work or serving in his vocation.

As long as man has worked for a living he has been more or less consciously guided in his work relations by a philosophy. For the great mass of mankind this philosophy always has been and still is a simple one. It is unwritten. It consists of tradition and custom. There is little or no freedom to choose a vocation under a hereditary social system, a static economy, or a totalitarian state. The philosophy of freedom of choice of a vocation is one of the latest freedoms to be recognized. It is a product of democracy and the American frontier. It applies to only a small proportion of the peoples of the earth.

Even when the occupational life of a people is ruled by custom and tradition the rule has the sanction of some authority. The authority may lie in religion, a ruling class, or in the myths and sagas of the people. Whatever the source of the principles of conduct, be they edicts, codes, or sagas, if they control the work life they are the philosophy of vocational guidance for that place and time.

The word "vocation" is an example of religious sanction. Early in the history of our country a person's vocation was also his calling. A person was "called to the ministry" or to medicine. In fact, one was called into any one of the professions. The word "profession" is derived from "I believe" or profess. The ethical concepts of the Christian religion made up a large part of our early philosophy of vocational guidance.

Two concepts have largely fashioned our national philosophy of vocational guidance; the faith of our people in America as a land of personal opportunity, and the authority of the scientist. Opportunity meant that personal success was a prize which could be won by any American youth who exercised wisely his freedom to choose the occupation thru which he would serve his fellow man, earn a living, engage in enterprise, win power, or amass a fortune. The scientist would cooperate with opportunity when problems of a personal nature would have to be met.

To many people philosophy connotes a stability, a permanence, which the present definition appears to exclude. A philosophy consisting of a body of concepts and scientific principles will change as the scientists contribute their discoveries. It is one of the functions of a useful and modern philosophy to assist the individual in keeping up with a changing world. It is not the function of a vocational philosophy to explain the construction of our occupational system as a rigid, stable, unchanging thing but rather to make the individual continually aware of its dynamic nature. Our occupational world is continually changing and at an accelerating rate.

When we reflect on the nature of our vocational philosophy we cannot isolate our thinking from the contemporary areas of living. Our vocational life is only one aspect of our total living. Each of the other aspects is as subject to philosophical reflection as the vocational. Some of these areas are: political, economic, home, social, education, religion, recreation, etc. Each of these areas of life influences each of the others more or less. Thus a philosophy of vocational guidance must be comprehensive. It cannot exclude the effect of recreation on the individual's work ability. It cannot escape the importance of a harmonious home life on a person's emotional stability on the job. It cannot overlook the importance of belief or disbelief in labor unions and the right to work in a closed shop community.

Early in the century the field of vocational guidance was limited to "the selection of one's life work." This is still a far too common concept. Maintaining an income throughout the productive years involves far greater personal problems for the average person than the original selection of his so-called life work. The concept is spreading rapidly that vocational guidance is needed throughout one's working life. If the average span of vocational life is forty years it is obvious that in a rapidly changing world casual concepts of the individual and vocations received in 1940 will be quite obsolete long before 1980.

There are now apparent certain economic and social trends which give definite promise of being maintained for many years to come. They may hold throughout the vocational life of today's young people. Acceptance of these trends could well form the structure of a philosophy yet the details would continually change within the framework. The foundation of this framework or structure is the accelerating complexity of our modern worldwide economy, the industrial organization necessary to support it and the governmental occupations necessary to service a highly organized society. It is the increasing complexity which gives rise to and supports the trends. These trends determine the nature of present and future occupations.

Very little of the literature in the field of vocational guidance deals with the factor of occupational trends or recognizes the changing nature of vocational life. Psychology, much of it out of date, supplies the major subject matter content in the field. The existing occupational information is almost entirely descriptive. Individuals and occupations are treated as separate and isolated phenomena. The main function of guidance according to prevailing opinion is to match the traits of the individual with specific job requirements. The classified descriptive available information about individuals and occupations does not contribute much toward an understanding of the nature of the individual or the occupation. Recently there has been considerable research on groups of occupations which require similar or related skills. A good many practical personnel administrators are of the opinion that there is entirely too much emphasis placed on skill and technical knowledge as a qualification for successful employment. Lack of ability to perform the work required is a comparatively rare charge for dismissal from employment. Personality difficulties, or excessive absenteeism and tardiness are the most common reasons for discharging an employee.

The trend toward a highly developed organization is changing the nature of an increasingly large number of occupations. Ability to work with others under managerial discipline as a member of a closely integrated production group calls for personality skill of a higher type than called for in the direct performance of the work. This shift in the changing nature of occupational skills is not yet generally recognized. Scientific studies in the field or organization and management are contributing much to an understanding of the nature of teamwork. Organized human relations call for highly developed personal qualities in workers—primarily the ability to adjust to one's fellow employees. The nature of these abilities is the same irrespective of the occupation or the size of the organization. The principles of organization are applicable to any group regardless of the size of the unit or the nature of the work. The principles were observed by Caesar, they are true today and they hold for the future. They are independent of the form of government. They are few in number. When applied they so clarify and simplify the specific work responsibilities of the worker that his burden of making technical judgments, of operating by himself as an individual, is greatly reduced. His problems are tied up with the problems of the group and under sound supervision they are solved as a group activity rather than an individual or personal matter. As organizations improve individuals of so-called mediocre capacity will have a greater opportunity to make good than the highly talented under deficient working conditions and management.

Very slowly we are learning that an individual's job interests and vocational satisfactions are tied closer to the conditions under which he works than the specific nature of the work he does. There are some grounds for the thesis that it is more important to choose one's employer wisely than one's occupation. The occupational information that will be of greatest future use to our youth will not be that which describes specific occupations, information that cannot possibly be reliable in the light of changing conditions, but information about the nature of all occupations in a highly organized society. Youth should be able to recognize the symptoms of good or poor supervision, capable or shoddy management, and to the extent that he has a choice, seek an employer who has favorably conditioned the occupational climate.

The study of history should give youth a sense of the social forces at work changing all professions and occupations. Geography should point out to him the relationship between natural resources, locality and the distribution of the different occupations. The sciences can contribute to his understanding of the relationships between discovery, invention, and the technical content of the trades and professions. He should see the relationships between the contributions of the scientist, and changes in job techniques with the consequent need for training in the application of the new techniques. He should gain a realization of the major rôle of the scientist as a creator of occupational changes. The practical application of the results of a single piece of scientific research may cause great changes in many lines of work, entirely eliminating some occupations, giving birth to others, creating training needs or revision of entrance qualifications. The biological sciences should show the student the conditions under which man does his best work. He should learn that there are optimum temperatures for efficient performance of various kinds of work, and the effect of color and light in the work place upon morale. The social sciences can show him how economic laws affect costs of production, job security, and earnings. Political science can reveal the nature of social needs and the services rendered by the government occupations. An important area in guidance is the nature of civil service employment compared to private employment. Sociology can reveal the nature of professionalism, unions, group loyalty, occupational customs, traditions, and ritual.

To the extent that the school curriculum provides for occupational interpretation in many of its subjects through much of the child's educational life it will be performing its main vocational guidance function. Guidance in the making of decisions in almost any area of life is founded on what we know about the area, and how well we understand or see clearly the facts and their meaning. Thus the function of the school is not so much to give vocational counsel as to furnish an opportunity for youth to learn the nature of occupations. If he could find out the ways in which all or nearly all occupations are alike just as he can now find out in a course in general biology the ways in which all living things are alike, he would be better equipped to make vocational decisions throughout his working life. This does not necessarily call for added subject matter courses, but rather new subject matter in the old courses. It calls for teacher application of special subject matter to a neglected area of life—the conditions which affect man at work and change the techniques of his work.

If the subject matter of the curriculum is to furnish guidance values in the form of vocational understanding, appreciation, and attitudes, the extra curricular activities because of their varied nature can supply facts about the individual's ability to fit into an organization or qualify as a member of a group or team. Group activity is quite the same whether on the schoolground or in business and industry. Some of the best vocational guidance today is taking place in the recreation departments of our public schools. It is not known as vocational guidance. The recreational leader is not conscious that he is guiding but as he assists a youth to take and follow out a team captain's orders more graciously, the result is the same—

learning to adjust and fit into the group as a whole. Any understanding or direction as to the way people work together, in communities large or small, in the professions, industry, agriculture, and business, can serve as vocational guidance.

Space does not permit adequate treatment of the implications of the point of view of those who believe that selecting a specific vocation or career is the major function of vocational guidance and counsel. Such decisions are important. They must be made and counsellors have the responsibility of giving advice and assistance. Their decisions are more important to those interested in the occupations which demand a long period of pre-entry training such as the older professions. However the vast majority of young people today and for a long time to come will choose their employer rather than their occupation. After they get their first few jobs, they will have some real facts upon which to make important decisions, facts about the different kinds of work they have seen people do, and most important of all, facts about their own interests and abilities. If the schools were able to contact their alumni in their early payroll years and help with youth's problem of "where do I go from here?" they could render a far greater counselling service than is possible before youth has been up against the vocational facts of life. This implies that the need for vocational counsel may be continuous throughout an individual's working years. A few school systems recognize this and have established counsellors in their adult continuation schools. Industry has recognized it by providing a counselling service in their personnel departments to assist workers and supervisors in making mutual adjustments.

At the end of World War II the United States faced the problem of assisting millions of returning veterans in their readjustment to civilian life. The reconversion of war industries to peacetime production resulted in the vocational maladjustment of millions of civilian war workers. The function of vocational counselling formerly restricted almost entirely to educational institutions became a major responsibility of numerous agencies of government from the Federal down to the local level.

During the war it was the policy of most large industrial organizations working on war contracts to provide employment counsellors in their personnel departments. These counsellors spent a considerable proportion of their time assisting employees in adjustment to their work. On occasion they recommended transfer to a more fitting type of work. Some of the organizations used objective tests for proper placement and guidance.

The armed forces developed many objective tests to assist in the effective assignment of personnel. Many of these will in time be available for civilian use. After the defeat of Germany, representatives of American military commissions searched Germany for information concerning personnel methods used in building the Nazi military machine. It is reported that several unique tests were found which were used to determine qualities of leadership, planning, and organization.

The meaning of vocational guidance undoubtedly penetrated deep into our National culture during the war. It will no longer be considered a responsibility associated solely with the lives of our young people. Adults will need vocational guidance throughout the span of their earning years as long as the economy under which they work is unstable and subject to rapid change.

B. E. M.

PHYSICAL ASPECTS OF THE GUIDANCE PROGRAM. A

guidance program cannot be adequately described in terms of its physical facilities and equipment. Nor can its effectiveness be evaluated in terms of the presence or absence of these physical factors. They constitute only one aspect of the program. Consequently description and evaluation must include consideration of other aspects such as the attitude, cooperation, and participation of the administration and faculty, the flexibility and adaptability of the curriculum, and the active rôle of the counselor and other guidance workers.

Effective guidance can be carried on with individual cases where there is no organized program or where the organized program is limited in physical facilities and equipment, but the effectiveness of the guidance worker in the efficient utilization of his time and in the number of individuals with whom he can work is thereby limited. Thus, the factors of physical facilities and equipment become important in planning and instituting an effective guidance program.

The guidance department should be located near the administrative offices. This location facilitates the use of records by the administration and the faculty and provides for a more adequate flow of information and personal checks between administrative personnel and the counselors. It also makes possible greater utilization of available clerical help. Furthermore, parents and others who desire to visit the department, will have less difficulty in locating it.

The guidance suite should include facilities for individual guidance, group guidance, individual and group testing, and conferences.

Provision should also be made for storing supplies and for displaying vocational and educational materials which can be selected by the students for individual perusal. Office space requirements will, of course, be dependent upon the size of the school, stage of development of the program and whether the program is being installed in a building which did not previously include plans for such a department.

There are certain physical aspects of any organized program which can be considered essential. A reception room or general waiting room, private counseling offices for each counselor, a room for group testing and group guidance, a small room for conferences and individual testing, and storage facilities for tests and supplies are recommended. Tests, office furnishings, and other supplies will also be necessary.

The waiting room or reception room should be comfortably and attractively furnished. Arrangement of furniture and the demeanor of the receptionist should be suggestive of informality and welcome to incoming students. In larger schools the reception room could serve both the guidance department and the health services. In smaller schools it may also be shared with the administration. The receptionist may be an office clerk who also serves in other office capacities. In some schools properly trained students may exercise this function, although this is generally regarded as a less desirable procedure because of the immaturity of the students and the confidential nature of the records, tests, and other guidance materials. Student personnel records maintained in a file which can be locked, should be kept here. Reading materials which provide information about vocations, colleges, and other guidance matters should be strategically placed on a reading table and in convenient display racks or shelves.

Each counselor should have a private office for interviewing purposes. These offices should be sound-proof, well-lighted, and simply but attractively furnished. Recommended size of these offices varies from a minimum of seven by seven feet [2] to an optimum of one hundred fifty square feet.[1] Necessary equipment includes a desk, a telephone extension, three chairs, a filing cabinet, and a bookcase. It is also recommended that a dictaphone be readily available in the counselor's office.

The group-testing and group-guidance room should be well-lighted and well-ventilated. It should be equipped with desks or with chairs provided with writing arms. A blackboard and a table which can be used for conferences or for working purposes should be located at the front of the room. A storage closet equipped with a lock should be provided for storing tests, supplies, and inactive files. This room can be used for group testing, group guidance, large conferences, and committee meetings. It should be located near the counselors' offices and the waiting room, and entrances should lead from both the waiting room and an outside corridor.

A small conference and individual testing room has many uses and should be provided. In addition to its use for testing individuals or small groups, it can be used for conferences with the counseling staff, faculty members, parents, visiting teachers or other professional workers, and committee groups. It also provides a room where faculty members may study personnel records, make out grade reports, or use guidance materials from the files and display shelves. It is recommended that the entrance to this room be made from the waiting room. A small blackboard, a conference table, and chairs are necessary equipment.

Bulletin boards for providing information about scholarships, training and other vocational and educational opportunities should be maintained by the guidance department. They should be placed in the reception room, library, and corridors, and should be attractively arranged with information and displays of current interest.

No single optimum plan for housing the guidance department can be promulgated for all schools. There are other considerations in addition to office space and facilities which must be taken into account before the guidance department can be set up or developed. Careful planning is necessary at every step of development.

Of primary importance is the factor of size of the school population at present and anticipated size in the future. Size of the building, its size in relation to the student population and the internal arrangement or plan of the building must be studied carefully, and necessary adaptations must be made. The school budget and the amount that can be expended for guidance is, of course, a very practical and potent factor. Considerable attention must be given to it, for it is through budget appropriations that sufficient facilities and supplies for the guidance department will be obtained. Lastly, even though all of these conditions have been met satisfactorily, the program will be doomed to failure or ineffectiveness unless the faculty is receptive to the idea.

Experience has shown that a simple beginning which avoids excessive expenditures for supplies and equipment is more likely to assure the success of the program than a ready-made program which is superimposed upon the school system. *The school must start where it is in establishing its guidance program.* Some of the furnishings can be obtained from available school equipment. Additional supplies can be purchased for relatively little if a modest beginning is planned.

Discussion here has been limited to describing and recommending physical facilities for a centralized guidance program in secondary schools or smaller institutions of higher education. In large institutions, guidance functions may be decentralized among the individual colleges or departments of the school, while the functions of admissions, housing, testing and guidance, placement, etc. are more or less independently performed under a general administrative head. In a program organized along these lines facilities for accurate and efficient exchange of information and cross-referral should be set up to function as a clearing house for all the personnel activities on the campus.

In large city school systems or in school systems organized on a county-wide or other geographical area basis, certain facilities such as the machine-scoring of tests can be located in the offices of the Board of Education where these services can be made available to the individual schools in the system. In the decentralized personnel program of a large university these services may be located in a clinical guidance and testing center or in that part of the program which would be considered the core activity.

References:

1. Corre, M. P. and Geiger, G. M. Building for school counseling. *Occupations,* 1946, *24,* 266–268.
2. Hahn, M. E. What price pupil-personnel work? *The School Review,* 1939, *47,* 374–381.
3. Russell, J. D. (Editor). *Student personnel services in colleges and universities,* Vol. XII, of the Proceedings of the Institute for Administrative Officers of Higher Institutions, 1940. Chicago: University of Chicago Press, 1941.
4. Williamson, E. G. and Hahn, M. E. *Introduction to high school counseling.* New York: McGraw-Hill Book Co., 1940.

W. F. J.

PHYSICAL CHARACTERISTICS. Physical characteristics cut across all major fields of work. For example, it cannot be said that certain physical characteristics are necessary in the professions generally. Part of the minister's stock in trade is a pleasant voice whereas muscular coordination and deftness of fingers are far more necessary for a dentist than a pleasant voice. However, in any field of work, there are jobs that, for the most part, fit a given combination of physical characteristics.

In the following material the chief physical characteristics usually connected with occupational choice are considered. Because of its briefness, this article is not all inclusive.

Age

Since age has a direct bearing on certain physical characteristics, it is included here. There are very few occupations that require any training whatsoever that are open to youth under the age of eighteen. There are a few notable exceptions. In some states, wiremen in the radio field, barbers, waiters and waitresses, and confectioners may be initiated into their work at the age of sixteen and the United States navy will enlist boys at the age of seventeen. On the other hand, many occupations require a more mature entrance age. A sampling of these are the airplane stewardess, the fireman, the hospital orderly, the pharmacist, the meter reader, service employees in the gas industry, the nurse, the telegraph clerk and soldier in the United States army. Some types of work require an even higher entrance age. For example, a fitter in the field of women's clothing must be over thirty; a civil engineer must usually be twenty-five; a railroad engineer must be forty-five; a railroad fireman or brakeman, thirty-five, the hostess on a steamer must be forty and a corsetier must be thirty years old.

There is also a maximum entrance age for a good many occupations. In the aeronautics field, the maximum age for entrance is twenty-two for a co-pilot, twenty-six for a stewardess and thirty for a mechanic's helper. A stock clerk in the clerical field may start when he is as old as fifty-five and so may service employees in the gas industry. In the needle trades, most of the jobs connected with power sewing have a maximum entrance age of thirty-five and laundry operators may enter as late as fifty.

Agility

For those vocations which require ladder-climbing, getting around in awkward places and bending a great deal, agility is necessary. Some jobs needing agility are the draper and fitter in the clothing industry; the fixture man, lighting wireman and low tension wireman in the electrical field, the fireman in the public service field and in the domestic and personal service field, the mopper, the vacuum operator and the window cleaner.

Ambidexterity

Cosmetology is a field in which ambidexterity is necessary. The all-round operator in a beauty parlor, the barber, the mortuary hair dresser, the permanent waver must all be able to use the left hand with almost as much skill as the right hand. This likewise is true of an elevator operator, male laundry workers, and in the manufacturing field, particularly the assembly line worker, the engine lathe operator and the transferrer. Motion picture studio workers and chauffeurs also need ambidexterity.

Charm

Charm is extremely important in such occupations as hostesses, models and stewardesses.

Cleanliness

Scrupulous personal cleanliness is essential in most jobs connected with the food industry, with certain jobs in the cleaning industry, for example, the fancy presser and the machine presser and for most jobs connected with the intimate care of the body as the doctor, the chiropodist, the pharmacist and the dentist.

Endurance

There are very few occupations in our modern world that do not call for endurance. An eight hour day in a factory or behind a counter, a five or six hour day in the schoolroom, the bending over a desk for eight hours in clerical work, the farmer working from sun-up to sundown, just to mention a few, all require endurance. However, some jobs require exceptional endurance. Some examples are the puddler and the rolling mill operative in the steel industry, the proof reader who must read aloud eight hours a day and the stoneman in the printing industry who must stand all day and handle heavy weights. In the professional field, the dentist, the dental hygienist, the doctor, the lawyer are examples. G men and state troopers in the public service field, the auctioneer and the domestic in a household all need abundant endurance to do their work efficiently.

Energy and Vitality

Employers require energy and vitality in the field of commercial art, art and industrial design. In the manufacturing field, these characteristics are essential to the machine operator, the all-round machinist, tool maker, the die maker, the die sinker and machine shop mechanic. In the sales field, restauranteurs who are most successful have an abundance of energy. The checker and the tester in the radio field must have exceptional vitality.

Eyesight

Average eyesight as endurance is required in the majority of occupations in every field. Some jobs can be held even if the incumbent has slightly below average eyesight. Examples are the upholsterer, the janitor, the elevator operator. There are some jobs in a tire factory in which the worker may have as little as 50% of normal sight.

Some occupations, however, require exceptional and very keen eyesight. Among these are the electrolysis operator, the make-up specialist, and the manicurist in the cosmetology field, the transferrer in the machine trades; the grainer in the painting and decorating field; the toolmaker and diemaker in the metal trades; the jewelry designer and engraver; the dental hygienist, the dentist, the physician, and the artist in the professions.

In connection with eyesight there are some occupations that require the ability to recognize colors. These may be found in almost every field of endeavor. Some of these are the forester and the gardener in farming; the buttonhole and buttonsewer in power machine sewing; the chainman in the building trades; the makeup specialist in beauty culture; the lineman in telephony; the creamery plant workers, the shoeshiner, the dentist, the chemist, the postal clerk, and the United States marine. No railroad man may be afflicted with color blindness.

For telephone operators who are totally blind, some telephone exchanges have special equipment. There are other jobs which the blind can do successfully, but space is too short to deal with them here.

Another facet of eyesight is depth perception which is extremely important for the commercial pilot.

Feet

Feet that can endure standing for long periods, or walking for long periods are necessary in many occupations. A few examples are the meter reader, the pattern maker in dressmaking, the line inspector, the allround operator in beauty culture, the postal carrier, the machine operator in the metal trades and the dentist in the professions.

Gracefulness

Gracefulness is an asset for the model, the draper and fitter in the needle trades, for the hostess and the airplane stewardess.

Hands

Dry healthy hands are important in the needle trades for the designer, the draper, the finisher, the fitter, and the maker. The all round operator in a beauty shop must have hands that are soft and pleasant to the skin. The telephone operator must have delicacy of touch. A great many occupations require dexterity of the hands. In fact, practically all types of work that are done by the hands require this characteristic. Nimbleness of fingers is demanded in a great many occupations, as for example the instrument maker, most of the jobs in telegraphy, the telephone operator, the barber, the waiter and the waitress, the typist, and many jobs in the printing industry and in the needle trades.

Health

Good health, at least good enough to keep people on their jobs regularly, is needed in every type of work. However, a great many occupations require better than average health. Some of these occupations are the forester, the G Man, the nurse, railroadmen, fishermen and miners.

In the food industry and creamery industry all workers must be free from communicable diseases. This is also true of workers dealing with the human body, as the nurse, the hospital orderly, the dentist, and the physician. In the public service field, the government has also set up this requirement for the postal carrier and the postal clerk, and the U. S. Navy. Chain stores also expect their clerks to be free of communicable disease.

Any sort of organic disease bars applicants from certain occupations. Some of these are the pilot in aeronautics, the fireman, the policeman, the U. S. Army, the U. S. Marines, the watchmaker and repairer in the industrial field, and the dentist in the professional field.

Anyone who tends toward bronchial or lung infections cannot enter mechanical dentistry, and those afflicted with hernia or asthma cannot be postal carriers or postal clerks.

Allergies too have a relation to occupational choice. A person who has allergies that cause respiratory diseases should not be a farmer who has to be in contact with plants and animals.

The chemist certainly should not be sensitive to chemicals, nor the dryspotter or fancy spotter in the cleaning industry.

Sensitivity to odors also has a place here. In the cleaning industry again the inspector and machine presser must have an immunity to odors.

Hearing

Average hearing is another common requirement for most jobs. However, there are some jobs in each field of work that need better than average hearing. The pilot in aeronautics, the forester in agriculture, the pipefitter's helper in the building trades, the stenographer in the clerical field, a good many jobs in radio, telegraphy, and telephony, operators of certain machines, most of the professions, many public service, sales jobs, and transportation jobs demand better than average hearing. Keen hearing is a necessity for the U. S. Marines, the low pressure operator, and the operating engineer in janitorial service. The hearing of the railroad man and the airplane dispatcher must be perfect.

In connection with the ears we have a characteristic known as equilibrium. This quality is essential for the private commercial airplane pilot.

Good ears for tone are a requirement for the piano tuner and the tester in radio work.

Muscular Control and Muscular Coordination

These characteristics are needed in jobs that cut across many general fields of work. The surgeon and the nurse must have a high degree of muscular coordination. So must the linotype operator in printing, the assembly line worker in a factory, the telegrapher, and the operator of a central or substation in the electrical field. The dentist and the make-up specialist in cosmetology must have muscular control.

Nerves

Nerve control is of first importance in certain occupations that again cut across the whole field of work. In design and drafting steady nerves are necessary. Other occupations where excellent nerve control is necessary are the elevator operator and the window cleaner in janitorial service, certain laundry workers, most of the jobs in the needle trades, many of the jobs in commercial art, most of the jobs in communication transportation, the electrolysis operators in cosmetology and in the professions, the doctor, the dentist, and the public school teacher.

Personal Appearance

Good personal appearance is especially important in those occupations in which close contact with the public is necessary. This is particularly true of the dentist, the surgeon, the teacher, the nurse in the professions; the labor inspector and the state trooper in the public service; the steward or the stewardess in the field of transportation; the merchandise manager, the buyer, the sales clerk in retail selling, and the model and the receptionist.

Physical Activity

All occupations that are not of a sedentary nature and which do not require standing in one position a long time require a good deal of physical activity. A lethargic person should not enter the building trades, certain jobs in every factory, janitorial service, personal or public service, sales service, or some of the professions.

Physical Disabilities

In most jobs that have to do with manual or mechanical work the free use of the hands is necessary. The farmer, the body and fender repairman, in the automotive industry; the bricklayer in the building trades; the telegrapher, the photographer, most factory workers are a few of the workers that must use both hands freely. Free use of both hands and arms are required in gardening, in many telephone jobs, in laundry work and many jobs in transportation, as well as in many others. Essential to such occupations as the chainman in the building trades, the sailor, the marine, is free use of hands, arms and legs.

Many occupations require a strict physical examination before an applicant is accepted. This is true in telegraphy, telephony, nursing and the public service field.

There are some occupations in which physical disability is not a handicap. For example, a slight paralysis or the loss of a finger is not detrimental in watch repairing; so likewise a leg or a back disability is no hindrance in mechanical engineering.

Posture

Good posture is important in certain lines of work both because the posture helps toward health and because the occupation can be more effectively executed because of it. Examples of jobs in which good posture is an asset are the stenographer, the telephone operator, armature winding in the electrical industry, certain machine operators, the dental hygienists, the teacher, the model, the stewardess and the railroad porter.

Stature

Medium stature is demanded in certain occupations because the worker has to work in awkward places or positions. Examples are the plumber, the steam fitter, certain positions in the needle trades, the dentist, the railroad porter and the truck driver.

For certain types of work height, weight, chest expansion, reach are definitely specified. A postal carrier (male) must be five feet, four inches tall and have a minimum weight of 125 pounds. A cable splicer in telephony must be five feet, one inch tall and must weigh 140 pounds; the telephone installer must be five feet, four inches tall and weigh 135 pounds; his reach must be normal for his height. An airplane stewardess must have a maximum height of five feet, five inches and must have a maximum weight of 125 pounds. The spinner in the textile industry must have a height of five feet four inches and his weight must be proportionate to his height. These are just a few samples; there are many others.

Laundry workers who do marking and distributing must be tall and so must shirt finishers. Some machine operators in factories must have long arms (rotary shear operator); some must be light in weight and slim in form (camber machine operator). In tire factory a worker's job depends on his height and weight.

Strength

All work demanding the lifting of heavy articles and gross muscular movements need strength. Strength is essential in the structural steel industry, in the building trades, in laboring jobs, in laundry work, in fire fighting, in mining, especially in coal and iron, and in fishing. The butcher, the railroad porter, often times the truck driver, the state trooper, the policeman all need strength of more than ordinary calibre.

Voice

A pleasant clear voice is a requirement in many occupations. A sampling of these are the receptionist, the telephone operator, the stenographer, the proof reader, the radio announcer, the teacher and the minister, the airplane dispatcher, the salesgirl and the railroad porter. None of these occupations tolerate speech defects. Neither can the postal carrier, the airline radio operator, nor the postal clerk have any type of speech defect.

Miscellaneous

Good teeth are important in the dentist and dental hygienist and men are often rejected in the Army and the Marines because of poor teeth.

Models and motion picture artists must be photogenic.

Righthandedness is important for telephone operators and dentists because the equipment they use is made for right handed people.

Although the foregoing material in no way exhausts this field, it is obvious that before making an occupational choice, it is extremely important to take into account the physical characteristics that the occupation entails as well as the physical characteristics of the person making the choice.

References:

1. Davis, Anne S. *Guidance Monographs*. New York: The Commonwealth Book Co., 1938.
2. De Schweinitz, Dorothea. *Occupations in Retail Stores*. New York: International Textbook Co., 1941.
3. Science Research Associates, Chicago: *Occupational briefs,* 1946.

                                                                    E. E. F.

PHYSICAL THERAPY, APTITUDE FOR. Physical Therapy is a relatively new profession, but a rapidly growing one. Marked attention was first given to it in this country during World War I. The growth of interest in this field from that time has been steady and was given renewed impetus during World War II by the important part which it played in the rehabilitation of the injured in our armed forces and in the accelerated return of injured industrial workers to the assembly line.

The American Physiotherapy Association, which is the professional association of qualified physical therapists, defines physical therapy as "The treatment of disability, injury and disease by non-medical means comprising the use of massage, exercise, and the physical, chemical and other properties of heat, light, water and electricity (except Roentgen rays, radium and electro-surgery)." The techniques of physical therapy are varied and interesting. The variety of patients is stimulating and the development of the entire field is so rapid that it is a challenge to any capable student. Physical therapy has been primarily a women's profession. It is important to note, however, that a number of men who had some training and experience as corpsmen in the armed services are seeking admission to the approved schools of physical therapy.

Students in physical therapy are selected on the basis of prerequisite training and experience, physical examination and evidence of suitable personality characteristics.

There are a number of four-year degree courses for which the prerequisite is graduation from an accredited high school. These courses are steadily increasing in numbers. By far the largest proportion of students take courses of nine to twelve months duration and are graduates of a degree course in physical education, an accredited school of nursing or offer a minimum of two years of general training, including biology and other sciences in an accredited college or university. These prerequisites are required by the Council on Medical Education and Hospitals of the American Medical Association which body approves the physical therapy schools. A few two-year students were admitted to schools during the war emergency but more maturity and educational background are desirable. Many students of physical therapy have entered school after several years of experience in teaching or nursing. Applicants over thirty-eight years are usually not accepted to the schools.

All of the schools require a physical examination. It is necessary that the therapist be able to read dials on the machines accurately, hear timing devices, assist the patient to adjust to his environment, etc. Therefore, vision and hearing are carefully checked. The work of a physical therapist is physically demanding as a considerable portion of the day is spent in standing and treating patients of all ages and degrees of disability. The weight of the patients' extremities in the process of muscle reeducation where the patient is lying on the treatment table or in bed, and assistance in standing and walking require a reasonable degree of strength. The condition of the therapist's feet, strength of the back and good body alignment are important considerations. Flexible, strong and sensitive hands are essential as much of the knowledge covering the patient's condition comes through the feel of the tisues under treatment.

The physical therapist must like people from all levels of the social strata; of all ages and races. She must be able to work as a responsible, cooperative member of the medical team. The therapist treats only under the prescription and supervision of the physician but the nature of the work is such that she must use imagination and initiative in the selection and presentation of the technique of treatment. She should inspire the confidence of her patients and should be understanding and sympathetic to the degree that will stimulate the patient to take active responsibility in the recovery process.

Intelligence, and the ability to do exacting and careful work, are of the utmost importance. Physical therapy requires the practical application of a considerable amount of theoretical basic science and medical knowledge. The best student of theory is not always the best therapist, but a poor student cannot meet the demands of the field. The treatment of the patient can only be as good as the ability, knowledge and skill of the therapist.

Physical therapy does not consist of routine procedures but requires knowledge, judgment and adjustment of technique for every patient. As the physical therapist has to meet all types and ages of patients, her general educational background and breadth of interests are useful tools in understanding and obtaining the cooperation of the patients.

Although there are at present no aptitude tests which have been devised for physical therapy, a number of groups are interested in the problem.

References:

1. American Physiotherapy Association. *Physical therapy, a service and a career.* 1945.
2. Elson, M. Physical therapy, a growing profession. Education for Victory, 1944, 3, 10.
3. Nesbitt, M. E. Physical therapy, a profession with a future. Journal of Health and Physical Education, 1945, 16, 12.
4. United States Department of Labor. Women's Bureau. *The outlook for women in occupations in the medical services: physical therapists.* Bulletin 203, No. 1. Washington: Government Printing Office, 1944.

C. W.

PHYSICS TEST, FULMER-SCHRAMMEL. The Fulmer-Schrammel Physics Test was developed in connection with the Nationwide Every Pupil Scholarship Tests. For about ten years one physics test for first semester testing and one for second semester testing had annually been provided. The results on these were analyzed in detail. Moreover, from time to time, a wealth of valuable criticism and suggestions from capable teachers in many different schools was received. These data were utilized in making the tests provided more valuable.

The forms provided in this series are based on textbook and course of study content; criticisms and suggestions offered by high school and college physics teachers; and analysis of scores and errors of students to whom the preliminary forms of the tests were given.

The battery of which this series of tests consists, and their general content, are the following. Test I, Forms A and B, covers mechanics, or the subject matter usually covered in the first semester of the course. Test II, Forms A and B, covers heat, magnetism, electricity, and sound, or the subject matter usually covered in the second semester of the course.

Authors and Publisher

The authors of this test are V. G. Fulmer, El Centro, California, and H. E. Schrammel, Director, Bureau of Educational Measurements, Kansas State Teachers College, Emporia, Kansas. The test is published by the Bureau of Educational Measurement, Teachers College, Emporia, Kansas.

Reliability

Between Forms A and B of Test I a reliability of +.77 was obtained. Between Forms A and B of Test II the reliability was +.72. The reliability of each test and form independently by the method of correlating scores on even numbered items with those of odd numbered items ranged between +.84 and +.86 with an average of +.85.

Administering, Scoring, and Interpreting

This test is simple to give and to take. The working time is 40 minutes for each division. Scoring of tests requires about one minute per paper. The test results are interpreted by use of percentile norms, computed from the scores of 7,682 students, both for mid-year and end-of-year testing.

H. E. S.

POLAND. The beginnings of the vocational guidance movement in Poland go back to the end of the First World War. As in many other countries these beginnings originated not with professional educators or psychologists but with a few public-spirited lay individuals. It was without any knowledge of similar earlier endeavors in the United States that in 1918 a few persons constituting the board of the Society for the Protection of Apprentices /Patronat nad Młodzieżą Rzemieślniczą/ in Warsaw became interested in guiding the vocational choices of youth along more rational lines. The immediate reason for awakening of this interest was a peculiar socio-economic situation. During the last year of the First World War food shortage motivated great number of youths to seek apprenticeship with bakers where bread was most easily available, while other businesses suffered from acute labor shortage. To remedy this abnormal situation some—of necessity amateurish—attempts at counseling were undertaken. At first they were directed mainly toward discouraging youngsters from entering the overcrowded occupation.

Only gradually a more positive approach has been worked out in order not only to stem an overflow into one occupation but also to direct the applicants to suitable jobs.

The techniques of counseling as they are known today were gradually developed in connection, however, at first not with vocational guidance proper but with vocational selection. All such activities require funds. The only money for this purpose was coming at that time from private businessmen who were interested in hiring the possibly best employees, reliably selected out of many applicants. The employers, however, were not particularly interested in the fate of those rejected.

The first laboratory of applied psychology in Poland, organized in Warsaw by Mr. Waclaw Hauszyld in 1922 under the auspices of the Society for Protection of Apprentices, served at the beginning almost exclusively the purposes of vocational selection. Factories and shops directed their young applicants to the laboratory where they had to undergo a series of examinations with the aid of psychological tests. A few lucky ones were proclaimed fit and employed, while the majority were simply rejected without any positive advice where to turn.

The limited social usefulness of such procedure was quickly grasped by the directors of this pioneer institution and soon the activities of the laboratory was supplemented by rather crude, at first, yet genuine positive counseling.

About the same time a few progressive elementary school teachers inspired by the news from abroad about the beginnings of the vocational guidance movement persuaded the authorities of the Warsaw school system to start on a very modest scale the first vocational guidance clinic for the graduating pupils of one suburban school. These endeavors received reinforcement from some young educators who studied abroad and brought back with them the ideas and experience of Claparède in Switzerland and of Decroly in Belgium.

The psychological testing practised by those teachers for the purpose of vocational guidance for grade school graduate was mostly of the paper and pencil variety with Stanford-Binet Revision dominating the field. On the other hand the tests used by the laboratory of the Society for Protection of Apprentices were mostly of the variety so popular at that time in German laboratories for industrial psychology best exemplified by the well-known laboratory directed by W. Moede at the Technische Hochschule in Charlottenburg.

The pioneer attempts of those two groups in Warsaw who soon entered into a friendly cooperation were shortly imitated by similar groups in other Polish cities, Cracow and Lodz among the first ones.

The growing interest among the industrialists, state agencies (notably the railroads) and city enterprises (streetcars and buses) in the possibilities of rationalizing the selection of employees gave rise to several laboratories of industrial psychology conducted with a limited purpose of vocational selection. This development had its very beneficial influence on the growth of the vocational guidance movement.

First, it created employment opportunities for the growing young generation of Polish psychologists. Second, it awakened the interest in applied psychology of the university professors who up to then were rather academically inclined.

This active interest in vocational psychology shown by the professors gave to the movement its decisive impetus through the stamp of official approval, increase in prestige, and—best of all—actual competent aid.

About 1926 there was already a group of scientifically trained psychologists actively engaged in practical work in some field of applied psychology, large enough to organize the Polish Society of Psychotechnics (Polskie Towarzystwo Psychotechniczne) in Warsaw. Its leaders began at once publishing the quarterly *Psychotechnika* which from the beginning devoted much space to the specific theoretical and practical problems of vocational guidance. The moving spirits of the Society and its journal were: Dr. Wladyslaw Witwicki, professor of psychology at the University of Warsaw, who aptly combined insistence on maintenance of scientific standards with keen insight and emphasis on intelligent, non-mechanical interpretation of test scores as well as humane approach to the problems of each individual; J. Wojciechowski, mechanical engineer, director of the Central Psychological Laboratory of the State Railroad System, and St. Studencki, psychologist and educator, director of the Psychological Clinic, maintained by the Ministry of Education for the secondary and college-type vocational schools.

The most vigorous stimulation to the Polish vocational guidance movement was given in 1928 by the arrival of the newly appointed professor of educational psychology at the University of Warsaw, Dr. Stefan Baley. Highly trained both in medicine and psychology, Professor Baley from the beginning brought into the vocational guidance movement not only his vast knowledge and talents but also an unusual enthusiasm, indomitable energy and great ability as an organizer. Dr. Baley at once became the editor of the quarterly *Polskie Archiwum Psychologji,* which in 1936 he renamed into the *Psychologja Wychowawacza* (Educational Psychology). Both journals were giving much attention to the problems of vocational guidance.

It was Dr. Baley who organized in 1928 The Vocational Guidance Clinic of the City of Warsaw, the first large institution of this kind in Poland, which almost at once became a model for similar clinics in other Polish cities and a training center where the rapidly growing ranks of vocational guidance workers, both counselors and clinical psychologists, received their practical experience.

The Vocational Guidance Clinic of the City of Warsaw was maintained by the School Division of the City Government and thus closely connected with the city school system. Its activities were many-sided.

Information about vocational training opportunities, occupational requirements, employment opportunities and their shifting trends was gathered and disseminated. Throughout the school year the members of the clinic's staff visited in turn the graduating classes of all elementary schools in Warsaw delivering talks on the problems of vocational choice and encouraging all those who could not solve their own problems to visit the clinic. Occupatinal films were shown and popular lectures on occupational requirements in several fields were given to larger groups of pupils.

Arrangements were made with school principals to send all the graduating pupils in need of guidance to the clinic. They reported there with a filled out exhaustive questionnaire concerning their socio-economic status and family relationships. As a first step all the applicants had to undergo a thorough physical examination by a physician trained in occupational hygiene. Only after that the applicants were given a series of psychological tests. These included a series of "paper and pencil" group tests to determine their I.Q. and a battery of special aptitude tests, most of which were devised to approximate as far as possible a true to life work situation (Arbeitsprobe). The group mental test and most of the clerical and mechanical aptitude tests were devised by Professor St. Baley; several standard American tests were adapted while only a few German tests were used.

After the completion of the aptitude testing the applicant had to fill out a vocational interest blank (very much like the one by Strong although independently developed). Not only occupational preferences, but also actual favorite activities, recreations, games and hobbies of each individual were disclosed.

In the last years before the war a comprehensive questionnaire concerning personality traits, not unlike, for example, Bernreuter's inventory, was also filled out by the applicants. Finally, an exhaustive personal interview was conducted.

The vocational advice given at the end of the applicant's visit to the clinic was thus based on the knowledge concerning: (1) socio-economic status and family situation; (2) physical and health data; (3) school records; (4) scores on the measurement of general intelligence, special aptitudes, achievements and interests; (5) rating of personality traits; (6) all other available information concerning occupational experience, special training opportunities, etc. In many cases presenting some special problem, social worker visited the homes of the children to check the information given by the applicant and elicit further data from the family.

This outline of the activities of the Warsaw clinic was, according to available facilities, more or less closely followed by other clinics which during the thirties were set up in several provincial cities. By 1939 most of the cities over 100,000 population had a vocational guidance clinic. Those institutions carried out their activities with varying degree of skill and success according to the ability and professional qualifications of their staffs. These were by no means uniform or everywhere satisfactory. The largest and outstanding for the quality of its work was the clinic in Cracow, maintained by the local Chamber of Commerce and Industry, which was directed by Dr. Bronislaw Biegeleisen. The vocational guidance activities conducted as a part of the educational guidance at the school system of the city of Katowice maintained a high standard as long as they were directed by Dr. Ludwik Goldscheider-Gorynski.

The severest handicap of the Polish vocational guidance was the lack of sufficiently trained workers. A remedy for this was sought in special courses in vocational guidance and clinical psychology given at the University of Warsaw since 1930 first by the present writer and later by Dr. Janina Budkiewicz.

There were several shortcomings of the vocational guidance activities in Poland. First, most of the applicants, who profited from them, were children in their last year of elementary schooling which in Poland was the fourteenth year of age. As it is well known, this is an age much too early for a rational vocational choice. The opportunities for expert and well-founded vocational counseling available to the older youth or adults were much too limited.

Second, there was lack of a uniform satisfactory organizational scheme. A variety of private charitable societies, city and state agencies supported financially the clinics under varying conditions. In most cases the financial support was insufficient, the salaries of the staff members were low which made very difficult the maintaining of high professional standards.

Third, with a few exceptions, there was as a rule no satisfactory coordination between the vocational guidance clinics and the placement agencies. Therefore counseling only too often was of little help to the individual and follow-up studies only very rarely were possible. These regrettable facts were due primarily to the severe unemployment from which Poland suffered—as did so many countries—in the thirties. Nevertheless, there were definite flaws in the organizational set-up which should be corrected in the future.

During the war and Nazi occupation of Poland all the hard won achievements in the field of vocational guidance were utterly destroyed by the invader as were all other Polish cultural institutions. No historical sketch of the Polish vocational guidance movement would be complete without a list of martyrs, persons connected in one or another capacity with this field, who were murdered by the Nazis. These are: Dr. Bronislaw Biegeleisen, Dr. Ludwik Goldscheider-Gorynski, Dr. Joanna Kunicka, Dr. Estera Markin, Ewa Rybicka, Zuzanna Stawska, Zofia Wajcman, Dr. Romana Wisniacka. There may be others whose death has not been ascertained yet.

The scanty news reaching at present (May 1946) from Poland indicates that the survivors of the holocaust are hard at work amidst ruins trying to rebuild and even expand their institutions. The Vocational Guidance Clinic of the City of Warsaw is active again under Professor S. Baley's directorship struggling with difficulties defying description. Against tremendous odds the resumed work is going on also in other places. This vitality and enthusiasm augur well for the future.

It seems reasonable to expect that the profound political, social and economic reforms which have taken place in Poland after the war will create new favorable conditions for the rebirth and further growth of vocational guidance activities. The now made possible industrialization of the country and man power shortage in the worse than decimated population have already created numerous opportunities for employment. Moreover the democratic reforms have opened up many positions restricted before for the few privileged ones. Satisfying new needs will require greatly expanded, expert and wise counseling services of the vocational guidance institutions.

References:

1. Polskie Archiwum Psychologji, Warsaw, 1924–1936.
2. Psychologja Wychowawcza, Warsaw, 1936–1939.
3. Psychotechnika, Warsaw, 1926–1939.

B. Z.

POLICE WORK, APTITUDE FOR. Greatest consideration in the selection of personnel for the police service is now essential. The means are at hand to evaluate the component attributes required to perform the many and varied duties of the police officer of today. Long range vision must be made in the initial selection of the police officer in order that stagnation hurdles, due to inherently slow advancement procedures, may be cleared. To say that the highest grade of intelligence is the only requisite for the job is by far insufficient. Intelligence alone will not surmount the long and difficult task that the law enforcement officer pledges his life to. In this respect, the vocational counselor must take into consideration a broad outline of the law enforcement field. The conclusions thus acquired will then indicate the attributes which promise the greatest public return and value in the selection of the police recruit. When this primary requisite is followed, we must evaluate the work to be done. The counselor must therefore ask himself the nature of the duties which we expect this prospective individual to perform and then measure him for the job.

What the policeman does should include a somewhat detailed outline of the work which that individual will be required to perform not only at the outset of his employment but also that which he will be required to carry on over a period of years. *What he should know* will include his formal education and acquired knowledge which should give an indication as to how he may fare in the wide knowledge of facts he will be required to retain and use. *What to look for* will entail an evaluation of the prospects, native and acquired attributes, and *how to find them* will conclude the broad outline of the counselor's task.

What He Does

At the outset of his employment, the prospect must be able to comprehend the value and intention of Line and Staff functions in organization and administrative affairs. These functions in the police field are not divergent from similar functions in other fields. They constitute accepted methods in organization and administration, finance, selection, training, public relations, and morale. In some instances in personal selection the emphasis upon selecting recruits for line functions with staff function abilities is not necessary; but, when we have surveyed the field of law enforcement, we readily see the advisability of such methods. Law enforcement is a career service and as such a recruit enters it faced with a long process of trials leading to situations at the top of the career ladder. If he is not able to cope with staff situations as he progresses through the promotional field, then he is stagnated and reverts to a lackadaisical attitude which is detrimental to the overall progress of the entire unit he represents. For it is true that the rookie patrolman of today is the executive head tomorrow. Our present day methods of police administration does not enable the executive head to choose adequately adapted personnel for administrative posts. Having to choose such leaders from among the lowest bracket of the field makes it mandatory that the selection of recruits must take into consideration the potentials of the individual in regard to administrative as well as functional possibilities. Such long range prognosis is very difficult but must be met if the standard of performance is to be increased in keeping with public demand.

An analysis of the police problem in a recent "beat survey" resulted in some concrete data upon which to base the average work load of the police officer in the field. The average time spent in routine observation and inspectional duties consumed approximately 55% of the patrolman's time. Investigational duties directly connected with cases accounted for the other 45% of his time.

If these observational and inspectional duties are evaluated, we find that they cover such potential CRIME HAZARDS as public, private and commercial *property*. Public hazards comprise such places as taverns, railroad stations, cheap boarding houses, card rooms, pool halls, gambling places, hotels and buildings. Private property hazards include such places as occupied and unoccupied residences, apartment houses and clubs. By far the largest category in this respect is the commercial property hazard which includes warehouses, service stations, restaurants, garages, supply houses, docks, parking lots, banks, new construction, theaters and stores of all kinds. *Traffic control* presents another major hazard to the law enforcement officer and his vigilance while on routine patrol must also be centered upon high incident thoroughfares and intersections with respect to accident contributory factors. *Gatherings* both large and small present their potential crime hazard problems to the police officer and his attention must be directed to such things as athletic events, political meetings, parades, conventions, disasters and amusement parks. The alert officer will not overlook the crime hazard presented by *people* themselves which includes such individuals as known criminals, alcoholics, peddlers, vagrants and canvassers. Certain *geographical locations* present their problem in the form of racial sections, low rent districts, foreign born population communities and parks. Conditional situations effect the division of duties due to such elements as high crime frequencies, high and low property values, seasonal situations, population density, and lighting.

He will be required to offer *information* pertaining to general subjects. In dispensing general information, he is required to advise individuals upon rights and wrongs concerning criminal actions and also where to look for guidance in regards to civil information and counsel. Location of buildings, areas, and routes are frequent requests. Relative to crime prevention, he must be able to advise the citizenry on how to protect their property and what safeguards to use. He must have at his fingertips, statistics on the most prevalent crimes, in what areas they are occurring, as well as the reason for such conditions.

Reporting and investigations which require approximately 45% of the officer's time will be spent upon felonies, misdemeanors, accidents, dependencies and the collection and preservation of evidence.

What He Should Know

For his knowledge requirements, the police officer must have a good comprehension of the Arts and Sciences. *Pure science* will enter into his occupational duties in relation to Medicine, Chemistry and Physics. First Aid, recognition of contagious disease and health safeguards encompass his daily routine. *Statistics* are his constant guide. He must be able to submit reports which yield proper information for statistical analysis of his problems. He must readily grasp the fundamentals of spot maps and apply corrective measures to alleviate hazardous situations. He must be fully able to grasp *records procedures* to enable him to use the store of material available to him. The use to which he is able to put the *Mechanic Arts* will often depend his success as an officer and investigator. He must be a skilled driver of cars and be able to impart proper driving techniques to others. In cases of catastrophes, he must be able to cope with erecting safety barriers or participate in rescue work with as quick decision and perfection as the emergency may require. In cases of accident investigation, he must recognize mechanical faults which may have been contributory factors as well as the apparent negligence of the parties involved. In this present day and age, he is provided with various pieces of mechanical equipment and devices, the malfunctioning of which he must be competent to recognize before serious damage results. In the rôle of investigator, he must be able to execute a workable drawing to illustrate the location of evidence and emphasize salient points of a case.

His recognition of *administrative and organizational* duties will enable him to save valuable time in seeking material, opinions and advice from cooperating staff agencies. In his investigative capacity outside of the organization, he must know the accepted methods used in business and apply it in seeking interviews and evidence the quickest and most desirable way. An understanding of *Psychology* will stand him in good stead for conducting his interviews, taking testimony, and in public relations.

If crime conditions are to improve, the police officer should possess a background of *Sociology*. He is in constant touch with the underlying sources of crime hazards and can well indicate to the proper agencies necessary treatments for their causes. He is the one who meets the juvenile long before he becomes a delinquent. The policeman is the one who can tell where and why crime prevention methods are working or not. The backbone of his work will be based upon his grasp of the *Law*. He must distinguish between civil and criminal cases. He must possess at the outset of his duties a full and thorough knowledge and training in the laws of arrest, search, seizure, felonies and misdemeanors. He must know the Federal and State statutes as well as the Municipal Ordinances.

What to Look For

After an appraisal of the job to be done and the necessary attributes which will be required to cope with this work, it is then necessary to reach out for those individuals who are most adapted for this task. No hard and fast yard stick has yet been devised which will insure a prognosis of success in any field. We may with good end results however approach this problem in a systematic and analytical way by use of the several methods of human analysis we have at hand. The future law enforcement officer must of necessity possess many of the qualities which can be measured collectively through: pencil and paper tests, a background survey, and a personal interview. The whole matter of choice may be stated in one sentence yet the process is one which should require ample time and much thought. At the outset, no one should be considered for this field who does not measure up to *intelligence standards* which groups them in the very superior brackets in terms of the Army Alpha or its equivalent. This would require a raw score of 135 or better. The marked advantages of this test to the counselor is in its component parts as they relate to the police field. It is extremely necessary that the law enforcement officer have the ability to: (1) follow directions; have good auditory memory, and the ability to concentrate on oral instructions. (2) He must possess arithmetical reasoning ability. (3) Practical judgment and ability to weigh facts and arrive at correct conclusions are an every day essential. (4) His vocabulary and ability to handle language must be above reproach. (5) His success as an investigator will depend largely upon his ability to recognize the relationship of easily recognizable parts to a given whole and interpret the concept. He must grasp ideas, have assembling ability and a general ability to systematize work. (6) If he is to meet changing requirements of his job, then he must have a mathematical capacity above average and an ability to handle statistics in order that he may apply corrective measures to indicated hazards. (7) Police officers must possess a great degree of adaptability, concentration, and continuity of mental effort. He must be able to discriminate and be free from suggestibility. (8) In perhaps no other field is it necessary to have such a broad range of interest and information as well as powers of observation and ability to acquire, retain and recall dissociated facts.

A police officer must be well *socially adjusted* and an index to this is possible to a certain extent through accepted testing methods. That a policeman must be truthful and honest is unquestionable. He must be contented, have a sense of wellbeing and a feeling that life is worth while. A sense of social membership acceptance and basic similarity with others is a needed consideration. Satisfactory social and emotional adjustment must be measured. The prospective peace officer must have a definite purpose in entering upon the field. Perhaps in no other field is it so necessary to manifest good impulse judgment. Only a brief survey of the duties which the police officer is required to perform is all that is necessary to realize that he must have a very satisfactory sense of self-control, self-regulation, and the ability to make and execute plans.

Many of the objectives which we seek in search of our vocation can not be indicated through pen and pencil tests. Our backgrounds and habits are good indexes to our behavior and desire patterns. The background picture should indicate his initiative and purpose manifestations and the degree to which he will expend himself. A survey of the places in which he has lived will indicate his environmental tastes. Many factors may be gained from the opinions of neighbors as to his conduct and character if such contacts can be made. His school records must be analyzed and specific emphasis placed upon those subjects in which he shows marked promise. For success in the police field, those who are mathematically or mechanically bent will probably result in the better choice. Clubs in which he has been associated will give an indication of his leadership qualities.

The *personal interview* will give you your last analysis of the individual and such things as his appearance, alertness, voice, speech, friendliness, emotional stability, judgment and ability to present ideas can almost readily be determined. Your first impression of him must be good. He must be healthy, energetic and clean cut. His voice and speech must be pleasant and non-irritating. His voice should be well modulated and his diction good. He must be alert and show friendliness by his politeness and likable manner. If, after he has met the foregoing standards, he is well poised, calm and self assured, exhibits good humor and self-control under stress, then he has aptitude for a police career.

References:

1. Adams, O.D. *Training for the police service.* U. S. Dept. of the Interior, Bulletin No. 197, 1938.
2. Beswick, J. C. *Instructional analysis of police service.* State of California, Department of Education, Bulletin No. 3, February 1, 1934.
3. Laird, D. A. *Psychology of selecting employees.* New York: McGraw-Hill Book Co., Inc., 1937.

D. F. McC.

PORTUGAL. (1) The history of institutions in Portugal devoting themselves specifically and with clearly defined programmes to the pursuit of theoretical studies and practical solutions of problems of vocational guidance and occupational selection is very recent history, since it only begins in the present century, or, more precisely, in 1925, the year of the foundation of the Institute of Vocational Guidance—Instituto de Orientação Profissional—in Lisbon.

This Institute was created, as is clearly shown by its name, with the explicit purpose of discovering and ascertaining by means of psycho-technical methods the innate abilities and propensities of young people, with a view to guiding them in the choice of professional activities best suited to their personal capacities. Nevertheless, the Institute has since its inception occupied itself also in tasks of direct selection of grown-up persons for certain services in the Portuguese Army and Navy, such as aviation, motorized services, etc., and in the occupational guidance of selective operations in private enterprise.

This many-sided activity of the Institute has been made possible thanks only to the very considerable income derived from the original bequest with the aid of which the Institute was established. This has permitted its equipment with abundant material for the necessary scientific research work and psycho-technical observation, and the provision of a numerous technical staff.

(2) From 1925 to 1940, all the scientific and practical work of vocational guidance in Portugal was carried out exclusively by this Institute. Its achievements thus became truly outstanding, not only as a result of its constant endeavors to propagate throughout the country the underlying principles and the most adequate working methods of efficient vocational guidance, but also to the professional aid given by it to Lisbon elementary, secondary and technical schools with which the Institute had been closely co-operating in various directions.

As regards elementary schools, the task of the Institute consists in observing the pupils of the last class with a view to giving them a clear idea as to the type and grade of the continuation-school best suited eventually to form and develop their natural aptitudes and tendencies. Thus, the Institute has been performing an intensive mission of educational guidance. In the secondary schools its work has particularly been to observe the pupils at the outset of each scholastic year, so as to obtain their best possible distribution into reasonably homogeneous classes, composed of groups of more or less the same mental level.

With regard to technical and professional schools or colleges the Institute has been trying its utmost to achieve a class selection according to the professional specialties best suitable to the capacities of the pupils who have just finished their preparatory course of technical initiation. But the most important part of the work of the Institute centers round its psycho-echnical consulting service to which quite a considerable number both of pupils and of grownups are having recourse in order either to obtain adequate advice on matters of educational and occupational guidance or to submit themselves to selective tests generally established for the various professional occupations and careers.

(3) In other places in the country no strictly scientific operations of vocational guidance have, so far, been undertaken since the organization of branch-establishments of the Lisbon Institute, provided for in its organic law, has as a matter of fact not yet been carried into effect. Nevertheless, quite an amount of good work in the field of vocational guidance has been done in almost all secondary schools of the two main types existing in the country (general education in lyceums and professional education and training in technical and commercial schools). This was mainly due to the better pedagogical preparation and training of the relative teaching staffs, acquired by them since 1912 at the Institutes or Faculties of

Education, created in that year in the Universities of Lisbon and Coimbra, where studies in educational psychology and pedagogical experiments by means of mental tests have since then been prosecuted in ever increasing proportions.

The greater possibility of transition from one type of secondary schools into another, increasingly favored by the relative legislation of the last two or three decades, has in its turn contributed towards the growing necessity for an appropriate selectional advice as regards the course of studies to follow, a necessity which is fundamentally the very vindication of educational guidance.

Finally, the various attempts made by the Ministry of National Education with a view to replacing the traditional procedure of scholastic selection, based upon purely subjective standards, by new methods best suited to determine it objectively and with a high degree of impartiality and accuracy, have to a large extent also favored the application of the fundamental principles of educational guidance in a more scientific manner and have in the course of time succeeded in convincing the parents of the pupils of the convenience, and even of the necessity, for them to take advice precisely of the teachers best prepared and competent to give them a considered opinion on matters of educational guidance.

(4) The diffusion, the progress and the achievements of an up-to-date technique of educational guidance have, naturally, created and consolidated the belief that in the course of time it would become possible to extend the application of its methods also into the field of vocational guidance proper, without going beyond the natural bounds of the school. Thus it has been thought, especially since 1940, that the particular scheme of vocational guidance, adopted and followed in Portugal at a time when only extra-scholastic Institutes were entrusted with the whole work of professional observation and guidance of young people about to enter a calling, trade, profession or career, was no longer the most efficient, or the most practical, or even the most economic of the possible schemes and that, consequently, it could be advantageously substituted by an explicitly scholastic system of vocational guidance, applicable in each individual school. It may be of interest to point out that it has been the Lisbon Institute of Vocational Guidance that has been advocating this same idea, in its various publications, and has been endeavoring to demonstrate that vocational guidance, while it can in no way be confused with the educational activity proper, constitutes nevertheless an operation which can, as such, be adequately carried into effect only in the school concerned. And this for the following reason: vocational guidance is a continuous

process requiring not only a persistent observation of the examinees and frequent experimental enquiries into their reactive behavior in response to situations either previously prepared for the purpose or incidentally arising from natural circumstances, but requiring also a complementary action of a pedagogical nature, the object of which is to strengthen the positive qualities ascertained in the course of experimentation and, at the same time, to atrophy or deviate their opposing forces. From this point of view, vocational guidance cannot therefore be envisaged as an operation of a merely informative character but as an operation which in order to be efficacious must also be constructive, creative or formative. Everything capable of limiting or of restricting its effectiveness, by withdrawing it from the natural sphere within which it should be performed—and that is the school proper—is therefore mere artifice and cannot lead to useful results.

The supporters of this view are therefore of opinion that a change in the present legal and pragmatic system of vocational guidance and its replacement by a scheme similar to that adopted in the United States or in Great-Britain are objects easily to be attained, as matters stand, and without appreciable financing expenses. For more than 10 years the Lisbon Institute of Vocational Guidance has been maintaining a special course for the formation of vocational counsellors, which has, so far, been frequented by scores of candidates. It would therefore not be difficult to find among the younger teachers of our lyceums and technical schools all the vocational counsellors that might be necessary in order to provide forthwith the principal secondary colleges with a competent personnel, familiarized with the necessary technique of psychological observation, carried out by means of mental, sensorio-motorial and sensorial tests or even tests of temperament and character. And neither would it prove difficult to find among them experts capable of performing, by adequate methods and means, an objective observation of the behavior of the examinees and of applying the necessary methods of statistical calculation to educational problems.

Thus, the extension of methods of vocational guidance, hitherto exclusively entrusted to one single Institute in one single town— Lisbon—to the great majority of elementary and secondary schools and colleges, both of general and of professional education, would not present a hasty imposition of new and consequently not sufficiently well known methods, but would mean, quite the contrary, a mere adaptation of long-practiced procedures, which are for this very reason still capable of appreciable improvements.

(5) However, if it is true that we may accept almost unreserv-

edly that all schools concerned, once conveniently provided with the competent psycho-technical staff and equipment, will be in a position to set up their own educational guidance system, with an efficiency corresponding to their relative pedagogical merits, it is nevertheless true that, on the other hand, we must make some restrictions as regards the problem of occupational guidance.

In fact, if there are colleges where this latter can be performed with considerable efficiency, on the condition that they are appropriately organized and equipped with all things necessary, other colleges there are where it will not be possible to carry out this task with the same degree of probability as regards the final results.

The first group is represented by technical schools of all grades, the activity of which is capable of being directly integrated into the professional activities of the place, of the district or of the country in which they operate. If these schools be organized and conducted in accordance with what by common consensus has been called the psycho-technique of the subject and of the object, and if, moreover, they do not miss properly to take into account the realities of economic life and the particular social circumstances of the place or province concerned, their task of occupational guidance can be carried into effect with such a degree of accuracy that it even may attain the full exactness of selective operations.

However, in order to secure this object, certain particular conditions must needs be taken into full consideration. First and foremost, it is necessary to organize the technical schools so as to establish in their programmes a clear separation between the apprenticeship of general technical education and that of a particular professional specialization. The former will have to take the strictest care of the methodical, precise and accurate structural articulation of technical attitudes, knacks and habitudes that are common to the whole series of professional operations proposed to be taught in the school. At the same time, it will endeavor to recognize and to ascertain, both by means of tests and of an adequate observation of the working behavior, the aptitudes and propensities that the apprentices might be disclosing as regards their various kinds of work.

The professional specialization, on the other hand, will have to perfect and to develop the aptitudes already revealed, in the direction of the speciality concerned, and, at the same time, will have to guide the apprenticeship towards the best possible perfection and economy of production, although without impairing in the least the physical and psychical integrity of the apprentice.

It is in the expectation that the Portuguese technical and professional colleges will be able to cope with this task that a project for their reorganization is at present under consideration, including the problem of their own occupational guidance.

As to the vocational guidance in schools which are merely a preparatory stage to professional colleges or schools of general education preparatory to a large number of schools of specialization, the problem presents aspects of a more difficult solution. No definite decision has therefore been reached as yet in this respect, especially as regards the methods that might be accepted and followed with full confidence of success, even though they are already beyond the preliminary stage of general experimentation.

J. J. O. G.

PRIMARY MENTAL ABILITIES, TESTS FOR. The construction of tests for primary mental abilities is based on the assumption that individual differences in mental endowment cannot be adequately described by any single index of intelligence. For many purposes a single index of intelligence is useful, but the practical work of educational and vocational counseling demands a profile of some kind for each individual. Two individuals may have the same index of average mental endowment as represented by a mental age or an intelligence quotient and yet they may be entirely different individuals as shown by their profiles.

In order to prepare a profile to describe an individual it is first necessary to determine the abilities or traits which are to be represented by the several columns in the profile. The methods of multiple factor analysis were developed specifically to solve this problem. So far, about 10 or 12 primary factors or abilities have been identified most of which are quite clear. A number of primary factors have been indicated but not identified with sufficient clarity to be incorporated in practical counseling tests. It is not known how many primary traits will eventually be required to describe the mental endowment and personality traits for purposes of counseling. Seven primary factors have been identified with sufficient clarity to justify their appearance in practical counseling, and additional factors will be added as they become known and reasonably well understood.

The 7 factors which are available in practical counseling tests at the present time are: The number factor N, the verbal comprehension factor V, the word fluency factor W, the space or visualizing factor S, the perceptual speed factor P, a memorizing factor M, and a reasoning factor R.

Children who are at the same general intelligence level differ remarkably in the ability to handle simple numerical work. The number factor is rather narrow. It represents facility in dealing with simple numerical relations. The ability to solve arithmetical reasoning problems is much more complex. Arithmetical reasoning represents in addition to the number factor N also verbal comprehension V, the space factor S and the reasoning factor R. Anyone who learns readily to do simple numerical tasks quickly, such as that of a cashier, is endowed with number facility. Other people of equal average intelligence would find this kind of task very difficult to learn. A person who does not have this ability can learn to do numerical tasks quickly but he will probably always find them fatiguing.

The most important factor for most school work is the verbal comprehension factor V. It is usually indicated by a large vocabulary and by facility in reading with comprehension. The word fluency factor W is concerned with the ability of the subject to produce appropriate verbal expression for his ideas. The two verbal factors, W and V, are quite distinct. A person who is high in V and low in W is capable of reading complex prose and he probably has a large vocabulary, but he is not fluent nor quick in his associations. A person who is high in W and low in V is verbally fluent with a limited vocabulary.

One of the most important of the primary factors is the ability S to visualize space. People who are good visualizers do much of their thinking in visual terms. They prefer diagrams and models. Those who are not endowed with this factor do their best thinking in verbal terms. The counselor meets rather frequently the child who is a non-reader or who is verbally retarded, but who can do good thinking in visual terms. Most fortunate are those individuals who are endowed with all or most of these abilities. Some of the practical applications of tests for the space factor are rather self-evident. For example, one can be sure that a boy who is a poor visualizer will not be happy as an apprentice draftsman.

Speed of perception P has been found to be a primary factor. Some otherwise bright people excel in this factor and some do not. These primary factors are useful but they are more practical in some occupations than in others. It has been found, for example, that inspectors need to be well endowed with the perceptual speed factor. It seems likely that speed of reading is determined partly by individual differences in this natural speed of perception.

Several memory factors have been indicated in factorial studies of memory. The ability to memorize paired associates is probably the factor that is conspicuous in most forms of memorizing. Poor memorizers are found among both bright and less gifted individuals. Some school subjects and some occupations are more demanding of this type of ability than others.

Experimental studies indicate the existence of several reasoning factors including facility for inductive and deductive thinking. These are combined for counseling test purposes in several tests of reasoning for children.

More than 20,000 profiles of the primary mental abilities of junior high school children have been examined and it has been found that all possible combinations of profiles occur in the school population.

Several profiles will be briefly mentioned here as examples. Some high school children will be found who are high in verbal comprehension V and low in space S and reasoning R. Such children are likely to have trouble with geometry and they may excel in the languages but not in the formal aspects of language. Some children have been found especially gifted in memorizing M and low in all the other primary factors. Sometimes they do acceptable school work although they are not bright. Naturally they do better in those courses which call for little more than memorizing. Children have been found who are low in everything except in word fluency W. Some of them succeed in talking themselves into good school grades. They frequently appear to be better mentally endowed than they really are. Several children have been found who are high in verbal comprehension V and low in all of the other abilities including reasoning R. Such exceptional children are good readers but they fail to do good work in subjects requiring reasoning with reading material. A common problem is a non-reader who is low in verbal comprehension V and in word fluency W and who is high in space S, reasoning R, and number N. Such cases are found quite frequently among boys.

Educational and vocational guidance consists in the intricate job of fitting the child's mental pattern to his school problems and vocational training.

Tests for primary mental abilities adapted for the junior and senior high school level are published by Science Research Associates, 228 S. Wabash, Chicago 4, Illinois. It has recently been found that essentially the same primary mental abilities can be identified in the kindergarten age. Non-reading tests of the primary mental abilities for 5 and 6 year old children have been prepared. It is expected that they will be published with norms in the fall of 1946.

References:

1. Thurstone, L. L. *Primary mental abilities.* Psychometric Monograph No. 1. Chicago: University of Chicago Press, 1938.
2. ————. *A factorial study of perception.* Chicago: University of Chicago Press, 1944.
3. Thurstone, L. L. and Thurstone, T. G. *Factorial studies of intelligence.* Psychometric Monograph, No. 2. Chicago: University of Chicago Press, 1941.
4. Wolfle, D. *Factor analysis to 1940.* Psychometric Monograph, No. 3. Chicago: University of Chicago Press, 1940.

L. L. T.

PRIMITIVE CULTURES.   The principal difference between vocational guidance in primitive and in modern societies lies in our classification of vocational guidance as education and guidance given by special non-familial agencies, whereas in primitive society most training and guidance are given by parents or other close relatives. Furthermore, the needs for vocational guidance and special vocational education arise when the parent's occupation, in its current form, no longer provides a model for the child of the same sex, which occurs in complex societies with division of labor, in societies undergoing rapid change so that the methods and techniques used by the children will differ from those used by the parents, or in which a definite effort is being made to divert individuals from one occupation to another, either for their own good, for that of society, because a given occupation needs more practitioners, or in an attempt to divert labor from one type of occupation to another.

Very few of these conditions which necessitate some form of formal vocational guidance and training obtain in those societies which we define as primitive because they lack the knowledge of a written language. With the exception of some of the higher civilizations of Central and South America, and Africa, which for purposes of this discussion can more profitably be classified with high civilizations (as they had a political and social structure usually associated with the keeping of records, etc.), most primitive societies have very simple divisions of labor, based first upon sex, then a simple locality basis, e.g. peoples living near the sea, fishing and exchanging fish for agricultural products, or people who lived near good clay deposits specializing in making pots, etc; occasionally on clan, caste or rank bases, so that members of hereditary kin groups were expected to be proficient in special occupations or avocations. In all of these simple forms of division of labor, the family still remained the training ground for the next generation, birth in a given family determined the choice of occupation, and slow imitation of the parents and elder brothers and sisters provided the learning situation. Under such circumstances, the most usual type of special vocational training for an individual would be, for instance, arranging for a nephew who showed signs of promise as a hunter to spend time with an uncle who had good hereditary hunting grounds, or for a youth who showed special interest in carpentry to work with some relative who was well known as a housebuilder or canoe builder, where such crafts were recognized as specialties. Occasionally, as on the North Pacific Coast and in certain Polynesian islanders, it behooved a man who held rank also to display extra skill and members of the chiefly family or their retainers might be detailed to teach a child of a chiefly family extra skills.

However, the prevailing picture is one in which each adult man or woman knew certain basic skills, and all the children were expected to acquire the skills appropriate to their sex. Acquisition of other skills, such as canoe building, special types of artistry, and the professions of therapeutic and religious procedure, mediumship, divination, midwifery, bone setting, interpretation of dreams, trepanning, etc. were all additional to the acquisition of the basic skills of life, and dependent either upon descent, special ability, or predisposing circumstances, as when recovery from certain sorts of illness made it obligatory to practice the appropriate behavior for curing that illness. The major shift in present day society is that we rely upon the family to teach the chief consumption skills, and upon schools, apprenticeship and work practice to teach production skills, while in primitive society the basic production skills were taught in the home.

Cultures varied in the extent to which special gift was regarded as dependent upon heredity, conditions of birth, both of which were actually extrinsic to the skill in question, or as simple individual variations which could be cultivated if not institutionalized. They also varied as to whether each or certain steps in learning the simple tasks common to every member of the society were marked by ceremonial or not, as among the Kwakiutl where a growing girl had heavy copper bracelets placed upon her arms, one of which was removed as she learned each appointed task, or among the Iatmul where parents might give a special feast in honor of a son or daughter's mastery of some step such as planting a yam or catching a tortoise. In a majority of societies learning the common adult skills was regarded as normal as learning to walk and talk, and deserving of as little special attention, and it was the failure in learning—the little boy who was afraid to take the cattle to the fields, or the girl who did not learn to weave who was commented upon and exhorted. For the most part the acquisition of extra skills was left to the volition of the individual, who himself, or with the help of his parents and with gifts, sought out a teacher. Very occasionally a society was regimented into age grades and certain occupations were expected from an age group.

Societies also varied in the sort of magical precautions which were taken at birth, as when a girl's umbilical cord was cut upon a bark cloth beater to make her a skillful bark cloth maker, or a boy's cord was cut on a digging stick, or a child's placenta was buried in some spot symbolic of skill in some adult occupation.

There was also wide variation as to whether the learning child performed a *miniature* version of the adult task, as when the small girl carried a small carrying bag on her head, or the little boy learned to manage a miniature canoe, or performed a *simple* version of the adult task, as when a child was allowed to use a punt in a large canoe under conditions of easy punting. This type of contrast extended also to the construction of objects. In some societies children were taught to make miniature objects in imitation of their elders, in others they learned by performing the simpler part of some construction operation, weaving the center of a mat before they knew how to begin or end the weaving. Less frequently, large complex operations, like housebuilding, or making an earth oven for a large household, were subdivided so that each aged child performed tasks commensurate with his strength and skill, the operation itself often being very simple, monotonous and partial rather than a simpler or miniature version of a complex adult task.

One rather striking contrast occurs between those societies which emphasize the *process* of carving a bowl, or weaving a mat where skill is regarded as something which is learned very slowly from long association with experts (as in Polynesia), and those cultures where the emphasis is upon the finished object, and an adult might undertake to duplicate an object when he was entirely ignorant of the way in which it had been made. In the former type of culture, a much higher degree of finish may be expected while in the latter the individual remains an indifferent but enterprising craftsman. The former attitude towards craftsmanship leads to such strong identification of a craftsman and his craft that sometimes members of a skilled craft were kidnapped as slaves, because it was not considered possible for the kidnapping tribe to master the skill. Contrasting attitudes such as these will be found to inform the whole learning period of childhood and youth and will be expressed also in the extent to which a child is allowed to perform any act, imperfectly and experimentally, or whether he is deterred from experimenting with a skill beyond his ability and encouraged to learn step by step.

Where any skill is regarded as inalienably bound up with status, as sex, or age or rank, or special type of birth or religious experience, there is likely to be a corresponding block on learning among all of those who are not of the appropriate status, as when women refuse to learn masculine skills, or people of inferior class or caste or rank fail to conceive of the possibility of learning the skills associated with the superior group. This phenomenon becomes specially important where primitive people come in contact with our modern civilization and attempts are made in schools to teach them the practices of modern technology, scientific agriculture, etc. In many instances the failure to learn is due neither to lack of skill or intelligence but rather to a failure to conceive of themselves as the sort of person who does the indicated task, such as typewriting, or running a tractor, or speaking a foreign language. Once this gap in identification is bridged and the child comes to believe that while not a member of the more civilized group, or of the sex which usually practices the skill, it is possible for him, an Australian aborigine, or North American Indian, to practice it also, the rest of the learning proceeds easily.

There are also very marked differences in the kind of learning characteristic of different cultures, whether it is rote learning, learning by step by step imitation, learning which is motivated by considerations of reward and punishment, learning in which the body of the learner—the carving hand or dancing limb is passive to the manipulation of the teacher, learning which is done "with the eyes," that is, based on a long period of observation in which no attempt is made to practice, or learning in which the adult breaks down the task into a series of steps and consciously and articulately directs each step. Whether the pupil is admired and rewarded for each step, or subjected to a long period of probationary hard work, such as the demand of the Mundugumor that the apprentice chew the pigments which the master painter uses, also varies. Some peoples take the position that any skill can be learned at any time during one's life and, like the Balinese, make virtually no distinction between the learning processes of a four year old and a sixty year old. Others regard the acquisition of a skill as essentially a pre-adult activity and the occasional adult learner in a child status. Very often there is a marked disassociation between the details of a skill on which attention is focussed, and the details which are necessary for the actual acquisition of the skill, as when an instructor concentrates on teaching a boy trapping magic while letting him learn to make the necessary traps and snares without any special instruction.

Comparative study of the methods of vocational guidance in primitive societies are mainly useful as a way of sharpening our imaginations as to the variety of ways in which individuals can learn, and throwing into relief our rather special cultural attitudes which rely upon vocational guidance to divert children from their parents' occupations or their parents' outmoded occupational practices, into occupations which either their innate abilities or the exigencies of the current division of labor indicate.

References:

1. Bateson, G. Social planning and the concept of "Deutero-Learning." Science, Philosophy and Religion, 2nd Symposium. (Conference on Sci., Phil. and Religion, New York, 1942), 81–97.
2. Bunzel, R. *The Pueblo potter.* New York: Columbia University Press, 1929.
3. Mead, M. Our educational emphasis in primitive perspective. *Education and the cultural process.* Edited by Charles S. Johnson, May, 1943.
4. Mead, M. Need for teaching anthropology in normal school and colleges. *School and Society,* 1927, 26, 466–88.
5. Reichard, G. *The Navajo shepherd and weaver.* J. J. Augustin, 1936.

M. M.

PROFILE GRAPH.   The profile graph is a means of showing the relationship between scores made on the various parts of a single test or standing on a series of tests. Non-comparable raw scores are converted into meaningful ratings such as standard or percentile scores. It is then possible to represent these scores on a single graph. It is customary to group tests of the same type together; for example, all the interest tests taken by a subject are presented in some orderly sequence. Test factors are equally spaced along one of the coordinate axes of the graph, and the percentile or standard scores along the other. A psychograph is then made by connecting related points on the chart. Some like to encircle points that represent total or summary scores.

Profile graphs are useful in that they make it possible to note quickly how subjects rank with reference to the norm group; thus deficiencies and proficiencies are emphasized. It must be remembered, however, that difference in the composition of norm groups may lead to marked discrepancies in standing on two tests of the same general type. For instance, converted scores derived from an intelligence test standardized on a representative sample of the general population might vary greatly from scores based on college norms.

O. J. K.

PROJECTIVE METHODS

War Experience, Projective Techniques and Vocational Guidance

The pioneer efforts in personnel selection on a large scale made necessary in World War I, were largely concerned with man's intellectual apparatus and led to the rapid and widespread use of intelligence testing in the 25 years which followed. The shortcomings of this onesided approach were becoming increasingly apparent with the realization that the height of the I.Q. did not necessarily correlate with vocational success.

One of the developments of this war from which business and industry may reap results, has been in the successful work carried out in selecting men for special jobs in which character and personality were equally, if not more, important than intelligence. New methods of selection developed under the urgent pressure of war proved better than any of those previously used.

The alert vocational counselor or clinical psychologist has become increasingly conscious of the disadvantages of the purely summative or dissective approach and has depended more and more on the qualitative analysis of traditional test results and his intuitive impressions. The subjective side of his evaluation has left loopholes for criticism from those who demand objective evidence. The development of a more dynamic concept of personality and the new techniques of diagnoses are beginning to replace the former trust in quantitative results.

Projective techniques for personality diagnosis take a medium position between clinical observation and psychometric devices.

Projective Techniques and the Specific Function of the Rorschach Method

Projective techniques differ from the usual psychometric procedures chiefly in one respect: the psychometric approach sacrifices everything (including the entity of the personality) to strictest requirements for standardizing the stimulus situation or the task that the subject has to fulfill. Projective techniques for the most part provide a situation that stimulates or even forces the subject to project his own thoughts, feelings, or way of handling life situations on to the particular situation at hand, as if it were a movie screen.

Considerations for standardizing the administrative procedure or mechanizing the techniques for interpreting these projections are secondary to this main goal.

It should be said that this point of view is common to both the projective techniques and the methods of clinical observation. In spite of this fact an essential methodological difference exists between these two procedures, namely, that all subjects of projective technique shall be exposed to one and the same stimulus situation, since this method alone permits quantitative comparisons of the many ways in which subjects react or project themselves.

In doing this, projective techniques attempt to avoid the negative aspects and hold on to the positive aspects of both approaches— the psychometric and the clinical—and enable the examiner or observer to get a picture of the "personality in action." In contrast to the psychometric approach it enables the examiner to observe the interplay of all the various emotional and intellectual functions, and, at the same time, facilitates the obtaining of objective evidence, which the experienced vocational counselor welcomes as a supplement to his subjective impressions and observations. The more experienced workers accept this diagnostic aid more readily than do the less experienced because they are unafraid of being checked.

For some time projective techniques have been using stimulus materials with various degrees of structuralization or meaningfulness. On the one extreme are Struve's cloud pictures (described by William Stern in [6] "Character and Personality") which use rectangular cuts of actual cloud photographs with no clear separation of figure and ground within the rectangle, no symmetry, and no determinants besides the various shades of gray produced by the clouds. On the other extreme are the pictures used in Henry Murray's "Thematic Apperception Test," * pictures of actual events with only slight blurring of outlines or other means of ambiguity.

During the last ten years, for both practical and theoretical purposes of diagnoses, the Rorschach method has played a more important rôle than any other of the projective techniques. The 1940 Yearbook of Tests and Measurements devotes more space to the Rorschach than to any other test. Its contribution is chiefly due to the particular kind of stimulus material that Dr. Hermann Rorschach, a Swiss psychiatrist, selected after his ten years of experimentation with the method (1911–1921).[5]

The reproductions of actual inkblot pictures, which are used on the ten stimulus cards, steer a careful middle course between the more structuralized and less structuralized materials mentioned above: (1) They are for all practical purposes symmetrical (the effect having been created by folding the paper so as to produce a similar blot on each half); (2) the inkblot material has spread itself over the white background of the cards in various forms, for example, there is a rather solid blot on some cards and a complete scatter of the blot material on others; (3) on half the cards the stimulus effect of the various gray shades is enlivened by ink of various bright color; (4) some of the blots resemble certain shapes so strongly that more than half of all subjects respond to them along the lines they suggest; others present greater difficulties in organizing the stimulus material for any interpretative purpose. All in all, the stimulus material offers the subjects the greatest possible variety for different techniques and procedures in responding to the standard instruction: "People see all sorts of things in these inkblot pictures. Now tell me what you see, what it might be for you, what it makes you think of."

Faced with this seemingly innocuous task in which he cannot guess what is expected of him, the subject is unable to fall back on his usual defences and thus reveals the underlying mental and emotional frame of reference by which he interprets his environment and reacts to it.

The Rorschach method does not aspire to disclose information about the life history of the subject and his environment, nor does it predict specific behavior in a particular life situation but it does make such behavior understandable by revealing the structural underpinnings, by explaining seeming contradictions and discrepancies, thus clarifying the total personality picture. Having discovered a consistent picture it is possible to plan more efficiently in helping the subject by recognizing structurally strong and weak points.

Among the most important of the structuralized aspects are: (1) The subject's mental approach to intellectual tasks, especially his preference for analytic or synthetic thinking; (2) his responsiveness to emotional stimulations both from without and within; (3) his preferred control mechanisms for the regulation of instinctual impulses; (4) the usual functioning of his imaginative thinking; (5) the form and level of his emotional adjustment and maturation.

The Rorschach method is not limited by discrepancies in the cultural or educational background. Naturally since the test is dependent on verbal expression, the educational background is visible. Moreover, the extent to which the subject draws on his cultural, educational or professional resources clarifies his structural personality picture. Vocationally determined content is usually recognized and may disclose the subject's present occupation or point to another which he would prefer. These associations, however do not appear to derive from the deeper sources in the personality.

With regard to age the range of applicability is almost as unlimited as it is in regard to cultural and educational background. Up to seven years the "age pattern" overshadows individual personality development. For children from seven to twelve years of age, adult standards of evaluation become more and more applicable. After puberty the significance of the chronological age is limited to problems of emotional and intellectual maturation and to the recognition of biological crises occurring at various stages of adult life.

The Special Contribution of Projective Techniques within the Field of Vocational Counseling

Projective techniques are not a substitute for aptitude tests. If the task is to discover among any number of applicants those who can use a specific skill most efficiently at this particular point in their lives, a specialized aptitude test is more efficient, but projective techniques are far superior to aptitude tests in the following situations:

(1) where the focus of interest lies in discovering any used or unused potentialities in an individual,

(2) where a complicated job demands not an isolated skill but a general maturity or superiority in personality development, and

(3) finally in a situation where it is important to screen out all those people who would be likely to fail in any task due to severe maladjustments or weaknesses in personality structure.

Personality and Vocation

One of the principles to be kept in mind in the field of vocational guidance has been put in the formulation that fifty per cent of the people can do fifty per cent of all jobs. Therefore the task is not that of picking out ready made personalities for ready made jobs but to discover the stresses and strains in particular jobs and the strong and weak points in the personality so as to get the best possible match between the two. For that reason in the use of the traditional screening devices for personnel selection, the intuitive impression of the examiner was found to be the best test.

Large-Scale Screening Techniques

Projective techniques do not lend themselves readily to large-scale application by untrained or semi-trained workers. However, the national emergency beginning in 1939 made more urgent than ever the problem of efficient utilization of human resources and served to emphasize the application of the Rorschach method as a device for the selection of personalities particularly suited for specific tasks. For example, the choice of satisfactory officer material and the screening out of personalities too unstable to withstand the rigors of army life were functions which the method was called on to perform.

Large-scale applications of the Rorschach method would have been utterly impractical without some modification of the traditional technique of administration and interpretation. During 1941, Molly Harrower [1] introduced a group method of administration which made possible a far more extensive use of the method than had heretofore been attempted. In the Harrower technique, the Rorschach pictures are reproduced on slides and projected onto a screen; twenty to fifty subjects view the blots at the same time, each subject writing his own responses to the blots.

Harrower's Multiple Choice test is another attempt to save the time of skilled examiners, but except in the hands of exceptionally highly-trained workers this seems only useful as a rough screening device for extreme misfits.

The introduction of abbreviated evaluation procedures, such as Piotrowski's [4] "sign" approach and Munroe's [3] "inspection technique" are further time-saving modifications of the original Rorschach method. These procedures do not attempt to construct individual personality pictures which shall be as complete as possible, but are aimed simply at selecting from the total Rorschach material the more conspicuous favorable or unfavorable patterns for particular selection purposes. Experimentation has revealed that the latter evaluation procedure can achieve a high degree of reliability and validity.

Marseille has recently introduced the "Rorschach Mail Interview," a booklet containing 16 inkblot pictures of his own design, but this is limited at present to use by the author as no figures are available and it is therefore without objective safeguards.

References:

1. Harrower, M. R. and Steiner, M. E. *Large scale Rorschach techniques; a manual for the Group Rorschach and Multiple-Choice Test.* Springfield: Charles C. Thomas, 1945.

2. Klopfer, B. and Kelley, D. M. *The Rorschach technique*. New York: World Book Company, 1942.
3. Munroe, R. The Inspection Technique: a method of rapid evaluation of the Rorschach protocol. Rorschach Research Exchange, 1944, Vol. VIII, No. 1, pp. 46–70.
4. Piotrowski, Z. A. Tentative Rorschach formulae for educational and vocational guidance in adolescence. Rorschach Research Exchange, January, 1943, Vol. VII, No. 1, pp. 16–27.
5. Rorschach, H. *Psychodiagnostics, a diagnostic test based on perception*. (Translated by Lemkau, P. and Kronenberg, B.) New York: Grune and Stratton, Inc., 1942.
6. Stern, W. Cloud Pictures, a new method for testing imagination, character and personality, 1937, Vol. VI, pp. 132–146.

B. K. & M. C.

PSYCHONEUROTICS. Vocational Guidance is used in the treatment of psychoneurotics as a therapeutic measure. Rarely is it the primary reason for such a patient seeking psychiatric advice. Most psychoneurotic patients are unaware of any maladjustment of a vocational nature when they seek psychiatric help or are referred to a psychiatrist for treatment. However, psychiatric investigation of the symptomatology presented by the patient, which means the study of the total personality and the environment in which it operates; investigation of the physical, social, vocational, family, sexual and other phases of problems presented by the patient, frequently brings to light the fact that the patient is vocationally maladjusted. He may not be intellectually challenged by his occupation or the particular work which he is doing is not giving him satisfaction, because while it might be a challenge to his intelligence, it is not of a character that meets his particular personality needs, or the patient's intelligence may be over-challenged by his job. It is seldom found that the emotional difficulty is primarily due to the vocational mal-placement. The usual reaction is that the vocational mal-placement aggravates the neurotic condition, intensifies the emotional maladjustment and the symptoms or makes them more frequent, and this in turn may be used by the patient for the creation of a few more symptoms which are centered around the vocational environment. In some cases, the patient projects the cause of his neurosis on to the vocational conditions, such as, a severe or unfair foreman, the noise in which the patient works, a disagreeable fellow-workman, the monotony of assembly line type of work, working with people of the opposite sex or of other nationality or color who are doing similar work, the hours of work required by the shift system and changing shifts which require a frequent change of hours of sleep, et cetera.

All psychoneurotic patients rationalize their symptoms and at times it is found that while the occupation of the patient meets his intellectual and personality requirements, he may unconsciously project on his vocational situation the blame for his troubles to such an extent that a temporary vocational change may be necessary until he secures enough knowledge of his problem and its cause to recognize the fact that he was acceptably well placed in the working world. Such a patient, during the period of treatment which precedes the recognition that his work did not cause his neurosis, can be placed in an occupation which will make him realize the advantages of the job upon which he placed blame for his difficulties. The dissatisfaction or lack of challenge in his new work may help in the development of the idea that the previous work was not at fault and that there were many things about it that gave him a feeling of success and satisfaction. If during the process of treatment the psychiatrist can help this attitude to develop, the patient has gone a long way toward lessening the need to find opportunities to project and rationalize the causes for his symptoms. He can sincerely accept the need to attempt the correction of the basic factors which have resulted in his neurotic personality. This attitude may create in him a desire to return to his first job and accept the need to go about the correction of the real cause of his neurosis.

There are patients whose work is suitable for their intelligence and personality needs, but whose occupation gives them opportunities or places them in situations which are undesirable because of their emotional instability. A commission salesman, for instance, may have wrecked many chances for success by prolonged alcoholic periods and seeks help to overcome his alcoholism. Some other job to satisfy the exhibitionistic, extroverted needs of such a man, and in which drinking is not a sales technique, must be found. This new vocational placement must be made on the idea that it will be permanent, not a temporary measure of therapeutic value during treatment. Such a patient must be permanently placed in a vocation where suggestion, example or accepted procedure will not be present to induce a return to alcoholic indulgence. This procedure is necessary even if, surprisingly, the psychiatrist is fortunate enough to eliminate the condition which caused the alcoholism which created the previous vocational failures.

The term "extrovert" is over-emphasized to such an extent that many people believe anyone to whom this term does not apply is abnormal. They fail to recognize that the audience is not only necessary but just as normal as is the actor. Such individuals, when they find themselves playing the part of audience and listening to the extrovert who comes to them to tell his new story, may envy him to such a degree that they either consciously or unconsciously try to copy this extrovert's activities. They may go to such an extent that they adopt his vocation. They have little recognition of the fact that their personality structure is such that they can only meet with failures, unhappiness and disappointment. The resulting loss of self-confidence and/or the development of depression in such an occupation may in turn make it necessary to seek psychiatric help. Here, a personality study brings to light such an individual's emotional structure. Then interpretation of the patient's personality needs, plus discussion of suitable vocational possibilities, produces a recognition of personal emotional normality and personality requirements and that one does not have to be vocal and active if one's personality is geared to less exhibitionistic types of work. Proper vocational placement can be expected to be followed by an acceptable emotional adjustment, satisfaction and success.

The child with too great an admiration for a parent or adult friend may copy such an individual to such a degree that as an adult that person's vocation is adopted and then find his work experiences so lacking in satisfaction that he unconsciously escapes by way of a neurosis. Children under the supervision of a dominating parent may as adolescents or adults be forced into a vocational choice for which they are in no way fitted and as a result they develop a neurotic difficulty that takes them to a psychiatrist. Such patients usually are emotionally immature. Proper vocational placement is only one of the therapeutic measures. While this phase of the treatment is important and necessary the problem would not be solved if this was the only treatment attempted. In such cases the primary problem is the personality difficulty.

During the war many patriotic adults as well as those who have been rejected by or discharged from the military services, have gone into war work for which they are not emotionally suited. The monotony of the assembly line work, et cetera, has produced psychoneurotic escapes when the worker's intelligence is too high for such labor, when the worker is emotionally unstable and not suited for the routine repetition required by his job, or when the work lacks interest or fails to give satisfaction. The federal requirements may prevent the suitable vocational placement of such a patient. The requirement that men leave non-essential jobs during war time and go into defense plants has caused many an emotional upheaval that would not have taken place had he been allowed to remain in the job that gave him opportunity to operate to advantage in terms of his personality drives. Placement of a man used to activity and frequently changing scenes, in a monotonous, repetitive situation, has produced neurotic behavior that would have been unlikely to occur if the man had not been forced to change his occupation. A production job may not be available in war industry that would be a challenge and that would give such a patient the satisfaction which he requires to be emotionally comfortable. If, however, in such a situation a position may be found which is no challenge to the patient's intelligence and does not meet the patient's personality needs, but which keeps him busy doing a variety of different things, each of which takes but little time, takes him into various parts of the plant and puts him in contact with many people —for illustration: a plant messenger, such a solution to the patient's vocational problem has definite therapeutic value as it not only keeps him in war industry and satisfies the federal or his patriotic requirements, but it lacks monotony and supplies many escapes from its lack of challenge.

Sometimes, because of the financial return, individuals get into positions for which they are emotionally unfitted. Sooner or later such misplaced individuals develop escapes of an undesirable character. Alcoholism or psychoneurosis are the usual reasons for such men seeking psychiatric help. Individuals in such situations, because of a feeling of insecurity and/or worry, frequently force themselves to spend much overtime meeting the requirements of their position. This over-application to their work eliminates healthy, conscious escapes and sooner or later the family physician and then the psychiatrist is called upon for help. To illustrate this situation: a man, who wanted to be an author, forced to take an office job for financial security—planning to write in his spare time—became valuable to his firm and was rapidly promoted into an executive position. His family responsibilities multiplied and he never secured financial security which would allow him to leave his position and devote his time to writing because the demands of his work increased to such a degree that he had no time to write. He escaped into steady, solitary drinking with the subsequent loss of his position. Placement in a position with regular hours, which gave him time to write week-ends and evenings, was indicated.

There are many other psychiatric situations that could be cited to illustrate the difference from that of the usual vocational guidance set-up, in the approach to vocational adjustment, which the psychiatrist working with psychoneurotic adults faces. Three things must be kept in mind: (1) that the psychiatrist is not often consulted by an adult for vocational placement; (2) that almost all such patients are working at the time they seek psychiatric help, and (3) that vocational guidance by a psychiatrist is used as one of several therapeutic efforts to correct the patient's psychoneurotic difficulties. Vocational Guidance is not used for the treatment of all psychoneurotic problems but it does become a therapeutic measure in a great number of cases.

When the psychiatrist finds the need of vocational adjustment he uses the techniques of the usual vocational guidance organization, but these are added to his other psychiatric efforts. The findings of the intelligence, aptitude and vocational tests are modified to meet the treatment needs of the patient and vocational recommendations based on test findings may be used or disregarded, depending upon the emotional condition of the patient. At times, vocational activities are prescribed which the psychiatrist knows should never be considered as permanent. In such cases, the patient is made aware of the temporary character and therapeutic value of such plans and advised that when the symptoms are corrected and the psychoneurosis improved, then patient will again be surveyed and new vocational activities considered.

There are situations, where there is no question about the vocational placement of the patient, in which vocational testing is of considerable value. Such a situation is that of an individual who spends his entire time between his work and his home; one who has no healthy conscious escapes into social, recreational or hobby activities and who as a result of his narrow routine life is developing emotional problems in his home, community or in his place of business. Such people usually become irritable, dissatisfied, faultfinding and unhappy. Verbal exploration by the psychiatrist may produce no evidence of interests that can be recommended as suitable escapes from the patient's routine. Vocational testing of such patients frequently brings to light possibilities which can be recommended as means of broadening the life and interests of such a patient.

To treat a psychiatric problem the psychiatrist must have not only a knowledge of his patient's immediate problems and symptoms, but also a thorough and detailed knowledge of the patient's physical condition and an exhaustive, specific and detailed history of the patient's entire life, his environment, educational and vocational experiences and the type of individuals—and their influence on the patient—with whom the patient has been in contact from his infancy. Conditioning, patterns and physical condition are all given serious consideration in all psychiatric efforts and even if the patient seeks psychiatric help for no reason other than a vocational study and recommendations, these things are given serious consideration before any recommendations are made.

Unfortunately, there are many pathologic organic conditions which may give no gross evidence of their presence, such as endocrine, cardiac or renal disease, and of which the patient may be unaware. Some of these may produce the neurotic symptoms which induces the patient to seek or be referred for psychiatric help, others may place severe limitations on vocational activities or may create emotional reactions because of physical discomfort, easy exhaustion, et cetera. Such physical conditions will have to be given great consideration when vocational activities are recommended.

Emotionally traumatic experiences in childhood or environmental patterns and experiences, may make it impossible for the patient to go into some vocation for which he seems at first to be admirably fitted. So, without a thorough knowledge of the patient's organic condition and his past experiences, a psychiatrist would be at a loss to function as a vocational guide.

In the Vocational Guidance literature, emotional maladjustment as a problem, when it is mentioned, seems to become apparent after the patient has failed and during the effort to work out a vocational adjustment for the patient. When this situation is encountered the patient is referred for psychiatric treatment and the vocational recommendations are rather indefinite, non-existent or dependent on the findings and judgment of the psychiatrist. In fact, the authors who mention emotional maladjustments as factors in need of consideration when advising about the vocational placement of an individual, seem to find the solution of the vocational problems of emotionally maladjusted individuals well outside the boundaries of the fields in which advice based entirely on testing procedure can be given with safety or certainty. Recent psychiatric pamphlet and magazine articles are beginning to include the positive value of psychiatry in the vocational placement of veterans discharged from military service for neuropsychiatric reasons. The near future can be expected to produce considerable definite and valuable information in this field of endeavor.

The psychiatrist working with psychoneurotics is usually consulted primarily because of the patient's emotional problem. Vocational adjustment may be one of several necessary treatment procedures. The usual testing procedure is of value, but the findings and recommendations are evaluated on the basis of the patient's therapeutic needs, emotional problems and organic condition.

E. W. F.

PSYCHOTICS. From a vocational standpoint, patients suffering a psychosis may have—and usually do have—impairment of working capacity. They may show severe disturbances in efficiency and concentration, so that participation in work may be extremely difficult for them. At times it may be impossible for them to work effectively. Most psychotic patients have to be sent to mental hospitals during periods of illness. The guidance of these patients in their capacity as workers, not specific methods for their treatment, will be discussed here.

Effective guidance resolves itself into giving the patient help in getting a better perspective of himself as a going concern. His personality, his reactions, and the situations in which these reactions occur, must be employed to aid the patient in living his life better, both socially and vocationally. Even his second-rate patterns of reaction must be used if need be. A constructive, appreciative evaluation and mobilization of his assets is the greatest aid in helping him gain perspective.

In helping the patient to do better, the hospital program usually includes medically directed participation in some type of work. Because work is reality, it provides a powerful aid in keeping the patient in touch with his surroundings. Concentration on given tasks demands attention. Absorption in a healthy activity tends to dispel disorganized thought, so that the patient redirects his energies toward checking his personality reactions as they affect others. He may learn to moderate these reactions, and make them acceptable; he may even use his reactions in a personal career of great social value. Society has need for persons of exaggerated trends. Clifford Beers in his "Mind That Found Itself" illustrates this point, as many others have done.

Techniques Utilized in the Hospital

A well-organized hospital treatment program, in which consideration to the patient's vocational needs is included, is a "team affair" in which every attendant, nurse, supervisor, social worker, occupational therapist, and physician plays his rôle. Many of the interests and basic needs of the patient are observed by workers other than the physician. An appreciation of these is frequently the starting point toward a patient's recovery. The effect of person on person must never be underestimated, and scientifically controlled interpersonal relationships are extremely important in this connection. To the trained observer, directly, or indirectly through his associates, this interplay of personalities gives indices of the patient's ability to function as a social unit. It gives leads as to his needs, clues as to how he may accomplish his tasks, and keys to his interests. It also makes possible a more comprehensive survey of his assets and liabilities. Participation by workers in the incidental interests of the patient arouses much inner response; it helps build emotional rapport between them that brings the recovery process into motion.

In his participation at various tasks with the patient, the occupational therapist can do much to aid the physician in the patient's psychotherapy. He not only elicits the patient's interest, but helps the physician observe how the patient tries to work in a real interpersonal relationship. Once interests are aroused, new enthusiasms are created, courage takes the place of discouragement, and the patient starts seeing his way clear to move ahead in socially acceptable activities.

If a psychosis has reached a point where a cure seems improbable, directed activity within the hospital provides a substitution which aids the patient toward a more comfortable adjustment to a long and indefinite period of hospitalization.

Some hospitals utilize the activities incidental to the operation of a hospital, as found in its shops, farm, garage, kitchen, bakery, etc. for treatment purposes and for purposes of vocational guidance, trial on the job, observations. The physician in charge makes or directs the making of job analyses, and acquaints himself with the supervisors in charge of the various jobs. He uses this knowledge along with the results of his interviews, the observations of the attendants and the occupational therapists, as well as the results of studies made by the psychologist and social worker in making the assignments. There again the patient is observed and his ability to perform in an actual vocational choice observed. The Institute of Living at Hartford, Conn. has for many years found the extension course service offered by colleges and universities throughout the country most promising in discovering and developing aptitudes and interests, which will be applicable in the individual's subsequent adjustment to his own community. "The individual's primary emotional drive, capability, and normal personality are given paramount consideration and then, on prescription of the medical staff, study is commenced on the course." [4] Thus in the hospital the patient's vocational guidance, trial at occupation (if not in utilizing his skills, nevertheless giving indices of his application and stamina) proceeds along with his medical treatment in preparing him to go back into the community.

Vocational Guidance in the Community

A small proportion of patients can return to their former occupations which are suitable for them and awaiting them. A large proportion are faced with legal restrictions, financial handicaps and the realities of community attitudes which apply to the discharged or paroled psychotic patient. Here the psychiatric social worker plays a most important rôle. It is most important that the psychiatric social worker as well as other agencies set up to help the recovered patient in making a psychiatric and vocational adjustment be utilized. The social worker helps find the jobs, obtains data on the physical, technical, intellectual, emotional as well as interpersonal requirements of the jobs and helps the physician correlate these with the needs of the patient. Perhaps the overall guidance studies indicate the job as a stepping stone to the vocation ultimately planned for the patient. His progress is watched. He is given therapeutic support. He is aided in finding his place in the larger sphere of human affairs, vocational, social, recreational, and physical. If a man has lived in a protected environment for several years he does not find it easy to take his place in the community and requires help as above indicated. We must remain cognizant of the fact that many patients can do a superior job in almost every line. The fact the public is afraid of them makes it difficult to get them into some community set-ups. If the patient has a relapse or becomes ill, usually his family or somebody else will take him to the hospital. When he has recovered plans can be made for him within the community.

Frosch [6] studied a group of 85 psychiatric patients of draft age who had been institutionalized in Bellevue Psychiatric Hospital and then discharged to the wartime community. Of the eighty-five patients used for study, thirty-three had been diagnosed as schizophrenic, thirty as neurotic, and the rest were divided among psychopaths, alcoholics, etc.

Fifty of these patients, of which twenty-one were diagnosed schizophrenic, and sixteen neurotic, had been placed in 4F Classification. A small percentage were working in defense industry, but most of them had not applied for such employment. A large number of 4F's were doing unskilled work in non-essential industry. Of these, few were technically skilled or suitable for technical training. Only fifteen per cent of the total group were unemployed, which was understandable in that they were still very ill. Very few of the patients had taken advantage of the agencies set up to help them in making a psychiatric or vocational adjustment.

Eccentric, erratic or borderline psychotic persons should be very carefully evaluated before allowed to enter the professional fields.

Intolerance of the recovered patient is the cause of many relapses. It requires considerable effort for any patient to return to face friends and neighbors before whom he may have "disgraced" himself by poor judgment or erratic behavior. If slighted or not accepted again as he is, then his problem is difficult. The community has a definite responsibility in the aftercare of mental patients to help them make a suitable adjustment. In Chicago, Recovery Inc., the association of nervous and former mental patients, was founded November 7, 1937 and tends to promote self-help among psychoneurotic and former psychotic patients.

Vocational Guidance in Industry

Both public and business must be educated so that the potentials of industry can be brought into action to take any of these individuals from the debit side as non-producers in mental hospitals, to the credit side as producers in industry. The answer to the challenge lies in its ability to coordinate vocational and psychiatric services for this purpose.

Brody[3] states that a psychiatric diagnosis by itself is of little use in industry. He relies chiefly on work record as far as employment prognosis is concerned. When a neuropsychiatric condition is present, consideration is taken of the acuteness of onset, duration of illness, adequacy of treatment, presence of affective features, whether or not improvement is continuing, presence of some degree of insight, and what the motivations are that determined return to work. He considers schizophrenics occasionally employable. Presence of asocial trends generally precludes employment. He points out that alcoholism is socially acceptable in certain types of work, particularly those which are dominantly masculine, involve bodily contact with the work, and offer a certain type of male rivalry and grueling hours. Where the ingestion of alcohol is excessive for the particular type of work, the applicant is rejected. For example, a certain amount of drinking is condoned in foundry workers, but none at all in test pilots. A patient with a paranoid trend which involves the company, supervisors, equipment or anything connected with the work situation is difficult to employ, however, certain others are perfectly compatible with employment as cited by Brody[3] and Thompson.[9] The patient recovered from a psychosis associated with a physical disease needs careful consideration from this standpoint and cooperation between the plant physicians and private physicians treating the case can do much in determining the person's usefulness to industry. For the manic-depressive patient, keeping at his vocation is of value if slowness and depression do not interfere with efficiency. To help him force his thoughts to some objective problem is important and he must continue at his occupation in order to avoid feelings of utter failure. The suicidal patient must be institutionalized. During periods of complete remission they can carry on in their chosen, suitable vocation. Selling [7] points out that both chronic schizophrenics and many manic-depressive psychoses seem able to work satisfactorily between episodes at routine jobs in industry. According to Dershimer,[5] in most plants of any size, a trained psychiatrist could find men who are psychotic. Yet some of these do their work faithfully for many years without disturbing anyone else. Under such circumstances, so long as they continue, the psychiatric condition is of no importance to the employer nor to his examining physician. As with a host of physical conditions, it is not a question of the presence or absence of disabilities at all, but of their severity and then weighing this against the requirements of various kinds of work, including the safety of the worker as well as the other workmen.

Guidance of Veterans

Individuals suffering chronic psychosis receive appropriate treatment by the army while awaiting disposition to the Veterans Administration. The policies governing rehabilitation of psychotics in remission are set up by Central Office of the Veterans Administration. In general it may be stated that the Veterans Administration considers that all neuropsychiatric cases, insofar as they are medically feasible for rehabilitation, should be given vocational counseling. The counseling procedures involves a thorough study of the veteran's background, experience, training, interests, special abilities, and aptitudes in order that no important factor may be overlooked. In addition to the interview, psychological tests are administered to appraise fundamental aptitudes, abilities and interests. Evaluation of material is made by the counselor and the possible employment objectives which are indicated are worked out from these data. The counselor and the patient review the possible employment objective; occupational information is given. Finally a satisfactory employment objective is agreed upon by the counselor and the counselee. The veteran is then formally entered into training in the appropriate educational institution or industrial concern. The veteran who needs further psychotherapy or personal adjustment counseling is provided the services of a psychotherapy clinic upon an outpatient basis. Psychotherapy is thus continued concomitantly with vocational rehabilitation training.

References:

1. Beers, C. *A mind that found itself.* New York: Doubleday Doran, 1921.
2. Bryan, W. A. *Administrative psychiatry.* New York: W. W. Norton & Co., Inc., 1936.
3. Brody, E. Neuropsychiatry and placement of industrial workers. *Connecticut State Medical Journal,* 1945, 9, 84.
4. Burlingame, C. C. Personal letter.
5. Dershimer, F. W. The employment examination for psychiatric casualties. Personnel copy.
6. Frosch, J. The psychiatric patient in a wartime community. *American Journal of Orthopsychiatry,* 1944, 14, 321.
7. Selling, L. S. Industrial psychiatry in wartime—employability of certain mental cases. *Industrial Medicine,* 1942, 2, 407-411.
8. Semrad E. and Wilkins, D. Occupational therapy as an aid to psychotherapy. *Occupational Therapy and Rehabilitation,* 1942, 6, 337-340.
9. Thompson, G. N. War engendered psychiatric problems. *Industrial Medicine,* Vol. 13, No. 9.
10. Veterans Administration, Washington, D. C. Communication to ARC, Consultation Service, Camp Wheeler, Ga.

E. V. S.

R

RADIO. Radio is recognized as an effective tool to serve the ends of vocational guidance. In the vocational guidance broadcasts of the past decade and a half there may be found illustrations of several objectives.

The first objective is that of promoting sound vocational guidance. The radio, with its ubiquitous voice is a superb medium for use in proclaiming the aims and purposes of vocational guidance. This was the aim of one of the first series of broadcasts, rendered through the weekly *National Youth Radio Conference* sponsored by the J. C. Penney Foundation in 1930–1931. Guests of honor presented to the radio audience over the National Broadcasting Company network included John Brewer, Emma Pritchard Cooley, O. Latham Hatcher, Anne Davis, and William M. Proctor. This also was the aim of the first series of six dramatic skits prepared by a Committee on Vocational Guidance of the National Advisory Council on Radio in Education. They were broadcast over the Columbia Broadcasting System nationwide network in the spring of 1932. The skits were accompanied by lectures clarifying the aims of vocational and educational guidance. The lectures were published in the October, 1932, issue of the *Vocational Guidance Magazine,* and the National Advisory Council on Radio in Education distributed a pamphlet containing the skits which bore the titles: "Choosing a Job in 1732 versus Choosing a Job in 1932," "What Kind of a Boy is Bill?" "Tom, Dick and Harry on the Job," "Planning Your Life Work," "At the Crossroads of Education," and "The Family Steps Out."

The second objective is to present information about the workaday world, both general information about the scope and variety of work that exists, and specific information about specific kinds of work. This has been the purpose of a number of programs. As early as 1931 a series of programs was broadcast each week by the Columbia Broadcasting System in which men outstanding in public life, in industry, or in the various arts and professions appeared before the microphone and told the listeners about the opportunities and problems to be met in the specific occupations in which they were engaged. Some of the men who appeared in this series were Secretary of State Stimson, who discussed the opportunities availing in public life; William Preston Beazell of the Pulitzer School of Journalism, who talked on the career of a journalist; and Colonel William Starrett, who had charge of the Government building operations during the First World War and whose company built the Empire State Building.

From 1934 to 1938 the American School of the Air, maintained by the Columbia Broadcasting System, co-operated with the National Occupational Conference in presenting weekly broadcasts on a wide range of occupations, using a different method of presentation. Programs were presented in dramatic form by professional actors during school hours. Examples of these scripts, prepared under the direction of H. D. Kitson, may be seen in *Occupations, the Vocational Guidance Magazine* for March 1935, May 1935, and February 1937, and in *Methods of Vocational Guidance*.[2]

From 1938 to 1940 the American School of the Air series was continued in co-operation with a committee of the National Vocational Guidance Association. Most of these programs featured "on the job" contact through interviews with workers in their shops, offices, or plants. Published under the title "Americans at Work" selected scripts may be found in some script libraries. The 1943–1944 series of the American School of the Air was entitled "Scientists at Work," each broadcast describing workers who use important scientific instruments such as the microscope, vacuum tube, spectroscope, microphone, battery, or weather instruments.

Another series featuring occupational information was called "On Your Job" a weekly public service feature of the National Broadcasting Company for two years, 1939–1941. Each program consisted of a drama built around some specific job or occupational problem. This was followed by an interview with a representative of the occupation and editorial comment by H. D. Kitson. Because the worker and the employer were named, the listener felt that the information was firsthand, direct, and authentic. Questions were prepared in advance and those pertinent to a vocational decision were discussed.

In 1945 a new technique in presenting occupational information by radio was introduced by WCAU in Philadelphia. Known as "The Career Forum" weekly forums were attended by senior students from one hundred fifty high schools. Nationally known leaders in twenty-six occupations were invited to preside at these forums and to open the discussions of opportunities, trends, and training. Students then asked questions by means of roving microphones, as many as fifteen students participating in a single broadcast. Under this plan the student has the advantage of speaking directly to the guest speakers while other students in the listening audience who are interested in the same subjects receive the benefit of the replies.

Several colleges pioneered in presenting occupational information on the air. Since 1935 the Iowa State College of Agriculture and Mechanical Arts, over its own station, WOI, has sponsored a weekly program entitled, "What Shall I Do?" These broadcasts are planned as teaching media for imparting occupational information and are broadcast during school time. Mimeographed materials are available for each of the topics covered. The material defines the occupation, indicates briefly the changing trends, outlines the qualifications necessary for entering upon and progressing in it, and includes a bibliography of reliable books and pamphlets.

Between 1938 and 1941, the University of Wisconsin College of the Air, over its station, WHA, broadcast a weekly program featuring "Your Job Outlook." Many of the topics were concerned with different phases of getting a job and the requirements needed in various fields of work. The College of William and Mary broadcast a series entitled "Your Career," stressing the need for integration of academic work and vocational choices. New York University broadcast a series entitled "Diplomas and Jobs" conducting interviews between University representatives and alumni.

Service clubs have sponsored radio programs giving information about the occupations represented in their membership. The Rotary Club of Buffalo conducted a program in 1940, discussing twenty-six occupations, and introduced an innovation by offering to any boy or girl the opportunity to have an interview with the radio speaker. The Rotary Clubs of Binghamton and New York City presented similar series and furnished scripts free of charge to all who requested them. The Altrusa Club of Austin, Texas, distributed reprints of broadcasts made by members on thirty-three occupations during 1938-1939.

In Oregon, the "Portland Dutch Uncles" series was produced weekly by KOIN through the cooperation of the service clubs and the vocational guidance department of the Portland Public Schools. It was designed for utilization by social studies classes in high school and upper elementary grades. Each broadcast was divided into three sections: an interview between a pupil and a Dutch Uncle (Portland business man), a transcribed trip with the pupil through the business, and a summarizing interview between the pupil and his vocational counselor. The pupil learned what qualifications the business demands of its employees, how one gets started, what opportunities are offered, and what kinds of work exist. In a conversation with the counselor the information is significantly pointed up through discussion of the character and personality traits of those succeeding in that particular business. A vocational guidance handbook is prepared and distributed by the school, and a field trip to the business is organized for those pupils who are interested in further information about its vocational possibilities.

Several school systems have produced vocational guidance broadcasts on municipal stations. One in Rochester, New York, consisted of a course in Occupations conducted over the radio by Mildred Lincoln and other teachers. A group of children in the studio held discussions under the direction of the broadcaster, while pupils in the schoolrooms discussed the same matters, pauses being made while they gave their responses to questions. By numbering pupils in the classroom, the radio instructor was able to call on particular pupils in the school to comment on certain matters. The classroom teachers served as discussion leaders of the topics proposed by the radio instructor. Examples of these scripts are presented in *Group Methods of Studying Occupations*.[1]

Cincinnati and Chicago public schools likewise developed vocational guidance broadcasts for classroom use.

A third objective of the vocational guidance programs is to assist in the placement of persons in a field of work in which one can contribute his best service and derive maximum satisfaction. This can not be achieved by radio, but some information about the kinds of openings available may be disseminated. In 1940, the United States Employment Service in eighteen states presented broadcasts on employment opportunities and requirements. For example in California State Employment Service broadcast fourteen series in seven cities in 1940. In Michigan, the Michigan Unemployment Commission sponsored a program entitled "I Want a Job" in cooperation with WWJ, Detroit News. In Nebraska, a program over WOW was called the "Job Clinic" and provided more than 600 jobs during one period.

Other aims are to offer inspiration to prospective workers, to broaden the understanding of interrelationships existing among many kinds of work, to call attention to printed sources of reliable information about occupations, and to encourage the study of occupational literature.

Two network programs of the Columbia Broadcasting System which possessed inspirational values were "It Can Be Done," conducted by Edgar A. Guest and "So You Want to Be a ——" conducted by various prominent figures in the fields of work discussed.

In the space provided it is not possible to present a complete history of vocational guidance broadcasts. One can cite only typical examples. In the school year 1939–1940 there were forty vocational guidance programs regularly broadcast by schools of the air, colleges, municipal stations, city school systems, employment services, service clubs, youth organizations and commercial sponsors in addition to the nation-wide network programs broadcast in the public interest. In order to encourage more complete and profitable use of these programs, several sponsors supplied manuals and guides, suggestions, bibliographies, and other study aids.

During the War years the programs were devoted to recruiting workers into wartime occupations, both military and civilian. With the announcement in 1945 that the Federal Communications Commission had made twenty channels, each 200 kilocycles wide, available for educational stations, it is expected that the number of educational programs will be increased manyfold, vocational guidance taking its proportionate share of the responsibility.

Several surveys have been made of the utilization of vocational guidance broadcasts. A questionnaire sent to listeners by WLW of Ohio brought requests for 663 scripts of "Guideposts to Living" series. In answer to the inquiry as to what related activities grew out of or supplemented the broadcasts, it was found that the programs were used in connection with forums, youth councils, job-finding clinics, and other group activities.

The results of a questionnaire sent to listeners of "Your Job Outlook" (University of Wisconsin) disclosed that one of the best-liked broadcasts of this series was "Meeting the Boss" in which a personnel manager was presented interviewing applicants for a job, suggesting valuable aids for young people in search of work.

From a survey made of methods of utilizing the vocational guidance broadcasts presented over the American School of the Air, 1934–1938, came many constructive suggestions. Inquiries were sent to the schools which had requested the weekly suggestion sheet on the utilization of these broadcasts. The 350 replies received from forty-two states presented substantial agreement that teachers should prepare their pupils in advance by giving appropriate readings and by orienting them to the problem to be treated. They also agreed that a post-broadcast discussion is highly important to intelligent listening and insures that the implications of the broadcast are thoroughly understood.

The methods of preparation for the broadcasts and the utilization of them included various uses of the reading lists; many ways of discussing the program and reporting on the assigned topics; uses of the blackboard, bulletin board, and visual aids; and many techniques for introducing the topic of planning one's career.

References:

1. Billings, M. L. *Group methods of studying occupations.* Scranton: International Textbook Company, 1941, Chapter IV.
2. Forrester, G. *Methods of vocational guidance.* Chicago: D. C. Heath and Company, 1944, Chapter III.
3. Kitson, H. D. Airways of guidance. *Occupations,* March, 1934, 26–28.

G. F.

RADIO ENGINEERING, APTITUDE FOR. Most of the knowledge concerning aptitude in the field of radio engineering has stemmed from experience during the war. Previous to the war very little literature relevant to the topic was available. Harrell and Churchill [7] have briefly summarized several studies on radio aptitudes. It is interesting that none of the data reviewed by them was collected in this country. The present discussion will necessarily be based on experience during World War II and will be limited to the problems studied in this brief period.

Several investigators have studied the factors relating to achievement in various radio, electronic and electrical training schools. Bolanovich and Goodman [2] and Bolanovich [3] have discussed the prediction of achievement of female engineering trainees in a ten-month electronic course at Purdue University. Frandsen and Hadley,[4] Hadley,[5] and Lawshe and Thornton [8] have studied factors relating to the achievement of Naval electrical and radio trainees. Both Army and Navy personnel research agencies [1][9] have been interested in this problem. In general the results of these various studies are in agreement. Although the data available concern only the prediction of achievement in training schools, it is assumed that these results will be useful in vocational guidance.

Frandsen and Hadley [4] conclude that the most efficient and economical combination of tests for predicting average achievement in a radio training school would be comprised of a mathematics test and a test of technical information in electricity. In this study the addition of an intelligence test and/or interest questionnaire did not improve the precision of the prediction. Lawshe and Thornton [8] report that the tests with the greatest predictive value are (1) ability to read simple measurements and solve simple arithmetical problems, (2) practical electrical information, and (3) mental alert-

ness. Using a regression equation derived from correlations of scores
on these tests, their predictions correlated .82 with achievement
scores. These authors also present curves indicating various cutting
scores on the tests and per cent success when these cutting scores are
used. Bolanovich [3] correlated various measures with grade-point
averages and reports the highest correlation was with scores on the
American Council on Education Cooperative General Mathematics
Test for High School Students (r = .55). Unfortunately he did not
employ any test of electrical or radio information in his study. However, the Wonderlic Personnel test (r = .50), previous school
grades (r = .50), fitness rating (r = .38) and personality rating
(r = .32) were correlated with grades.

The Army Personnel Research Section [1] reports eleven tests
which showed promising correlations with electrical course grades.
"The eleven tests showing best relationship with grades in electrical
courses (r = .41 to .68) were the Army General Classification Test;
Mechanical Movements (Air Corps); General Electrical Information (Signal Corps); United States Employment Service, C–40–A
Radio (part score); C–40–A Electricity (part score); C–40–A
(remaining parts); the mechanical information tests, Shop, Physics,
Electricity, and Mathematics; and Physics (Columbia). Of these
eleven, four—the Army General Classification Test, C–40–A
(Radio), mechanical information, Electricity and Mathematics
sections—gave a multiple correlation coefficient of .75 with the
average grade of 5 electrical courses."

The Staff of the Test and Research Section of the Training,
Standards and Curriculum Division, Bureau of Naval Personnel [9]
reports validity coefficients for their basic test battery in ten types
of Elementary Naval Training Schools. The validity coefficients for
two schools—electrical and radar operators—are tabulated below:

Test	Electrical School	Radar Operators School
General Classification	.52	.60
Reading	.52	.67
Arithmetical Reasoning	.59	.61
Mechanical Aptitude	.44	.50
Mechanical Knowledge		
(Mechanical Score)	.35	.35
(Electrical Score)	.49	.38

The highest validity coefficients for combination of two tests
are as follows:

For the electrical school—Arithmetical Reasoning and Mechanical Knowledge (Electrical Score): multiple r = .63.

For the radar operators school—reading and arithmetical reasoning: multiple r = .70.

The Navy [10] has recently reported on a Radio Technician Selection test. The various forms of this test include the following uniform content: Mathematics, 20 items; General Science, 20 items; Shop Practice, 10 items; Electricity, 15 items; Radio, 15 items. All items are of the five-response multiple-choice type. Each item in the mathematics section is given a weight of two points while items in the other sections count one point each, for a total score of 100 points. This test, again, is essentially an achievement examination designed to ascertain whether personnel have the necessary background and previous interest in the scientific subject matter. The forms of the test appear to have very satisfactory reliability but the data on validity is very meager. The use of the test as a selection instrument has resulted in a reduction in personnel attrition in the Navy schools.

In general the best predictive devices seem to be measures of mathematical ability and tests of electrical or radio information. The armed services have withheld the exact names of the tests used in some of the studies reported. However, several tests have been used and the results on all are relatively uniform.

It is doubtful whether a test of intelligence would add materially to precision of prediction achieved by tests of mathematical ability and electrical or radio knowledge. However, it is apparent that a certain level of intelligence is necessary for success in the field of radio engineering. This is particularly true if the individual being counselled contemplates study of an advanced or technical nature. Tiffin and Lawshe [10] report that trainees who earn high grades obtain significantly higher Adaptability Test scores than trainees who earn low grades. The correlation between grades and scores is .64. The intelligence test adds little to prediction because of its high intercorrelation with other tests concerned. Frandsen and Hadley [4] have found this to be especially true of mathematics tests. The mathematic tests give greater accuracy of prediction when used in combination with other tests. In the absence of mathematics tests a fair degree of accuracy might be achieved with intelligence tests. Some informal observations have indicated, however, that differences in intelligence within a group possessing above average intelligence will not discriminate between different levels of achievement.

Interest (as usually measured) does not appear to be a promising factor for the prediction of achievement in a training situation. However, Hadley [5] has reported that certain instances of failure to succeed may be eliminated by the selection of only those who are definitely interested in this type of specialized training. Bolanovich and Goodman [2] report that the Kuder Preference record shows some promise as a device for eliminating those who would be likely to drop out before completion of the course. Although little specific data are available it appears safe to conclude that interest in radio engineering should correlate highly with job satisfaction and should be considered in counselling. It is possible that factors of previous radio experience, activities as a radio amateur and related activities are as valid, if not more valid, than traditional interests tests or inventories in the evaluation of radio interest.

Little information is available concerning the relationship between radio ability and scores on tests of mechanical ability and mechanical comprehension. Some unpublished data, in addition to those previously reviewed, indicate that the correlation of such tests with achievement at radio training schools is very low. However, the correlation of mechanical ability and comprehension tests with performance in laboratory or shop is quite satisfactory.

Hadley [5] has studied the relation of certain personal data to achievement in radio training. Comparisons were made between the achievement of those who reported some previous radio experience and those who reported no such experience. When the groups are matched upon the basis of pre-test scores of electrical information the difference in achievement is not significant. The important factor seems to be the knowledge of electricity and not the mere possession of experience. Experience is helpful, especially in laboratory or shop work, if accompanied by knowledge but is not essential.

When men over 26 years of age are compared with those under 26 years of age the differences are insignificant.

When comparisons are made between men enlisting specifically for radio and those selected from the ranks, the differences in achievement are significantly in favor of the former group. The percentage of those selected from the ranks transferred from the school for failure to achieve was approximately three times the percentage of those enlisting specifically for radio training. Instructors report that those enlisting are more cooperative and generally better students. However, again when the groups are matched upon the basis of electrical knowledge the difference does not approach statistical significance.

In all of the comparisons above, the group with lower average scores on the intelligence test is the group with the higher average achievement. This fact supports the findings previously reported by Frandsen and Hadley [4] relative to the predictive significance of intelligence as compared with mathematical and electrical knowledge.

College training is definitely advantageous although it is possible for an individual to succeed very satisfactorily without such training. When a group possessing some college training is compared with a group with no college training the college group excels. This difference is maintained when the groups are matched upon the basis of electrical knowledge.

No consideration of the aptitude for learning radio code is included in this article. Since it may be desirable, although not necessary, for the radio engineer to be familiar with radio telegraphy certain references to this problem are included in the bibliography.[1 6]

In summary and conclusion—upon the basis of our present limited fund of information: aptitude for work in radio engineering can best be predicted from mathematical ability and electrical knowledge. The studies reviewed in this article have employed tests of mathematics and arithmetic reasoning which in most cases can be considered as ability or aptitude tests rather than achievement tests. On the other hand, the tests of practical and technical electricity employed in the various studies have been information tests. Obviously the individual who has had little opportunity to learn will not obtain a very high score on such a test. The vocational counsellor should weigh results on such tests in terms of the opportunity for the acquisition of technical information. A test of the aptitude for learning electrical and electronic principles is sorely needed. The counsellor should give consideration to any cues to this aptitude which are available to him. Intelligence is important to the extent that average or above average mental alertness is desirable. In the case of the individual contemplating advanced study it is a serious consideration. However, an individual may be very successful as a radio technician or shop worker even though his intelligence test score is below average. Interest (as usually measured) is of limited value in the prediction of success in training. On the other hand, completion of training and happiness with work is definitely related to interest. Mechanical ability and/or comprehension is important only to the shop worker, not necessarily to the engineer. Factors of age, sex and personality do not appear important providing the basic abilities and knowledge are present.

References:

1. Adjutant General's Office. Personnel Research in the Army. IV. The selection of radio-telegraph operators. *Psychol. Bull.*, 1943, *40*, 357–371.
2. Bolanvich, D. J. and Goodman, C. H. A study of the Kuder Preference Record. *Educ. Psychol. Measmt.*, 1944, *4*, 315–325.
3. Bolanovich, D. J. Selection of female engineering trainees. *J. educ. Psychol.*, 1944, *35*, 545–553.
4. Frandsen, A. N. and Hadley, J. M. The prediction of achievement in a radio training school. *J. appl. Psychol.*, 1943, *27*, 303–310.
5. Hadley, J. M. The relation of personal data to achievement in a radio training school. *Psychol. Bull.*, 1944, *41*, 60–63.
6. Harmon, F. L. and Dimichael, S. The development of the H-D Code Aptitude test: A preliminary report. *Psychol. Bull.*, 1943, *40*, 601–604.
7. Harrell, T. W. and Churchill, R. D. The classification of military personnel. *Psychol. Bull.*, 1941, *38*, 331–353.
8. Lawshe, C. H., Jr. and Thornton, G. R. A test battery for identifying potentially successful Naval electrical trainees. *J. appl. Psychol.*, 1943, *27*, 399–406.
9. Staff of the Test and Research Section, Training, Standards and Curriculum Division, Bureau of Naval Personnel. Psychological Test Construction and Research in the Bureau of Naval Personnel: Validity of the Basic Test Battery, Form 1, for selection for ten types of elementary Naval training schools. *Psychol. Bull.*, 1945, *42*, 638–644.
10. Staff of the Test and Research Section, Bureau of Naval Personnel. Psychological test construction and research in the Bureau of Naval Personnel V: Navy radio technician training program. The American Psychologist, 1946, *1*, 80–90.
11. Tiffin, J. and Lawshe, C. H., Jr. The adaptability test: a fifteen minute mental alertness test for use in personnel allocation. *J. appl. Psychol.*, 1943, *27*, 152–163.

J. M. H.

RATING SCALES. When the vocational counselor attempts to predict vocational aptitude or to give educational or vocational guidance, he is most likely to prefer information which is available through standardized tests and objective biographical data. However, these sources of data frequently fail to yield all that he needs for his purposes. He needs, in addition, the opinions of teachers, employers, fellow employees, parents and friends on those traits, subjective in nature, for which there are no adequate tests or for which there is no "truth" except as it exists in the opinion of others. Examples of such subjective traits are initiative, emotional control, cooperation with colleagues, appearance, moral attitudes, and originality. In order to estimate such traits and the many others which are equally subjective in nature, the counselor uses rating scales.

A rating scale is an instrument designed to record in regular and systematic fashion opinions and estimates regarding an individual's character and personality traits. Its special province is the field of traits which do not lend themselves well to more objective measurement. These estimates and opinions are gathered from a sample of people who know the ratee in a variety of circumstances and situations, and who meet certain other qualifications as to length of acquaintance, nature of acquaintance, objectivity of viewpoint, and impartiality of judgment.

It is recognized that subjective estimates may or may not be valid. Ratings are only opinions about an individual. Such opinions may, however, be significant factors in the vocational success or failure of an individual. A man's usefulness is often influenced by what people think of him, as well as by what he does or can do. However, the major value of rating scales in guidance is not in what they reveal about the effects of people's opinions regarding an individual, but in what they reveal to the counselor who seeks to obtain a complete inventory of the significant facts about the advisee.

The use of rating scales requires three persons: a rater, a ratee, and an intermediary such as the vocational counselor or personnel man in industry. Ratings are used far more extensively by industrial personnel men than by vocational counselors. Among the terms used by industry for ratings are merit rating, personality rating, service rating, progress report, personnel review, and others. Industrial personnel men have found the less easily measured traits of the employee so important that they have developed thousands of different rating scales. The most common kinds of scales used in industry and occasionally in vocational guidance are very briefly described.

1. *The graphic rating scale.* This consists of a list of general traits or activities, five to fifty or more in number, to be rated by placing a check mark at the adjective or descriptive phrase which denotes the ratee's grade or position in the specified trait or activity. The general trait or activity is usually defined and a line opposite the definition is marked off to indicate degrees of possession of the trait or activity. In some instances, a numerical score is assigned to each division of the line on the scale. Adjectives may be unequally spaced and numerical values may be adjusted accordingly.

Accuracy in work as defined by freedom from errors:	10	8	5	3	0
	|	|	|	|	|
	no errors	very few errors	aver- age		many errors

The graphic scale is the most frequently used in industry because it is easy to understand and can be quickly filled in by busy supervisors.

2. *Descriptive or multiple choice scale.* This form of scale is quite similar to the graphic scale. The main difference is that descriptive adjectives or phrases are used in the manner of a multiple choice question without a line to indicate gradations.

3. *Order-of-merit scale.* This type of scale is applied only to employees or members of the same group or department. The rater arranges all the members of the group in order of merit regarding a trait, placing the best member at the top of the list, the poorest at the bottom, and other members in their proper ranks between the two extremes.

4. *Alphabetical scale.* The rater judges each ratee in terms of letter grades to indicate degrees of excellence in much the same manner as teachers grade pupils. "A" may stand for excellent, "B" for good, "C" for average, "D" for low average, and "E" for poor.

5. *Numerical scale.* This is similar to the alphabetical scale except that figures are used instead of letters. A rating of 100 or 10 assumes the highest possible degree of excellence and 0 indicates a complete absence of the trait in the ratee's behavior.

6. *Man-to-man scale.* This is often called the Army officer scale because it became well known during World War I as an instrument for rating officers. Its use required the rater to first set up for each considered trait a standard scale that contained the names of officers who represented five all-inclusive degrees or levels of possession of the trait. The ratee was then compared with the five men on the standard scale and given a rating on the basis of recognized similarity to some one man on the standard scale.

When instructions in the rating technique were followed closely and the raters did their work conscientiously, degrees of useful accuracy and uniformity were obtained through the use of the man-to-man scale. The main reason for its lack of use today is its cumbersomeness and the need for high intelligence on the part of the raters.

7. *Specific-instance scale.* The man-to-man scale requires the rater to compare the ratee with personally known individuals whom he has chosen to represent the various degrees of possession of a

given trait. Actual persons represent the degrees on the scale. In the specific instance scale, specific acts indicate degrees on the scale. Specific examples of behavior are used instead of men.

The specific-instance scale is similar to the scales used in the educational field for rating drawings, compositions, and handwriting. This type of scale has not won wide usage because of the difficulty in finding specific instances that would yield clear-cut differentiations. When vagueness in the definitions of typical instances is overcome by means of more highly specific instances, the scale sets up a narrowness which limits its use.

A few researchers have overcome some of the difficulties inherent in the specific instance scales through application of the statistical treatments often used for the study of attitudes. Numerical values are assigned to the statistically significant instances.

8. *Outstanding traits.* One of the most widely used rating scales in the public service and one that is especially useful in vocational counseling is the kind developed by J. B. Probst. He has developed a number of "service reports," each of which contains about 100 descriptive items concerned with character traits, work qualities, habits, and personality. All the items are outstanding traits and were selected after considerable experimental testing. The form of the report is illustrated by the following excerpt:

Place an x mark next to each of the items in this column which you know from your own experience will describe or fit this person.

Check columns

1	2	3	
——	——	——	Lazy
——	——	——	Slow moving
——	——	——	Quick and active
——	——	——	Minor physical defects
——	——	——	Indifferent; not interested
——	——	——	Talks too much
——	——	——	Too blunt or outspoken
——	——	——	Too much self-importance
——	——	——	Good team worker
——	——	——	Not a good team worker

In the Probst method of rating, each employee is first rated by his immediate superior. The same blank is then given to the next higher level of officer and the latter rates the employee with the first ratings before him. Thus, in the form shown above, the foreman may mark his x in column 1, the department head in column 2, and the superintendent in column 3.

In vocational counseling, it is not practicable for several raters to use the form that has been filled in by another rater. It is important, however, for the advisee to be rated by three or more acquaintances and this can be done by asking each rater to send his ratings to the counselor. The counselor can easily place on one summary sheet the check marks of the several raters. Some counselors ask the advisee to rate himself and the counselor places on the self-rating sheet all the check marks of the several raters.

Raters can be encouraged to give additional information about the person rated. Such comments or "behaviorgrams" on the back of a rating sheet are very illuminating to the counselor because they narrate instances, explain assigned ratings, and portray significant features of the individual's personality.

Many efforts have been made to develop an ideal rating scale, but a scale that is perfectly satisfactory to most raters has never been developed either in industry or in vocational counseling. The major reason for this failure is the way in which the instrument must be used. It is always used by a counselor with a unique personality who has learned to make interpretations of other personalities in terms of his own mental habits. The information elicited by a rating scale must fit the counselor's patterns of thinking. He tends to interpret his own diagnostic instruments and develop his concepts regarding the individual whom he analyzes in terms of his own personality and the basic approaches to personality used by him. As an illustration: the counselor who is steeped in statistical facts concerning individual differences would find useless a rating scale that might be very helpful to a counselor who is a member of one of the psychoanalytical schools. Each of these counselors would need a different rating scale and each might use his own scale advantageously.

This limitation in the use of rating scales also indicates that the value of a scale increases in the extent to which the counselor uses some basic pattern or conceptual approach in his vocational counseling. No counselor can develop an effective scale for his own use before he has developed a basic working concept concerning the dynamics of human personality. Once he has learned to think in the terms of Sigmund Freud, Alfred Adler, Kurt Lewin, or in some other fundamental pattern of his own invention in his approach to the study of human personality, he can develop and use a rating scale that is helpful to him in the systematic interpretation of the ratee's personality. The information obtained by means of his unique scale becomes significant to him and improves his diagnoses and predictions. This applies particularly to the clinician or clinically-minded adviser.

Of course most industrial personnel men have had no clinical training, nor have they developed academically recognized basic concepts regarding the dynamics of human personality. They have, however, developed excellent "frames of reference" for their thinking about the traits of the employee. The experienced industrial rater uses in his frames of reference factors such as the requirements of the job and the ways in which certain characteristics of employees tend to mesh with the supervisor's outstanding personality characteristics. The rater in industry is likely to have basic frames of reference empirically developed, which are to him more definite than the relatively vague bookish principles of the immature vocational counselor.

Few vocational counselors use rating scales because only a few have learned to think in terms of some basic conceptual pattern for the study of human personality and its dynamics. Most counselors prefer to use objective tests because they supply information that has been statistically treated for validity and reliability. Tests, however, are exceedingly limited in their powers to reveal certain significant facts about the advisee. To make a comprehensive case study of an advisee, test findings, scholastic records, and biographical data should be supplemented by means of an instrument such as the outstanding trait rating scale.

Many extensive studies of ratings have been made to produce statistically correct scalings and to discover correlations between subjective ratings and objective measurements such as job levels, salaries, and production records. Few such studies, however, have produced results of significance to the vocational counselor.

One reason for such lack of significant correlations is that measuring instruments have been developed, in so far as is possible in the present stage of science, for objective criteria. By its very nature, a rating scale is an instrument that should be used when more objective measuring devices are unavailable.

Numerous rules for the effective use of rating scales in vocational guidance might be stated. Some of these rules are:

1. Obtain ratings from three or more acquaintances, preferably seven raters.

2. Consider as significant only those outstanding traits checked by at least two raters.

3. Know the relationship of each rater to the ratee. Is the rater parent, employer, fellow student or sweetheart?

4. Use the ratings to elicit reactions from the advisee in order to clarify his appraisals of himself.

5. Discuss the ratings with the advisee in order that he may appreciate the effects of his personality traits on others. Most advisees gain much encouragement from such discussion with a wise counselor. When used in this manner, a rating report becomes a powerful stimulus in motivating the advisee.

6. If ratings are to be shown to the advisee, express the phrasings on the rating form with due regard for his feelings. The form of the statements should not be so cold, brusque or discouraging as it is in many rating scales now in use. John G. Watkins, Alabama State Personnel Department, has shown how the phrasings of a rating scale may be changed to improve the effect on the feelings of the ratee.

OLD FORM

QUANTITY OF WORK:
- —— Unusually high output.
- —— High output.
- —— Normal output.
- —— Limited output.
- —— Insufficient production; unsatisfactory.

NEW FORM

QUANTITY OF WORK:
- —— Exceptionally high output. Keep it up.
- —— Better than average. Good going.
- —— Meeting our requirements.
- —— You could do more. Try harder.
- —— You could do a lot more. Try harder.

7. Do not divulge to the advisee the specific ratings made by any one rater. Let the advisee see only the summary or recapitulation of all raters' checkmarks and comments. When behaviorgrams are used, they should be re-phrased by the counselor before reporting them to the advisee. Thus the advisee will be unable to identify the rater who had made adverse comments.

Other factors, vital to the effective use of rating scales, have been reported in numerous publications.

References:

1. Burtt, H. E. *Principles of employment psychology.* New York: Harper and Brothers, 1942, Chapter 12.
2. Fuller, S. E. Goodyear Aircraft employee counseling. *Personnel Journal,* 1944, October and November.

3. Halsey, G. D. *Making and using industrial service ratings*. New York: Harper and Brothers, 1944.
4. Hepner, H. W. *Psychology applied to life and work*. New York: Prentice-Hall, 1941, Chapter 12.
5. Moore, H. *Psychology for business and industry*. New York: McGraw-Hill Book Co., 1942, Chapter 8.
6. Poffenberger, A. T. *Principles of applied psychology*. New York: D. Appleton-Century Co., 1942, Chapter 14.
7. Traxler, A. E. *Techniques of guidance*. New York: Harper and Brothers, 1945, Chapter 7.

H. W. H.

READING ABILITY, RELATIONSHIP TO SCHOLASTIC AND OCCUPATIONAL APTITUDE. It is well known that reading ability is related to scholastic aptitude and to success in many vocations. Studies have shown that the correlations between reading ability and general aptitude for school work is comparatively high. For example, in one study the correlation between the scores of 200 eleventh-grade pupils on the Iowa Silent Reading Test and their total scores on the American Council on Education Psychological Examination, 1945 edition, was found to be .759 (2:61).

This rather close relationship is due in part to the fact that the total scores on most tests of general scholastic aptitude are heavily saturated with a verbal factor. When general scholastic aptitude is separated into linguistic and quantitative aptitude, or into language and non-language aptitude, there is, as one might suppose, a significant difference between the correlation of reading ability with these two aspects of aptitude. Correlations of the linguistic and quantitative scores of 190 eleventh-grade pupils on the American Council Psychological Examination with their scores on the Iowa Silent Reading Test were respectively .817 and .611 (1:56). The language I.Q.'s of 108 eighth-grade pupils on the California Test of Mental Maturity were correlated to the extent of .755 with their total scores on the Traxler Silent Reading Test, whereas the correlation of non-language I.Q.'s of these pupils with total reading scores was only .423 (3:66). The breakdown of scholastic aptitude into a variety of mental factors in the manner of the Chicago Tests of Primary Mental Abilities would result in further differences in correlation with reading ability.

The relationship of reading ability to achievement in school work varies from subject to subject.[4] In general, the correlation of reading comprehension scores with achievement test scores tends to be high in English, substantial in social studies, science, and languages, statistically significant although not high in mathematics, and probably low in fine and practical arts, although objective evidence concerning the relationship in the last two fields does not seem to be available.

The relationship of reading ability to vocational aptitude and success depends, of course, upon the extent to which reading is used in the occupation concerned. It is obvious that for certain manual occupations reading is of little or no importance, while for others, such as law, success in the occupation would be impossible without high reading ability of the reflective and analytical type. Very few studies reporting actual correlations between reading test scores and scores on vocational aptitude tests have been reported.

In view of the significant relationship between reading ability and success in most school subjects and in many vocations, the correction of reading deficiencies is an important aspect of a complete guidance program in any school. As soon as the purposes of the remedial work are clearly in mind, the first step in a remedial reading program is to give a reliable survey test of reading ability throughout the school. The second step is the identification, on the basis of the reading scores and other information such as that furnished by teachers' reports, of the individuals who need remedial instruction. Reading test scores will not automatically separate individuals into two groups—normal readers and remedial cases. The distribution of reading scores is a continuum ranging from very high to very low. Any decision concerning what individuals should have remedial help is partly a subjective one. It should be made not only upon the basis of the grade norms, but also in the light of the reading ability in the local school and of the school course and vocation for which each individual is preparing, as well as the resources of the school for carrying on the remedial work. In general, all pupils who are two grades or more retarded in total reading achievement and others who are extremely low in specific aspects of reading are suitable candidates for remedial help.

The third step is the diagnosis of the reading difficulties of the pupils who have been selected for remedial attention. This calls for a review of all available information about each pupil including school history, home background, personality, scholastic aptitude, and study habits. The administration of additional reading tests and of an intelligence test may be required in connection with this step. Special attention should be given to the discovery of physical handicaps, such as deficiencies in vision and hearing, to associational difficulties that may have a neurological basis, and to personality maladjustments. As a result of careful diagnosis, a few pupils may be identified whose reading retardation clearly arises from physical limitations, obscure failure in central associative processes, or personality factors. These pupils should be separated from the rest for individual attention or referral to the proper specialists. The great majority of the retarded readers in a usual school group, however, evince difficulties which are in the field of learning and which can be relieved by group corrective teaching with a certain amount of individualization of instruction.

The corrective instruction may be organized either on the basis of small groups of pupils with similar difficulties meeting at free periods or after school hours or in the form of regular classes meeting each day and conferring credit toward graduation. The opinion of reading experts and the experience of remedial teachers indicate that the latter type of organization is preferable.

The objectives and techniques of the remedial teaching should be determined by the needs of the individuals in the group. Among the procedures which may be employed are (1) free reading to stimulate interest; (2) training in work-study skills such as finding facts, identification of main ideas, and supporting details, sequential reading, skimming, and identification of large divisions in longer selections; (3) reading test lessons and keeping a record of scores in order to note improvement from week to week; (4) training in general and technical vocabulary; (5) analysis of check lists of study habits and planning of improved study programs; (6) training in thoughtful, critical, and analytical reading; and (7) oral reading in an audience situation. The remedial help should be carried on long enough for new reading habits to be developed and made relatively permanent. Usually this type of work should be continued for at least one semester.

The last step in the remedial program for a group of retarded readers is an appraisal of the progress made by each individual during the period of training and recommendations concerning future remedial work. Comparable forms of tests used in the beginning should be administered at the end of the instruction period to measure growth and again several months later to note retention of gains. All individuals who have been in the remedial group, even those whose reading has apparently been brought up to or above average, should be kept under observation for at least a year and their progress in school work rechecked at intervals.

References:

1. Seder, M. The reliability and validity of the American Council Psychological Examination, 1938 Edition, *1938 Fall Testing Program in*

Independent Schools and Supplementary Studies, pp. 51–58. Educational Records Bulletin No. 26. New York: Educational Records Bureau, January, 1939.

2. Townsend, A. A Summary of correlations based on the use of certain fall tests, *1945 Fall Testing Program in Independent Schools and Supplementary Studies*, pp. 58–63. Educational Records Bulletin No. 44. New York: Educational Records Bureau, January, 1946.

3. Traxler, A. E. Some correlation data for the California Test of Mental Maturity, *1938 Fall Testing Program in Independent Schools and Supplementary Studies*, pp. 63–69. Educational Records Bulletin No. 26. New York: Educational Records Bureau, January, 1939.

4. ————. Reading and Secondary School Achievement, *1946 Achievement Testing Program in Independent Schools and Supplementary Studies*. Educational Records Bulletin No. 45. New York: Educational Records Bureau, June, 1946.

A. E. T.

Emporia Silent Reading Test

Purpose and Validity

The Emporia Silent Reading Test is the result of several years experimentation in reading test construction in connection with the Nation-wide Every Pupil Scholarship Tests. The paragraphs for this test were carefully selected from a large variety of sources. The aim was to include material whose content would interest the pupils for whom the test is designed. Before their final selection, the paragraphs were critically checked in respect to quality and difficulty by several supervisors and teachers of reading.

The validity of the test was further checked by setting up an independent criterion. Three nationally known reading tests of recognized merit and one form of the Emporia Test were administered to the same pupils in grades IV, V, and VI. The pupil's total score on the four tests was considered the criterion of reading ability. Intercorrelations were made for each of the three grades. The average of the coefficients between the Emporia Test and the criterion was $+.86$. The mean average for the other three tests versus the criterion was $+.85$. The average of the r's between the Emporia Test and the other tests of the criterion, individually, was $+.72$. Thus the test ranks high in respect to validity.

Reliability of Tests

By the odd-versus-even method of computation on Form A, reliability coefficients ranging between .82 and .93 were obtained for grades III to VIII, inclusive. The average of the six coefficients was

.88. On Forms A and B the average coefficient obtained was .71 for grades IV to VI. Later studies showed Form C and Form D equivalent to the earlier forms in validity and reliability.

Authors and Publisher

The authors of this test are H. E. Schrammel, Director of Bureau of Educational Measurements and Head Department of Psychology, and W. H. Gray, Associate Professor of Psychology, Kansas State Teachers College. The test is published by the Bureau of Educational Measurements, Teachers College, Emporia, Kansas.

Administering, Scoring, Interpreting, and Use of Results

There are four equivalent forms of this test. The time limit for taking it is 15 minutes. It is simple to administer and to score. It is recommended for grades IV to VIII, but norms are provided for grades III to VIII for both mid-year and end-of-year testing. The percentile norms which are set up in four concise tables are based on scores made by 25,000 pupils. Suggestions for using the test results are provided.

Reference:

1. 1940 Mental Measurements Year Book, p. 341.

H. E. S.

READING TESTS

Gates Series of Reading Tests.   The Gates Series of Reading Tests includes the following:

1. Gates Reading Readiness Tests for kindergarten and the early stage of Grade I. One form, five subtests.

2. Gates Primary Reading Tests (revised). Three forms, three subtests, as follows: (1) word recognition, (2) sentence reading, (3) paragraph reading. For use in Grades I and the first half of Grade II.

3. Gates Advanced Primary Reading Tests. Three forms, two subtests: (1) word recognition, (2) paragraph reading. For use during the second half of Grade II and through Grade III.

4. Gates Basic Reading Tests (revised), silent reading tests. Four forms, four subtests: (1) Type A, general significance; Type B, outcome of events; Type C, following directions; Type D, reading for details. For use from the middle of Grade III through Grade VIII.

5. Gates Reading Survey. Two forms. Each booklet contains tests of (a) speed of reading; (b) vocabulary; (c) comprehension. For use in Grades III to VIII.

6. Gates Individual Diagnostic Tests. Includes a set of reusable test cards; two brief exposure cards; a twelve-page pupil's record booklet; and a manual. For use for individual diagnosis, Grades I to VIII, inclusive.

The series test is designed to provide a coordinated program of group testing and individual diagnosis throughout the range of the elementary and junior high school. Each test is accompanied by a comprehensive teacher's manual which gives certain technical details, such as reliability coefficients, etc. For example, the manual for the Gates Basic Reading Tests, page 18, lists the self-correlation of each of the four tests and all the intercorrelations of the test in the case of each of ten different school groups in which the number of pupils ranges from 42 to 400. The correlations were based on grade groups. The self-correlation of two forms of the test in the case of Type A range from 83 to 93; for Test B, from 80 to 94; for Test C, from 76 to 94; and for Test D, from 88 to 94.

A. I. G.

Iowa Silent Reading Tests. The Iowa Silent Reading Test, Elementary and Advanced (developed by H. A. Greene, University of Iowa, V. H. Kelley, University of Arizona and A. N. Jorgensen, University of Connecticut), is designed to measure economically, accurately and reliably the proficiencies of pupils from grades four through the junior college in doing silent reading of the work-study type. Economy implies that it must be relatively inexpensive in proportion to the information it furnishes, and that its time consumption must be in keeping with the reliability of the results. Accuracy and reliability imply that it must consistently reveal the actual study and silent reading abilities of the groups of pupils for which it is designed. In the main these aims have been realized.

The Iowa Silent Reading Tests go far beyond the ordinary general survey of a single phase of silent reading abilities. The test is designed to cover a wide range of the skills known to be indispensable to effective reading of the work-study type. The test measures three broad general areas of silent reading abilities; namely, (1) Rate of Reading at a Controlled Level of Comprehension, (2) Comprehension of Words, Poetry, Sentences, Paragraphs, and Longer Articles, and (3) Ability to Use Skills Required in Locating Information.

The Advanced tests were administered in seventeen communities in eleven states, and the elementary tests were given in nineteen communities in thirteen states widely distributed geographically in order to complete the standardization. Grade percentile norms for each sub-test and the total, and age and grade equivalents for the total are available based on approximately sixty thousand cases. Standard scores make possible comparison of scores on the several tests, forms, and batteries. Scoring is by means of a simplified stencil key.

The reliability of the test was obtained by correlating the odd and even scores and correcting the resulting coefficient by application of the Spearman-Brown formula to yield an estimate of the whole test. The reliability coefficient for the Advanced test was .918 and the Elementary test was .930. Reliability coefficients for each of the sub-tests are also given. In addition to the reliability coefficients data are presented showing the probable error of measurement for each of the sub-tests and the test as a whole.

Validity for the test was secured first by analyzing the situations calling into play the skills or abilities which experienced observers consider fundamental to success in reading. The analysis of what these situations are naturally forms a basis for the development of an effective course of study and by the same logic provides the most defensible basis for the validating of silent reading tests. The authors of the test attempted to secure validity by paralleling test items in a number of work type reading situations.

Every item in the four forms, both Elementary and Advanced, of these tests has been carefully tried out under experimental conditions. The items in the several test parts are arranged in order of difficulty, and the sub-tests in the four forms are carefully balanced as to difficulty. In general the percentage of pupils responding correctly to items in consecutive grades shows the expected increases.

The Iowa Silent Reading Test can be given satisfactorily by any teacher or principal who is willing to adhere conscientiously to the directions and who is reasonably skillful in discipline.

One of the most important functions of these silent reading tests lies in the fact that their use in a class provides the teacher with a rather exact estimate of the level of development of a number of important elements of silent reading abilities in the class, as well as with specific information in certain important skill areas concerning the limitations of the individuals comprising the class. By comparing the results obtained from a class with the norms, a clear idea of the general ability of the class in silent reading of the work-study type can be obtained. By analyzing the scores made by individual pupils on the various parts of the tests, certain of the specific weaknesses or strengths of individual members may be discovered. It is only on the basis of such an analytical approach that a really constructive remedial program can be developed.

The publisher of these tests is the World Book Company, Yonkers-On-Hudson, New York.

V. H. K.

Schrammel-Gray High School and College Reading Test

Nature and Purpose of the Test

The Schrammel-Gray High School and College Reading Test consists of two equivalent forms, A and B, each of which is composed of twenty-five paragraphs followed by three to five objective questions concerning the content. The total number of questions on each form of the test is 100. The test was planned and constructed with the purpose of providing both survey and diagnostic measures. It measures efficiently reading rate, general reading comprehension, and comprehension efficiency on the junior and senior high school and college-freshman levels. The aim is to provide a test of adequate length so that survey measures will be reliable as will also any remedial measures based on its diagnostic value.

Since the test yields three significant scores, it is not only a valid survey measure, but also one of considerable diagnostic value. All three of the scores which it yields contribute to a thorough analysis of the student's reading ability. The gross-comprehension score consists of the total items answered correctly on the paragraphs read. This score is interpreted by percentile norms for each grade. The rate score is a measure of the number of words read per minute for the 25-minute period and is likewise interpreted by percentile norms for each grade. The comprehension-efficiency score is the most valuable of the three scores which the test yields; but all three scores are important. The comprehension-efficiency score is a ratio between the student's gross-comprehension score and his rate score. It is indicative of his efficiency in reading based on the quantity read. It is also interpreted by reliable percentile norms for each grade.

Authors and Publisher

The authors of this test are H. E. Schrammel, Director Bureau of Educational Measurements and W. H. Gray, Associate Professor of Psychology, Kansas State Teachers College, Emporia, Kansas. The publisher of the test is the Public School Publishing Co., Bloomington, Illinois.

Validity of the Test

The paragraphs composing the forms of this test were carefully selected from a wide variety of sources on the reading level commonly reached by high-school and college students. A conscious attempt was made to select paragraphs which would prove interesting to students of each level. The difficulty value of the vocabulary was checked against the Thorndike Word Lists. Both the paragraphs and questions were tried out several times on classes, and studies and revisions were made until the two forms were equated for various ability groups.

Correlations between college-freshman scores and composite decile ranks computed from scores on tests in intelligence, English, vocabulary, spelling, mathematics, reading, and current history, yielded the following coefficients; Gross-comprehension score in reading and decile rank .73 ± .01, reading rate score and decile rank .67 ± .02, and comprehension-efficiency reading score and decile rank .87 ± .01. These coefficients are indicative of the high validity of this reading test and, since reading ability is a most vital factor in determining scholastic efficiency, denote that this test possesses marked predictive value as regards scholastic success.

Reliability of the Test

Various reliability studies of the test were made. Table I shows a representative sample of some coefficients which were computed from scores made by a homogeneous ninth-grade group.

TABLE I

Reliability Coefficients

Correlation Between	No. of Cases	Reliability Coefficients	P. E. of Score
Form A and Form B, Rate........	272	.86 ± .011	9.3
Form A and Form B, Gross Comprehension	266	.86 ± .011	4.1
Form A and Form B, Comprehension Efficiency	272	.65 ± .024	
Form A, Gross Comprehension and Comprehension Efficiency	266	.63 ± .025	
Form A, Gross Comprehension and Rate	266	.82 ± .013	

These coefficients are sufficiently high to show a satisfactory degree of reliability. The probable error of a score means that a student's true score, in fifty per cent of the cases, does not diverge from his obtained score by 9.3 points or less in case of rate, by 4.1 points or less in case of gross comprehension, and by 4.7 points or less in case of comprehension efficiency.

Administering, Scoring, and Interpreting

Simple directions for administering the test are provided. The working time is 25 minutes. Scoring is accomplished by use of a printed key. Machine scoring of this test is also possible. The total items answered correctly comprises the gross comprehension score. The rate score is read off the test blank at the last line the examinee read. The comprehension efficiency score is obtained from a table which is provided. It is the ratio between the number of items answered correctly and the amount read. Each of the three scores is interpreted by use of percentile scores which are provided for each grade VII to XII and the four years of college.

Reference:

1. 1940 Mental Measurements Yearbook, p. 365.

H. E. S.

READING TESTS IN A GUIDANCE PROGRAM. An important aspect of a guidance program is a school-wide, systematic testing program. Because of the known relationship of reading ability to achievement in school and in many vocations, one of the several kinds of tests which should be used regularly in such a program is a silent reading test.

Reading is a complex and unitary process in which the apprehension of the visual symbols, the central associative processes, and the comprehension of meanings take place almost simultaneously. Attempts to measure reading as a whole or the various aspects of it necessarily use test situations which are somewhat artificial and which, at best, can only roughly approximate the natural reading situation.

There are three general types of silent reading tests. The first and oldest of these is the kind of test which yields only one or two scores and which is designed for survey purposes only. Some of these tests can be administered within a brief working period of five to fifteen minutes. They are not long enough to be very dependable for use in studying the reading ability of individual pupils, but they are helpful in the appraisal of the reading achievement of groups. The Monroe Standardized Silent Reading Tests and the Whipple High School and College Reading Test are illustrations of this type.

The second and most widely used type consists of survey reading tests with diagnostic features. The working time for this kind of test is usually about one class period. It provides scores for several aspects of reading ability and a total or median score which is a measure of general reading achievement. Some of the part scores obtained with these tests are not high in reliability, but they are somewhat useful for the discovery of possible strengths and weaknesses in reading which call for further investigation. The total scores on these tests usually indicate overall reading ability with rather high reliability.

Reading tests of the third type are intended to form a basis for the analysis of the reading process and to yield valid and reliable diagnostic measures of different aspects or factors in the total reading achievement of individuals. The working time for a test of this kind is necessarily long, and it may include as much as three or four hours.

A few of the available reading tests are now being used each year with thousands of junior and senior high school pupils throughout the United States. Among these are the Cooperative Reading Comprehension Test, the Iowa Silent Reading Tests, the Nelson-Denny Reading Test, the Traxler Reading Tests, and the Van Wegnen-Dvorak Diagnostic Examination of Silent Reading Abilities. The first four tests belong to the second of the three general types of reading test, and the last one is the best example of the third type.

The Cooperative Reading Comprehension Test is one part of the Cooperative English Test. It is available either separately or in a "single-booklet" edition along with the other two parts of the English test. There is a lower level, known as C_1, which may be used in the junior and senior high school grades, and an upper level, C_2, which is available for use in the last two or three grades of senior high school and in college. Each level provides Scaled Scores for vocabulary, speed of comprehension, and level of comprehension, as well as a total Scaled Score. The reliabilities of the scores at the 50-point on the Scaled Score distribution, estimated from the publishers' data on standard errors of measurement, are: vocabulary, .91; speed of comprehension, .84; total score, .94. The median of seven correlations of total scores on this test with school marks in English was found in one study to be .605 (4:43). Since the relationship between reading and achievement in English is known to be substantial, this coefficient indicates considerable validity for the test. A factor analysis of the Cooperative Reading Comprehensive Test was made by Davis.[2] He found that word knowledge and reasoning in reading were the most important factors in the scores yielded by this test. The test exists in five forms: Q, R, S, T, and X, at each level.

The Iowa Silent Reading Tests consist of an elementary test for Grades 4–9 and an advanced test for Grades 9–12. The revised new edition of these tests contains four forms on each level, Am, Bm, Cm, and Dm. The advanced form of the test contains nine subtests including rate, comprehension, directed reading, poetry comprehension, word meaning, sentence meaning, paragraph comprehension, and location of information, including use of the index and selection of key words. The elementary form does not have the poetry comprehension section and contains a subtest on alphabetizing instead of one on selection of key words. The reliability coefficients reported in the manual of directions are above .7 for all parts of the advanced test except rate and poetry comprehension and for all parts of the elementary test except comprehension and sentence meaning. A study by Townsend [3] tends to verify these reliabilities. The same study, however, indicates that the standard scores on the elementary and advanced tests are not directly comparable and that some of the parts are so highly correlated that their diagnostic value is somewhat limited.

The Nelson-Denny Reading Test contains just two forms—A and B, each of which measures vocabulary and paragraph comprehension. The scores on the two parts are combined, in each form, into a total reading score. The test is suitable for Grades 9 to 12 and junior college students. The reliability has been reported by the authors of the test as .91. Aside from the data given in the manual of instructions, there seems to be little information on the reliability and validity of the Nelson-Denny test, notwithstanding the fact that this is one of the oldest of the reading tests now being used. A study by Davis (1:371) indicates that the factors determining the total score obtained with this test are mainly word knowledge and speed of reading, and thus implies that its validity as a measure of general reading ability is not especially high.

The Traxler Reading Tests include the silent reading test for Grades 7 to 10 and the high school reading test for Grades 9 to 12. The first test consists of four forms designed to measure rate of reading, vocabulary, story comprehension, paragraph comprehension, and total comprehension, and to provide a total score for overall reading ability. There are just two forms of the second test which provides scores for rate, story comprehension, main ideas in paragraphs, and total comprehension, and also yields a total score. The reliability coefficients have been reported as follows: silent reading: rate, .82; story comprehension, .65; vocabulary, .85; paragraph comprehension, .74; total comprehension, .81; total score, .92. High school reading: rate, .90; story comprehension, .72; main ideas, .80; total score, .93. The reliabilities of the rate, vocabulary, total comprehension, and total scores are fairly satisfactory, but the story comprehension and paragraph comprehension scores are not reliable enough to warrant their use in the study of individuals. Total scores on the silent reading test were correlated to the extent of .56 with average school marks and .88 with composite scores on a battery of other reading tests.

The Van Wagenen-Dvorak test is an examination which requires about three hours of administering time and is intended to be thoroughly diagnostic. There are three levels of this test—an intermediate division for Grades 4 and 5, a junior division for Grades 6 to 9, and a senior division for Grades 10 to 12 and college. The test is designed to form the basis of differential diagnosis of rate of comprehension, ability to perceive relationships, vocabulary (words in contest), vocabulary (isolated words), range of information, grasping central thought, retention of clearly stated details, interpretation of content, integration of dispersed ideas, and drawing inferences from content. The test also provides a reading index which may be compared in a general way with the I.Q. The only available study of this test is one published in Educational Records Bulletin No. 31.[5] The results were not very favorable to the diagnostic value of the test. The range of corrected Spearman-Brown reliability coefficients for the Junior Division was .471 to .924, with a median of .758; the range for the Senior Division was .431 to .787, with a median of .689. The intercorrelations among the parts tended to be high when corrected for attenuation. Notwithstanding the limitations suggested by this study, the Van Wagenen-Dvorak test is still the most promising diagnostic test now available.

At this writing, a new diagnostic reading test is being constructed by an independent committee working under a small subvention provided by the Blue Hill Foundation. The first form of this test should be available for general use by the fall of 1947.

The results of the regular use of reading tests in a guidance program should be recorded with other test data on individual cumulative record cards and used constructively both as a basis of identification and correction of reading weaknesses and as an aid in the advising of students concerning the choice of school courses and vocations.

References:

1. Davis, F. B. Two new measures of reading ability. *Journal of Educational Psychology,* 1942, 33, 365–372.
2. ———. Fundamental factors in comprehension in reading. *Psychometrika,* 1944, 9, 185–197.
3. Townsend, A. A study of the revised new edition of the Iowa Silent Reading Tests. *1944 Fall Testing Program in Independent Schools and Supplementary Studies,* pp. 31–39. Educational Records Bulletin No. 42. New York: Educational Records Bureau, January, 1945.
4. Traxler, A. E. The Cooperative English Text, Form Q: Correlations with school marks and intercorrelations. *1940 Achievement Testing Program in Independent Schools and Supplementary Studies,* pp. 42–50. Educational Records Bulletin No. 30. New York: Educational Records Bureau, June, 1940.
5. ———. A study of the Van Wagenen-Dvorak Diagnostic Examination of Silent Reading Abilities. *1940 Fall Testing Program in Independent Schools and Supplementary Studies,* pp. 33–41. Educational Records Bulletin No. 31. New York: Educational Records Bureau, January, 1941.

A. E. T.

RECORDS, FORMS FOR KEEPING

Richardson Entrance Questionnaire and Experience Record

The *Entrance Questionnaire and Experience Record,* prepared by H. D. Richardson, is designed to furnish high school guidance workers with information about individual students who enter the secondary school that is essential in helping them to become satisfactorily oriented and happily adjusted in a new school environment. The questionnaire serves indirectly to help the student to better know and understand himself, to become acquainted with important factors in his experience background, and to anticipate some of the new problems and experiences with which he soon will be faced. Similarly, the questionnaire provides a means by which parents may assemble and review knowledge pertaining to the growth and development of their children and use it in thinking and planning for new problems that lie ahead.

In Part I of the questionnaire is summarized the information on the home and family background of the student, his interests, school and out-of-school activities, health and physical condition, past school history, tentative plans for further education, and a selected first year high school program of studies. Part I of the questionnaire is to be filled out by the student and his parents. While eighth grade students can supply most of the information in Part I in reliable form, parental cooperation and participation are desirable.

Part II of the questionnaire provides a check list of behavior patterns for an appraisal of the personality and character of the student. Space is also provided for an informal statement about the student's personality and how the new school can be of greatest help in furthering his rounded personal and social development. This part of the questionnaire is to be filled out by the student's elementary school principal or his eighth grade teacher.

The validity of the questionnaire has been demonstrated empirically in its use in pre-high school admission, registration, and orientation programs, in individual counseling situations, and in group guidance activities. No statistical data on validity and reliability have been made available, but experience has shown that the questionnaire yields valuable and dependable information in convenient and easily accessible form for guidance workers.

The publisher of the *Entrance Questionnaire and Experience Record* is Science Research Associates, 1700 Prairie Avenue, Chicago, Illinois.

Reference:

1. Hamrin, S. A. and Erickson, C. E. *Guidance in the secondary school.* New York: D. Appleton-Century Company, 1939, pp. 127–37.

H. D. R.

Richardson Individual Guidance Record

The *Individual Guidance Record,* developed by H. D. Richardson, is a guidance tool for the study and understanding of an individual high school student by his homeroom adviser. The record provides a means for assembling and using, over a five year period, pertinent information in each of the following areas of personal and social development: home and family background; health and physical condition; personal interests, attitudes, and recreational experiences; personality ratings and observations; educational plans and achievements; and vocational interests, goals, and plans.

The record is so designed that the student, as well as his adviser, may participate actively in assembling the information and in its interpretation and use. It is not only a record of a student, but by and for him as well. Its value for the student is largely in the making of it, for through his participation he gains insight and understanding of himself and his developing personality pattern—his interests, abilities, and personal characteristics; his strengths and weaknesses—and how all factors are inter-related and integrated in the "whole." With this kind of understanding of himself, he becomes increasingly self-responsible and self-directive.

It is this dynamic concept of record making and keeping as a continuous means by which the homeroom adviser may study the "whole" student, and by which the student may progressively learn to know himself, that gives distinctiveness of purpose and function to the *Individual Guidance Record*. The validity of the record must be judged in terms of this distinctive purpose and the related criteria of a good homeroom record for guidance purposes—viz., usability both in the sense of convenience and accessibility; comprehensiveness in scope, reflecting the integrated character of the individual; and cumulative in form, revealing the developmental trends and pattern of the individual. The actual tested use of the record over a number of years in high school home rooms indicates that its major purpose can be realized by both advisers and students.

The Individual Guidance Record is published by Science Research Associates, 1700 Prairie Avenue, Chicago, Illinois.

References:

1. Hamrin, S. A. and Erickson, E. C. *Guidance in the secondary school.* New York: D. Appleton-Century Company, 1939, pp. 77–83.
2. Richardson, H. D. An individual guidance record for home room advisers. *School Activities*, 1939, 10, 245–247, 283.
3. ———. *Analytical devices in guidance and counseling.* Chicago: Science Research Associates, 1940, pp. 25–46.

                                                              H. D. R.

RELIABILITY

The reliability of a test is the relative freedom from error of the measures or scores which it yields. Since all measurements in psychology are subject to a number of chance or variable errors (dependent on psychological factors such as fluctuations in interest and attention, shifts in emotional attitude, and on environmental disturbances, etc.), no single obtained test score represents the individual's "true" ability in regard to the trait measured. A "true" score is obtainable only from a very large (theoretically infinite) number of measurements of the given trait under identical conditions, and is therefore never secured in actual practice. The measures or scores yielded by some tests, however, approximate more closely than do others the "true" scores in the given trait. On the closeness of this approximation, which can be estimated, depends the reliability of the test.

A commonly used index of the reliability of a test is its self-consistency or self-correlation (the coefficient of reliability). The size of this correlation coefficient will depend on the amount of the true score that is common to the test and the alternate form or other comparable measure used, assuming that the errors of measurement are entirely independent and therefore uncorrelated. Thus a reliability coefficient of .95 may be interpreted to mean that 95 per cent of the score represents the ability measured by the test whereas 5 per cent of the score is attributable to errors of measurement.

There are three methods of determining the self-correlation of a test, as follows:

1. repeating the test and calculating the correlation coefficient between the two sets of scores;
2. testing the same group on alternate or parallel forms of the test and correlating the two sets of scores;
3. the split-half method of dividing the test into two equivalent parts (usually by grouping odd-numbered items into one half and even numbered items in the other), correlating scores on these half-tests, and by means of the Spearman-Brown prophecy formula, estimating the reliability of the whole test from the calculated reliability of the half.

The use of alternate forms or the split-half method is generally preferable to repetition of the same test, for in the latter case memory and practice factors tend to make the reliability coefficient higher than it should be. The split-half method also has a disadvantage, however, in that the subjects are tested on only one occasion, with the result that relatively temporary influences (e.g., attitudes, feelings, etc.) affect the scores on both halves in the same way, resulting in a reliability coefficient that is too high.

If a test is to be used as a basis for conclusions regarding individuals, its reliability should be .90 or more. In order to distinguish between groups, on the other hand, a lower reliability coefficient may be adequate. In evaluating a test, factors such as validity and the quality of the standardization must be taken into account, for they are at least as important as reliability.

In general, the greater the number of items in a test and the longer the test time, the clearer and more definite the items, and the less susceptible to guessing, the more reliable the test.

Instead of the coefficient of reliability, the index of reliability is often used. This index which is simply the square root of the coefficient of reliability provides an estimate of the correlation between the obtained scores and true scores on the test.

One caution needs to be observed in the use and interpretation of both the coefficient of reliability and the index of reliability. It must be remembered that, like any correlation coefficient, the coefficient of reliability varies according to the range of ability represented in the group. The more heterogeneous the group and consequently, the wider the range of talent, the higher the self-correlation. In evaluating a given reliability coefficient or in comparing the reliability of two tests, therefore, the size and range of the groups on whose scores the coefficients are based must be taken into account.

Because it is free from the disadvantage cited above—i.e., because it is independent of the range of ability in the group tested— the standard error of measurement is frequently used to indicate the reliability of a test. The formula for the standard error of measurement ($\sigma_1 \infty$) which is a measure of the probable divergence of an obtained score from its corresponding true score, is as follows:

$$\sigma_1 \infty = \sigma_1 \sqrt{1 - r_{11}}$$

If for example, for a given test, $\sigma_1 \infty = 3$, 68% of obtained scores on the test do not differ from their corresponding true scores by more than ± 3 points.

Finally, the standard error of estimate of a true score, the formula for which is $\sigma^\infty = \sigma_1 \sqrt{r_{11} - r^2_{11}}$ gives the width of the zone or band within which the true score probably lies. Thus, for an estimated true score of 50, if $\sigma^\infty{}_1 = 5$, the chances are 68 in 100 that the true score lies between 45 and 55.

References:

1. Bingham, W. V. D. *Aptitudes and aptitude testing.* New York and London: Harper and Bros., 1937.
2. Garrett, H. E. *Statistics in psychology and education.* New York: Longmans, Green and Co., 1941.
3. Guilford, J. P. *Psychometric methods.* New York and London: McGraw-Hill Book Co., Inc., 1936.
4. Scott, I. D. *Manual of Advisement and Guidance.* Washington: United States Government Printing Office, 1945.

I. C.

RELIGIOUS APTITUDE, WILSON TESTS OF. Thirteen thousand four hundred thirteen people in 875,493 separate religious reactions had a part in the tests of religious aptitude constructed by

Matthew H. Wilson. These persons lived in about 700 widely scattered towns.

In addition to the ordinary total grades which are given with tests, the average grade is also stated for each item of each test. Scores generally appear for junior and senior high school students, junior and senior college students, and adults 35 years of age and older.

These tests measure the capacity or the talent of man for religious experiences. The reliability of the Composite Test of Religious Aptitude is .92 + both for non-Christians in India and our own people at the same age level. A purely scientific analysis of man's aptitude for religion has great practical value for all human beings.

People need to know what they actually are as human beings in order to orient themselves as individuals, groups, and nations.

Because each individual needs his moral strength increased in order best to accomplish his tasks, he should understand his own capacity for religious experiences. Contrary to a rather wide spread belief that many people are without religious experiences, each person has religious support in his moral struggles; and it follows that each person should know clearly where such encouragement is most likely to come to him.

These tests show, in a proportionate way, those drives that largely cause people to behave as they do. The tests reveal those inner urges which produce progress in human relations. These tests demonstrate that essential religious experiences strengthen morality, increase stability, and lessen instability.

These tests are not only measurements of the capacity of each human being to experience religion, but they also give a detailed statement of what the main religious experiences of a human being actually are. By means of the methods used in modern psychology, a chart of those channels through which the persuasive power of religious experiences is released is carefully drawn. The implications of this chart are far reaching. Now each person, if he will take these tests at his own age level, is able to understand this inner meaning of his own life.

The C. H. Stoelting Scientific Company, 424 North Homan Avenue, Chicago, Ill., publishes the first three of these religious aptitude tests:

A Test of Religious Aptitude (exploratory). Reliability. .90+
Religious Aptitude Concerning People. Reliability. .93+
Religious Aptitude Concerning Nature. Reliability. .90+

The Bureau of Educational Measurements, Kansas State Teachers College, Emporia, Kansas, publishes the next six tests of religious aptitude with one Manual for all of them.

Religious Aptitude Concerning Parents.	Reliability.	.88+
Religious Aptitude Concerning Friends.	Reliability.	.89+
Religious Aptitude Concerning Trees.	Reliability.	.95+
Religious Aptitude Concerning Flowers.	Reliability.	.94+
Religious Aptitude Concerning Prayer.	Reliability.	.95+
A Composite Test of Religious Aptitude.	Reliability.	.94+

Note that the Composite Test of Religious Aptitude is composed of the best items taken from the eight other tests of talent for religion. This particular test is the most important of these measurements of aptitude for religion. The other tests supplement this main test.

References:

1. Wilson, M. II. *An ethical discrimination test and manual.* Chicago: C. H. Stoelting Company.
2. ———. *Scales of stability and instability, and manual.* Emporia: The Bureau of Educational Measurements, Kansas State Teachers College.

M. H. W.

ROTARY CLUBS. Rotary International is the organization of 6,000 Rotary Clubs in 75 countries, which have a membership of 300,000 business and professional executives. In whatever country they are located, Rotarians are active in civic work, in community welfare, in leading boys and girls into good citizenship, in raising the standards of their businesses and professions, and in working together for the advancement of international understanding, good will and peace.

Rotary Clubs throughout the world are deeply interested in programs of occupational information and guidance for young people, and are carrying on activities in various phases of this important field.

Rotary International as an organization engages in no direct activity in the field of occupational guidance, and therefore has no official guidance program. Individual Rotary Clubs are free to choose their own fields of endeavor and generally select those types of occupational guidance activity best suited to their communities.

Rotary International makes suggestions to Rotary Clubs as to how their members may assist young people in finding their life work, and encourages Rotarians to share their business and professional experience with students on an informational basis, but makes no recommendations as to the particular type of activity to be carried on.

In the furtherance of this program, Rotary Clubs throughout the world have developed various types of occupational information and guidance programs dealing with those phases which may best be handled by persons not specifically trained for guidance work, in cooperation with organizations and persons trained in such programs.

The general purpose of most programs of occupational information and guidance sponsored by Rotary Clubs is to provide high-school students (and in some cases college students and other adults) with information which will assist them to develop an understanding of their interests and abilities, and to help indicate the studies and outside reading best suited to fit them for the careers in which they are interested.

Such programs are especially valuable in small cities and towns where guidance programs are not part of the regular school curricula. This program seeks to provide the student with all the necessary information about the career in which he is interested, but makes no attempt to advise or persuade the student to take certain courses, or in any way influence decisions in regard to careers.

Nearly all such Rotary Club programs of occupational guidance and information are developed in cooperation with the Board of Education and/or Superintendent of Schools or School Principal in the community in which the Rotary Club is located. A number of Clubs also cooperate with local and state guidance agencies and with other organizations interested in similar programs, such as the library, boys clubs, and so on.

Generally speaking, the activities of Rotary Clubs in occupational guidance may be divided into four groups—

(1) individual information and counseling programs carried out in cooperation with the Board of Education or other groups
(2) programs of occupational guidance involving aptitude testing, also carried out in cooperation with the Board of Education
(3) rural vocational agricultural projects, carried out in cooperation with local Farm Bureau, 4-H Clubs, F.F.A., etc.
(4) miscellaneous projects, including occupational bookshelves, industrial tours, talks in the schools on occupations, etc.

The simplest type of program carried out by Rotary Clubs consists of counseling with young people regarding occupations. Each Rotarian in the program is an expert in his own business or profession, and is able to provide information concerning his occupation in all phases—required education, nature of work, obtaining employment, financial rewards, drawbacks and risks, and the future of the business. He invites questions and answers them frankly, but makes no attempt to influence a decision in regard to a course of study or choice of career.

Many Rotarians serve regularly as counselors in this type of activity, cooperating with the local high school in providing this service.

A number of Rotary Clubs have cooperated in the development and operation of occupational guidance programs which involve aptitude and preference tests, serving in a counselor relationship in this more technical application of the program.

A large number of Clubs have maintained "occupational bookshelves" in their community or high school library, keeping on the shelves for the use of high-school students the latest books, pamphlets, and periodicals on those occupations in which the students have shown an interest.

Some Clubs sponsor talks and discussion forums in the schools; others arrange tours through industries, and provide tools and machinery for the use of vocational classes.

Many Rotary Clubs cooperate with their local Farm Bureaus, 4-H Clubs, Future Farmers and similar organizations in vocational agricultural projects, furnishing equipment, seed, and pure-bred animals to young farmers to assist their study of modern farming methods.

P. L.

S

SALESMANSHIP, APTITUDE FOR. "Just before the war broke out there was an army of three million workers in the United States who earned their living by one form or another of salesmanship. This total does not include 1,400,000 store owners and shop keepers who very often double as salesmen in their own establishments." [4] Sales workers fall roughly into three major groups: the *salesmen* (such as insurance and real estate agents), the *salespersons* (such as specialists in furniture, radio, etc.) and *clerks* in stores, who are essentially order-fillers. In this particular article the term salesman shall be used in its generic, rather than technical sense of the word, i.e. "the middle man between producer and retailer or consumer."

Considering the rôle salesmanship plays in the industrial world, and in vocational guidance, an analysis of the factors that enter into the make-up of a successful salesman is imperative.

Warren defines [15] aptitude as "a condition or set of characteristics regarded as symptomatic of an individual's ability to acquire with training some (usually specified) knowledge, skill, or set of responses, such as the ability to speak a language, to produce music, etc." Traxler holds [13] that there are three basic assumptions underlying such a definition: (1) Few, if any individuals have equally strong aptitudes in all directions, (2) individuals differ from one another in every aptitude they possess and (3) the difference among individuals and within individuals tends to persist within limits. Hull holds that generally speaking, on a scale of vocational aptitude efficiency, one's best potentialities are approximately three times as good as his worst. Considering the above definition and its underlying assumptions the question may be raised whether there exists an entity which could be designated as an "aptitude for salesmanship," or whether successful salesmanship is really a conglomeration of several relatively independent traits and attributes. Salesmanship, or the ability to sell successfully has been considered as a single trait by some, as a unique combination of several characteristics by others, as an "instinct" by G. R. Schaeffer,[10] while A. F. Dodge actually speaks of a "sales personality." [5]

It is interesting to note that the Dictionary of Occupational Titles does not even define the term "salesman" in its generic sense, but devotes considerable space to the definitions of specific kinds of "salesman." The term salesman has been defined elsewhere as "a man who is so skilled in the understanding and technique of handling people that he is able to get them to buy what he has to offer—at a profit to himself and to his company—to the enduring satisfaction of the buyer." The emphasis on the "technique of handling people" is so important in successful salesmanship that the immediate sale may be actually overlooked for the sake of a good rapport —"The modern viewpoint in selling is to make a customer rather than a sale." [3]

A study of the attributes that go into the make-up of a successful salesman reveals some of the following traits: a certain minimum level of general intelligence, ability to express oneself clearly and convincingly, a personality make-up enabling one to enter into amicable relationships with people, ability to judge others, a sense of humor, attractive appearance, and interest in the work. This by no means exhausts the list of factors that contribute to success in the field. The actual "amount" of these characteristics and the particular pattern which they form may determine the specific nature of salesmanship. It is quite apparent that the skills and abilities utilized by a barker at a side show are quite different from those of a life insurance salesman. Both may be excellent salesmen in their respective areas although if their positions were reversed there is a likelihood that neither would succeed. The difference between the two is due not so much to a difference in the components, but rather to the difference in their amount and the manner in which they are combined.

From the above it becomes quite apparent that an attempt to measure "aptitude for salesmanship" is by no means a simple task. Two methods of investigation suggest themselves quite readily, (a) the measurement of individual components that go into the make-up of a salesman (such as interests, personality traits, etc.), and (b) a total empirical evaluation of individuals known to be successful in the selling field. Both techniques have been used repeatedly with varying degrees of success.

Experiments designed to measure sales-ability objectively yield somewhat conflicting results. This may be due to the difference in techniques employed and to the difference in statistical sampling. A common procedure is to administer a battery of tests to a known group of salesmen and to correlate the obtained scores with supervisors' ratings of the individuals in the group. Sometimes the responses on the personality inventories and interest questionnaire are examined qualitatively in order to determine what general type of a reply may be characteristic of a successful salesman.

Attempts to measure sales aptitude *per se* did not prove too successful because of at least two inherent difficulties: [2] the specificity of the salesman's work, and the difficulty of localizing and measuring the personality attributes. Further problems associated with the measurement of salesmanship lay in the difficulty of establishing a satisfactory criterion of success. It was found that wages or volume of business were poor indices of success because they were subject to fluctuation and influence by factors other than the ability to sell. For example, the question of supply and demand and competition, the season of the year, purely local conditions such as the culture and habits of a particular community, the advertising campaign behind the product, etc., may all have a profound influence on the earnings and the volume of sales of a particular salesman almost irrespective of his sales "aptitude."

Some workers were moderately successful in selecting potential salespeople on the basis of the Strong and Bernreuter scores, but here again the findings are by no means in complete agreement. It was found, for instance, that although salespeople as a group tend to attain high scores on the Bernreuter B4-D scale (social dominance), the B4-D scores, when used alone, cannot differentiate between successful and unsuccessful salesmen.[6] Ghiselli, in using the Strong Interest Inventory came to similar conclusions by stating ". . . the validity of a test is not necessarily demonstrated by the fact that a given group of workers earns higher scores on it than would be expected on the part of a random sample of the population." [7] When other tests were employed such as the Humm-Wadsworth and the Bell, the results again were influenced by the methods of statistical procedures in use. These findings raise a fundamental question whether it is possible to measure sales-aptitude by means of personality questionnaires.

In the field of life insurance the technique of testing was refined at least by some workers, to the point where by assigning letters to the scores on the "index," the examiner could predict with considerable certainty whether the candidate is or is not likely to earn a certain minimum amount. Using the same data it is possible to express numerically the value of each man in terms of business obtained. For example, a single "letter A" man may be expected to bring in as much business as $2\frac{1}{4}$ average or "letter C" men and almost five times as much business as a "letter E" man.[12] However, not all the studies in the field of salesmanship yield quite such satisfying results. Furthermore, an empirical method for the selection of sales personnel still casts very little light on the theory underlying the nature of "aptitude for salesmanship."

Despite these rather obvious limitations imposed upon an accurate selection of selling personnel the problem of choosing the right people is both common and concrete. Larger concerns frequently employ the four means of selection which proved to be among the most effective ones in the choice of salesmen.[12] They are: personal history blanks, personality questionnaires, interest inventories, and interviews. Frequently the written part is assembled into one booklet of several pages, and is usually considered by the applicant as a single test.

A typical questionnaire usually consists of several parts arranged somewhat as follows: questions pertaining to the socio-economic background of the applicant; his personality characteristics as revealed by the "yes," "no," "?" type of questions; a self-rating scale of adjectives "which you think fit you best"; and finally a preference rating scale of interests and activities set within a social frame of reference. In one instance a test designed to select insurance agents purports to measure such traits or characteristics as ". . . self-confidence, self-assertiveness, dominance, emotional adjustment, and understanding of people." The component parts may be scored and weighted by the employer to yield a total score. The test findings are generally considered as a supplement to the interview which is the *sine qua non* of most employment procedure.

A comprehensive treatment of the interview may be found in Bingham and Moore "How to Interview." The interview, as indicated, is the most frequently employed single factor in determining the suitability of a prospective salesman. At the same time the interview is perhaps the least objective method of determining sales aptitude. Although the interview affords considerable latitude and flexibility in obtaining information, a written questionnaire may serve even better to that end for the questions are usually more concise and direct. It may be argued that an interview permits an observation of the "intangibles," but that is precisely where it fails as an objective instrument. Preconceived ideas and deeply ingrained attitudes on the part of the interviewer, are bound to have their effects on the final evaluation of the applicant. Since the interview is frequently conducted by the employer himself, its objective value is further lowered because as often as not the interviewer lacks the technical knowledge and skills of a professionally trained worker. The Vocational Monograph [14] suggests several "characteristics most frequently associated with those who have been most highly successful in the merchandising vocations." It may be well to center the interview around these characteristics which are: *"Social Behaviors:* Having other people always about him. Interest in all kinds of people. Ready acceptance by others. Accurate analysis and judgment of others. Ability to manage people. Working in and through groups. Skillful co-operation. *Mental Behaviors:* Thinking in confusing surroundings. Skill in use of spoken language. Some facility in mathematics. Planning ahead. *Emotional Behaviors:* Use of methodical procedures. Close confinement to one place. Working for concrete results. Working under pressure. *Physical Behaviors:* Being much indoors. Working in noise and confusion."

These points are by no means intended as a blue print for interviewing. They may aid in interpreting test results and may serve as a rough nucleus around which the employment interview may be centered.

Summary

A study of the literature dealing with the measurement of "aptitude for salesmanship" reveals a rather contradictory picture. Although it is empirically recognized that the presence of certain interests and personality characteristics is conducive to effective salesmanship, the quantitative measurement of these traits does not always enable one to make an accurate prognosis. There is also disagreement among the workers in the field as to the very nature of the entity that is being tested. Whereas some maintain that salesmanship is an arithmetic summation of several identifiable elements, others imply that it is an "emergent" aspect of personality itself.

Objective studies tend to show that some aspects of salesmanship are more readily measurable than others. In the field of life insurance, for example, a test designed to measure the social background, interests, and certain personality traits of the applicant, when combined with an interview, yield a satisfactory degree of prediction.

Studies employing some of the well-known interest and personality questionnaires, suggest that testing in the areas of personality, interest, and general ability, are helpful in the pre-selection of sales candidates.

The interview, although perhaps the least objective single method for the determination of sales-aptitude, is used extensively as a major factor in personnel selection.

References:

1. Bingham, W. V. and Moore, B. V. *How to interview.* New York: Harper Bros., 1934.
2. Bolanowich, D. J. and Kirkpatrick, F. H. Measurement and selection of salesmen. *Educational and Psychological Measurements,* 1943, 3, 333–339.

3. *Business as a career.* New York University Bulletin, Volume XLV, Number 31, 1945.

4. *Career News,* August 1945, B'nai B'rith, Washington, D. C.

5. Dodge, A. F. Social dominance and sales personality. *Journal of Applied Psychology,* 1938, 132–139.

6. ———. *Ibid.*

7. Ghiselli, E. E. The use of the Strong Vocational Interest Blank and the Pressey Senior Classification Test in the selection of casualty agents. *Journal of Applied Psychology,* 1942, 26, 793–799.

8. Kurtz, A. K. Recent research in the selection of life insurance salesmen. *Journal of Applied Psychology,* 1941, 25, 11–17.

9. Lovett and Richardson. Selecting sales personnel; the significance of various types of test material. *Personnel Journal,* 1934, 12, 248–253.

10. Schaeffer, G. R. *Retail merchandising.* Chicago: University of Chicago, Board of Vocational Guidance, 1931.

11. Steward, V. *Selection of sales personnel.* Los Angeles: Verne Steward and Associates, 5471 Chesley Ave., 1936, pp. 48.

12. *The value and use of the Aptitude Index.* Life Insurance Sales Research Bureau, Hartford, Connecticut, 1945.

13. Traxler, A. E. *Techniques of guidance.* New York: Harper and Bros., 1945.

14. *Vocational Monograph.* Number 21, The Quarrie Corp., Chicago, Illinois, 1943.

15. Warren, H. C. *Dictionary of psychology.* Boston: Houghton Mifflin Co.

H. S.

SELLING APTITUDE TESTS

Detroit Retail Selling Inventory

This inventory, constructed by Harry J. Baker and Paul H. Voelker, was published in 1940 and designed to aid in the selection of suitable personnel for retail selling.

The inventory consists of questions to estimate the following elements which are important in retail selling: arithmetic skill, accuracy in checking names, numbers, and letters; certain personality factors, and two parts which indicate a partial measure of intelligence. These parts consist of word opposites and verbal analogies.

A score may be computed without the intelligence sections if a more complete intelligence test is desired. The personality sections require no time limit. Total time for administration is about thirty minutes.

Validity was established by determining the degree to which the inventory differentiated 205 successful sales clerks from 107 less successful ones.[1] These groups were selected upon the basis of sales records of each clerk. No report is given by the authors about the specific sales groups from which subjects were drawn.

A preliminary test battery was constructed based upon the findings of a job analysis of the salesclerks' duties and results of previous experimentation in the field. The preliminary test battery was administered to a criterion group of 312. Each item in the personality traits portion of the test was tabulated separately for the superior and inferior clerks. A critical ratio was computed for each item and only those items revealing a standard error of three or more were retained in the final draft of the inventory. Then each item was given a weight based upon its ability to discriminate between the criterion groups as shown by the standard error. The weights were assigned, test papers scored, and percentile ranks computed. The same procedure was followed for the other parts of the test except that each item was not considered separately but the entire portion as a whole. In the criterion group, twenty-six per cent of the superior group of salesclerks fell in the upper quartile while only four per cent of the inferior group obtained scores in this level. Twenty-five per cent of the inferior group scored in the lowest quartile while only six per cent of the superior group fell in this classification.

Reliability estimates, investigated by the split-half technique and test-retest method, show coefficients of .86 for personality, .76 and .80 for the two pages of intelligence questions, .98 for checking, and .77 for arithmetic.

The directions for administering and scoring are self-explanatory. Percentile ranks are available for the four subdivisions and total score of all tests as well as total score omitting the intelligence test.

In vocational guidance this inventory may be used as one of several methods for evaluation of individuals who have an interest in retail selling. The authors indicate that those who fall below the twenty-fifth percentile should not be selected as potentially successful salesclerks. Chances of obtaining superior salesclerks are greatest if only those scoring at the seventy-fifth percentile or above are selected. It is probable that critical scores for superior and inferior salesclerks will vary according to the specific retail sales areas for which they are being considered.[2]

The publisher of this inventory is the Public School Publishing Company, Bloomington, Illinois.

References:

1. Baker, H. J. and Voelker, P. H. *Examiner's Manual for the Detroit Retail Selling Inventory.* Bloomington: Public School Publishing Company, 1940.
2. Flemming, E. G. and Flemming, C. W. Qualitative approach to the problem of improving selection of salesmen by psychological tests. The Journal of Psychology, 1946, 21, 127–150.

LaV. H. R.

Moss-Wyle-Loman-Middleton Test for Ability to Sell

This test was constructed by Fred A. Moss, Herbert Wyle, William Loman and William Middleton to measure innate ability to become a successful salesperson, the test being aimed particularly at salesmanship in department stores.

There are six sub-tests in which the subject is required to (1) choose the best of four possible solutions in twelve typical selling situations, (2) memorize twelve names and faces, and subsequently identify them in a series of twenty-four faces, (3) determine the truth or falsity of thirty statements concerning human behavior, (4) study three advertisements and subsequently answer ten questions concerning the products advertised, (5) follow directions in filling out a sales check and (6) solve five arithmetical problems.

In administering the test, the subject is given ten minutes to study the advertising material and the twelve names and faces. The answer booklets are then distributed with thirty-five minutes allowed for answering all questions. The reliability of the test, as reported by the authors is .91, by the Spearman-Brown formula.

The test was validated by correlating test scores with efficiency ratings for 100 salespersons. Efficiency ratings of salespersons were based upon the number of sales, number of errors made, amount of merchandise and ratings by the buyer, floor manager and personnel officer. The resulting correlation was .54.

From each of twenty-five departments the best and poorest salespersons were chosen. The best salespersons made an average score of 112, and the poorest, an average score of 70.5. In every instance the best salesperson scored higher than the poorest in the same department. However, there was some overlapping, with the poorest salespersons in some departments scoring higher than the best salespersons in other departments. From this the authors conclude that a salesperson whose selling ability is too low to make a good salesperson in one department may render satisfactory services in another department where the requirements are lower.

The reviewer feels called upon to point out that these salespersons were not equated for age, education, intelligence or any other criteria. Since the test does contain many elements commonly found in tests of abstract intelligence, it is felt that this relationship should be further investigated.

Norms are presented, not only for salespersons, but for junior high school students, senior high school students and college students. In all, the norms are based upon a thousand cases.

The test is published by the Center for Psychological Service, George Washington University, Washington, D. C.

Review based on abstract prepared by Center for Psychological Service, George Washington University from:
"The Use of Objective Tests in Selecting Employees— (author not given) Store Management, April 1929.

L. S. R.

SCANDINAVIA (Denmark, Finland, Iceland, Norway, Sweden) With reference to vocational guidance activities the Scandinavian countries fall into three groups. In Finland and Iceland little need has been felt up to the present for any systematic professional guidance in the selection of occupations by young people. Denmark, Norway, and Sweden each has a Juvenile Exchange as a branch of the Municipal Employment Exchange located in their respective capitals, and in some instances in connection with exchanges in a few of their larger cities. Private organizations in these countries are also interested in vocational guidance work. In Denmark and Norway psychotechnical and medical examinations form a part of the vocational guidance procedure. In Sweden, however, little use has as yet been made of these examinations for guidance purposes.

All of the Scandinavian countries have facilities and many types of schools for training in the various occupations of the country concerned.

Denmark

An organized vocational guidance program was begun in Copenhagen in the 1830's through the cooperation of the Juvenile Employment Exchange, a municipal institution supported by state funds, and the Copenhagen Municipal Polytechnic Institute.

The usual procedure in the case of an elementary school graduate who wishes assistance of the Juvenile Employment Exchange, is for the Exchange to send a questionnaire to the school asking for information as to the applicant's ability, interests, industry, health and marks made. A second questionnaire is given to the applicant to fill out at home requesting information as to his leisure time interests and activities, associations, habits and other personal characteristics. The applicant is then sent to the Psychotechnical Institute for a psychotechnical and physical examination. Applicants who already have decided on the trades they wish to enter are given tests of capacity for learning their respective trades. Those who do not know what they wish to do are tested for general ability. On the results of these examinations the Institute gives its opinion as to choice of occupation.

After receiving the advice of the Institute the applicant returns to the Juvenile Employment Exchange for a thorough discussion of his occupational problems on the basis of the information obtained from the school, the home, and the Psychotechnical Institute. The Exchange then assists the applicant in finding a suitable place of apprenticeship or training.

The Juvenile Employment Exchange also gathers factual information about the various trades and occupations including for each the nature of the work, requirements for admission to apprenticeship, the duration of apprenticeship, technical school training and future prospects. This data is available not only at the Exchange but at schools and other centers where young people may apply for information.

The schools aid in vocational guidance by informing pupils about the work of various information services such as the Juvenile Employment Exchange. Each year also the pupils of the graduating class and their parents are given opportunity at least once to attend a lecture on "What are you going to be?"

A few years ago the Danish Ministry of Education issued a 22-page booklet on *Vejledning vedrörende Deltagelse i Ungdomsundervisning* (Guidance concerning participation in the instruction for youth), which opens with the statement:

"Completion of school does not mean the end of learning. You are about to learn your trade, but so much is now demanded of all the citizens of a community that you must in addition improve yourself in every way in order that you may be able to fill to the best of your ability the position to which you are assigned.

"It is important, therefore, that you make use of the opportunities for further education afforded every young man and woman."

Brief accounts follow giving pertinent information about various schools such as schools for young people between the ages of

15 and 18 years, continuation classes, evening schools, agricultural instruction, and the folk high school.

Finland

Finland, as already indicated, has no systematically organized work in vocational guidance. The country is small, largely agricultural, and professional opportunities relatively few. No real need, therefore, has so far been felt for professional vocational guidance.

Young people discuss the problems of future occupation with their parents and friends and undoubtedly in some instances with their teachers. The final choice as to occupation, however, is made by the boy or girl and the parents with practically no assistance from outside.

After the decision as to occupation has been made the young man or woman enters an apprenticeship, or attends the type of school which offers the necessary preparation for the life work planned.

News of shortage or opportunities within a trade or profession spreads quickly in a small country and is marked immediately by higher school enrollments within the field concerned. The news of a surplus becomes known equally fast and is marked by a corresponding decrease of registration in the given trade or profession.

Iceland

Up to the present vocational guidance with reference to choice of occupation is unknown in Iceland. To meet the needs of its industries Iceland has, however, a complete set of schools such as:

> Bunadarskóli (School of Farming)
> Gardyrkjuskólinn (School of Horticulture)
> Handidaskóli (Artisan School)
> Idnskóli (Trade School)
> Styrimannaskólinn (Nautical School)
> Verzlunarskólinn (Commercial School)
> Vélskólinn (School for Marine Engineers)

The schools offer occupational instruction on secondary school level which in some instances is supplemented by apprenticeship or practical work. Young people enter these schools after their choice of occupation has been made.

The University of Reykjavik has a Student's Information Bureau (Upplysingaskrifstofa Studenta) for the advice and guidance of college students. One of the main functions of the Bureau is to assist Icelandic students with reference to study abroad.

Norway

Systematic and practical work in vocational guidance has been given in Oslo through various agencies since the middle 1920's. Through the Psychotechnical Institute of the Oslo Employment Exchange under Helga Eng and the Juvenile Employment Exchange, boys and girls under 18 receive vocational guidance analogous to that offered by the Juvenile Employment Exchange and the Psychotechnical Institute in Copenhagen. As in Denmark the guidance is based on information gained from the applicant, the home, the school, and the scientific analysis of the individual.

The Oslo Trade and Preparatory School has been giving vocational guidance for boys in manual trades through interviews with the boys and their parents. Effort is made to give information about the nature of the work in a given trade, the duration of apprenticeship, the conditions of pay, and future prospects. Further, the boy is encouraged to visit the school and the workshops and to talk with persons in the trade. The school also conducts a program of psychotechnical testing for aptitudes and abilities.

Posters and literature on vocational guidance have been published by the Occupational Training Committee for Manual Work, a state organization which also provides direct guidance.

Other organizations rendering vocational guidance are the Social Exchange for Youth in Rural Areas and the Norwegian Association for Social Work.

A law on vocational and trade schools passed on March 1, 1940, but which was not put into operation because of the war, provided for various types of vocational schools. Among these types were preparatory schools in manual work and industry (Forskoler for håndverk og industri). The preparatory schools were to give from ½ to 1 year of instruction in preparation for apprenticeship. They were to be organized so as to serve also for vocational guidance (yrkesveiledning). Preparatory schools could be arranged for trades with a need of at least 5 apprentices but the number of pupils in a class could not exceed 15. For admission to a preparatory school the applicant was to be at least 14 years of age and have completed the elementary school.

In January 1944 the Royal Norwegian Government appointed a Committee on vocational training. In its report to the Government in October 1944, the Committee included among its recommendations that the law on vocational and trade schools be put into force.

A comprehensive publication or calendar on Norwegian schools and instruction (Norsk Skole- og Undervisningskalender) edited by

B. W. Areklett was published in 1938, for the aid of young people desiring further education in preparation for their lifework. It is intended particularly for elementary school graduates faced with the problem of selecting the vocation they are to pursue and of how they may most easily and quickly obtain the necessary training after their choice of lifework has been made.

Sweden

In addition to the work of the Juvenile Exchange in Stockholm many publications have been issued for the purpose of assisting Swedish youth in its vocational planning.

In 1937 the seventh revised edition of *Vad Vill du Bli?* (What do you wish to be?), a booklet on the choice of occupations for girls was published under the sponsorship of the Stockholm Board of Elementary Education. The following year the eighth revised edition of a similar booklet entitled *Gossarnas Yrkesval* (Boys' Choice of Occupations) was published by the same educational authority.

Following a brief discussion about the choice of continued education after graduation from the elementary school and immediate entry into practical work, the booklet for boys tells about various types of schools, about vocations from among which a choice may be made, and the selection of a vocation. It closes with a series of three graphic presentations, one each on the average wage per hour within certain vocations, the duration of training and wage conditions within certain trades, and a graph on the educational system of Stockholm. The discussion about schools includes also schools leading to the *real* or modern examination. In Sweden this examination marks completion of the lower stage of secondary education and qualifies for middle positions in the Civil Service, industry and commerce.

Illustrative of another type of publication which aims to serve young people in general as well as their advisors is *Skolor och Utbildning* (Schools and Education) by Rudolf Farhaeus. This book gives a comprehensive picture of the various types of schools in Sweden and of the educational opportunities they afford.

For young people interested in professional work and vocations requiring higher education the Directors of the United Student Organizations of Sweden (Sveriges Förenade Studentkårers Styrelse) issue with the assistance of a State subsidy a Swedish Student Calendar (Svensk Studentkalender). The seventh annual edition which was that for 1938–39, gives information about the various types of institutions of higher education in Sweden, their requirements for admission, duration of study, costs, examinations, and future prospects.

References:

1. Areklett, B. W. (redaktr). *Norsk Skole- og Undervisningskalender.* Oslo: Olaf Norli, 1938.
2. Bahnsen, P. The Scandinavian countries. *Vocational guidance through-the world,* by Franklin J. Keller and Morris S. Viteles. New York: W. W. Norton & Company, Inc., 1937, 427–439.
3. Barck-Lagergren, K. och Söderberg, G. *Vad Vill Du Bli?* Flickornas Yrkesval. Anvisningar till Flickorna och deras Föräldrar i Fråga om vissa Yrken och Utbildnings vägar. 7:e upplagan. På uppdrag av Stockholms Folkskoledirektion. Stockholm: Hesse W. Tullberg, Esselte AB., 1937.
4. Eliasson, H. *Lög og Reglur um Skóla- of Menningarmál á Islandi sem í Gildi eru í Marzlok 1944.* Gefid út af Fraedslumálastjórninni. Reykjavík: Ríkisprentsmidjan Gutenberg, 1944.
5. Fáhraeus, R. *Skolor och Utbildning.* Bonniers praktiska böcker. Stockholm: Albert Bonniers Förlag, 1933.
6. Hesslen, G., Ljungberg, G. and Willers, U. (editors). *Svensk Student-kalender 1938–39.* Sjunde årgången. På uppdrag av Sveriges Förenade Studentkårers Styrelse och under medverkan av talrika fackmän. Lund: C. W. K. Gleerups Fölag, 1938.
7. Pehrson, A. T. and Eriksson, L. H. *Gossarnas Yrkesval.* Korta anvisningar rörande vissa yrken och utbildningsvägar. 8:e Delvis omarbetade upplagan. På uppdrag av Stockholms Folkskoledirektion. Stockholm: Am. Hasse W. Tullbergs boktryckeri, 1938.
8. *Vejledning vedrörende Deltagelse i Ungdomsundervisning.* Udgivet paa Undervisningsministeriets Foranstaltning. Köbenhavn, J. H. Schultz A/S Universitets-Bogtrykkeri, 1943.

A. M. L.

SCHOOL GRADES, USE OF. In spite of the fact that research workers during the last fifty years have demonstrated over and over again that the grade assigned to a student in a class has little reliability or validity, school grades are frequently consulted by practically all guidance officers.

Unless a large amount of additional information is available, the fact that a high-school senior was marked 80 per cent in English does not supply any definite information about his abilities or his achievements. He may have been the best student in his class, or the poorest. No one can be sure what a given school grade means. Even the teacher who assigned the grade would be unable a few years later to say confidently what she intended it to mean, unless she were told the name of the student and remembered a great many facts about the class that no one else could possibly know. The mark or grade recorded for a student's performance in a class is extremely subjective and relatively meaningless to anyone except, perhaps, at the moment to the teacher who assigned it.

School grades are used by some guidance officers because they do not realize the inadequacy of grades as evidences of an individual's characteristics. Others examine a student's grades when more valid data are not available regarding him, or when it seems desirable to supplement other data by checking on the general impression which the individual may have made on his teachers. Unless a counselor is fully aware of the unreliability of school grades, he is in danger of basing upon them suggestions that are quite unjustified or that may be, in some cases, contrary to the best interests of the individual.

The deficiencies of school marks as measures of an individual's characteristics arise from the utter confusion that exists in the minds of teachers as to just what a grade should indicate regarding a pupil. One teacher tries to mark her pupils in terms of their status with relation to some personal concept of perfection, using 100 per cent to mean that the student has, in her judgment, learned all that was taught, as much as could be expected of pupils in that class, or as much as could be expected of the particular student when his own intellectual and other handicaps are fully understood. Another teacher attempts to assign grades to the different pupils in terms of their relative current status in knowledge, in skill, in effort made, or in attitude toward the subject, the teacher, or the generally-accepted rules. The comparisons may be with the other pupils in the same room, or with all pupils in the same grade in that school, or in that city school system, or with pupils of the same grade throughout the state. Still other teachers attempt by means of the marks they assign to indicate a pupil's current status in relation to his status at the beginning of the year or at some other previous time. Most teachers use indefinitely understood combinations of several or all of these criteria, along with still others which they may have developed for themselves without being fully aware of their own intentions.

There is no uniform plan or purpose in assigning school grades. Even if all teachers had agreed upon what a grade should indicate, their abilities to judge by that criterion differ so widely that the marks they would assign would still be very unreliable evidences of the pupil's actual status. Many studies using objective tests of knowledge and skill have revealed that the pupils having the highest test scores in one class actually have distinctly lower scores than the pupils having the lowest scores in another class of the same grade. A pupil who would be marked "A" by one teacher would be marked "Failure" by another equally efficient teacher of the same subject in the same grade. The marks made in school are not reliable or valid as measures of an individual's abilities or achievements.

In spite of their indefinite meaning and general unreliability, school grades should be consulted when they are available to the counselor. If an individual's school grades are uniformly high, that fact may be taken as a general indication that his teachers approved of him as a student, and as a suggestion that other teachers would probably feel toward him in much the same way if he continued in school. In like manner, if an individual's grades have been uniformly high in a particular school subject, but only average or low in other subjects, that fact may be taken as a rough indication that teachers of that subject have felt more favorable toward his abilities than have the teachers of other subjects. When it is important to know just how much a student knows or just what he can do in a given field, it will be necessary to administer a well-validated objective test in that field. When the evidence from objective tests agrees with the suggestions obtained from examining school grades, the counselor may have a reasonable degree of confidence in his data.

The suggestions obtained about an individual from examining his school grades are, of course, more often useful in giving educational counseling than in giving vocational guidance. In any type of guidance the evidence obtained from carefully administered objective tests is likely to be more useful than that obtained from examining school marks. The professionally competent counselor will, however, use every bit of evidence he can obtain regarding an individual, but will always interpret the data obtained in the light of its known limitations and of its relationships to other important facts.

Reference:

1. *School Records and Reports.* Research Bulletin of the National Education Association, Vol. V, No. 5 (November, 1927), pp. 267–273.

M. R. T.

SCHOOL HABITS, NEW YORK RATING SCALE FOR. This scale was developed as an aid to teachers in making more objective ratings of pupil traits important for adjustment to school work. The scale was devised by Ethel L. Cornell, Warren W. Coxe, and Jacobs S. Orleans. Nine traits are described in terms of average and extreme performance. The teacher rates a pupil on each trait in terms of the descriptions provided and obtains a profile of pupil traits. This is not a general personality rating but a rating on traits such as attention, persistence, stability, as they apply to school work. It is intended primarily as an informal aid to teachers and counselors in discovering specific needs of pupils whose school adjustment is inadequate. It can be used to secure a numerical rating if this is desired for survey purposes or for cumulative records. The rating line for each trait is ten centimeters in length. A rating from 1 to 10 can, therefore, be made by using a centimeter scale.

Published by World Book Co., Yonkers-on-Hudson, N. Y.

E. L. C.

SHORTHAND APTITUDE TESTS, EVALUATION OF. (See also articles under heading of "Stenography.") The limited experimentation that has been done in the measurement of aptitudes for shorthand learning has not revealed the abilities and characteristics needed by students for the mastery of the subject. Therefore, before educators can undertake the task of advising students to study shorthand or not to study shorthand, with any degree of certainty that their advice is of much more value than personal opinion, the factors that relate to shorthand success must be discovered. The task of exploring all the elements involved in learning shorthand and all the human influences that affect the student's achievement in shorthand, is one that will require the combined efforts of many research workers. The complexity of the task is one of the reasons that the field is practically unexplored.

Prognostic Tests in Shorthand

Prognostic tests in shorthand are few in number, and studies have shown that they are in the experimental stage. At present there is no prognostic test that will give consistently reliable data for individual prognosis or for group prognosis. The data that are available for one of the best known and oldest tests of this kind, The Hoke Prognostic Test of Stenographic Ability, indicate that this test has never been particularly effective. One of the most extensive experimentations with the Hoke Prognostic Test of Shorthand Ability was made by Blanchard.[1] His investigation was carried on in twenty-six cities in the United States and scores were obtained for 1,279 beginning students in Gregg shorthand. The correlation between the scores on the Rollinson Diagnostic Shorthand Test on Lesson 4 of Gregg Shorthand, which was used as the criteria for measuring achievement in shorthand learning, was .23.

The correlation between the Hoke Prognostic Test of Stenographic Ability and the final semester grade was .24, which is also very low.

The Turse Shorthand Aptitude Test is a more recent test that is available for school use. Research workers in the field have not reported data to substantiate claims made by the author. Tuckman's study [3] of the Turse Shorthand Aptitude Test revealed, on the basis of correlations obtained between test scores, that there is a great deal of community between intelligence as measured by the American Council of Education Psychological Examination and the Turse Shorthand Aptitude Test. At present, the inefficiency of intelligence tests as a single factor in predicting shorthand success is quite widely accepted by educators. An analysis made by the writer [2] (p. 4) revealed that the correlations obtained between the criteria of shorthand achievement and the intelligence tests employed in eleven published investigations ranged from $-.59$ to $.50$, with a median of .36. From the standpoint of prediction, none of these correlations indicate enough control to make the prediction valuable.

Other investigations that have been undertaken in an attempt to settle some of the questions in connection with prognosis in shorthand involve relationships between a variety of tests and shorthand achievement. These tests include analogies, arithmetic, best answer, cancellation, character traits, classification, clerical, coding, coördinates, directions, English, handwriting, identification, information, logical selection, memory span, mixed sentences, motor control, number series, reading, sentence meaning, spelling, substitution, temperament, and vocabulary. A detailed summary of the studies that incorporated these tests and a tabular survey of the correlations reported in the research are given in a study made by the writer [2] (pp. 4–28). In summarizing, suffice it to say that none of the investigations produced a criterion for vocational guidance or the selection of students for shorthand learning.

Another factor that has received consideration in connection with shorthand prognosis is school marks. Even though relatively high correlations have been reported between shorthand achievement and teacher ratings in English, penmanship, typewriting, foreign language, etc., caution must be observed in recommending school marks for use in prediction of shorthand ability. School marks are often influenced by factors that are extraneous to learning. Teachers admit that they permit such factors as effort, enthusiasm, attitude, conduct in class, industry, neatness, courtesy, attendance, and originality to influence their marking to an extent that is greater than these factors would normally have on achievement in the subject. The emphasis that is put on the extraneous factors obscures the meaning of the marks and makes them practically useless in predicting success. Any criterion that has the aspect of subjectivity that exists in school marks cannot be considered a reliable factor in securing accurate research data.

Summary of a Recent Research Study in Prognosis

A statistical study made by the writer [2] (pp. 1–58) gives additional information on the area of research in shorthand prognosis. The problem was to make a comprehensive study of the value of certain psychological tests in the prediction of the shorthand achievement of secondary school students. The selection of the psychological tests was based on their value as measures of psychological factors which are pertinent to shorthand learning and on the promise that the tests had shown under other investigators. The Shorthand Learning Test used as the shorthand criterion of success is one of a series of tests constructed and partially standardized by Carmichael for measuring achievement in shorthand learning. The test is valid, the coefficients of reliability for the four subtests range from .88 for the dictation test to .97 for the transcription test, and the intercorrelations of the various subtests suggest that they are measuring a commonality of shorthand ability.

Of the five psychological tests used in the investigation, the Otis Self-Administering Tests of Mental Ability rank first in size of correlation with the criterion of shorthand achievement (r.3765). The correlation of .3765 indicates that some degree of relation exists between intelligence and shorthand achievement, but it also means that superior intelligence does not assure high achievement in shorthand and that low intelligence does not preclude high scores. In other words, the ability used by an individual, not necessarily the ability possessed by the individual, is the important factor in achievement. The correlation between intelligence and shorthand achievement suggests that success in shorthand is conditioned by intelligence to a lesser degree than success in academic subjects.

The relationship of the Iowa Silent Reading Tests and the I.E.R. General Clerical Test, C-1, to shorthand achievement is practically the same as that of the Otis Self-Administering Tests of Mental Ability (r.3577 and .3757 respectively). The correlation of the Revised Minnesota Paper Form Board Test with the shorthand criterion is the lowest of the complete test series (r.0754), and a comparatively low correlation exists between the Gates Visual Perception Tests and the shorthand criterion (r.0905).

The inefficiency of these instruments in predicting success is also indicated by the square of the multiple correlation .4350 (.189225). This suggests that these factors account for approximately 19 per cent of the variance of the shorthand cases, which leaves approximately 81 per cent unaccounted for. From the standpoint of prediction, this is not enough control to make the prediction valuable except in the negative sense.

The skills measured in the study are limited to those learned early in the second semester of shorthand training and do not include numerous other abilities that a stenographer needs, such as ability to produce an acceptable typewritten transcript, to take dictation at a rapid speed, and to work in the environment of a business office. These are still unexplored problems in the field. Although this study indicates that the relationship between intelligence and shorthand achievement is low, it does not suggest that high intelligence is not required in secretarial positions.

Need for Additional Research

There is no disagreement with the statement that a battery of tests is more effective in eliminating failures and in predicting success than any single test. Up to the present time, however, no battery of tests that gives a reliable criterion for vocational guidance in the field of shorthand has been reported in educational literature. Personal traits such as persistence, desire to excel, interest, and emotional stability influence shorthand learning to a great degree. Shorthand learning also requires quick response to auditory and visual stimuli. A study should be made of these functions as they relate to shorthand success.

Typewriting is one of the phases of the complete secretarial process and must be considered as a component involved in transcribing shorthand notes. Almost all poor typists will be poor stenographers, but not all good typists will be able to learn shorthand. We do not know what characteristics the good typists who can succeed in shorthand have in common with the good typists who do not succeed.

Shorthand is a language skill, and consists of reading, writing, and transcribing a highly symbolic language. An analysis of the techniques used in foreign language investigations may provide suggestions for shorthand prognosis.

It is evident that further analysis of the abilities and characteristics needed in learning shorthand will reveal that there are other components involved in learning shorthand that may be subjected to research. The few research studies that have been made have given valuable suggestions for improved methods and procedures, and point the way for the discovery of a reliable criterion for vocational guidance in the field of stenography.

References:

1. Blanchard, C. I. Results of Hoke-Rollinson Research Study. American Shorthand Teacher, 1928, 9, 37–39.
2. Osborne, A. E. *The relationship between certain psychological tests and shorthand achievement.* New York: Bureau of Publications, Teachers College, Columbia University, 1943.
3. Tuckman, J. A. A study of the Turse Shorthand Aptitude Test. Journal of Business Education, 1943, 19, 17–18.

A. E. O.

SHORTHAND APTITUDE TEST, TURSE

Construction of the Test

An analysis of the abilities for stenographic aptitude suggests that a good shorthand prognosis test should include measures of each of the following: manual dexterity; ability to write, carry matter in the mind, and listen for new matter simultaneously; ability to learn and combine abstract symbols; ability to associate the correct literal spelling of a word with its phonetic form; ability to discriminate between words having similar or identical shorthand outlines; spelling ability; and the ability to construct entire words from incomplete or ambiguous shorthand outlines.

Validity and Reliability

Tests were prepared in each of the areas mentioned above and were subjected to preliminary experimentation on two small groups of high school pupils after one year of instruction.

Correlations for each of the sub-tests with various shorthand Achievement Tests were as follows: (49 cases)

Sub-Test	Correlation	Validity Criterion
Stroking	.61	
Spelling	.72	
Phonetic Association	.78	Rollinson Shorthand Achievement
Symbol Transcription	.55	Test
Word Discrimination	.68	
Dictation	.84	
Word Sense	.82	
Total Test (unweighted)	.68	
Total Test (unweighted)	.49	Blackstone Stenographic Proficiency Test (Form B)

Total Test (unweighted)   .54   Turse-Durost Shorthand Achieve-
                                  ment Test (Form A)
Total Test (unweighted)   .63   Turse-Durost Shorthand Achieve-
                                  ment Test (Form B)

In order to determine more adequately the predictive value of the battery, a revised form of the test was administered to approximately 800 children in eleven high schools who were just beginning the study of shorthand. At the end of the one year of instruction, a shorthand achievement test was given to a random sampling of 163 of these pupils. This test consisted of transcribing three letters. The correlation between the verbatim transcript of these three letters and the Aptitude Test for 163 cases after one year of shorthand was .50. The correlation between the total aptitude score made by the same pupils in correcting a prepared transcript of the three letters dictated (Turse-Durost Shorthand Achievement Test) was .67.

To compare the predictive efficiency of the Aptitude Test with that of certain other measures, scores on the Turse-Durost Shorthand Achievement Test, given at the end of one year of instruction, were also correlated with I.Q.'s and with ninth-grade English marks. A correlation of .35 based on 194 cases, was found between achievement scores and I.Q.'s (derived from Otis Self-Administering Tests and Terman Group Test of Mental Ability). The correlation between achievement scores and English marks was found to be .33, based on 174 cases.

It seems obvious from these data that the Aptitude Test was a more efficient instrument for predicting shorthand achievement at the end of one year's instruction than either ninth-grade English or I.Q.

At the end of two years it was possible to retest 268 cases of the original 780 pupils who took the Aptitude Test before beginning the study of shorthand. A second form of the Turse-Durost Shorthand Achievement Test, comprising four letters instead of three, was used for validating purposes, and a correlation of .67 was obtained. The split-half reliability coefficient for the entire test based on 337 cases was found to be .98.

Other Uses of the Test

While the Turse Shorthand Aptitude Test has been prepared chiefly for prognostic purposes, it may be given as a diagnostic test to pupils who have already begun the study of shorthand. The tests composing the battery—Stroking, Spelling, Phonetic Association, Symbol Transcription, Word Discrimination, Dictation, and Word

Sense—may yield valuable information to teachers regarding deficiencies of failing pupils. Even for successful pupils, unusually high scores in the stroking or dictation test may give some indication of the pupil's potentialities for newspaper, civil service or court reporting, or other types where high speed or sustained verbatim reporting is required. The test may also be used as a classification test where it is desired to place pupils in homogeneous groups for more effective shorthand instruction. The test may be used for all the above purposes in connection with any modern system of shorthand, including machine systems.

Published by World Book Company
Yonkers, N. Y., 1940

P. L. T.

SCIENCE, APTITUDE FOR.

New Requirements for Scientifically Trained Manpower

The dramatic speed with which science has intruded into nearly every phase of modern living has cast an aspect of urgency on our national situation with regard to encouraging, developing and training a "corps" of scientists. The late war was in many respects a scientific war and the Allied victory was enabled if not actually won by the achievements in laboratories and research centers mobilized by Allied science. Postwar developments in weapons of war and counter-weapons and in the peaceful expansion of manufactures, housing, transportation, communication and social welfare have raised the requirements for scientifically trained personnel to a new high.

Vocational Guidance versus Haphazard Selection

Most scientific fields as well as those fields more specifically recognized as the professions, require somewhat lengthy preparation. This fact alone has frequently operated as a method of selection—only those who can afford the necessary time and money generally obtaining entrance. The result, from the standpoint of both the student and society, has been far from satisfactory. This haphazard method overlooks many who are qualified and also rejects, frequently after much wasted time and effort, many unqualified aspirants at one or another stage of training. Such social waste and the accompanying individual frustrations and disillusionment could be avoided by the adoption of more systematic methods of selection and guidance and adequate standards for admission to educational institutions for scientific and professional training. The adoption of such methods and standards would also safeguard society by meeting the increased needs for scientific manpower through more efficient utilization of educational resources and by eliminating inefficient students and practitioners. From the standpoint of the vocational guidance profession, the problem of manpower recruitment and training for the sciences has been oriented to success in educational and professional institutions as a criterion rather than to success in later life. While this may at first appear to be a compromise with expediency, it is both a reasonable and a valid procedure. Success in courses can be measured with some uniformity and accuracy, while there is considerable doubt as to the meaning of success in the practice of a profession. Fortuitous personal, social and economic factors affect the employment, productivity and advancement of the practitioner to a far greater extent than they affect the student. Furthermore, the validity of such factors as earnings, publications, honors and positions, to the extent that they can be quantified is more difficult to establish than the measures of scholastic success. Nevertheless, the two goals are not unrelated. Educational institutions have constantly directed their curricula toward the realization of practical outcomes and there is much evidence that scholastic success is a good predictor of high standing in later practice.

General and Specific Attributes of Aptitude for Science

Candidates for all scientific fields must have the general prerequisites of intellectual development, interest, scholastic ability and character development essential to scientific study, research and work. Specific requirements in personality traits and specific skills and interests vary as between specific fields.

There is little validity, however, in the stereotype of a scientist as a person of high intellectual and academic attainment but preoccupied, unsocial, introverted and impractical, if not improvident. Social awareness, responsibility, and participation are as essential to scientific work as to any other field of endeavor and in some respects more essential. Scientific men and women have taken their places in positions of responsibility in government, industry, education and military organizations as well as in laboratories or universities.

It may be argued that standards of selection which place undue weight on personality and character development, interests and social attitudes may reject the infrequent and improbable genius who, though lazy, shy, uncooperative, socially irresponsible and truant, might nevertheless one day contribute a great discovery.

Such a contingency should, however, be of little concern to vocational guidance. This errant genius is, first of all, a rara avis, and second, he will develop, if he does, without benefit of formal educational assistance.

Research on the Prediction of Scientific Aptitude

The validity of a test, of a scholastic grade, of ratings by teachers, or of an interest measure as a predictor of success in a particular function is indicated by its correlation with that function or with a criterion which represents it.

Much research has been published dealing with the establishment of correlations between tests or other measures and college grades in scientific studies as criteria. In general, measures of final scholastic standing in high school and tests of general intellectual development and general scholastic attainment show a positive correlation with scientific studies. The significance of these results is comparable to that of the general findings with respect to aptitude for higher educational training, however, and they do not discriminate specially qualified candidates from others.

Several tests have been developed for the specific purpose of measuring aptitude for success in scientific studies. These consist generally of work samples covering component skills closely related to the criterion. Examples are the Stanford Scientific Aptitude Test, the (Moss) Medical Aptitude Test, the Minnesota Medical Aptitude Test, and the Iowa Physics and Mathematics Aptitude Tests. Although positively correlated with grades in respective subjects, these tests by themselves are generally not sufficiently discriminatory either to afford a basis for advising an individual student or for selecting the best candidates from a group. However, in conjunction with other measures, such as high school or college grades and other specialized indicators, they may form the basis for a combined predictor battery of considerable value. For example, MacPhail and Foster obtained a multiple correlation of .76 between grades in elementary college chemistry and a battery consisting of Iowa Chemistry Training test scores, high school rank and scores on the Cooperative General Mathematics Tests. Douglass obtained the best predictor combination for medical school success (a multiple correlation of .66) with premedical honor point ratios and certain sections of the Minnesota Medical Aptitude Test; and Mercer obtained a multiple correlation of .71 between freshman engineering grades and a battery consisting of a number completion test, an English usage test, science information and arithmetic problems tests, the MacQuarrie Block test, the Thurstone-Jones Sketching Test and the Detroit Pulleys test.

Because curricula, student sources, and other conditions vary between schools, such prediction equations are specific and may not be applicable if transferred directly for use elsewhere. For the same reasons their validity in the same school may vary from year to year. For maximum efficiency it is necessary to refine and restandardize them constantly, adjusting to changing conditions and changing individual test elements. Tests must also be varied in specific detail because of the danger of coaching if their content should become known.

In developing a predictor battery for predicting success in any scientific field, the general principles of test construction and validation apply. A detailed analysis of skills, interests, and subject mastery should precede the selection and tryout of predictor elements. Specialized tests should then be tried out which are related to the desired outcomes. For example, while tests of spatial relations, mechanical ability and finger dexterity have been found to be generally unrelated to college physics grades, it has been reported that these same items contribute significantly to a battery for selecting candidates for a dental school.

Another type of test of value in selecting scientific talent, particularly at the high school level, is the interest inventory. Some interest inventories have been based on choices between a series of alternative activities representing the subjects or fields involved; others on choices between key words selected from the vocabulary of different academic subjects; still others are related to choices between vocational situations. Interest tests, used in conjunction with other predictors, are of particular interest to vocational counselors and grade advisors in advising individual students in the choice of curricula.

Professional Selection Programs in Medicine and Engineering

Outstanding progress in the development of formal standards and procedures for the selection of candidates for professional study has been achieved in medicine and engineering. In both cases, strong professional organizations and close relationship between these and professional training institutions has been a primary motivating force. The excess of candidates over educational facilities, especially in medicine, has likewise been a factor.

Medical aptitude tests have today been almost universally adopted by medical colleges. The Moss and the Minnesota tests are best standardized. Despite their widespread use, however, there still remains considerable variability among schools in standards of admission.

Studies of aptitude for engineering have continued over a long period under the sponsorship of the Society for the Promotion of Engineering Education. The general trend of these investigations seems to indicate that the outstanding single predictor of success in a college engineering course is mathematical ability. Here again, however, it is recognized that to get a complete, rounded basis for evaluating the student, not one test, but a comprehensive battery of predictor elements is needed.

The Annual Science Talent Search

One of the most comprehensive developments in techniques for selection of scientific talent is the work of Edgerton and Britt in setting up and administering the procedures for the Annual Science Talent Search. This institution was inaugurated in 1942 as a scholarship contest conducted by the Science Clubs of America to discover boys and girls with scientific ability. It is limited to boys and girls who are seniors (12th grade) in a secondary school.

In the development of criteria of selection emphasis was placed on such attributes as intellectual ability, interest in some branch of science, social competence, initiative, resourcefulness and leadership. Their picture of a potential scientist suggested a person intellectually capable, interested in science, and a leader among his fellows.

The annual contest is conducted in local schools. The procedure is that of "successive hurdles" consisting of six successive steps, with elimination of candidates at each step. The survivors of all six hurdles are the winners. It is claimed that the successive hurdles are applied in decreasing order of validity. They are as follows:

1. Science Aptitude Examination—to select those who have the aptitude to study science in colleges and universities, but without too heavy a premium on previous knowledge of science.
2. High School Record—a transcript of the high school record and a statement of the contestant's rank in the senior class, indicating the number in the senior class.
3. Score on recommendations furnished by high school teachers. Ratings were made on the basis of ten categories or "families" of traits: Attitude—Purpose—Ambition; Scientific Attitude; Work Habits; Resourcefulness; Social

Skills; Cooperativeness; Initiative; Responsibility; Mechanical Ability and Special Abilities.

4. Rating on an original essay on a scientific subject.
5. Rating by a committee of judges in a personal interview. A standardized interview was used. Each of three judges used the same form and sought to rate the candidates on the same traits, which included Academic Background; Social and Personal Competence; Interests, Hobbies and Activities; and Motivation.
6. Score on a Social Attitudes Test, scored so as to reflect clarity of thinking in terms of democratic ideals.

The Science Aptitude Examination is of particular interest because it demonstrated the value of a comprehensive instrument of its type at the twelfth grade level. It was developed as a paragraph reading test, set up so as to be practically self-administering. A time limit of 2½ hours was given, which permitted practically all candidates to finish. Eighteen paragraphs were included, each followed by a group of questions which could be answered on the basis of information in the paragraph. All of the paragraphs were composed of science materials selected from various publications in the fields of geology, physics, chemistry, physiology, mathematics, agriculture, and psychology. Two of the paragraphs were diagrams, one of a rotary pump and the other of a simple gear system. The following paragraph illustrates the type of material used:

Paragraph Number 2: About 3,000 stars are visible with the naked eye at any time under the most favorable conditions. To a first approximation the stars appear to be fixed relative to one another on a celestial sphere which makes one revolution around the pole star in 23 hours, 56 minutes, and 3 seconds. On the sphere appear also the sun, moon and planets. These continually change their positions with respect to the stars. The moon moves eastward on the celestial sphere about 12° per day, the sun moves eastward about 1° per day, and the planets move mostly eastward but sometimes westward at varying rates. Except for the sun and moon most objects in the sky fall within a range in brightness of approximately 500 to 1. The average of the 20 brightest stars is only 100 times as bright as the faintest star that can be seen by the naked eye. Some stars are blue white, others white, some yellow, some orange and some red. The planets other than Mars are yellow, and their light resembles that of the sun.

Questions on Paragraph 2:   *Answers*

5. A clock which keeps star time would have to
   1: run more slowly than our ordinary clocks;
   2: run at the same rate as our ordinary clocks;
   3: run faster than our ordinary clocks; 4:
   have a different type of construction than our
   ordinary clocks.

☐ ☐ ☐ ☐
1 2 3 4

6. For the sun to return to the same position in
   the celestial sphere (relative to an observer
   on the earth), it will take 1: more than one
   clock year; 2: less than one clock year;
   3: slightly more than one clock day; 4: one
   clock day.

☐ ☐ ☐ ☐
1 2 3 4

7. The celestial sphere is 1: the locus of the
   earth's rotation; 2: the periphery of the solar
   system; 3: a synthetic concept; 4: the locus
   described by the major constellations.

☐ ☐ ☐ ☐
1 2 3 4

8. To an observer on the earth, the celestial
   body which retains its absolute position is
   1: the sun; 2: the moon; 3: Mars; 4: the
   pole star.

☐ ☐ ☐ ☐
1 2 3 4

9. To an observer on the earth, the celestial body
   showing the greatest relative change of position is 1: the sun; 2: the moon; 3: Mars;
   4: Polaris.

☐ ☐ ☐ ☐
1 2 3 4

10. The brightness of the sun is to the brightness
    of the faintest visible star as 1: 500 to 1;
    2: 100 to 20; 3: 1 to 20; 4: indeterminate.

☐ ☐ ☐ ☐
1 2 3 4

References:

1. Douglass, H. R. Prediction of success in the medical school. *University of Minnesota Studies in Predicting Scholastic Achievement*, 1942, 2, 1–16.
2. Edgerton, H. A., and Britt, S. H. The First Annual Science Talent Search. *American Scientist*, 1943, *31*, 55–68.
3. Kandel, I. L. *Professional aptitude tests in medicine, law and engineering.* New York: Teachers College, Columbia University, 1940.

4. MacPhail, A. H., and Foster, L. S. New data for placement procedures. *Journal of Chemical Education*, 1941, *18*, 235.
5. Mercer, M. An analysis of the factors of scientific aptitude as indicated by success in engineering curricula. *Pennsylvania State College, Abstracts of Studies in Education*, 1940, *Part IX*.
6. Sells, S. B. Measurement and prediction of special abilities. *Review of Educational Research*, 1944, *14*, 38–54.

S. B. S.

SCIENCE TEST, McDOUGAL GENERAL
Purpose and Content

The McDougal General Science Test was constructed for use as an achievement test in high school classes pursuing work in a first course in general science. Test I is designed for use at the completion of one semester's work and Test II for use at the completion of a year's work. Two equivalent forms, A and B, are available for each test.

Test I covers: liquids, pressure, light, environment, air, foods, narcotics, hygiene, clothing, diseases, housing, sanitation, heat, temperature, fire, water, and the heavenly bodies.

Test II covers: heavenly bodies, air, weather and climate, foods, plant life, water, water power, hygiene, health, physiology, fire and heat, rocks, soils, building materials, machines, electricity, light and lighting, sound and communication, matter and energy, transportation, and heredity, together with natural selection.

Author and Publisher

The author of this test is Clyde R. McDougal, Superintendent of Schools, Sun City, Kansas. The test was edited and the manual of directions was provided by H. E. Schrammel, Director, Bureau of Educational Measurements. The Publisher of the test is the Bureau of Educational Measurements, Teachers College, Emporia, Kansas.

Validity of Test

The distribution of the content of the divisions of this test is based on an analytical study of textbooks, courses of study, student errors on preliminary editions, and constructive criticisms made by science teachers.

Reliability of Test

The reliability of each division of the test is approximately .90. The P. E. of scores for Test I is 4.90, and for Test II, 4.42. The P. E. median of the two divisions respectively is .34 and .28.

Administering, Scoring, and Interpreting

This test is easy to administer, to score, and to interpret. Simple directions are provided for these procedures. The time limit for taking the test is forty minutes for each division. Percentile norms computed from the scores of 11,822 students are provided for interpreting the test results both for mid-year and end-of-year testing.

Use of Test Results

It is suggested that the test results may be profitably used in a number of ways: for determining student achievement; for checking the efficiency of instruction; for assigning school marks; for analyzing student and class weakness; and for motivation of student effort.

H. E. S.

SOCIAL BACKGROUND FORMS

Social Background Data Sheet. The Social Background Data Sheet was constructed by J. Wayne Wrightstone, and was published in the *Journal of Educational Sociology,* April, 1934. This questionnaire, or data sheet, provides an index of selected social and economic factors, based primarily on the home background of the individual. It correlates highly with the Sims Score Card for Socio-Economic Status.

The scores derived from this data sheet may be used to provide a basis for classifying individuals in terms of such social and economic factors as the parent's occupation, type of home, and ownership of such items as radio, piano, books, automobile and telephone.

It may be filled out by individuals who have fourth grade or higher ability in reading. The directions for administration are self-explanatory. The data sheet calls for recording the occupation, title and general nature of the individual's or, if a minor, the parent's occupation. It requires, also, an indication of the number of persons living in the home and the number of rooms in the home and a designation of "yes" or "no" about the ownership of a radio, piano, number of books, automobile and telephone. A scoring key for weighting numerically the various responses is provided. The administration of the data sheet requires approximately ten minutes.

The data sheet was standardized on elementary, junior high and high school pupils. The scores are stated in deciles and a table for comparison of the scores on the data sheet with the Sims Score Card for Socio-Economic Status is available. The correlation between the Social Background Data Sheet and the Sims Score Card is .90.

Validity has been demonstrated, first, by the correlation with the Sims Score Card for Socio-Economic Status and by an actual check on approximately 100 pupils who filled out the questionnaire and whose answers were later checked by a visit to the home.

The reliability has been investigated by re-administration of the data sheet and has been found to be .93. This data sheet is not distributed by a commercial publisher. Permission to reproduce the data sheet, however, may be obtained from the author, J. Wayne Wrightstone, Board of Education, 110 Livingston Street, Brooklyn 2, New York.

J. W. W.

American Home Scale.   This scale, constructed by W. A. Kerr and H. H. Remmers, is designed to obtain valid and reliable measurements of the socio-economic status of individuals and groups. Knowledge of such a factor is an important consideration not only for purposes of psychological and sociological research, but also for vocational and educational planning and guidance, since home environment plays such a strongly determining rôle in ultimate vocational choice and educational opportunity.

This scale yields a total score and sub-scores on one general and three specific aspects of environmental background which may be defined as follows: (1) cultural environment includes the contacts an individual has with books, magazines, and other literature, contacts with other people and groups, and education; (2) aesthetic environment includes natural surroundings such as trees, flowers, and birds as well as various forms of art and artistic expression; (3) economic environment includes all factors which contribute to material welfare—basically, shelter, food, and clothing—all of which determine to some extent an individual's capacity to benefit from his total environment. The general or miscellaneous factor contains items which are independent of the other factors, but which nevertheless contribute to the total score of over-all socio-economic status.

Construction

The scale was constructed after a careful review of relevant scientific literature. Each item was subjected to the criticism of a group of 14 competent judges. First administration of an experimental form of the scale was made on 1300 Gary, Indiana, high-school seniors. Intercorrelations were computed between all items and an intensive statistical analysis followed. Altogether, 1225 intercorrelations were used in performing a profile analysis which was later validated with a partial factor analysis. As a result of this analysis, three aspects of environment were found to be measured by the scale, average intercorrelation among these three clusters of items being .61 when corrected for attenuation. The fourth section is a miscellaneous one which adds reliability to the scale and also includes a meaningful cluster of organization membership items which do not correlate highly with the remainder of the scale.

Two methods of investigating item validity were utilized—first, the upper and lower 27 per cent method [1] and second, a check on the ability of each item to discriminate between six sociological areas in a large American city.

Validity

In addition to determining item validity the scale was further validated by teachers visiting the homes of pupils and filling out the scale by interviewing the parent. The teachers did not know the scores obtained from measuring the pupils in the classroom. The correlation between home-call scores and group administration scores was .915 ± .01. This coefficient is an underestimate in that it is not corrected for either restricted range or attentuation in the criterion (home-call) scores.

Reliability

Reliability of the scale was determined in three ways. First, the Kuder-Richardson *t* formula [4] yielded a coefficient of .91 ± .01, second, the scores of twenty-six pairs of twins and siblings yielded a coefficient of .84 ± .02 and third, a split-half reliability of a random sample of 217 papers yielded a coefficient of .89 ± .01.

Reliabilities (split-half Spearman-Brown) for the four sections of the scale are as follows: Cultural .670, economic .675, aesthetic .682, and miscellaneous .670. Reliability of the mean magazine cultural score [3] for 29 pairs of twins and siblings was .82 ± .04.

The directions for administration are self-explanatory. There is no time limit but about 90 per cent of eighth grade pupils in 42 American cities finished in 35 minutes.

The scale may be scored by hand or by machine.

The scale was standardized on 16,455 eighth grade pupils in 42 cities in 28 states. Norms for the four different parts and for the total are given in percentile and standard score equivalents.[5]

The scale is published by Science Research Associates, 1700 Prairie Avenue, Chicago, Illinois.

References:

1. Arnold, J. N. Nomograph for determining validity of test items. *Journal of Educational Psychology*, 1935, 26, 151–153.

2. Kerr, W. A. The measurement of home environment and its relationship with other variables, *Studies in Attitudes, Series V, Studies in Higher Education XLV, Bulletin of Purdue University,* June, 1942.

3. ────── and Remmers, H. H. The cultural value of 100 representative American magazines, *School and Society,* 1941, 55, 476–480.

4. Kuder, G. F. and Richardson, M. W. The theory of estimation of test reliability. *Psychometrika,* 1937, 2, 151–160.

5. Remmers, H. H. and Kerr, W. A. Home environment in American cities, *American Journal of Sociology,* July, 1945.

H. H. R.

SOCIOLOGY TEST, BLACK-SCHRAMMEL

General Statement

The Black-Schrammel Sociology Test was constructed for use as an achievement test in high school and junior college classes pursuing introductory courses in this field. The test covers such problems as customs, folkways, mores, traditions, and social problems in education; immigration; poverty; government; religion; marriage; and divorce.

The test items were selected from the basic content of several leading textbooks which cover this field. All items were subjected to a careful checking by subject matter and test construction specialists.

For determining the reliability of the test, the papers of sixty-two junior college students were used. Scores on the odd-numbered items were paired with those on the even-numbered items, correlated, and extended by the Brown-Spearman formula. By this method a reliability coefficient of .81 ± .03 was obtained.

Authors and Publisher

The authors of the test are William A. Black, State Supervisor of Junior Colleges, Olympia, Washington, and H. E. Schrammel, Head, Department of Psychology and Director, Bureau of Educational Measurements, Kansas State Teachers College. The Publisher is the Bureau of Educational Measurements, Teachers College, Emporia, Kansas.

Giving, Scoring, and Interpreting

This test is easily administered. The working time limit is 40 minutes. There are two equivalent forms available. Scoring is accomplished by use of a printed objective key. The scores are interpreted by use of reliable percentile norms.

H. E. S.

SOCIAL WORK, APTITUDE FOR. Due to the historical development of social work, the terminology of the profession has had many meanings, and since former practices and ideologies have survived alongside more modern ones and the same terminology used for both, there is much general confusion today. In spite of this confusion in terms, however, social work has emerged as a profession with a body of knowledge and techniques of its own.

There are six general areas in which social work practice is carried on today—social case work, social group work, social research, social welfare planning (or community organization), social welfare administration, and social action. These areas of practice may be carried on in various settings such as homes, hospitals and clinics, custodial institutions, courts, schools, labor organizations, industry, etc., and may be under various auspices such as public and private social agencies, churches, fraternal organizations, business concerns, labor unions, etc.

Social work aims toward a satisfactory adjustment between men and their environment. This involves not only the capacity of the individual to adjust to his environment but also "implies the attainment of a social and economic structure which will afford every individual opportunity for the maximum development of which he is capable." [6] Basic, therefore, to all social work is social case work which consists "of those processes which develop personality through adjustments consciously effected, individual by individual, between men and their social environment." [4] Social case work is a relationship rather than a technique, wherein the case worker, trained in the use of the professional self, employs her knowledge of the human personality to help the individual mobilize his own resources to cope more adequately with his environment to the end that he can live a more adequate and satisfying life. Interest in people for their own sake, a warm, out-going personality, sufficient objectivity to see others' points of view and to understand their feelings, and enough respect for personality to leave each individual free to determine his own life goals are the first requirements of a social worker. To these must be added knowledge of human nature and of social institutions and understanding of the interaction between the two under which individuals must live and grow.

Social group work deals primarily with individuals in their group relationships. It "is a method of personality development in which the group itself is utilized as the chief tool," [5] the interaction of one personality upon another being guided by the leader in a way that will make for the fullest possible development of each individual in the group. The term "group work" usually applies to most of the activities carried on by settlement houses, community centers, character-building agencies such as the Y's, Scouts, 4-H Clubs, etc., and to rapidly expanding "group therapy" activities sponsored by institutions, clinics and case work agencies.

In addition to knowledge of the arts and crafts, of the various cultural backgrounds, and of program planning for various age and interest groups, the group worker needs an understanding of the human personality in its social relationships, of the interaction between individuals in a group, and ways in which those interactions may be modified and utilized in furthering the social adjustment of the individual.

Social planning (or community organization) involves the principles of case work and group work but in a much broader setting. Here the emphasis is upon intergroup processes with social betterment as the aim. While social planning is to some extent a part of all social work activity, it is for the most part carried on by welfare federations, coordinating councils and similar organizations. The social worker responsible for social planning needs not only understanding of the human personality, of social institutions, of group interactions, etc., but in addition he needs special skills in bringing together various interests in the community, and in molding those interests into a common purpose eventuating in social action.

In attaining a social and economic structure which will afford every individual maximum opportunity for development, the social worker must work toward the reshaping of social and economic institutions which are failing to fulfill their functions and the creating of special services for groups of individuals whose needs are not being met. The achievement of these goals involves social action. The four steps in social action cover fact finding (or social research), interpretation of need, the mobilizing of public opinion and stimulation of legislative or other formalized action.

Capable leadership is the first requirement for social action. Such leadership should be flexible, courageous, informed as to goals and processes, with a keen sense of strategy and timing.

The basis for social planning and the development of new philosophies and skills in case work and group work is social research. The research person needs not only considerable education and experience in social work but in addition he needs skills in methods of research and the use of statistics. While all social workers are continually in touch with social data, the primary function of the research person is the bringing together and the analysis of facts. All types of social agencies, public and private, engage in research, and many of the larger agencies such as councils of social agencies and state departments of public welfare have permanent research departments.

Social administration in the executive or managerial sense involves "the determination and clarification of funtion; the formulation of policies and procedures; the delegation of authority; the selection, supervision, and training of staff; and the mobilization and organization of all available and appropriate resources to the end that the purposes of the agency may be fulfilled." [3] The administrator should combine a technical knowledge of social work with a mastery of generic administrative skills. To do this, he should have first learned through study and practice the basic knowledge and skills of social work, and should then add to these the additional knowledge and skills pertaining to administration.

Preparation for social work consists first of a broad background in the social subjects—economics, sociology, political science, biology, history, psychology, literature—as a basis for the more specialized professional training. More and more colleges and universities, desiring to make their contribution to the training of social workers, but unable for various reasons to offer training on the professional level, are setting up pre-professional curricula approved by the American Association of Schools of Social Work.

At the present time, there are 47 graduate schools of social work accredited by the A.A.S.S.W. offering professional training, 7 of which offer only the first year of the regular two-year course leading to a master's degree in social work.

Qualifying for employment is done in various ways at this stage of the development of professional social work. Positions under public auspices are usually obtained through civil service examination, both assembled and unassembled. State and county residence are usually required for minor positions while top positions are open to persons outside the state. Ratings are based upon written tests of the nature of intelligence tests coupled with tests of knowledge of specific programs, personal evaluations of applicants by former employers obtained through letters of reference, and oral interviews by the examiners. Qualifications for positions in private agencies are based upon education and training, past performance and personal adjustment as indicated by references, and membership in professional organizations of which there are three: American Association of Social Workers, American Association of Medical Social Workers, and American Association of Psychiatric Social Workers.

Satisfactory methods of determining fitness for social work and competence in practice have not yet been devised but various groups of professional social workers, The United States Civil Service Commission, state merit systems and others are giving considerable thought to the development of such tests with the ultimate aim of nationwide registration and certification of social workers. In the meantime the professional schools of social work are counseling prospective students, where possible before enrollment in the pre-professional curricula but in every instance before acceptance in the graduate schools, in an effort to encourage those individuals who are emotionally and intellectually suited to social work to enter the profession and to redirect to other fields those persons whose qualifications seem to lie in other directions.

References:

1. Brown, E. L. *Social work as a profession.* New York: Russell Sage Foundation, 1942.
2. Fink, A. E. *The field of social work.* New York: Henry Holt and Co., 1942.
3. Mayo, L. W. Administration of social agencies. *Social work yearbook.* New York: Russell Sage Foundation, 1945, p. 15.
4. Richmond, M. *What is social case work?* New York: Russell Sage Foundation, 1922, p. 98.
5. Sullivan, D. F. *Social group work. Social work yearbook.* New York: Russell Sage Foundation, 1945, p. 421.
6. Towle, C. Social case work. *Social work yearbook.* New York: Russell Sage Foundation, 1945, p. 415.

H. H. W.

SPASTICS: See Speech Defectives.

SPEECH DEFECTIVES.   The purpose of this vocational study in the field of speech pathology is to clarify some of the outstanding problems which have always been with us, but which are particularly timely now, due to the emphasis which is being placed upon the rehabilitation of veterans.

Following World War II there are many veterans returning from military service who need not only physical and vocational aid, but who are faced with serious problems of psychic readjustments such as have never before faced veterans of any wars in history. For those whose difficulty includes also an organic or functional disorder of speech, it may be necessary to seek an entirely new field of vocational interest. To make this difficult adjustment it will require not only all of the determination and energy of the veteran himself, but much skill, patience, and exploration on the part of vocational counselors to enable the ex-service man to find his place in the scheme of things, after his return from military service.

Since the vocational problem of the speech-defective in civilian life is not materially different from that facing the returned soldier with a similar defect, it seems desirable to review briefly the main types of speech defects which are found in various hospitals, university clinics, and schools or privately operated speech clinics, to find the relationships which exist between them, and to prescribe certain remedies. Much constructive help in this direction will be needed for the next few years, and it should prove useful and economical of time for both counselor and service man if this information is readily available.

We shall consider only those defects which appear most frequently in the adult speech clinic and those which may be expected to occur following World War II. Many of them are the result of diseases of the central nervous system; some were present at birth, others have been acquired in civilian life or in military service, and some have persevered since infancy or childhood. These may have figured in the poor adjustment of the individual.

Abridged Classification of Disorders of Speech

I. DYSARTHRIA

Defects of speech due to lesions of the central nervous system.

Main types:

a. Anarthria—Inarticulateness.
b. Bradyarthria—labored speech (as in spastics).
c. Mogiarthria—ataxic speech (as in locomotor ataxia and in some cases following encephalitis).

II. DYSLALIA

Main types:

a. Agitolalia—cluttered speech (excessively rapid).
b. Alalia—mutism.
    a. Dysaudia or speech of the deaf.
    b. Delayed speech in childhood.
    c. Physiologic mutism.
c. Barbaralalia—foreign dialect.
d. Idiolalia—invented language.
e. Paralalia—lisping.
f. Uraniscolalia—cleft-palate speech.

III. DYSPHASIA

Impairment in the power of expression by speech, writing, signs, or of comprehending spoken or written language.[1]

Main types:
a. Alexia or word blindness.
b. Auditory aphasia; word deafness.
c. Motor aphasia.
d. Nominal aphasia.
e. Semantic aphasia.
f. Agraphia; loss of written language.
g. Mixed aphasia.
h. Amnesia—Broca's; inability to recall spoken words.
i. Amnesia—Verbal; inability to call words to mind.

IV. DYSPHEMIA

Nervous speech disorders.

Main types:
a. Aphemia—dumbness
  1. hysterical attack or illness.
  2. due to fright or intense anger.
  3. voluntary muteness.
  4. spasmodic or transient dumbness.
b. Paraphemia—neurotic lisping.
c. Tachyphemia—excessively rapid, tense speech.
d. Spasmophemia—stuttering; stammering.

V. DYSPHONIA.

Defects of voice.

Main types:
a. Aphonia; complete loss of voice.
b. Transitory loss of voice, as in fear, anger, pain.
c. Trachyphonia—hoarse voice.
d. Metallophonia—metallic voice.
e. Hypophonia—whispered speech.
f. Microphonia—weak voice.
g. Pneumaphonia—weak voice .
h. Rhinophonia—nasal voice.
i. Tremophonia—tremulous voice.
j. Dysphonia—due to injury to vocal cords, or to the laryngeal muscles or cartilages.
k. Spasmodic Aphonia.

Dyslalia (II) includes some of the speech defects of infancy and early childhood, but its persistence into adult life is often found, and with the advancing maturity of the individual the recognition of such a defect and the knowledge of its effect upon his career, may be a cause of serious maladjustment, loss of self-confidence, and gradual withdrawal from social activities. Men are found in the army, who have been fairly successful in civilian life, in spite of marked dyslalia, but in the army the persistence of "baby-talk," so called—or mutilated, inaccurate speech due to poor speech habits in infancy, poor environment or poor auditory perception, has actually led to neuroses necessitating removal from certain types of military duty and transferral to other branches of the services where the speech defect would not be embarrassing or especially noticeable to a man's companions.

Dysarthria

Dysarthria (I) or speech in which there exists some lesion in the brain or spinal cord, is fairly common in the adult speech clinic. Paralytic strokes, various forms of paralysis involving the speech mechanism, through the peripheral or central nervous system often lead to seriously impaired utterance. Spastic speech is an example of dysarthria in which the muscles, not only of face and neck, but also of the limbs, with impaired gait, often cause the layman to misjudge such a person and to think him subnormal in intelligence. This is a serious error in most instances, as the spastic is often very intelligent, but lacks the muscular ability to express himself normally, due to neuro-muscular involvement, as a result of birth paralysis. His spasticity may have come about later in life, due to infantile paralysis or to cerebro-spinal meningitis, or to encephalitis.

The autobiography of Earl Carlson is illuminating on this point.[1] He mentions his embarrassment at being unable to eat alone in public until he was eighteen or nineteen years old, as he could not relax before strangers.

Due to misunderstanding on the part of family and friends, he was deprived of simple recreation and found school work terrifying in the large city schools, but found himself at ease in a small sectarian academy. Becoming interested in science, he turned to electricity, experimenting with bells, wires, buttons and batteries until, at the age of fifteen, he was able to wire a building. His ability to secure a license from an electrical company after passing the necessary tests, was one of the early vocational successes which helped to determine his career. He gained more self-confidence on this job than on anything he had done previously, and saved money, which he used to further his college training.

He learned to operate a car, and showed ingenuity in starting a car without a key. His inventiveness and unswerving determination to continue his formal education resulted in his attending a small college, his success there being reflected in his good grades. Later he attended the University of Minnesota, and persisted in spite of numerous discouragements and failures, until he obtained his degree. With the aid of friends he obtained a position as librarian in one of the Eastern universities and after a severe struggle to convince his instructors of his ability to do the work despite his handicap, he at length entered medical college. Upon graduation he attained the ambition of his lifetime, in establishing a school for spastics and other similarly handicapped young people. He was also made a member of the Neurological Institute at the New York Medical Center. The story of his life is one of the most inspiring ever written by a handicapped individual, and shows in countless ways the effect of education and motor training. Carlson believes that motor representation of ideas is an important factor in the education of the handicapped, and his conviction is shown in the type and extent of motor-sensory training given to the pupils in his school.

Dyslalia is a less serious speech defect than dysarthria as in this type of defect the central nervous system is not involved. However, it may lead to more serious difficulty than is generally believed. Many children are delayed in learning to talk until long past the time when the natural tendency to express oneself is usually apparent. Because of the late period at which speech begins, such a child may continue to mutilate words, express himself in incoherent or almost unintelligible speech; this leads to misunderstanding, often to ridicule by other children, and the individual's personality is warped at the very outset. The writer has trained adult men whose speech defect, originating in childhood, has persisted throughout life. Even though they were able to make a fair economic adjustment in civilian life, they took refuge in a neurosis, when faced with the necessity of conversing daily with their buddies in military service, or having to give orders, or to verbalize in other ways in a group situation.

Lisping and cleft-palate speech are two types of Dyslalia which are easily recognizable, the former frequently having no organic cause, while the latter is a form of nasality due to a cleft or perforation in the hard or soft palate, allowing air to escape in an unnatural way. This often makes the individual self-conscious and unsocial. It is important to him and to his family that the organic basis of his difficulty should be early recognized, the cleft repaired and speech training instituted as soon as possible, in order to clear up this excessive nasality, and to enable the patient to speak freely and easily, and without fear of ridicule, or misunderstanding.

Dysphasia will undoubtedly become increasingly common, following World War II, because of modern methods of warfare, larger injuries sustained and new types not known in previous wars. Speech defects of the types described, as well as Dysphonia or voice defects were described in the literature following World War I, and throw some light upon what we may expect in such cases. It is impossible to furnish detailed data regarding the present status of speech defectives in World War II, due to its recency, and because it is the custom of the government to restrict the use of such data until after the official publication of its history by the War Department.

In his compilation of case histories following World War I, Southard [5] mentions many cases of hysterical aphonia, aphasia, word-deafness or word-blindness, following intensive bombardments, and although we are still too near to the recent conflict to be able to use such information as has been gained from the war, in the field of speech handicaps incident to warfare much is being done in various centers in speech rehabilitation. The work for the deafened veteran has been under way for many months, through centers in various parts of the country. An example is found in the work for the deafened veteran at Deshon State Hospital, Pennsylvania. The work for other types of speech defectives is somewhat more scattered, depending as it does upon the psychological and speech-pathological training of army-navy personnel. We know something of what Germany has done in speech clinical service, because of writings which have been published in various magazines in that country during the recent war. Articles are appearing in various American journals which touch upon some of the problems, but as yet the bulk of this material is not available, because of the war situation. During World War I, Eder, of the British Army, reported that most of the cases in the Gallipoli campaign came under the head of hysteria, anxiety neuroses and psychasthenia. Symptoms and various conditions described by him include anaesthesias, paralyses, asphasia, aphonia, stuttering, hysterical deafness and blindness, tics, tremors, respiratory and cardiac disturbances. The therapy most successfully used was suggestion and hypnosis. The inclusion of a well trained and efficient group of vocational counselors or advisors available during and following the recent war, will enable veterans to receive a more thorough check-up, and to find without delay better opportunities, better training and greater personal satisfaction than could possibly be the case, under the former system. The large number of returning veterans, the fact that the war has engaged men from the east and from the west, as well as from the central region of the country, has scattered those centers where work may be found. This has made information more difficult for the individual to obtain, because of the distance and the time involved in seeking personal service unaided.

Yealland,[8] a British physician, describing cases which came to his attention during the first World War, found the use of electro-therapy beneficial to many patients, especially in cases of hysterical seizures, aphonia and stuttering. Kretschmer attributed the disinte-gration of the speech function to nervous stress and strain which caused man to revert to more primitive types of behavior, the cortex giving way to thalamic control and emotions governing the intel-lect. Exhaustion and prolonged stress and strain often led to actual pain symptoms and to neurasthenia, especially in officers. In other men the psychic symptoms of great restlessness, anxiety, mental tension and sleeplessness led to psychasthenic reactions in the sufferer.

Among the methods of treatment employed were rest, relaxa-tion, recreation, physical therapy, occupational therapy, psycho-therapy through suggestion and counseling, nutrition and massage. In World War II, new methods have been added, such as number and types of new occupational courses, vocational training, change of military location, and vocational service which includes not only the service man himself, but which undertakes counseling as a serv-ice for an entire family if desired—at least until such time as the veteran is satisfactorily located or readjusted to civilian life and to his family. Such aid should have far more satisfactory conse-quences than any previous rehabilitation program ever undertaken.

Menninger has discussed the types of personalities most liable to be found among the psycho-neurotics and psychotics in the adult psychiatric clinic. As these are practically all to be found in any adult speech clinic, in the course of time, it would be useful to review them.[2]

Crippled personalities as in organic disease.
Stupid personalities as of the hypophrenic type.
Lonely personalities of the isolation type.
Queer personalities of the schizoid type.

Moody personalities of the cycloid type.
Frustrated personalities of the neurotic type.
Perverse personalities of the antisocial type.

Many of these persons cannot accept defeat and take refuge in fantasy or in unreality, eventually terminating in a psychosis, or they become confirmed alcoholics or drug addicts. Such patients eventually must be treated in our State or government hospitals. Milder cases of those who remain in touch with essential realities, may become hysterics, psychasthenics or neurasthenics, but they are much more hopeful from the standpoint of rehabilitation, and it is with many of this type that our speech clinics have had to deal in the past. We should be prepared to treat them on a more extensive scale now and in the future.

According to Sadler, rehabilitation in these and similar cases must include the following mental hygiene principles, for success: [4]

1. The ability to face reality honestly and without fear.
2. Cultivation of social outlets.
3. Recognition of and redirection of one's neurotic tendencies into safe channels.
4. Recognition of the possibility of mental disorder and learning how to deal with it.
5. Assuming that the unhappy are always wrong.

He stresses the following points as necessary for rehabilitation:

Work. It is less important what it is than that one works at something which one can do.

Re-education. Facing one's problems and learning to manage them.

Mental Hygiene and active therapy.

Psychoanalysis.

These are the methods often used by the staffs in charge of speech clinical patients, as not only must the medico-physical aspects be included, but also psycho-therapy under direction of the psychiatrist, and educational work undertaken by trained workers including the occupational therapist, as well as the speech therapist.

Cases of advanced speech defects are not usually accepted for service, but many draft boards have allowed men to be drafted, evidently through the unfamiliarity of board members with such defects. Those who have qualified for service have often become liabilities; others have justified the appointment by rendering a high quality of service despite the handicap. Many who never stuttered before the war, are returning with severe impediments, due to war-shock as well as to physical injuries sustained in the discharge of duty.

Following the last war the four main avenues for preparing the disabled for useful employment were:

1. By means of physical rehabilitation.
2. By mental catharsis, in case of a psychosis or psychoneurosis.
3. By vocational counseling and advisement.
4. By helping the veteran to become established in business or occupation.

Many stutterers who have been obliged to give up certain branches in order to assume other types of military service, have been fitted into the plans more rapidly and more easily during this war, because of the fact of occupational counseling, possibility of transfer, and special aptitude tests which further aid in settling their adjustment problems.

Light has been thrown on the adjustment of the spastic and other orthopaedic patients by a recent survey of patients enrolled in the Speech Clinic of the Orthopaedic Hospital at Los Angeles, during the years 1933–42. Many cases of excellent vocational adjustment were discovered. The number of cases of former patients who had not become at least partially self-supporting in adulthood, was surprisingly small. Fifty-three Speech Clinic patients were studied intensively, representing those patients treated during an eight year period, and who returned for a re-check during the year 1942. It was found that most of the parents of these patients came from Group III on Barr's Occupational Rating Scale; that is, the Skilled Worker Group. The next largest number came from the semi-skilled and the unskilled labor groups or Group IV and V on Barr's Scale. Very few of the patients came from Occupational Groups I and II, professional and executive backgrounds. Most of the referrals came from social agencies, physicians, nurses or friends, rather than from parents or patients themselves.

In nine cases where retests on the Revised Stanford Binet were given, the I.Q. remained constant in a few cases, there was deterioration in one, while the majority showed an advance of from five to thirty percent. In one case the I.Q. advanced from 119 to 150 within five years, and in another from 92 to 142 within a similar period.

Educational status ranged from no schooling at all to graduate work of the university level, although there were none who had taken advanced degrees. The majority were making normal school progress, despite their handicaps. The median grade placement was Grade 7, which is rather surprising for handicapped individuals, as it assumes an average chronological age of 13 years, and an educational age of thirteen. Four per cent of the number attained college status, and compared favorably with non-handicapped students in their educational progress.

Among special talents found in this group, in order of frequency were:

> Drawing and reading.
> Strong mechanical interests.
> Piano playing and musical knowledge.

Less frequently were listed interest in arts and crafts, domestic science, music appreciation and radio, and training in singing. They were definitely not interested in arithmetic, manual training, engineering, library work, nursing, playing musical instruments other than piano; physics, social studies, spelling or writing.

Detailed questionnaires and personal interviews by members of the staff, especially in the Social Service Department, as well as by the State Department for Rehabilitation of Handicapped Adults, aided greatly in the vocational guidance of many of the older patients, upon completion of their hospital treatment.

From the standpoint of mental hygiene, a study of the comments of the hospital psychiatrist on the selected cases showed that about twenty-five per cent were well adjusted, with good personalities in adult life. Four to ten per cent had exhibited traits of a less fortunate type such as temper tantrums, stubbornness, emotional immaturity, hyper-emotionality, hyper-excitability, extreme self-consciousness, undue submissiveness, often traceable to a poor environment in school or home. The fact that about one-fourth have made a very good adjustment, is indicative of the possibility of rehabilitation for the handicapped individual. Dysarthria, dyslalia and dysphemia (especially stuttering) were the chief speech defects in this group.

One boy in this group had presented rather an unfavorable history at the outset, and was stuttering badly, partly because of his fear of an alcoholic father. A few years later, when the parents had been divorced, this lad's I.Q. took a surprising turn, mounting from 92 to 142 within a period of approximately five years. He was living with his mother, attending high school and making a number of good social contacts at last report.

The writer personally spent the better part of three forenoons with one spastic patient (at the Employment Agency established by the State during the depression). This young man was an expert radio worker, drove a car, was quite an expert in toy making, and could have obtained work with a local toy-concern. He also had a social security card and number. However, it was impossible to convince the authorities that the boy was worth the expenditure of government funds to help to establish him at a certain toy center, and the project was given up. This youth then proved to himself and to his critics his real worth by securing a job in a grocery store where he successfully waited on customers, marketed some of the supplies from downtown wholesale centers, drove his car, and eventually married. His wife was also slightly handicapped, but possessed a marketable musical talent, so that together they have earned an excellent income for the past two years.

The adult handicapped youth is often a great surprise to his parents. From a rather helpless, dependent state, he often emerges and in some cases, like that of a boy called Tim, returns the help given by the parents one-hundred-fold. When Tim's father's health failed, during the depression of 1930–1937, the family was in sore straits, and had it not been for Tim's wages, they would have been unable to keep up the payments on their home and might have lost the only tangible security they had acquired during their working years. Tim's speech defect was a minor one, and did not detract from a winsome, fairly aggressive personality, which enabled him to make friends readily, and to succeed in his vocation, as well as to marry the girl of his choice.

Stutterers and those with similar speech defects may obtain aid by applying to the American Speech Correction Association, through its secretary, D. W. Morris, Ohio State University, to obtain competent teachers in the veteran's own state. For vocal difficulties, veterans may require the services of medical specialists. Clinical centers may be located through the State's Rehabilitation Service.

The American Speech Correction Association has established contacts with the Veterans' Administration and the Vocational Rehabilitation authorities, and the extent to which the speech-defective veteran is judged to be eligible for rehabilitation is indicated by the following quotation from a letter from one of these organizations to the Coordinator for wartime services, of our Speech Association— Dr. Herbert-Koepp Baker.

"It is our feeling that when it can be established that a speech defect operates in a significant way to handicap a veteran either in his vocational training or on the job, such a speech defect constitutes a legal condition for re-education attention by a specialist in this field."

Typical Case Material

Jane, a young woman, found it difficult to make her way in the world because of her stuttering. Being ambitious and desiring greater success, she undertook to correct her stuttering with a teacher's assistance. After a year's work she became employed in the business office of one of our largest movie industries in Hollywood.

Helen had such a severe lisp that she was unable to carry major speaking rôles in high school plays. This was such a disappointment that she decided to do something about her speech. She had set her heart upon a stage career, and so consulted a speech clinician. Perseverance and hard work soon overcame her speech defect. She is now a well known actress on Broadway.

Harry, a six-year old boy, had never learned to talk. A medical examination showed that he was in excellent health, and his mental tests revealed that he was far above average in intelligence. After studying the case, the logopaedist found that Harry had never felt it *necessary* to talk. Because the boy's mother had died when he was an infant, an aunt had become his foster-parent. She did not require the boy to ask for what he wanted. Instead he merely grunted or pointed at an object. Harry felt no need for articulate speech. Because of his superior mentality, he was leading his class in school within eight months' time, largely as a consequence of his speech training. Harry became an officer in the armed forces during the recent war.

Max was obliged to leave high school in his senior year, due to some maladjustment and to his severe stutter. He took a temporary job requiring early rising and commuting from the suburbs in the city. He was often late, and eventually lost his job, became disappointed, grouchy and an unhappy lad, much misunderstood by his family. At the time when he consulted the speech teacher, he was contemplating suicide. That summer the boy worked unceasingly in a university speech clinic, audited economics classes, and in the fall entered a boy's preparatory school, which enabled him to continue his speech correction. Two years later he was accepted by four outstanding universities. He chose Harvard, and at the end of one year, was in the upper fourth of a large class of college men. Due to excellence in his work he was enabled to spend his junior year abroad, and later graduated with honors. He entered the banking field, married the girl of his choice, and could scarcely ever be identified as a former stutterer by anyone unacquainted with his history. It took fully two years of constant effort and alertness to master the difficulty in this case, and his is a good example of the time element usually necessary for successfully coping with adult stuttering. Even then it may be unsuccessful, if too firmly ingrained and if the person has lost flexibility of mind and purpose. The time element varies with the nature of the case, and pupils respond differently to different methods of instruction and to different teachers.

We should avail ourselves of every possible legitimate aid in order to clear up neurotic speech difficulties as soon as possible, as they are but the outward manifestations of a deep underlying cause which is often remediable. A speech "sign" or symptom is often the outward manifestation of a deep-seated emotional conflict or a fear or phobia so strong as to unfit a person for a useful life, until the causal factors are analyzed, understood by the patient himself, and his psychic disturbance has been relieved by active therapy. This may require the services of the psychiatrist. It may be a matter best handled by the psychologist, or it may be completely relieved by speech correction in the hands of clinically trained personnel. It may require the service and the cooperation of all three. In any case, it often yields large dividends to the patient, and rehabilitates him for civilian, economic life.

References:

1. Carlson, E. *Born that way.*
2. Menninger, K. *The human mind.* New York: F. Crofts and Co., 1931.
3. Ogilvie, M. *Terminology and definitions of speech defects.* New York: Bureau of Publications, Teachers College, Columbia University: 1942.
4. Sadler, W. S. *Psychiatric educational work.* St. Louis: American Psychiatric Association, 1936.
5. Southard, E. H. *Shell shock and neuropsychiatry.* 1919.
6. Stinchfield-Robbins and Russel. *Dictionary of terms dealing with disorders of speech.* Boston: American Speech Correction Association, 1931. (Revision in press)
7. Thomson-Fatherson. *Speech bibliography.*
8. Yealland, L. R. *Hysterical disorders of warfare.* London: 1918.

The author wishes to express her appreciation to the following persons for reading and offering suggestions in regard to this article: Major Arthur R. Casey, Jr., Chief, Neuropsychiatric Section ASG Regional Hospital, Pasadena, California; Hollis P. Allen, formerly Major, U. S. Army Air Forces and now Veterans' Counselor and Professor of Education, Claremont College, California. She also wishes to acknowledge the case history notes supplied by Dr. Mary C. Longerich, Speech Pathologist, Los Angeles, California.

S. S. H.

STANDARDIZATION. Standardization of a test, upon completion of the selection, experimental try-out, validation and scaling of the items to be included, has two major aspects, as follows:

1. establishment of uniform procedures for administering and scoring the test;
2. development of appropriate norms.

The first of these steps is far more easily accomplished than the second. By means of further experimental try-out, tentative instructions to subjects are revised so as to eliminate ambiguity, time limits are established, and alternative scoring methods explored. The procedures finally determined upon are embodied in the manual of directions to accompany the test.

The development of appropriate norms requires the application of the test, in its final form, to large numbers of individuals who are truly representative of the group for which the test is designed. Since norms provide the frame of reference against which individual scores on the test are to be evaluated, it is essential that the standardizing sample (i.e. the population used in deriving the norms) be large enough to yield stable means or other constants, and possess characteristics approximating in range and quality those of the general population to whom the test is subsequently to be applied. Securing samples of adequate size does not pose as great a problem as does random selection of representative cases. It might seem at first glance, for example, that standardization of a test of mental ability for ages 6 to 14 might be readily accomplished by examining sufficient numbers of elementary school students of each sex and age. Standardization on the elementary school population alone, however, would exclude individuals within the age range whose mental ability is so low that they are not in school and those bright 12, 13, and 14 year olds who have gone on to high school. The sample must, therefore, be extended to include those extremes. Furthermore, in selecting the sample, care must be taken to include scholastically and economically "good," "average" and "low" schools in sufficient proportions.

The characteristics which must be taken into consideration to assure representative sampling are those which are related to the trait or ability being measured and, therefore, vary for different kinds of tests. In standardizing tests of intelligence, for example, factors such as age, education, occupational and economic status, sex, and race should be taken into account, for they are known to influence intelligence test results. Ideally, separate norms should be derived for each category of these factors as, for example, for various degrees of educational achievement, for males and females, whites and negroes, various age levels, etc. Practically, however, this is often not feasible in regard to certain characteristics; in such cases, the best the test-maker can do is to select his standardizing group so that the general level or character of the group as a whole approximates that of the population for whom the test is designed.

The size of standardizing samples necessary to produce reliable norms is readily determined by means of appropriate statistical formulas; the characteristics which must be taken into account to assure representativeness, however, must be determined by the test-maker on the basis of his psychological knowledge and judgment. The user of standardized tests will do well, therefore, to consider carefully the quality of the standardization and the adequacy of the test norms when using individual scores as data on which to base vocational or other decisions.

Reference:

1. Wechsler, D. *The measurement of adult intelligence.* Baltimore: Williams and Wilkins, 1944.

I. C.

STANDARD SCORES. It is frequently necessary to compare scores obtained by an individual on two quite different types of measures. Suppose, for example, one wishes to know an individual's relative ability in mathematics and English as measured by two achievement tests; the two raw scores are, say, 85 and 126 respectively. The two scores obviously cannot be directly compared, since they are probably not based on similar units. The mathematics test might be composed of 100 free-answer questions of varying degrees of difficulty, while the English test might be composed of 200 items of various types which tend to be relatively easy.

Knowing that one of the scores obtained by the individual is above average and the other is below average does not help much. We need also to know *how much* below and above the averages are the two scores. The distance of each score above or below its mean can be defined, using the standard deviation of the distribution of scores as the unit. The deviation of a raw score from the mean of its distribution, expressed as a multiple of the standard deviation of that distribution, is the *standard score* or *z-score*.

If X is the raw score, M is the mean of the distribution and σ is the standard deviation of the distribution, then the computation of the z-score is shown by the formula

$$z = \frac{X - M}{\sigma}$$

Such a distribution of standard scores will have a mean of 0 and a standard deviation of 1. Most of the scores will fall between —3 and +3, if the distribution is normal (or approximately normal).

Suppose the mean of the mathematics test in our example is 80 and its standard deviation is 10; then the individual's standard score is

$$\frac{85 - 80}{10} = \frac{5}{10} = .5$$

If the mean and standard deviation of the English test are respectively 151 and 25, the standard score in English would be

$$\frac{126 - 151}{25} = \frac{-25}{25} = -1.0$$

The scores of .5 and —1.0 are comparable scores, and we are now justified in concluding that the person is more able in mathematics than in English, as measured by these two achievement tests. We are also able to state that the difference in ability is fairly large, amounting to 1.5 σ.

Standard scores have the disadvantages of involving negative numbers and the use of decimal points. These disadvantages may be avoided through the use of the device known as the T-score. The T-score is obtained simply by multiplying the z score by 10 (to eliminate the decimal) and adding 50 (to avoid negative values).

$$\text{T-score} = \frac{10\,(X - M)}{\sigma} + 50$$

A distribution of T-scores will have a mean of 50 and a standard deviation of 10. The T-scores will not ordinarily go below 20 or above 80.

The T-score on the mathematics test in our example is

$$\frac{10\,(85 - 80)}{10} + 50 = 55$$

and the T-score for the English test is

$$\frac{10\,(126 - 151)}{25} + 50 = 40$$

The values of 10 and 50 are of course purely arbitrary. By using other values, one could obtain distributions with a mean of 100 and a standard deviation of 20, a mean of 500 and a standard deviation of 100, or any other values desired.

In using standard scores for the purpose of making individual comparisons, it is important that two precautions be observed. First, *the distributions from which the two scores are obtained should be of similar shape.* If the two curves differ in the amount of "piling up" in the center of the distribution (kurtosis), the range from plus one to minus one standard deviation from the mean will include a larger proportion of the cases for one distribution than for the other, and hence the unit of the scales (the standard deviation) will differ from one to the other. Or if the two distributions differ in amount or in direction of skewness, the means will be placed differently with respect to the distributions, making the points of origin dissimilar; hence the standard scores will not be comparable.

Secondly, *the samples on which the distributions are based should be similar.* If in our example the mathematics test distribution had been obtained from high school freshmen and the English test from college freshmen, the comparison of the two scores would be meaningless.

As an alternative to the use of standard scores, percentile ranks are frequently employed. The percentile rank is a type of score based on the percentages of cases which lie below certain points in the distribution. Percentile scores have the advantage of being easily understood and explained. The principal disadvantage is that the units are unequal. Many more raw-score points occur between the first and the tenth percentiles than between the 46th and 55th percentiles, since few cases fall in the tail of the distribution as compared with the middle. Only in the middle range of the distribution are the units of a percentile scale relatively uniform in size. As a consequence of this inequality of units, percentile scores do not lend themselves to arithmetical manipulations. Standard scores, on the other hand, can be added and averaged without introducing errors due to inequality of units.

Norms for standardized tests are usually expressed in terms of standard scores or percentiles. When such a test is administered to a person who was not a member of the standardization group, one is strictly justified in using those norms only if that person is a member of the larger population of which the standardization group constituted a sample.

N. F.

STATE OCCUPATIONAL INFORMATION AND GUIDANCE SERVICES. The federal and state governments have cooperated in the development of effective programs of vocational

education in public schools since the passage of the Smith-Hughes Act in 1917. In 1937 the George-Deen Act provided for the further expansion of this program. It was clearly recognized by leaders in this field that the effectiveness of vocational education depended on the development of effective programs of guidance. Hence, provision was made in 1937 [5] for the use of federal funds for the employment of state supervisors of occupational information and guidance. The Occupational Information and Guidance Service in the United States Office of Education was established in order to give leadership to this movement.

By 1946, 32 states and territories had accepted the provisions of the federal acts and had established such services. These states and territories are: Arkansas, California, Colorado, Georgia, Hawaii, Illinois, Indiana, Iowa, Kansas, Kentucky, Louisiana, Maine, Maryland, Massachusetts, Michigan, Minnesota, Missouri, Montana, Nebraska, New Jersey, North Carolina, North Dakota, Ohio, Oregon, Pennsylvania, Puerto Rico, Rhode Island, South Dakota, Washington, West Virginia, Wisconsin, and Wyoming.

In addition, several states and the District of Columbia have established similar services but are supporting them entirely from state funds. These include: Connecticut, Delaware, Idaho, New Mexico, New York, Utah, Vermont, and Virginia.

The Program at the State Level

In most states the program comprehends the development of guidance services throughout the public school system and is not confined to the service of vocational schools or classes. As described by the Commissioner of Education [4] "The emphasis of the Service will be placed upon cooperation with state and local authorities in making occupational information and guidance really function in the education of boys and girls, youth and adults, in city and country. The Office of Education hopes thereby to render an important service in the further development of a movement which the laws of economics and sociology seem to indicate can no longer be denied as one of the essentials in any modern program of education."

The nature of the program envisioned at the state level is indicated by the following excerpts from a typical state plan: [1]

"Functions of the Service shall include the following:

"Studies and investigations:
    "Studying employment conditions in the State as a guide to occupational information.
    "Surveying the school facilities of the various communities

to ascertain the best means for establishing programs of occupational information and guidance suited to the individual communities.

"Preparing material for distribution to individuals, schools, and other agencies, describing successful studies, surveys and investigations in occupational information and guidance.

"Promoting in cooperation with other vocational services throughout the State, follow-up studies of graduates and former students in secondary schools and particularly all vocational schools and classes in order to reveal from the experience of such school-leavers better ways of serving the individuals in the schools and of adjusting school programs to individual needs, both in wage-earning and non-wage earning occupations.

"Promotion

"Consulting with school authorities, such as superintendents, principals, and supervisors, desiring information regarding establishment of programs of occupational information and guidance and aiding in the organization of such programs as have been approved by the local authorities.

"Making special studies of the needs of rural and semi-rural school units with relation to occupational information and guidance, with a view to promoting a program suitable to these needs. Investigating the possibilities of cooperative effort in providing personnel, equipment, and occupational information and guidance programs in rural school units which, because of small enrollments or other reasons, may be unable to provide complete programs for themselves.

"Supervision

"Supervising the occupational information and guidance programs in public schools of secondary grade in the State, with particular attention to vocational schools and classes, and programs for persons no longer enrolled in full-time schools.

"Studying means of improving the professional preparation of teacher-counselors or other persons who are designated in individual schools to carry on programs of guidance. Promoting means of in-service training of teachers and counselors, as well as the work of teacher-training institutions in guidance."

The Program in the School

Within the local school or school district the program involves six basic services:

1. *Individual inventory of each pupil*

   This necessitates the securing of information about each pupil which will portray his abilities, aptitudes, interests, needs, and other characteristics useful in appraising him as an individual. It requires further that this information be recorded from semester to semester in an orderly system which permits analysis of the evolving patterns.

2. *Occupational information*

   This information may be of an educational, vocational, or personal character. It must be local, regional, and national in scope. It must have background as well as recency in order to portray trends. It must be disseminated in regular classrooms and special groups, by audio-visual methods, by interview, and by primary exploration and investigation.

3. *Individual counseling*

   This function has been termed "the heart of guidance." It is the means by which the individual is given help in appraising himself on the one hand and his opportunities and restrictions on the other, and in developing plans of action which have maximum probabilities of success. It is a continuous and not merely a predictive function.

4. *Vocational training*

   The discovery of individual and community training needs and cooperation in the development of plans for meeting these needs is a part of the guidance program.

5. *Placement*

   This may involve placing an individual on a job, in a school, a class, an exploratory or vocational activity. It is a task not only of referral but also of induction and assistance in breaking in to the job. In carrying out this responsibility the school may well make full use of other agencies and services.

6. *Follow-up*

   The guidance service has as one of its major responsibilities the maintaining of contacts with those who leave school, whether they be graduates or drop-outs, for the purpose of rendering further service to them as well as forming a basis for the evaluation of educational services.

Appraisal

This program has tremendous possibilities for the improvement of public education. It has just made a beginning. State supervisors report some progress. More schools are providing counseling services. Appraisal techniques and cumulative records are improving. In-service training programs are increasing the competence of counselors. Many useful information materials have been developed. There is need for much improvement. Inadequate provision is made for valid diagnosis and treatment of intellectual and emotional problems which block learning and adjustment. Inter-relationships of guidance and curricular programs are not clearly defined and served. Many assigned to counseling duties are poorly selected and inadequately trained. Coordinated use of all school and community resources for guidance is seldom attained. Little effort is made to validate guidance methods by thorough, well-planned, and controlled follow-up studies of graduates and school leavers.

Leaders of these organized state programs give evidence of being aware of these deficiencies and research needs. Colleges, universities, special research agencies, and individual students are being encouraged to undertake evaluative and developmental work on specific problems. It is the purpose and the task of national and state supervisors of occupational information and guidance to stimulate and coordinate such research activities and to give leadership to implementing the findings.

References:

1. Commission for Vocational Education, California State Department of Education. *California state plan for vocational education.* Sacramento, September 1, 1945. mimeo.
2. Occupational Information and Guidance Service. *Occupational Information and Guidance Service.* 1941–1942. Washington: U. S. Office of Education.
3. *Proceedings of the Sixth National Conference of State Supervisors of Occupational Information and Guidance.* Voc. Div. Bulletin No. 235. Washington: U. S. Office of Education, 1945.
4. Studebaker, J. W. The new national Occupational Information and Guidance Service. Occupations, November, 1938, p. 104.
5. U. S. Office of Education, Division of Vocational Education. *Statement of policies for the administration of vocational education.* Bulletin No. 1. Washington: Government Printing Office, 1937.

H. B. McD.

STENOGRAPHIC ACHIEVEMENT TEST, TURSE-DUROST.

In constructing the Turse-Durost Stenographic Achievement Test, the authors had in mind four essential requirements. In the first place, the test must satisfy the criteria of validity, both from the point of view of the common sense interpretation of what the test measures and also from a statistical point of view. Secondly, the test may be used to measure shorthand, independent of typewriting ability, ability to space a letter properly, etc. The dictated material subsequently may be transcribed in the traditional way to provide a measure of typewriting, letter spacing, etc. Thirdly, the test must give proper emphasis to errors falling into three major categories; namely, errors involving language skill, errors caused by poor short-hand penmanship, and errors caused by lack of mastery of shorthand principles. Finally, the test had to be in a form to permit easy and rapid scoring by use of a strip key rather than the traditional laborious scoring of a verbatim transcript.

This test has been so constructed that it may be used with individuals in all stages of development and experience in shorthand beyond the point of initial experience in transcribing connected discourse. In a public school situation it is not recommended for use earlier than toward the end of the first year of instruction. It has great value as a terminal test for first-year students (or with business school students with equivalent training). It also may be used very helpfully during second-year work and as a terminal test for second-year students.

In its present forms, it is the third experimental edition through which the test has gone in process of development and a considerable body of information concerning the test is now at hand. For example, the split-half reliability coefficient of the test for a group of approximately 200 second-year students was .94. The intercorrelation of Forms A and B for the same group was .83. In another experiment involving 149 cases a correlation of .67 with teacher's marks was obtained. This value is unusually high, since these were the regular term grades and not marks based upon shorthand proficiency alone.

In an additional study involving 100 second-year high school pupils, the correlation of Forms A and B was .81. Correlation of the test with lateral verbatim transcripts of the same material yielded correlations ranging from .69 to .89.

The tests may be scored so as to obtain diagnostic sub-scores. This is especially valuable in the case of first-year students who must be advised concerning their future program. The total score on the test may be used as the basis for term marks in stenography achievement. Local percentile norms may be set up to be used in employment records and in connection with job recommendations.

P. L. T.

STENOGRAPHY, APTITUDE FOR.   A great deal of study has been devoted to the determination of aptitude for stenographic work. Such study has been stimulated by the following facts:

1. vocational statistics in normal times reveal that four to five times (or more) as many students enroll in stenographic classes than existing opportunities for employment in this field
2. the class enrolment mortality in secondary and private business schools ranges from 25% to 60% for Shorthand

It is, therefore, evident, that large numbers have pursued the study of stenography who have been unable to find employment as stenographers; and that large numbers beginning to study, for one reason or another, fail to complete it. This comparatively high enrolment mortality suggests lack of aptitude on the part of many individuals.

Aptitudes are so elusive in nature that one cannot be too sure of the abilities or capacities measured by any "aptitude" test in spite of the care with which it may have been constructed. Investigators of shorthand aptitude have looked into many fields which on the surface seem to be vaguely or remotely associated with shorthand learning. Research studies are therefore reported on the predictive value of such diverse measures as motor reactions, spelling, symbols substitution, speed of handwriting, quality of handwriting, memory, intelligence, English marks, foreign language marks, scholastic standing, sex, motility, will-temperament, speed of reading, comprehension of reading, clerical aptitude, speed and comprehension of reading, vocabulary and at least fifty other measures.

Of all the factors investigated, those which measure certain types of verbal skill seem to be the most promising, i.e., vocabulary, spelling, "word sense" and phonetic association. While the average high school student may be able to satisfactorily pass a shorthand course, studies reveal that the *average employed stenographer* has an I.Q. of 112.

On the basis of the limited samplings frequently investigated, no sweeping inferences as to the hopelessness or as to the promise of aptitude testing in shorthand can be made. For example, a review of 30 studies in shorthand prognosis reveals that 11, or more than one-third of this number were finally concerned with less than 100 cases for experimentation. Literature frequently has appeared reporting experimental data based upon as low as 39, 55, 73, 40 and 59 cases.

Since vocational shorthand is generally a two-year course, it would seem that any really authoritative study should be concerned with several hundred properly sampled cases, followed through two years of training, with a statistically valid and reliable transcription test providing the greater part, if not all, of the criterion measure. A shorthand study of such scope and with such validated achievement measures seems to be quite rare.

While most of the experimental data in shorthand prognosis shows discouragingly low validity correlations, aptitude authorities seem to agree that combined tests correlating .50 to .60 with true criterion measures have more than negligible value. In fact, most of the useful aptitude tests now in general use show correlations within these limits.

The purpose of a shorthand aptitude test is primarily to eliminate those who are unfit to pursue the study of shorthand and not to predict with a high degree of accuracy, the relative standing of those who continue the study. Considered from this point of view, and keeping in mind the disparity between employment possibilities and enrolments, as well as the abnormal drop-out rate, the distinct usefulness of a test correlating .60 with achievement should be apparent. Obviously, any individual prognosis for this subject should not be made without consideration of other factors such as, interest and incentive, general intelligence, verbal intelligence, etc.

In addition to their use for predictive purposes, tests of shorthand aptitude may be used for purposes of diagnosis, classification and self-appraisal.

P. L. T.

STENOGRAPHIC APTITUDE TESTS

ERC Stenographic Aptitude Test. This test, constructed by Walter L. Deemer, Jr., was devised to determine ahead of time the probable performance of pupils studying shorthand. The performance is predicted in terms of accuracy of transcription and speed of transcription. The results of the test may be used to eliminate potential failures among students considering the study of shorthand, and to separate large first-year classes into groups according to probable learning rate.

In the construction of the *ERC Stenographic Aptitude Test,* a subjective study was made to determine in which of their various activities the more efficient stenographers would probably be superior to the less efficient. An effort was made to devise tests that would predict achievement in these activities; after tryout of various tests and items, a test consisting of five sub-tests was constructed. No knowledge of shorthand symbols is needed to take the test. The sub-tests are:

1. *Speed of Writing.* A two minute speed test of copying in longhand familiar and fairly simple material. This test was selected to measure the gross ability to move the hand rapidly when writing.
2. *Word Discrimination.* A seven minute test of the ability to choose the right word for the context from two or three choices with the same or similar pronunciation. This test was selected to measure the ability of the stenographer to select from the context the right word when the shorthand note stands for more than one word.
3. *Phonetic Spelling.* In most shorthand systems words are written phonetically. The phonetic spelling test (eight minutes) was designed to measure the ability to recognize words from their phonetic spelling and to spell them correctly. This test does not have any context to help in the choice of words.
4. *Vocabulary.* In writing outlines for words during dictation a large vocabulary will probably be of value. A large vocabulary will also be an aid during transcription, contributing to both accuracy and speed. The vocabulary test (nine minutes) contains fifty-five choice items.
5. *Sentence Dictation.* This is a test of the ability to write in longhand from dictation as the individual gets farther and farther behind the dictation. This test parallels very closely the situation of taking notes in shorthand from dictation, the only difference being that in the test the student is writing in longhand instead of shorthand.

Norms are available based on scores made by 10th and 11th grade beginning shorthand students.

Validity

The validity of the *ERC Stenographic Aptitude Test* has been investigated over a three year period, during which shorthand achievement of pupils who took the test at the beginning of their shorthand courses was carefully measured.

Accuracy of transcription at the end of two years of shorthand study may be predicted before shorthand courses have been started with a precision indicated by a multiple correlation of .68 for material dictated at 80 words per minute or less and a multiple correlation of .70 for material dictated at more than 80 words per minute. Tables are available for predicting scores of accuracy of transcription and of rate of transcription.

The publisher of this test is Science Research Associates, 228 S. Wabash Avenue, Chicago 4, Illinois.

W. L. D.

Bennett Stenographic Aptitude Test. This test is designed to predict ability to acquire the skills in shorthand and typewriting. The process tested is one of writing and transcribing intrinsically meaningless symbols. A second portion of the test measures spelling ability.

The present form is a second revision of an unpublished test developed in 1934 and used in the prediction of success in high school classes of shorthand and typewriting. The results then obtained indicate that this measure is appreciably superior to previous academic grades or intelligence test scores as an index of future achievement in secretarial courses. The first revision, published in 1937, confirmed the earlier findings. Standardization of the present form on a population of approximately 1500 is in progress.

Administrative problems are reduced to a minimum. The substitution and transcription portions require a total of twelve minutes time, including instructions. The spelling section occupies only ten minutes. The entire test can be scored in about 60 seconds by a reasonably skilled person.

The transcription test consists of two parts. In the first part, the digits from 1 to 5 appear in a random order. There are 10 digits on each line. In the center section, the student writes the symbols corresponding to the numbers. The key to be used in this substitution is printed at the top of this section. The right section is also blank. The student writes the numbers corresponding to the symbols he has written in the center section. The same key is used for writing and transcribing symbols.

A manual of directions presents complete instructions for administering and scoring the test; data concerning intercorrelation of the parts of the test and correlation with Revised Army Alpha, Form 5; and norms for several kinds of students.

The coefficient of consistency for an earlier form of the transcription test was computed for 126 subjects by correlating the scores made in odd minutes with those made in even minutes. The reliability of the whole test was found to be .975.

The consistency coefficient for the spelling test was computed for 185 applicants to schools of nursing by correlating the scores on the first half of the test with those on the second half. The reliability of the spelling test was found to be .913.

Validity coefficients, using success in a secretarial school as the criterion, were determined for 211 students with some previous experience in either stenography or typewriting, and 296 students with no such experience. The following coefficients were found:

	Experienced	Not Experienced
Spelling vs. Success	.47	.47
Transcription vs. Success	.27	.27
Spelling and Transcription vs. Success..	.54	.55

The publisher of the test is The Psychological Corporation, 522 Fifth Avenue, New York 18, New York.

References:

1. Bennett, G. K. *Differential aptitude prognosis,* 1935. Unpublished Doctoral Dissertation filed Sterling Memorial Library, Yale University, pp. 85–114.
2. ————. Psychological factors in secretarial success. Transactions of the New York Academy of Sciences. Series II, Vol. I, pp. 100–103.

G. K. B.

STUDY-HABIT INVENTORIES. Of the many types of tests that are now available, perhaps, study-habit inventories have received comparatively little attention. There can be no doubt that the cultivation of good study habits at as early an age as possible is highly desirable, and, as a preliminary to this, some attempt at measurement is important. The basic consideration here, as elsewhere, is to determine the components of a standard upon which to base our comparison. Just what constitutes a good student? What habits or practices characterize him as opposed to the mediocre student? The usual criterion in a test of this type is the relationship existing between the possession of the study habit and success as a student. Thus most of the inventories that we have are made up of items that have been selected because they significantly characterize the behavior of the good student or the poor student. Perhaps, in the limited space available for our discussion, some consideration of a few such inventories as typical would be desirable.

An example of a study-habit on the higher level is the *Study-Habits Inventory* by C. Gilbert Wrenn. It is suitable for use in the twelfth grade and in colleges. This inventory consists of twenty-eight items, classified under four major groupings; (A) Reading and Note-taking Techniques, (B) Habits of Concentration, (C) Distribution of Time and Social Relationships in Study, and (D) General Habits and Attitudes of Work. The items are weighted, being given correspondingly high or low positive or negative scores, as the items differentiate good or poor students. There are three possible answers to each item, as, for example, the statement "I study with others, rather than by myself" may be answered by checking any one of the three following responses: (1) Rarely or never, (2) Sometimes, (3) Often or always. A check of number one or three carries more weight than number two. While a total score is derived from the test by computing the algebraic sum of the weights, the results of individual answers as indicating good or bad practices are most significant. The inventory is untimed and self-administering.

The author recommends that the inventory be used with entering groups of students as a possible basis for remedial work, as a means of aiding students in learning their own weaknesses, as a basis for counseling, and as an aid for high school seniors in learning study habits which they possess and their significance for college work. The overall purpose is to cause students to think in terms of specific habits rather than in generalities. The warning is given that, even though one's total positive score is high, he may possess some very undesirable habits that should be corrected.

The items in the inventory were first selected as a result of a study involving 110 pairs of undergraduate male students of Stanford University. They were selected on the basis of scores upon the Thorndike Intelligence Examination, field of study, academic level, and length of time in the University. Then they were paired, one for each pair ranking in the highest ten per cent, and the other in the lowest twenty per cent of the student body. From a list of sixty-nine statements, twenty-eight were selected as receiving significantly different answers for the two groups of students. In 1939–40 Wilbur J. Humler made an additional study of this inventory at the University of Minnesota, and he included women as well as men subjects. Here the selection was on the basis of the American Council Psychological Examination. A further analysis was made of the responses of men and women. It is interesting to note that women were found to differ less than men in their study habits.

The author states in the manual of Directions that there is no known method of determining the reliability of a test of this type, and also that ordinary methods of determining validity do not apply. The care with which the individual items were selected is the chief means of validation. The inventory has been in general use since 1935.

On the lower level, *A Test of Study Skills* by J. W. Edgar and H. T. Manuel will serve as an example. This inventory is designed for grades four to nine inclusive, and was constructed in coopera-tion with the Texas Commission on Coordination in Education. The inventory consists of two parts. Part I deals with Finding and Understanding Printed Materials, and Part II with Critical Think-ing in the Use of Printed Materials. Part I is intended to test ability to discover and interpret information from printed sources, such as the sources to which one may go for information, the meaning of various abbreviations, the understanding of diacritical markings, use of the index, and interpretation of tables, charts, graphs, etc. Part II is designed to test the pupil's ability to understand the material read, and to relate it to other fields.

The only claim that the authors make as to validity is that the selection of items was carried out with considerable care. A coeffi-cient of correlation determined on the basis of a small number of pupils, less than a hundred, between the two forms of the test was .92. Norms are to be made available; however, users of the inven-tory are cautioned against undue emphasis upon comparisons of individual pupils with group norms.

Part I consists of fifty-six and Part II of forty-six items, which are of the multiple-choice type. The maximum time permitted is thirty minutes on each of the two parts. The inventory provides a separate answer sheet, and is machine scorable.

The Iowa Every-Pupil Tests of Basic Skills include two tests of Work-Study Skills, the elementary battery for grades three, four, and five, and the advanced battery for grades five to nine. The ele-mentary battery can be administered in a single period of fifty-five minutes, or two periods of about thirty minutes each. The advanced battery requires a single period of about ninety minutes, or two periods of approximately forty-five minutes each. The batteries are divided into five sections, the first four of which are map reading, use of references, use of index, use of dictionary, and for the ele-mentary battery, alphabetization, and for the advanced battery, reading graphs, charts, and tables. The items are principally of the multiple-choice type, but one section consists of questions to be answered.

Norms are provided in terms of grade-equivalents, chronological age-equivalents, and percentiles. Any of these norms may be read directly from conversion tables. Profile charts are available. The manual of directions includes specific suggestions for the use of the battery in remedial work.

As may be concluded from this discussion of three typical tests, study-habit inventories do not lend themselves to the degree of standardization that achievement tests do. There is rather general agreement as to the types of skills that should be tested, but no means of objectively determining the relationship of those skills to successful achievement, or the lack of it. In the final analysis the inventory contains items that are generally thought to be pertinent. The warning is generally given that these tests serve their main purpose as instruments for individual diagnosis, that is, for determining specific habits or abilities in order to discover those that should be corrected. One should not accept an average score as indicating an acceptable degree of skill, if undesirable habits or inabilities are indicated.

Evidence of desirable study-habits might indicate a type of individual who would do well in occupations requiring efficient work methods. The student who gives evidence of inefficiency probably should avoid the type of vocation which requires attention to detail. A study of the relation between scores earned on study-habit inventories and results of interest inventories would be a worthwhile and interesting project. At present any deductions that can be drawn are purely subjective.

C. W. T.

STUDY HABIT INVENTORIES

Wrenn Study-Habits Inventory. The Inventory was devised by C. Gilbert Wrenn, Lieut. Comdr., USNR (on leave from University of Minnesota) assisted in the original edition by R. B. McKeown and in the revision by Wilbur J. Humber. It is published by Stanford University Press, 1933 (Rev. Ed.), 1941.

The *Inventory* is a weighted check-list of specific study habits which distinguish students of high scholarship from those of low scholarship even though they may possess equal ability on scholastic aptitude tests. It has long been known that so-called "good" students and "poor" students possess different methods of attack upon their studies but the question of different levels of intelligence and its influence upon study habits has often confused the issue. The *Inventory* was constructed in such a way as to include only those habits of study that distinguished college students in the upper 10 per cent of scholarship from those in the lower 20 per cent of scholarship who had been matched on intelligence test ability, pattern of college work, length of time in college, sex, and scholastic load. In other words the attempt was made to hold these latter factors "constant" while varying only the specific study habits used by high and low achievement students.

The original edition grew out of a study of 4,000 Stanford University students while the revision was conducted upon University of Minnesota students. The revision re-validated all of the original items, tested out many new ones, and determined the items that were valid for women as well as men.

The *Inventory,* of which well over a quarter of a million copies have been sold in the past ten years, is used in the following ways:

1. Given to entering classes or other large groups of students in order to determine the particular study weaknesses that are most evident for the group as a whole, so that class work, remedial assistance, and counseling assistance can be provided with the proper emphasis in the educational program of the institution.
2. Given to classes or other groups of students and the scored Inventories returned to them individually so that each can see the particular habits which he needs to modify.
3. Given as a part of any comprehensive battery of tests the results of which are to provide the basis for clinical study and individual counseling. The specific nature of the Inventory items makes it particularly helpful as an introduction to counseling interviews upon study habits.
4. Given to classes of high school seniors for their own information as to the significance of the study habits they possess and as a basis for pre-college assistance and individual counseling on study.

The *Inventory* is most useful in making students think of study habits in a specific rather than a general sense and in motivating them to attack specific habits for development. In 1941 the *Inventory* was included in a combined diagnostic and remedial booklet, *Studying Effectively,* published by Stanford University Press. This booklet enables the student to take the *Inventory,* score it, and then immediately relate his weak points to the appropriate remedial section of the booklet.

The *Manual* of the *Inventory* contains full information upon the construction of the test, the weighting methods used, and various validation studies that have been made. Since the *Inventory* is a check-list of specific study habits of unknown degrees of discretion, rather than a test in the ordinary sense of the word, none of the ordinary methods for determining total-test reliability can be applied. Likewise a sound criterion of validity is difficult to find. The algebraic sum of the weights, however, gives a quantitative score that may be used for comparison with quantitative grades. Various such studies have provided a range of correlation coefficients, the most typical of which is a Pearsonian "r" of .42 between *Inventory* scores and grade-points. This dropped only .03 when aptitude test scores were held constant. The resulting coefficient of .39 is about as high as the maximum one could expect, when it is remembered that study habits are only one of several major factors that affect scholastic achievement.

C. G. W.

SUPERVISORY TESTS

How Supervise?   How Supervise? was constructed by Quentin W. File and edited by H. H. Remmers. This instrument is designed to aid industrial management in obtaining a clear picture of its supervisors' understanding of the more important general aspects of their jobs. It has been found to be a valuable aid—

1. in selecting individuals for upgrading,
2. in selecting candidates for supervisory training,
3. in measuring the outcomes of supervisory training programs,
4. in checking the attitudes of present supervisors for areas of weakness,
5. as an indication of how supervisors feel about related company policies,
6. in the counseling and interviewing of supervisors.

Two alternate forms of the test are available. Each form consists of seventy items which are divided into the general areas of Supervisory Practices, Company Policies, and Supervisor Opinions. Both forms are hand scored from keys provided with the manual.

Both percentile and standard-score norms are provided for individual forms and for the two forms combined. These norms are based on an experimental sample of 577 supervisors from ten industrial concerns of varied size, type, and geographical location.

The validation of *How Supervise?* was accomplished by administering an experimental edition of two forms of 102 items each to approximately 750 supervisors in the industries mentioned above. Best answers to the items were obtained by having the test answered by thirty-seven members of the supervisory staff of the government's Training Within Industry program and by eight individuals who have written recognized articles or books in the field of industrial relations or mental hygiene. The responses most frequently given by the two groups combined were taken as the correct answers. The correlation between the modal answers of the two groups was .91 where five possible responses to each item were provided.

The validities of the items retained were calculated with respect to a primary criterion of total scores on the test and a secondary independent criterion of four ratings of each supervisor by members of management at or above the supervisor's organizational level.

The form vs form reliability of scores on the experimental edition of *How Supervise?* was .86. Elimination of ambiguous items and the equating of the two forms with respect to item difficulty and item variability is believed to have appreciably increased this value.

The overall validity of the test is indicated—

1. By studies in individual plants in which supervisors of recognized ability averaged significantly better scores than individuals who had been by-passed for promotions because of lack of ability.
2. By the repeated ability of the test to measure improvements in supervisory quality which result from supervisory training. Alternate forms of the test were administered before and after training. Material content of the programs was either organized by other universities or through the government's Training Within Industry program and were in no way related to the development of *How Supervise?*
3. By the nature of the test's construction in which only those items that were important in the opinion of the experts and that discriminated between supervisors with respect to the primary criterion were used.

How Supervise? is published by The Psychological Corporation, 522 Fifth Avenue, New York 18, N. Y.

References:

1. File, Q. W. The measurement of supervisory quality in industry. Journal of Applied Psychology, 1945, 29, 323–337.
2. ———. *Manual for "How Supervise?"* (Development, directions, and norms), 1945.

Q. W. F.

SWITZERLAND

I. *History of the Development of Vocational Guidance*

In Switzerland vocational guidance was initiated by teachers and pastors. Towards the end of the nineteenth century, certain Public Utility Societies founded Apprentices' Patronage Committees with a view to Vocational Guidance and Aid to apprentices. Gradually religious and political societies, as well as government authorities began to show an interest in this movement. The first and most important object of the Apprentices' Patronage Committees was the general welfare of these youths, and, in the course of time, their activities developed into regular vocational guidance and assistance in finding the employers, who were willing to engage the apprentices; they also provided apprenticeship stipends for suitable cases. As legal regulations for apprenticeship did not yet exist, they acted as mediators in conflicts arising between employers and apprentices, advising the youths and their parents. In 1902 these committees amalgamated into the Swiss Association for Apprentices' Patronage. Later on this association changed its name into "Swiss Association for Vocational Guidance and Apprentices' Aid," which may be considered as the leading union of all the groups or movements concerned with this problem. This Association produced the strongest impulses for the systematical introduction and propagation of professional guidance.

II. *The Present Organization of Vocational Guidance*

There are, at present, no legal ordinances of the Swiss Government concerning the organization of vocational guidance. The latter is mainly supported by Cantonal decrees by which this organization is established and more or less minutely controlled. In almost each of the 25 Swiss Cantons there is a special Office, which is either exclusively or partially charged with vocational guidance, in the latter case as a complement to its dealing with questions of apprenticeship in general. Besides these offices there are regional advisers, i.e. usually local teachers, who are members of the Swiss Association for Vocational Guidance and Apprentices' Aid.

Most of the regional advisers were only appointed during the last decade; their appointment was probably suggested by the Swiss Federal Act of 1930 concerning professional training, which provides State subsidies for institutions of vocational guidance. According to this Act, Federal subsidies can be granted to:

(a) Societies for the Promotion of vocational guidance, whose sphere of action covers a large part of the country;

(b) Vocational Guidance Offices;
(c) Instruction Courses for vocational advisers;
(d) Tests of Aptitude, so far as they are necessary in the interest of professional training and are efficiently conducted.

On the whole, the Swiss Federal Government limit their cooperation, as we see, to subsidize the institutions of vocational guidance; however the Act of 1930 also contains further provisions in support of this cause. One of these provisions refers to the so-called Pre-apprenticeship Courses, which serve as a preparation for, or introduction to particular crafts or groups of crafts and may be useful as a means of revealing the potential aptitude of the youth for a profession. Various factors may commend such an introduction of young people to a vocation. Some of them may e.g. lack in self-confidence or the necessary judgment, and may have arrived at a decision to choose a certain trade, because they were so advised. In this case the pre-apprenticeship course is calculated to reveal the actual aptitude of a youth, to let him discover pleasure in a profession and, after his aptitude has been determined, to procure a definite apprenticeship agreement.

However there are professions which, for various reasons, are avoided by young people and which are consequently at a disadvantage. Now the holding of pre-apprenticeship courses is an excellent means of awaking an interest for such a vocation, to dispel prejudices and to help solving the problem of professions, that are badly in need of apprentices. At the same time a sufficient number of suitable workshops should be held at the disposal of those, who are about to begin their apprenticeship. Moreover pre-apprenticeship courses may be desirable in the case of professions, in which for various reasons the systematical initiation of apprentices meets with technical difficulties. Finally the holding of pre-apprenticeship courses for particular groups of vocations may be desirable. Such courses are possible, when similar vocations are in question, the training for which can be based upon one and the same program of tuition.

If professional associations submit a proposal to the competent government authorities, demanding that the attendance of pre-apprenticeship courses in their vocations should be made compulsory for apprentices, such a proposal may be given effect. As a rule, the pre-apprenticeship courses will be reckoned as part of the apprenticeship period. Their duration depends on their program of instruction; it can extend to several weeks, or up to five months as a maximum. Government subsidies are granted for such courses, if they keep strictly to the rules laid down by the above-mentioned Act.

III. *The Main Objects of Vocal Guidance and the Manner of Their Attainment*

The chief object of vocational guidance is to aid parents and youths, to choose a profession according to personal aptitude and inclination, and with due regard to the economic situation and the chances of making a living. It would not conform to Swiss democratic principles to make use of pressure in any direction, or to go so far as to prescribe the vocation, in which the youth should be trained. In every case the decision and the responsibility concerning the choice of a profession rests with the youth and his parents. They are entirely free to avail themselves of every kind of advice, which, as a rule, is free of charge.

The actual vocational guidance has its complement in a well-organized *Employment Agency*. Already fifty per cent of all apprenticeship agreements in Switzerland are due to organized vocational guidance. Finally, the latter is also prepared to procure contributions to the apprenticeship *expenses* for young people, who are not well off.

The activities of the 150 regional advisers of Switzerland are directed by the Swiss Association, which in 1946 counts some 600 members, many of whom represent whole societies. Its Central Secretariat endeavors to obtain the results desired by the following means:

1. Instruction Courses and Conferences for vocational advisers, men and women, subsidized by the Federal Office for Industries, Crafts and Labor (Office fédéral de l'Industrie, des Arts et Métiers et du Travail). Also aid in creating further offices or finding representatives for vocational guidance.
2. Publication of Literature concerning the choice of a profession, vocational guidance, aid for apprentices and advice about careers. Personal Information, free of charge, concerning all question of choice of a profession, vocational education and apprentices' aid.
3. Information of the general Public (by radio, press, pamphlets, lectures, lantern-slides and graphs for lecturers) concerning the importance of a careful choice of the vocation.
4. Extension of aid by a further development of Insurance, of Stipends, as well as Homes and lodgings for apprentices.

The success of vocational guidance greatly depends on the special talent, training, personal interest in this kind of work and a sense of duty of the advisers. The association is therefore intent upon the right choice, training and continual technical, pedagogical and psychological instruction of these persons. They must keep in contact with the economic life of the country, which will enable them to facilitate the adaptation of the youths, who leave school, to the existing training possibilities and to find those suiting their inclinations. New vocational advisers are prepared for their work by special courses of instruction, while continuation courses are organized for those, who have already done work of this kind for some time. Regular conferences are held for a thorough discussion of important problems and an exchange of personal experiences.

The Swiss Association for Vocational Guidance and Apprentices' Aid also publishes a large monthly periodical, as well as so-called "Types of Vocations" (Berufsbilder) and "Information sheets on particular vocations" (Berufskundliche Merkblätter). The publication "Berufsbilder" ("Types of Vocations") contains data on particular vocations, their requirements and the necessary aptitude or qualifications, also the standard principles of a vocation and the chances it may offer. The great value of these types is their uniform basis, which makes them comparable among each other. On the other hand they have the advantage of an impartial description, which makes no attempt at a prognosis. Another important aid is offered by the Apprenticeship Regulations for 154 vocations, concerning professional education and tests of the youths' regulations which have so far been edicted by the Federal Economic Department. These Regulations contain tuition programs as well as the minimum requirements for the final tests, held at the end of the apprenticeship. From these data conclusions about the physical and intellectual requirements of a vocation can be drawn by all persons interested.

As a rule the vocational advisers collaborate in the tests for professional aptitude or themselves arrange for such tests. Quite a number of middle-sized and, above all, big firms only employ apprentices, who have successfully passed such tests.

Psychotechnical institutes, a great number of which exist in Switzerland, are often entrusted with these tests.

During the year 1945, roughly 250 Swiss vocation advisers have treated nearly 34,000 cases, 56% being boys and 44% girls.

Federal Office for Industries, Crafts and Labor
Berne, Switzerland

T

TEACHING, APTITUDE FOR. What qualities should a teacher candidate possess? The combination of traits necessary to teaching has been the subject of extensive research. Such traits must include qualities that make for success in any field, and to these must be added qualities that pertain to teaching only, as for instance that inborn facility that certain instructors have for imparting knowledge clearly and logically.

There is no common pattern by which to judge the qualities of successful teachers, and authorities do not agree on all traits that are suggested. Nevertheless the findings of such researches as, "The Commonwealth Teacher-Training Study," a 5-year project directed by W. W. Charters and Douglas Waples (Chicago Press, 1929), includes a comprehensive view of traits of teachers. As a premise it is stated in this study of teacher qualifications that, "Any determination of personal traits is at present dependent upon *judgment*." A group of competent judges then listed and defined 83 teacher traits, and by grouping these reduced the number to 25. Without giving further details, the list shorn of definitions includes the following traits:

Adaptability, attractive personal appearance, breadth of interest, carefulness, considerateness, cooperation, dependability, enthusiasm, fluency, forcefulness, good judgment, health, honesty, industry, leadership, magnetism, neatness, open-mindedness, originality, progressiveness, promptness, refinement, scholarship, self-control, and thrift.

The sum of these traits in any one person would produce a dynamic, cultured, progressive individual desirable not only in teaching but in any line of work. It will be observed that many of these same traits apply equally well to a sales clerk in a department store, or to a stenographer in an office. A teacher with all of these traits would be an inspiration to young people in any classroom. Due to individual differences, however, it is doubtful if any teacher would have all of these qualities. One teacher might be extremely adaptable but personally unattractive because of poor health. Another might be forceful and fluent, but inconsiderate of the feelings of others. Teachers in the classroom are expected to exercise their good qualities, and to inhibit their faults, especially if the faults tend to cancel certain good traits. A teacher candidate, for example, might have many excellent traits and yet be unfit for classroom work if she were emotionally unstable.

Teachers and other workers in professional classifications should have the following general qualifications: Ability to undertake special projects that involve individual initiative, imagination, and planning work; qualities of leadership as evidenced by offices held in clubs, participation in committee work, and other activities requiring planning and executing work cooperatively with others; ability to deal with people, mental ability above the average; and ability to do creditable college work. In school work particularly parents demand teachers of good character, cultured, and personable if they work with children in the classroom and engage in community work.

Studies show that pupils like teachers best who are: Helpful with school work; explain lessons and assignments clearly using examples in their teaching; cheerful; happy, good natured; jolly; can take a joke and have a sense of humor; human; friendly; and companionable. Students also believe that those teachers are most effective who are: Exacting in standards of work; strict in marking; explain lessons well; plan their work; and know their subject thoroughly.

On the negative side, T. L. Thorgerson in Review of Educational Research (June, 1937), points out that nearly 500 research studies have attempted to secure a more adequate knowledge of the factors that condition success in teaching. While the problem is still largely unsolved, the findings reveal much about teachers and teaching. For instance such factors as age, experience, salary, and skill in handwriting are *not* related to teaching success. On the other hand scholarship and intelligence although moderately related to success in teaching cannot be depended upon as measures for predicting success.

Teaching is a profession that every educated adult comprehends. Every individual who has been through school or college has, through his own experience, a basis for opinion as to what qualifications good teachers have, what teacher traits are desirable, and what personality factors constitute assets or handicaps in teaching. Most adults can name outstanding teachers that have influenced their lives for the better, and can tell what traits made these teachers outstanding.

Likewise, teaching is a profession that every school child can observe and understand. At a very early age a child may form an opinion about teaching and sometimes will make a definite decision to become a teacher, or not to become a teacher. Child attitudes change, however, as occupations are studied with a view to employment, and as high school graduation approaches. For this reason alone it is important that young people interested in teaching have the advantage of a personal interview with a good counselor.

The school counselor helps young people to understand better the occupation of teaching. The counselor is able to view teaching both from the classroom standpoint and from the training angle because he has had to qualify for his own job through the field of education. He is able not only to discuss teacher traits, but to give information on the general background necessary for teaching, on the time and money required for training, and on specialization, experience and other factors which contribute to success in teaching. It is his duty to present and interpret facts in a given situation from an unbiased viewpoint without neglecting needs in particular fields, or overemphasizing shortages in others. Pupils who come to him for advice about teaching as a career are entitled to impartial information without any attempt to recruit teachers.

One of his duties, therefore, is to point out to young people qualities which seem to indicate they would make good teacher candidates, or handicaps that might prevent them from becoming successful teachers. He is not a soothsayer, and makes no claims of predicting whether an individual will, or will not, become an effective teacher. He uses the best judgments available about teachers and helps students to decide for themselves about continuing their training in a teachers college.

With these factors in mind, how is the school counselor equipped to make selections? What techniques and procedures will enable him to discriminate between those who should be encouraged to prepare for teaching and those who should be encouraged to enter other work?

In interviewing teacher candidates, a good observer will recognize certain personal characteristics that may affect a career in teaching, for example, posture, poise, manner, grooming, general appearance, features, voice, and other objective traits that can be seen and described. Subjective traits must be probed.

Seriousness of purpose of a candidate may be determined through such leading questions as: Why did you choose teaching? When did you first become interested in teaching? Who first advised you for this work? Did you choose it in preference to all other occupations? Do you have relatives who teach? How long do you expect to teach? Are you using teaching as a steppingstone to some other occupation?

During such interviews the counselor helps the pupil to pull together the evidence obtained about his suitability as a teacher. In the process, the counselor explains what is required of teachers in general, what teachers' college demands of a students, what types of students have succeeded in the past, what types have failed, and what caliber of former student is now in teacher training.

The counselor will also explain that when a pupil applies for entrance to a teacher training institution, further selective techniques will be applied. At the end of the sophomore year, he will be examined to determine his qualifications for continuing in the junior and senior years. In one institution students are selected at the end of the sophomore year after continual individual study, and those who continue in the junior and seniors are selected on the basis of five factors: (1) Physical fitness, (2) desirable personality, (3) professional attitudes, (4) mastery of the elements of general education, and (5) satisfactory college record for the first two years. Upon graduation selection again takes place, when only one applicant out of a group is selected to fill a vacancy. During employment the teacher's efficiency is checked for renewal of contract, or for promotion.

The counselor may also make use of several devices in identifying teacher qualifications in young people who arc considering teaching as a profession. Such indicators or aids include cumulative records; questionnaires, personality records, and tests.

Criteria are needed for each individual in the form of records of school work kept over a period of years. The cumulative record, or the pupil's individual inventory consists of a file of records kept from year to year to reveal evidence of abilities and readiness for a training program; data on family background; personal history; physical and medical history; test results; school marks; extra-curricular activities; special talents; personality records; and anecdotal records. The use of this inventory in counseling will help to determine the direction of the pupil's interests, and furnish reliable estimates of his educational and vocational possibilities. Discussion and use of the cumulative record may be found in: "Minimum Essentials of the Individual Inventory in Guidance," by Ruch and Segel, U. S. Office of Education, Vocational Division, Bulletin No. 202, Washington, D. C.

If the school does not maintain cumulative records of pupils, the counselor must assemble one the best way he can for each senior interviewed. By devising a questionnaire that each senior can fill out, certain pertinent information may be obtained that is useful in the interview. This student questionnaire might contain questions similar to the following:

Occupational preference:	Do you expect to teach?
	What other occupations interest you?
Home responsibilities:	What regular duties do you have at home?
School grades:	Best grades were in ....
	Poorest grades were in ....
School activities:	Mention offices held, teams made, honors, etc.
Private lessons:	Mention any in music, dancing, art, etc.
College:	Do you plan to enter college next fall? Where
Leisure time activities:	
Reading:	Newspaper, magazines, books

Such a questionnaire is helpful in revealing occupational choice and qualifications for such a choice.

Some counselors use personality records on which preliminary ratings on pupils in school are indicated. The ratings are judgments of teachers and others who are acquainted with the students. They are not tests, and there are no right or wrong answers. The ratings summarize briefly the esteem in which young people are held by adults who know them. They are useful in discovering maladjustments, in helping boys and girls to overcome certain limitations that they may possess, and in making helpful recommendations in the case of teacher candidates.

Several personality forms are available commercially including: H. M. Bell's "Adjustment Inventory" published by the Stanford University Press, and the "Personality Record" published by the National Association of Secondary-School Principals of the National Education Association, Washington, D. C.

Or personality record forms may be devised by the counselor. A few important characteristics are usually listed. The number of such characteristics should be kept under 10 and each may be rated on a brief 5-point scale similar to the following:

I. Seriousness of purpose: (1) Purposeless ....
(2) Vacillating .... (3) Potential ....
(4) Limited .... (5) Purposeful ....

The teacher makes a check on the scale where he or she believes the pupil is best characterized. Allowances must be made for age factors, growth, development, and training because young people change in their habits and attitudes as they grow older. Judgments are not final but should be altered as conditions demand, and may be made at different age levels.

Another aid for the counselor is the testing program. Testing programs common in many school systems where special testing services are maintained, provide certain measurements of ability and aptitudes of individual pupils in the high school. There is no test that will reveal the *one* occupation that a person should enter, but batteries of tests are given to predict large fields of work or major interests—not occupations. If no testing service is provided, the counselor may take the initiative and give the tests himself, or he may secure assistance in the work of giving, scoring and recording tests, from another qualified staff member, or from one of the members of the guidance committee.

For guidance purposes, tests may be grouped as follows: Scholastic aptitude or general intelligence tests helpful in predicting school success or failure, especially when combined with previous scholarship records; achievement tests, given for trade skills and for educational achievement; and special aptitude tests in art, music, manual, clerical, and other activities. Interest inventories show the direction of a person's interests.

In this work of testing, classification and selection, four references will be found helpful: "Aptitudes and Aptitude Testing" by Walter V. Bingham (Harper Bros.); "Student Guidance Techniques" by Paterson, Schneidler and Williamson (McGraw-Hill); "Testing and Counseling in the High-School Guidance Program" by John G. Darley (Science Research Associates, Chicago); and The Dictionary of Occupational Titles, Part IV "Entry Occupational Classification" (U. S. Government Printing Office, October, 1944, 35¢).

As to the tests themselves, a few are mentioned below as typical of the instruments available. These are suggestive only and a counselor may select one from each of the two groups:

1. *General Intelligence.* These tests are devised to measure scholastic ability or capacity of an individual to do school work of a verbal or academic nature.

    American Council on Education (D. C.) Psychological Examination for High School Students

    Otis Quick-Scoring Mental Tests. (World Book Co.)

    Henman-Nelson Test of Mental Ability, Form B. (Houghton-Mifflin Co.)

Terman-McNemar Test of Mental Ability, Grades 7–12. (World Book Co.)

2. *Achievement Batteries.* Achievement test scores are predictive indicators of what a student is likely to accomplish in a special field of work:

Metropolitan Achievement Tests, Advanced Battery. (World Book Co.)

Progressive Achievement Tests, Advanced Battery. (Calif. Test Bureau)

Stanford Achievement Test, Advanced Battery, Revised 1940 (Psychological Corporation, N. Y. C.)

Cooperative General Achievement Tests. (Coop. Test Service, N. Y. C.)

Interpretation of ratings and test scores is by far the most important and most difficult part of the testing program. As soon as tests are scored and recorded, the performance of one pupil may be compared with that of the group and certain estimates may be made of probable success or failure in the areas tested. In the hands of a trained specialist test scores may be interpreted to reveal both positive and negative factors that are likely to influence the individual's future. Test scores therefore must be translated into information that will help the individual tested.

Discovering factors involved in aptitude for teaching is not accomplished through any single means nor at any one time. The process involved is long and includes all the phases and devices of a good guidance program. Even during training in a teachers college the process continues in an effort to determine suitable candidates for the teaching profession.

W. J. G.

TEACHING APTITUDE TESTS

Coxe-Orleans Prognosis Test of Teaching Ability.   This test is a combination of two tests which were devised by Warren W. Coxe and Jacob S. Orleans to assist in selecting students for the ten normal schools of New York State. After being tried out for this purpose they were revised and given their present form.

"Teaching ability" is given a limited meaning in this test. It is the ability to do the work of the normal school, not necessarily to become a successful teacher. This limitation is made because it is believed that successful teaching depends upon more factors than could be measured with this type of instrument. Although the purpose of the test is primarily to assist in selecting students for teacher training institutions, the test has been used to rate candidates for teaching positions in a number of cities. Analysis of this and other tests has recently been made by Seagoe. She concludes that the Prognosis of Teaching Ability Test is a valid indicator "of teaching success when administered on admission to the first course" and should be given at the beginning of professional training.

The results of first use in New York State show low correlations with teachers' marks in teacher training and with measures of later success. However, this test correlates higher than marks with measures of teaching success. The correlations of the test with a comprehensive achievement test given at the end of the first year varied in the different normal schools from $r = .551$ to $r = .839$. Presumably higher correlations would be found in later years when more professional work had been included.

The test has five parts. Part I is a test of general information. Part II measures the extent the student has observed classroom practice. Parts III, IV, and V sample the kinds of professional subject matter the student may be expected to encounter in his teacher training courses.

The total time for administering the test is approximately three hours. Norms are not available and it is thought that they are not of great significance because it has been found that schools differ greatly in respect to the kinds of students they attract and in respect to the character of their offerings. No measure of reliability is available.

The publisher is the World Book Company, Yonkers, N. Y.

References:

1. Coxe, W. W. and Cornell, E. L. *The prognosis of teaching ability of students in New York State Normal Schools.* Albany: The University of the State of New York Press, 1934.
2. Coxe, W. W. and Orleans, J. S. *The manual of directions.* Yonkers: World Book Company, 1930.
3. Seagoe, M. V. Prognostic tests and teaching success. Journal of Educational Research, 1945, 38, 685–690.

W. W. C.

Moss-Hunt-Wallace Teaching Aptitude Test. This test was devised by Fred A. Moss, Thelma Hunt, and F. C. Wallace in cooperation with various educators in order to measure the native ability necessary to become a successful teacher. There are, according to the authors, five different important factors which constitute aptitude for teaching. These factors are (1) ability to recognize attitudes, states of mind or emotions in others, (2) comprehension of teaching situations and judgment in solving them, (3) comprehension and retention, (4) relevant information, (5) the ability to observe details of a situation and to recall what has been observed.

Consequently, the test consists of five parts, each purportedly measuring one of the five factors. In taking this test the subject is required to (1) choose the best of four possible solutions to 30 typical problems which might confront a teacher, (2) determine the truth or falsity of eighty statements concerning school problems or educational psychology, (3) study a fairly difficult paragraph and then answer twenty questions on the material studied (4) match descriptive terms of mental states with ten pictures, mostly of children with different facial expressions, (5) answer ten questions concerning a picture of a school fight which had been studied at the beginning of the test.

Each of the parts of this test is timed; hence it cannot be self-administered. The entire working time is 37 minutes, which includes the nine minutes used to study the paragraph and the picture of the school fight before actually answering any of the questions.

The reliability of this test, as determined by the Spearman-Brown formula is .91, based on a group of 100 teacher college students. Intercorrelation of the various sub-tests are reported (1) to be low "except for a moderately high relationship between Parts I and II" (judgment in teaching situations and knowledge of school problems).

This test was validated [1] by correlating test scores with grades in teacher- training courses. The resultant correlation was about .50. It was also pointed out that this test shows a slightly higher correlation with grades than do the tests of abstract intelligence. The predictive value is even better for educational and psychology courses than for the more academic courses. When the test was administered to summer school teacher college students it was found that experienced teachers scored distinctly higher than teachers without any experience, and that teachers in better schools scored somewhat higher than teachers in poorer types of schools (rural, one-room, etc.).

Hunt presents norms based on a total of 2,978 cases for experienced teachers, city and rural, teacher college students and normal college students in various grades, and for high school seniors. The scores on this test have no relationship to age, but females show a slight superiority over the males. Correlations of .57 with abstract intelligence and .60 with social intelligence lead the author to believe that these, too, are important components in teaching ability.

In a critical study [2] of this test it was found that the correlation between grades in practice teaching courses and test scores was .117 ± .056. For the five sub-tests, the correlations ranged from .147 to .003. In the same study a correlation of .60 was reported between teaching aptitude test scores and scores on a test of abstract intelligence. The correlation between abstract intelligence and grades in practice teaching was .07 ± .06.

Markt and Gilliland [2] confirm Hunt's finding that experienced teachers score higher than those with no experience. Hunt thought that this was probably not due to experience as such, but that the teaching profession acted as a selective factor, forcing out the least capable teachers. On the other hand, Markt and Gilliland, after pointing out that the non-experienced group scored higher on a test of abstract intelligence, feel that the scores are markedly influenced by teaching experience.

The conclusions of Markt and Gilliland are that as a test of teaching aptitude the test has little validity, that it is probably a much better test of abstract intelligence, and that it does not test native ability since the scores are influenced by teaching experience.

The publisher of this test is the Center for Psychological Service, George Washington University, Washington, D. C.

References:

1. Hunt, T. Measuring teachers aptitude. Journal of Educational Administration and Supervision, 1929, 15, 334–342.
2. Markt, A. R. and Gilliland, A. R. A critical analysis of the George Washington Teaching Aptitude Test. Journal of Educational Administration and Supervision, 1929, 15, 660–666.

L. S. R.

Stanford Educational Aptitudes Test. This test was constructed by Milton B. Jensen. Its purpose is to measure differences between abilities in three major fields of education: School Administration, Educational Research, and Teaching. It indicates whether the individual is more or less capable as a school administrator than as an educational research worker, as a school administrator than as a teacher, and as an educational research worker than as a teacher, or whether ability is equal in any two or all of these fields. Since the test is intended as a measure of relative rather than absolute abilities it is most useful with individuals who already have selected education as a career. It has been used most widely in schools of education, teachers colleges, normal schools and by workers in education and allied fields who were considering further training or specialization in some field of education.

The test is self-administered and requires about thirty minutes to complete. Scores are interpreted in chances per 1,000 that they are significant. It is hand scored. Scoring procedures are somewhat complicated for ordinary clerical help.

Validation was by means of the responses of 205 eminent American educators rated by from one to seven of their peers as being much more or less capable as school administrators than as educational research workers, as school administrators than as teachers, or as educational research workers than as teachers. Product-moment correlation coefficients of the weighted ratings of these 205 individuals with their scores on the test were in the neighborhood of .85. Among professional students in education test scores were found to bear no significant relationship to sex, age, years of professional experience, nor to years of professional training. Among professional workers in education with five or more years experience test scores correlated .73 + .03 with self-ratings as to the field or fields of education in which they were most capable.

By product-moment correlations of comparable halves the author found reliability coefficients as follows: Administration vs Research, .91 + .01; Administration vs Teaching, .85 + .02; Research vs Teaching, .94 + .01.

This test is published by the Stanford University Press, Stanford University, California.

M. B. J.

TESTS, ADMINISTRATION OF. The method of administering tests is exceedingly important. If they are not administered properly, the results obtained, even from the best and most reliable ones, can be misleading or incorrect.

Tests are administered individually or in groups. Where time and cost are the most important considerations, the group method is usually chosen since hundreds of persons can be tested simultaneously at a fraction of the cost of individual testing. Where it is essential to observe the performance and reactions of an individual or where it is desirable to obtain a more accurate measure of his abilities than can be obtained by the group method, individual testing is the better choice.

Individual testing and group testing have much in common, but there are important differences between them. Both similarities and differences will be considered here with regard to administrative personnel, environment, materials to be used, and techniques.

Individual Testing

The administrator of a test always should have a kindly and agreeable personality with sufficient firmness to control any situation. He should enunciate clearly, with a pleasing voice. The rasping complaining type of voice which ends sentences with rising inflections is out of place in a testing situation. A great deal of confidence and and rapport can be established with the testee by means of the voice alone.

The attitude of the administrator should be that of trying to help the testee to do the best he possibly can, to encourage him and to give him the impression that the examiner wishes him to make the best showing possible. The administrator should not act as if he were trying to impress the testee or to find out how many mistakes he makes. Some people come to a test with an idea, which is not unnatural, that the examiner is trying to catch them in an error to disclose their weaknesses. One way to avert such suspicions is to give directions without insinuating that the person cannot perform the task requested. As an illustration the examiner, if permitted by the author of the test, should say "Do this" instead of saying "I want to see if you can do this."

The experienced examiner must be a good actor. He should never show surprise, amusement, or annoyance at what the examinee has done. He should never lose his poise and certainly never lose his patience no matter what happens.

In addition the examiner should be so familiar with the directions for giving a test that he will not hesitate and, above all, will not depart from standard practice. One way to accomplish this technique is for him to take the test himself. Such an experience will enable him to associate the test with the directions, as he will then appreciate the necessity for the various procedures.

Individual testing should be done alone with the examiner. All spectators, particularly relatives and friends, should be excluded. Many persons are self-conscious or distracted in the presence of others and hence cannot give their whole attention to the task in front of them.

The room should be quiet, well lighted, and well ventilated. It should be situated so as to assure privacy and freedom from interruptions. To avoid distractions it should be furnished like a comfortable office or room in a home. Imposing wall charts, scientific instruments, and other strange objects should be out of sight, preferably stored in a closet. The room should have an appearance of neatness and orderliness. An untidy desk or a table littered with an assortment of objects can cause distraction, particularly with emotionally disturbed persons or with those of low mentality.

All the materials for the test should be at hand where they can be reached at once. Before a test is given, a check should be made to see that no articles are missing. The materials necessary for giving tests should include pencils, paper, screens, and timing devices, in addition to the material necessary for the particular test. Several pencils should be available which have been sharpened in advance and which have clean erasers. If the tests are paper and pencil tests which are to be machine-scored, a check should be made to see that the pencils are the special ones required.

Where timing is necessary a very satisfactory device to use is a cumulative stop watch with a sliding lever near the stem. This operates noiselessly and allows the examiner to obtain both partial and total times and to take out time for interruptions. A watch which springs back to zero before it can be started again is not adapted to measuring time in a testing situation. Stop watches with a narrow range of time for one complete cycle, such as 15 minutes, should be used only in connection with a fairly reliable watch. The watch should be used to check the correct multiples of 15 minutes and the stop watch used to secure accuracy within a second. All timing devices, whether used for individual or group testing, should be checked periodically for accuracy.

A screen of some sort should be provided on the desk so that the testee cannot see either the stop watch or the examiner performing the act of writing. Nothing is more distracting to a person being tested than to begin to wonder what the examiner is writing about him. This means that the examiner should practice writing without looking at the paper. If notes are transcribed immediately after the examination, no loss in accuracy should occur.

If several tests are to be given the easiest one should be given first, and a very brief explanation should be given of the purpose of the test. This helps to get the examinee over the first hurdle of nervousness. The order of the tests should be such as to encourage the testee and keep his interest at a high level. This end can be achieved by occasionally following a difficult test by an easy one and by mixing interest and manual tests with achievement and aptitude tests. Critical and difficult tests, such as intelligence tests and some speed tests, should not come at the close of the day when fatigue is a factor and apt to lower the scores significantly.

Directions should be followed rigorously. No explanations should be given except those indicated in the directions for the test. Timing is particularly important on timed tests, since conclusions and interpretations are otherwise apt to be invalid. The examiner should be aware of all possible sources of error so as to eliminate them from his administration of the test.

During the examination a great deal of valuable information which is extraneous to the tests can be secured by observation, but not by staring directly at the testee. The experienced examiner gets this data without making the testee aware that he is being watched. Such things as endurance, resourcefulness, energy, concentration, awkwardness, unusual answers, and emotional control may be significant factors in vocational guidance. Sometimes during the test it becomes apparent that the testee needs psychiatric assistance. A notation of all of these facts should be made at the time of the examinations for future reference. An excellent check list of what to observe and how to interpret what is seen, can be found in Occupations, volume 14, 1935 on pages 115–122. This is a translation by F. J. Keller of an article on "Die Tastmethode" by Franziska Baumgarten.

At the end of some tests it is advisable to give some words of praise. Such encouragement must be given judiciously. If given wisely, it keeps the testee at a high performance level. If given indiscriminately, it is likely to arouse resentment at the implications suggested.

Group Testing

Group testing, in comparison with individual testing, presents other problems, particularly when the number to be tested is large or when it is necessary to give the same battery of tests to several groups, either simultaneously or at different times. In any event it is essential that all testing be done uniformly.

The administrator should be the type of person who has a pleasing but firm personality and is so familiar with the nature of his task that he instills confidence in the testees. His voice should reach with clearness the people in the last rows. He should be able to read directions in a natural and well modulated tone of voice which keeps the interest of his listeners. To avoid the effect of artificiality the administrator must be a good oral reader, and above all he should avoid reading rapidly or in a monotone. His speed of reading should never be faster than that at which everyone can easily hear and follow. Public address systems are so common these days that such devices should be used whenever possible. They enable an administrator to speak in an ordinary well modulated tone and still have his voice carry distinctly to all parts of the room.

Proctors can be relatively untrained individuals provided they have good sense, are alert, and are able to follow directions. If the proctors are untrained, they should be called together before the test is given and instructed as to their duties and the things to watch out for in the examination. At the same time they should take at least some parts of those tests which are the most difficult to administer and to proctor.

One proctor is sufficient for every 20 to 40 students. In performing their duties proctors should move around noiselessly and inconspicuously. Shoes which squeak, or wooden heels on wooden floors, are out of place in a testing room. The help which proctors give to students should be confined to seeing that they are following directions and that they are comfortable, away from drafts and out of poorly lighted corners. Proctors should never give any aid on examinations, except possibly on practice exercises; but they should always be ready to give assistance if a student needs another pencil or shows signs of illness. As for the things they should not do, a good rule for them to follow is never to do anything which they would resent if they were taking the tests.

The rooms in which tests are given should be well lighted, well ventilated, and free from extraneous noises. Seats should be far enough apart or so arranged that students cannot accidentally see the answers on each other's papers. The fact that it is possible to see a neighbor's paper is often distracting. Tables, such as those used in drafting rooms, make ideal desks on which to write. Because this kind of equipment is seldom available, recourse must be had to the usual school room chairs which are equipped with arms. These arms should be smooth and of sufficient width to accommodate the answer sheets used so commonly with machine-scorable tests. Nothing is more disconcerting than to poke a hole through an answer sheet into a depression on a desk top.

For timing the tests where split second accuracy is not a necessity, devices are available which can be set so that a bell is rung at the end of a pre-determined time interval. After the alarm has been sounded a few times, students soon become conditioned to it. In any case the timer should be set well away from the microphone. Such a timer is exceedingly convenient since it obviates the necessity for the administrator continually to watch the hands of a clock. Furthermore it eliminates the common accident of absentmindedly giving too long a time for the completion of a given test. Where it is not available, the next best thing is a good clock, a good watch, or a stop watch. If an ordinary watch is used, the administrator should record on a paper the exact time, minute and second, when a test is begun, add to that the time necessary for the test, and then stop the test immediately when the terminal time is reached.

If uniformity of results are to be obtained, whether several groups are to be tested simultaneously or at different times, it is essential that the same directions and the same information should be given to each group. To accomplish this, a manual should be prepared where every word which the administrator says is predetermined. In preparing such a manual, it is a wise precaution always to give directions in positive terms. If negative directions are given, such as "Do not write on the pages of your test booklet," these should always be preceded by positive directions, such as "Put all your answers on the answer sheet."

Just before beginning a test, proctors should be assigned to the area they are to cover and requested to inform the head proctor of the number of students under their supervision. The head proctor, if the test is machine scored, gives to each proctor the correct number of pencils, and then hands him the correct number of tests for his section.

The first information given to the group should be such as to assure them of the benign purpose of the examination and to explain to them the nature and purpose of the tests they are about to take. Since the manual is prepared in advance, the phraseology can be so chosen as to secure the maximum of good will and cooperation on the part of the listeners. Any apprehensions which the group being tested might have, should be put at rest by explaining to them how they will benefit from the test and by assuring them that the test will not be used against them. Whatever is said will be influenced to a certain extent by the directions for the test.

When the materials are distributed, the pencils should be passed out first. If these pencils are of the mechanical type, each person should be asked to check his to be sure it is in good working condition. Proctors should be supplied with extra pencils so that as little time as possible is lost if a pencil becomes defective during the examination. Next all the test booklets should be distributed, title page up but reversed. This is an excellent method of passing out tests: it keeps up the morale of the persons who receive their tests last, since it assures them that those who received their tests first do not have an unfair advantage; it also keeps those who have already received their tests occupied, since they invariably try to read the tests upside down.

After the directions for a test are read, some tests invite the testee to ask questions. Although the administrator should be prepared in advance for any emergency, he should be particularly prepared to answer such questions frankly and quickly without hesitation. Uncertainty and doubt on the part of the administrator may cause confusion in the minds of some members of the group. Above all the administrator should know the directions so thoroughly that he will not unconsciously give help which should not be given.

As soon as the testing procedure is under way the proctors should be alert to see that the students start when they should, stop when they should, keep on working when a part of the test covers several pages, are working on the correct page of the test and the correct side of the answer sheet, are making marks heavy enough and long enough if the test is to be machine scored, are erasing properly, and are not copying from each other. On the whole proctors should interfere as little as possible and make themselves inconspicuous. Nevertheless if machine scorable tests are used, students should not be allowed to jeopardize their scores through faulty mechanical operations.

At the close of a test proctors should make sure that every one stops immediately. Recalcitrant individuals can be quickly cured by drawing a line through that part of the test which is worked on after time is called, but this seldom is necessary.

If several tests are given during the course of one session, rest periods should be provided. If the tests are short, it frequently is sufficient to have students stand at their seats for a few moments, without moving about. If longer rest periods are considered necessary, they should never be so long that the energy level of the testees begins to drop.

Every precaution should be taken to see that test questions are not circulated outside the examination room. Every test booklet should be accounted for. Scratch paper should not be used in an examination unless the test calls for it. When it does, every bit of scratch paper should be collected at the same time as the test booklets.

An examiner who gives heed to the directions as indicated will be fairly sure to secure reliable results. Furthermore, since the testee is likely to suffer from poor test administration, it is only fair to him to do everything possible to help him secure a reasonably true score.

W. C. K.

TEST PUBLISHERS

1. Bureau of Educational Measurements, Emporia, Kansas
2. Bureau of Educational Research and Service, University of Iowa, Iowa City, Iowa.

3. Bureau of Publications, Teachers College, Columbia University, New York.
4. Center for Psychological Service, George Washington University, Washington, D. C.
5. California Test Bureau, Los Angeles.
6. Chicago University Press, Chicago.
7. Cooperative Test Service, New York.
8. Educational Test Bureau, Minneapolis, Minnesota.
9. Ginn & Company, Boston.
10. Houghton Mifflin Company, Chicago.
11. McKnight and McKnight, Bloomington, Illinois.
12. National Institute of Vocational Research, Los Angeles.
13. Psychological Corporation, 522 Fifth Avenue, New York.
14. Psychological Institute, Washington, D. C.
15. Public School Publishing Company, Bloomington, Illinois.
16. Sheridan Supply Company, Box 837, Beverly Hills, California.
17. Science Research Associates, 228 S. Wabash Avenue, Chicago.
18. Stanford University Press, Stanford University, California.
19. World Book Company, Yonkers-on-Hudson 5, New York.

California Test Bureau, 5916 Hollywood Blvd., Los Angeles 28, California. The California Test Bureau was organized in 1926 for the purpose of publishing and distributing standardized and diagnostic tests of abilities, interests, aptitudes, personality or temperament, and achievement. The authors of the various test publications are, for the most part, nationally-known authorities in educational and psychological research and guidance. Many of them are engaged professionally in vocational and educational guidance and in personnel selection and placement activities.

The following list of publications, reviewed elsewhere in this *Encyclopedia,* are illustrative of the areas for which standardized instruments for appraisal and controlled interview are published by the California Test Bureau:

California Test of Mental Maturity
California Test of Personality
Johnson Temperament Analysis
Lewerenz Test of Fundamental Abilities of Visual Art
MacQuarrie Test for Mechanical Ability
Mental Health Analysis
Occupational Interest Inventory
Prognostic Test of Mechanical Abilities
Progressive Achievement Tests

Survey of Mechanical Insight
Survey of Object Visualization
Survey of Space Relations Ability
Survey of Working Speed and Accuracy

In addition to the publication of tests and inventories, the California Test Bureau publishes occasional descriptive and analytical bulletins and reports, of which the following are typical:

Educational Bulletin No. 7. Conducting High School Guidance Programs.

Educational Bulletin No. 12. Use of Tests and Inventories in Vocational Guidance and Rehabilitation.

Educational Bulletin No. 13. Use of Standardized Tests in Correctional Institutions.

Educational Bulletin No. 14. The Proper Use of Intelligence Tests.

Educational Bulletin No. 15. Vocational Guidance for Junior and Senior High School Students.

Industrial Bulletin No. 1. How to Use Employment Tests.

W. W. C.

Educational Test Bureau. *History.* The Educational Test Bureau was founded in 1926 by S. C. Bolstad, one of the first men in the Middle West to recognize the significance of the emerging movement in psychological measurement.

The Brueckner Diagnostic Arithmetic Tests, the Brueckner-Cutright Geography Cards, and other tests were published the first year. The first edition of the now famous Kuhlmann-Anderson Intelligence Test was published the second year.

The Middle West was originally served from a basement room across the street from the University of Minnesota campus. The Eastern Office was opened in Philadelphia in 1931 and the Southern Office was opened in Nashville in 1936. The Home Office is now located at 720 Washington Avenue Southeast in Minneapolis.

Services. The Educational Test Bureau publishes psychological and educational tests for use in schools, in business, and in industry. This includes group tests and individual tests, achievement tests and skills tests, ability tests and aptitude tests, as well as rating scales and interest inventories. With modern, high speed equipment the Educational Test Bureau does its own typesetting, photo-engraving, printing, folding, and binding, and manufactures all the psychological apparatus it sells.

The editorial staff advises and assists authors in item analysis and other phases of test construction. The Trade and Industrial Advisory Service cooperates in the development and installation of specialized employee selection tests. As Educational Publishers, Inc., the firm publishes text and reference books for professional and classroom use. As the County School and Office Supply Company, the firm publishes a wide variety of school record and report forms.

G. L. B.

Psychological Corporation.   The Test Division of the Psychological Corporation was formally opened in 1935 and since that time has been engaged in four kinds of activities in its services to psychologists and persons engaged in various forms of educational, vocational, and personal guidance.

These functions are as follows:

1. *Publication of Tests and Related Books.*

   These publications of tests and books have either been submitted to the Division for publication by psychologist-authors or have been developed within the organization by the research staff of the Division.

2. *Sale of Tests and Related Publications.*

   The main function of the Test Division is to sell its own publications. However, the Division is also a distributing agency for most of the standard publishers of tests as well as for individual persons who have published their tests themselves and desire a sales outlet.

3. *Test Advisory Service.*

   The Test Division has a permanent staff of professional psychologists who are specialists in test construction and the application of tests in education, social work, counselling and guidance, employment, clinical psychology and other fields. Much of this advisory service is incidental to the sale of tests. It is carried on by mail and in personal conferences in the office. The Division also carries on advisory services on a consultant basis with all kinds of organizations who wish special help in problems of testing. This consultant work may range from such simple things as setting up a pre-employment testing program to the construction of special tests for large industries.

4. *Research*.

The research work of the Division primarily involves the standard statistical work required in the construction of new tests, ranging from item analysis through standardization and validation. Along with this psychotechnology, the staff engages in more fundamental research in the field of psychometrics.

The Division of Testing for Schools of Nursing is a unit of the Psychological Corporation which has as its function the testing of applicants to nursing schools. Over three hundred schools of nursing use this service. The testing is conducted in announced places throughout the country from time to time during the year, and all applicants to these schools take the tests under the supervision of local psychologists or educators or members of the home staff.

The tests are scored in the New York office and reported with interpretive norms to the school of nursing to which the applicant indicates she wishes the reports sent. No results are sent to the applicant. The fee for the testing is paid by the applicant.

The Division carries on research studies to improve the battery of tests which is used and also validation studies, both with respect to the success of the applicants in schools and their later success as practicing nurses.

H. S.

Science Research Associates. As a leading educational publisher in the field of occupational information and guidance, Science Research Associates serves as a clearing house for vocational and educational guidance material and information used in colleges, schools, and libraries. Working closely with various professional organizations, such as the American Council on Education, the National Vocational Guidance Association, and prominent guidance people in various states, the activities of Science Research Associates have been instrumental in furthering the wide-spread development of the guidance movement in recent years. From its inception, it has worked constantly through its research facilities and publications to bring before educators the importance of effective guidance work with students and has directed its efforts toward establishing and developing functional guidance programs in schools.

To this end it has also, during the war, cooperated with the Examinations Staff of the United States Armed Forces Institute in developing a comprehensive series of tests of educational development and subject matter mastery, and has also furnished Army

Service Forces with a large volume of pamphlets and ephemeral occupational information material.

When first organized, there was an urgent need for reliable occupational research and information to be made available to young people, and the organization made investigations of employment trends and conditions, presenting reports written in terms understandable to the layman. From this work has developed the magazine, *Vocational Trends*; regularly published *Occupational Reprints* of articles from not-readily-available sources; the *American Job Series* of Occupational Monographs, a library of booklets covering broad occupational fields and vocational success subjects, and the *Occupational Briefs of Postwar Job Fields,* a series of four-page, factual reports on special occupations. Providing such materials is one of the major activities of the Science Research Associates program and will continue to be the hub around which the organization turns.

As experience was gained, however, a need for other types of materials directed toward helping counselors, teachers, librarians, and school administrators became apparent. To better serve in the broad field of guidance, other activities were begun, and today Science Research Associates also provides a number of professional aids for counselors, such as John G. Darley's *Testing and Counseling in the High-School Guidance Program,* which is widely used as a pattern for setting up effective guidance programs in schools. In the fall of 1944, publication of a *Guidance Newsletter,* interpreting and reporting guidance developments and serving as a medium of exchange for new ideas in the area of guidance, was begun. The *Occupational Filing Plan* for classifying pamphlet materials has proved to be a usable system of organization for an occupational information library and is being adopted by many schools and libraries. In many instances it has served as a stimulus for schools to set up such a library. The *Guidance Index,* published monthly, is a specialized bibliography listing current vocational and occupational publications.

Closely coordinated with the program of providing guidance people with both the "tools of the trade" and professional aids is the organization's work in testing. As publishers of a variety of tests—intelligence, interest, aptitude, achievement, and vocational—Science Research Associates has been instrumental in promoting the use of tests giving counselors scientific evaluations of students, which in turn can be used in advising students more wisely. These and many other tests are described in detail in another section of this Encyclopedia.

In an effort to promote the development of more reliable tests, Science Research Associates publishes new, as well as established tests, aiding authors in working out norms and in standardization. To further strengthen the place testing is gaining in schools, it established a professional journal, *Educational and Psychological Measurement,* in which appear reports of research on the development and use of tests and measurements in education, government, and industry; descriptions of testing programs being used for various purposes; and discussions of problems of measurement. By advocating better testing in these ways, Science Research Associates has won a reputation as a progressive, forward-reaching organization, and test authors now look upon it as a sounding board for their ideas and for advice in advancing their work.

By means of specialized publications, such as those described above, Science Research Associates has done much to elevate counseling to a professional level, and has also considerably augmented the scant body of occupational information literature of a few years ago.

J. R. Y.

World Book Company. The Division of Research and Test Service of the World Book Company serves the users of its tests in a dual way. In the first place, the experience and specialized training of the director and the editorial staff are utilized to insure that the tests published are prepared in a form for the most effective, reliable, and economical use. The second function is that of direct test service—service to users in the way of advice and assistance, comparable to that provided by the manufacturer of a mechanical device.

Through the Division of Research and Test Service the Company endeavors to contribute to the sane and useful application of test results. Test users are encouraged to call for any suggestions or guidance they may need. Users and prospective users of tests frequently request information regarding the choice and use of our tests, the interpretation of results, the method of attacking educational problems by means of testing, the handling of special cases, statistical calculations, and many other similar problems. All questions are answered as fully as possible.

From time to time the division issues Test Service Bulletins and Test Method Helps of practical value.

In so far as it is feasible members of the division go into the field to aid in planning testing programs and in the proper interpretation and use of test results.

B. C. W.

TEST RESULTS, INTERPRETATION OF. The specific interpretations to be placed on any test score will depend upon a number of factors, general and specific. General factors to be considered are the purpose of the testing, the nature of the tests, and the relation of test results to relevant information obtained from other sources. Specific factors to be considered are the nature of the score, the significance of the score, the pattern of scores obtained from several tests, and the nature of the criterion used in validating the test.

General Factors

The most common reasons for the administration of tests are: survey, diagnosis, selection, guidance or placement, and research. When examinations are administered for survey purposes, the major interest is in the discovery of the performances of groups, usually on a number of different tests or traits. For example, intelligence and achievement tests may be administered to all pupils in the second, fifth, and eighth grades of an entire school system. By comparison of mental ability and subject achievement it will be possible to determine whether the groups are learning at the rate that should be expected from their ability. If the actual subject matter achievement is also compared with the expected achievement at each grade level, some basis is obtained for determining whether the progress of the pupils is normal, accelerated, or retarded. By studying mental ability, subject achievement, and grade level, the educational system may be evaluated in terms of its utilization of the potential ability of the pupils.

In a school system where the average mental ability of the pupils was above the national average, it would be reasonable to expect achievement to be similarly above the average. If the achievement test scores indicate that this is so, then the conclusion would be that the schools were adjusting instruction to the level of the ability of their pupils. If the achievement scores are not above the average, then we must search the curriculum, the instructional methods, or other factors, for the source of the discrepancy.

Survey examinations may also be used in comparing the instructional methods employed in different schools within the same system, or by different teachers within the same school. Similarly, in industry, survey tests may be used to study the general level of ability or achievement of applicants for employment. This may help to measure the effectiveness of recruiting procedures, or may be used to help determine the type of person to be selected for employment, or may be used in guiding the level of training within industry.

The broad survey test battery may also be used for the purpose of detecting specific weaknesses in an instructional program. If a survey of apprentices shows that achievement is satisfactory in four of the five areas of training, but deficient in the fifth, it may be found that instruction in this area is being neglected, is poorly presented, or that the subject matter has for some reason not kept pace with developments in the other areas.

For the analysis of individual performance the more specifically diagnostic test should be employed. Weaknesses in group progress, training, or achievement may be indicated by the survey type of examination, but the diagnostic test is constructed to reveal strength and weakness in the specific skills, habits or information which are deemed essential. For example, the survey examination might indicate that an individual is a little below the average of other apprentices in knowledge of machine shop, but the diagnostic examination might indicate that he was superior in understanding of the uses of tools, but very deficient in shop arithmetic. It is especially important in the interpretation of diagnostic test scores to relate the individual scores to opportunity and instruction, and to the possibility of remedial instruction.

Test results are frequently used to select individuals for employment, or for admission to a class, school, or training program. As it is quite unlikely that any test will yield scores which will unequivocally separate the eligible from the ineligible, an element of judgment must be employed in the interpretation of the data. Judgment will be based, among other factors, on the relation of test scores to success in the work for which the individuals are to be selected.

As a fairly typical example, it may be assumed that a test has been administered to several hundred applicants for a certain type of work, and that over a period of time there have been obtained reliable measures of each individual's subsequent success on the job. Grouping the individuals with similar test scores, there may then be determined for each score the per cent of applicants who will be successful, and the per cent who may be expected to fail. It is quite likely that at every score there are some who are successful, and some who fail. By careful examination of the distribution of scores there can usually be found the score *above* which there is the greatest per cent of success, and *below* which there is the greatest per cent of failures. This score is called the "critical score" or "cut-off score."

It must be emphasized that the critical score is not a fixed point, but is arbitrarily determined, and that its value fluctuates in response to a number of factors, particularly the validity of the test, the number of applicants from whom the selection is to be made, and the per cent of satisfactory workers already employed.

Tests are widely used in the vocational guidance or placement of individuals. Here the emphasis is not on finding those who have a reasonable chance for success, but in finding an occupational objective which offers the highest degree of probability for success.

For this reason, in order to receive favorable consideration, test scores should be above the average of the population with whom the individual is to be compared, and should certainly be significantly higher than the critical score which may be used in eliminating individuals for consideration in such occupations. It is desirable in most cases that the score should be at least one standard deviation above the mean.

However, the total range of ability found in any occupation, as indicated by the distribution of test scores, needs also to be considered. Where a wide range of ability in the trait in question is found among workers already engaged in a specific occupation, it may be assumed that other factors or abilities may be used to compensate for some deficiency in this trait, or that the trait is relatively unimportant in that particular occupation. Where a very narrow range of the ability is found, it may be assumed that some factor or factors are operating to limit the selection or retention of workers in the occupation, and that a certain minimum level of ability in the particular trait is a necessity. In this case, test scores indicating possession of ability in this range assume a great deal more significance.

In either case there is indicated the necessity of considering all pertinent data which may be obtained from other sources. Test results should be used to supplement such other guidance techniques as the interview, personal history, educational record, vocational experience, and medical record. Factors of opportunity, energy, ambition, work habits, perseverance, personality, and the like, will need to be considered in connection with the ability which has been found.

The significance of the test score depends not alone on the purpose of measuring an individual, but also upon what is being measured. The achievement test measures the amount of skill, or the amount of knowledge, which the individual possesses. The aptitude test measures the latent capacity of the individual to acquire the information or develop the skill if given training. The achievement test may be used as an aptitude test where a number of individuals have had exactly the same amount of training or experience, as the one with the greater aptitude will profit more from the training. The achievement test may also be used as an interest test where there has been little or no formal training, as it may be assumed that in these circumstances the one who knows more than others in the group about a specific kind of work has had an interest in that work, and has explored the field on his own initiative. Thus a superior knowledge of tools may indicate mechanical interests, and a superior vocabulary in the biological sciences may reveal both interest and reading experience in the scientific occupations.

Tests of information are used also as measures of skill in certain manual occupations. It is assumed that the worker who is able to meet specified standards of interpretation, nomenclature, and description of job experiences or tools is also able to perform those tasks adequately. This assumption may not always prove to be correct, but it is quite safe to assume that the worker who cannot name the tools, describe the operation, or explain why certain things are done, has had too little experience with the task to be a competent workman.

Measures of interest are inventories, or catalogs of preferential responses, and are not tests. Although there is some evidence to indicate that ability and interest tend to be associated, this association is far from perfect, and it is unwise to assume that interest in an occupation, no matter how clearly indicated, is an evidence of aptitude for that occupation. It is also true that interest may vary inversely with the amount of information the individual has about the specific occupation. It is usually desirable to include some measure of information in addition to interest inventories and aptitude tests, when considering vocational choices.

It is well to keep in mind, too, that responses to interest inventories can be manipulated by the individual to produce desired patterns. The amount of reliance to be placed in these scores will therefore be influenced by the motivations of the individual, and the purpose for which the tests have been administered. Considerably more weight may be given to the scores when the tests are taken voluntarily for purposes of guidance, than when they are used as part of an employment procedure.

Much the same considerations apply to the interpretation of personality inventories or questionnaires. These are not tests, but are, in one way or another, self-ratings on a variety of traits. The many prevalent misconceptions of personality are responsible for some additional problems in the interpretation of these results.

Certain personality types are popularly regarded as highly desirable, and consequently the individual responding to the questionnaire may indicate, not the type of person he actually is, but the sort of person he would like to be or would like the counselor to believe he is. There is an added problem in that it is difficult to evaluate accurately the personality of another, and even more difficult to evaluate oneself. The individual may be thoroughly sincere in his responses to the questionnaire, but the adjustment behavior which he there indicates may be quite at variance with reality. For these reasons, responses to personality questionnaires must be interpreted cautiously, and should be weighed against as much other evidence as is available. Because the tendency is to emphasize the desirable aspects of personality, or of interests in relation to a specific job or type of training, we should be less willing to accept, without independent confirmation, very favorable ratings on personality tests. In general, the more unfavorable the rating, the more reliance may be placed on its accuracy.

Specific Factors

The raw score alone is useless for purposes of selection or guidance. To be useful it must be compared with something else in such a way that it expresses a meaningful statement of the individual's performance. This type of expression may be obtained by relating the position of the score to the total distribution of scores obtained from known and described groups. These groups may be children of a specified age, freshmen admitted to colleges in a given year, males applying for work in mechanical trades, females employed in retail sales positions, and so on.

The two most widely used devices for expressing the relationship of a single score to the group, are the percentile rank and the derived score. The percentile rank expresses the position of the scores in the total distribution, in terms of the proportions of the group below that specific score. The differences between percentile ranks are not equivalent, and the percentile scores may not be added, multiplied, averaged, and so on. For example, the difference between percentile ranks of 90 and 95 is much greater than the difference between percentile ranks of 50 and 55. In comparing the performance of individuals where differences are expressed in percentile scores, greater weight should be given to differences which lie toward either extreme, and less weight to differences found toward the center of the distribution. The derived score is an expression of the distance of a given score from the mean, in terms of the standard deviation of the total distribution. Differences between these scores are equivalent, and the derived scores may be averaged, multiplied, divided, and so on. When differences are expressed as derived scores, differences are equally significant throughout the distribution.

The nature of the norm group is extremely significant in those cases where we are predicting future performance. For example, an intelligence test score may be expressed as the 50th percentile, indicating average mental ability. The value of this score in predicting opportunities for success in a specified profession, however, will be greatly affected by our knowledge of whether the performance was compared with those in the same 17 year age group, with high school seniors, college freshmen, third year medical school students, or graduate physicians. So far as possible, the scores obtained from tests should be compared with those obtained by others of the same age, sex, educational and social status, and also with the scores obtained by those who have reached the contemplated goal.

In the example just cited, it is also important that we know whether the ability which we have measured is static or is growing, and if the latter, the kind of growth which may be expected. If the mental ability represented by the 50th percentile is static, then as we compare the individual with progressively more selected and older groups, we may expect the relative ability to decrease rather sharply. On the other hand, if the ability in question is one which is still maturing, and is maturing at a normal rate, then as he grows older we may expect him to maintain his relative position with respect to older groups, but to show some decline in comparison with the groups more selected in educational achievement.

We have assumed so far that the test score is an entirely accurate one. The importance of the score for purposes of guidance and selection will of course depend upon the reliability of the measurement. That is, the more certain we can be that the individual would receive the same score if the test were repeated at another time, the more assured we can be in our interpretation of its significance. As no test is entirely reliable, we may always expect some variation in scores if the test is repeated. The amount of variation which may be expected is usually expressed in terms of the probable error of the score. The smaller the probable error, the greater the confidence we may have in the accuracy of the specific measurement.

In evaluating the importance of the score we will need to know not only that our score on this trait is accurate, but also that the deviation from the performance of others is significant. That is, given an accurate measure of performance, expressed in terms of its deviation from the performance of those of a known group, the counselor must now consider whether deviations of such magnitude, for other individuals, have been associated in any significant fashion with achievement in any particular occupation.

The score and its deviation should also be considered in relation to the performance of the individual in other traits. A significant deviation in a specific trait may become unimportant when compared with an even greater deviation in a second trait which offers perhaps greater possibilities, or is for some reason more desirable. The deviation may also be below the mean, in a trait closely associated with the first, and may thus completely nullify the importance of the first.

Few, if any, occupations depend entirely upon a single ability, but are determined rather by a combination of skills, aptitudes, and interests, all of which must be considered in the selection and in the guidance of individuals. There are, however, a few traits which do not permit compensation in some form. If it is assumed that for a particular occupation traits A, B, C, D, and E are all necessary, and that minimum scores have been determined in each of these traits, the individual may be measured for his performance in these traits to determine whether he is above the minimum level necessary. Assuming further that his performance in trait A is below the minimum, the possession of superior abilities in B, C, D, and E becomes unimportant if a definite minimum level in A has been accurately determined, and if A is an absolutely necessary trait. On the other hand, trait A may be desirable, but not necessary. In this case superior performance in B or C may be found able to compensate for a deficiency in trait A.

It is fairly safe to assume that superior performance on a test indicates possession of the trait which is being measured. The opposite, however, cannot be assumed: that a poor performance on the test indicates a lack of whatever trait the test measures. A great many extraneous factors will affect test results, and will need to be evaluated from personal history, interviews, and personal records. Nor is it always certain that the cause of weakness or failure in a test is due to a lack of ability in the trait measured by the test: i.e., failure in a written test involving the comprehension of arithmetical problems may be due not to an inability in computational processes or intellectual understanding, but may be the result of a deficiency in vocabulary or to reading disability and this, in turn, may be the result of emotional factors extending far into the childhood of the individual.

Although there are numerous variations in the ways in which the validity of a test is determined, the two most common methods basically depend upon either the agreement of the test with certain theories or assumptions of the author, or an agreement with specified external criteria. In either case it is necessary to examine critically the nature of the criterion employed, for if this has not been wisely chosen, the validity coefficient of correlation may be impressively high, but will also be misleading. Thus it is possible for a test to be a reliable measure of one trait while purporting to be a measure of another. Users of a test will study carefully the nature of the author's validating criterion, and will also examine carefully the criteria used by others in subsequent investigations or experiments in which the test is employed.

References:

1. Greene, E. B. *Measurements of human behavior.* New York: Odyssey Press, 1941.
2. Jones, A. J. *Principles of guidance.* New York: McGraw-Hill, 1934.
3. Traxler, A. E. *Techniques of guidance.* New York: Harper & Bros., 1945.

G. S. S.

TESTS, SELECTION OF.* Tests in vocational guidance depend for their value on their relation to the whole guidance process. Thus their selection requires a brief consideration of the other elements of the process, so that tests, as a particular psychological technique, may be employed with maximum utility.

The purpose of counseling may be for direct placement on the job, as in a state or federal or private employment service; in that case tests which are of maximum validity in determining immediate success on that job are very useful. However, if the individual is to undergo a period of training before placement, as in a school or college or in a vocational rehabilitation program, it is of more importance that a suitable training program be selected; the counselor's attention will then be directed toward the individual's training potentialities. If the agency has a very large number of persons to serve with a small staff, a limited battery of tests that are short and simple to administer would be indicated. If the agency has the facilities for a more intensive study of a smaller number of individuals, then a more extensive and complex set of tests may prove useful. If the individuals are adults with aptitudes fully matured,

* The point of view, judgments, and opinions expressed herein are purely those of the writer. Nothing in this paper is to be construed as reflecting the official policy of the Veterans Administration.

some tests might be used which would not be applicable with adolescents.

The data available to the counselor may be limited to that obtainable from the counselee himself, or it may be much more extensive, from school, employment, hospital, or social agency records or from field investigation. Many important variables of personality can only adequately be assessed by the historical method—by repeated or prolonged observation. Where records of such observations are not available, a much greater burden is placed upon the "cross section" methods of tests and interviews. The time available for counseling may vary extremely, from an agency whose policy and procedure may require that counseling be condensed into a period of a day or a few days to one where the practice may be to extend the process over a period of several days or even weeks. During this time there is provided plenty of opportunity for directed reading and vocational exploration, which, with its attendant interviews, may provide the counselor with a great deal of information; without this exploration, more extensive testing, particularly of interests and personality, may be necessary.

The individuals who do the counseling and who administer and score the tests constitute one of the most important factors in determining which tests will be useful. Some counselors are not qualified to interpret the tests, and must depend for their interpretations on a report by a psychologist who is himself not directly involved in the counseling process. In other agencies counseling is done by psychologists who may be very extensively trained in psychometric techniques, and who may or may not administer the tests themselves.

The importance of each of these elements arises from the fact that, to be of maximum value, the tests should be integrated into the whole counseling process in such a way that they supplement rather than duplicate the other information. The factors which determine the value of any test or battery of tests, including reliability, validity, norms, ease and practicality of administration, and cost, require careful consideration.

Two aspects or kinds of reliability must be considered. Some tests with a high degree of internal consistency as far as a given series of trials at one sitting are concerned, may show considerably less stability over a long period of time. Other tests which have a lower intra-test consistency at any given point in time will show good consistency over a span of years. The question involved here is one of actual changes which occur in the individual over a span of years. The prediction which the test user seeks to make is therefore the important consideration—whether the prediction is for a short-term or long-term objective. The data made available regarding the test's reliability should furnish the prospective user with information as to the kind of "reliability" described and the manner of its determination.

The validity of a test, customarily defined as the fidelity with which it measures that which it is presumed to measure, involves, for vocational guidance purposes, psychometric problems of considerable complexity. Validity is ordinarily determined by (a) the test's ability to discriminate between various occupational groups or (b) the correlation with some criterion of job success. These two methods yield quite different results; a test with excellent validity by one method may be poor by the other. The reason, as with the matter of reliability, is that two different problems are being solved, and the test user must carefully determine which problem he is trying to solve by use of the test. In the first instance, adjustment is sought by an *individual* who wishes the job-field that will prove most suitable to him. In the second method of validity determination, the focus is rather on the job, and on the selection from a group of available applicants of the individual most likely to perform proficiently on that job. In the typical vocational guidance situation, the counselor is looking to the best adjustment of the individual; yet occasionally he will wish to apply the same selection techniques as would a prospective employer, in order to give a refined basis for judgment between several feasible occupations. The selection of tests, and the kind of validity data required of tests, thus will depend upon the function performed by the counselor.

There are many tests on the market which appear to have excellent potentialities, but upon which adequate normative data is quite lacking. Although this would be unimportant in an experimental situation, it becomes crucial for the vocational counselor who must know, before he uses a test, the frame of reference within which the test may be interpreted. An example of deficiency in this regard is a personality test published a few years ago with only the statement that it was standardized on "adults near Los Angeles." No information on the selection of these adults, their numbers, sex, ages, or problems, was provided. The normative basis for a test may thus afford evidence of the care or lack of care with which the test is constructed and the appreciation by the test constructor of the problems with which the counselor is faced. Ordinarily a vocational counselor working in a general community situation is most in need of general population norms. However, in a college situation extensive norms may be available on several academic groups, and these norms will be of utmost importance to the college counselor. Similarly, specific norms for a variety of occupations may be necessary in some employment counseling situations.

Various practical matters in test administration deserve consideration because the main reason for using tests is that they aid in providing practical answers to guidance problems. The cost of a test, apart from the time employed in its administration and interpretation, is usually a relatively small matter, although there are significant variations also in material costs. With a few important exceptions, all available guidance devices require only a quiet, well-lighted room free from distraction. The important item of practicality, therefore, is that of the skill and training required by the individual who administers, scores, and interprets the tests. Some tests, highly valid and reliable, require for their administration and interpretation so much time of a highly skilled psychologist that their practical clinical usefulness is seriously impaired. Many tests may be adequately administered by a carefully trained and intelligent clerk working under the close supervision of a skilled psychometrist, and the scoring time for such tests is frequently a matter of minutes. As a practical matter, most guidance services find it advisable to rely chiefly on those tests which can be handled in groups. Individual tests, when required, are then administered by the psychologist, psychometrist, or by the counselor himself.

In this discussion of the use of tests, the assumption is made that the counselor is seeking the information about the individual that is necessary for a thorough-going "vocational diagnosis." This implies that the purpose of guidance is not merely to determine whether the individual has the minimum capacities required for the job he is seeking, or for which he is being considered, but to assess more comprehensively his potentialities for the vocational field as a whole. The level and type of job for which he is best fitted by reason of native endowment, experience, training, interests, and personality attributes—these are the elements of a thorough vocational diagnosis. Testing constitutes one of the techniques for the performance of this diagnosis. Tests do not themselves provide a diagnosis, any more than the stethescope, X-ray, or laboratory tests of the physician provide a medical diagnosis. The counselor, like the doctor, must weigh the evidence from many sources and evaluate its significance. The attitudes, training, and experience of the counselor will therefore be of determining significance in the selection from available tests of those most useful to him. Although a test may be designed to provide a rather carefully-described kind of information, experience in guidance agencies indicates that there are enormous differences among competent counselors in the amount of information which may be derived from a particular test or test battery, school record, or social service report. Such differences, largely due to variations in training and clinical experience and familiarity with various kinds of data, may be expected to diminish as the literature of vocational psychology grows and wider common bases of experience and understanding are developed. It should become practical to translate, more readily than now, the results of one test into the terms of another. No such process, however, will entirely eliminate the variations due to individual preferences. And these preferences themselves, resulting in varying attacks on a complex problem, are the stimulus to valuable research. The following description of the kinds of tests found to be most useful in vocational diagnosis would probably not be universally agreed upon; it represents a sincere attempt to state general principles upon which many clinicians will agree.

In measuring academic ability in the typical vocational clinic, an untimed test is desirable from the standpoint of clinical practicality; a test where several sections must be separately timed is exceedingly awkward in a testing-room where many people are working on a variety of tests. Some counselors prefer to have both timed and untimed tests of academic ability. An omnibus test, with a single over-all time limit, is the most practical from the psychometrist's standpoint, and several good tests of this nature are on the market, while only a few untimed tests are at present available.

Few satisfactory tests of clerical aptitude are available. Some are so heavily weighted with general mental ability that they contribute very little information that does not overlap that of a good test of "mental alertness." Some that appear to be potentially good are marred by inadequate directions for administration and scoring, and by norms of very limited utility. A satisfactory test in this category should be relatively brief, simply administered and scored, and should measure a kind of perceptual speed and accuracy involved in typical routine clerical operations, with a minimum correlation with mental ability.

Validity studies have clearly shown that the skilled mechanic or craftsman is primarily dependent upon ability to perceive spatial relationships and upon knowledge of mechanical principles and practices. Many tests of mechanical functions in both group (paper-and-pencil) and individual (apparatus) form are available; both timed and untimed tests of mechanical comprehension are on the market. Scrutiny of published validity data should readily indicate to the discriminating user which of the many available tests will best meet his needs.

Many tests of manual dexterity are on the market, and few tests are so frequently over-interpreted. In spite of the experimental studies which have been almost universal in indicating that dexterity is a secondary or tertiary factor in most of the skilled trades, counselors are prone to put much weight on tests of manual dexterity. The error is a perfectly understandable one because it is easy to "see" the deftness with which a skilled craftsman manipulates his tools. The more important aptitude, which cannot be "seen" by direct observation, is the complex of intellective and perceptive abilities which guide the nimble fingers. In the semi-skilled, routinized jobs which may be learned in a few hours and in which success depends upon speed of performance of a standardized operation, dexterity is undoubtedly important. The counselor's problem is complicated, however, by the fact that there are many kinds of dexterity, all having low intercorrelations, and that few tests have been validated against job criteria. The counselor concerned with the placement of workers in these occupations may be aided by a battery of dexterity tests; in most guidance situations, however, the selection of such a job will be indicated rather by the absence of higher-level abilities which might better be utilized in jobs of higher skill.

Interest measurement offers some hard choices for the typical counselor. The only test which to date (April 1946) has been extensively validated, is difficult to score. Among the alternatives, careful scrutiny of the method of construction, norms, and occupational validation is required for a choice. Experience with available interest inventories indicates that great caution must be exercised in interpreting those in which the items have not been directly validated by their ability to discriminate between defined occupational groups.

Personality as a factor in vocational success cannot be doubted. Personality tests of proven occupational significance are not, however, available at this writing. It is necessary for the counselor to utilize personality measurement primarily for the purpose of determining areas or kinds of maladjustment, and then utilize this information as the individual case data may suggest, in determining its vocational significance. It follows from this that the criteria that apply in selecting a personality test are those of the field of personality evaluation, rather than vocational guidance *per se*. As with interest measurement, however, the test will prove most useful in which the items have been directly validated by their ability to discriminate specified kinds of personality disorders.

This paper has dealt largely with principles; little with specific tests. Its thesis is that there can be no universal prescription of a suitable battery of tests for vocational guidance. Selection must be made from the hundreds of published tests in accordance with a few fundamental principles of test construction, some particular factors applying in the vocational clinic, and finally in accord with the peculiar needs and capacities of the individual vocational counselor.

L. R. H.

THINKING, TESTS OF

Goldstein-Scheerer Tests of Abstract and Concrete Thinking. Five different performance tests have been constructed for these purposes:

1. To detect impairment of abstract behavior, to assess the degree and the extent to which different performance fields are thereby affected.
2. To establish criteria for diagnosing the behavioral symptoms of pathological concreteness.

The testing procedures are based on clinical and experimental findings in brain injured patients, in feeble-minded and in deteriorated psychotics, as established in various studies by the authors and other investigators. These findings suggest that the nature of the intellectual deficit in such dements and aments consists in a restriction of the total personality to a simpler level of functioning. This restriction expresses itself in an impairment of the abstract and an abnormal preponderance of the concrete level of behavior. Normally the two levels (or attitudes) are operative in adjustive interaction and the individual can shift according to the demands of the task.

Abstract behavior as elaborated elsewhere [5] encompasses the conscious and voluntary formation of a range of mental sets through which our cognitive performances are executed as, e.g.: we grasp essential relations in a given whole, analyze it into parts and synthesize the parts; we comprehend different aspects of the same situation or object; we shift from one aspect to another. We evolve common denominators, hierarchic concepts; we reason in categories—symbolically. We give verbal accounts of acts. In concrete behavior we do not transcend the immediate reality and uniqueness of a given stimulus or specific aspect of a situation. Our performances and corresponding mental sets are not guided by conscious volition but we respond to our experiences without reflection. Thinking and acting are governed by immediate claims.

The tests present tasks where proper solution requires the abstract attitude, and failure or errors reveal "concretization." Each test probes a different performance field. The combined results indicate which fields have suffered, and to what extent.

1. In the cube test colored designs must be reproduced with 4 colored cubes. The design is to be analyzed into four "arbitrary" parts, i.e. imaginary squares. The corresponding block sides must be found and combined into a whole. After failure, simplified models are given, e.g. the design is divided by lines into 4 squares. It is crucial whether the S. can learn from these aids.

2. In the color sorting test the S. has to sort a variety of colored woolen skeins according to a color sample or a named hue. S's with impaired abstraction cannot sort (conceptually) by color categories but show abnormally restricted choices and other anomalies, including rejection of presented correct groupings.

3. In the object sorting test the S. must sort a variety of objects and shift from grouping concretely (e.g. practical use) to the conceptual abstraction of common properties—color, material, shape, etc. Impaired S's cannot shift, and also fail on "abstract" groupings, when presented.

4. In the color form test the S. must discover how to sort 12 figures according to color and also form. This requires conceptual orientation towards both color *and* form. The S. must shift from one to the other when told to group differently (but not "how"). Impaired S's fail and may reject correct groupings when presented.

5. In the stick test the S. must copy and reproduce from memory meaningless geometric designs with sticks. This requires an abstract grasp of spatial relations. Impaired S's succeed only on designs which make concrete "thing" sense. Failing a simple design of 2 sticks (e.g. right angle), they may succeed on a 9 stick design of a house.

The publisher of the Monograph by K. Goldstein and M. Scheerer is the American Psychological Association, Inc., Massachusetts and Nebraska Avenues, Washington, D. C.

The distributor of the test materials and scoring blanks, etc., is the Psychological Corporation, 522 Fifth Avenue, New York, N. Y.

References:

1. Bolles, M. M. The basis of pertinence, *Archι Psychol.*, N. Y. 1937, No. 212, 1–51.
2. ——— and Goldstein, K. A study of the impairment of "abstract behavior" in schizophrenic patients. *Psychiat. Quart.*, 1938, *12*, 42–65.
3. Goldstein, K. *After effects of brain injuries.* New York: Grune & Stratton, 1941.
4. ———. *Human nature in the light of psychopathology.* Cambridge: Harvard University Press, 1940.
5. Goldstein, K. and Scheerer, M. Abstract and concrete behavior: an experimental study with special test, *Psychol. Monogr.*, 1941, *53*, 2, 1–151.
6. Hanfmann, E. and Kasanin, J. Conceptual thinking in schizophrenia. *Nerv. Ment. Dis. Monogr.*, 1942, 67.
7. Hanfmann, E., Rickers-Ovsiankina, M., Goldstein, K. Case Lanuti: Extreme concretization of behavior, etc. *Psychol. Monogr.*, 1944, 57, 4, 1–72.
8. Kasanin, J. S. *Language and thought in schizophrenia.* Berkeley: University of California Press, 1944. (Collected papers.)
9. Nadel, A. B. A qualitative analysis of behavior following cerebral lesions. *Arch. Psychol.*, N. Y., 1938, No. 224, 1–60.
10. Rashkis, H., Cushman, F., Landis, C. A new method for studying disorders of conceptual thinking. *J. Abn. Soc. Psychol.*, 1946, 1, 72–74.
11. Reichard, S., Schneider, M., Rapaport, D. The development of concept formation in children. *Am. J. Orthopsychiatr.*, 1944, 14, 156–161.
12. Rylander, G. *Personality changes after operation on the frontal lobes.* London: Oxford University Press, 1939.
13. Scheerer, M., Rothmann, E., Goldstein, K. A Case of "Idiot Savant": An experimental study of personality organization. *Psychol. Monogr.*, 1945, *58*, 4, 1–63.
14. Strauss, A. A. and Werner, H. Disorders of conceptual thinking in the brain-injured child. *J. Nerv. Ment. Disorders*, 1942, 96, 2, 153–172.

M. S.

Watson-Glaser Tests of Critical Thinking. These tests, constructed by Goodwin Watson and Edward Glaser, are designed to measure ability to think critically at the high school, college and adult levels. The tests are arranged in two batteries, each battery consisting of a booklet of four tests. Battery I, entitled "Discrimination in Reasoning," includes tests which measure the ability to draw warranted generalizations, to make sound inferences, to discriminate between strong and weak arguments, and to recognize unstated assumptions. Battery II, entitled Logical Reasoning," includes tests of logical reasoning and logical consistency. The Batteries may be given either separately or in combination.

The test results may be used in one or all of the following ways:

1. As a means of obtaining quantitatively as well as qualitatively a measure of the students ability to think critically with regard to problems involving interpretation of data, drawing inferences, making warranted generalizations, discrimination between strong and weak arguments, recognizing unstated assumptions in reasoning and other aspects of critical thinking.
2. In evaluating a local curriculum.
3. In evaluating the relative effectiveness of different methods of instruction which are intended to develop the ability to think critically.
4. As source material for classroom instruction (after they have served their purpose as evaluation instruments).
5. For individual guidance and remedial teaching.

All items in the tests have been carefully validated by a jury of fifteen competent judges and by extensive experimental tryout. In general, the tests are appropriate for persons whose reading comprehension level is equivalent to 9.0 grade or higher on a standardized reading test. There are no time limits for the tests. It is presumed that in general the two batteries will require four sittings, each thirty and thirty-five minutes. Scoring is facilitated by the use of an attached answer sheet which may be scored with a stencil key. Detailed directions for stencil scoring and for interpreting results are given in the Manual of Directions.

The publisher of these tests is World Book Company, Yonkers-on-Hudson, New York.

B. C. W.

TRADE TESTS

Purpose

Like all other tests used in guidance and personnel work, trade tests are used to measure individual differences known to exist. These tests are closely related to aptitude tests, but they serve a different purpose. Aptitude tests are designed to measure potentiality for development along certain lines or to estimate success expectancy *after training,* and are useful in making choices between occupations and the training therefor. Trade tests, on the other hand, are designed to measure occupational readiness or the ability to perform the work of a specific occupation. Some trade tests may be used as measures of attainment in vocational education, but their chief use is in the selection and placement of workers whose skills and abilities must be matched against known job requirements, to the end that human resources may be used most effectively, maximum production obtained, and worker dissatisfaction reduced to a minimum.

Origin and Development

Trade tests, as we now know them, had their origin in the first World War. Each man who entered the army or navy was required to state his previous occupation. As our first mechanized military force mushroomed in size, men were assigned to the various trade and technical jobs on the basis of these statements. It was soon found, however, that these statements were grossly unreliable. Men who gave their previous employment in a certain occupation ranged all the way from the novice who knew very little about the occupation to the expert worker. It was necessary to classify those in the different occupations, so that when a worker of any grade was needed, he could be selected and assigned at once.

A group of psychologists, engineers, trade teachers and expert tradesmen were hurriedly set to work on the problem. They developed a series of written, oral, picture, and performance tests for over eighty different trades. By means of these tests four grades of workers could be differentiated: the novice with practically no trade skill or knowledge; apprentices with a fair degree of proficiency in the trade; journeymen who could do most of the jobs of the trade satisfactorily; and master workmen who could be relied upon to meet any emergency in the field.

During the depression years the U. S. Employment Service found itself confronted with a never-ending list of applicants for employment, mostly in skilled and manual occupations. It was relatively easy to obtain from these applicants such information as age, weight, height, color, sex, place of residence, amount of schooling and the like. But when it came to obtaining accurate and reliable information concerning such important factors as work history and specific occupational skill and knowledge, they were confronted with a puzzling situation.

Recognizing that effective occupational counseling and placement service can be rendered only when the counselor has at hand adequate information concerning *individuals* and *occupations,* the Employment Service, through its Worker-Analysis Section, set out to develop the needed techniques. First, they revised and adapted the Army Trade Tests to the task at hand. Later, they developed a series of new trade tests, mostly of the oral type.

During the recent war the various branches of the armed services, the War Manpower Commission, and many private industries made use of trade tests. Millions of service men and war production workers were assigned to specific jobs on the basis of these and other tests. It can be expected that many new and improved trade tests developed during the war will eventually be available on a commercial basis to schools, employment offices and to private business and industry.

Requirements of Trade Tests

If trade tests are to be truly useful in matching human assets and liabilities against job opportunities and requirements, they must meet the following fundamental requirements:

1. The test must bear a positive relationship to the successful performance of the occupation. That is, it must be evaluated and standardized in terms of sound criteria of occupational success.

2. The test must differentiate the most proficient workers in the occupation from those workers of less proficiency. These differences should be expressed in terms which are readily understood—such as novice, apprentice, journeyman and master workman.

3. The test must differentiate, as far as possible, between the skills and characteristics of workers in dissimilar occupations. That is, the test must contrast the required traits of workers in different occupations or job families.

4. The test must be so constructed and worded that it can be used effectively in various parts of the country. That is, the content, the terminology and the norms must apply to the whole country rather than one locality or section.

5. The test must be comprehensive enough to insure a reasonably wide sampling of fundamental core elements of the occupation, yet brief and simple enough to be administered, scored and interpreted in a short time.

6. The results of trade tests must be interpreted and used in terms of known job descriptions and occupational duties, not merely occupational titles. This means that the person using the test must be well-informed as to specific job requirements.

Written Trade Tests

The original trade tests developed by the War Department were in the form of objective written questions and statements which could be administered to soldiers in groups. These, however, soon proved to be unsatisfactory. It was found that many men with long trade backgrounds and high degrees of skill in their occupation could not read well enough to do themselves justice on a written test. Written tests were, therefore, abandoned in favor of other types.

Despite their unsatisfactory use in the Army, written trade tests may be used to advantage with groups which are not handicapped by reading difficulties. Vocational schools especially may find them helpful in measuring the achievement of students in various trade courses. They may find them useful also in classifying students, particularly adults, for training purposes. Finally, both schools and personnel departments may find the use of written trade tests advisable in obtaining placement data from groups of students or workers.

Oral Trade Tests

The easiest trade test to use on an individual basis is undoubtedly the oral test. Such tests usually include from twelve to twenty well-chosen and carefully-stated questions and can be administered and scored in from four to ten minutes. The U. S. Employment Service was using this type of test almost exclusively before the war to measure occupational proficiency. Their tests, as reported by Stead and Shartle, who were instrumental in developing them, include eight kinds of questions, as follows:

1. Questions dealing with *definitions* and calling for short, descriptive answers.
2. Questions dealing with *modifications* and *limitations* of tools, materials and machines used in the trade.
3. Questions dealing with the *use* of the tools, materials and machines of the trade.
4. Questions dealing with *procedures* by which the worker goes about doing the operations of the trade.
5. Questions dealing with the *location* of things used, processed and assembled in the trade.
6. Questions dealing with *proper names* of tools, materials, machines, parts and processes.
7. Questions dealing with the *purpose* for doing things, using things, locating things and the like in trade practice.
8. Questions dealing with *numbers* as related to tools, parts of machines, materials and the like.

The U. S. Employment Service has standardized sets of questions of these types covering a hundred and twenty-six or more of the most common skilled and semi-skilled occupations, with instruction manuals for their administration and scoring. These tests are not suited for the measurement of student achievement in vocational classes, because there are not enough questions in each test, because they are standardized for individual presentation, and because the tests are based on the assumption that the verbal knowledge measured by this technique is associated with actual experience in the trade, not pre-employment training.

In using these tests, it is recommended that they be administered only after a complete work history has been secured. Then, the tests should serve three purposes as follows:

1. Elicit supplementary work history.
2. Check knowledge of occupation in which skill is claimed.
3. Provide, along with other data, a basis for estimating occupational potentialities.

Picture Trade Tests

A third type of trade test consists of a series of pictures showing fundamental tools, machines, materials and processes of the trade, together with a carefully selected series of questions which the examiner asks as he presents the pictures one after the other. The questions are designed to reveal the individual's knowledge of the items presented in the pictures and thus indirectly to classify him as novice, apprentice, journeyman or master. Norms for these tests are established by a process of experimentation with workers of various degrees of proficiency in the trade.

Since things which have been seen are usually more easily recalled than those which have been heard, it is probable that the picture trade test has some advantage over the oral trade test. However, it is more expensive to prepare and somewhat more difficult to administer. If the pictures and questions are synchronized on a sound film, it is possible, with the aid of score cards on which to record answers, to give the tests to large groups, thus saving a great deal of time for the counselor or personnel worker.

Performance Trade Tests

In many respects the best test of trade proficiency is the performance test, wherein the person being tested actually does certain typical operations or jobs of the trade or occupation. Such tests are really measures of speed, accuracy, trade knowledge, and procedure. When properly related to the successful performance of the trade, the performance test may be used in measuring progress and attainment in vocational training as well as trade proficiency for purposes of employment.

On the negative side, however, is the difficulty of administering performance tests. They usually require special equipment, which is often bulky and expensive. More time is required to take the tests and consequently fewer people can be tested. The conditions under which the tests are given are usually not actual trade conditions and this may influence the results obtained.

Performance tests have been developed in many occupations. Among them are those of the typist, stenographer, tool maker, gun smith, pattern maker, truck driver, aircraft riveter, welder, plumber, telephone operator, lathe operator, sheet metal worker, street car motorman, painter, and many others. Extensive use was made of many of these tests during the recent war in both training schools and war production plants. Aside from tests of typing, shorthand and a few trades, performance trade tests are not available on a commercial basis. Such tests, however, should appear in the near future as an outgrowth of war experimentation.

Limitations of Trade Tests

In using trade tests it must be remembered that at best they measure only present proficiency in skill and knowledge. Taken alone, they provide no indication of the individual's possibility for future improvement in the trade. The length of time he has spent in preparing for his trade, his intelligence, any special aptitude he has shown, and such personal qualities as initiative, ambition and perseverance must be considered in estimating an individual's possibilities for future development in the trade.

Since trade tests do measure only trade skill and knowledge, a person's trade status, for purposes of placement, should be determined not only by his responses to trade test questions, but also by a judicious interpretation of work history data, interview impressions, and any other valid data at hand.

While it is a truism in vocational guidance that the best predictor of future success in any activity is prior success in that activity, this principle is often of no value to the vocational counselor or placement officer. Frequently he must deal with individuals whom he may never have seen before and who lack either occupational experience or training, or both. Others may misrepresent their work experience and their occupational proficiency to him. Confronted with this situation, one, if not the best, technique available to the counselor is the trade test.

When properly constructed, used and interpreted, trade tests provide the vocational counselor or personnel worker with valid objective data concerning the occupational readiness of individuals, which may be matched against occupational opportunities and requirements in the placement of workers in jobs where their resources can be used to the best advantage of themselves, their employer, and the nation.

References:

1. Chapman, J. Crosby. *Trade tests.* New York: Henry Holt & Co., Inc., 1921.
2. Stead, W. H. and Shartle, C. L. *Occupational counseling techniques.* New York: American Book Co., 1940.
3. Thompson, L. A. and Others. *Interview aids and trade questions for employment offices.* New York: Harper and Brothers, 1936.

H. H. L.

TUBERCULOUS.   In counseling a person with a history of tuberculosis, the responsibility of the counselor to his client and to the community is more than usually serious. Sound counsel may prove a substantial factor, not only in improving the economic adjustment of the client, but in conditioning his life expectancy. The competence and pertinence of counsel may help to determine whether the disease is conquered or whether it flares once more into a fresh activity, destructive to the client and, because of its bacillary cause, also communicable to others. Pulmonary tuberculosis is notoriously a recurrent and reactivating type of disease. However, thousands of patients who have made successful and permanent recovery from pulmonary tuberculosis in our time, justify the observation that these characteristics of the disease often may be effectively neutralized by intelligent social treatment. Social malpractice, including ill-considered counsel, obviously increases the hazard of recurrence inherent in characteristics of the disease.

This heightened responsibility in the counseling process calls for five basic preparations and procedures when serving the tuberculous. Each of these has some counterpart in service for persons with other disabilities, but each is definitely indispensable in service for the tuberculous. First comes as much understanding of the disease and its treatment as the layman can assimilate, coupled with careful study of the individual medical case history. Second, the counselor needs a versatile command of job objectives which will enable him to suggest a variety of occupations within the physical limitations imposed upon the client by his history. Third, especially because of the impact of diagnosis and treatment upon the patient and his family, the counselor needs a detailed study of the individual personality and of his family group. Fourth, effective counseling of the tuberculous cannot be conducted in a vacuum; the means for applying the outcome of consultation are as vital as the counsel itself. Access to facilities for further orientation, conditioning, try-outs, training and placement are practical essentials. Finally, systematic follow-up may provide further aid to the client and a clue to the further improvement of guidance method. Some plausible techniques seem to work famously as far as the counselor's door.

While the total subject of tuberculosis is a life-time study, there is no health field today in which so much informative material in so many forms has been made readily available to the layman who will make use of it. Popular folklore on this subject is a dangerous basis for counsel. Much of it is not merely uninformed; it is misinformed. All too often, popular legend promotes a belief directly opposite to the fruits of research and clinical experience. A wide gamut of publications, ranging from the simplest of leaflets to exhaustive medical texts, may be consulted in any but the most obscure communities.

Each of the state and local tuberculosis associations offers local workers a wide choice of educational literature, much of it free. Educational motion pictures on various phases of tuberculosis present portions of this material in visual terms. These are also available from tuberculosis associations, as are teaching institutes for those who work with the tuberculous or plan to do so. In spite of the appalling additional burden which the war has heaped upon them, many specialists in this field, particularly sanatorium physicians, give their time generously in teaching the lay workers who serve their former patients. Anyone who attempts to counsel the tuberculous should be completely familiar with *Diagnostic Standards and Classification of Tuberculosis*,‡ published by the National Tuberculosis Association and available from its state and local affiliates, in order to obtain an understanding of everyday diagnostic and prognostic terminology consistent with that employed by the physician.

It is essential for the counselor to know, not only how extensively the disease progressed before its inroads were checked, but also to note with some particularity the patient's *capacity to cope with his disease*. The nature of the treatment employed may condition further the future terms of training and employment; hence,

‡ Diagnostic Standards and Classification of Tuberculosis, 1940 Edition. National Tuberculosis Association.

the counselor cannot safely function with only a vague notion of this part of the medical history. The best practice is, not merely to read and consider all available medical information, but also to make the physician who is best acquainted with the patient's clinical progress a co-partner in the counseling process. Deference to the physician's expert knowledge of the physical problem usually results in a reciprocal respect for the expert equipment of the counselor regarding the extra-medical factors involved.

This cooperation is often facilitated by hospital and sanatorium physicians. Many of them utilize the therapeutic potentialities of at least some preliminary counseling relatively early in treatment. Some plan for ultimate readjustment induces many patients to accept treatment with less anxiety and depression than when their future remains wholly unchartered. Because patients' departures from hospitals against medical advice may frustrate both treatment for tuberculosis and the control of the disease in the community, intelligent counsel can be medically as well as socially valuable. Therefore, some physicians answer the question, "When should counseling service begin?" objectively by calling for a first interview not very long after diagnosis. Scores of patients have indicated the reconstruction possibilities of the long period of enforced leisure which is inseparable from the treatment of this disease, by making, with or without counsel, a plan for the future. By reading and studying in preparation for things to come, they have made treatment more bearable and the future less hazardous. Precedent is not wanting; it has been abundantly supplied. In terms of guidance, early contact with the client has the advantage of continuous treatment, provided that the working relationship established at that time be maintained by the counselor.

Whether the opportunity for counseling is arranged during treatment or during convalescence, the item of job objectives should be influenced by extensive and considered information, never by folklore. Folklore led some employment interviewers of an earlier day to refer all male applicants with a history of tuberculosis to farm jobs, on the theory that outdoor work was less hazardous. Considered information taught these workers eventually that the facts were, once more, the exact opposite of folklore—that most outdoor jobs are physically exhausting, involve exposure to every variety of inclement weather and usually increase, instead of diminishing, the hazards of the ex-patient. Folklore led an inexperienced interne to quench the interest of a girl patient in future stenographic work on the ground that typing would call for "too much arm movement." His medical chief directed the young man's attention to the relaxed touch-typing performance of their medical secretary and asked him "what arm movement?"

Valid generalities regarding the possible range of job objectives are few. A general statement by Alice Klein, made in 1927, has stood the test of time and states the facts clearly and compactly. She said:

> "There are no industries in which all jobs are suitable for the ex-tuberculous and only a few industries which have no suitable jobs." *

On the negative side, the counselor eliminates jobs which are physically exhausting, which involve exposure or long hours or extra-hazardous environmental conditions. The more the counselor knows, or can find out, concerning the physical demands of each job or job family, the better his equipment to assist the client in the selection of an occupational target. Discussion with the client is likely to be chiefly in terms of required skills and the means for their acquisition. The client's physician is, very naturally, far more intent on the physical demands of that job or job family.

It is essential for the counselor to remember, however, that physical exhaustion may be produced by non-manual causes. A worker at a sedentary assignment who attempts responsibility for office detail without commensurate clerical aptitude may be as weary at the day's end as if he had worked on a shipping platform at loading trucks. An unadjusted introvert, thrust into such continuous contact with others as outside selling requires, is often as exhausted in a short interval of sales resistances as if he had loaded pig iron. The matching of job requirements with the patient's physical and vocational aptitude patterns is properly a precision assignment. Accordingly, in counseling the tuberculous, the range of jobs to be considered should be as wide as possible, and the job analysis should be as minute as possible. Similarly, the exploration of the client's aptitudes should include as much objective evidence as can be obtained—school records, previous employment performance, a record of observations by the occupational therapist, and a full battery of occupational aptitude tests.

In any list of completed rehabilitations of the tuberculous, there should be nearly as many job objectives as there are clients, for, if the counsel is tailored to the client, about that much variation may be expected in most groups of clients with such a disability. A pre-

---

* Klein, Alice C. "Placement and Rehabilitation of the Tuberculous," Transactions of the National Tuberculosis Association, 1927, p. 316.

ponderance of placements in watchmaking, office machines, barbering or hairdressing, for example, indicates that clients are being subjected to a kind of vocational processing which does not include true counseling procedure. They suggest reversion to the archaic pattern of categorical selection, job A for men with one arm, job B for men with one leg, job C for the hard of hearing, and the like.

Personal service occupations may well be next to last choice in counseling the tuberculous. In most regions, they involve exhausting work conditions. Furthermore, should a customer who has been served by the ex-patient develop tuberculosis, the worker and his employer are shining targets for litigation and abuse, whether or not the source of infection was wholly different.

One factor in job selection which is important to many ex-patients is the stability of the job. A few ex-patients are quite happy in casual employment. The majority, however, appear to hold their own more surely in jobs where reasonable tenure and eventual opportunities for advancement are present. For those who can qualify for examinations, the civil services supply this employment factor. However, continuity of employment is not limited to "white collar" employment. Many manufacturing, processing and utility employers take pride in the long tenure of their mechanical personnel. These are far better placement targets for persons with a history of tuberculosis than concerns inflated by an ephemeral market.

Throughout this article it is assumed that the counselor is sufficiently proficient in his calling to supply his client with the materials for intelligent choice instead of attempting to choose for him. Persons with a history of tuberculosis who are manipulated into a training inharmonious with their own personal convictions, are exceedingly likely to drop out of training arranged for them or to seek unrelated jobs upon its completion. Unless the client is incapable of choice, dictation by the counselor is an invitation to failure in the counseling function.

Counseling which takes into major consideration only the experience, or the test scores, or the ambitions of the client himself is especially hazardous when he has a history of tuberculosis. Each of us is conditioned by family ties, past or present. What pattern has the family group stamped into the intellectual and emotional patterns of the client? Have they shared with him a fear or a fatalism which must be cleared up before he can make a sensible adjustment of his future? On the other hand, do his familiars consider his illness as a closed chapter, regarding no further precautions warranted? Are his home responsibilities, whether in terms of chores or play, likely to undo the opportunities provided by wholly suitable employment?

Has the counselor utilized, in addition to his own equipment, the continued and skilled observation of professional workers qualified to appraise and evaluate such factors? The contribution of the trained social worker may substantially increase the validity and effect of counsel.

It is an axiom among some phthisiologists that former patients squander their strength and hard-won resistance dangerously quite as often on ill-selected recreation as on the demands of a job. Many patients relapse following suitable work but wholly unsuitable recreation. All too many treatment institutions have failed to provide their patients with any affirmative substitute for their old, violent forms of amusement, depending entirely upon education which begins with DON'T admonitions, which, as counselors learn, are less reliably controlling than habit patterns. In order to counsel a former patient so that he may eliminate unsuitable forms of recreation, it is often necessary to provoke an interest in forms of recreation which make more moderate physical demands and allow opportunity for adequate hours of rest.

As these conditions indicate, counseling the tuberculous is seldom an undertaking for solo performance. The counselor who calls upon the special skills and knowledge of the physician, the occupational therapist, the job analyst, the social worker, the teacher, multiplies the probability of successful result and diminishes hazards otherwise present. The counselor's essential function is to enhance continuity in his client's planning and action from the initial interview to the job. Interim discussions which maintain the progress of the client, are as much a part of guidance as any exploratory process.

Finally, the counselor should have established in advance an array of facilities through which the tuberculous client may begin to apply some part of their joint conclusion. In the fully arrested case, a choice of training courses is apparent enough. If, on the other hand, the patient is in an earlier stage of convalescence, some means of beginning to apply counsel without too much delay is indicated. This may take as simple a form as guided reading. Or, if occupational therapists and teachers are available, mechanical and other tryouts may be introduced. By such means the client appraises counsel as reality instead of another fragment of the fantasies which have helped to beguile his enforced leisure.

Such pre-vocational exercise does more than to increase the client's certainty regarding his acceptance of counsel; it also conditions him to carry on the specific vocational training or placement selected when he has reached a clinical stage at which this is medically approved. The client and his physician are both free from further apprehension because they have physical tryout to verify clinical findings. Necessary habits of study and application are gradually established. One knows what the client can do because he has done it while maintaining satisfactory clinical conditions.

H. H.

TURNOVER, LABOR, AND JOB SECURITY IN THE MAJOR OCCUPATIONS. Throughout the ages there has been a perpetual conflict between those forces making for change and progress in our economic life (and incidentally undermining its stability) and those other contending forces designed to provide protection and security for various classes and groups of people affected by such changes. Sometimes this conflict seems to take the form of a struggle of people as human beings against machines and impersonal forces, whether these latter are the inventions and processes of the engineers or the economic forces of the market place, such as a competitive development of new firms and new industries displacing the old. In a very real and important sense this is one form of the conflict—too often in the past the advantages and profits of change have, in the short run, been captured by the few (if at all), while the costs and the losses have been borne by the millions of common people who are unable to adapt themselves quickly to new situations.

When we go more deeply into the issue, however, it readily becomes apparent that the conflict is fundamentally one between one group of people and another, between some individuals and other individuals. For example, there is the perennial battle of youth and age. Youth wants opportunity and may, therefore, welcome a "shake out" which will displace some of the oldsters who are clinging doggedly to precarious pinnacles of economic status. Age, on the other hand, wants security above everything else, because change for them in our society all too frequently means loss of position, and even possible penury.

On second thought it also becomes apparent that the significance of labor turnover and job security vary markedly from one time to another. For example, during the war we had high labor turnover rates throughout industry, but these were due in large measure to the voluntary quitting of workers.[2] This, in turn, reflected the flood of job offers which were available to ambitious, capable men and women. Labor turnover which reflects this climbing of the economic ladder to bigger and better jobs during prosperity periods is a happy symptom of economic health. But let the economy plunge in the other direction (toward a major depression) and labor turnover becomes a Frankenstein monster which terrorizes the entire working population. Under these circumstances labor turnover expresses itself in a rising lay-off rate. It is the lay-off initiated by the employer which throws the worker into unemployment and destitution.

As we stand facing the future in these crucial years, what is the outlook? Which features of this age-old problem will dominate our lives in the next 5 years, in the next several decades? As a background for the consideration of this question, we must first analyze the conditions under which the American economy is likely to operate in the future. What are the basic trends which will condition the operation of the contending forces?

First, there is the factor of fluctuating economic conditions—prosperity and depression, full employment and mass unemployment. The short-run outlook is for an expanding and prosperous post-war economy in the United States. Not only do we have a long list of war-time shortages to make up, but there are even longer-range deprivations from the great depression of the 1930's. The needs are great; the financial and industrial resources appear adequate; the results should be at least a temporary period of high employment, high earnings and a rising standard of living. This means also a flow of job opportunities for workers.

Later on, the Nation must face the possibility that after the boom period there may occur a deep and prolonged major depression, such as has normally followed former wars. In the long run, the Nation will have to make some major industrial shifts and readjustments to correct the war-time and post-war dislocations. We may succeed in achieving those readjustments with a minimum of waste in human and technical resources and without undue hardships for the working population. It would be against all experience, however, to assume that the conditions of the early post-war years will last indefinitely.

Second, entirely apart from the business cycle, we shall probably experience as never before the impact of rapid and continuous change in our economic life. The atomic bomb is only a symbol of the far-reaching inventions and discoveries which have been, are being, and will be made in science and industry. New processes were developed during the war, new materials have been brought to new uses, new applications of old methods have been successfully achieved. It is difficult to envision the speed and extent of change in our industrial life during the years immediately ahead.

Third, the war intensified the shifting of industry and the migration of labor from one part of the Country to the other. During the war, interstate migration reached abnormally high levels.[4] The Bureau of Census has calculated that by March 1945 there were 15.3 millions of persons living in communities other than those in which they lived prior to December 1941. Of these, a little more than half had moved across State lines in the course of their migration. During the war period, a total of nearly 2.5 million individuals migrated from one State to another on the average each year. This is almost twice the interstate migration rate that existed in the period 1935–40. In general, this migration was from the interior of the Country toward the sea coasts (including the Great Lakes), but more particularly it was to the West Coast and to certain States on the Atlantic Coast. The great Mississippi Basin, particularly States west of the Mississippi River and extending through the Rocky Mountains, nearly all lost population. New plants and new industries were established on a large scale in various parts of the Country. These developments are being modified, but not reversed, in the post-war period. The likelihood is that migration on a large scale will be a feature of American industrial life for some years to come. Furthermore, the perennial movement from the farms to the cities, further stimulated by the war, will receive a new impetus in the years immediately ahead. Labor-saving machinery is invading farming areas where hand labor and the hoe have been dominant for a century.

Fourth, the industrial expansion of the immediate future is in the direction of instability. Let us look ahead, say, some 5 years. It has been estimated that in 1950 the total labor force of the Nation may approximate 60 million persons, and that, making allowance for frictional unemployment and for service in the armed forces, there will be somewhat more than 55 million workers available for civilian employment.[5] One estimate of job opportunities ranges from 55 to 58 million. It is significant, however, that some industries and occupations will actually show decreases as compared with 1940 (the last pre-war year), while others will show marked increases. Agriculture, for example, will show a marked decline in workers as compared with 1940. Domestic service will decline as compared with 1940 (though there will be some increase from the war-time low). On the other hand, as compared with 1940, manufacturing will use more than three million additional workers; employment in building construction will increase considerably and may even double; retail and wholesale trade will absorb more than a million; and Government (Federal, State, and local) about half a million. Independent work and self-employment (non-agricultural) should increase by more than a million workers. Since most of the independent business ventures are highly unstable, this portion of the labor force will be characterized by high labor turnover, although the consequences are not shown in the usual labor turnover data, which are based wholly upon employed workers. It should also be noted that the industrial group having the greatest rate of expansion (building construction) is the most unstable of all our industries, and the group having the greatest absolute increase (manufacturing) is more unstable than the service industries.

Fifth, the almost inevitable consequences of the above trends will be the continuation of the high war-time rates of labor turnover into the post-war years. Labor turnover rates may not be as high as in war-time, but certainly higher than we have been wont to consider "normal." For a decade or so in the future there is likely to be widespread shifting of industries and workers, at first under prosperity conditions, and later, perhaps, in depression. The prospect is one of change, migration, and fluctuation.

I. *Pressure for Job Security*

One reaction to this situation is to intensify the drive for job security on the part of many groups of workers. The threat of change strengthens the quest for stability. The forces designed to provide job security are unquestionably being strengthened at the present time.

One expression of this, brought about by the war, has been the expansion of veterans' preference, not only in government, but in private industry as well. We have not yet seen the end of this movement. A period of even moderate unemployment could result in its further extension. Furthermore, the ex-servicemen of World War II are approximately three times as numerous as those of World War I; therefore, the individuals involved in these preferences may constitute a majority of the male workers in certain industries and a large minority of the total labor force of the Nation. There might possibly be industries and occupations in which non-veterans would have very little opportunity for jobs or advancement.

Second, labor unions are putting increasing emphasis upon strict seniority as the determining factor in layoffs and in rehiring. The great depression of the 1930's left a deep imprint of insecurity upon the minds of American workers and undoubtedly stimulated the drive toward seniority. Union membership has expanded dramatically during the last decade, and unions seem destined to hold or extend their gains during the post-war period. Consequently, we may expect that the seniority principle will be greatly strengthened throughout the major American industries.

Third, for some decades past the Nation has become increasingly conscious of the increasing proportion of older workers in the labor force. In the census of 1940, it was found that 31.3 per cent of the male workers under 65 were between the ages of 45 and 64. By 1960 this proportion will have increased to about 34.0 per cent. In the 1930's, in the midst of mass unemployment, the aged became pension-conscious, but the employment opportunities of the war have revived their interest in holding on to their jobs. A typical device for achieving protection by older workers is the placing of limitations upon the entry of new younger workers into the trade or occupation, either by limiting apprenticeships or by other means. We may expect an intensification of the efforts to limit new entries or to check their advancement.

To what do all these add up? Will the sum total of all these efforts have the effect of creating a labor market in which status and job rights will have greater weight than competence and potential capacity?

In my judgment, the answer to this question is, no. Weighing the strength of the forces making for change in turnover against those protections described above, it would seem that the forces of change will prevail. The economy of the future cannot be circumscribed by such devices.

II. *Dynamic Security*

What then is the outlook for the worker, particularly the young worker who wants to develop his potentialities and carve out a career? Is the individual to be tossed helplessly and aimlessly, buffeted by forces he cannot master? Not at all; there are two major protections on which the worker can now rely and which can be still further developed in the future. One of these is community action designed to assist the individual; the other is individual action designed to fit the individual into the economic world in which he finds himself.

The community action which is significant for this purpose is that whole complex of activities designated by the term "social security" in its larger sense. This does not mean social security in terms of the particular programs that now exist or the organization which goes by that name.

Social security in the broad sense means protection of the individual and his family against the major hazards of economic life. It provides certain minimum income security when the worker cannot find work, and it enables him to support his family during periods of unemployment. It also provides services designed to assist the individual in adjusting himself to changed conditions.

The social security program is barely 10 years old, although certain features of it go back much further. It was not fully effective during the last depression, but in the future it will have an important part to play. If it is revised and extended, it may become a more significant factor in the life of the average worker than job security as outlined previously.

There is space only for a brief listing of the basic elements of social security. Of primary importance for this discussion is the existence of a Nation-wide public employment service, organized for the purpose of assisting employers to find workers and workers to find jobs. During war time, the United States Employment Service, by virtue of labor-market controls, came to play a most significant part in regulating the movement of labor from industry to industry and from place to place. In peacetime, however, there will normally be other types of placement activities to take care of the majority of workers; the more important of these are the personnel departments established by employers, and the placement functions of labor unions. The public Employment Service has the residual job of filling in where other types of placement are not effective. Further, it has the difficult task of working with that fraction of the unemployed who are most difficult to place, who may require retraining and readjustment. In conjunction with the schools, the Employment Service can assist in vocational guidance and placing of younger workers starting their careers.

Failing to find a job, a worker may be entitled to unemployment benefits. In 1945, some 37 million workers in the United States earned sufficient wage credits to be eligible for benefits under the Federal-State systems of unemployment compensation or the railroad unemployment insurance system. In addition, some 15 million servicemen were potentially eligible (upon demobilization) for servicemen's readjustment allowances, which is a form of unemployment benefits. For short-run unemployment in the future this program can and will provide protection for millions of industrial workers and their families in future years.

For those too old to work and for the families of wage earners who die, there is a program of old-age and survivors insurance. In this program nearly 50 million earned wage credits in the year 1944, and Congress is considering an amendment of the law to provide coverage for servicemen. In addition, Congressional consideration is being given to extending the coverage to provide for the inclusion of the major groups of workers not now in the system. Eventually, perhaps, every group of gainfully-occupied workers (other than some which have retirement systems of their own) will be included in one comprehensive national system of old-age retirement and survivors insurance.

In this connection, it is important to note the effect a single system of this kind has in facilitating the shifting of workers from industry to industry or from occupation to occupation. The specialized retirement systems for a given industry or occupation tend to tie the older workers to their jobs, because a shift may mean the loss of pension rights. Plans are being considered for relating the specialized retirement systems to the general one so that workers who do shift their jobs will be able to retain their rights.

Another feature of social security which is still in the early stages of development is the protection against accident or illness, whether in the form of public health services and preventive medicine or in the form of cash—sickness benefits and health insurance. Public health is one of the oldest of social security activities, but the full flowering of community action in this area is still to come. However, the movement is underway. The rapid extension of voluntary plans and the legislative consideration of compulsory plans in both the State and Federal Governments are evidence of a great future development in this field.

Finally, there is the oldest of all social security programs—public assistance, which provides service and financial aid to individuals and families in need. This is the basic and residual program designed to pick up those who fall through the other programs or exhaust their prior rights.

The outlook is for increasing community action in the form of social security in all its aspects. In an economic system in which rapid change is the key characteristic, there will be urgent need for security measures. By lessening the absolute dependence of a worker upon a particular job and by providing a worker with more freedom of choice in obtaining jobs best suited to his capacities, and by providing income to individuals when they cannot work—in all these ways social security helps people to adjust themselves to a dynamic economic system.

Last of all, there is the field of individual actions. In what direction should vocational guidance point the younger workers streaming into the labor force every year? In my opinion, it is a hopeless task to attempt to find the industries and occupations in which a worker may find stability of employment, job security, and opportunity for advancement. The chances are that the shifts in occupations will be more frequent than ever before, and that the length of time an occupation or skill remains unchanged will become shorter and shorter.

During the war, it was discovered, both in the armed forces and in industry, that short periods of training were all that was necessary. The training requirements for pilots in the Army Air Forces were for a period of not more than a few months; yet flying an airplane is an extremely highly-skilled job. In industry, it was found that young workers could be trained to the highest skills, mostly on the job, and in a comparatively short period of time. Perhaps the most significant factor in this entire experience is the dominance of aptitude in determining occupational success. The implications for the future are that more attention should be paid to discovering the aptitudes of our younger workers and pointing them in the direction of those aptitudes, without too much regard to the labor supply-and-demand situation of the moment. There are not promising occupations, but rather promising individuals.

But if occupations change frequently, then there is another factor which individuals should develop to the highest possible degree. That is the factor of flexibility and adaptability—capacity to change jobs and occupations easily.[2] The young man and young woman of this present generation must anticipate the possibility that he or she will experience a high degree of mobility during working life. A general educational background will be better than a highly-specialized one. Adaptability may be the best security. It is to be hoped that industry will also make a positive contribution to this objective —the acquiring by the worker of a diversified work experience.

References:

1. Clague, E. *The economics of war and peace—the problems of prosperity and security in the world of the future.* Pennsylvania School of Social Work of the University of Pennsylvania.

2. United States Department of Labor, Bureau of Labor Statistics *Monthly Labor Review,* January 1946 (or any other issue), Vol. 62, No. 1, Labor Turnover Section.

3. Williams, G. R. *The price of social security.* New York: Oxford University Press.

4. Woytinsky, W. S. Interstate migration during the war. *State Government,* March, 1946, pp. 81–84.

5. ———. Post-war economic perspectives. *Social Security Bulletin,* December 1945, January and February, 1946.

E. C.

U

UNEMPLOYED. Unemployment is a problem which is ever with us, and much of it is unnecessary, inefficient and preventable. Although its economic waste is recognized and actual experience has shown the real productive value of some individuals labeled "unemployable," many employers still retain their prejudices against hiring persons who have been out of work for a long time. No adult member of society unless completely incapacitated by illness, should be forced to remain long unemployed; rather, efforts should be made to salvage him in the early stages of his unemployment or, better still, to prevent his unemployment in the first place. While this is not always possible, it is nevertheless known that enforced unemployment results eventually in physical deterioration, loss of essential skills, mental decline, emotional disturbance and social inadequacy.[2 4 5 7 9 10] Of course, in some persons these factors have been the cause rather than the result of loss of a job but even in these cases, the deterioration in all areas has been hastened in direct proportion to the length of the period of unemployment. It therefore behooves us, not only from an humanitarian but an essentially practical point of view, to salvage as many individuals as possible and thus lessen the great economic load which the unemployed place upon the productive members of society.

Few persons are really unemployable, but those who long have refrained from any productive activity will require a planned program of rehabilitation before they will be ready to take their place in a group and compete successfully with their fellowmen. This program involves the rehabilitation of the whole individual. It is not just finding a job for a man but so ameliorating his physical, mental and emotional conditions, improving his social outlook and developing his skills that he will function happily and effectively in the job for which he is found to be best suited.[3] The emphasis of the rehabilitation program will necessarily vary with the needs of the individual and the basic reasons for his unemployment. Individuals may be unemployed for various reasons, personal and otherwise, but the ones who concern us here are those long unemployed because of fundamental inadequacy (fundamental physical, mental or emotional inadequacy), physical handicaps, mental disorders and advanced age. Certain aspects of the rehabilitation program, particularly those of a mental hygiene nature, will be applicable to all of these groups but in addition, each group will also present its own special problems for the counselor to solve.

General Considerations for the Counselor and His Client

The counselor in this field must be an understanding person of broad background. He must have not only the feeling within himself which is necessary to help these people but also the practical knowledge and skill which are essential to helping them effectively. As he himself can not be an expert in all fields, he must be flexible enough to seek the cooperation of other specialists where their need is indicated in helping certain individuals to effect a satisfactory adjustment. This means that he must be thoroughly familiar with all community resources. He must know where he can secure needed medical care, both free and paid, where he can send his client to procure sensory aids and prosthetic appliances without or at minimal cost, and where he can get psychiatric treatment.

a. *Mental Hygiene in Rehabilitation*

The counselor must be thoroughly trained in mental hygiene and in dealing with people, particularly maladjusted people. Unemployment leads to increased emotional instability and lowered morale so that great skill on the part of the counselor is often necessary to establish that good rapport which is the basic step in adjustment. Individuals differ in their emotional and social reactions to unemployment, and the counselor who is aware of his client as an individual rather than a case will be alert to his reaction patterns. Some unemployed persons become openly rebellious and anti-social in their attitudes and behavior; some become resigned so quickly that they soon lapse into apathy and indifference. Many develop feelings of degradation, uselessness, bitterness, irritability, resentment and hostility; others become anxious and insecure and develop feelings of inadequacy, dependency, fear, indecision and distrust. Some lose their self-reliance, anticipate disaster and have a bad outlook on the future. Over-concern with his personal problems often results in an introspective individual who is not fit for group living, let alone for gainful employment where he must form relationships with fellow-workers and employers.[1][2][5][7][9] The well-trained rehabilitation counselor will be able to cope adequately with most of these problems and lead his client to an understanding of his own assets and liabilities and of the importance of learning to live and work with other people. With others he will require psychiatric assistance.

b. *Psychological Tests in Vocational Rehabilitation*

Full understanding of tests and measurements is essential to the vocational rehabilitation counselor. If he himself is not a qualified psychologist, the counselor should arrange to have these tests administered and interpreted by a qualified clinical psychologist. Batteries should include tests of general intelligence and of the efficiency of mental functioning, motor tests, tests of aptitudes and special abilities, measures of scholastic achievement, personality tests (both projective and non-projective techniques), trade and occupational tests, and interest inventories. The items included in the aptitude test batteries for different occupations, such as those developed by the Division of Occupational Analysis in the War Manpower Commission, should be available for use. Evaluation and interpretation of these tests with knowledge of the individual's life history, including his background, educational and vocational history, early skills and habits, and his avocational interests, will lead to a basic understanding of the client's assets, liabilities and further rehabilitation needs.[3]

c. *Job Finding*

Finally, the counselor must know what is available in the way of vocational training, both public and private, and he must know jobs. He should be familiar with the physical, mental and emotional requirements of many different types of jobs and be flexible enough to see relationships between skills which might enable his client to utilize his obsolete skills in an entirely different kind of work. While he should not find the job for his client, as this is an important part of the client's own rehabilitation experience, the counselor should know what job possibilities there are in the community and what firms are willing to employ aged workers or those suffering from physical or mental handicaps.[3] As ego-building is such an important part of the rehabilitation program, every precaution should be taken to avoid having the client's first job-seeking experience met with the destructive effects of abrupt and discouraging rejection based on his handicap. The counselor should seize every opportunity to assist in the re-education of prospective employers to the usefulness of handicapped workers. He should never seek employment for his clients on the basis of sympathy and he should send only applicants who have a good chance of adjusting on the job, remembering that employers are interested in finding men for jobs, not in filling jobs for the sake of charity. As one poorly placed employee may result in a firm's wholesale rejection of similarly situated applicants, the importance of the counselor's wise selection of individuals can readily be appreciated. The fact that there are some individuals who are unemployable and incapable of being rehabilitated must be faced squarely.

The vocational rehabilitation worker should keep abreast of the research and practical work being done in his field. He should be familiar with the work of the Veterans Administration, the United States Employment Service, the Division of Employment Service and the Division of Occupational Analysis of the War Manpower Commission, the Vocational Rehabilitation Division of the Federal Security Agency and the State Vocational Rehabilitation Services and know how to use these and other agencies when necessary. Familiarity with and free use of available occupational tools will prove invaluable aids to the counselor. The Dictionary of Occupational Titles, particularly Part IV which has classification of entry fields of work, supplies useful information in outlining training programs and courses. The Physical Demands Analyses, Occupational Classification and Information, Operations Manual for Placement of the Physically Handicapped (United States Civil Service Commission), Job Descriptions (United States Employment Service) and Job Family Series (War Manpower Commission) will be found to be indispensable tools. The job families, which have been developed from job analysis schedules and worker characteristics forms on which are indicated the amounts of worker traits needed for successful performance of the job, will prove especially helpful to the counselor. They include traits such as strength, dexterity and memory and they show the nature of the work on different jobs, describing the machines, the tools and the materials used.[6]

The Problem of Fundamental Inadequacy in Unemployment

Some individuals enter the ranks of the unemployed because they are fundamentally inadequate—inadequate physically, mentally or emotionally. They experience difficulty in finding employment and they are the first to lose their jobs in lay-off periods. Although without discernible organic defect, the physical inadequates lack energy, tire easily, suffer from nutritional difficulties and lose much time from work because of minor illnesses, injuries and industrial accidents. Mental and emotional inadequacies often accompany physical inadequacy, so that high grade mentally defective, dull, alcoholic and psychopathic individuals will be found in the group. Certain epileptics might also be included because their convulsive seizures have resulted in a social inadequacy which handicaps them in the vocational field. Some, although physically healthy, lack the efficiency, the stability or the perseverance to remain on a job. Because of their very inadequacies, these individuals do not respond well to rehabilitation and are difficult to adjust vocationally. The first step in their rehabilitation program is to secure a complete life history, including a report of illnesses, accidents, education and work history. This should be followed by a complete medical examination with correction of existing, modifiable physical defects and improvement of diet and health habits. Psychological examination can then determine the individual's general intelligence, efficiency of functioning, skills, weaknesses, personality traits and interests. Further vocational training, development of basic skills or job possibilities which are in accord with his peculiar abilities and needs can then be decided upon. Because of their trouble-making characteristics, caution must be exercised in permitting some of these inadequates to attempt work which involves dealing with people; they will be more effective in working with materials. These individuals will also need many interviews with either the vocational rehabilitation counselor or a case worker who will help them to establish a beneficial routine of living, improved morale and suitable goals and then keep contact with them until these new habits become firmly fixed. However, it must be remembered that where fundamental inadequacies exist, the prognosis usually is not good and jobs of responsibility should not be the goal.

Physical Handicaps and Unemployment

Where prolonged unemployment is due to a definite physical handicap the basis of the vocational rehabilitation program must necessarily be physical rehabilitation. In these cases not only a physical examination is important but also expert medical attention to the specific physical defect. Prosthetic appliances and sensory aids, such as glasses and hearing devices, should be provided where needed, and the client should be taught the most efficient use of these aids. His life history, intelligence, education, personality, interests and basic skills should be studied psychologically and the job possibilities open to him, either with or without further training, analyzed. The Operations Manual for Placement of the Physically Handicapped should prove helpful in this connection. If he has never been employed, has been unemployed a very long time, has a severe physical defect or is emotionally disturbed, it might be advisable to give him first a period of occupational therapy or perhaps employment in a sheltered workshop rather than subject him immediately to the competitive industrial world. Mental hygiene will be an important part of the rehabilitation program of this group. The client must be helped to make as presentable an appearance as possible, to accept his handicap, to face the future with confidence, to get away from introspection and develop objective, stimulating habits of thought, and to be ready to meet his fellow workers with the assurance that accompanies security in the knowledge of one's skills. Acquaintance with the reports of the satisfactory service given by handicapped workers should prove stimulating to those who suffer from discouragement, timidity and anxiety.

Mental Disorders and Unemployment

Every year more individuals suffering from major mental disorders are being returned to the community from mental hospitals as cured or improved. Many of these individuals are employable, but no vocational rehabilitation program should be instituted without direct psychiatric consultation. This also holds true for those psychotics who have not been hospitalized. Most of the hospitalized clients will already have been given psychological examinations, and the counselor's duplication of this work will often be unnecessary if he can secure adequate reports of these examinations. It may be advisable, though, to make some further study of the individual's special skills and interests. It will also be helpful to know what occupational therapy he has had while in the hospital. Every effort should be made to develop in the person who is or has been mentally ill the feeling that the counselor understands his feelings and anxieties and has the greatest confidence in his ability to succeed. Care should be taken to see that his first job is challenging but at the same time not work which will place too great a strain upon him. The development of feelings of usefulness and accomplishment is extremely important. The same general principles apply in the minor mental illnesses—the psychoneurotics who have not been hospitalized but who have been unemployed for long periods because of their psychosomatic complaints. Both physical and psychiatric care of such individuals is essential but with these assisting consultants, the counselor often has the opportunity to do a fine job of vocational rehabilitation.

Old Age and Unemployment

Although it is estimated that ultimately 35% of our total population will be 50 years of age and over, many employers are still so loath to employ older workers that this group usually makes up most of our unemployed population. Yet, as with physically handicapped workers, it has been found that older workers being more mature in their outlook, have less absenteeism, smaller turnover, fewer accidents and less breakage of materials.[4][8] However, it is known that prolonged unemployment of this group does bring about a sharp decline in efficient functioning. It also intensifies existing maladjustments and the tendency toward introspection, self-centeredness, dwelling in the past, fears and feelings of inadequacy, self-distrust and hopelessness. Nevertheless, most old people are employable and are much healthier physically, mentally and emotionally when they are engaged in productive activity. After the usual appraisal of the individual's life history, physical condition, mental ability and efficiency, skills, personality and interests, the counselor's main problem will be one of mental hygiene. He will have to help the old person to look, feel and act alert, to keep up to date and look forward to the new instead of dwelling in the past, to think of the other fellow instead of himself, and to choose goals which will help him to grow instead of stagnate and deteriorate mentally and socially. L. J. Martin's Handbook for Old Age Counsellors [7] offers valuable suggestions in this field.

Summary

Prolonged unemployment results in physical deterioration, loss of essential skills, mental decline, emotional disturbance and social inadequacy. The majority of it is preventable, as relatively few persons are unemployable.

Persons may be long unemployed for various reasons, among which are fundamental inadequacy, physical handicap, mental disorder and old age.

Vocational rehabilitation of these persons involves rehabilitation of the whole individual—physically, mentally, socially and emotionally—but the emphasis on various aspects of the program will depend upon the basic reasons for the unemployment. Many old workers and those with physical and mental handicaps are good possibilities for vocational rehabilitation, but those who are fundamentally inadequate are the most difficult to adjust.

The rehabilitation counselor should have a knowledge of physical conditions and handicaps, a good background in mental hygiene, full understanding of psychological and trade tests and he must know jobs and job possibilities in his community. He can assist in the re-education of employers to the economic value of hiring certain handicapped workers.

He should be acquainted with existing occupational tools and their uses and have an awareness of the special needs of the unemployed groups he is trying to rehabilitate. Above all, he must have a thorough knowledge of community resources so that he will know where to secure needed medical care, psychiatric treatment, vocational training and job openings.

References:

1. Davis, J. S. An introduction to the problem of rehabilitation, Men. Hyg., 1945, *29*, 217–30.
2. Eisenberg, P. and Lazarsfeld, P. F. The psychological effects of unemployment, Psychl. Bull., 1938, *35*, 358–90.
3. Elliott, R. M. Occupational and vocational rehabilitation. Psychol. Bull., 1944, *41*, 47–56.
4. Gilbert, J. G. Senescent efficiency and employability, J. Appl. Psych., 1936, *20*, 266–72.
5. Ginsburg, S. W. What unemployment does to people; a study in adjustment to crisis, Am. J. Psychiatry, 1942, *99*, 439–46.
6. Marquis, D. G. (Ed.) Psychology and the war, Psych. Bull., 1943, *40*, 687–718.
7. Martin, L. J. *A handbook for old age counsellors.* San Francisco: Geertz Printing Co., 1944.
8. Rusk, H. A. Hope for our disabled millions, N. Y. Times Mgn. Jan. 27, 1946.
9. Watson, G. Morale during unemployment. *Civilian morale.* Boston: Houghton Mifflin, 1942, pp. 273–348.
10. Vié, J., Fail, G. and Opolon. Chrômage et psychopathie, Bull. Acad. Med., Paris, 1940, *123*, 624–31.

J. G. G.

UNEMPLOYMENT RATES IN THE MAJOR OCCUPATIONS.

All qualitative analysis and comparison of changing rates of unemployment for various occupational groupings suffer from lack of adequate empirical data. (1) There are no comprehensive statistics on unemployment *per se,* Federal, state or local. Unemployment must be inferred from data on employment, estimates of persons attached to various industries and trades, sample studies, and limited information supplied by unemployment insurance figures. (2) Before the WPA began its monthly estimates in April of 1940, there were no regularly compiled official Federal estimates of unemployment. Two states, Massachusetts and New York, had previously kept up local estimates of unemployment in certain trade unions for limited periods of time. The American Federation of Labor and the National Industrial Conference Board had compiled annual estimates based on a miscellany of sample data of both employment and unemployment for the country as a whole since the early 'twenties. (3) Adequate historical data on persons attached to various industries and occupations, or of movements amongst occupations do not exist. Furthermore, classifications used in various estimates are in many respects non-comparable between census intervals, between industrial classifications, and from one country to another. (4) Such data as exist do not permit of ready comparison between producers' goods and consumers' goods, durable and non-durable goods, and other categories of importance for analytical purposes. (5) Finally, until quite recent times most data and estimates appear as annual figures or for irregular intervals, making it very difficult to separate seasonal, cyclical, secular, and other influences.

The picture abroad is better in some respects, and worse in others. Wherever comprehensive social security programs exist, including unemployment compensation, and wherever a large percentage of employment is handled through national exchanges, as in England and Germany, unemployment coverage is more nearly complete. Occupational statistics, however, are apt to be confused by even less consistency in classification than is to be found in the American data. Other sources of confusion in the foreign data lie in such factors as high chronic unemployment after the first world war due to serious dislocations in international industrial and trade relations, the employment role of government works projects, and the manipulation, particularly in the case of Germany after 1933, of unemployment data for political purposes.

Despite these handicaps there are certain broad conclusions which may be drawn from individual studies, estimates, and official statistics with some degree of certainty. In general, over a long period of time, all over the world, and for all levels of economic development, the following hold:

Seasonal unemployment is highest for agriculture, forest products, industries using agricultural raw materials, the building industry in the colder climates, and in industries heavily influenced by model and fashion changes as in certain branches of the durable consumers' goods industries, notably automobiles. The determining factors are seasonal climatic changes and fashion. Both may be influenced by improved employment services. These increase labor mobility, spread the transition period in model changes, or modify various social habits such as the common termination of leases in New York City in October, which concentrates moving over a two months span.

Cyclical unemployment shows an almost equally definite pattern. It is highest during periods of depression in the heavy and producers' goods industries, and lowest in the consumers' goods industries. It is high in construction and in those branches catering to investment demand. It is relatively high in consumers' durable goods industries, and low in the soft goods—textiles, leather goods, etc.—and foodstuffs industries.

Employment in industries catering primarily to basic standard of living necessities declines in most cases less than in the bulk of the luxury trades. Employment in large-scale enterprises fluctuates much more widely than in the small, and in concentrated and metropolitan areas than in smaller towns and the countryside. Personal and professional services show practically insignificant change.

Secular and long range unemployment associated with changes in the structure of the national economy are more difficult to summarize, and show less regularity in pattern. It is found, in general, in industries, regions, and countries which, for one reason or another, are undergoing expansion at an unevenly low rate, or which are actually declining, and where these changes are associated with either, or both, disproportionately high population growth and immobility of labor. An example is supplied by the coal mining industry, where production declined from an average of around 560 million net tons at the close of the first world war to around 450 million net tons during the later 'thirties. This decline was caused in part by substitution of other fuels and energy, such as oil, gas, and hydro-generated power; but the more important reason was higher thermal efficiency in the use of coal. Better boilers, generators, engines, and heating apparatus, coupled to widespread chemical breakdown and by-product utilization account for the change. According to the estimates of Prof. Paul Douglas, the number of coal miners in the U. S. rose steadily from 398,000 in 1897 to reach a peak of 863,000 in 1923, yet the percentage of unemployed never declined below 16.1 (during the war year of 1918), and it has fluctuated on an average between 20 and 40 per cent for the entire interval between 1897 and 1926. Since then, as the data supplied by Lubin in the Prologue of the Temporary National Economic Committee reports show, there has been further secular decline in the industry, while the number of persons "attached to the industry" has remained about the same.

Much the same holds for agricultural labor. Added to the seasonal pattern of unemployment is the swift increase in migratory and casual farm labor due to dust storms and "tractoring out" in the prairie states. This non-seasonal agricultural unemployment is on the increase. Conservative estimates anticipate an increase of half a million ex-farmers and farm laborers who will fall in this category during the first decade after the recent war because of advancing mechanization in the corn, cotton, wheat, and sugar beet belts.

Somewhat the same picture may be repeated in many other industries, such as chemicals and heavy metals, where mechanization, flow production, and supporting methods are being rapidly introduced. The president of the CIO has estimated that the automatic strip mill "has already thrown forty thousand workers out of their jobs" in the steel industry. A chemical process which formerly required 126 men now needs but six. Such changes, of course, do not necessarily mean unemployment. So long as mobility of labor and capacity to absorb elsewhere exists, technological displacements can only mean increasing overall national productivity. It is for this reason that the phrase "technological unemployment" lacks meaning, since failure of absorption is a social, not a technological, fact.

Regional and international changes may produce a like chronic secular unemployment. It is feared, for example, that some forms of internal migration, such as that from the Middle West to California and of Negroes to the North during the war, will create surplus pools of labor for long periods to come. After the first World War chronic unemployment remained high in Germany due to loss of foreign markets and investments, industrial dislocations, loss of merchant marine, and other changes brought about by subsequent reparations settlements. England suffered in a similar way because of inability to compete in many markets due to technological obsolescence and the migration of many important British industries, chiefly in textiles, to Empire outposts.

Although there are notable exceptions—as in the case of the atrophying of the British cotton gray goods industry in the face of Japanese and Indian competition—most long-run and cyclical unemployment is found in investment goods, durable and luxury goods, construction and construction materials, and in large scale centrally located industries. Typically, either these industries supply consumers' goods which are dispensable in the short run, or the demand for their products is derived from changing consumer demand in such a way that employment is severely affected.

The case of durable consumers' goods, housing construction and materials supply, and luxury industries is obvious. If the consumer has any reason for curtailing expenditures whatsoever, durable goods will be made to last longer. They will be repaired instead of being replaced, new models will not be purchased, and the luxuries enjoyed when times are flush will be foregone. New houses will be built only when necessary. Residential construction, for example, declined from $4.5 billion in 1926 to $270 million in 1934. Employment for carpenters, foundation men, plasterers, roofers, electricians, etc., declined in proportion, and unemployment rose in a like manner in cement, brick, lime, lumber and other building supply industries. Lumber production declined from 40 billion board feet in 1925 to 10 billion in 1932. While employment for the United States as a whole declined by 28 per cent between 1923–25 and 1932, the drop in durable goods industries was 53 per cent.

The demand for producers' goods is derived from the demand for consumers' goods. Its two components are the supplying of consumers' goods industries for operation at current levels, and the requirements for expansion of both consumers' and producers' goods industries. Consequently, any tendency for the rate of expansion to diminish in the consumers' goods industry, causes not only tapering off, but actual decline in the producers' goods industries. If consumers' goods industries suffer an actual decline in demand, the effect upon producers' goods is both multiplied and accelerated. Unemployment may appear suddenly, and without apparent cause. Conversely, when demand begins to rise in the consumers' goods industries, the reabsorption of labor is apt to be equally swift and unexpected.

Consequently, any policy or practice which adversely affects the flow of consumer purchases will cause a degree of immediate unemployment in durable and luxury consumers' goods industries and will, through the multiplying effect upon the producers' goods industries, create severe unemployment. This will, in turn, still more heavily curtail consumer expenditures. Thus national income, consumption, savings, investment, and full employment are bound together in our society in such a way that an interruption or marked distortion of these interlaced flows immediately threatens economic stability which is always to the relative disadvantage of employment in the strategically vulnerable heavy industries. Keynes worked out these interrelationships in an interesting manner in his *General Theory of Employment, Interest, and Money*. From his formulation, it follows that one essential condition to the maintenance of full employment is stability in the investment goods industries. This requires continued growth of productive capacity in the economy as a whole at an even pace. Thus the program of government "compensatory spending" arises as a plan to make up for any deficit caused by failing consumer purchasing power to the amount needed to promote normal investment expansion. This stimulation is calculated to add directly or indirectly to the demand for the products of the investment goods industries, and may be supplemented by measures to better the profit position of their leading concerns, and otherwise improve investment prospects.

At this point a number of developments have caused many economists to take a pessimistic view of the future of employment in the major heavy goods industries. Among these developments, four closely related considerations are of particular interest:

(1) Declining population growth, particularly emphasized by Hansen, tends to mean a reduction in the rate of growth of basic consumer requirements and hence a disproportionately large decrease in the demand for investment goods. *Per contra,* decline in the rate of population growth is not being fully compensated for by increase or change in the structure of *per capita* demand because of the failure of the standard of living to rise with sufficient rapidity.

(2) Unionization has swept the heavy industries, bringing with it a demand for high wage scales. The effect has been to accelerate the introduction of labor-saving devices. These developments are particularly spectacular in the mining, chemicals, fuels, metallurgical, component parts, machinery, and assembly industries, and in certain branches of textiles (notably rayon). They tend to create large pools of chronically unemployed similar to those in the coal mining industry alluded to above.

(3) These pools are not being drained by reabsorption, due to expansion of demand, as rapidly as they are being filled. This is largely because of the growth of monopolistic and restrictive policies, chief of which are common resort to price fixity and to high price policies. Price rigidity tends to unstabilize production, and hence to accelerate changes in employment, and high price policies tend to limit demand. Both have been widely adopted in most major capitalist countries, and are instrumented by a series of policies which adversely affect both domestic and international trade. Many of these are now legal, having been sanctioned by state and Federal resale price maintenance, fair trade practices, and similar laws— most of which are patterned after the policies that dominated the NRA and AAA during the early 'thirties. Such policies have permitted the swift cartelization of strategic segments of the American economic system.

Finally, (4) if *per capita* income increases without an accompanying downward redistribution of income from the upper brackets, the national "propensity to consume" will be lowered. Such a relative lowering of consumer demand tends to depress the producers' goods industries. It follows that high employment in these fields will be threatened even under conditions of moderate prosperity.

The consideration of these interdependent factors is common to most of the full employment proposals for overcoming the foregoing difficulties. *The Winning Plans in the Pabst Postwar Employment Awards* all emphasized one angle or another of these problems. Nourse, in his *Price Making in a Democracy,* makes a strong plea for a return to a low price policy. Thurman Arnold and the Anti-Trust Division see the answer in wholesale elimination of monopolistic controls. In general, most theorists tend to divide into those favoring (a) stimulation of consumption, and (b) stimulation of investment. New Deal sympathizers and the trade unions are usually found in the former camp. The National Association of Manufacturers favors the latter. The Committee for Economic Development favors a middle course leaning toward the latter.

But all are agreed that with some sort of workable solution is bound up the uneasy alliance of the business system on the one hand, and political democracy on the other. The recent history of Europe seems to demonstrate that chronic and recurrent unemployment in the heavy industries ultimately creates social disturbances which lead to civil war initiated from either the right or the left. The problem of varying rates of unemployment, therefore, has important political repercussions, and may not be solved outside of such a frame of reference.

References:

1. Burns, A. F. *Production trends in the United States since 1870.* New York: National Bureau of Economic Research, 1934.
2. Clark, J. M. *Strategic factors in business cycles.* New York: National Bureau of Economic Research, 1935.
3. Douglas, P. H. *Real wages in the United States, 1890–1926.* Boston and New York: Houghton Mifflin Co., 1930.
4. Fabricant, S. *Employment in manufacturing, 1899–1939.* New York: National Bureau of Economic Research, 1942.
5. Kuznets, S. *Seasonal variations in industry and trade.* New York: National Bureau of Economic Research, 1933.
6. U. S. Bureau of Labor Statistics. *Handbook of labor statistics, 1941.* Washington: 1941.
7. International Labor Office. *Year book of labor statistics, 1941.* Montreal: 1942.

R. A. B. and J. H. D.

UNION OF SOCIALIST SOVIET REPUBLICS. Achievement of maximum production and a satisfactory worker adjustment are the twin objectives of vocational guidance activities in the Soviet Union. The needs of the nation as well as the interests, traits and aptitudes of individuals are given consideration in order to insure a distribution of labor which fits in with the requirements of a planned economy. Viteles [2] has indicated that demands for labor sometimes take priority over guidance findings; this was no doubt particularly true during the critical war years.

Chief responsibility for counseling and worker selection seems to fall upon the All-Union Central Council of Trade Unions (VTzSPS), which has carried on an extensive program of guidance throughout the U.S.S.R. In 1937 the Council operated approximately eighty vocational guidance bureaus (Profconsultatzia) devoted to direct guidance activities and incidental research, five regional laboratories devoted primarily to research and supervisory functions, and a Central Laboratory of Vocational Guidance and Placement in Moscow. The Central Laboratory has exercised a good deal of control over methodological procedures used by the other units, has helped in the direction and integration of research, and has had a voice in fiscal matters affecting the entire system.

Often carrying on counseling activities in the same areas served by the All-Union Central Council of Trade Unions centers, but dealing with other groups of children, are bureaus sponsored by local Commissariats of Health, local plants, and by the Commissariats for Heavy Industry, Light Industry, Agriculture, and Transportation. Apparently, the Commissariats of Education play a comparatively minor role in guidance activities, although they participate in such work. There is some cooperation between the various agencies active in the counseling field.

Most attention is directed toward children in the seventh grade of the general school, who average about fifteen years of age. These youngsters are given assistance in selecting from among the following alternatives: (1) entering a factory apprentice school; (2) matriculation in one of the technicums; (3) enrollment in the second division of a secondary school. This work is performed by bureaus staffed by educational specialists (pedologists), physicians, clerks and statisticians.

Surveys of individual development are undertaken with emphasis upon social origins and political beliefs. School records, including the results of mental and physical examinations, grades, and extracurricular activities are carefully scrutinized. In addition, consideration may be given to the ratings made by members of the Komsomol organization, and by foremen or apprentice school instructors with whom students have worked. Students are asked to write essays on their occupational interests and to complete interest inventories of various kinds. A very complete medical examination is required. A considerable number of psychological tests have been employed, including adaptations of such well known American examinations as the MacQuarrie Test for Mechanical Ability and the Minnesota Paper Form Board Test. Intelligence tests have also been used, but they have been criticized because of their emphasis upon individual differences.[1][2] Many original manual and mechanical aptitude tests have been devised in the Soviet Union, designed to predict performance in various skilled fields. Because of the many language groups, it has been found necessary to translate verbal tests into Ukrainian, Russian, Yiddish and other languages. Interviews with counselors play an important role in shaping the advice given to the students.

After the complete record has been compiled and evaluated by a Commission of Preliminary Review, which includes a physician, psychotechnician, and a pedologist, recommendations are made and discussed with both the child and his parents. Sometimes the decision is placed in the hands of a Final Commission consisting of members of the Preliminary Commission and representatives of the Parents Association, the Komsomol, the school, and the enterprise which maintains the school with which the child is affiliated. As might be expected, guidance and placement go hand in hand.

Guidance activities have been more highly developed in urban and industrial areas than in isolated rural sections; this seems to be true of countries all over the world. Some clinical work of the personality type has been carried on at such centers as the Institute for Occupational Diseases in Moscow. Some guidance is provided adults in connection with the personnel activities of the steel, chemical, transportation and other industries, and there is counseling within factories leading to the specialization of workers. Distribution of occupational information has not been as widespread as some Soviet educators would like, but this has been partially overcome by conferences, visits to plants, motion pictures, and polytechnical education. Courses for the training of counselors have been organized and such subjects as economics, physiology, and psychotechnics prescribed. Some research has been carried on in Kharkov, Moscow and Leningrad with reference to the advisement of tenth graders and even more advanced students. The writer has been unable to obtain information regarding the status of vocational guidance in the U.S.S.R. in the post-war period.

References:

1. Razran, G. Education in the Union of Socialist Soviet Republics, in *Encyclopedia of modern education,* edited by Rivlin, H. N. and Schueler, H. New York: The Philosophical Library, Inc., 1943, pp. 852–855.
2. Keller, F. J. and Viteles, M. S. *Vocational guidance throughout the world.* New York: W. W. Norton and Co., 1937, pp. 200–260.

O. J. K.

UNION OF SOUTH AFRICA.   Vocational guidance activities in South Africa have largely been carried on under the sponsorship of the Juvenile Affairs Boards. These Boards assist in finding jobs for young people, collect and maintain statistics, provide vocational counseling, and carry on research on employment problems affecting youth. They work closely with parents in establishing job objectives. The local Boards have a high measure of autonomy with regard to operations, concerning themselves to a large extent with local occupations and problems. Psychological tests are used in guidance work. The smallness of school populations makes possible an intimate acquaintanceship with pupils and facilitates the giving of sound advise. Apprenticeship Committees aid in the absorption of young people into industry and the trades.

References:

1. Rowe, O. H. and Hanley, A. M. South Africa, in *Vocational guidance throughout the world.* Keller, F. J. and Viteles, M. S. New York: W. W. Norton and Co., 1937, pp. 469–473.
2. Todd, L. P. Education in Union of South Africa, in *Encyclopedia of modern education,* edited by Rivlin, H. N. and Schueler, H. New York: The Philosophical Library, Inc., 1943, pp. 855–858.

O. J. K.

UNITED STATES ARMED FORCES INSTITUTE EXAMINATIONS

The United States Armed Forces Institute

During World War II and continuing during the period of demobilization, the United States Armed Forces Institute at Madison, Wisconsin, has offered correspondence-study courses to men and women in service. This Institute has offered the best educational materials and instructional services that could be commanded in the face of urgent demands for such instruction from service personnel at all points of the globe. Some of these courses do not differ from correspondence courses that have always been offered through regular university extension courses; many of them are radically different.

The majority of students who have had such courses will not present themselves for "educational credit." They took the courses for intellectual entertainment, and the acquisition of "credit" may mean nothing to them. The Institute was not established with the accreditation purpose in mind, and it does no educational accrediting.

The National Advisory Committee

Recognizing the need for a more rational plan (1) for placing members of the armed forces on their return to education institutions, (2) for granting appropriate credit for educational attainment while in military service, and (3) for motivating the educational work of the soldier and sailor, a special committee of educators recommended to the Armed Forces Institute that a procedure be provided which would enable members of the armed forces to demonstrate their educational attainments so that educational institutions might give proper recognition and fair credit. This committee, chairmanned for four years by Dr. E. G. Williamson of the University of Minnesota, has been known as the Advisory Committee. It has enlisted the support of the American Council on Education and the National Association of Secondary School Principals. Through these two organizations the interest and scrutiny of nineteen major accrediting groups were directed to the program. The complete summary of recommendations of the Advisory Committee has been published in the form of a handbook that is an indispensable item in the counselor's library. It is entitled, *A Guide to the Evaluation of Educational Experiences in the Armed Services.*

The Examinations Staff of the U.S.A.F.I.

The Advisory Committee envisioned early in its planning the eventual desire of students of the Institute to receive formal credit, and they devised plans to safeguard such awards. Under the direction of Dr. Ralph W. Tyler, a civilian Examinations Staff was established at the University of Chicago. This staff developed approximately 500 end-of-course tests to be used with the Institute courses, approximately ninety subject examinations broader in scope than the end-of-course tests, and a high school and a college battery of Tests of General Educational Development. A corps of instructors and examiners was employed through the Board of Examinations of the University to construct these examinations. Additional consultants and critics supplemented this staff with services *in absentia*. Altogether, several hundred high school and college instructors figured in this one aspect of the program.

The U.S.A.F.I. End-of-Course Tests

The U.S.A.F.I. end-of-course tests are taken upon completion of an Institute course while the man is still in service. They are not available for civilian use. The report which the Institute issues describes the course taken and indicates either that it was "successfully completed with no end-of-course or subject examination taken," or a report of test scores is given. The *Guide* makes a recommendation of how much credit should be allowed if the end-of-course test has been successfully passed. When the man wants to get educational credit, it is necessary for the counselor to have his local institution establish a policy concerning acceptance or nonacceptance of the Committee's recommendation, as given in the *Guide*. The end-of-course tests are considered to be the equivalent of a comprehensive examination for a course, and their content is limited to that of the textbook used for the course. They have not received tryouts, and standards of passing for them were arbitrarily fixed by consultants.

The U.S.A.F.I. Subject Examinations

The subject examinations differ from the end-of-course tests in that they (a) are more comprehensive; (b) are more carefully constructed; (c) apply to no set course; (d) have norms based on civilian cases; (e) have civilian forms; (f) were prepared with the accreditation purpose in mind; (g) represent the combined judgment of several or more persons.

The list of subject examinations follows:

High School Level	*College Level*
Elementary Algebra	Astronomy (Introductory)
Second-year Algebra	General Chemistry
Advanced Arithmetic	Qualitative Analysis
Solid Geometry*	Quantitative Analysis
Plane Geometry	Organic Chemistry
	Zoology*
General Biology	General Biology
General Chemistry	General Botany

High School Level	*College Level*
Meteorology	General Physics
General Physics	
Radio (beginning)*	Engineering Drawing
General Science	Surveying
Senior Science	Engineering Mechanics
	Aviation Engines*
French Reading, Grammar, Vocabulary at the lower level	Machine Design
French Reading, Grammar, Vocabulary at the upper level	Diesel Engineering
	Electricity and Magnetism
German Reading, Grammar, Vocabulary at the lower level (only)	Electron Tubes and Circuits
	Engineering Electronics
	Advanced Engineering Electronics
Spanish Reading, Grammar, Vocabulary at the lower level (only)	Fluid Mechanics
	Radio Engineering
	Advanced Radio Engineering
Italian Reading, Grammar, Vocabulary at the lower level (only)	Strength of Materials
	College Algebra
	Analytic Geometry
Business English	Plane Trigonometry
Business Arithmetic	Differential Calculus
First-Year Typewriting	Integral Calculus
Second-Year Typewriting	
First-Year Gregg Shorthand	Economics*
First-Year Bookkeeping and Accounting	American History
	Modern European History
Second-Year Bookkeeping and Accounting	American Government*
	Elementary Psychology
American History	
Civics	Commercial Correspondence
Problems of Democracy	English Composition
Modern European History*	English Reading and Literary Acquaintance
World History	
Mechanical Drawing	French Reading, Grammar, Vocabulary at the lower level
Auto Mechanics*	
	French Reading, Grammar, Vocabulary at the upper level
English Composition (Grade 10, 11 or 12)	

High School Level	*College Level*
English Reading and Literary Acquaintance (Grade 10, 11, or 12)	German Reading, Grammar, Vocabulary at the lower level (only)
	Spanish Reading, Grammar, Vocabulary at the lower level (only)
	Italian Reading, Grammar, Vocabulary at the lower level (only)

* No B forms were constructed.

Several hundred each of high schools and colleges have cooperated in the programs to establish standards for the subject examinations. *Criterion scores* for each, representing a satisfactory level of achievement at which to allow credit, are reported in the *Guide*. Percentile ranks for the distribution of part and total scores of the confidential military Form A examinations have been obtained, along with equivalence data for equating Form A and B scores. At present these data are available from Veterans' Testing Service only, although it is expected that they will soon be more generally available.

The Tests of General Educational Development

There are two batteries of the *Tests of General Educational Development,* one at the high school level and one at the college level. Both measure chiefly the student's ability to do mature analytical reading in the natural sciences and social studies. The Tests, *Correctness and Effectiveness of Expression* and *Interpretation of Literary Materials,* measure the more traditional informational type of educational outcome. At the high school level the *Test of General Mathematical Ability* is a test of achievement in mathematics considered most useful in daily life. At the college level, it is recommended that the college subject examinations in mathematics (*College Algebra, Analytic Geometry, Trigonometry*) be employed.

Like the subject examinations, all of these tests have civilian B forms. Two additional confidential forms are now in preparation. The norms are comprehensive, having been derived from civilian high school and college populations throughout the country. The high school norms are reported separately in six regional distributions. The college norms are reported separately for three types of institutions defined by their median scores on the *American Council Psychological Examination.* Recommended standards for accreditation are given in the *Guide*. A more complete report on these norms is included in the *Manual* which is distributed with the B forms. A supplementary statement pertaining to their application and interpretation has been written by Dr. E. F. Lindquist.

The Veterans' Testing Service

The Veterans' Testing Service is a supplementary service of the Commission on Accreditation of the American Council on Education. It is a testing agency, established for the purpose of assisting in the interpretation of the U.S.A.F.I. examinations and in making available the confidential military forms of the U.S.A.F.I. examinations for the testing of veterans. It issues the military Form A examinations, under restricted conditions of use, according to two plans: (1) Plan I, the Individual Application—whereby any school officer may obtain sealed examinations for stated individuals and have all scoring and interpreting done by the Service; (2) Plan II, Group Rental where any approved educational agency with trained personnel may rent a small stock of examinations and process them locally. It is expected that many thousands of veterans will be tested through VTS for the purpose of evaluating their claims to educational credit for educational experiences in service.

Sources

The parallel forms of the subject examinations and Tests of General Educational Development are available to civilian purchasers from the Cooperative Test Service, 15 Amsterdam Avenue, New York City 23, and from Science Research Associates, 228 South Wabash Avenue, Chicago 4, Illinois.

The Guide to the Evaluation of Educational Experiences in the Armed Services is available from the American Council on Education offices of the Cooperative Study of Training and Experience in the Armed Services, 363 Administration Building, University of Illinois, Urbana, Illinois.

The descriptive statements of the Plans for Veterans' Testing Service can be obtained from its office at 6010 Dorchester Avenue, University of Chicago, Chicago 37, Illinois.

References:

1. Detchen, L. Appraisal of military training and experience: continuation report. *Journal of the American Association of Collegiate Registrars*, 1945, *20*, 231–237.
2. ———. The educational counselor and the United States Armed Forces Institute Examinations. *Journal of the American Association of Deans of Women*, 1945, *9*, 19–26.

3. Lindquist, E. F. The use of tests in the accreditation of military experience and in the educational placement of war veterans. *The Educational Record*, 1944, *25*, 357–376.
4. Tyler, R. W. Appraisal of military training and experience. *Journal of the American Association of Collegiate Registrars*, 1943, *18*, 345–352.

L. D.

UNITED STATES EMPLOYMENT SERVICE.   The role of the United States Employment Service in vocational guidance has been primarily the classification, selection, and referral of workers to job openings. During the depression when there was a surplus of workers, vocational counseling was undertaken in many offices particularly for youth. More recently counseling programs have been initiated to aid veterans and displaced war workers in finding suitable jobs. The United States Employment Service performs an important function in developing and supplying occupational information, labor market information and other occupational techniques and tools which are widely used both within and outside the Employment Service offices.

The present United States Employment Service was established by the Wagner-Peyser Act in June, 1933. The Act called for state administered public employment offices, affiliated with the United States Employment Service, a bureau in the Department of Labor. In addition there was established the National Re-employment Service administered by the United States Employment Service to operate local employment offices in communities which were not served by the state operated offices. As the state offices expanded under the Wagner-Peyser Act, the National Re-employment Service was withdrawn and was terminated July, 1939 when the United States Employment Service was moved from the Department of Labor to the Social Security Board, and was merged with the Bureau of Unemployment Compensation. The new Bureau was called the Bureau of Employment Security. Shortly after Pearl Harbor, President Roosevelt issued an executive order removing control of local offices from the states and establishing a national system which in 1942 was transferred from the Social Security Board to the War Manpower Commission.

The purpose of the United States Employment Service and its affiliated State Agencies was to operate a nation-wide system of public employment offices whereby persons seeking work could locate job openings and through which employers could obtain qualified workers for positions. In the early days much of the employment service activity was involved in supplying workers to government work projects. This activity gave the erroneous impression that the Employment Service was a kind of relief agency rather than an agency which referred workers on the basis of their qualifications to private industry as well as to government work projects. During the period July 1, 1935 to June 30, 1936, the Employment Service made nearly six million placements about 80% of which were for public employment or on relief work. By 1941 the picture had reversed and 80% of all placements were in private industry.

During the war the program of the United States Employment Service has been altered by the changing manpower situation. Because of the scarcity of labor and the willingness of employers to hire most anyone the local employment officers were "streamlined." The taking of applications was largely eliminated and referrals were made as quickly as possible with a minimum amount of interviewing and record keeping. There was a great increase in labor clearance whereby arrangements were made for the transfer of workers to localities where the manpower situation was most critical. The local offices were called upon to handle certain manpower controls and to participate in aiding war plants in better utilization of manpower. The offices also participated in vigorous recruiting campaigns to motivate more workers to take war jobs.

Vocational counseling developed in the United States Employment Service Offices during the depression when persons could not be immediately placed in jobs and it was necessary for many persons to discuss their occupational plans with an interviewer or counselor. The National Youth Administration supplied counselors in many offices, particularly to aid in the counseling of youth who were having difficulties in obtaining work. Several hundred offices before the war had counseling services.

During the war when jobs were plentiful, counseling in the offices in the Employment Service decreased and was finally discontinued altogether. However, with the return of veterans, counseling again became important and in 1943 experiments in the counseling of veterans were initiated and no doubt with the end of the war vocational counseling will be carried on extensively in the offices of the United States Employment Service.

The type of counseling carried on in local offices is known as "placement counseling," for the chief role performed by the Employment Service is the placement of workers in jobs.

Counseling is and has been carried on principally in the larger offices. One or more persons is selected and assigned counselor and is given special training in counseling methods. In some offices one or more counselors devote their entire time to veterans. Also in some offices there is a counselor who deals primarily with handicapped job seekers. Employment service counselors have also been assigned to naval hospitals and Army Separation Centers.

In local offices the counselor sees only those applicants who are found to have problems requiring counseling service. Such applicants are referred to the counselor by an interviewer who has talked to the applicant and found that he needs special attention in regard to his occupational problems. Persons with little occupational experience, individuals displaced from their jobs, handicapped persons, and veterans seeking advice about civilian jobs are the most frequent cases referred. If the applicant has a problem outside the scope of the employment service such as medical, legal or social service, he is referred to the community agency giving such service.

Counseling in the Employment Service involves obtaining full information regarding the applicant's occupational problems, giving him information about the duties and qualifications of jobs and opportunities for work; also informing him about his capabilities for certain occupations as indicated by occupational tests and giving such other facts as the counselor may have which will be of assistance. The counselor attempts to ask questions and to give facts to aid the applicant in making his own occupational decisions.

Applicants who are counseled are classified occupationally so they may be referred to suitable jobs as openings occur. If the applicant has occupational experience he is classified according to the *Dictionary of Occupational Titles, Parts I and II*. His application card bears the code number of his occupation and is filed according to the *Dictionary* code structure. Applicants lacking work experience are classified according to fields of work as specified in *Entry Occupational Classifications* (also known as Part IV of the *Dictionary*).

The relationship of counseling in the Employment Service to that conducted by other community agencies has been studied particularly in a joint project of the Employment Service and the American Youth Commission in 1938–1939. As a part of the Occupational Research Program, Community Research Centers were established in Baltimore, Providence, St. Louis and Dallas. Various arrangements for counseling were tried out. In St. Louis for example, counselors employed by the school system were located in the local Employment Service office and in Providence persons on the Employment Service payroll worked in the school counseling service. From these experiments no set pattern was recommended for it appeared that the pattern should be set in relation to the particular counseling resources in each community. With the returning of veterans in 1943, community cooperation in counseling was again stimulated. In a number of communities committees were established with representation from the various agencies interested in the veterans.

Special emphasis has been given by the Employment Service to the counseling and placement of the handicapped. The "physical demands" approach to job analysis was developed whereby jobs are analyzed from the standpoint of the physical requirements of the jobs.

Vocational Testing in the Employment Service was begun in 1936 and reached its peak as an aid in placing war workers in 1941 when nearly three quarters of a million job seekers were given either trade or aptitude tests. Although testing was abandoned almost entirely during 1942 and 1943, it began to return in 1944 as a tool for counseling discharged veterans.

A noteworthy development in the United States Employment Service was the establishment in 1934 of the Occupational Research Program which later became the Division of Occupational Analysis. This program was initiated to develop occupation information and other interviewing and counseling tools to aid in the effective placement of job seekers. These tools have also been adopted by many government agencies and are used extensively by schools and employers. The most widely used tool is the *Dictionary of Occupational Titles* which defines and classifies over 20,000 separate jobs. This document was introduced into the Employment office in 1940 and has been amended and enlarged by supplements from time to time. A Part IV of the *Dictionary* known as the "Entry Occupation Classification" is used in counseling and classifying persons who have limited work experience. This document was revised and enlarged in 1944. The Employment Service has also prepared numerous volumes of job descriptions and has developed and standardized trade tests and aptitude test batteries for several hundred occupations. More recently the Employment Service has developed tables of related occupations which show the relationship of military occupations to civilian occupations. These tables are widely used in the counseling and placement of veterans.

The Employment Service plays an important role in determining labor supply and demand. Employers are visited periodically and information is obtained regarding future labor needs. During the defense and war periods Employment Service statistics regarding available job seekers were used extensively as aids in assigning the locations for government contracts.

More recently the Employment Service has prepared "industry" and "area" manpower statements which give pertinent information regarding labor demand and supply. These statements are prepared especially for the use of counselors and are also widely distributed outside the Employment Service.

Although the Employment Service has been absorbed by the War Manpower Commission and some of its program has lost its identity as an employment service function, there is considerable opposition to its remaining a Federal service after the war. Unless the Wagner-Peyser Act is amended the Employment Service will eventually return to the control of the States and, as before the war, it will be administered by the States in conjunction with the state programs of unemployment insurance.

Editor's Note: The U. S. Employment Service was transferred from the War Manpower Commission to the Labor Department, and on November 15, 1946, the Service was turned over to the States.

References:

1. Bell, H. M. *Matching youth and jobs.* Washington: American Youth Commission, American Council on Education, 1940.
2. Shartle, C. L., Dvorak, B. J., Heinz, C. A. and Others. Ten years of occupational research. *Occupations,* 1944, *22,* 387–446.
3. Stead, W. H. and Masincup, W. E. *The occupational research program of the United States Employment Service.* Chicago: Public Administration Service, 1941.
4. Stead, W. H., Shartle, C. L. and Associates. *Occupational counseling techniques.* New York: American Book Co., 1940.

C. L. S.

U. S. OCCUPATIONAL INFORMATION AND GUIDANCE SERVICE.

The Occupational Information and Guidance Service is administratively a part of the Vocational Division of the U. S. Office of Education, Federal Security Agency. It was inaugurated in 1938, when for the first time the Office of Education provided a staff devoted entirely to the area of occupational information, guidance programs, and related problems. Previous to that time a single specialist had been assigned part-time to these duties.

Origins and Early History

A number of events supplied background for the initiation of this Service. One was the report of the President's Advisory Committee on Education published in 1938. In the volume on vocational education [3] the index records twelve references to vocational guidance, and in the volume containing the condensed report of the Committee [1] there were sixteen references. These recommendations ranged from a few sentences to a number of pages, and reflected the growing national importance of guidance as a distinct field of educational effort.

At the same time the National Occupational Conference [2] which for a number of years as a private foundation had been carrying on promotion of vocational guidance objectives throughout the United States, was about to bring its activities to a close. The Director of the National Occupational Conference, Dr. Edwin A. Lee, and his board of directors, turned to the Office of Education for a continuity of this country-wide effort.

Other currents moving in the same direction which had some effect on the inauguration of the Service were those set in motion by the American Youth Commission, by the experiments in counseling of the U. S. Employment Service, and by the continuous efforts of the National Vocational Guidance Association. The National Youth Administration and the Civilian Conservation Corps emphasized guidance in their Nation-wide programs. Economic conditions made vocational guidance take on new importance as an implement of individual adjustment.

To meet needs from so many directions, the Commissioner of Education, Dr. J. W. Studebaker, organized the Occupational Information and Guidance Service.[5] The new Service was supplied with a substantial amount of money by the National Occupational Conference to expedite activities which otherwise would have evolved more slowly through Government procedures. Its Federal budget was met mostly from funds available through the Smith-Hughes and George-Deen Acts.

Early direction was given to activities of the Service by the many individuals and organizations consulted as the program took its form. Richard D. Allen of Providence, Rhode Island, was the first consultant. Such well-known authorities as Walter V. Bingham, Paul W. Chapman, Giles M. Ruch, L. S. Hawkins, and David Segel served for nearly a year on its staff. Numerous organizations, institutions of higher learning, State and local school departments, and professional groups from both general and vocational education were brought into conference at numerous times during the first year of its existence. From this varied background emerged even the very name of the Service, as well as its principles, purposes, and plan of action.[6]

Four General Objectives

The program of the Service contemplates several distinct objectives. One of these is the extension of programs of occupational information and guidance throughout the country with the assistance of funds available through the Smith-Hughes and George-Deen Acts, the so-called Federal vocational education statutes.[4]

States may use Federal money to reimburse in part the salary and other necessary expenses involved in supervision of occupational information and guidance programs. This money has been available for supervision only, and does not include reimbursement for counselor trainers or for local directors and counselors. A State program is free to follow the pattern which a State may adopt, subject only to approval by the U. S. Office of Education to determine that it is in accordance with the Federal statutes. The breadth of the program and its ability to vary according to the needs of the individual State may be judged from the following quotation. This statement was included in the first proposals from the State of Maryland in 1938, and has become practically standard among all the States:

Properly selected pupils are among the prime essentials of efficient vocational schools and classes.

The selective process, to avoid waste of vocational education funds, should take place before the pupil enters upon vocational training. It follows that the pupil must make his choice on a basis of information about his own interests and abilities, and about wages, working conditions, and possibilities of continuous employment, acquired before the critical moment of his choice of specific training for an occupation.

Enrolling officials in vocational schools and classes can likewise function efficiently only if they also possess similar knowledge of occupational information and pupil inventory before acceding to, or directing, the enrollment of a pupil for specific training.

The vocational school itself will, in turn, continuously utilize related kinds of information during the process of training, placing, and following up its pupils. In addition many other persons in school and out will defer or change their decisions with regard to their occupations. Further problems in occupational information and guidance are presented by this group.

From these premises, it follows that "providing for the further development of vocational education in the several States and Territories," to quote from the opening sentence of the George-Deen Act, requires first, the improvement of the ability of teacher counselors, both in schools from which vocational classes draw their pupils, and in vocational schools themselves, to secure and use facts about occupations, and facts of occupational significance about their pupils; and, second, the improvement of these teacher counselors in the use of the necessary techniques in applying these facts to the wise counsel and guidance of pupils.

In the seven years since the establishment of the Service the number of States which have officially provided for supervision has grown from one to thirty-eight, of which thirty are using Federal funds and eight are supporting their programs entirely from State appropriations. Field service is supplied from Washington to aid these State departments.

A second objective of the Service is to serve as a clearinghouse on the Federal level for guidance activities throughout the Nation. This is accomplished in numbers of ways:

1. Bulletins resulting from research and from studies in areas of current interest are issued at frequent intervals.
2. Relationships are maintained with other Government agencies which have activities directly or indirectly related to the guidance field. Such agencies often ask assistance in securing contacts with States and with school systems. On the other hand, information of interest to States and school systems is frequently secured from these agencies. This information is passed on through publications, conferences, and other communications with the field.
3. Members of the staff of the Service are frequently called upon to work with national organizations interested in guidance work, to address their meetings, to assist them in their publications, and otherwise to perform clearinghouse activities.
4. Counselor training and certificating agencies in the States are supplied with services to aid them in developing counseling as a profession and in increasing the supply of persons who may be regarded as experienced and well-trained counselors.

A third objective is the integration of the principles and practices of guidance work within the Office of Education itself. The Service is the focal point of these activities in the Office, and, in accordance with the stated purposes of the Commissioner of Education, maintains close contacts with those Divisions in the Office which deal with elementary and secondary education, vocational education, higher education, and educational relationships with other countries.

A fourth objective is to serve individual correspondents of professional status who write from every State and from abroad. Many thousands of these letters are received annually. Disposing of them requires much direct service. In addition, the policy of referring as many as possible to State and local authorities tends to build up the prestige and influence of the latter and to enlarge their activities.

The Purpose and Implementation of a Guidance Program

The method of arriving at a definition of the field, and the purposes and plans of work, of the Service has been described previously. The basic philosophy and principles on which the Service operates have gone through a process of evolution, but have not changed their general direction, since they took form under the advice available at the inception of the Service.

The Service believes that the objective of guidance activities is to help the individual make choices which lead to a reasonable state of adjustment both as a worker and as a member of society. Since this may be considered the objective of education itself, and there should be some clear delineation between the whole and any of its parts, the guidance program is defined as a group of activities which are merely tools in the total educative process. Of these tools, individual counseling is the most critically essential, and affects the individual most directly, but counseling cannot be used successfully unless other implements are available.

The activities commonly carried on in a guidance program include:

Individual Inventory—the process of identifying, recording, interpreting, and utilizing the facts about the individual's physical, mental, and personal traits, in cumulative form.

Occupational Information—the process of accumulating, disseminating, and interpreting for class and individual use material of occupational significance. This material concerns the number and kinds of occupations, the qualifications they demand, the conditions of training and entry, and their relation to the individual's ability to secure placement in them. The term "occupation" is used comprehensively, from the unskilled level to the professions. Therefore, the entire range of education, preparation, and training is within the scope of necessary information.

Individual Counseling—the personal assistance to an individual in aiding him to identify and solve his problem, and in increasing his ability to solve future problems. It includes matching characteristics and occupational opportunities, but must contemplate many problems of a seemingly unrelated nature, to which specialized professional medical, social, and other help must be summoned, often from outside the school or counseling office.

Utilization of Training and Try-Out Experiences—the discovery and use of many experiences, often outside the curriculum, to develop aptitudes, try out abilities, build up attitudes, or to give specific training which will make for better choice preparation and adjustment.

Placement and Adjustment—the responsibility for aiding the individual directly, or through other established agencies, to enter successfully his next phase of experience. This may mean another grade, another kind of school, training for a vocation, college, a job, or some other sphere of adult life. The principle involved is the continuity of the guidance process until adjustment is approximately attained.

Follow-up and Other Evaluative Procedures—following the individual for a period of time after he leaves the jurisdiction of his counseling sponsorship to discover the quality of his adjustment. The objective includes finding out whether the individual requires further guidance services, which may be supplied through adult counseling centers, the existence of which is implied in the comprehensive program advocated by the Service. But a distinct product should be the discovery and accumulation of facts derived from information supplied by the former counselees themselves, that is, all school leavers. These facts will concern the number and kind of jobs, wages, promotion requirements, adjustment to civil life and to employment conditions, and any ascertainable effect of the guidance program and of the curriculum on the individual. These facts, accumulated and analyzed, will be of the utmost importance to the school administrator as he plans the continuous evolution of his entire educative process to serve better the individuals he instructs and the community which supports the school system.

Implications for the Institution and the Administrator

When, as a result of a guidance program in action, individuals make choices as a result of counseling, an implied obligation springs up for the educative process to aid him in following through successfully. This, again, involves education of a kind, at a rate, and to a level adapted to the individual's needs. The same tools, then, which help the individual to make his decisions wisely, are essential to the school administration itself to determine what kind of persons are being taught, the objectives which they can be helped to reach, and the content and method of the curriculum which is evolved for these purposes. Guidance activities, therefore, affect the individual very directly through counseling. They affect him no less potently by supplying administrators with the facts for continuous revision of the school program in every aspect of administration, supervision, and instruction.

It is further held that the activities which together compose a guidance program are specific, require skill, and demand recognitior by school administrators in terms of time, place, staff, and equipment. All teachers will participate in and utilize the guidance activities. One or more of them will require special skills to perform tasks which are different from other tasks in the roster of school duties.

The Integrity of the Guidance Process

This program should serve the individual from his earliest years, through adolescence and adulthood until he requires no further assistance. It will find itself housed in schools, colleges, or community offices. Problems which it handles will include those of education, mental hygiene, vocation, health, recreation, social relations, and many others. But the principles are unitary. The individual must always be approached by a counselor who contemplates without prejudgment a personality whose problems will appear during the counseling process in their proper relation and importance. There are no special kinds of counseling, a process which is universal in its attack. There are many kinds of problems.

The counselor is much in the position of the physician who is to give a thorough general examination: he makes no assumptions, and realizing such interrelations as that a malfunction of the stomach may have its cause in an emotional conflict, searches for all symptoms, and is ready to refer the patient to a specialist if such a course is indicated. By the same analogy, the counselor discards such evidence of prejudgment as labeling his program or his counseling as "vocational," "moral," "health," "educational," or "social," adjectives applicable to the term "problem," rather than to "guidance" or "counseling." The counseling must retain a universal point of view in order to identify and clarify for the counselee the problems with which he is really grappling and their due relationship and order of importance and attack. When the counselor has once identified the problem, he may then call on many resources for their solution, including at times the physician, the psychiatrist, the welfare worker, or even a general attack by these and the family, school, and community.

Relationship of Service to State and Local School Administration

Although the philosophy and principles just briefly described are accepted by the Occupational Information and Guidance Service, the following statement made by the U. S. Commissioner of Education in 1938 accurately describes the attitude of the Service:

It will not be the purpose of the Office of Education to advocate any particular pattern of organization or administration for a Guidance Service nor will the Office seek to secure uniformity with reference to the variety of specific functions to be performed by the several State, local, and school guidance organizations. All of these matters will be dealt with by the Office of Education in the way in which it deals with similar problems in other fields. It is anticipated that the organization of guidance in a State will be supported by funds and other assets which may be available to the State. The form of organization, the functions, and the methods of administration are all matters which are to be determined by the State authorities.

Organization of the Service Staff

The present staff of the Service is assigned to responsibilities in the following categories: (1) Field service, especially in Federal-State relationships, and in the administrative aspects of establishing and maintaining guidance programs; (2) Counselor training, with emphasis both on institutional method and content, and on in-service training of counselors who are employed; (3) Occupational information, including all phases of accumulating, evaluating, and disseminating facts, making source material available, exploring visual and other supplementary aids, and using occupational facts in class work or counseling; (4) Methods and techniques used in guidance programs, such as counseling, cumulative records, tests and measurements, and follow-up studies.

References:

1. Advisory Committee on Education. Report of the Committee, February, 1938.
2. National Occupational Conference. *Occupational adjustment: interim report.* New York: National Occupational Conference, 551 Fifth Avenue, 1938.
3. Russell, J. D. and Associates. Staff Study No. 8, prepared for the Advisory Committee on Education, Washington: U. S. Government Printing Office, 1938.
4. Studebaker, J. W. Inauguration of a program of occupational information and guidance. Office of Education, U. S. Department of the Interior, C. L. No. 2107. October 28, 1938.
5. ————. The new national occupational information and guidance service. Occupations, 17, No. 2, November, 1938.
6. ————. The occupational information and guidance service: a report of progress. Occupations, 17, No. 7, April, 1939.

H. A. J.

V

VALIDITY. The validity of a test is the extent to which the test measures what it purports to measure. Test validity is determined, whenever possible, in terms of the relationship between results on the test and some other objective measure of the trait or ability which the test is designed to gauge. The latter measure is called the criterion. Thus, for example, school grades, teachers' ratings for intelligence, or academic honors may be used as the criteria against which to validate a test of general intelligence. Frequently, an existing test believed valid is used as a criterion. The correlation between criterion and test scores is the validity coefficient.

Validity and reliability are related aspects of test efficiency. A valid test cannot be unreliable, for its correlation with a criterion is limited by its own reliability coefficient (and, it should be remembered, by the reliability of the criterion). A test may, however, be highly reliable—i.e. self-consistent—without being a valid measure in the sense of yielding a high correlation with outside independent criteria or measures of performance.

Many widely-used tests of vocational aptitude have relatively low coefficients of validity. Often, however, this is not to be construed as indicating that the test is not a satisfactory measuring instrument. Rather, it reflects the fact that adequate and reliable criteria of occupational success against which to validate tests are difficult to define and measure. It is difficult, for example, to determine a suitable criterion as to what constitutes success in the practice of medicine—any single criterion, such as income, is influenced by a number of extraneous factors, such as the individuals' policy regarding fees. The criterion measures are also likely to be rough and subject to error. Furthermore, a number of factors, in addition to aptitude, determine vocational success. A one-to-one correlation between aptitude for and subsequent success in an occupation can therefore hardly be expected.

No arbitrary standard can be set as the minimum for a satisfactory validity coefficient. The vocational or educational counselor must evaluate the size of the coefficient in the light of the comprehensiveness, adequacy and reliability of the criterion and in addition must rely on his own appraisal of the suitability of the content of the test and the experience which he and others have had with its use.

References:

1. Bingham, W. V. D. *Aptitudes and aptitude testing.* New York and London: Harper and Bros., 1937.
2. Garrett, H. E. *Statistics in psychology and education.* New York: Longmans, Green and Co., 1941.
3. Scott, I. D. *Manual of advisement and guidance.* Washington: United States Government Printing Office, 1945.

I. C.

VARIABILITY OR DISPERSION. In describing a set of statistical data the first descriptive measure stated is an average of some type such as the arithmetic mean, the median or the mode. Whichever one of these is stated has presumably been selected as being the most typical of the items of the set. While this average value gives something of a picture of the set of data, the picture will be more complete if it is known, in addition, how the items differ from the stated average. In general, the items of a set of data differ from the stated average by variable amounts. This quality of variability is termed "dispersion" by statisticians and measures of dispersion of various types and their calculation will be found discussed in any standard textbook of statistical methods.

To illustrate how series having the same arithmetic mean may have different dispersions consider the three series:

A: 50,   50,   50,   50,   50,   50,   50.
B: 35,   48,   49,   50,   51,   52,   65.
C: 35,   40,   45,   50,   55,   60,   65.

The arithmetic mean ($\overline{X}$) of each series is 50. 50 is the most typical of the items in series A since each item has the same value, that of the mean. There is no dispersion or variability in this series and any calculated measure of dispersion would have a zero value. In series B most of the items lie close to the mean and the dispersion is not great. In series C the items are scattered further from the mean and the dispersion or variability is greatest in this series.

The Range

The range of a set of data is the arithmetic difference between the highest and lowest items of the set. While this may be used as a measure of dispersion, it is the least satisfactory, or weakest, of all such measures since it does not take into consideration the relative

1332 ENCYCLOPEDIA OF VOCATIONAL GUIDANCE

positions or magnitudes of items between the two extremes of the set. For the two sets B and C given above the ranges are both 30 but the dispersion of B is less than that of C. This measure of dispersion is also an unsatisfactory one for comparing the variabilities of two different sets of data, especially if the total frequency of the two sets differ greatly. For range is apt to increase with frequencies, but dispersion does not necessarily do so.

Quartile Deviation or Semi-Interquartile Range

The quartile deviation measures dispersion somewhat better than the range. It is calculated by the formula $Q = \dfrac{Q_3 - Q_1}{2}$ wherein Q is the semi-interquartile range, Q_3 is the upper quartile and Q_1 is the lower quartile. The difference $(Q_3 - Q_1)$ is the interquartile range. By definition, Q_1 is that score below which one fourth of the items of the set lie, and Q_3 that score above which one fourth of the items of the set lie. Therefore, one half of the items of the set lie between Q_1 and Q_3 and $(Q_3 - Q_1)$ gives the range within which half of the items in the central portion of the distribution lie. The narrowness of this serves as a measure of concentration; a small range, in comparison with the total range, indicating that the central half of the items differs but little from the mean or median. If the distribution is a symmetrical one then $Md - Q = Q_1$ and $Md + Q = Q_3$, where Md represents the median score (that score below which and above which half of the items of the data lie).

While the quartile deviation is a better measure of dispersion than the range it has the weakness that, like the range, it is a positional measure. That is, its value depends upon the relative positions of scores within the set rather than upon their magnitudes.

Average Deviation or Mean Deviation

The average or mean deviation is the arithmetic mean of the absolute values of the deviations of the individual scores from some average. "Absolute value" means that the algebraic signs of the deviations are to be ignored. In other words, the arithmetic difference between each score and the median score, or between each score and the arithmetic mean is found. Then the arithmetic mean of these differences is calculated. By mathematical analysis it can be shown that the mean of these deviations is least when they are taken relative to the median. However, because the mean is so frequently the average stated as typical of the set, the mean deviation from the mean is the most commonly calculated.

The computation is illustrated for series B and C given above.

B:	X	IXI		C:	X	IXI
	35	15			35	15
	48	2			40	10
	49	1			45	5
	50	0			50	0
	51	1			55	5
	52	2			60	10
	65	15			65	15
		36				60

$$\text{M.D.} = \frac{\Sigma \text{IXI}}{N} = \frac{36}{7} = 5.14 \qquad \text{M.D.} = \frac{\Sigma \text{IXI}}{N} = \frac{60}{7} = 8.57$$

For each series the mean $(\overline{X})$ is 50. The absolute values of the deviations of the individual scores from the mean are designated by IXI. If those scores below 50 were assigned negative deviations and those above 50 positive deviations the sum of the deviations would be zero. The purpose of the computation, to secure the magnitude of the average deviations, would then be defeated. Consequently, in the calculation all the deviations are taken as positive.

The calculation of the mean deviation from the mean is not as simple as that illustrated here if the mean is a decimal quantity or if the data is classified into a frequency table. However, of the measures of dispersion which take into account the magnitude of every item in the set the mean deviation is about the simplest to compute. This measure of dispersion has the advantage that meaning is easily assigned the result of the calculation. Set B is less variable than set C because the mean of the deviations of the scores of set B from their mean is 5.14 while the corresponding mean deviation for set C is 8.57.

The reason this measure of dispersion is not more widely used is that it cannot be used as a link in further mathematical analysis of the set of data. This is because it is not truly algebraic in form, the algebraic signs of the deviations being ignored as stated above.

The Standard Deviation

The standard deviation is by far the most used measure of dispersion. The symbol used for it is almost universally σ. To calculate it from unclassified data the following steps are necessary:

1. The deviation of each score from the true arithmetic mean of the set must be found (x).
2. Each deviation must be squared, (x^2).
3. The squared deviations must be summed (Σx^2).

4. The sum of the squared deviations must be divided by the number of scores in the set, thus finding the mean squared deviation, $(\Sigma x^2/N)$.

5. The square root of the mean squared deviation must be taken

$$\sqrt{\frac{\Sigma x^2}{N}}$$

The formula is, therefore, $\sigma = \sqrt{\dfrac{\Sigma x^2}{N}}$. This measure is sometimes called the "root-mean-square-deviation" which, by comparison with the steps indicated above for its calculation, will be seen to be a very good descriptive name. The process for series B and C is illustrated below.

B:	X	x	x^2	C:	X	x	x^2
	35	−15	225		35	−15	225
	48	− 2	4		40	−10	100
	49	− 1	1		45	− 5	25
	50	0	0		50	0	0
	51	+ 1	1		55	+ 5	25
	52	+ 2	4		60	+10	100
	65	+15	225		65	+15	225
			460				700

$$B: \sigma = \sqrt{\frac{\Sigma x^2}{N}} = \sqrt{\frac{460}{7}} = \sqrt{65.72} = 8.1,$$

$$C: \sigma = \sqrt{\frac{\Sigma x^2}{N}} = \sqrt{\frac{700}{7}} = \sqrt{100} = 10.0$$

As indicated by the mean deviation, calculated in a previous section, the standard deviations for series B and C show series B to be more concentrated than series C.

Note that the magnitude of every individual score is involved in the calculation of σ as in the case in the calculation of the mean deviation. There is this important difference, however: in the calculation of σ the algebraic signs of the deviations are retained. The calculation of σ is, therefore, more truly algebraic than that of the mean deviation. Because of its mathematical nature the standard deviation becomes an important measure in conjunction with further mathematical analysis of sets of data. This will be appreciated at once if reference is made to any discussion of the normal curve of probability. All of the important characteristics of the normal distribution are known and tabled in terms of σ. From a table of areas under the normal curve we find, for example, that 99.73 percent of the area under the curve lies between ordinates located 3σ below and 3σ above the central or mean ordinate; that 95.45 percent of the area lies between ordinates 2σ below and 2σ above the mean ordinate; and that 68.27 percent of the area lies between ordinates one σ below and one σ above the mean ordinate. σ is not only used in the process of fitting normal curves to sets of data where such fitting is applicable, but is used in the fitting of asymmetrical curves as well.

Any particular measure of dispersion, such as mean deviation from the mean, will have different values when calculated from different samples of the same kind. This fluctuation, termed "sampling fluctuation" will be found treated in any discussion of Reliability. The important point to note here is that the standard deviation is, in general, more stable or less subject to sampling fluctuation than any other measure of dispersion. This fact is one of the strongest recommendations for its use wherever psychological or educational data are to be submitted to careful analysis.

The Coefficient of Variability

The range, interquartile range, mean deviation, and standard deviation are measures of absolute dispersion. When it is desired to compare different sets of data as to variability, it is often necessary to have a relative measure of dispersion. For this purpose the coefficient of variability is the most commonly used measure.

Direct comparison of σ's of series of data would be misleading in either of the following circumstances: (1) If the data of the sets being compared were expressed in the same units but had very different means. Thus, if it were desired to compare the variability of length of men's feet with variability of width of men's thumbs, both being measured in inches, no direct comparison of σ's could be made since the arithmetic means of the two series would be so very different. In the set for length of foot one would expect σ to be greater since the mean length of foot is certainly greater than the mean width of thumb. (2) If the data of the sets are expressed in entirely different units a direct comparison of the σ's would be meaningless. Thus if variability of human oral temperature is to be compared with variability of weight no direct comparison of σ's should be made since temperatures would be measured in degrees Fahrenheit while weights would be measured in pounds.

To meet this need for a comparative measure a coefficient of variability is calculated by dividing the standard deviations of each set by the arithmetic mean of the set. The quotient is generally multiplied by 100 so that the result can be expressed conveniently as a percent. The formula is $V = \dfrac{\sigma}{X} \, 100$ where σ is the standard deviation and $\overline{X}$ is the arithmetic mean. By using this coefficient it becomes possible to compare the variabilities of sets of distinctly different data, or of sets of the same kind (such as sets of scores) having different means.

R. E. W.

VETERANS. The war veteran returning to civilian life will face many readjustments to family, schools, associates, neighborhood and civilian life in general. All of these readjustments are of great importance in terms of the morale of the individual concerned. But the problem of vocational readjustment will take primacy in the thinking of most veterans. This concentration upon vocational problems stems from the fact that, upon entering military life, veterans were either in the process of completing their vocational training or had just begun their employment careers. A prolonged interruption at such a time in the life of a young person produces serious results, especially when interpolated experiences are in some cases not convertible into peacetime equivalent experiences. Because of these and of certain morale factors to be discussed later, vocational readjustment presents difficulties. Unless this readjustment is made smoothly and early upon return from war, later unemployment and vocational maladjustment may result when increased competition and a swollen labor market lead to the replacement of semi-trained and untrained veterans by those who have completed their vocational training. The effect of these and other related factors is to force the veteran to concern himself at once with getting a job—in many cases the first job offered or at least the one which pays the most money.

Thus it is that the counseling of veterans will take place within the framework of vocational orientation, reorientation and readjustment. Vocational counseling thus deserves a high priority with respect to the needs and demands of the individual war veteran. It should be noted too that vocational counseling provides a readily acceptable means of leading from one type of counseling to another. A veteran who consults a counselor with respect to getting a job may gradually find himself discussing certain personal and emotional problems, which, if not properly taken care of early in his readjustment period, will produce vocational maladjustment at a later period or may even block immediate adjustment.

It should be pointed out in this discussion of vocational counseling that, contrary to popular opinion and even to the expressed opinions and expectations of the war veterans themselves, making an immediate vocational decision and getting an immediate job are not always or necessarily equivalent in many cases to adequate or satisfying vocational adjustment. Many human beings seek for over-simplified solutions of their adjustment problems and war veterans are no exception. As was true of the youth surveyed in Maryland by the American Youth Commission,[1] *getting a job* appears to be a simple and completely adequate way of solving one's adjustment problems. "Give me a job and I will do the rest" appears to be the attitude of many war veterans and, indeed, the point of view of veterans' needs by many citizens who organize so-called vocational counseling services for war veterans. As will be seen later in this discussion, however, getting a job is oftentimes only the first in a long series of steps required for adequate vocational readjustment. *In many cases it should not be the first step but should be preceded by certain types of orientation and personality counseling* which are preparatory and prerequisite to adequate vocational adjustment and even to getting an immediate job.[2] Job placement is not necessarily the same process as employment counseling.

Outline of Steps Involved in Vocational Counseling
Reasons for Seeking Counseling

War veterans, and indeed all individuals should, and in most cases do, seek vocational counseling partly because of a desire for more information about occupational opportunities, training requirements and similar questions. Sometimes the counseling is sought because of confusion experienced by war veterans as they seek help from community agencies which compete for the opportunity to aid veterans to readjust themselves to civilian life. An equally important although less well-understood need for vocational counseling comes from our incomplete knowledge about our own abilities, aptitudes and interests. Relatively few individuals can be sufficiently objective with respect to their own qualifications for vocational placement to make a satisfactory diagnosis of their capabilities. And if the individual himself is objective or at least suspects his own true status, then perhaps his parents, his teachers or his fond uncles and aunts may cloud his own understanding of his capabilities.

Still a third reason for seeking vocational counseling lies in the fact that many war veterans will possess personal and emotional impediments to adequate adjustment and to reemployment or, in some cases as a result of military experience, will have become overly dependent upon others to make their decisions. These three reasons for counseling influence or determine the character of counseling as will be evident in the following discussion.

Two Major Steps in Counseling

Vocational counseling consists essentially of two major steps with many sub-steps: first, the use of certain analytical techniques to discover what capabilities an individual possesses; and, secondly, the cooperative use of certain procedures designed to enable an individual to develop fuller understanding of himself and the world within which he must find satisfactory and satisfying adjustments. When deeply laid emotional experiences and feelings are involved, specialized therapeutic procedures must be integrated with the above two basic steps in vocational counseling.

Analytical techniques consist of valid and dependable ways of finding out for which jobs success can be predicted for a veteran or for any other individual. These ways are really samplings of aptitudes and interests. They consist of paper and pencil tests, performance and oral tests, interview observations and an analysis and evaluation of experience and training. Interpretation of test scores and experiences should be in terms of definite predictions of vocational adjustments for particular individuals. The vocational counselor can aid the individual by avoiding overestimates and underestimates of probabilities of successful and satisfying adjustments.

The giving of occupational information to an individual so that he may see more clearly and evaluate more clearly his own capabilities in the light of the demands of different types of work is a very important procedure. In the case of veterans who show symptoms of rejecting their civilian's responsibility for their own decisions, care must be exercised to avoid fostering this dependency attitude through freeing them from all responsibility for obtaining information about jobs. Other veterans must be aided to obtain and use adequate information by helping them to adjust to an over-reaction against civilian independence. Such an over-reaction might cause them to underestimate the value of information. Such individuals in many cases make the mistake of being satisfied with the first job offered, the old job or any new job. The use of these simple therapeutic procedures, when integrated with vocational counseling, makes it possible for the individual to give free expression to his feelings and to organize his vocational plans in terms of his attitudes and feelings as well as his ability and aptitude. Sometimes it is necessary for the skillful counselor to help the individual to achieve this free expression even when he may not at first see its importance and may desire to have the counselor tell him in a straight-forward manner what job he should and can get.[3]

Occupational Rehabilitation

Certain special factors must be given consideration in the vocational counseling of veterans. Among these special factors is the obvious one of physical disabilities. The number of physically disabled individuals seeking and needing vocational rehabilitation through retraining, reorientation and counseling will probably run into hundreds of thousands. Fortunately, governmental aid is available to these disabled veterans through the Public Law No. 16, Training and Service Act of 1940, and through the various laws establishing the Federal Office of Vocational Rehabilitation. The necessary legislative and financial facilities, therefore, appear to be provided for the reorientation, counseling and readjustment of disabled veterans.

In counseling rehabilitation cases, the vocational counselor needs to know about the various factors involved in this work, such as an understanding of the nature and variety of physical disabilities. He needs more to know about the techniques of counseling these physically handicapped veterans. The counseling of these individuals does not differ greatly in general type of procedure and in the essentials from the counseling of able-bodied persons. But the counselor must give special consideration to emotional disturbances and mental states brought about by habitual brooding and depression associated with the thought of being handicapped and by the inability to see any hope for readjustment and for overcoming the handicap. The counselor must also be able to see the relationship of the disability to the training and vocational objective and must appraise the physical handicaps of the individual in terms of his desired vocational objective. In this respect, the counselor should help the individual to center his attention on his abilities rather than on his disabilities by helping him face openly his disability and his feelings about it.

In counseling physically handicapped veterans, as is true of other individuals, an analysis of capabilities must be made through a comprehensive analysis of capacities, interests, personality and other factors, using psychological tests and the other analytic techniques mentioned above. Furthermore the counselor will find it necessary to become oriented and informed with respect to the varieties of jobs open to individuals with certain physical disabilities. This information will be useful in cases where individuals with handicaps aspire to vocational goals beyond the limits of their physical capacities. In such cases, the counselor must be well-informed about occupational outlets in order to aid the disabled veteran to find a satisfactory *equivalent* vocational goal which is within his physical range of possibilities.[4]

In counseling disabled veterans, the counselor must also be fully informed about the various agencies and special organizations available for counseling such persons and should make use of them by referring the individual veteran. These agencies include the United States Veterans Administration, United States Employment Service, the Federal Security Agency, the Office of Occupational Rehabilitation of the Federal Security Agency and various state and local welfare agencies.

Psychiatric Complications

In giving vocational counseling to veterans, the counselor should be prepared for a higher incidence of psychiatric complications than is usually found with civilian clients. This arises from the extraordinary stress and strain experienced by the veteran himself during military service and also because of the extra strain which is sometimes experienced in making the transition from military to civilian life. These factors call for very close integration of the work done by the psychiatrist, and other psycho-therapeutists, and the vocational counselor. The counselor should be alert at least to the gross psychiatric symptoms and should become sufficiently oriented in the fields of psychiatry and abnormal psychology to understand the common manifestations or symptoms of maladjustments. Moreover, the vocational counselor will need to adapt his procedures to individuals in emotionally disorganized states both with respect to the testing of aptitudes and the use of occupational information in the process of helping the individual choose ana occupational goal.

Older Clients

War veterans are older than the usual type of client given vocational counseling. This older age status introduces complications in the counseling process, such as anxiety induced by and associated with delayed economic independence and postponement of marriage and the establishment of a home. To many veterans, taking further time out to complete occupational training seems like adding too many years to the delay already induced by the war. Many veterans will prefer to get their training on the job, and many counselors will be ready to encourage such a *practical* move because of the great success of the war program of Training Within Industry. The counselor should take care to make clear, however, that the greatly accelerated and overly simplified training programs made necessary by the urgency of the war may not be fully satisfactory for the preparation of war veterans for life careers which demand flexibility and great personal resources rather than the ability to do a simple operation at a particular time in an emergency period. Moreover many such emergency training programs, set up to train workers in a great hurry, were abandoned at the close of the war.

The older age status of the war veteran who decides to go back to school to complete his training may produce additional complications in counseling because of the age difference between the veteran and the younger person who goes through the school in the regular sequence. Fitting the school situation to the mature veteran may cause some difficulties because of the social psychology involved. In many cases, the counselor may need to help the veteran find refresher courses, accelerated courses and special curricula which complete his training in less than the normal period of time, without serious sacrifice in quality of learning of vocational and general education values.

Reconversion Through Counseling

Two special factors must be considered to gain a deeper understanding of the veteran's problem in converting himself from military to civilian life. The first is directly related to the question of choice of occupation. The individual veteran needs the counselor's assistance in determining the significance of previous civilian training and experience in relation to service training and experience. The evaluation of both types of experiences will be influenced by the individual's present goals as related to his pre-war goal. To give this counseling aid, the vocational counselor needs to use the special aids prepared for determining equivalents of military and civilian occupational experiences.[5] These tables of equivalents permit the counselor to make the individual aware of the salvageable aspects of his military training and experience and the type of jobs to which he may transfer his skills acquired in military life.

Young war veterans whose only occupational experience prior to service was in an unspecialized job may experience considerable feelings of conflict between their present aspirations and their prospects. In civilian life, the adolescent ordinarily expects to wait a long time and to go through a prolonged period of being dominated vocationally by older, more established men. Now, many veterans may find it difficult to accept this rôle after having attained positions of considerable responsibility in the service. This problem is sometimes illustrated by the hypothetical colonel in the Air Force who at age twenty-one returns from war to his messenger's job in Wall Street.

These feelings, growing out of military service, are the second factor necessary to an understanding of the veteran's reconversion problem. There will be those feelings directly related to the way he looks at himself in the occupational world. But there will also be more generalized morale and temperamental factors which will influence not only his general adjustment to civilian life but also the manner in which he makes use of, or does not make use of. the reconversion possibilities in his military experiences.

As has been pointed out elsewhere,[6] veterans as a group will tend to have certain feelings related to their change of personal rôles. Most will have feelings of loss in being deprived of a comradeship rarely duplicated in civilian life. Some will feel guilty for being released from war responsibilities before the job is done. Others will experience the inevitable feeling of relief which comes from removal from danger. Many will find that the long period of planned and supervised activity has left conflicting habits—for civilian life—of needing continuous activity but of relying on someone else to plan it.

Job Placement and Reconversion

Unfortunately those in charge of some community agencies have an overly-simplified understanding of this reconversion and readjustment process. They appear to feel that if the individual finds a civilian job which utilizes what he has gained in the way of experience and skills in the army, then he is prepared to be vocationally adjusted. In many cases individuals, because of the feelings that have been discussed above, would rather do anything than what they did in the army or would prefer almost any job other than the one they had prior to service. It is at this point that the counselor needs all the training possible with respect to the understanding of subtle and disguised human motives and effective ways of aiding individuals to use them constructively. Many veterans, if not properly counseled at this point, will be so thoroughly disgusted that they will take the first job open to them. These may well be the individuals who are the first to be discharged when the labor market changes from a manpower shortage to a job shortage.

Still another special factor involved in the counseling of war veterans is found in the framework of governmental regulations within which the veteran must find his occupational objective and select and secure any necessary retraining. Particularly the procedures in use by the United States Veterans Administration must be understood and used by the counselor and the veteran. Legal restrictions, involuntary counseling, the pressure of a short time to make a decision and the impediment of filling out governmental forms—all may present such psychological obstacles as to compel some veterans to discontinue counseling and go to the nearest employment office for immediate placement regardless of the long-term deficiencies of a job for them as individuals. Effective counseling can still be done despite all of these obstacles and difficulties surrounding the veterans. But the counselor of veterans must develop a resourcefulness and ingenuity not always found among those who counsel civilians in normal circumstances.

Special Features of Programs and Organizations for Vocational Counseling of Veterans

It is essential that vocational counseling be organized in an integrated manner with other services available to veterans. The United States Veterans Administration, itself, has established its counseling services for disabled veterans and others in an integrated and coordinated well-rounded program. Reference is made to the relations of vocational counseling to medical treatment, to employment placement and to the training programs within industry and in educational institutions. Unfortunately, veterans not eligible for vocational rehabilitation service may not be handled in as integrated and well-rounded a manner, since, under Public Law No. 346, initial vocational counseling by the United States Veterans Administration is not obligatory upon the individual veteran. Such veterans may resort to self-counseling, to advice from friends and relatives or from untrained advisers in community social agencies and veteran organizations as well as in training institutions. Insofar as this type of sub-standard counseling results in the selection of inappropriate goals and training courses, it will have made a contribution to the subsequent maladjustment of the veteran. The vocational counseling needed by the veteran, if he is to have the greatest probabilities of satisfactory and successful long-term vocational adjustment, must be of the highest possible caliber. Hasty and ill-advised programs improvised for the moment to get the veteran back to work and off the unemployment compensation rolls or relief rolls are never justified in terms of human or any other type of values. Planning for the individual's long-term objectives in terms of his basic aptitudes, capabilities, attitudes and feelings is of major importance not only to the individual but also to society as a whole. But the decision as to what type and quality of vocational counseling shall be provided in every community goes beyond the realm of vocational counseling and is the responsibility of society. Counselors, as citizens, believe that society should provide adequate services for the reinduction of its members so as to bring the best possible adjustment to the individual and the greatest possible gain to the group of which he is a member.

References:

1. Bell, Howard M. *Youth Tell Their Story.* Washington, D. C., American Council on Education, 1938.
2. *Employment Counseling in the Public Employment Service* in United States Employment Service Manual; Part II, Performance of Employment Service Functions. War Manpower Commission, Bureau of Placement. Washington, D. C., Sept. 1944.
3. For fuller discussions of counseling procedures, see: Williamson, E. G., *How to Counsel Students.* New York, McGraw-Hill Book Company, Inc., 1939. Rogers, Carl R., *Counseling and Psychotherapy.* New York, Houghton Mifflin Company, 1942.
4. See the following: Davis, John Eisele, *Principles and Practice of Rehabilitation.* New York, A. S. Barnes and Company, Inc., 1943. Doherty, William Brown, M.D., and Runes, Dagobert D., Ph.D., *Rehabilitation of War Injured,* New York, Philosophical Library, 1943. Pintner, Rudolf and Eisenson, Jon and Stanton, Mildred, *The Psychology of the Physically Handicapped,* New York, F. S. Crofts & Co., 1941.
5. *Special Aids for Placing Military Personnel in Civilian Jobs,* Washington, D. C., War Manpower Commission, 1944. *Special Aids for Placing Navy Personnel in Civilian Jobs,* Washington, D. C., War Manpower Commission, 1943.
6. Waller, Willard, *The Veteran Comes Back,* New York, The Dryden Press, 1944.

E. G. W., E. S. B. & L. H. H.

VETERANS ADMINISTRATION. The Veterans Administration is the agency of the United States Government responsible for providing advisement and guidance services for disabled veterans who are eligible to vocational rehabilitation under Public Law 16, 78th Congress, as amended by Public Law 268, 79th Congress, and for all veterans who are entitled to and request educational and vocational guidance under Title II of the Servicemen's Readjustment Act of 1944, Public Law 346, 78th Congress, as amended by Public Laws 268 and 190, 79th Congress.

Under Public Law 16, counseling is provided to help the veteran who is in need of vocational rehabilitation to overcome a vocational handicap resulting from a disability incurred in the active military or naval service, to select an employment objective and such course of training to prepare for it as will restore the employability lost by reason of the handicap through qualifying the veteran for employment in an occupation suitable to his residual abilities and vocational interests and compatible with his disability. Under Public Law 346 any veteran eligible for education or training is entitled to be supplied vocational and educational guidance services by the Veterans Administration with reference to making plans for pursuing either vocational training courses or educational courses under the provisions of the Act.

Counseling Services Are Comprehensive

Vocational and educational guidance are not the only counseling services provided veterans under the plan of the Veterans Administration. The counseling program has been developed with most careful regard to placing emphasis upon abilities rather than disabilities, but with full recognition of the fact that veterans will have greater assurance of achieving their educational or occupational goals when mental conflicts, emotional maladjustments, and other types of personal problems, are alleviated through proper counseling being given prior to or parallel with training. For many veterans, guidance in the selection of an occupation or of an educational objective is all that is required. Other veterans need assistance in handling personal problems, in resolving mental conflicts, in attaining emotional stability or in learning how to secure and hold employment. The Veterans Administration furnishes all the kinds of counseling service which are needed by an individual veteran. He is guided in making intelligent use of other clinical and professional services, available to him through the Veterans Administration and other agencies, for the purpose of assisting him in making and maintaining the mental, emotional, and social adjustment essential to the attainment of his objectives. Each veteran is counseled as a person, regarded as a complete entity with reference to his needs, and educational and vocational guidance are not given without full consideration of all problems which may affect the life of the individual.

When the V. A. counseling program for World War II veterans was initiated in 1943, the counseling services were provided in fifty-three regional offices. As the number of veterans increased this service has been decentralized to about 300 Veterans Administration guidance centers established in educational institutions and is now being extended to the sub-regional offices located in areas in which it has not been found practical to establish guidance centers in educational institutions. Steps are being taken to establish Veterans Administration counseling units in Army and Navy hospitals so as to supply counseling services to disabled persons before they are discharged from such hospitals.

Vocational advisement and educational counseling by Veterans Administration Advisers for blinded servicemen of World War II who were patients in Army hospitals was established at Valley Forge General Hospital, Phoenixville, Pennsylvania, in May, 1943, and was extended in August 1943 to Old Farms Convalescent Hospital, Avon, Connecticut which was the Army's center for the protracted convalescence and orientation training of blinded servicemen. Similar services were established for Navy cases at the Philadelphia Naval Hospital, Philadelphia, Pennsylvania in September 1943. The purposes to be achieved by these services were to (a) inform the patients of their rights to the benefits under the federal laws; (b) assist them in effecting social adjustment to the disability; (c) to help them determine their vocational plans; (d) prepare for their proper reception at home following their discharge from the hospital; (e) make preliminary arrangements for getting them started in their training or employment programs; and (f) render any or all such additional services as would contribute to their vocational rehabilitation.

Early in 1945 the Veterans Administration took action to expand its program for providing vocational advisement to patients in Veterans Administration hospitals. Under the plan previously in effect the regional offices rendered advisement services at an increasing rate to patients in hospitals, while those, who for special reasons were not so counseled were referred for advisement to the regional offices after discharge from the hospital. On December 17, 1945, the establishment of Vocational Rehabilitation and Education Sections was authorized for all Veterans Administration hospitals having a case load of 25 or more patients desirous of and medically ready to receive counseling services. The regional offices were instructed to render such services to all hospitals having a monthly case load of less than 25 patients desirous of and ready to receive advisement. In either case full coordination is established between the hospital and the regional offices of the areas to which the patients return after discharge from the hospital.

Employment objectives for the severely disabled hospital cases, as in all other instances, are selected with due consideration of: the individual's capacities, aptitudes, and interests; his present and potential work tolerance; his record of employment and related experiences; the nature of his home and community background;

general vocational fields appropriate for the veteran, and specific local opportunities that exist or may be developed; the demands of the job, the possibilities of adapting the job to the individual, and the environmental and work conditions of the job; the type of disability; the diagnosis and prognosis of the individual's condition; his acceptance of and adjustment to his handicap; the differences that exist among persons having the same general disability.

In cases where persons discharged from hospitals must continue their convalescence at home or wait for a considerable period of time before they can assume the duties of job or school training, special personal and social adjustment programs may be arranged on an out-patient basis to suit individual needs and to combine therapy with vocational rehabilitation. If the patient who is confined at home is interested in a job objective requiring courses of study, such courses are provided by correspondence supplemented by tutorial or reader services and by such mechanical and electronic equipment as may assist in overcoming the veteran's handicap.

In general, it may be stated that every possible vocational rehabilitation service is offered the patient as soon as he is able to respond to advisement. Furthermore every effort is made to coordinate all steps so that the rehabilitation process may be continuous from hospital to home and into training or employment.

Group Guidance

There is also being developed a group guidance program to be conducted in connection with the advisement and guidance of veterans in Veterans Administration hospitals and in communities at large. The group guidance methods will supplement the regular individual counseling procedures and will in no way be used to supplant them. Through the medium of appropriate types of group sessions, such as forums, panels and discussion groups, conducted by trained Vocational Advisers, often with the assistance of selected community agencies, there will be accomplished for groups of veterans such of the basic steps in the advisement and guidance process as are common to all individual advisement and can be effectively achieved through group methods. These steps include informing the veteran of the nature and function of vocational advisement, supplying him with occupational information, and giving him insight into the need for analysis of his abilities and traits through the use of psychological tests, etc. As a means of stimulating veterans to seek individual advisement and of disseminating necessary information and developing appropriate attitudes, the group guidance program will constitute an important adjunct to the individual counseling provided by the Veterans Administration.

Counseling for Personal Adjustment

Another of the special types of service is counseling for personal adjustment. The purpose of personal adjustment counseling under the Vocational Rehabilitation and Education program is to provide assistance in meeting the personal and emotional problems of veterans which are of such a nature that vocational readjustment cannot be successfully effected without such assistance but which are not sufficiently serious to require the services of a psychiatrist. Such problems often become manifest to the Vocational Adviser during the initial vocational counseling relative to the selection of the employment objective. Sometimes the problems become evident after the veteran has entered upon his course of vocational training. The Personal Counselor who is responsible for carrying on personal adjustment counseling is a technically trained person who has an understanding of the dynamic mechanisms that function in producing the various symptoms found in the maladjusted personality. He applies this technical knowledge in such a manner as to assist the veteran in gaining such insight as may serve to relieve the conflicts which block adjustment and therefore are a great cause of hindrance to the veteran in achieving total rehabilitation. The personal counselor's work is differentiated from the services performed by a Doctor of Medicine or Psychiatrist to whom cases having serious mental or emotional disturbances, and particularly cases having an organic involvement, are referred for appropriate treatment.

Counseling Integrated for Occupational Planning

It is, of course, necessary to integrate and coordinate the various types of counseling service, including personal counseling, with the vocational and educational guidance services so that all the counseling services rendered in any case will be directed toward accomplishing the purposes authorized by law. On this basis, the primary object of the guidance services furnished a veteran must be to assist him in selecting the employment objective or educational goal and training courses designed to effect his readjustment to civilian life, having special regard to the importance of occupational adjustment as a factor in this process. Counseling for the attainment of this purpose must necessarily stress vocational advisement. Accordingly, the Veterans Administration's "Manual of Advisement and Guidance" was prepared with a view to providing a procedure which would place emphasis upon the application of the basic principles of vocational counseling but at the same time insure that they would be supplemented by and coordinated with other types of counseling according to the needs in the individual case. The Manual therefore sets forth first the major procedural steps believed essential to the accomplishment of vocational advisement in all cases regardless of whether they may require the application of the more specialized techniques such as those of personal adjustment counseling. These major steps are summarized below:

(a) The first step is preliminary to those comprising the actual counseling process but is so related to them with respect to the necessity of its being taken before the counseling of an individual is initiated that it must be given precedence in this presentation. It is to assemble and organize occupational information covering the nature of the work done, the training requirements, the working conditions, the employment requirements and outlets with respect to the occupations comprising the fields affording employment for the disabled and the non-disabled. This step also includes systematizing information as to what educational and training facilities may be utilized to prepare persons for meeting the employment or educational requirements essential to attain their occupational or educational objectives.

(b) The next step is to ascertain through recognized counseling techniques the veteran's interests, aptitudes, attainments, and personality traits, which have the greatest significance in determining the occupational fields and the educational pursuits in which he may have the greatest possibility of success, considering also the limitations imposed by physical or mental disability. The counseling techniques include interviewing, the review of records of school training, and of military or naval service, the survey of work history, and the use of objective tests. The tests used include interest tests, personality inventories, mental ability tests, achievement tests, special aptitude tests and trade tests. These tests provide a means for the counselee to demonstrate objectively the possession of abilities, aptitudes, and interests previously unrevealed especially in the fields unexplored because of the person's restricted opportunities for activities within such fields.

(c) Having the information regarding the occupational requirements and training facilities, and the information respecting
the veteran's potentialities and attainments, the next step is
to make a direct application of one to the other. This includes comparing the veteran's occupational capacities with
the occupational demands of employment objectives, the
veteran's educational potentialities with the educational
achievement required for the attainment of educational
objectives, and the determination as to the adequacy and
suitability of suggested employment objectives in the light
of the veteran's aptitudes, interests and abilities. During a
conference with the Adviser when all these matters are considered the veteran is usually able to make a tentative selection of an occupational goal and of the education or training courses necessary to reach it.

These major steps involve many actions by the advisement and
guidance personnel such as those relating to assembling and digest-
ing information, interviewing, administering and interpreting tests
of aptitude, interest and ability, referring counselees for special
services, etc. In order to integrate the counseling process it was
necessary to establish some definite procedure for coordinating these
activities with one another and with other related activities such as
training and medical. There are set forth in the Manual, therefore, certain procedures which specify standardized forms to be
used in systematically recording the data regarding the various
factors to be considered during the counseling process, the results
of the evaluation of such data and the conclusions based thereon.
When properly executed these forms comprise the complete "Vocational Advisement Record." Each form has been devised to serve
a specific purpose which makes it possible to divide the counseling
work among personnel so that specialized skills of Advisers or Appraisers may be utilized to best advantage.

These procedures would, if applied routinely, tend to control
to an undesirable extent the order in which the counseling functions are performed and to limit the number of factors which may
be covered by the advisement record. No such control is intended
nor is there any intention to limit the number of interviews or the
time required to complete the counseling in any case. The Adviser,
is free to consider any pertinent factors respecting which he obtains
information during the interview or from any reliable source and
he may attach as many additional sheets to any record form as he
may desire. The Manual, and the forms are necessary guiding and

procedural devices which are intended to preserve uniformity in recording the results of the counseling. It is important that the records be as uniform as possible and that the data be recorded on the forms under captions having the definite meanings assigned to them in the Manual, because the records may be transferred many times and used by many different employees before the veteran's training is completed. With the exception of stating some specific principles to be applied in vocational advisement the Manual does not prescribe any special techniques to be used in the different kinds of counseling.

Counseling the Individual Veteran

When a veteran applies for vocational rehabilitation under Public Law 16 or for educational and vocational guidance under Public Law 346 an appointment letter is mailed to him and a "Rehabilitation and Education File" is prepared for his case. In this file are placed pertinent papers from his service records, abstracts of medical and social data that may be necessary for counseling and if the veteran is disabled there is included a copy of his Veterans Administration Disability Rating Sheet. Transcripts of school records and statements from former employers are secured if necessary for counseling purposes.

Before the veteran reports for counseling the Adviser assigned to the case reviews all the material that is in the counselee's "Rehabilitation and Education File." When the veteran reports he is introduced to his Adviser who explains to him his rights and benefits and what to expect from the advisement procedure. During the initial interview with the veteran the Adviser secures factual data which he records on one of the forms which have been designed to constitute the "Vocational Advisement Record." The data include among other items the veteran's family status, employment status (preference for employment and training), work history and vocational outlook. With this material as a guide to help decide what tests the veteran should take, the Adviser confers with the psychometrist and arranges for testing. The psychometrist administers and scores the tests, records the test results and prepares a "Test Record and Profile Chart." These results together with any special comments which may be helpful in interpreting the test data are transmitted to the Adviser and if necessary the psychometrist again confers with the Adviser.

The Adviser now has the information necessary to provide a basis upon which to proceed in taking the steps which relate more closely to assisting the veteran in selecting an employment objective and the course or courses of training to prepare therefor. The Adviser studies the information assembled in the Vocational Advisement Record and evaluates that relating to each of the factors to determine their significance with reference to the selection of the educational or occupational objective. He discusses the various factors with the veteran, making any explanations which are necessary to give the counselee insight into their significance and in so doing gives special attention to supplying any occupational information which will help the veteran to make his own determinations as to the choice of his occupational or educational objectives and training courses. During this interview the Adviser is expected to refrain from making directive statements but to do everything possible to improve the veteran's own understanding of the problems confronting him so that he may be induced to make his own decisions.

When a tentative selection has been made the physical demands and the environmental factors of the chosen objective are studied carefully in order to ascertain whether any activity may overtax the veteran's capacity and whether there may be any condition under which he should not work. The personal characteristics which are necessary for success in the chosen employment objective are also considered. These checks are made by the use of special devices provided in the forms. A conference is then conducted to consider the adequacy and suitability of the chosen employment objective. Included in the conference are the veteran, the Vocational Adviser, a Training Officer and when necessary a Medical Consultant. If the selected employment objective is found not suitable the Adviser proceeds to assist the veteran until a suitable one is chosen. When the employment objective is agreed upon the Adviser prepares a "Summary of Vocational Advisement Record" and includes therein any special recommendations to the Training Officer who is to continue to assist the veteran throughout his period of training.

This counseling procedure complies with the intent of the legislation by focusing attention upon encouraging the veteran to consider fully and carefully the factors which relate to accomplishing his occupational adjustment. This emphasis is desirable since nearly all veterans who will be counseled under the provisions of either enactment will be adults or will be regarded as adults, and should give paramount consideration to their occupational adjustment because this is, for the great majority of adults, the most important aspect of any satisfactory adjustment as useful members of society.

Where Counseling Is Available

In order to make the advisement and guidance services available to veterans at points near their homes the Veterans Administration has employed a staff of competent, professionally trained and otherwise well qualified persons to administer its counseling service. A very large number of qualified counseling personnel (more than 1,400 at the present writing) is made available in the Branch Offices, regional offices and sub-regional offices to serve veterans throughout the nation. The counseling services have also been further distributed by the establishment of several hundred guidance centers in educational institutions spread over the country. This arrangement makes it possible for a large number of well-qualified people in colleges and universities who would not wish to sever their relationship with their educational institutions but who are able to contribute highly valuable service in the counseling of veterans, to participate in the Veterans Administration counseling program.

The fact that a veteran is requested to report for counseling at a Veterans Administration guidance center located at any particular institution places no obligation upon him to take educational or training courses at that institution. For example it would be possible for a veteran to be counseled at a guidance center in New York and to take his training in an approved educational institution or industrial establishment in California if that seems to be the best way to secure the education or training which he needs and desires. In most cases veterans select training institutions or establishments near their homes, but the location of the Veterans Administration guidance center at which a veteran receives counseling should in no way limit or influence his selection of an educational or training course or a place of training. The guidance center plan which locates a great part of the practical work of counseling in educational institutions which provide counselor training is in many respects ideal. Such colleges and universities not only are able to train counselors through their usual classroom instruction, but they are also in a position to combine with this instruction observation of the actual counseling procedure. As the new counselors develop, they are given closely supervised practice in counseling techniques. Thus the established guidance centers not only provide veterans with the services of well-qualified and experienced counselors, but they also serve to increase the number of trained counselor personnel.

Since facilities vary in educational institutions, three kinds of guidance centers have been approved. Under one plan the educational institution provides complete counseling services and space and other facilities for the Veterans Administration personnel assigned to the center. Under another plan the institution provides testing services but other functions relating to counseling are accomplished by Veterans Administration personnel; and under a third plan space and certain facilities are provided but all counseling activities, including testing, are accomplished by Veterans Administration personnel. Under this arrangement many colleges that would otherwise be eliminated, may cooperate in providing services relating to counseling.

At each guidance center the Veterans Administration has at least one Vocational Adviser and one Training Officer. The members of the faculty of the educational institution who are assigned to counsel veterans at guidance centers are called "Vocational Appraisers" in order to distinguish them in the records, from the Veterans Administration Vocational Advisers. The Veterans Administration Vocational Advisers are selected from lists of professional counseling personnel certified by the United States Civil Service Commission, and the counselors who are employed by the educational institutions to render service to veterans in Veterans Administration guidance centers have similar professional qualifications.

In deciding to decentralize the counseling service to veterans by utilizing qualified personnel in colleges and universities the Veterans Administration has adhered to the point of view that the counseling of veterans should be of the highest professional level and should utilize the most competent, well trained, and highly qualified persons available. It was felt that colleges and universities were the best source of potential advisers since among their faculty members could be found many persons with graduate training in the fundamental fields of psychology, industrial personnel administration, public personnel administration, labor problems, labor market analysis, tests and measurements, social work and community organization, education, rehabilitation of the handicapped, vocational psychology, mental hygiene and psychiatry. In addition, a number of the persons so trained have had practical experience in counseling students and adults in the community. Experience thus far has shown that the plan to establish guidance centers was a wise one, and it is hoped that this policy will continue to pay dividends in the high quality of service rendered veterans. The emergency has required a lowering of standards in many areas, but the Veterans Administration is hopeful of maintaining high standards of professional qualifications for the people who are performing the complex function of dealing with the human relationships of the veterans whose lives and plans have been so sorely upset by our wartime society. Even the most highly qualified professional counselors are finding the job a challenge for their technical skills, personal abilities, and most ingenious efforts.

References:

1. Scott, I. D. *Manual of advisement and guidance of the Veterans Administration.* Washington: U. S. Government Printing Office, 1945.
2. ————. (Included in the address of Hon. Harry R. Sheppard) *Veterans Administration Program for the Counseling of Veterans.* U. S. Congressional Record, May 9, 1945, Proceeding and Debates of the 79th Congress, First Session.
3. Ward, C. E., and Schneidler, G. *The counseling program of the Veterans Administration.* Educational and Psychological Measurements. Vol. 5, No. 2, 1945.

I. D. S.

VETERINARY MEDICINE, APTITUDE FOR. The veterinarian safeguards the livestock industry by insuring better health of farm animals. In so doing, human health and wealth are strongly influenced. There are many variations of this work.

About 60 per cent of all veterinarians engage in private practice, where the primary effort is the detection and treatment of the diseases and injuries of domestic animals, such as cows, horses, pigs, sheep, and poultry; vaccination of animals to prevent the spread of diseases; and the prevention of cruelty to animals. In a general practice, these men will encounter all of the animals mentioned; and possibly also dogs and cats, such fur-bearing animals as foxes, mink, muskrats, and rabbits, and at times wild game and fish. In rural areas, all farm animals will be patients, but a specialized practice may be developed for any one species. In the larger cities, the household pets and breeding kennels will provide the greatest source of income, while individual effort may bring any group to a position of primary importance.

The United States Department of Agriculture, employs more veterinarians than any other agency. In this field, the chief problems are disease eradication and meat inspection. In disease eradication, cattle are tested for tuberculosis and brucellosis, inspected and dipped for ticks; sheep are examined and dipped for mange or scabies; and there are programs against other diseases. In meat inspection, emphasis is placed upon the public health problems associated with food products of animal origin; chiefly the inspection of meat-producing animals before, at the time of, and after slaughter. Other opportunities in the Department include stockyards and packing house supervision, enforcement of import and export regulations, and laboratory or research work in animal diseases, animal husbandry, biochemistry, virus and serum control, and parasitology.

In addition to these two main classes, a few veterinarians specialize in state and municipal health work, extension work for universities and colleges, research work for public and private institutions, commercial preparation of serums and vaccines, the Army Veterinary Corps, conservation of fur-bearing animals either in the wild state or under domestication, the health of zoo or circus animals, the propagation and care of laboratory experimental animals, and even the diseases of fish.

The work performed will vary with each field, but in all cases it will demand a knowledge of the structure and normal actions of the body organs, of the nature of changes produced by diseases, and of methods of correcting faults or abnormalities either by surgery or the use of drugs and/or biological products.

Qualifications

In order to carry on these types of work one must possess some special qualifications. Good health and stamina are essential. An understanding of animals through close association is desirable, because animals can sense fear in an attendant; and because fear overcomes gentleness, which is important in caring for the sick. The prospective student of veterinary medicine must also possess good powers of observation, and must be able to interpret what he sees, hears, and feels. As the animal cannot answer questions, diagnosis must be based on objective phenomena.

Health and vigor are important because the veterinarian puts in long hours of hard, physical work in all kinds of weather, and works under a wide range of disagreeable or uninviting conditions, oftentimes hampered by insufficient assistance, limited facilities, and monotonous routine. Good understanding of animals helps to avoid personal injuries, and proper interpretation of careful observations prevents unpleasant experiences and unfavorable results.

Because of the physical demands upon the body, veterinary medicine has been almost exclusively a man's profession. The exceptions are so uncommon that they assume headline importance.

With all of these qualifications there must go the ability to study and master the difficult subjects of the college curriculum.

Course of Study

The study of veterinary medicine requires more than average ability, because the five-year course begins during the pre-veterinary year with the study of such subjects as zoölogy, chemistry (general and physiological), physics, English, history and a foreign language. The next two years comprise (1) anatomy (macroscopic and microscopic) of normal tissues of all species of animals and all ages from embryo to adult; (2) physiology, including all stages of digestion and metabolism of foods, actions of the organs of the body, and movements of the muscles and joints; (3) pathology, a study of abnormal body tissues; (4) bacteriology, a study of the disease-producing agents which cause tissues to be abnormal; and (5) materia medica, a study of drugs and their actions, including the botany of medicinal plants and their extracts.

The last two years comprise largely clinical work on the ailing animal, observing deviations from normal, recognizing the cause, and learning to administer the appropriate medicinal or surgical treatment, and correcting errors of feeding and housing. Obstetrics, the study of the reproductive process, dentistry, toxicology, meat inspection, postmortem technique and parasitology are included.

R. C. K.

VISION, MEASUREMENT OF. Optometry the art of measuring and correcting visual anomalies is based upon the sciences of physics, physiology and psychology.

The physical aspect of optometry concerns itself with the control of light both from the standpoint of adequate illumination and of the application of suitable lenses to produce upon the retina of the wearer the very best optical image of external objects that he is capable of forming.

The physiology of vision has to do with; the functioning of the visual apparatus in the conversion of light impulses into nerve currents, the action of the auxiliary focussing mechanism which adjusts the eyes for clear vision at various distances and the activities of the ocular muscles which so direct the two eyes that similar images may fall upon corresponding areas of the two retinae; thus fulfilling the requisites for single, simultaneous, binocular vision which is a result of the mental blending (fusion) of the two images into a single impression which in any pair of normal eyes is richer and more satisfying for reasons somewhat akin to those by which the golfer is better able to direct his club and ball with the double grip which use of both hands affords.

Visual perception may be considered from three standpoints involving:

(1) *The light sense* which in primitive organisms consists in the bare ability of recognizing the presence of light or shadow. In the human eye there are two separate mechanisms, the rods (130 million in a normal eye) which occupy the paracentral and peripheral retinal areas and which are acutely sensitive to movement and function at very low illumination levels. Their principal service to the human animal is to keep him in touch with his surroundings, to apprise him of the presence of things in his surroundings which may be of interest to him or offer a threat to his well being or safety.

(2) *The form sense* resides in the retinal cones (seven million of these) which in the center of the retina are closely packed much like the cells in a honeycomb. The ultimate in form vision is the ability to discriminate two adjacent point images as two discrete sensations. It is the form sense with which the optometrist mainly is concerned since as its name implies it is the interpretation of the shape and relative size of the parts of an image that enables the individual to recognize the object looked at.

Obviously the first requisite for clear seeing is a good retinal image and the first concern of the optometrist is to correct optical defects and produce the best possible retinal image.

(3) The third aspect of vision is *color perception* which involves the judgment of wave lengths of light which range from 375 to 750 millionths of a millimeter or vibrations ranging from 400 to 800 million per second. While some training may improve the perception of color as also of form there is no known cure for real color blindness, although training may be of benefit to some who are merely color weak.

The necessity of measuring light perception is rarely of much concern to the optometrist, although it does afford a clue to Vitamin "A" deficiency. Measurement is done with a biophotometer, adaptometer or glarometer. The patient is pre-exposed for a few minutes to a uniformly illuminated field. The illumination is turned off and a very subdued illumination capable of gradual and consistent increment is introduced until the patient can determine the outline or direction of a rectangular aperture, when a record of sensitivity is made, based upon the minimum amount of light which produces a visual response.

Form vision involves a record of patient's naked vision and measurement of errors of refraction, although preceding such measurement the case history is taken to ascertain the cause of complaint or any diagnostic symptoms.

Examination

Following the recording of the patient's history and symptoms his naked vision and vision with his own distance glasses is recorded.

Visual Acuity may be regarded as a measure of the faculty of receiving (by the lens system and retina), transmitting (by the optic nerve), and mentally interpreting (by the visual centers in the brain) retinal impressions. Visual Acuity measurements usually are made at 20 feet from a chart first developed by Snellen. The various letters are designated by distances at which each would subtend an angle of 5 minutes (1/12 of one degree) over all, each limb and space occupying one minute of arc.

The 20 foot letter is 8.7 millimeters in height and width. The 40 foot letter is twice as large and the 200 foot letter usually the largest on the chart is ten times as large or 87 millimeters.

The Snellen fraction is not a fraction at all, merely a statement of fact. The person with normal vision is supposed to read the 20 foot letter at 20 feet recorded as 20/20 or in meters as VI/VI.

Many persons have more acute vision than that, reading the 15 foot letter at 20 feet distance, sometimes a 10 foot letter at 20 feet recorded as 20/15 or 20/10 respectively. Sometimes a person will read a line missing say two letters or perhaps an entire line with say two letters on the next line. These would be recorded as 20/20–2 or 20/20+2. 20/30, 20/40, etc., must never be regarded as two-thirds or fifty per cent vision respectively.

Scientific tests show that 20/40 indicates a loss of visual efficiency of only 16.3 per cent; in other words instead of 50 per cent vision it represents 83.6 per cent Visual Efficiency.

A word of warning is in order regarding the limitations of the Snellen Test. In the absence of other more discriminating tests it suffers from two serious defects. Children and young persons most likely to be under a strain whenever they use their eyes, instead of exhibiting impaired acuity on the Snellen chart, usually show up better than normal.

Secondly, a test at 20 feet gives no indication of the individual's ability or efficiency at near work. The latter is not determined by any test as simple as reading letters since it necessitates an investigation of the muscle status which, while desirable at far, is positively necessary at near.

Following the record of vision O.D. (right eye) O.S. (left eye) and O.U. (both eyes) a thorough inspection is made of the eyes, eye lids, eyelashes, cornea, sclerotic and contiguous parts. Some of the commoner conditions indicating reference to the eye-physician are as follows:

Conjunctivitis (Pink Eye) an inflamed condition of the conjunctiva of the eyeball and eyelids which may be mild or serious according to its cause and severity. It is frequently prevalent in the spring and fall especially among children and being infectious may spread through a class or an entire school. One of the predisposing causes is an uncorrected error of refraction. If the condition persists more than a day or two or if the eyeball and blood vessels surrounding the cornea appear inflamed and engorged medical care is in order. In fact it is always better to be safe than sorry.

Blepharitis Marginalis, inflammation and matting together of the margins of the lids is another concomitant of uncorrected errors of refraction. Its immediate cause is bacterial infection.

Styes. A reddish swelling near the roots of the eyelashes indicates need for examination and correction of visual defects. The cause is stoppage of one of the glands of Moll or Zeiss which secrete the oily fluid which lubricates the eye.

Chalazion. (Greek, hailstone). Is a hard nucleus in the lid over which the skin moves freely. It may or may not give rise to discomfort. The preferred cure is incision and evacuation of the nodule.

Pterygium. (Greek, a small wing). Is a triangular growth whose base is usually near the nose, the apex extending towards, and if neglected actually encroaching upon, the cornea and over the pupil. In the latter case vision may be completely ruined. It is specially prevalent among habitues of the desert, miners, Indians, etc. The cause, irritation of the tissues by wind and sand. The cure dissection and tucking in of the apex of the growth so that if it develops further its development will be away from the pupil. Sometimes the condition may be quiescent for years but an active inflammatory condition calls for immediate medical or surgical care.

Trachoma. Perhaps the most dangerous and serious external condition. Also known as Granulated Eyelids. It consists of small pustules covering the inner surface of the lids spreading over to affect the cornea. In its early stages it is not easy to differentiate from a simple catarrhal conjunctivitis, but in its second stage the inner surface of the lids are raw and look very much like a strawberry. It is most prevalent among backward people and those who do not observe the niceties of cleanliness and hygiene. It is widespread among the Indians and the farm population in some of our central and southern states.

Ophthalmoscopic Examination

Following an external examination of the eye and adnexa the optometrist projects a small diffuse illumination into the eye approaching quite close so that looking through the patient's pupil he uses the patient's lens system as a simple magnifier to inspect the interior of the eye to determine whether or not it is a healthy eye properly subject to optometric care or if it is a sick eye calling for reference to the eye-physician.

The construction of the ophthalmoscope is such that it enables the user to project light into the eye while allowing the returning light an unobstructed path into the eye of the observer.

Some of the commoner conditions indicating reference to the eye-physician are as follows:

Conditions within the eye diagnosed by inspection with the Ophthalmoscope include; cataract, a clouding of the crystalline lens usually a condition of advancing years, although occasionally present at birth and sometimes resulting from a severe blow.

In its incipiency the lens swells and in many cases enables the patient to discard his lenses, reading without them. This is the condition known as "second sight." The next stage is the clouding which if it occurs late in life may be insufficient to cause marked visual impairment. In other cases the lens becomes practically opaque and the only remedy is removal of the lens and substitution of strong spectacle lenses for far and near since the eye is now a fixed focus camera.

Normally the interior of the eye presents a pinkish appearance, lighter or darker as the patient is blond, brunette or negroid. Arteries and veins are seen branching out from the Optic Disc which is the name given to the entrance of the optic nerve. Departure from the normal usually is indicative of pathology. Internal pathology includes such conditions as: Optic nerve atrophy, retinitis, choroiditis, etc.

One of the most serious conditions is Glaucoma (Greek, glaukos —sea green) from the appearance of the pupil. It is a condition of hypertension due to a blocking of the normal drainage of the eye. Like cataract it is a condition of adulthood. In acute primary glaucoma, it attacks without warning, is accompanied by severe pain and calls for immediate attention. A rapid loss of vision is one of its signs. There is also a chronic glaucoma unaccompanied by the symptoms described, also a secondary type which need not concern us here.

There are very many other conditions of greater and lesser

severity and variations of the conditions mentioned, also ocular reflexes of systemic conditions which do not fit into an article of this nature. Suffice it here to say that the part of wisdom is always to seek advice whenever any situation arises in which there is the least element of doubt.

Keratometer and Retinoscope

The next step is the use of a Keratometer or cornea meter. The purpose of this instrument is to measure the meridians of least and greatest curvature of an assymetrical cornea, the difference constituting the condition known as astigmia or astigmatism. This condition is at once the most prevalent and the most disturbing of the visual anomalies.

With the keratometer in skilled hands differences in the radii of the principal meridians of the order of a two hundred and fiftieth part of an inch are measurable.

Next in sequence is the retinoscopic examination. The instrument employed differs from the ophthalmoscope in that in the latter we desire a large area uniformly illuminated whereas now we desire as nearly as possible a bright point of light as near as we can get to the macula or visual center of the eye. The aim being to form an image of that luminous retinal point at a convenient distance in front of the patient.

Assume for example that without any lens the emergent light focuses at one meter, then one meter is his "far point" and anything beyond it is blurred. It is a simple matter to take a negative lens of one meter focal distance which will cancel out the excess power and put the eye in adjustment for seeing distance objects. On the other hand if it took a convex lens of one meter focal distance to bring the emergent light to a focus at one meter, remove it and the eye is in a position to focus light from a distance upon the retina without effort.

Other conditions are measured by determining the lens needed to bring light to a focus at a predetermined distance and then calculating the correction for infinity or any point within infinity.

With the data thus assembled we are ready to proceed to the subjective examination which in modern optometry is done with a phoro-optometer. The optometer consists of a battery of convex and concave spheres and of cylindrical lenses with which literally thousands of combinations can be achieved, the quest being to determine that lens or combination of lenses with which maximum visual acuity is possible with each eye individually and with the two eyes together.

Then follows the subjective examination in which indications revealed by the keratometer and retinoscope are subjected to the acid test of trial on the test chart and the refinements of the cross cylinder and other check tests.

Description of Errors

A brief description of the various visual defects and the terminology employed will be of interest.

The unit of lens power and of visual defects is the Dioptry usually designated the Diopter. A convex lens whose focal length is one meter is known as a "plus" one diopter lens written + 1.00. A concave lens of equal but opposite power (i.e. diverging instead of converging) is a minus one diopter lens, written — 1.00 D. A two diopter lens has a focus of half a meter and a half diopter lens a two meter focal distance.

Lenses of equal power and opposite sign neutralize one another.

Visual defects are divided into two classes—Spherical: Hypermetropia (Hyperopia) (far sight)in which the eye at rest is deficient in power and must draw on its reserves (accommodation) normally used only for near vision—and Myopia (near sight) in which there is excess of power, so that objects at a distance are imaged forward of the retina and only objects at near distances can be focussed on the retina.

The extent to which the Hypermetrope can draw upon his accommodation depends upon his age. In any case such a draft is likely to be exhausting. In young children this sometimes leads to a convergent squint which if taken in hand promptly, frequently can be corrected by the wearing of appropriate convex lenses, perhaps with a few weeks or months of vision training, but if neglected may result in loss of vision in the squinting eye. An operation will straighten the eye but will not restore vision. Myopia is a condition demanding rigorous attention to visual hygiene. Correction of the defect with lenses—erect posture—rest periods and restricted near work for children—large objects. Good illumination—the best of health care. In any case of visual disability of children it is highly important that parents, teachers and friends shall refrain from discussion of their defects with them or in their presence. Control must be exercised with the utmost of tact and by indirection lest an inferiority complex be induced. Glasses should be substantial but as attractive as can be.

The second and more prevalent class of defect is astigmia (astigmatism), of which there are five varieties. In one sense all five are identical; namely, there are meridians of least and greatest dioptric power at right angles each to the other. Such a lens system produces two line images at different distances, and at right angles to each other, for each external object point. In such an eye the material available for the construction of the retinal image is (1) an aggregation of lines all in one meridian (all vertical, all horizontal or all oblique), (2) an aggregation of ellipses in one meridian or (3) an aggregation of circles (euphemistically called circles of least confusion). With such image materials only a line in the appropriate direction can have a sharp image on the retina.

It is the location of this line which enables the optometrist to locate the principle meridians and determine the appropriate cylindrical lens power to bring both meridians to a common focus.

Two classifications, simple hypermetropic and simple myopic astigmia have one meridian in focus (emmetropic) and require a lens which in one meridian (the axis) has no power and in the opposite meridian at right angles to it the plus (convex) or minus (concave) power indicated. Compound hypermetropic astigmia and compound myopic astigmia are conditions in which the eye is hypermetropic or myopic in all meridians, but with maximum and minimum errors in opposite meridians. The fifth type is mixed astigmia, a condition of excess power in one direction and of deficiency in the meridian at right angles.

Perhaps it should be noted that the principal meridians may lie in any pair of mutually perpendicular meridians, although in general the higher power is usually at or near the vertical, 90° meridian, calling for a plus cylinder with axis in this direction or a minus cylinder at right angles thereto, as + 1.00 x 90, + 1.00 sphere + 1.00 cylinder x 90 or —.75 x 180, — 1.25, —50 x 165.

Irregular astigmia does not lend itself to rigid rules, nor can it be fully corrected by spectacle lenses whose curves are always regular. A slit is rotated to the meridian of best vision and lenses applied until maximum vision is secured. The slit is rotated 90° and the process repeated. The two values are then combined in a single lens.

If the condition is confined to the cornea a contact lens may be of service, as for other special needs, actors, naval officers whose spectacles are likely to be clouded with spray.

It is impossible that contact lens ever can fulfill the role of spectacle lenses, for one thing they cannot be made in bifocal or trifocal form.

Presbyopia (old sight) is a condition of impaired auxiliary focussing power (accommodation) occasionally present in younger persons. The correction being added plus power. For an eye otherwise perfect, the condition manifests itself at 45 to 50 years of age. The sign is putting the book or newspaper farther and farther away.

Muscle Tests

Following this part of the examination two types of tests are made at the 20 foot distance to determine

(1) The posture of the muscles whose function it is to direct the eyes to the object of regard and
(2) To ascertain the breadth of fusion control.

From the first of these we may learn much about the functioning of the ocular economy.

Farsightedness leads to abnormal effort of the focussing apparatus to sharpen the focus. This in turn tends to over stimulate the normal convergence (in turning) muscles. In fact in early childhood such effort may produce a convergent squint with abandonment of vision in one eye. Such cases respond readily to appropriate lenses if cared for early in life but if not so cared for will result in loss of vision and the disfigurement of squint which latter may be overcome by surgery but not the loss of vision which is permanent.

The second stage of distance muscle testing consists of displacing the image horizontally and vertically to ascertain how much ability the individual has to follow such displacement, this having an important bearing upon his comfort in prolonged use of his eyes at distance.

Next comes a series of similar tests at near distances and this part of the modern visual examination is optometry's contribution to the visual efficiency and comfort of that large and growing section of the community who appreciate the vital importance and benefits accruing from scientific eye care.

It is axiomatic among optometrists that the only really satisfactory way of measuring any visual function is to make the measurements while the eyes are engaged in a task involving normal use of the particular elements involved.

In an earlier day it was thought that the really important tests were those made at a distance, and they are important for distant vision, but we now know that it is not enough to add to the distance lens an added power to care for the nearer distance. We must not only know what the distance or distances are for which the eyes must adjust themselves but in addition we must learn about that most important interrelation: namely, that between the focussing mechanism of each eye and the muscles which direct the two eyes to objects at near distances. (Accommodation and convergence.)

If there is incoordination here, visual training may be in order or if the individual is past the time of life where training promises much benefit he must be provided with such lenses as will supplement his impaired focussing power and also will reduce the effort necessary to direct both eyes to his reading or other near work.

There is much popular misconception regarding orthoptics or vision training. We hear talk of weak eyes and weak eye muscles. The muscles of the eyes are a hundred times stronger than the physical turning of the eyes demand. The prime function of orthoptics is so to stimulate visual perception that the presence upon the two retinae of images of an object that interests us will arouse prompt and accurate direction of the two eyes to the object and equally efficient operation of the focussing mechanism.

Furthermore there is no question that visual perception can be sharpened and speeded up by practice. Every Psychologist is familiar with flash cards and the tachistoscope which at the moment is enjoying quite a vogue among orthoptists.

The old throw away your glasses cult is still going strong. Relaxation and relaxed attention to detail is their stock in trade. Training in visual perception is valid as an adjunct to glasses in many cases but never as a substitute therefor, which is not to say that all cases require glasses but when they are needed there is no substitute. In such cases training may teach a person the better to interpret poor images which like our war imposed use of recapped tires is an inferior makeshift.

This brings to mind another aspect of visual care. There are cases benefiting from tinted glasses, notably persons of a very light complexion or with abnormally large pupils and all persons with incipient cataract.

Such glasses to be of maximum benefit should be worn only when exposed to excessive light. To wear them continuously is like wearing outdoor wraps indoors, thus losing the benefit of the extra protection when needed.

Muscular Imbalances

Muscular imbalances doubtless are as prevalent as errors of refraction, which latter by some authorities are said to affect 87 per cent of the population in this country.

Muscular imbalances usually are latent conditions overcome by a strong desire for single vision. A tendency to overconvergence is designated esophoria. A lag of convergence, also overcome by the fusion sense, is called exophoria, while tendencies to vertical deviation are known as right or left hyperphoria.

Squint or strabismus is of two kinds, functional (concomitant) which is the manifest deviation present when above conditions can no longer be overcome and known as eso- exo- or hyper-tropia, and paralytic squint in which paralysis affecting one muscle or a group of muscles movement is restricted in the direction of their action. In other directions movement is normal and vision is retained in both eyes, the head being turned in the field of action of the paralyzed muscle.

In concomitant squint both eyes move, maintaining a constant deviation. Vision in the squinting eye is lost, although there is one more classification alternating squint in which first one, then the other fixes but never both together for more than a brief moment.

E. A. H.

VISION, PARTIAL. The first successful vocational guidance program for partially sighted students in public schools was initiated in 1935, under the inspirational leadership of Mr. George F. Meyer, then Supervisor of Sight Saving and Braille Classes of the Minneapolis Public Schools. Prior to that time all partially sighted high school students or those aged sixteen or over leaving from the Sight Saving Department of the Minneapolis Public School System became the responsibility of the State Department of Vocational Rehabilitation for industrial training and placement. Because it became apparent that neither the schools nor the office of rehabilitation at that time possessed the facilities conducive to successful industrial placement for the partially sighted youth of the city, a program termed the "Applied Industries" came into being. This program is instituted while the pupil is still in school—in the twelfth grade. After graduation from high school all sight saving students are subject to the supervision of the State Rehabilitation Department. That there may be continuity of planning the Applied Industries Program operates in cooperation with the State Department of Vocational Rehabilitation.

Who Are the Partially Sighted?

According to physical standards set up for recipients of rehabilitation services by the Federal Security Agency, a person must have at least a 25 per cent loss in visual efficiency. Generally speaking, useful vision is determined on the basis of a visual acuity of 20/60 in the better eye after the best correction has been obtained. A notation of 20/60 means that a person sees as well at a distance of 20 feet as a person with normal vision sees at 60 feet. In other words he has a 30 per cent loss of visual acuity. If there is a difference in acuity for reading (near vision) and for distance, the greater loss is used in determining eligibility for rehabilitation. If loss of acuity for near vision is the determining factor, acuity must be 14/42 or if Jaeger notation is used J–10 is the dividing line.

A common practice for admission to sight saving classes is an acuity rating of 20/70 or less in the better eye, although the diagnosis as well as the prognosis and any peripheral field defect are considered in the recommendation for placement.

Instances may be cited in which pupils are regarded as eligible for rehabilitation and still are not in need of the services of a sight saving class: A person who has lost one eye and who has normal vision in the other eye is eligible for rehabilitation services but usually is not admitted to a sight saving class.

All youth are in need of vocational counseling and especially the youth with serious loss of visual acuity. Therefore, persons with visual acuity with correcting lenses ranging from 20/70 in the better eye to travel vision (ability to count fingers at 3 feet) are considered as partially sighted.

Causes of Loss of Visual Acuity

Causes of loss of visual acuity may be divided into three general groups: diseases of the eye; defects of the muscles of the eye; and defect in the shape of the eye itself.

Diseases of the eye may cause an opacity or other defect which blocks or blurs the rays of light as they enter the eyeball, or they may render the retina and optic nerve powerless—the retina to receive the visual image and the optic nerve to carry that image to the brain. The most common diseases of the eye are conjunctivitis, trachoma, keratitis, iritis, cataract, retinitis pigmentosa, glaucoma, and amblyopia exanopsia.

Defects in the external muscles of the eye may cause double vision or loss of vision in the faulty eye—this condition is known as strabismus.

Defect in the shape of the eye causes errors of refraction. The common errors of refraction are hyperopia (farsightedness), myopia (nearsightedness), and astigmatism.

The above general information should be considered essential knowledge for any one working with the partially sighted. The degree to which the vision of an individual should be used depends upon the diagnosis and should be determined by the ophthalmologist.

Vocational Guidance—A Cooperative Enterprise

Vocational guidance at its best requires the cooperation of all who touch the life of the child. One might almost say: All who have touched the life of the child because he is what he is, due to his inheritance plus the experiences he has had since coming into the world. If this statement is true of youth with normal visual acuity, it is especially true of the partially sighted youth. Much depends upon how his loss of visual acuity has been handled and the effect made upon him. Therefore, the cooperation of the youth himself is the first to be obtained in helping him to make the best possible decisions with reference to his life work. Both his parents and his teachers have a share in this program. Community organizations must also share this responsibility.

The parent of a partially sighted child by being overprotective, overindulgent, or both, can become a definitely deterrent factor to the successful life of his child. On the other hand if he gives him all the usual experiences of childhood and youth, striving always to make him as independent as possible and remembering always that there is no handicap so great as the child's non-acceptance of his difficulty, he has started him well on the road to success.

The teacher of a sight saving class also has a definite responsibility for vocational guidance. She must be alert to every opportunity for making care of the eyes habitual, for providing a setting for his mental health, for establishing desirable work habits, for guiding him in his working relationships with those who have more normal vision and for seeing to it that, in so far as he is capable, that he achieves a mastery of the basic tools of learning. In addition she cannot emphasize too strongly the importance of punctuality in keeping appointments, regularity of school attendance, independence in traveling to and from school or about the school building. Personal appearance and grooming must be considered as definite assets in future vocational placement and therefore, receive due consideration early in the child's life.

The classroom teacher too has a share in this responsibility. She can do much to make him one of her group. She can do much to prepare the normally sighted children of her group to accept the child with low vision who must bring to class the large clear type books, lessons prepared on a larger scale whether executed in script or by using a typewriter. She must give the child with low vision responsibility and expect his contribution to the group in order to give him the feeling of belonging—so essential to his normal development.

Both teachers are responsible not only for teaching the skills and the formation of desirable attitudes and habits which will be of value in the world of work, but they must see to it that these young people are ready to take responsibility as citizens of this country.

It is not enough that the youth leave the schools of today fully aware of the social and economic changes taking place about them, but they must also know how to meet them constructively.

The responsibility of the community is implied in that it furnishes the special educational facilities which will enable the partially sighted child to take his place among his more normally sighted contemporaries throughout his school life—but does not end there. The community also has a responsibility for furnishing an opportunity for making him economically secure provided his performance is on a competitive basis. Upon that basis, and that only should a partially sighted person be accepted in industry.

The liaison officer between the schools and industry is the vocational guidance worker, counselor, or coordinator. He must have followed the student from the time he enters junior high school until he is ready either for higher education or for industrial placement.

The partially sighted student with a high intelligence rating, social maturity, emotional stability, and outstanding scholarship has a fair chance of taking higher education with satisfaction. Even though the economic status of his parents presents a handicap, he may still avail himself of a college education with the aid of scholarships and funds from the State Rehabilitation Department if it can be proven that he is eligible for such aid. The testing program and case history taking is also essential for the students of higher intellectual attainment. That preliminary work, however, is usually done by the testing bureau of the institution of higher learning. The guidance program still continues but in the case of the partially sighted is usually assumed by the State Department of Rehabilitation.

To do a satisfactory job in the industrial placement of a normally sighted person the counselor must thoroughly know and understand the person in question. Low visual acuity further complicates the situation.

Information to be Assembled

Most school systems have some form of cumulative record which follows a pupil through school. Much information found on these records is valuable to the school counselor. For students in Sight Saving Classes up-to-date ophthalmological records, physical records, psychological records, attendance records, as well as records of academic achievement are available. To the data mentioned above, the counselor must obtain from the teacher of the Sight Saving Class such additional data as: estimates of personality, adjustments made or not made, pupil participation in school activities, in extracurricular activities, and in ability to get along well with others. He should read the visiting teacher's records of home visits; or better yet, visit the home himself that he may better understand the contribution of the home to the situation.

Before the pupil has completed the tenth grade, a complete battery of tests should be given. Preferably the psychological tests including the manual dexterity test should be given by a psychologist from the Child Study Department of the schools. The battery of tests should include intelligence tests, achievement tests, interest inventories, manual and finger dexterity tests, and a personality rating scale.

Tests

Among the intelligence tests which have been found helpful are: The Individual Stanford Binet, The I.J.R.—Intelligence Examination for the Visually Handicapped, and the Otis Self-Administering Test of Mental Ability—Higher Examination, Form B.

Any recognized, standardized achievement tests in reading and arithmetic may be used. The Stanford Achievement Tests are excellent as the test for Reading covers Paragraph Meaning, Word Meaning, Language Usage, and Spelling from Dictation. The Arithmetic Tests give results in Arithmetic Reasoning and Computation. To save the psychologist's time the other tests may be administered by the counselor himself or by the teacher of the Sight Saving Class after transcription into clear type has been made. All tests should be scored and interpreted by the psychologist.

An assembly of all data as indicated above constitutes rather a full case study of the individual which is reviewed with interpretations by the psychologist at a conference of all school workers directly concerned (the teacher of sight saving class, counselor or coordinator, visiting teacher, director of special education), any social workers if active on the case, and the representative of the State Rehabilitation Department.

At the conference tentative plans for industrial placement are made which are discussed with the student and his parents as the

1372 ENCYCLOPEDIA OF VOCATIONAL GUIDANCE

cooperation of both is paramount to the successful culmination of
the plans.

Programming for the last two years in high school should be
aimed toward the same goal reached in the conference. Every effort
should be made to make the experiences of those two years both
complementary and supplementary to the conference plans. Two
years so planned affords an opportunity for filling in the gaps
brought to light through the testing and conference periods. In the
twelfth year it is advisable to arrange for a period of orientation in
industry for the partially sighted student as a supplemental measure.
It is in the twelfth year, therefore, that the coordinator takes over
the supervision of the case.

In a small school system the counselor may act both as counselor and coordinator or a qualified teacher may act in that capacity.

It is essential at this point that the coordinator works very closely
with the State Rehabilitation Department as the partially sighted
person becomes the responsibility of that department for guidance
and placement upon leaving school.

Survey of Local Industries

Before the plan for orientation in industry can become effective a
survey of local industries must have been made by the coordinator
with reference to possibilities of employment and analyses of specific
jobs that might be considered for possible placement.

All the preceding information concerning the individual student
must then be reviewed in light of the industrial situation and the
two fitted together like parts of a puzzle. Even then the coordinator
may expect some problems to arise as he is dealing with human
beings.

Placement for Learning

Such a placement should be considered by all concerned (the
student, the school, the coordinator, and the employer) as a learning situation. The student should not replace a regular worker, the
school could well issue two vocational credits in lieu of such training, the coordinator should supervise the industrial situation to see
that the student is getting the necessary experience and that the
employer fully understands and appreciates the situation.

Before an industrial placement can be made, however, much
ground work has to be done in establishing a thorough understanding on the part of the employer. Lasting and workable relationships
are established only when placed upon a business rather than an
emotional basis. No placement should ever be made which does not

give promise of benefiting both the employer and the student worker.

Cooperation of labor organizations is also essential to a successful placement program. It is the opinion of those who have had experience with the problem of industrial placement of the partially sighted (vision 20/70 or less), that remuneration during the learning period is not desirable as these students take longer to acquire the speed of a paid worker. If however, placement is made with any firm engaged in interstate commerce a minimum wage must be paid. All placements should be made in accordance with state and federal laws regulating employment.

Placement for Living

If the temporary placement has given satisfaction, the student has made himself indispensable to his employer and after graduation from school is taken on as a paid worker. The coordinator still continues to give counsel if necessary. He places the student's name on the inactive list only when he is sure that satisfactory progress is being made. If dissatisfaction arises the contributing factors should be determined and as far as possible ruled out in the second placement.

An opportunity to become a self-supporting member of society should be offered to every partially sighted person in any community. All the steps as outlined above are necessary, however, if he is to enjoy the satisfaction which comes from a life of achievement.

Follow Up Work

A Follow Up Program would be exceedingly valuable from the standpoint of conservation of effort and elimination of erroneous practices. It is a waste of time to preserve a pattern of performance if it does not net desirable results. Follow up work in the future should not be hampered by lack of funds. Human lives are too precious.

Types of Employment in Which the Partially Sighted Succeed

An adequate analysis of industrial situations in relation to placement of the partially sighted has not been made. On the other hand no general statement with reference to types of employment found successful for the partially sighted can be made as so much depends upon the personalities of the individuals concerned, the thoroughness with which the groundwork has been laid, the attitude of the worker toward work and the demands made upon the worker by the employer.

Types of employment as listed below offer possibilities for successful placement for partially sighted boys and girls with high school education:

BOYS	GIRLS
Assembly Worker	Assembly Worker
Baker	Cafeteria Worker
Barber	Clerical Worker (if work is sufficiently varied)
Dish Washer	
Machine Feeder	Florist
Maintenance Worker (Drug Store)	Grooving Machine Operator
	Marker
Office Boy	Retail Sales
Packer	Sewing Machine Operator
Retail Sales	Sorter in Laundry
Shoe Repair	Supervisor of Mailing Room at Wholesale House
Stock Boy	
Truck Driver's Helper	Telephone Operator

To the partially sighted person with a college education, who has the required personal qualifications added to specific training such fields as law, music, secretarialship, ministry, teaching, or lecturing may be found avenues worthy of exploration.

References:

1. Allen, F. J. *Principles and problems of vocational guidance.* New York: McGraw-Hill Book Co., Inc., 1927, p. 5.
2. American Association of School Administrators. *Paths to better schools, 23rd yearbook.* Department of National Education Association of the United States, 1945.
3. Educational Policies Commission. *Education for all American youth.* National Education Association of the United States and the American Association of School Administrators, Washington, D. C.
4. Gruber, K. F. *The vocational training program for the visually handicapped in the Minneapolis public schools.* New York: National Society for the Prevention of Blindness.
5. Haas, K. B. *Distributive education.* New York; Chicago: The Gregg Publishing Company, 1941.
6. Lorwin, L. L. *Youth work program, problems, and policies.* Prepared for the American Youth Commission, American Council on Education, Washington, D. C., 1941.
7. May, C. H. *Manual of diseases of the eye,* Sixteenth Edition. Baltimore: William Wood and Company, 1939.

8. Norton, T. L. *Education for work*. The Regent's Inquiry. New York: McGraw-Hill Book Company, Inc., 1938.
9. Report of the Committee of the National Vocational Guidance Association, Occupations. *The principles and practices of educational and vocational guidance*. The Vocational Guidance Magazine, 1937, 16, pp. 772–778.
10. U. S. Federal Security Agency, Instructions for use and interpretation of Medical Report Form R-3c. *Visual disabilities*. Office of Education, Vocational Rehabilitation Division, Washington, D. C., August 1942.

M. E. B.

VISUAL REQUIREMENTS OF THE PRINCIPAL OCCUPATIONS.

Probably the most common pre-employment test in industry is some kind of vision test. More applicants for jobs have had to take a vision test than any other single pre-employment test. Most frequently this test has been nothing more than the traditional letter chart on the wall twenty feet away—a test that measures one aspect of vision, and does not disclose individual differences in the variety of visual skills that are important in different degrees on different jobs. Yet this test is found in many employment offices where no other test is used. Because of the widespread use of vision tests and visual requirements, it is important for vocational counselors to be informed in this field. Vocational aims may be thwarted and vocational training wasted if the student cannot meet the visual qualifications for the job he has chosen.

Such relatively widespread use of pre-employment vision tests reflects the common recognition that vision is important. Even on operations that are primarily manual, direction or control of the manipulations usually depend on seeing. Some operations, such as inspection of a product for appearance, are primarily visual. Dimensional control, while it is a matter of mechanical measurement, usually requires visual interpretation of scales, gauges, and meters. General control, including scheduling, cost accounts, specifications, instructions, and so on, depends chiefly on various paper forms that must be interpreted visually. Any job that cannot be done by a blind man unaided requires some sort of visual application.

Visual Requirements for Specific Jobs

Over and above minimum general visual requirements that are established by management policy, individual differences in visual ability are responsible to some extent for success or failure on most jobs in industry. Only since 1940 has there been any systematic investigation of visual requirements for specific jobs. This investigation is being carried out in the Occupational Research Center at Purdue University and in many industries that are participating. The results already are conclusive that visual requirements differ on different jobs. Individual differences in vision are such that one person may be particularly qualified for one job, while another is not at all qualified for that job but is well qualified for a different job. Visual aptness or ineptitude for a job makes a difference in production, earnings, quality of work, scrap or waste, accidents, absences, job tenure, training cost, learning time—in any of the different measures of successful and satisfactory employees. It makes a difference also in the ease and comfort with which workers do the job.

The visual requirements for specific jobs are being discovered by a standardized fact-finding procedure. This procedure discloses the visual abilities that are important for the job not by analysis of the job but by analysis of workers on the job—contrasting the visual characteristics of the most successful workers with the visual characteristics of less successful workers, or contrasting the visual skills of fast and slow learners on the job. Job descriptions are used also, but for the purpose of identifying similar and dissimilar jobs in different plants so that visual requirements for various jobs may be checked against each other.

Each year an increasing number of additional companies enter upon this project. Visual requirements that are specific for a job are adopted as minimum requirements for placement on that job. Even on similar jobs in different plants the minimum requirements may differ, since differences in population may make a single set of visual requirements too severe at present in one area, although they are quite suitable in another area. What the visual requirements are for their different jobs must be learned directly from these plants. It is their responsibility to make known their own particular visual requirements for placement on different jobs.

Visual Skills

Vision is not a simple or unitary function. It is a complex of varied visual skills. Therefore, vision cannot be classified simply as "good" or "bad." Visual skill or visual performance may be adequate in some respects and inadequate in other respects. Furthermore, adequacy of vision must be considered always in terms of specific job requirements. One person's vision may be satisfactory for one job and inadequate for another. "Good vision" is whatever kind and whatever degrees of the various visual skills are necessary for optimum performance on a given job.

The measureable characteristics of vision that are important for job success are the primary visual functions of accomplishment—what one can see or accomplish with his eyes. How he does it is a secondary problem, one that is of interest chiefly to professional eye men. Tests of primary visual accomplishments, or visual skills, have been recommended for use in industry by committees of the American Optometric Association, American Medical Association, and American Academy of Ophthalmology. These primary visual skills are usually catalogued as follows:

(1) Visual Acuity: The ability to see small detail. This skill is sometimes subdivided according to the type of discrimination required—such as micrometer vision. Tests of visual acuity are perception threshold tests. Visual acuity is not constant for different distances and cannot adequately be predicted at one distance from test results at a much different distance. It must be measured, therefore, at least at two distances, one representing distance seeing (beyond arm's reach or contact) and one representing near seeing (within easy reach). Acuity is measured for each eye separately and for both eyes together.

(2) Depth perception or stereoscopic acuity: The ability to perceive small differences in the distance of objects from the eyes. A test of depth perception is a measure of the difference threshold of perception of distance. The major cue for depth perception is that the two eyes see things differently because of their small difference in point of view, and these differences are integrated into perception of things in three dimensions.

(3) Color discrimination: Ability to perceive small differences in color. A test of color discrimination is also a measure of a difference threshold, sometimes subdivided for qualitative differences of color. Color discrimination is of direct importance on some jobs and of indirect importance on many others.

(4) Indirect or peripheral vision: The ability to perceive in other directions while looking or fixating in one direction. A test of indirect vision is also a measure of threshold of perception, and is often subdivided for stimuli that are different quantitatively (size and brightness) and qualitatively (color and motion). Indirect vision has not been studied extensively in relation to job success, chiefly because it requires special equipment and special training to give the tests.

(5) In addition to these true visual skills, certain postural characteristics of the eyes are important in relation to job success. Under artificial testing conditions in which any demand for two-eye coordination is eliminated, individual differences in eye posture are

quite marked. Variations in eye posture, called "phorias," are measured laterally and vertically. Phorias, like visual acuity, are not constant for different distances and must be measured at least at two distances.

These visual characteristics, while they may be thought of as separate elementary performances, are really complex integrated functions. Complex as they are, they are subject to change. With increasing age all these functions change, usually in the direction of deterioration. Also it is possible for these functions to be changed by professional eye care, through the medium of optical aids or visual training. The instability of these functions over a period of time raises problems of maintenance of visual skills that are desirable on a job, but it also makes it possible for most persons to achieve the visual skills they need for a job.

Visual Test Battery

For the large scale investigation of visual requirements on specific jobs, as described above, a battery of vision tests was carefully selected, improved and standardized. Each test in this battery had to meet three requirements: reliability, valid relations with success on a variety of jobs, and ease of administration in the hands of lay testers delegated in industries to conduct the tests. These tests are incorporated in a single instrument, the Ortho-Rater, manufactured by the Bausch and Lomb Optical Company of Rochester, New York. The tests are made at two distances (produced optically in the Ortho-Rater)—26 feet and 13 inches. The tests included are:

FAR (26 feet)	NEAR (13 inches)
1. Phoria, Vertical	1. Acuity, Both Eyes
2. Phoria, Lateral	2. Acuity, Right Eye
3. Acuity, Both Eyes	3. Acuity, Left Eye
4. Acuity, Right Eye	4. Phoria, Vertical
5. Acuity, Left Eye	5. Phoria, Lateral
6. Depth	
7. Color	

While this repertory of tests does not include all tests that can possibly have some relation to success on particular jobs, it includes those that are most useful and that meet the criteria described above. Since this battery is the basis for the only systematic study of visual requirements on specific jobs, the visual requirements on various types of jobs can best be described in terms of these tests.

Different Types of Visual Requirements

Jobs differ in their visual demands in terms of a number of factors, which factors are emerging from the nation-wide investigation. Similar jobs have similar visual requirements. However, the similarity of jobs cannot be assumed from a similarity of job titles. A drill press operator in one plant may be on a production operation simplified by means of jigs, fixtures, and automatic controls and safeguards to the point where a blind person could do the work. In another plant a drill press operator may do lay-out and set-up operations requiring precise visual skills.

Different jobs may have quite different visual requirements. Mending hosiery at a very close distance obviously requires a different combination of visual skills from those required to operate a push-truck safely and efficiently. These differences in visual requirements are not always so obvious nor easily guessed from casual observation on the jobs.

Figures 1 to 6 show sample patterns of visual requirements on several typical jobs. The background of each pattern is a matrix showing all possible scores on each of the twelve Ortho-Rater tests. The first seven lines are the FAR tests, the last five lines the NEAR tests. These scores are simple numbers and do not of themselves describe the visual characteristics that they measure; they simply classify individual differences in these characteristics. One person's "visual profile" is indicated by a series of circles around his scores on the tests. Figure 1 shows one person's scores on these tests. On the phoria tests (first two and last two lines) "normal" scores are in the middle range, anomalous conditions represented by the extremes. On the other tests larger numbers represent higher degrees of visual skill.

Figure 2 shows the pattern of visual requirements on a very close job—mending and embroidering in a hosiery mill. Scores that are characteristic of the less successful operators are shaded out as being undesirable. On this job the near skills are important, distance skills unimportant. As a matter of fact, distance acuity often has a *negative* relation to success on such very close jobs. Looping, another very close job in a hosiery mill, has similar visual requirements.

Figure 3 shows the pattern of visual requirements on a distance job requiring only modest degrees of visual skill—loading and push truck operators. Only the far skills are critical on this job. This is in marked contrast to the visual requirements illustrated in Figure 2.

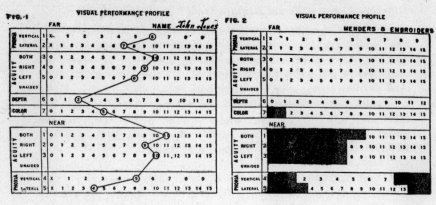

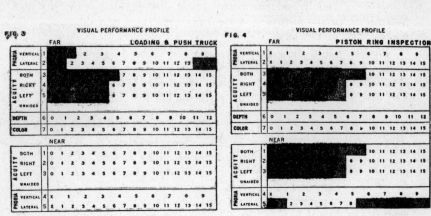

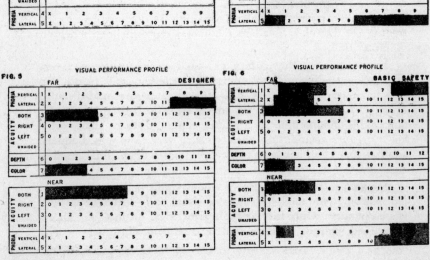

Figure 4 shows the requirements on a job of inspecting polished surfaces—piston rings. The polished surfaces seem to act like mirrors, multiplying the visual working distances. Both far and near visual skills are important on this job.

Figure 5 shows visual requirements that can be met by one-eyed persons, in this case for the job of designing.

Figure 6 shows a generalized pattern of visual requirements for safety in heavy industry, particularly on physically active jobs. This pattern illustrates also a case of asymmetric requirements on phoria tests; on the second far test low scores are unsafe, on the fifth near test high scores are unsafe.

These examples illustrate the different types of visual requirements for different types of jobs. Actual minimum requirements for specific jobs are available only from the plants where such requirements have been set.

As similar visual requirements are discovered on different jobs, the common factors in the jobs themselves can be identified. One major factor is the visual working distance. Sometimes several visual working distances are involved in the same job. Another factor is the manipulative nature of the operation—what is being done. It may involve only a single flat surface, such as drafting, writing, or reading. It may involve positioning and assembly of parts in three dimensions. Or it may involve manipulative control in one field and visual control in another field, as in typing or piloting vehicles. The type of visual judgments required varies infinitely on different jobs. A third factor is posture—body, head, and eye posture with respect to the work. Abnormal posture requirements (such as a head tilt) produce abnormal visual characteristics and sometimes asymmetric visual requirements. Illumination may affect the degree of visual skills required and yet may not affect the kind or pattern of visual skills required. Jigs, and fixtures, on the other hand, help to reduce the complexity of visual requirements. Optical aids, such as magnifiers, microscopes, loupes, and projectors, may have their own peculiar visual requirements. With all these factors affecting visual requirements, it would obviously be impossible for anyone but a visual expert to look at a job and guess accurately what the specific visual requirements are. But by means of the fact-finding procedure described above, it would be possible to determine scientifically the visual requirements on specific jobs or job groups.

Visual Requirements in Transportation

Minimum visual requirements are most elaborate and rigid in the field of transport—chiefly in the operation of public carriers such as trains, aircraft, trucks, and buses—and in some branches of the armed forces. These requirements are largely in the interests of public safety. Visual requirements on such jobs are specific with different operating companies, just as visual requirements for motor vehicle operator's licences are specific in the different states. Visual examination for jobs in transport is part of a general physical examination and is conducted by doctors who are designated or appointed by the operating companies to make such examinations. For an applicant to find out whether he can meet the visual requirements for any of these jobs, he must be examined by the company's doctor. These companies as a rule conduct periodic re-examination of transport crewmen and require them to maintain their visual characteristics within the same tolerances or limits that are prescribed for initial employment. While these visual standards are somewhat arbitrary, and there has been some question as to the validity or genuine value of certain phases of them, they are prescribed for employment on these jobs, and applicants must meet these requirements or not be hired.

The Blind, Near-blind, and One-eyed Persons

On some jobs, a one-eyed person is not handicapped, if his vision is adequate in the one eye. A number of industrial jobs in scattered plants have been modified so that blind employees can perform them. No doubt other jobs will in time be adapted for blind workers. Several agencies are working toward more opportunities for the blind. Blindness by industrial standards includes any degree of vision that is no better than what it takes to see the big E of the letter chart twenty feet away.

There are fewer blind persons than there are near blind or severely handicapped in vision, but for this latter group there is perhaps even less industrial opportunity than for the blind. The most common serious handicap is lack of vision in one eye. A person may be one-eyed because

   (a) he has lost one eye
   (b) one eye cannot see and cannot be made to see
   (c) one eye habitually does not participate in seeing, although by itself it can see or could be made to see.

Industries have had special concern for one-eyed and seriously handicapped persons, and in normal times many plants refuse to hire them. Such a policy may be defended as protecting the safety and efficiency of the plant personnel, but there is also an immediate economic problem in connection with employer liability for workmen's compensation. Legal provisions, and therefore company policies also, differ in the different states. Employment restrictions of this sort are most common among the larger and newer industries. As a rule only one visual function is involved in these medico-legal restrictions: perception of small detail at a distance, such as is measured by the letter chart at twenty feet. The legal aspects are probably not important for vocational counselors, except when they must explain why a person cannot expect to qualify for a certain type of work. It is important, however, for counselors to know the employment policies, with respect to visual handicaps, of employers in the community so that they will not be encouraging others in vocational aims that cannot be realized because of visual limitations.

References:

1. Coleman, J. H. Vision tests for better utilization of manpower. *Factory Management and Maintenance,* July, 1944.
2. Shepard, C. F. Visual skills. *Optometric Weekly,* January 27, 1944.
3. Stump, N. F. Spotting accident-prone workers by vision tests. *Factory Management and Maintenance,* June 1945.
4. Tiffin, J. *Industrial Psychology.* New York: Prentice-Hall Inc., 1942, Chapter 6.
5. ———— and Wirt, S. E. Determining visual standards for industrial jobs by statistical methods. *Transactions of the American Academy of Ophthalmology and Otolaryngology,* November–December, 1945.
6. ————. Near vs. distance acuity in relation to success on close industrial jobs. Supplement to *Transactions of the American Academy of Ophthalmology and Otolaryngology,* June, 1944.

S. E. W. & N. C. K.

VOCATIONAL COUNSELING OF COLLEGE STUDENTS.

Need

It has been amply demonstrated that undergraduate students in colleges and universities need vocational counseling. The many studies of the problem that have been made during the past two decades show that: over two-thirds of college students give occupational preparation as a motive for attending school; while the greatest enrollments are in vocational curricula, nevertheless, from twenty-five to seventy per cent of entering students and at least one-third of college seniors have made no specific vocational decision, and from among those who have made a choice, over half change their decision once or more during their college careers; of the problems listed by students as being of greatest importance, vocational ones lead the list; in selecting an occupation, students tend to show little regard for either their own aptitudes or abilities or the practical possibilities of obtaining a position in their chosen fields.

Even though many liberal arts colleges and universities do not include vocational objectives among their aims, the students frankly proclaim their practical purposes in attending, and vocational curricula have been provided for them. Perhaps nothing more permeates, dominates and determines a person's type of living than does his occupation. Furthermore, most men and an increasing number of women enter careers upon graduation, and they expect their colleges to give them practical assistance in deciding upon, training for, and entering an occupation. This was true even before World War II and particularly so since. College graduates of today enter a wide variety of types of occupations and the rapidly shifting occupational pattern demands of them great flexibility. Consequently, vocational decision and preparation is no longer the relatively simple problem it once seemed to be.

The vastly larger number of students who now go to college, their altered reasons for attending, and the complexity of the problem of finding their places in a rapidly changing society impose inescapable responsibilities upon higher education, not the least of which is that of assisting each student wisely to choose and prepare for an occupation suitable to his talents and to the needs of society.

Vocational counseling, since its inception at Stanford University in 1911, has extended and improved in quality throughout the colleges of the nation. When effective vocational guidance is made available, college students readily seek it.

Organization

Educational and vocational counseling of students are so closely akin that they are almost always discussed together in professional writing and research. The student's vocational plan and the selection of his courses are functionally interrelated.

The two distinct patterns of organization of vocational counseling are the *faculty advisory* system, which is predominant, and the *central staff* system. An entering student, under the faculty advisory system, is assigned to a faculty member who advises him on selection of courses and problems of vocational decision during the first and sometimes second years, until he selects a major, at which time the head, or designated member of the major department, becomes his advisor. In small institutions a variation may be the designation of one or more faculty members to advise each of the classes, i.e., freshman, sophomores, juniors, and seniors. While these faculty advisors may be chosen because of their interests and special aptitude for counseling, they seldom are trained in personnel procedures. In the central staff system, the bulk of advising on vocational and educational problems is done by a group of specially trained officers variously designated as deans, personnel directors, counselors and placement officers.

In recent years, a combination of the two systems is becoming more prevalent, with specially trained workers assuming responsibility for the direction, coordination and over-all planning of the program, and for the treatment of cases which require intensive care. There is a tendency for vocational advising to be concentrated at the freshman and senior levels. In some instances, students are required to consult counselors at designated times, in others, they are left free to come when they wish, with the exception of conferences at registration time.

Threlkeld has summarized the more common practices in vocational and educational guidance as follows: (a) guidance extended into high schools, by visiting representatives, publications, programs, and summer camps; (b) varying emphasis upon the vocational problem during freshman orientation work; (c) recognition given vocations in lectures for freshmen continued during the year; (d) vocational lectures and conferences for all students; (e) courses in occupation; (f) extra-curricula activities; (g) part-time and summer employment; (h) placement.

Whether or not specifically charged with vocational counseling responsibilities, many different persons and groups participate in vocational guidance programs. These include: (a) faculty members who are designated as counselors; (b) deans of men and deans of women; (c) registrars; (d) personnel directors; (e) student committees; (f) senior student advisors; (g) placement officers; (h) heads of departments.

Originally stimulated by the need in World War I, and greatly augmented by World War II, has been the development of refined procedures and techniques so that the counselor in college has a rich storehouse of resources upon which to draw. To the pioneering efforts of the American Council on Education the profession is indebted for invaluable work in developing cumulative records, aptitude, achievement and interest tests, rating scales and occupational information monographs.

In vocational advisement at college as well as at other levels, several steps are essential. First, the student's aptitudes, potentialities, desires and general background must be accurately determined and understood both by himself and by the counselor. Fairly reliable and valid instruments are available to assist in this phase of the task. Among these are such tests as the American Council on Education Psychological Examination and the Ohio State University Psychological Test, the Cooperative Achievement Tests, the Strong Vocational Interest Blank, the American Council Personal Rating Scale, and Bell's Adjustment Inventory. Colleges are increasingly making the results of such tests easily available through a testing bureau or personnel department which assumes the burden of administration, scoring and recording. Greatly improved cumulative record procedures are also being employed to assist the counselor in obtaining an accurate picture of the student. Secondly, both student and advisor need to have reasonably accurate and comprehensive knowledge of the world of work in which the student must find his place. They need to be informed of occupational trends, new job opportunities, over-crowded fields, particularly as they apply to college graduates. There are now available occupational information monographs which outline for specific occupations, the nature of duties, qualifications required, methods of entrance and advancement, earnings and other compensations, trends and miscellaneous considerations. A vocational shelf or room in the library is frequently provided so that students may find occupational information. Lectures to freshmen and courses in occupation for all students are offered to assist in obtaining a realistic picture of the world of work. The third and, in many respects, the most critical step in vocational advising is the integration of the knowledge gained in the first two steps and its personal application in reaching a tentative decision and planning an appropriate program of training. Herein lies the heart of the vocational counseling process. For some students, this step may be already accomplished by the time they enter college, with need only for periodic review. For others, it may be a long, laborious process involving hours of conferences with many persons. In still other instances decisions will be made and re-made many times in four years in college. There is no standardized procedure by means of which all students may be brought at a given time to the point of vocational choice and program planning. The counseling procedure most heavily drawn upon in this phase of vocational advising is the *interview* which only recently has begun to emerge as a delicate well-tempered tool. The final step in vocational advising is placement and follow-up in which the student is assisted in entering his first position in the field which he has chosen and for which he has prepared himself, and in making necessary adjustments so that he may progress in his employment.

Effectiveness

Since the beginning of vocational counseling in colleges and universities, improvements have been made, but a critical scrutiny of the effectiveness of current programs is not encouraging. There has been little scientific appraisal of the results of counseling. This is both disappointing and surprising in view of the fact that concrete results are probably more easily observed in this than in some other areas of counseling. From the few studies that have been made, it appears that as yet, only a relatively small number of students have available comprehensive vocational counseling service and that students' decisions on vocational problems tend to be made with little regard for their own aptitudes and abilities, the training opportunities available in the colleges, and for occupational trends. One writer has referred to the "persistent tendency of students to yearn for unachievable goals *despite* possession of occupational information." Students, in appraising the type of help they receive on various problems, rate that on vocational problems as least effective. It may be seriously questioned whether or not the help in this area is least effective or whether the pressure of vocational problems is so insistent that students feel deeply concerned about them irrespective of the type of counseling they receive. The North Central Association accreditation studies reveal that the better institutions generally have superior cumulative records, reports and testing programs. They fail to find a predominance of either the faculty advisory or the central staff organization in the superior institutions.

Trends and Conclusions

It is encouraging that an increasing number of colleges and universities are providing for vocational counseling. There is a tendency away from the traditional dean-of-men and dean-of-women organization of personnel service toward a coordinated program under the direction of a dean of students or a director of personnel with various specialists providing vocational counseling. At the same time, there is an attempt to draw more of the faculty into counseling activities under the direction of a staff of experts in order to overcome the weaknesses inherent in both the faculty advisory and the central staff systems. In-service education of faculty members in counseling procedures is beginning to be provided.

Vocational counseling is properly coming to be considered as integral to the total collegiate program with recognition of the fact that problems in this area cannot be considered apart from those in the emotional, social and academic realms. Nevertheless, at the present time, it must be concluded that for most under-graduates, in both colleges and universities, vocational problems, even though they are among the most insistent and perhaps the easiest types upon which to advise, are being dealt with rather ineffectively.

The influx of students, many of whom are veterans of World War II, to campuses is forcing a recognition of the need for wise vocational decision, and vocational advisement units are being established. While funds from the United States Veterans Administration have been widely drawn upon, it is to be anticipated that these services will become locally supported as an integral part of the collegiate program. Many of these schemes follow a rather rigid outline. It is hoped that it will be recognized that students change during their college careers, that the occupational outlook is variable, and that the older idea of trying to fit each peg into an allotted hole is inappropriate. Flexibility of plans and programs is necessary if students are to be adjustable and prepared to cope with the demands of a swiftly-moving age.

References:

1. Bingham, W. V. and Moore, B. V. *How to interview.* New York: Harpers, 1934.
2. Blaesser, W. W., Chairman. Student personnel work in the post-war college. *American Council on Education Studies,* Series VI, Student Personnel Work, Number 2, Volume III, April 1939.
3. Gardner, D. H. V. Student personnel service. *The evaluation of higher institutions.* Chicago: University of Chicago Press, 1937.
4. Cowley, W. H., Hoppock, R. and Williamson, E. G. Occupational orientation of college students. *American Council on Education Studies,* Series VI, Student Personnel Work, Number 2, Volume III, April 1939.
5. Hawkes, H. E., Chairman. *Measurement and guidance of college students.* Washington: American Council on Education, 1933.
6. Maverick, L. A. *The vocational guidance of college students.* Cambridge: Harvard University Press, 1926.
7. Sparling, E. J. Do college students choose vocations wisely? Teachers College, Columbia University, *Contributions to Education, No. 639,* 1935.
8. Threlkeld, H. The educational and vocational plans of college seniors. Teachers College, Columbia University, *Contributions to Education, No. 639,* 1935.
9. Williamson, E. G. and Sarbin, T. R. *Student personnel work in the University of Minnesota.* Minneapolis: Burgess Publishing Co., 1940.
10. Wrenn, C. G. and Bell, R. *Student personnel problems.* New York: Farrar and Rinehart, Inc., 1942.

R. N. B.

VOCATIONAL SERVICE FOR JUNIORS. Incorporated under the laws of the State of New York as a philanthropic organization, Vocational Service for Juniors is directed by a Board of Managers and an Advisory Board drawn from the ranks of business, education, labor, the professions and interested laymen. It supplies information regarding training opportunities and seeks to further a satisfactory adjustment between the interests and abilities of young people and the requirements of their vocational work. For further information, address Vocational Service for Juniors, 95 Madison Avenue, New York, N. Y.

Reference:

1. Vocational Service for Juniors. *Directory of opportunities for vocational training in New York City.* New York: Vocational Service for Juniors, 1943.

R. Z. K.

VOCABULARY TESTS
Schrammel-Wharton Vocabulary Test

General Statement

The Schrammel-Wharton Vocabulary Test is a survey achievement test for use in measuring the vocabulary efficiency of high school and college students. Since scholastic success depends to a large extent on adequacy of vocabulary this test may be profitably used, along with other measuring instruments, for determining scholastic aptitude, or for diagnosing scholastic weaknesses.

The authors of the test are H. E. Schrammel, Director, Bureau of Educational Measurements, and La Verna P. Wharton, formerly Test Technician, Bureau of Educational Measurements, Kansas State Teachers College. The publisher of the test is the Bureau of Educational Measurements, Teachers College, Emporia, Kansas.

Validity

This test consists of two equivalent forms, A and B. The words comprising the test were selected from the Pressey Lists of basic vocabulary in a large number of high school subject fields, and other supplementary lists. An attempt was made to select words from the various fields in the same proportion as they appear in these lists. All words were checked against the Thorndike Word lists in order to insure an equitable distribution according to difficulty and frequency of use.

After the preliminary forms of the tests were constructed they were administered to a number of classes and studies of responses were made in order to detect weaknesses and needed modifications. For all items more responses were provided in the preliminary forms than appear on the final test. This made it possible to eliminate the less desirable ones. The final forms were used in the 1938 Nation-Wide Every Pupil Tests of January and April.

Reliability

This test processes high reliability and correlations between scores and later academic success yield significantly high coefficients. Both forms of the test were administered to a class of 72 unselected college juniors and seniors. The distribution of scores yielded a reliability coefficient of .85 ± .02, and the P. E. of scores was 2.61.

Both forms of the test were also administered to 61 college freshmen. The distribution of scores from this group yielded a reliability coefficient of .94 ± .01, and the P. E. of scores was 1.62. Form A was also administered to 100 college freshmen. By the split-half method of computation these scores yielded a reliability coefficient of .90 ± .01, and a P. E. of scores of 2.13.

Administering, Scoring, and Interpreting

This test is practically self-administering. The time limit is 40 minutes, but most students finish in much less time so that it really is a work-limit test. Scoring is entirely objective and can be accomplished in about one minute per paper. The scores are interpreted by use of percentile norms for each grade, VII to XII and college freshmen, both for mid-year and end-of-year testing.

Use of Test Results

It is suggested that the test results may be profitably used in a number of ways: for determining pupil achievement; for checking the efficiency of instruction; for analyzing pupil and class weaknesses; and for motivating pupil efforts.

Reference:

1. 1940 Mental Measurements Year Book, p. 142.

H. E. S.

O'Connor English Vocabulary Test. The Human Engineering Laboratory (Johnson O'Connor Research Foundation) has found that a measure of English vocabulary is essential in vocational guidance.

While vocabulary seems to have little in common with the inherent aptitudes now measurable in the Laboratory, research indicates that there is a pronounced relationship between an individual's vocabulary and his possibilities for success in a vast majority of occupations and professions. (Books 1, 2, 4, 6, Technical Reports 2, 8, 90, 102) For example, in typical industrial companies which the laboratory has studied, those in charge, from the president down to the lead men, have much the same inherent aptitudes. They differ mainly in vocabulary. Each executive scores higher than the average of the group he supervises.

Also, laboratory researches have repeatedly shown that there is a pronounced relationship between vocabulary and school success. (Books 6. Technical Reports 1, 2, 4, 17.) In this same connection, the acquirement of general English vocabulary facilitates the acquirement of the technical vocabulary necessary to success in most fields. (Books 1, 2, 6.)

The vocabulary tests constructed by the Human Engineering Laboratory have been designed to apply to three general levels of word knowledge; these levels fall into ranges roughly classifiable by school year and age. (See Vocabulary Test Forms.)

Although the vocabulary tests can be given to a group, whenever circumstances allow it, individual administration is recommended. Individual administration is essential for children of thirteen or under.

Since a vocabulary test which requires the taking of 150 words is long, and yet an attempt at that many words is necessary for accuracy, the laboratory has arranged the words in order of difficulty. The difficulty of each word has been determined by a statistical study of the number of persons missing it. The words have then been arranged in ascending order of difficulty, words from group one being the easiest, and words from group ten, the hardest.

With the words arranged in this manner, it is possible to confine the examinee's work on the test to groups neither too easy nor too difficult, so as to get a meaningful sample of his vocabulary. The only remaining problem is to determine at which level he is to start. This level the administrator can find approximately by the use of the introductions, which consist of one-word samplings of the level of difficulty of each group in the test.

It is essential that the vocabulary test be selected and the administration handled by a trained examiner who has studied *Administration of Vocabulary Tests* (Books, 6), which also includes interpretation of the results and norms.

Laboratory research shows that the rate of increase in vocabulary can be speeded up by the conscious effort of the individual, and the speeding up brings with it a parallel acceleration of improvement in his general work. (Books, 1, 2, 3.)

Because of this, the laboratory has found it important not only to measure vocabulary accurately, but also to find ways for building it. Thus far, five rules for learning vocabulary are known. (Books 1, 2, 3, 6.) In this connection, the laboratory offers the *Johnson O'Connor English Vocabulary Builder,* in which the laboratory lists 1100 words in the order in which they should be learned by one desirous of speedy acquisition of vocabulary.

Vocabulary Test Forms

Applicable fifth grade to second year high school.
> Junior English Vocabulary, Worksample 176, Form AC
> Junior English Vocabulary, Worksample 176, Form BA

Applicable first year high school through college.

> English Vocabulary, Worksample 95, Form AD
> English Vocabulary, Worksample 95, Form BC
> English Vocabulary, Worksample 95, Form CC
> English Vocabulary, Worksample 95, Form DB
> English Vocabulary, Worksample 95, Form EB

All of these may be obtained through the Human Engineering Laboratory Incorporated, 347 Beacon Street, Boston 16, Massachusetts.

References:

BOOKS

1. O'Connor, J. *Ideaphoria.* Human Engineering Laboratory, 1944.
2. ———. *Too Many Aptitude Woman.* Human Engineering Laboratory, 1941.
3. ———. *English Vocabulary Builder.* Human Engineering Laboratory, 1937.
4. ———. *Psychometrics.* Harvard University Press, 1934.
5. ———. *Born That Way.* Williams and Wilkins, 1928.
6. ———. Administration of Vocabulary Tests. Human Engineering Laboratory, 1929.

TECHNICAL REPORTS

Number   English Vocabulary
5. *First Revision of Form E of the English Vocabulary Test,* Worksample 95 (1935).

11. Filley, Mary E. *Construction of the English Vocabulary,* Worksample 95, Form DB (1939).

33. Alfano, Marie V. *English Vocabulary Distributions for Twenty-nine Secondary Schools.* Worksample 95, Form EA (1939).

35. ———. *Variation of Vocabulary Scores with Age and Schooling.* Worksample 95 (1939).

36. ———. *Variation of Vocabulary Scores with Age, Sex, and Schooling.* Worksample 176 (1939).

72. Sidserf, Edward H. *Index to Test Words of Vocabulary Worksamples* (1940).

73. Filley, Mary E. *Test Words and Mislead Classifications of Vocabulary Forms G, H, I.* Worksample 95 (1940).

84. Sidserf, E. H. Report I—*The 95 EA Scale and the General Scale for the English Vocabulary Tests;* Report II—*Relation between Recognition and Active Vocabularies.* (1941).

93. McLanathan, F. L. *Learning Process in English Vocabulary as shown by Words of Similar Sound.* (1941)—Vol. I.

94. ———. *Learning Process in Vocabulary shown in Opposite and Malapropistic Misleads* (1942)—Vol. II.

95. ———. *A Graphical Analysis of English Vocabulary.* Worksample 95, Form D. (1943).

VALIDATION

1. Characteristics of Graduate Nurses (1934).

2. The English Vocabulary Scores of 75 Executives (1935) (out of print).

4. Comparative Scores of Two Groups of Graduate Nurses (1935) (out of print).

8. A Two-Year Follow-up of Student Nurses (1936).

17. First Analysis of the Traits of Fifty-six Secondary School Boys (1937).

27. Ferry, M. E. Preliminary Study of 20 Problem Students (1938).

46. Horton, S. P. Relationships Among Nineteen Group Tests and Their Validity for Freshmen Engineering Marks (1939).

90. Seeley, L. C. An Analysis of the Worksample Scores of 101 High-School Teachers (1941).

101. ———. Analysis of the Worksample Scores of 109 Engineers (1942).

102. Luqueer, M. O. Preliminary Study of the Relationship of Test Scores to Success or Failure in School (1942).

107. Horton, Samuel P. Report to the U. S. War Department on Tests for Trainability in the War Industries Training School (1942).

K. M.

VOCATIONAL EDUCATION. Vocational Education is that education which prepares directly for entrance into a specific occupation or which increases the proficiency of workers in their present occupation. According to the popular conception, the term vocational education applies only to preparation for the skilled trades and for other occupations for which college training is not required. This narrow conception of vocational education is erroneous, as the education given in a medical school or a law school is as truly vocational as the education given in a trade school. Actually, the term vocational education covers a very broad field. Any course, whether offered by a public or a private school which prepares directly for entrance into any of the thousands of different occupations or which increases the proficiency of workers already in any of these occupations, is vocational education. In this article, however, especial emphasis will be given to the fields of vocational education in which college training is not required.

History

Vocational education is a prerequisite for even the crudest type of civilization. In order for mankind to progress, it must be possible for one generation to pass on to the next the skills and knowledge necessary for survival and for the gradual transformation of man's environment. At first, such skills and knowledge were acquired informally, but very early in the history of man there must have been attempts to teach the vocational skills in an organized manner. The Babylonian Code of Hammurabi (B.C. 2200 or earlier) contained sections regulating a type of apprenticeship which was evidently already in existence at that time. Before the Christian era indentures or written apprenticeship contracts were used to bind the agreements between master and apprentice. A number of such manuscripts have been preserved intact until the present time.

This institution of apprenticeship, by which the learner or apprentice agreed to work for the master for a period of years and the master agreed to teach the apprentice an occupation, was the only type of vocational education for most occupations from the dawn of civilization until the beginning of the industrial revolution.

The introduction of machinery and the assembling of large numbers of workers in factories led to the breakdown of those trades which were involved in factory production. Employers hired unskilled children who in a few weeks were able to learn specialized skills representing fractional parts of a trade. By means of this subdivision of labor, employers were able to substitute semi-skilled child labor for the all-round skill of the journeyman. These semi-skilled youths were often incorrectly called apprentices even though the employer had no intention of teaching them all the skills of the trade.

In the United States, the industrial revolution started later than in England, but by the beginning of the nineteenth century textile production was being rapidly converted to a factory basis. During this century the production of more and more types of goods was placed on a factory basis. Wherever this occurred the subdivision of labor resulted in the substitution of semi-skilled workers for the skilled journeymen formerly employed. Under the factory system the employer saw little need of training journeymen skilled in all phases of the trade, and consequently the number of true apprentices continued to decline.

But the institution of apprenticeship has never entirely disappeared. Certain trades, among them the building trades, have not yet been taken over by the factory system and even in the factory organization certain skilled trades are required for the making of tools and dies and for maintenance of plant and equipment. For such trades, apprenticeship is still recognized as a desirable method of training future craftsmen. A Federal Committee on Apprenticeship, established in 1937, has set up certain approved standards and is attempting to revive apprenticeship by a program acceptable to both labor and employer.

The industrial revolution with the subdivision of labor and the substitution of semi-skilled child labor for skilled journeyman labor was one of the causes of the growth of trade unionism. Trade unions from their early beginnings attempted to restrict the number of apprentices an employer might hire. Employers fought these restrictions and in some cases set up schools for training so-called apprentices. In general, these employer-sponsored schools trained workers only in limited phases of a trade and did not turn out all-round skilled mechanics. As a result, few skilled workers were trained, and by the end of the nineteenth century it became evident to labor leaders as well as employers that a shortage of skilled labor was imminent unless immediate steps were taken for the thorough training of all-round skilled workers in the various trades.

To remedy this condition some of the larger corporations set up true apprentice training programs. Some of the earliest of these company-controlled programs were: Hoe and Co. 1872, Westinghouse Machine Co. 1888, Baldwin Locomotive Co. 1901, and General Electric Co. also started in 1901.

Labor leaders, suspicious of company-owned schools, began to advocate trade training as a part of our public school program. In 1911, the American Federation of Labor, at its annual convention, adopted a committee report recommending a program of vocational education under public supervision and control.

The recommendations contained in this report were very specific. Ten clear-cut, brief statements described the type of program desired by the Federation. It is interesting to note that these recommendations were followed with practically no change, when Congress finally, in 1917, through the Smith-Hughes Act provided funds for the promotion of vocational education as a part of our public school system.

The history of vocational education as so far described in this article may seem to be confined to trade education only. To clear up any possible misunderstanding, it should be pointed out that in the early days, practically all occupations, professional as well as industrial, business and agriculture, were entered by the path of apprenticeship. In certain occupations, however, which required the learning of many facts and principles, there was a tendency to set up formal schools for the teaching of such knowledge. Probably the first of such schools were for the preparation of priests. Schools for the training of priests are known to have existed among the ancient Egyptians and the Hebrews. The early universities of medieval Europe established schools for medicine and law as well as theology. These three occupations were the first to be recognized as "professions" requiring a "higher" education in college or university. As scientific knowledge has increased, its application to other occupations has become evident and additional occupations (teaching, engineering, etc.) have been raised to the rank of professions requiring college training.

The Manual Training which was introduced into the public schools of the United States about 1880 was primarily thought of as general education, but there were many who believed that manual training was of value in preparing workers for the skilled trades. Very early in the twentieth century, however, it became evident that manual training was contributing very little to trade training and a small group of school men associated with representatives of a few of the larger and more progressive industrial organizations began to advocate specific trade training as a responsibility of our public schools. These leaders organized the National Society for the Promotion of Industrial Education in 1906, which was later to develop into the present American Vocational Association. In 1907, Charles R. Richards, secretary of this society, addressed the convention of the American Federation of Labor, requesting the support of organized labor. The action of the A. F. of L. at its 1911 convention, giving full support to this movement, presented for the first time a united front of school men, employers and union labor in a drive for trade training in our public schools.

Federal Aid

Long before the beginning of this concerted drive for trade training in our public schools a precedent for federal aid to vocational education had already been established. The Morrill Acts of 1862 and 1890 established the Land Grant Colleges and provided federal aid for instruction in "agriculture" and the "mechanic arts." This, it should be noted, was on the college level and resulted in the development of college courses in agriculture and engineering.

The movement for trade training in our public schools as sponsored by the National Society for the Promotion of Industrial Education and the American Federation of Labor, advocated federal aid at the secondary school level. The desired legislation took the form of the Smith-Hughes Act of 1917. This act provided federal aid for the promotion of vocational education "of less than college grade" in the fields of agriculture, homemaking and "trades and industry." This aid was in the form of reimbursement for one-half the teacher's salary provided certain standards set by the act were observed. The instruction must be under public supervision or control, and designed to meet the needs of persons over fourteen years of age in order to fit them for useful employment.

Three types of classes were provided for: the full-time day class designed to prepare boys and girls still in school for entrance into specific occupations; the part-time class designed to provide either vocational or civic training for a minimum of four hours each week to working boys and girls; and the evening class designed to increase the vocational proficiency of workers already established in some occupation. The minimum age for evening school pupils was set at 16 years.

The act provides that all-day students in the agricultural courses must engage in supervised practice in agriculture on a farm for at least six months each year. All-day students in trades and industry courses must spend at least half of their instruction time, or a minimum of three hours each day, on "practical work on a useful or productive basis." The act also provides that at least one-third of the amount appropriated to each state for salaries of trade and industrial teachers, if expended, must be spent for part-time classes for working boys and girls.

Under the stimulus of federal aid, enrollment in these public school vocational classes increased from 164,000 for the year ending June 30, 1918 to 1,497,000 for the year ending June 30, 1937. In 1936 the George-Deen Act was passed, which provided additional annual funds for the original three fields of agriculture, home economics, and trades and industry, and also provided funds for a fourth field, distributive occupations. Aid in the distributive field is limited to part-time and evening classes only and distributive occupations are defined as those followed by workers directly engaged in merchandising activities, or in direct contact with buyers and sellers.

Enrollment in these federally-aided vocational classes continued to increase after 1937 and reached a peak of 2,630,000 in the year ending June 30, 1942. Enrollment in this year was divided as follows abong the four fields: agricultural 610,000; trade and industrial 851,000; home economics 954,000; distributive 215,000. As to types of classes, this enrollment was divided as follows: evening classes 803,000; part-time classes 622,000; all-day classes 1,205,000.

Although the federally-aided vocational programs of the three fields of agriculture, homemaking and trades and industry were established by the same legislation and have been administered by the same agency, nevertheless, there are significant differences among these programs. The agricultural and the homemaking programs have many points of similarity, but these two programs differ in many ways from the trades and industry program.

Students enrolled in the all-day classes of the industrial or trades and industry program must attend shop classes for a minimum of three clock hours each day, whereas students enrolled in similar programs in agriculture or homemaking may satisfy the requirements by attending these vocational classes for 1½ clock hours each day. This means that students enrolled in vocational agriculture or homemaking are able to elect a greater number of non-vocational subjects than students enrolled in the industrial program. On the other hand students in agriculture and homemaking are required to carry on certain work projects outside of school hours either on a farm or in the home, while no such outside work is required of the students enrolled in all-day trade classes as provision is made for teaching all the necessary trade knowledge and skills in the school shop.

Teachers of all-day classes in vocational agriculture and homemaking in general are required to have completed a four year college curriculum in agriculture or homemaking which includes certain required courses in education. At least two years experience on a farm after the age of 14 is usually required of vocational agricultural teachers, but after school and summer work on the home farm is often accepted as satisfying this requirement. Practical experience is recognized as valuable for vocational homemaking teachers also, but work in the home is often accepted as providing the necessary experience.

In the field of industrial education the skills to be taught can be acquired only by actual work in the trade. For this reason, trade teachers are required to have had at least two years experience in the trade beyond apprenticeship. Because of the difficulty of finding skilled journeymen who are college graduates, it is common to accept four years, or even less, of high school work as satisfying the requirements for formal education. Courses in teaching methods and other professional courses are often carried to such teachers through extension courses.

In agriculture and homemaking the enrollment in all-day classes is much larger than the total enrollment of both part-time and evening classes. In trades and industry the emphasis is on the part-time and evening classes, with the enrollment in the part-time classes alone greater than the enrollment in the all-day classes.

The field of distributive education, for which no federal funds were provided until the passage of the George-Deen Act in 1936, differs in many ways from the other three federally-aided vocational fields. This program contains no all-day classes. Practically the whole program is centered around the training of adult workers already employed in distributive occupations. In the year ending June 30, 1943, over 100,000 such workers were enrolled in short unit courses meeting during working hours and nearly 200,000 were enrolled in similar courses meeting outside of working hours. The only phase of the distributive education program designed to meet the needs of youths of high school age is the cooperative part-time class, enrollment in which is usually limited to high school seniors. High school students who enroll in such classes must be employed in a distributive occupation a minimum of 15 hours per week. Enrollment in such cooperative part-time classes for the year ending June 30, 1943 amounted to 14,500.

War Production Training

In 1940 the stepping-up of production both in industry and on the farm in the interests of national defense disclosed a shortage of trained men. In order to improve this condition, Congress, as an emergency measure, authorized the setting up of a defense training program, and voted funds for carrying it on. This program, later called the war training program, was composed of two parts: courses of college grade and courses of less than college grade. Courses of college grade approved for this program are short engineering courses designed to meet the shortage of engineers, chemists, physicists, and production supervisors in fields essential to the national war effort. This part of the program has come to be known as

ESMWT (Engineering, Science, & Management War Training) and such courses are offered by degree-granting colleges and universities whose educational property is exempt from taxation and by public degree-granting educational institutions.

The less than college grade part of this war training program is composed of two parts: vocational training for war production workers and food production war training. Vocational training for war production workers comprises courses designed to provide training for skilled and semi-skilled industrial occupations essential to the war effort. Under the food production war training program, courses are offered in the production, conservation and processing of farm commodities and in the repair, operation and construction of farm machinery and equipment.

Federal funds provided for the war training program do not require matching by state or local funds, as is the case of funds provided under the Smith-Hughes and George-Deen Acts. Also federal funds for the war training program may be spent not only for teachers' salaries but to a certain extent for rent for additional school shop space and for purchase or rental of additional equipment.

The whole war training program is administered by the United States Commissioner of Education and the classes organized under the less than college grade part of the program are administered on the state level by the individual state boards for vocational education, which, since 1918, have been responsible for such administration of all vocational classes receiving reimbursement under the Smith-Hughes and George-Deen Acts.

It is believed that the war training program deserves much credit for the rapid conversion which industry was able to make from civilian to war products. In the classes training war production workers, the most important phase of the war training program as measured by enrollment, the enrollments amounted to nearly a million for the year ending June 30, 1941, nearly two million for the year ending June 30, 1942, and over two million for the year ending June 30, 1943. Much of this phase of the training was carried on in school shops already in use for Smith-Hughes classes. In fact, this rapid expansion of industrial training would have been impossible without these school shops. Some of these shops during the emergency were in continuous operation for 24 hours a day.

Table I shows the enrollment in each of the three phases of the war training program for the first four years. The ESMWT and the training for war production workers reached peak enrollments the third year, although enrollments in the food production war training continued to increase the fourth year.

TABLE I

New enrollments by fiscal year in each of the three war training programs

	July 1, 1940 to June 30, 1941	July 1, 1941 to June 30, 1942	July 1, 1942 to June 30, 1943	July 1, 1943 to June 30, 1944
ESMWT	121,000	439,000	596,000	412,000
Training for War Production Workers	888,000	1,864,000	2,304,000	1,507,000
Food Production War Training	255,000	410,000	1,030,000	1,341,000

Industrial Arts Education

Industrial arts education is not vocational education, although there is confusion in the minds of many individuals as to the distinction between industrial arts classes and vocational industrial classes. This confusion is due largely to the fact that both types of classes are conducted in school shops equipped with machinery and tools such as are used in industry. In fact, both types of classes are sometimes conducted in the same shop and use the same equipment although at different hours. The essential difference between these two types of classes is the purpose or aim of the course. The aim of the vocational-industrial or trade class is to prepare for entrance into a specific industrial occupation or trade. The industrial-arts class, on the other hand, is an integral part of general education, and its purpose, stated in broad terms, is to give the student an intelligent understanding of the present industrial environment. Courses in industrial arts are sometimes organized with especial emphasis on one or more of the following specific objectives: (1) to make more intelligent consumers of industrial products, (2) to teach such elementary tool skills and knowledge of industrial materials and products as should prove of value to most individuals regardless of future vocation, (3) to aid in intelligent choice of future occupation.

Because of the difference in aim, there are necessarily differences in the conditions under which these two types of classes are conducted. Each member of a vocational industrial class has already chosen a specific industrial occupation as his future vocation. Members of industrial arts classes have not made this choice and may have no intention of choosing any industrial occupation for a vocation. Class hours for vocational industrial classes are usually 15 hours each week, whereas the industrial arts classes are usually scheduled for from 2 to 7½ hours per week. Vocational industrial classes are planned to give individual members intensive training in a single occupation. Industrial arts classes are planned to give individual members experiences in as wide a range of industrial fields as possible with emphasis on the skills and knowledge which are likely to prove of value to the individual regardless of future occupation.

Although industrial arts classes are an integral part of general education, and should be clearly distinguished from vocational industrial classes, nevertheless, an industrial arts program provides a most valuable foundation on which to build a vocational industrial program. A good industrial arts program not only assists pupils to make an intelligent choice of their future industrial vocation, but it provides a broad knowledge and understanding of the present industrial environment which should prove of great value to all industrial workers, regardless of their specific trades. Industrial arts classes may be offered anywhere in the school program, but are most commonly organized for pupils 12 to 16 years of age inclusive. Vocational industrial classes should be limited to those who have chosen as their future vocation the occupation for which training is given, and who will be qualified to enter that occupation upon the completion of their training. Therefore, vocational industrial classes are planned for the last few years of the students' school life.

The above discussion has been confined to the industrial field, but the same relationship exists in other occupational fields—in agriculture, home economics and the distributive occupations for example. Thus there are two types of courses in each of these fields; vocational agricultural courses, and agricultural arts courses; vocational home economics courses and home economics arts courses, for example. The term "practical arts" is used as a general term to include general education courses in the fields of trades and industry, agriculture, home economics, distributive occupations, and similar occupational fields. For example, industrial arts and agricultural arts are two of the practical arts fields.

Attitude of Labor Toward Vocational Education

Since the beginnings of labor organizations in this country in the early part of the nineteenth century, labor has consistently advocated free public education. About a century later, after many years of hostility toward privately financed vocational industrial schools, the American Federation of Labor voted to support vocational education as an integral part of our free public school education, and used its influence to secure the passage of the Smith-Hughes Act.

In general, labor has been well pleased with the results of this federal aid for vocational education of less than college grade. The part-time classes and the evening classes, because they are designed to improve the efficiency of individuals already working in some occupation, have the hearty approval of organized labor. The full-time trade-preparatory classes, however, have been the subject of occasional criticism. Analysis of such criticisms reveals two common fears; first, that an over-supply of workers may be trained in certain trades and second, that the goods or services produced by these classes may be sold in the open market and reduce the work opportunities of union members. Organized labor recognizes that no effective training is possible except through the production of marketable goods, but labor would like to have a voice in determining how such products can be disposed of with the least disturbance to commercial markets. Probably all criticism would cease if local advisory councils consisting of equal representation from labor and management were set up wherever full-time trade classes are established. Such advisory councils are advocated by organized labor and recommended by the U. S. Office of Education.

Relation of Vocational Education to Vocational Guidance

Vocational education and vocational guidance are very closely linked to each other and were introduced into our schools at approximately the same time as part of a common movement to make the education of our schools more "practical" and to introduce the "life career motive." No vocational training can be effective unless each student before starting his training has been helped, through some form of vocational guidance, to make an intelligent choice of his future vocation. Also every student receiving vocational training in our public schools should be helped to secure a work opportunity in the occupation for which he has been trained and should be followed up and helped to adjust and to advance in that occupation. This is not only for the benefit of the student, but also as a check on the efficiency of the training program and as a means of keeping the program in line with present needs.

The Report of the Massachusetts Commission on Industrial and Technical Education (1906) is often credited with initiating the beginnings of our present vocational education movement. This report also mentions some of the problems of vocational guidance, referring to the problem of "the choice of a vocation for which the child is fitted."

The report of the Committee of the American Federation of Labor (1911) which endorsed vocational education, also contained an endorsement of vocational guidance: "A system of vocational guidance should be established to determine the child's aptitudes."

But in spite of the need for coordination between these two movements, there was a period when there seemed to be a tendency for them to grow apart. The Smith-Hughes Act contained no reference to vocational guidance and the National Vocational Guidance Association holds its annual convention at the same city and just prior to the National Education Association Convention, rather than at the time and place of the American Vocational Association Convention.

Recently, however, there are signs of a reversal of this tendency. In 1938 the U. S. Commissioner of Education interpreted the George-Deen Act as authorizing the expenditure of federal funds for State Supervisors of Occupational Information and Guidance, although this act makes no specific reference to vocational guidance. By May, 1944 thirty-two states had appointed such supervisors and there is evidence to indicate that these supervisors working through the local schools have been effective in securing closer coordination between vocational guidance and vocational education.

References:

1. American Federation of Labor. *Guide for vocational education.* Washington, D. C.: American Federation of Labor, 1938.
2. ———. *Reports of the Executive Council of the American Federation of Labor to the annual conventions.* Washington: American Federation of Labor.
3. Lee, E. A. *Objectives and problems of vocational education.* New York: McGraw-Hill Book Co. Inc., 1938.
4. U. S. Office of Education. *Digests of annual reports of State Boards for Vocational Education.* Washington: U. S. Government Printing Office.
5. ———. *Statement of policies for the administration of vocational education, Vocational Education Bulletin No. 1.* Washington: U. S. Government Printing Office, 1937.
6. *Report of the Massachussetts Commission on Industrial and Technical Education.* New York: Teachers College, Columbia University, 1906.

A. F. D.

VOCATIONAL HIGH SCHOOLS. "A vocation means nothing but such a direction of life's activities as renders them perceptibly significant to a person, because of the consequences they accomplish, and also to his associates. . . . An occupation is the only thing which balances the distinctive capacity of an individual with his social service. . . . An occupation is a continuous activity having a purpose. Education *through* occupation consequently combines within itself more of the factors conducive to learning than any other method." [2] It is this continuity, this purpose, that makes vocational *guidance* so necessary and so fruitful in a program of vocational *education.* The very factors that are so conducive to learning are equally conducive to orientation. For the subject matter and skill taught in a vocational school provide experiences closely paralleling those in adult life. They are the realities out of which valid decisions are made.

While the pupil often, though not always, enters the vocational school with a fixed vocational objective in view, he changes his views and his purposes as he grows older, and there is no such period for change as that of adolescence. So guidance is an important phase of the vocational school program.

Obviously, the guidance program in a school on any level can be effective only as it is integrated with the programs for schools on other levels. The school systems must be organized for continuity. It is especially important that all those orientation devices used in the elementary and junior high schools to help the pupil to select his high school course should be effective. The success of both teaching and guidance in the vocational high school is dependent upon the success of the guidance program in the schools from which the pupils come.

In one sense, it may be said that the guidance program in a vocational high school is no different from that in any other type of high school. However, the modifications and emphases in the vocational high school are so marked that they produce almost another kind of guidance. The following paragraphs are an attempt to make clear just what these variations and deviations are.

The avowed purpose of vocational education makes it imperative that the new pupil shall be assigned to the course that will best train him for success in the occupation he will enter after graduation. Therefore the admission, placement, and follow-up services must be effectively rendered. Cooperative liaison with the source schools, coordination with the employers, and repeated contact with industry for several years after graduation, are indicated as special tasks of the vocational high school guidance program.

For many adults, certainly in the earlier years, all employment is tryout. People feel their way into vocations. Sometimes the process is happily brief, at other times it goes on for years. So, occupations in the vocational high school, although organized primarily for instruction, always have tryout value. The pupil learns to like or dislike a trade. The teacher observes the pupil's success and failures, and counsels accordingly. But this is not enough. Positive, analytical approaches must be made to discover the pupil's adaptability to his chosen work. Tests of all kinds must be given, but especially those that reveal aptitude, personality, and physique. Bodily characteristics that, at home or in an academic school, may be only objects of tender sympathy, in the vocational high school become conditions of success or failure in particular occupations. Defective color vision, flat feet, vertigo, allergies, to mention only a few, are specific data for orientation.

The "whole child" and "continuity of personality" are pedagogical commonplaces. However, they are more often mentioned than managed. The most effective device is the permanent advisory system. (q.v.) Briefly, it provides for the assignment, upon admission, of a pupil to an advisor (sponsor, section officer, home room teacher) whom he retains as his personal counselor throughout his school career. He meets this teacher every day during a home room period. The teacher is responsible for him as a person and a pupil, in all his school and home relationships. He is in loco parentis. The teacher gets expert advice from the psychologist, the physician, the principal, from any one who has the knowledge, but, as an advisor to the pupil, he is responsible for the pupil's whole life during his entire stay in school.

To aid in this continuous sponsorship, the advisor keeps the pupil's accounts in the cumulative record, for the cumulative record with all its authorizations and visas, is the pupil's passport to all the new domains of knowledge and experience that he will explore.

In academic high school occupational information is taught for guidance purposes. In vocational high school it is taught primarily as preparation for a vocation. However, in view of what has been said about changing adolescent interests, such information should have particularly useful guidance value.

Since the vocational high school is a school with a purpose, this must be very clear in the minds of both the pupil and the teacher. Such clarification appears automatically in "graduation requirements." If the pupil can be recommended for a type of full-time employment which will permit self-support, the school should also be able to certify to a well-rounded general education, special abilities gained through out-of-school experiences, favorable personal traits, sound physical development, general intelligence, persistence, and so on. These traits should be guiding stars by which the pupil may orient himself throughout his school career.

The vocational high school is especially responsible for flexibility of programming so that the individual may receive the instruction for which he is best fitted. It is such flexibility that makes it possible to put into operation the good counsel resulting from the guidance program. Practical implementation of good advice is as important here as in all other phases of life.

As in all other fields, the function of research in vocational guidance is to make better guidance possible. In the vocational high school, in additional to the usual school services, research must range over the whole field of industry and commerce and, ideally, must answer all the questions about the adaptation of the individual to life. Specifically, it will tend to make all of the foregoing services more effective and, naturally, will lead to better teaching. Thus may vocational guidance be ever renewing itself and better serving the boys and girls who come under its influence.

References:

1. Bingham, W. V. *Aptitudes and aptitude testing.* New York: Harper & Bros., 1937.
2. Dewey, J. *Education and democracy.* New York: Macmillan, 1916, pp. 358–361.
3. Hoppock, R. and Luloff, N. Chapter on Vocational Guidance in *Vocational Education, Forty-Second Yearbook* of the National Society for the Study of Education. Chicago: Department of Education, University of Chicago, 1943.
4. Keller, F. J. and Viteles, M. S., *Vocational guidance throughout the world.* New York: W. W. Norton, 1937.
5. Kitson, H. D. Chapter on Trends in vocational guidance, in Prosser and Allen's *Vocational education in a democracy.* New York: D. Appleton-Century Co., 1945.
6. National Society for the Study of Education. *Guidance in educational institutions, Thirty-seventh yearbook,* Part I. Bloomington: Public School Publishing Co., 1938.
7. Snedden, D. *Vocational education.* New York: Macmillan Co., 1920.

F. J. K.

W

WESTERN PERSONNEL INSTITUTE. Western Personnel Institute, unique in the educational personnel field, is a non-profit cooperative research association maintained by and for colleges and universities in the eleven western states. It serves as a regional clearing house of information useful to personnel workers and to students in its member colleges. It reports on developments in methods of student personnel work and on information and trends in occupations of interest to college students.

Growing out of a need felt in 1930 by a small group of western colleges for a central research agency to assist them with their student personnel problems, Western Personnel Service developed into an incorporated association supported by institutional memberships, individual sponsor memberships and special grants.

Western Personnel Service is the only regional organization west of the Mississippi which is affiliated with the national Council of Guidance and Personnel Associations and the American Council on Education. Its research is carried on under the direction of an Academic Council, made up of faculty representatives appointed by the presidents of its member institutions.

In servicing its member institutions through an over-all program of research, Western Personnel Service

> *Studies* national and regional trends in education, agriculture, business, industry and the professions;
> *Collects and Evaluates* data on occupational changes, training requirements and opportunities and methods of student personnel work;
> *Classifies and files* data for resource material in counseling students;
> *Maintains* a clearing house for all this information for use of the colleges, with a larger and better selected library than individual institutions can afford;
> *Plans* with the Academic Council how information can be used effectively on campus through improved student personnel programs, better student counseling and curriculum changes.

All these regular procedures are basic to the publications issued by Western Personnel Service, to special research and service projects, to consultation work, and to an in-service training program. A continuous flow of information is provided from Western Personnel Service to its member colleges through the following publications: "Tomorrow's Job" (Bulletin of Occupational News), Occupational Briefs, Occupational Reading Guides, Personnel Methods Bulletins, Personnel Methods Reading Guides, and Special Bulletins.

The occupational research service provides original studies of selected occupations with special attention to western states, up-to-date information on changing occupational trends, evaluation and selective distribution of occupational information issued in book or pamphlet form, and evaluation and selective distribution of governmental findings and statistics. Personnel methods bulletins include reports of regional and national meetings, student personnel plans and programs of other colleges, summaries and reprints of technical and professional articles, tests and measurements (their developments and dangers), and information about other phases of student personnel work. Special services to colleges include consultant work, field work on campuses, special technical studies made at the request of individual colleges, conferences, and occasional institutes.

In 1939 an in-service training program in advanced personnel work was started at Western Personnel Service whereby one or two graduates of member institutions were selected each year to serve a ten months interneship period in the headquarters office. Special fellowships or grants-in-aid are available for this work. The training course provides a general overview of the field of personnel work in education, industry and government. It is planned toward the maximum development of each student, and insofar as possible the work of each trainee is adapted to his special interests in a particular phase of personnel work. Experience is given through study and reading in literature and techniques of personnel work; supervised work in student personnel methods research and occupational research, including library research, field investigation, interviews, writing for Western Personnel Service publications, and classification of materials; practice in office procedures; and individual projects at WPS headquarters or in other personnel offices in education, industry or government.

During the war special projects have been developed for college students in the armed forces, and now Western Personnel Service is helping its member institutions plan and enlarge student personnel programs to meet increasing needs of returning service men and women.

W. H.

WILLOUGHBY (Clark-Thurston) **PERSONALITY SCHEDULE.** Measuring neurotic tendencies, the Schedule can be completed by most literate subjects in less than fifteen minutes. Subjects indicate their answers on a five point scale, thus avoiding the negative attitudes engendered by Yes-No inventories. The test is very easy to score, since all that is required is the adding of the circled responses.

Women generally achieve higher neurotic scores than men; percentile tables are presented for both men and women. The percentile tables are based largely on college samples. Reliability of the schedule, as calculated by the split-half method, varies from .82 to .97 in different groups, with an average of .91; test-retest reliability is .89. Willoughby,[3] describing the method of derivation, states that it involved criteria for inclusion of items of discriminatory power, cohesiveness, and correlation with physiological syndromes. Information on the validity of the scale has been published by Bernreuter [1] and Galton.[2]

Persons who achieve very good adjustment scores on the test are thought of as fitted for exasperating human relationships, such as are likely to be encountered by the classroom teacher, the salesman and the business executive. Those with high neuroticism scores have a higher probability of success in research, individual teaching, and creative art. Persons with high neuroticism scores may also be in need of psychiatric treatment. No evidence is presented with regard to the relationship between test scores and occupational success. Scale scores are not related to mental ability.

The test may be purchased from the Psychological Corporation, 522 Fifth Avenue, New York 18, N. Y.

References:

1. Bernreuter, R. G. Journal of Social Psychology, 1934, 5, 184–201.
2. Galton, H. B. Psychological Bulletin, 1936, 33, 620.
3. Willoughby, R. R. Journal of Social Psychology, 1932, 3, 401–424.

R. Z. K.

WOMEN. Like the techniques of any other profession, those of vocational guidance do not vary with the sex of the specialist who employs them nor with that of the individual for whom they function. In this art which is concerned with the best possible occupational adjustment of the individual, particular stress is placed upon individual differences rather than upon group characteristics of sex, nationality, or race. Nevertheless, some programs have been established and a considerable body of occupational literature has been prepared for the particular vocational guidance of girls and women.

The distinct literature may be attributed in part to the marked concentration of most women in a relatively few principal occupations often called "women's occupations." Although this concentration is gradualy being diluted and although some women are engaged in almost every occupation known to man, as recently as 1940 there were only 11 principal occupational groupings reported by the U. S. Census as employing 200,000 or more women as compared with some 40 for men. Special books and pamphlets have also been prompted by the fact that undifferentiated occupational literature has frequently been written with opportunities for men in mind, so that the variations in employment, earnings, advancement, and training likely to be encountered by women in the same fields have not been considered except perhaps in an incidental paragraph or chapter. In any case, numerous occupational pamphlets and books have been written over the years for use in the vocational guidance of women and the current demand indicates their continuing usefulness.

Usually vocational guidance services in the public schools, public employment offices, and other community agencies make no differentiation in services to girls and boys, men and women. However, special group informational conferences may be arranged or special facilities used for one sex group or the other sometimes in cooperation with women's or men's organizations offering to supplement these community services. Where separate programs of vocational guidance for women exist, they have been primarily in schools or agencies which serve only girls or women, such as women's colleges or girls' schools and in women's organizations such as the YWCA. They are a result of circumstance rather than of difference in purpose and employ the customary techniques for vocational guidance which are discussed elsewhere in this volume.

Although efforts to assist girls and women in planning their education and employment have never been confined to a single place nor can be said to have begun at a particular time, the earliest organized attempt in the United States to provide vocational guidance to meet their particular needs was made in Boston. As early as 1906, the Research Department of the Women's Educational and Industrial Union (which since its founding in 1877 had included placement assistance among its activities) recognized the need for information on occupations for trained women other than teaching "since many women who are unfitted for teaching drift into it because it is the vocation with which they are most familiar." Its

296-page book "Vocations for the Trained Women: Opportunities
Other than Teaching" published in 1910 resulted from its first
attempt to meet this need with a series of introductory papers
written by some 80 men and women on 70 occupational fields.
While this material was being prepared, the Union began to register
college seniors for placement and to work directly with the women's
colleges in the Boston area in supplying information and counseling
to students. The reorganization of its Appointment Bureau, later
called the Bureau of Vocational Advice and Appointment, in 1910
recognized this new function in its statement of purpose "to offer
vocational advice to women and to place trained women in positions
other than academic teaching."

Following the pattern of the Boston Bureau, college alumnae in
other cities established similar bureaus such as those in New York
(1911), Philadelphia (1912), Chicago (1913), Los Angeles (1913),
Pittsburgh (1915), and Minneapolis (1917). To coordinate the
work of these bureaus a National Committee of Bureaus of Occupations was organized in 1917. A 1923–24 leaflet of this Committee
outlined the functions of the bureaus as follows:

    I. "They find employment for trained women workers in their
       own localities; . . . exchange information . . . ; pro-
       mote among employers an interest in the desirability of
       trained workers.
   II. They study continuously the work of women in their own
       localities and watch their developing opportunities for
       training and work.
  III. They visit schools and colleges to give vocational advice
       and information to students—prospective workers. They
       offer similar service to great numbers of women who
       call at their offices.
  IV. They seek to open up and develop new lines of work for
       women.
   V. They cooperate . . . with local, State, Federal agencies
       and departments by supplying employment statistics and
       other information concerning their special groups of
       workers, and in other ways."

A number of related organizations were at work, as were these
bureaus, in adding to the information on occupational opportunities for trained women. In 1913, the Association of Collegiate Alumnae (which later became the American Association of University
Women) published a pamphlet which listed "institutions training
educated women for occupations other than teaching." The South-

ern Women's Educational Alliance at Richmond and the Women's Occupational Bureau of Tennessee at Nashville studied women's employment in the South. In 1927, the Alliance published a book on "Occupations for Women" based on studies of women in Atlanta and Richmond. The Bureau of Vocational Information organized in New York City in 1919 as a national organization "to serve as a definite connecting link between the education of women and their vocational activities and to bring about . . . a closer correlation between the two," published a 742-page training directory, a series of occupational studies, and a semi-monthly news bulletin. In 1923, its director reported inquiries from individuals or organizations in 45 States and 13 foreign countries.

Following the discontinuance of the Bureau, work of a similar nature was undertaken by the Institute of Women's Professional Relations. Its first publication in 1929 was a bibliography on "Occupations for College Women." A clip sheet under the title "Women's Work and Education" has been issued quarterly since March 1930. Conferences are sponsored periodically by the Institute for deans of women and personnel officers and other interested persons at which occupational and educational problems of college and professional women are considered.

Conferences at which speakers discuss a number of occupational fields and at which the problems of occupational planning are presented to women students have been employed from the beginning as a part of vocational guidance programs in colleges and secondary schools. The proceedings are often published and added to the literature. In 1913, for example, a bulletin of the University of Wisconsin which presented a set of papers given at its second vocational conference for women was used to answer "repeated requests for information and guidance both from women in the university and from women throughout the State." The need for occupational information was also recognized by the trade schools for girls confronted with the problem of informing pupils and their parents concerning outlets for their graduates and also that of adapting courses to current needs. A full-time vocational assistant to study occupations and counsel with girls and parents was appointed in the Girls' Trade School in Boston as early as 1910.

Special literature for girls appeared at the start, as vocational guidance services developed for pupils in the public schools in a number of cities and for those who left school to go to work. In Boston, for example, the series of pamphlets published by the Vocation Bureau on "Vocations for Boston Boys" was supplemented by a similar series on "Vocations for Boston Girls" prepared by the

Girls' Trade Education League, which not only engaged in research but also conducted a vocation office to help girls decide upon the particular work for which they were best fitted, to place them and follow them up. Telephone operating, bookbinding, dressmaking, stenography and typewriting, and nursing were among the occupations included in this series. Industrial studies by such organizations as the Women's Educational and Industrial Union of Boston and Russell Sage Foundation in New York added to the early literature of this type, used by schools, employment bureaus, and others in giving vocational guidance. "Women in the Bookbinding Trades" (1913) published by the Foundation and "The Boot and Shoe Industry in Massachusetts as a Vocation for Women" (1915) prepared by the Union and published by the U. S. Department of Labor are examples of these early studies.

The Federal Government had become interested in the vocational guidance movement even before World War I. In 1911, a chapter of the 25th annual report of the Commissioner of Labor was devoted to the subject. But the war resulted in the establishment in 1918 of a Woman in Industry Service to advise the Secretary of Labor on all matters affecting the employment of women. In 1920, this temporary service was succeeded by the Women's Bureau, established as a permanent agency in the U. S. Department of Labor. In carrying out one of its functions "to advance the opportunities of women for profitable employment," the Bureau has over the years published information on industries and occupations in which women are engaged. "The New Position of Women in American Industry" the report of a study directed by the Women's Bureau and financed by the War Work Council of the YWCA, and "Industrial Opportunities and Training for Women and Girls" were among the early bulletins of the Bureau. During World War II, the occupations of women in war industries have been described. The most recent studies along the lines of occupational opportunities being published in 1945 describe the outlook for women in occupations in the medical services. The Bureau of Labor Statistics has also from time to time published statistical reports on the employment of women which combined with the Bureau of the Census statistics given by sex have been used by vocational counselors as a primary source of statistical data on the industrial and occupational distribution of women. The Women's Bureau has summarized these data in periodic reports on the trends in women's employment.

Federal agencies concerned with education and training, like those concerned with employment, took an early interest in vocational guidance. In 1918, the Bureau of Education, then in the De-

partment of Interior, published a bulletin on Vocational Guidance
and the Public Schools. In 1921 and again in 1925, the Federal
Board for Vocational Education (which later became the Vocational
Division of the U. S. Office of Education) published extensive bibliographies on vocational guidance. Separate bibliographies on the
vocational guidance of women have been published by the Vocational Division of the U. S. Office of Education covering the years
since 1925, the latest ones bearing the titles: References and Related Information—Vocational Guidance for Girls and Women
(1941) and Wartime Work for Girls and Women (1944). The
U. S. Civil Service Commission, and the War Manpower Commission, are among other Federal agencies which have issued publications on occupations in which women are employed.

From the beginning, national women's organizations have played
an active part in initiating programs of vocational guidance and in
supplementing and assisting them in a variety of ways. The National
Board of the YWCA cooperated with the Bureau of Vocational
Information in 1919 in publishing "Vocations for Business and Professional Women." A number of local branches of the YWCA provide counseling services with or without placement assistance. For
some time the National Board had a specialist on vocational guidance on its staff to coordinate service in this field and to give
assistance to local branches which conduct vocational conferences
for high school girls and cooperate with the schools in vocational
guidance programs for girls of this age-group.

The interest of the American Association of University Women,
as noted earlier, dates back to the time of its earlier existence as the
Association of Collegiate Alumnae. Many of its local branches carry
on some form of vocational guidance work in cooperation with the
public schools and colleges, usually supplying information or arranging conferences. The National organization has aided local groups
by advising on such activities and has cooperated at the national
level with the American Council on Education, the Women's Institute of Professional Relations, and other groups and agencies in research and informational activities related to occupational opportunities for college women. Mortarboard Fraternity and the Women's
Professional Panhellenic Association are among the many other organizations of college women which have interested themselves in the
vocational guidance of college students and graduates. Since 1938,
the National Association of Deans of Women has published annually
a guidance bibliography which includes a section on vocational
guidance.

Women's service organizations, too, have taken an active part in assisting in the vocational guidance of girls. The first of these, Altrusa International, in 1924, voted to encourage each club to adopt vocational guidance as its general service activity in the community. Its pamphlet "Vocational Guidance at Work" published in 1936 describes the types of projects local groups undertake. Most of the local clubs of Zonta International also engaged in vocational guidance work supplementing the programs of the public schools and other agencies. Quota, Pilot, and the Soroptimist clubs report similar activities on the part of some of their local groups although these activities have not been especially promoted by the national organizations.

The National Federation of Business and Professional Women's Clubs soon after its organization in 1919 became involved in projects related to vocational guidance and over the years has cooperated in and conducted studies of its membership which have contributed to the body of available information on working women. As a result of its experience in administering loans and scholarship funds for girls needing additional preparation before entering business, in 1928 it undertook a 3-year survey of vocational facilities for girls, beginning with a study by local clubs of the vocational literature available in libraries. Cooperation with the public schools was stressed in suggestions to local clubs to participate in supplementing local programs and a vocational kit was prepared for local groups. *Independent Woman,* its periodical, has for some years had a vocational editor who summarizes news of interest in vocational guidance and arranges for occupational articles which appear in each issue.

Professional nurses have been the first women's occupational group to plan a nation-wide counseling service for those in the profession and for those contemplating entering it. In 1944, a personnel consultant was engaged by the American Nurses' Association to map out such a program in cooperation with State and district nurses' associations and nurses' professional registries.

The General Federation of Women's Clubs, and many other national women's organizations have aided vocational guidance activities of local groups even though there is no formal program of vocational guidance or no special stress on this activity at the national level. The Girl Scouts, the Camp Fire Girls' and similar organizations of girls have published vocational guidance units in their program outlines or have issued handbooks for local groups on such topics as "vocational exploration."

Just as the special occupational literature for women has resulted from their circumscriptions in the labor market so special vocational guidance services have emerged in a number of communities for those who experience additional handicaps in employment. For example, physically handicapped women and those with age or personality handicaps were given special attention by the Women's Educational and Industrial Union in Boston which early established a Bureau of Occupations for Handicapped Women. The needs of older women, especially during the depression of the thirties, were served by special projects sponsored by women's organizations. Articles on suitable occupations, on training, and on job-finding resulted from this interest as well as the organization in a number of communities of Job Clinics or Job Councils to aid older women (over 40 or 35) to find employment. Many of these were sponsored by women's organizations acting jointly as for example the President's Council Guidance Bureau in San Francisco, the Women's Job Clinic of the District of Columbia, the Senior Guidance Council in Philadelphia.

The special needs of rural girls prompted the Southern Women's Educational Alliance in the twenties to study their needs and publish such reports as "Rural Girls in the City for Work." Later this organization centered its activities on the needs of rural boys as well as girls and became the Alliance for the Guidance of Rural Youth.

One of the earliest efforts to supply a much-needed but difficult service resulted in the establishment of the Vocational Adjustment Bureau for Girls in New York City in 1921, to give vocational advice and to find suitable work for young girls who were subnormal mentally, or presented problems of behavior, or were neurotic or psychopathic in their tendencies. The work of this Bureau, too, was later extended to boys as well.

Such programs, like the special literature on occupations for women, have been designed not to duplicate but to supplement existing programs and literature, which, because of the tremendous needs have not yet been able to meet the total need. Some of the projects too, have grown out of the service motivation of public-spirited women who wanted to help other women, less favored. Many of these special programs for women have met the need for which they were established so well that they have been expanded or taken over by the community and enlarged to meet similar needs of men or boys, and have lost their special identification with service to women.

Most of the evidence at hand indicates that there should be no special problems inherent in the vocational guidance of women that are not also characteristic of the vocational guidance of men.

Sex differences in aptitudes, attitudes, and interests important in occupational selection which were assumed at the start, over the years have been found to be either nonexistent or of less significance in vocational guidance than the likenesses. Programs of vocational guidance, therefore, should not be separate for men and women, except where the circumstances of numbers or geography or of sponsorship or facilities or other local conditions make a separate program for women desirable and feasible. The methods in any case are the same. However, until we reach in reality that equality of occupational opportunity toward which steady progress is being made, it will be necessary to continue supplementing vocational guidance programs and materials with aid and information to enable women to continue their progress.

The only fundamental difference between men and women significant in planning their work life is women's child-bearing function. That this function should be recognized and provided for with all the skill of social planning is essential to the welfare of the Nation. That it should interfere with rather than complement the other contributions women make as workers and citizens is not a sound assumption. Nor are there sound reasons for assuming that such contributions interfere with rather than complement the maternal function. Conflicts of this sort arise from attitudes and traditions rather than from physical facts. Children strong in body, mind, and purpose and living in happy homes are more likely to be found together with equal opportunity for women to utilize their work capacities and interests in a culture than to thrive at the expense each of the other.

In dealing with this problem, the vocational guidance of women should strive primarily to assist them in working out the best possible combination of their roles as homemakers and as contributors in the job market. This adjustment will vary with the individual and her circumstances. To work out such a plan may be more difficult but is sounder than to evade the realities of life by encouraging girls to make a choice between "marriage" and "an occupation." It calls for the most skillful type of individual planning and assistance which the term vocational guidance implies.

In its larger sense, vocational guidance must also be concerned with improving the conditions which limit the occupational adjustment of the individual. It is, therefore, interested in changing attitudes toward women who work outside the home and in making it possible for a woman to bear and rear children well without unnecessary sacrifices of her services to the community or of set-backs to her maximum development. Those who are interested in the vocational guidance of women will continue to supplement programs and information with special assistance and information. But their major task lies in the elimination, through realistic information and counseling, of conflicting attitudes on the part of individual women and on the part of the society in which they live and work.

F. S. M.

Y

YMCA SERVICE, QUALIFICATIONS FOR PROFESSIONAL.

The Young Men's Christian Association, organized in London, June 6, 1844, is now entering its second century of service. Organized and operating in sixty-six different countries, it is a world-wide organization for the development of character and international understanding among the youth of the world. Through its Army and Navy Department and War Prisoners Aid programs, it serves young men in military service and prison camps.

Toward its goals of developing Christian personality and the building of a Christian society—the YMCA uses the following methods:

1. Organizes groups around school, vocation, neighborhood, friendships, leisure time, and other social relations that furnish a medium for mutual helpfulness and provide experience in democratic living and cooperative action.
2. Conducts group programs embracing a wide variety of activities, including music, dramatics, hobbies, outdoor pursuits, discussion groups, citizenship, public affairs, vocational guidance, educational classes, forums, lectures, religious education, health clubs, swimming, recreation, athletic activities, and camping.
3. Provides individual counsel to men and boys where there are problems in their living, school, work, religion or other relationships.
4. Provides service buildings with opportunities for wholesome recreation, education, and health for the youth of the community, and residence facilities for those away from home.
5. Conducts camps providing opportunities for outdoor life with training in leadership and democratic living.

In achieving these goals, the following list of skills is practiced by the professional worker: locating the needs and interests of youth; counsels individuals; organizes and supervises group activities; directs informal educational activities; conducts social activities; directs recreation and physical education; directs a camp; develops a membership constituency; enlists, trains, and supervises volunteers; guides committees at work; administers organizational and business affairs; raises funds and manages budgets; keeps accurate records; manages a building; interprets the Association's purposes and programs; interprets the Christian faith; cooperates with churches and other community agencies.

Many of these skills are practiced primarily with definite age and occupational groups—for example; younger boys, older boys, students, young men, industrial workers, and adults.

The personal qualities which are expected of the YMCA secretary include fundamental integrity of character; vital Christian purpose; capacity for spiritual life and growth; an integration of thinking and experience around a Christian philosophy of life; an interest in working with people for their personal and social growth irrespective of race, creed or economic status; a personality which commands confidence and respect; emotional stability and poise; initiative, self-reliance and resourcefulness; above average intelligence and alertness; cooperativeness; and social sensitivity.

For registration as a professional worker, the following qualifications must be met:

Age
Twenty-one years of age or older.

Education
A general college preparation, graduation from an accredited college or a carefully defined equivalent.

Religion
Membership in a Christian church or signing the authorized personal statement of faith.

Health
Satisfactorily passing a standard health examination.

For advancement to full professional status as secretary, the following qualifications are required:

Competence

Those able to receive satisfactory competence rating by Board of Certification, which, in addition to a review of all of the previous items, is based especially upon a record of two years' successful experience in actual service.

Educational Requirement

For those persons employed on or after May 1, 1945, thirty semester hours of accredited study in professional subjects in such areas as principles and techniques of religious leadership, counseling and guidance of individuals; leadership of informal groups; supervision and training of volunteers; community organization; administration of social and religious agencies; history, organization, objectives, program and administration of the YMCA; and appropriate field work is required for Certification.

It is important for candidates for the secretaryship to have as significant a content and quality of training and experience as possible. In planning undergraduate courses for YMCA service, preference should be given to such studies as religion, philosophy, history, psychology, biology, economics, sociology, political science, government, education, and modern literature. Professional training should supplement general education as indicated.

Further preparation should equip the secretary for the particular type of position or the age level with which he prefers to work, such as boys' work, young men's work, physical education, adult education, religious education.

The YMCA has two colleges—George Williams College in Chicago, Illinois, and Springfield College in Springfield, Massachusetts—both of which provide specialized professional preparation. The names of other educational institutions offering training for the secretaryship may be secured upon request.

As an aid in determining the aptitude and qualifications for the secretaryship, the following tests will be found useful, YMCA Personal History Record, YMCA Confidential Achievement Rating Form, standard intelligence test, Strong Vocational Interest Test.

References:

1. *Professional Opportunities in the Y.M.C.A.* New York: Association Press, 1945.
2. *Qualifications and Training for the Y.M.C.A. Secretaryship.* New York: Association Press, 1945.

L. J. T.

YUGOSLAVIA. It has been impossible to obtain information regarding vocational guidance activities in Yugoslavia. Sime Balen of the Yugoslav Embassy in Washington states that there were a few vocational guidance bureaus in his country prior to the war, but the destruction has been so extensive that activities at present are greatly impaired.

O. J. K.